The Development of the British Economy

Fourth Edition
1914–1990

Sidney Pollard

Professor Emeritus of Economic History, University of Bielefeld, Germany

Edward Arnold
A division of Hodder & Stoughton
LONDON NEW YORK MELBOURNE

© 1962, 1969, 1983, 1992 Sidney Pollard

First published in Great Britain 1962
Reprinted 1963, 1967
Second edition, revised 1969
Reprinted 1970
Reprinted as a paperback 1973
Reprinted 1976, 1979
Third edition 1983
Reprinted 1984, 1985, 1988, 1989
Fourth edition 1992

Distributed in the USA by Routledge, Chapman and Hall, Inc.
29 West 35th Street, New York, NY 10001

British Library Cataloguing in Publication Data

Pollard, Sidney
  The development of the British economy 1914–1990
  —4th ed.
  I. Title
  330.941082

  ISBN 0-340-56185-8

Library of Congress Cataloging-in-Publication Data

Pollard, Sidney
  The Development of the British economy, 1914–1990 / Sidney Pollard.—4th ed.
    p.   cm.
  Includes bibliographical references and index.
  ISBN 0-340-56185-8 : $22.50
    1. Great Britain—Economic conditions—20th century. I. Title.
  HC256.P62 1992
  330.941′082—dc20   91-35786 CIP

Typeset in 10/11 pt. English Times Compugraphic by
Butler & Tanner Ltd, Frome, Somerset.
Printed and bound in Great Britain for Edward Arnold,
a division of Hodder and Stoughton Limited,
Mill Road, Dunton Green, Sevenoaks, Kent TN13 2YA

Contents

Preface

The difficulties of writing recent history are well known. Much of the material is not yet available, the monographs and autobiographies have not yet been written, and many of the actors are still alive, to refute the most ingenious theories. Above all, we are still too close to the events, and too emotionally involved, to see them in their historical perspective.

But the pitfalls of writing recent history are as nothing compared with the pitfalls of teaching it, for it is here that the gap between the generations is at its most unbridgeable. What are everyday events and terms to the teacher are strange mysteries to the student, who finds the nuances, the background, the flavour of events, so familiar to the teacher as to be not worth making explicit, lost on him in a welter of unrecognizable references. The teaching of recent economic history has its own special difficulties, for it enters into the subjects of complex theoretical debate of yesterday, much of which is still unfinished. Yet teaching there must be, if the student is not to carry away with him a blank in his mind regarding the period when 'history' ends and when 'current economic problems' begin – precisely the period in which the minds of his elders were formed, and which some of them, alas, have never succeeded in leaving.

This book arose out of my desire to teach present-day students something about the no-man's land between history and applied economics or current affairs, and my difficulty in finding suitable general introductions, as distinct from specialist treatises and polemical works, of which there are probably too many. The usual tributes paid by the author in his Preface in this case must go to my students who unwittingly, and most likely unwillingly, forced me to write it. It is intended primarily for University students of Economics, Modern History and related subjects, and it assumes a modicum of knowledge of economic terms and institutions, such as any regular reader of the more intelligent weekly press could also command. It is hoped that it may also be of some use to their teachers and, further, to those interested members of the public, graduates, perhaps, in the subjects named here, and now active in business or public affairs, who require some knowledge of recent events to make up their own minds, believing with the author that the infallibility of our professional economic Oracles is by no means assured, even though they conform to their Delphic ancestor's habit of speaking in riddles, and regularly improve on it by speaking with several different voices at once.

A special word needs to be said about the bibliography. Traditionally, books designed mainly as textbooks have their reading lists either at the end of each chapter or at the end of the volume. Both suffer from similar limitations, for while the earnest student will be exasperated by not finding further reading hints on the pages on which his subject-matter occurs, the idle one will be too discouraged by the length of the reading list to make a start at all. Here, therefore (apart from a few general works mentioned at the end), the bibliography occurs in the form of footnotes to the text. These notes, even where they have the ostensible object of referring to the origins of quotations, statistics or unusual views, are all primarily intended as hints to further reading. It follows that the student's reading should extend beyond the page or chapter of the work quoted, according to the demand of his interests.

Each sectional chapter division has been treated as self-contained for the purposes of the bibliography, in the sense that full references are given again, even if the work has been mentioned in earlier sections or chapters. The statistical examples have been chosen deliberately from a wide range of sources, and conflicting series are occasionally given side by side in order to teach a healthy scepticism about economic measurement. The literature has been chosen so that the sum of the footnote references to each section forms the complete bibliography of the section and the sum of the references in each chapter, the bibliography of that chapter. It has, further, been chosen so as to make the student familiar with a wide selection of reading matter available, including books, reprints of documents, articles in learned journals and other periodicals, and official papers and statistics.

S. P.

In this second impression, the bibliography has been brought up to date, and some minor corrections to the text have been made. For some of the latter I am much indebted to Dr Walter Stern and Mr C. G. Hanson.

S. P.

7 August 1963

The enlarged edition brings the present volume virtually up to date. The new final chapter runs an even greater danger of showing all the weaknesses of writing on contemporary history, for not only may it stand too close to the events to recognize all the facts, but it may also fall into the trap of taking sides in the controversies. Yet to leave a widening gap between itself and the present would progressively diminish the value of the rest of the book. Amendments and additions to the rest of the book have been kept to a minimum, and mostly concern the literature published since the last revision.

S. P.

31 May 1968

In this third edition, the book has once more been brought up to date, ending formally in 1980 but extending in some respects to 1982. The final chapter of the last edition, which covered 17 years, would have had to cover 30 years in this, and it has therefore been split into three by topics, each covering the whole period, in parallel with the chapters covering the inter-war period. To preserve the same total length, the earlier chapters have been correspondingly shortened, and have been largely re-written to incorporate the literature and some of the controversies that have appeared in the course of the past 20 years or so. As before, the most recent events have been the most difficult to describe, and in the face of an economics profession split down the middle between monetarists and Keynesians, each of several different hues, a bland neutrality would have been even more difficult to attain than on former occasions, and has not been attempted.

S. P.

31 October 1982

The fourth edition follows tradition by shortening the earlier chapters in order to make room, without enlarging the whole, for the final chapter that brings the account up to date. Earlier chapters have also been re-written in part to incorporate the findings contained in the recent literature and, in a very few cases, even manage to substitute certainty for conjecture as new data have come to light, or as econometric manipulation has affirmed or rejected earlier guesswork. The final chapter, covering the years 1979–90, stands alone and is not spliced by topics into the other post-1950 chapters. This is done in tribute to the deliberate radical departure in economic policy in the Government's intention, even if not always in its execution.

S. P.

15 June 1991

Abbreviations used in Footnotes

References

Amer. Econ. Rev.	American Economic Review
B. of Eng. Qtly. Bull.	Bank of England Quarterly Bulletin
Bull. Oxf. Inst. Stat.	Bulletin of the Oxford Institute of Statistics
Bus. Hist. Rev.	Business History Review
Econ. Hist. Rev.	Economic History Review
Econ. J.	Economic Journal
Expl. Econ. Hist.	Explorations in Economic History
Geog. J.	Geographical Journal
J. Econ. and Business History	Journal of Economic and Business History
J. Econ. Hist.	Journal of Economic History
J. Royal Soc. of Arts	Journal of the Royal Society of Arts
J. R. Stat. S.	Journal of the Royal Statistical Society
J. Transport History	Journal of Transport History
Manchester School	Manchester School of Economic and Social Studies
Nat. Inst. Econ. Rev.	National Institute Economic Review
Oxf. Bull. Econ. Stat.	Oxford Bulletin of Economics and Statistics
Oxf. Econ. P.	Oxford Economic Papers
QJE	Quarterly Journal of Economics
Rev. Econ. Studies	Review of Economic Studies
Rev. of Econ. and Statistics	Review of Economics and Statistics
Scot. J. Pol. Econ.	Scottish Journal of Political Economy
Yorkshire Bulletin	Yorkshire Bulletin of Economic and Social Studies
HSWW	(Official) History of the Second World War
NS	New Series
RC	Royal Commission
SC	Select Committee
2nd S.	Second Series

Note: In references to articles in journals the convention has been followed where possible of separating volume and issue numbers by an oblique stroke: thus 3/13 means Volume 3, Number 13. The date afterwards refers to the date of the number, not necessarily of the whole volume.

In accordance with the practice which has become increasingly common in recent economic literature, the word 'billion' is used throughout in the American sense of a thousand million, and *not* in the traditional British sense of a million million.

1

The End of the Long Peace and the First World War, 1914–1918

1 British Industry and its Position in the World

The popular ideas about a country and an age, the ideas which are so all-pervasive that men find it largely unnecessary to express them on paper, take a long time to mature, and they take a long time to eradicate. The ideas which the British citizen imbibed in the last years of the century of peace which came to a close in 1914, as he watched the areas of red spread across the map, and saw fresh technical marvels introduced every year, were based on the experiences of the past two or three generations. These contained a dual promise of progress: the promise that science and industry would continue to improve material conditions of living, and the promise that Britain would continue to be at the head of this march of improvement.

Yet there were misgivings. One source of doubt about the prospects of progress is to be found not so much in its general direction, but largely in the glaring inequalities in income and wealth: in 1911–13, it has been estimated, 170,000 persons, or 0·85% of the population, owned 65·5% of the capital in the country, while at the other extreme, over $16\frac{1}{3}$ million, or 87·4% of the property-owning population, owned only 8·5% between them.[1] But inequality, of at least the same or even greater extent[2] had existed before. What was new was the fact that real wages were no longer rising, as they had been to 1900, and the diversion of much of the new wealth to classes who had not learnt the 'double bluff' of pre-war society noted by Keynes,[3] that capitalists were allowed to appropriate a large part of the nation's wealth, in the face of bitter poverty among the rest of the population, only on condition that they did not enjoy it, but re-invested it in their concerns. Altogether, a spirit of restlessness appeared to pervade the last years of the Long Peace.[4]

Moreover, weaknesses had begun to appear in the British industrial structure before 1914, though they were not yet visible to many contemporaries. Total industrial production was still growing and 1913 was a peak year on any reckoning. Between 1900 and 1913 gross domestic product (GDP) of the United Kingdom at factor cost was still growing at the rate of 1·7% a year, and even

---

[1] H. Campion, *Public and Private Property* (Oxford, 1938).

[2] Peter H. Lindert, 'Unequal English Wealth since 1670', *Journal of Political Economy* 94/6 (1986).

[3] J. M. Keynes, *Economic Consequences of the Peace* (New York, 1920), pp. 18–22.

[4] The atmosphere of those years is captured most aptly in Geo. Dangerfield, *The Strange Death of Liberal England* (1936), a book to be recommended more for its intuitive perception than its historical accuracy. Also G. D. H. Cole and R. Postgate, *The Common People, 1746–1938* (1938), chapter 37.

output per head was rising at an average of 0·7%.[5] Exports were also rising, but at no more than 0·93% per head p.a.[6] and they showed a dangerous concentration on a narrow range of industries: the old 'staple trades' coal, iron and steel, machinery and vehicles, ships and textiles between them contributed two-thirds of all exports in 1911–13. Some of them were no longer buoyant. Thus the output of coal per miner had been falling since the early 1880s, and in the Lancashire cotton and Cleveland pig iron industries real costs had not been reduced at all since 1885.[7]

Coal mining, the most basic of industries, providing the fuel and determining the location of the others, was still expanding. From 223 million tons at the turn of the century, production had increased to 287 million tons in 1913, of which over 94 million tons was for export and bunkering.[8] However, technically the industry was falling behind other countries. Only 8% of the coal was cut mechanically in 1913, and even less was mechanically conveyed underground; in the use of electricity, concrete, even steel, British pits seemed backward, though the geography of the British fields and the nature of the seams might explain the delay in the introduction of methods which were not yet fully proved.

In the pig iron and steel works, a sector of basic importance for an industrial country, a considerable growth in British outputs had been overtaken by the faster growth of Germany and the USA. In 1913 the USA produced 31 million tons, Germany 16·5 million, and Britain 10·3 million of pig iron; in steel production, by 1913 the American output was of the order of 13 million tons, the German of 7 million, and the British of 5 million. British units were smaller and less efficient. Britain adopted the cheaper basic processes only very slowly, and the final change-over even from puddled iron to steel took place long after it had been completed elsewhere.[9]

In general engineering and shipbuilding Britain was also losing her early lead. In some respects she was paying the penalty for being the pioneer. In her period of supremacy, over much of the nineteenth century, success in industry depended to a large extent on the skill of craftsmen, their use of tools and machinery, their knowledge of their materials. Britain had a race of craftsmen second to none, and it was precisely the lack of such craftsmen in sufficient numbers in the USA which forced American employers to pioneer automatic and foolproof machinery, mass-produced articles using interchangeable parts as well as 'scientific management'. These, again, turned out to be the methods of the future, but they were resisted here both by masters and men,[10] and adopted only slowly, if at all, before 1914. The lag behind Germany in electrical engineering, as well as

[5] C. H. Feinstein, *National Income, Expenditure and Output of the United Kingdom 1855–1956* (Cambridge, 1972), T. 18.

[6] C. K. Harley and D. N. McCloskey, 'Foreign Trade, Competition and the Expanding International Economy', in Roderick Floud and Donald McCloskey (eds.), *The Economic History of Britain Since 1700*, vol. 2, *1860 to the 1970s* (Cambridge, 1981), p. 51.

[7] G. T. Jones, *Increasing Return* (1933). Some of the results of this classic work have recently been questioned. E.g. Lars Sandberg, *Lancashire in Decline* (Columbus, Ohio, 1974), chapter 5.

[8] H. Stanley Jevons, *The British Coal Trade* (1915).

[9] Peter Temin, 'The Relative Decline of the British Steel Industry, 1880–1913', in H. Rosovsky (ed.), *Industrialization in Two Systems* (New York, 1966).

[10] David A. Hounshell, *From the American System to Mass Production 1800–1932* (Baltimore, 1984); E. H. Phelps-Brown, *Growth of British Industrial Relations* (1959), pp. 94–6.

in chemicals, pointed to another hangover from earlier days: the neglect of university-trained scientists.[11]

As a result of these and other factors, British achievements in the engineering branches were mixed. In motor cars, office equipment, most machine tools, agricultural machinery and electrical machinery the record was poor; clock making was almost wiped out. By contrast, British did well in the older manufactures of steam engines, textile machinery and heavy machine tools, and the newer manufacture of bicycles. In shipbuilding, the United Kingdom still built 60% of the world's mercantile tonnage over the whole period 1900–14.[12] All told, engineering exports by 1911–13 had increased threefold in value since the early 1880s. Engineering output is notoriously difficult to measure, but one estimate put the British share of world machinery production in 1913 at 11·8%, compared with the USA, 50%, and Germany, 20·6%.

The textile industries formed the remainder of the old staple trades, which Britain had pioneered and on which her exports still largely depended. Of these, the cotton trade was still by far the most important exporter. In the years 1911–13, it accounted for an average of £123 million, compared with £54 million for all other textile exports combined. Both output and exports (especially of piece goods) were still on the increase, and there were some signs of technical improvement, but British firms failed to adopt the key cost-reducing innovation, the ring spindle.[13]

There was one other old staple industry, though it had long since ceased to figure in the export statistics: this was agriculture, the chief victim of the Free Trade policy of the nineteenth century. Cheap freights and unrestricted imports reduced the home output of wheat, but meat production found growing home markets, and since 1870, the proportion of cultivated land under permanent pasture had risen from 42% to 53%. Market gardening was another occupation which made economic sense, in a population now largely urban, and the crisis in agriculture may be said to have been over by 1910.[14]

By contrast with these old staples, some newer industries promised well for the future by their rapid rate of growth, though they were still relatively insignificant. Among them, electrical engineering and supply were based to a considerable extent on British inventions and discoveries, but Britain lagged sadly behind Germany and even America in their development. The gas engine, and the motor car industry, its chief user, were equally the fruits of foreign,

[11] J. H. Clapham, *An Economic History of Modern Britain*, vol. 3 (Cambridge, 1938), chapters 1 and 3.

[12] S. Pollard, 'British and World Shipbuilding', *J. Econ. Hist.*, 17/3, 1957; *Report on Engineering Trades after the War* (1918, Cd. 9073); S. B. Saul, 'The Market and the Development of the Mechanical Engineering Industries in Britain, 1860–1914', *Ec. Hist. Rev.*, 20/1, 1967; idem, 'The Engineering Industry', in D. H. Aldcroft (ed.), *The Development of British Industry and Foreign Competition 1875–1914* (1968), R. A. Church, 'Nineteenth Century Clock Technology in Britain, the United States, and Switzerland', *Ec. Hist. Rev.*, 28/4, 1975; A. E. Harrison, 'The Competitiveness of the British Cycle Industry', *Q.J.E.*, 22/3, 1969; S. B. Saul, 'The Motor Industry in Britain to 1914', *Business History*, 5, 1962.

[13] Lars G. Sandberg, *op. cit.*, William Lazonick, 'Factor costs and the Diffusion of Ring Spinning in Britain Prior to World War I', *ibid.*, 96, 1981; idem, 'Production Relations, Labor Productivity and Choice of Technique: British and US Cotton Spinning', *J. Econ. Hist.*, 41/3, 1981.

[14] A. D. Hall, *A Pilgrimage of British Farming* (1912); Lord Ernle, *English Farming, Past and Present* (4th ed., 1927), chapters 18 and 19; T. W. Fletcher, 'The Great Depression of English Agriculture, 1873–1896', *Ec. Hist, Rev.*, 13/3, 1961.

rather than British, enterprise. The British chemical industry also appeared increasingly unable to keep pace, despite its early lead, being handicapped by the lack of scientists and by being wedded to older processes, e.g. the Leblanc, rather than the Solvay, process of making soda. The war quickly showed up the serious shortcomings in the making of organic chemicals, such as high explosives, the shortage of oleum, one of their basic raw materials, and the neglect of the recent methods of producing fertilizer.[15] These industries were among the most rapidly expanding ones, together with the allied rubber,[16] oil refining, airplane, artificial silk and scientific instruments industries.

The industries enumerated so far employed some 40% of the occupied population between them. Changes in other sectors, including commerce, distribution, building, the professions, and central and local government, contributed equally to the growth in consumption and living standards, though they were less easy to capture in the statistics.

By the standards of the mid-twentieth century or those of contemporary USA[17], industrial amalgamation and combination in the last years of peace had not proceeded very far. There were, in effect, two distinct, even if related, movements: a simple growth in size, and an attempt to restrict competition. The former usually took place in order to obtain economies in working, administration, marketing or finance, while the latter was, more often than not, directed towards raising prices to consumers. Both tended to occur in slack times when markets were difficult.[18]

Combinations of this kind began to be viewed with apprehension wherever they obtained control over a significant share of their markets; thus in the case of railways, from the 1850s, and the banks in 1918,[19] official policy became expressly opposed to permitting any further reduction in the small number of competing units. The authorities did not, however, intervene to curb the activities of private combinations to restrict competition.

In some industries the typical form of organization was an association of independent producers, agreeing on common prices, and often developing common sales organizations and restriction schemes on output in order to protect their prices. These associations were most notable in the iron and steel industry, and side by side with single-firm monopolies, the building materials industry. It was calculated that in 1914 one-quarter of the cost of a cottage was fully price controlled, and a second quarter partially so.[20] The shipping conferences or 'rings' which had been flourishing since the 1870s were normally limited to liner companies which stood to lose heavily if their ships sailed empty

[15] Cf. S. B. Saul, *Studies in British Overseas Trade, 1870–1914* (Liverpool, 1960), pp. 37 ff.; T. I. Williams, *The Chemical Industry* (1953), chapter 6; L. F. Haber, *The Chemical Industry during the Nineteenth Century* (Oxford, 1958), chapter 9; *idem, The Chemical Industry 1900–1930* (Oxford, 1971), pp. 135 ff.; Peter H. Lindert and Keith Trace, 'Yardsticks for Victorian Entrepreneurs', in Donald N. McCloskey (ed.), *Essays on a Mature Economy: Britain After 1840* (1971).

[16] Wm. Woodruff, *The Rise of the British Rubber Industry during the Nineteenth Century* (Liverpool, 1958).

[17] Alfred D. Chandler, Jr, *Scale and Scope* (Cambridge, Mass., 1990).

[18] Leslie Hannah, 'Mergers in British Manufacturing Industry, 1880–1918', *Oxf. Econ. P.,* 26, 1974, p. 9; Lance Davis, 'The Capital Market and Industrial Concentration: The US and UK, a Comparative Study', *Ec. Hist. Rev.,* 19/2, 1966, p. 266.

[19] Treasury Committee on Bank Amalgamations, *Report* (1918), in T. E. Gregory, *Statutes, Documents and Reports Relating to British Banking,* vol. 2 (Oxford, 1929).

[20] *Report of the Committee on Trusts* (1919. Cd. 9236). Some of the unpublished material on which this Report was based was used by Clapham, *op. cit.,* chapter 5.

at their advertised times, and they brought to perfection a weapon adopted later by other associations: the deferred rebate.[21]

Some associations took the ultimate step of a complete merger to obtain monopolistic powers in this period, especially in the chemical and the textile industries. Among chemical firms the Salt Union (1888), the United Alkali Co. (1881), Brunner Mond & Co. (1881), Borax Consolidated (1899) and the Nobel Dynamite Trust were the most prominent. In textiles, J. & P. Coats (1890) and the English Sewing Cotton Co. (1897) stood out, together with the following associations, each formed of numerous small constituent companies: Fine Cotton Spinners' and Doublers' (1898), Calico Printers' (1899), Bleachers' (1900), Bradford Dyers' (1898), and Woolcombers' (1900). In other industries were found Imperial Tobacco (1901–2), British Oil and Cake Mills (1899), the Distillers' Company (1907) and Associated Portland Cement (1900).[22]

A different method of organization making remarkable progress in the years before 1914 was that of the co-operative society. With a membership of 3 million, the 1,385 societies had total sales of nearly £90 million, and had been transformed from insignificant local associations to a major factor in retail distribution and a few related fields. They were an important factor in the pioneering of large-scale enterprise in retailing, in promoting the campaign for wholesome and unadulterated food, and in providing convenient facilities for working-class savings.[23]

While there were modern traits to be found in industrial and commercial organization, the skill and enterprise of the British entrepreneur of that period have been called in question. In particular, the failure of the economy to grow at the rate of the USA, of Germany and most other continental countries, and the failure to modernize certain key industries and to develop others, have been seen as part of a general decline in enterprise. Against this, it has been argued in several detailed studies, the British entrepreneur behaved rationally in obeying the market signals that he met. In many fields he stayed indeed on top of the world; in others, he was not to be blamed if the market misled him into actions which, in the long run, turned out to be inhibiting for British progress. The debate is still unresolved, and it turns largely on the functions and range of the entrepreneur. How many years ahead should he plan for? Which among the economic data surrounding him should he consider as given, and which should he endeavour to change if necessary?[24] How far was he to blame for the British 'over-commitment' to slow-growth industries?[25]

[21] *S.C. on Shipping Rings* (1909. Cd. 4668, 4669, 4670, 4685).

[22] Hermann Levy, *Monopolies, Trusts and Cartels in British Industry* (2nd ed., 1927); F. W. Hirst, *Monopolies, Trusts and Kartells* (1905); Henry W. Macrosty, *The Trust Movement in British Industry* (1907).

[23] G. D. H. Cole, *A Century of Co-operation* (1944).

[24] D. H. Aldcroft, 'The Entrepreneur and the British Economy 1870–1914', *Ec. Hist. Rev.*, 17/1, 1964; Donald N. McCloskey, 'Did Victorian Britain fail?', *ibid.*, 23/3, 1970; Donald N. McCloskey and Lars G. Sandberg, 'From Damnation to Redemption: Judgements on the Late Victorian Entrepreneur', *Expl. Ec. Hist.*, 9 (1971); D. H. Aldcroft, 'Technical Progress and British Enterprise, 1875–1914', *Business History*, 8, 1966; William H, Phillips, 'Induced Innovation and Economic Performance in late Victorian British Industry', *J. Econ. Hist.*, 42/1, 1982. S. Pollard, 'Reflections on Entrepreneurship and Culture in European Societies', *Transactions of the Royal Historical Society*, 5th Ser. 40 (1990).

[25] H. W. Richardson, 'Over-commitment in Britain Before 1930', *Oxf. Econ. P.*, 17, 1965.

2 The Banks, the Money Market and Foreign Investment

Among the many changes in the forms of economic organization in the generation before 1914, those in the field of banking were among the most significant. The swallowing up of the private banks by the joint-stock bank engaged in branch banking, 'a trickle in the middle decades of the century, ... had become a headlong rush as the century neared its end. In the new century amalgamations continued to follow one upon the other, and they were now amalgamations between banks already greatly enlarged by earlier absorptions.'[26] This process was all but completed by 1914, when the several hundred private banks had shrunk to fewer than a score, but there now were 20 joint-stock banks with over 100 branches each (the largest, the London City and Midland, having over 700), besides 20 or so with fewer than 100 branches each and local connections only. Between them, they maintained about 7,000 offices in England and Wales. In Scotland, where joint-stock banking had a longer tradition, there were eight banking companies in 1914, with just under 1,200 branches between them. In the 'race' of amalgamations, the objective was increasingly seen to be national coverage for each firm. In the process, any existing gaps were filled by opening new offices and sub-offices, which increased in number year by year.[27]

The process bespeaks an increasing banking habit of the population: between 1906 and 1914 alone, bank deposits per head of population rose from £18·8 to £23·4, and clearings from £292 to £359. Its consequences were far-reaching. The circulation of private bank notes virtually disappeared, except for Scotland, the cheque system became all but universal, and Bank of England notes were mainly used for wage payments and small retail purchases only,[28] while inland bills were rendered largely obsolete:[29] bills were now used mostly for foreign traffic only.

A further result of amalgamation was to make banking much safer as resources and reserves were increased. The accumulation of 'private' gold reserves by the banks (the Midland alone held £8 million by 1914, and the others probably £16 million between them) made it easier for them to defy the central bank, had they so desired,[30] though in fact collaboration with the Bank of England became closer, and a liaison committee between them was set up in 1911.

The strengthening of the English banking structure by amalgamation also altered the role of the Bank of England as the central bank and banker of last resort. An internal drain having become unlikely since there were very few country banks with their own note issue left, it would appear, to judge from the evidence given to the US Monetary Commission, that the Bank was almost

[26] R. S. Sayers, *Lloyd's Bank in the History of English Banking* (Oxford, 1957), p. 241.

[27] J. F. Ashby, *The Story of the Banks* (1934); P. W. Matthews, *The Banker's Clearing House* (1921), chapter 7; J. Sykes, *The Amalgamation Movement in British Banking, 1825–1924* (1926).

[28] Evidence of Governor and Directors of the Bank of England to US National Monetary Commission in 1910, reprinted in T. E. Gregory (ed.), *Selected Statutes, Documents and Reports Relating to British Banking, 1832–1928* (Oxford, 1929), vol. 2, p. 309; also First Report of Cunliffe Committee, quoted in *ibid.*, pp. 335–6.

[29] W. T. C. King, *History of the London Discount Market* (1936), pp. 271–5.

[30] E. Victor Morgan, *Theory and Practice of Central Banking 1797–1913* (Cambridge, 1943), pp. 210–12.

exclusively concerned with the foreign exchanges, and with safeguarding the gold reserve against the dangers of a drain abroad.

The Bank's two main weapons in carrying out its obligations as a central bank were the bank rate and open market operations. The former could sometimes be accompanied by greater selectivity in the kind of paper the Bank would accept for rediscounting; the ideal, however, was to lend freely, but at high rates, in times of need. A rise in the bank rate achieved its primary object if it led to a general rise of interest rates in London. These were then expected to call forth an influx of foreign funds including gold, on the one hand, and to discourage enterprise, lead to a reduction of stocks and to general deflation at home on the other, thus reversing the outflow of gold which was the usual ground upon which the high bank rate policy had been put into operation. 'Open market operations' covered a variety of actions with which the Bank experimented in this period to supplement its bank rate policy by making money scarce or plentiful in the City. They ranged from purchases and sales of securities to influencing market rates (as distinct from bank rate) and the gold market, and included the increasingly effective 'hint from headquarters' to the clearing banks.[31]

Several circumstances combined to turn the imperfect control of the Bank of England over the market which existed in 1890 into the smooth and perfect instrument of the last years before 1914.[32] In the first place, the gold reserve rose after the mid-1890s, when the vast quantities from the new goldfields of Alaska and South Africa began to arrive in London.[33] Secondly, the Bank could count on the support of other strong institutions, including foreign central banks and the joint-stock banks and it could use the growing funds of Colonial Governments and British local authorities to back up its policies.

Above all, the powers of the Bank over the City depended on the growth of London as the leading money market in the world. Most of the world was on a gold standard by the end of the nineteenth century, but the premier position of London ensured that an attractive rate would bring gold from the four corners of the earth. This power of a high rate to attract gold was demonstrated in 1907, when, after a serious loss of gold to America, a 7% bank rate brought in speedily £19 million in gold from 24 countries.

In the years before 1914, the facilities in London for raising capital for British industry were limited and badly co-ordinated. Local authorities, railways and public utilities could use the London money market, and their securities were freely quoted on the Stock Exchange. For the rest of the domestic capital needs, however, the Stock Exchange was of little help: in the years before the war, only 10% of real investment in this country was made by issues of industrial firms

[31] R. S. Sayers, *Bank of England Operation, 1890–1914* (1936), and 'Open Market Operations in English Central Banking' in his *Central Banking after Bagehot* (Oxford, 1957); *idem, The Bank of England 1891–1944*, 3 vols. (Cambridge, 1976), vol. 1, chapter 3; P. Barrett Whale, 'The Working of the Pre-War Gold Standard', *Economica*, 1937, reprinted in T. S. Ashton and R. S. Sayers (eds.), *Papers in English Monetary History* (Oxford, 1953); A. G. Ford, 'Notes on the Working of the Gold Standard before 1914', *Oxf. Econ. P.*, NS, 12/1, 1960; Donald N. McCloskey and J. Richard Zecher, 'How the Gold Standard Worked 1880–1913', in Donald N. McCloskey, *Enterprise and Trade in Victorian Britain* (1981).

[32] W. E. Beach, *British International Gold Movements and Banking Policy, 1881–1913* (Cambridge, Mass., 1935), chapters 7–9.

[33] R. G. Hawtrey, *A Century of Bank Rate* (1938), pp. 46–8.

through the London Stock Exchange, and only 3% by new industrial firms. As a result, capital for industry had to be found largely by personal connections, in provincial centres, and by ploughing back the firms' own profits.[34]

By contrast, the market for investing abroad was extremely well organized. Particularly active were the merchant banks which floated foreign loans, acted as agents for foreign governments and public corporations, accepted foreign bills and engaged in foreign exchange operations. In consequence foreign investment in the last years of peace had reached an astonishing level. According to Imlah, capital assets abroad owned by British citizens amounted to about £2·4 billion at the turn of the century; by the outbreak of war, they had risen to £4 billion.[35] Further, the pace of foreign investment tended to increase from an average of under £50 million per annum in 1901–5 to about £150 million per annum in 1907–10 and £200 million per annum in 1911–13. From 1907 on, annual investment abroad appears to have exceeded the total of real net investments at home.

How was this vast capital export, amounting in the last years to about one-third of the total export trade, financed? Britain, it must be remembered, showed a substantial unfavourable balance on merchandise trade of the order of £150 million annually. This negative balance, to which must be added (net) bullion imports and tourist expenditure abroad of about £20 million, was almost exactly counterbalanced by large and rising credit terms for net invisible exports: banking, insurance and shipping earnings. The surplus was provided by dividends and interest rising from about £100 million to £200 million between 1900 and 1913, and it was these which allowed Britain to increase her foreign investments at an equally rapid rate. This was not merely a statistical coincidence: a large part of the foreign investment was, in fact, direct re-investment of earnings abroad.[36]

There were clearly marked cycles in these large movements, booms in capital exports coincided with booms in the exports of capital goods and with a high tide of emigration from the United Kingdom, particularly to the countries which received a large share of the British capital, alternating with periods of an exactly opposite character.[37] The years before 1914 formed the second half of the last,

[34] A. K. Cairncross, *Home and Foreign Investment 1870–1913* (Cambridge, 1953), chapter 5; F. Lavington, *The English Capital Market* (1921); and the controversy in A. R. Hall, 'A Note on the English Capital Market as a Source of Funds Before 1914', *Economica*, NS, 24/93, 1957; A. K. Cairncross, 'The English Capital Market Before 1914', *ibid.*, 25/98, 1958, pp. 142–6; A. R. Hall, 'The English Capital Market Before 1914 – a Reply', *ibid.*, 25/100, pp. 339–43. But see Lance Davis, 'The Capital Markets and Industrial Concentration: The US and UK, a Comparative Study', *Ec. Hist. Rev.*, 19/2, 1966, p. 262.

[35] A. H. Imlah, 'British Balance of Payments and Export of Capital, 1916–1913', *Ec. Hist. Rev.*, 5/2, 1952; reprinted in *Economic Elements in the Pax Britannica* (Cambridge, Mass., 1958). Other broadly similar estimates are summarized in E. Victor Morgan, *Studies in British Financial Policy, 1914–1925* (1952), p. 328; J. H. Lenfant, 'Great Britain's Capital formation, 1865–1914', *Economica*, NS, 18/70, 1951; C. H. Feinstein, *National Income, Expenditure and Output of the United Kingdom 1855–1965* (Cambridge, 1972), p. 205. But see D. C. M. Platt, 'British Portfolio Investment Overseas before 1870. Some Doubts', *Ec. Hist. Rev.*, 33/1, 1980, pp. 14–16.

[36] A dissenting view will be found in A. G. Ford, 'The Transfer of British Foreign Lending, 1870–1913', *Ec. Hist. Rev.*, 11/2, 1958.

[37] Brinley Thomas, *Migration and Economic Growth* (Cambridge, 1954); Cairncross, *op. cit.*, chapter 8; P. L. Cottrell, *British Overseas Investment in the Nineteenth Century* (1975), chapters 5 and 6.

and perhaps most powerfully marked, of these cycles.[38] At the same time British investment, as well as British migration, went increasingly to areas within the Empire. Thus in 1901–10 an annual average of 85,000 migrated from the United Kingdom to Canada, and 23,000 to Australia and New Zealand. In 1911–13, the figures were 189,000 and 85,000 respectively. The proportions of British emigrants making for territories within the Empire were 28% in the 1890's, 63% between 1901 and 1912, and 78% in 1913.

When we note, further, that the years before 1914 were also marked by a general rise in world prices, in which food and raw materials, the main British imports, tended to rise faster in price than the manufactured goods which Britain exported,[39] it may now be possible to discern a distinct pattern in the heavy reliance of the staple industries on exports, the export boom in capital goods, the lag behind other countries in technical equipment and progress, the concentration of the City of London on foreign lending, and the downward pressure on real incomes (except for profits), in the last years of peace. Do they all add up to the statement that Britain invested too much abroad, to the detriment of her own industrial future?

The question admits of no easy answer. The direction of the British investment programme was not the outcome of a deliberate decision, but of the choices of innumerable investors. It has long been assumed that they invested abroad because the returns were higher, but even that seems no longer certain, particularly when the risks are added in. It may well have been that the smoothness of the City operations channelled funds abroad that might have earned more at home. Even if foreign returns were higher, it mattered for Britain's future whether they were earned in equipping complementary economies, supplying raw materials and food, as had largely been the case earlier, or whether they were equipping competing economies with such items as textile machinery, as was increasingly the case in the early twentieth century.[40]

The destination of the funds thus sent abroad was significant.[41] By 1910, when foreign investments totalled some £3¼ billion, about £1,550–£1,650 million was invested within the Empire, virtually all of it in four regions, Canada, Australia–New Zealand, Africa, and India–Ceylon, holding just under £400 million each. The United States and the rest of America came next, with over £600 million each, and other areas shared the remainder. By 1913, 47% of British overseas investment was in the empire. The importance of the Empire stands out, particularly, since, with South America,[42] it formed the area of the fastest increase of investments.

Modern Imperialism has many roots. It was fed by nationalism and jingoism, perhaps the most potent beliefs in the advanced countries of the West before

[38] C. K. Hobson, *The Export of Capital* (1914).

[39] H. A. Imlah, *Economic Elements*, pp. 87–8; also 'Terms of Trade of the United Kingdom 1798–1915', *J. Econ. Hist.*, 10/2, Nov. 1950; Cairncross, *op. cit.*, p. 206; W. W. Rostow, 'The Terms of Trade in Theory and Practice', *Ec. Hist. Rev.*, 3/1, 1950, and 'The Historical Analysis of the Terms of Trade', *ibid.*, 4/1, 1951.

[40] S. Pollard, 'Capital Exports, 1870–1914 – Harmful or Beneficial?' *Ec. Hist. Rev.*, 38/4, 1985.

[41] For recent summaries, see Morgan, *Studies*, p. 328; Saul, *op. cit.*, chapters 8 and 9; Matthew Simon, 'The Pattern of New British Portfolio Foreign Investment 1865–1914', in A. R. Hall (ed.), *The Export of Capital from Britain 1870–1914* (1968).

[42] J. Fred Rippy, *British Investments in Latin America, 1822–1949* (Minneapolis, 1959), chapter 4.

1914; it owed much to the inspiration of soldiers, poets, missionaries and explorers; and often colonies were sought for their strategic value. As far as there were economic roots, these did not lie so much in the search for trade, but rather in the promise of relatively protected investment opportunities, and second, in the promised relief for social and economic pressures at home.[43] The British electorate turned down Joseph Chamberlain's drive for Empire preference, in trading, and as far as the colonies were concerned, the only effective protectionist measure was the prohibitive export duty on Malayan tin ore in 1903, which kept the smelting capacity within the Empire.[44] Recent research seems to show that, taken as a whole, the Empire represented an economic loss, rather than a gain, to Britain.[45]

3 Pre-War Incomes and the Standard of Living

In the second half of the nineteenth century it became one of the unspoken tenets of all classes that total national output per head would rise in the long run and that those performing some useful economic function would normally share in the increased wealth. Long-term upward movements do not, however, exclude movements in the opposite direction for substantial periods of time, and in the first 14 years of this century, while the total national product increased as before, the real wages of labour remained stationary or declined.

According to Feinstein, the index of industrial production rose from 80·1 to 100·0 between 1900 and 1913, both of these being peak years. 'Unearned' income in the form of interest and dividends from abroad rose even faster. Total national income at constant prices, according to Prest, grew by 20·3% between 1900 and 1913.[46] Real national income per head rose by about $8\frac{1}{2}$%,[47] and productivity per worker employed rose by 7% in those years.

This increased national output was not necessarily reflected in increased personal consumption, for the price rises occurred largely in food and textile raw materials, the bases of consumer's expenditure, while the relative prices of capital goods fell. Thus the volume index of total consumers' expenditure stood at 111·4 in 1911 and 111·7 in 1912, 1900 being 100, so that it was only just keeping pace with the growth in population.[48] Wage-earners stood to lose most by the relative movement of prices, since about seven-tenths of their incomes were spent on food and clothing.

[43] J. A. Hobson, *Imperialism* (1st ed., 1902; 3rd ed., 1938); also V. I. Lenin, *Imperialism, the Highest Stage of Capitalism* (1916, repr. in *Selected Works*, vol. 5, 1936); Clive Day, *A History of Commerce* (New York, 1907), chapters 37, 38, 53; W. Ashworth, *A Short History of the International Economy, 1850–1950* (1952), chapter 6; D. K. Fieldhouse, *Economics and Empire 1830–1914* (1973); P. J. Cain and A. G. Hopkins, 'The Political Economy of British Expansion Overseas, 1750–1914', *Ec. Hist. Rev.*, 33–4, 1980.

[44] S. B. Saul, 'The Economic Significance of "Constructive Imperialism"', *J. Econ. Hist.*, 17/2, 1957.

[45] Lance Davis and Robert Huttenback, *Mammon and the Pursuit of Empire* (Cambridge, 1986).

[46] C. H. Feinstein, *National Income, Expenditure and Output in the United Kingdom, 1855–1965* (Cambridge, 1972), T. 24–5; J. Kuczynski, *A Short History of Labour Conditions in Britain, 1750 to the Present Day* (1946 ed.), p. 121; A. R. Prest, 'National Income of the United Kingdom, 1870–1946', *Econ. J.*, 58/229, 1948.

[47] Prest's figures as corrected by C. H. Feinstein yield an increase of 4% only: 'Income and Investment in the United Kingdom, 1856–1914', *Econ. J.*, 71/282, 1961.

[48] A. R. Prest and A. A. Adams, *Consumer Expenditure in the United Kingdom, 1900–1919* (Cambridge, 1954).

To make matters worse, wages were falling relatively to other incomes, declining as a proportion of total incomes, from 41·3% in 1900 to a bare 36·2% in 1913.[49] Thus real wages failed to rise at all, though average wages have been calculated to have risen by 0·29% a year owing to a shift in the labour force to better-paid jobs.[50] Contemporaries thought that over the whole of the period 1902–12, real wages were well below the levels reached in 1899–1901.[51]

Statistics of this kind should not be credited with too great an accuracy, but the general trend of real wage indices is established beyond doubt. Within these general figures of wage changes, however, three developments stand out: differences in the payments for different jobs, differences as between families of varying sizes, and the incidence of unemployment and cyclical variation of employment.

The difference between the nominal weekly wage rates of skilled and unskilled men was exceptionally wide in this period. The unweighted average of unskilled wages in five industries (coal, cotton, engineering, building and railways) was 60% of the skilled wage in 1886 and 58½% in 1913.[52] Artisans' wages were in the region of 40s. to 50s. per week in all but the smallest towns, and labourers' still round the 25s. mark.[53] Women's industrial wages were around one-third to one-half of a man's wage.

The differences in the wage rates between the skilled and the unskilled were widened by the fact that it was often the labourers' jobs that were the most irregular, employers preferring to keep their skilled crews together. Families were getting smaller but there were marked class differences, the lower the social status of the family, the larger being the number of its children. The life of householders who belonged to that half of the labour force which brought home an average of 20s. or less per week, or who had an unfavourable ratio of dependants, was bound to be a life of economic hardship or distress.

Charles Booth found in London that about one-third of the population lived below a standard which kept them physically efficient, later called the 'poverty line'. This discovery was soon confirmed by other inquiries, made in York in 1899 by B. S. Rowntree, and in the four towns of Northampton, Warrington, Stanley and Reading, undertaken in 1912–13 by A. L. Bowley and A. R. Burnett-Hurst.[54] Among the men who in 1911 received less than 25s. if in regular work, there could not have been fewer than 2 million who were married and who would have dependent families, numbering 8 million souls all told. All of them were 'underfed, under-housed and insufficiently clothed. The children among

[49] Feinstein's figures are: 41·5% and 37·8% respectively. Cf. also A. L. Bowley, *The Change in the Distribution of the National Income, 1880–1913* (Oxford, 1920).

[50] C. H. Feinstein, 'What really happened to real wages? Trends in wages, prices and productivity in the United Kingdom, 1880–1913', *Ec. Hist. Rev.*, 43/2, 1990.

[51] J. A. Hobson, *Gold, Prices and Wages* (1913), chapter 7 produced these index figures for real wages: 1895–163; 1900–179; 1910–161.

[52] K. G. J. C. Knowles and D. J. Robertson, 'Differences Between the Wages of Skilled and Unskilled Workers, 1880–1950', *Bull. Oxf. Inst. Stat.*, 13/4, 1951, p. 111.

[53] J. F. W. Rowe, *Wages in Practice and Theory* (1928), chapters 1, 2 and 3 and Appx. 1: Board of Trade, *Report on Earnings and Hours of Labour* (1911. Cd. 5814).

[54] E. H. Phelps-Brown, *Growth of British Industrial Relations* (1959), pp. 19–20; Ch. Booth, *Life and Labour in London* (1904 ed.); B. S. Rowntree, *Poverty, a Study of Town Life* (1902); A. L. Bowley and A. R. Burnett-Hurst, *Livelihood and Poverty* (1915); *Report of Inter-Department Committee on Physical Deterioration* (1904. Cd. 2175).

them suffer more than the adults. Their growth is stunted, their mental powers are cramped, their health is undermined.'[55]

Unemployment fluctuated round an average of 4% among trade union members, but in the very worst years it rose up to 11%; in 1908 and 1909, for example, it was over $8\frac{1}{2}$%. In such years, standards of consumption would deteriorate still further and debts would have to be incurred.[56]

Unemployment relief, the responsibility of the basic Poor Law administered by the elected Guardians of local 'Unions' of parishes, had been found increasingly ineffective in dealing with cyclical unemployment. As a result, local authorities, subject to increasing pressure from their working-class voters, had begun to supplement the work of the Guardians by supporting Public Relief Committees and providing public works in slack periods. The Unemployed Workmen Act passed in 1905 by the Conservative administration attempted to regularize such aid by establishing Distress Committees in all the large towns of over 50,000 inhabitants and by encouraging local labour exchanges and the provision of work. The appointment of the Royal Commission on the Poor Laws and the Relief of Distress at the end of 1905 symbolized the widespread conviction that a new approach to this, as to several other social problems, was now required: 'measures which only 10 years ago would have been dismissed as impracticable were now (1906) debated seriously'.[57]

In addition to the causes of this change that have been mentioned already, i.e. the discovery of widespread poverty by the new social science and the stagnation of real wages, there was also the cumulative effect of the power of civil servants, health and factory inspectors, and local government officers, who had a professional interest in further reform. Their influence must not be underrated, as 'England was becoming bureaucratic': employment in local and central government rose from 104,000 in 1891 to 226,000 in 1911.[58] Over-riding all these was the workmen's suffrage, granted by the Reform Acts of 1867 and 1884, which the working classes had learnt to manipulate.

The Labour Party, it is true, which was founded in those years, was established only as a minority pressure group, with no agreed policies of its own other than those relating to the interests of labour. Nevertheless, politicians of the two main parties began more consciously to address themselves to the new electorate. Above all, labour was to be propitiated by welfare provisions. This preoccupation subtly and imperceptibly changed the attitude of Governments: the initial drive may have been the concern to secure votes, but the effect was nonetheless that for the first time in British history 'the poor' were considered to be full citizens. What had been a matter of charity to one's inferiors was becoming a matter of rights to one's equals.[59]

[55] (Mrs) Pember Reeves, *Round About a Pound a Week* (1913), p. 214. Also see Standish Meacham, *A Life Apart: the English Working Class 1890–1914* (Cambridge, Mass., 1977).

[56] A. C. Pigou, *Unemployment* (1913); W. H. Beveridge, *Unemployment, a Problem of Industry* (1909, repr. 1930 as Part 1 of a new edition).

[57] E. H. Phelps-Brown, *Growth of British Industrial Relations* (1959), p. 253.

[58] E. Halévy, *A Short History of the English People in the Nineteenth Century*, vol. 6, *The Rule of Democracy*, Book 1 (1952 ed.), p. 262. On a different calculation, excluding 'industrial' employment, such as in dockyards, post office, gas and water works, but including teachers, the central and local authorities employed 632,000 persons in July 1914.

[59] See, in general, Gertrude Williams, *The State and the Standard of Living* (1936), esp. chapters 1 and 4.

In 1897 the Workmen's (Compensation for Accidents) Act was passed, as one of the fruits of Joseph Chamberlain's attempts to win the Conservative Party for social reforms.[60] Though limited in scope, the Act introduced a new principle, 'that the right to compensation of any person injured in the ordinary course of his employment is a public right and a national obligation'.[61] Thus what had been a private contractual relation was transformed into one of public concern. In 1899 agriculture, and by a further Act in 1906 virtually all employments, including now also many very small firms were, brought in while compensation for certain industrial diseases was also enacted. This added 6 million workers to the $7\frac{1}{4}$ million encompassed by the existing legislation.

Another one of their early subjects for legislation was the relief of the old. As a rule old age held the terror of destitution for all those who earned their bread by manual work. The existing Poor Law and its institutions were so feared and detested among respectable workmen, that the greatest hardship was suffered before resort was had to them. The Old Age Pensions Act, passed in 1908, provided for non-contributory payments, since under any sound contributory scheme at least 20 years would have had to elapse before the first pension was actually paid. All respectable persons over 70 years of age whose income did not exceed £21 a year were to receive 5s. a week (7s. 6d. for a married couple), and those with incomes of £21 to £31, proportionally smaller pensions. The 'tests' of respectability were inevitable relaxed, and by 1913 three-fifths of the population over 70 was in receipt of pensions.

In contrast with old age pensions, the two main welfare provisions embodied in the two parts of the National Insurance Act of 1911, covering health and unemployment insurance respectively, caused considerable controversy. The disagreement was in part about principles. At one extreme was the view of Sidney and Beatrice Webb, expressed in the Minority Report of the Royal Commission on the Poor Laws and the Relief of Distress (of which Beatrice was a member), favouring the 'break-up of the poor law', i.e. the provision of separate and functionally different institutions for the able-bodied unemployed, the sick, the old, the orphans and the lunatics. It also favoured a 'national minimum of civilized life', open to all, provided by the State, a kind of safety net to offer security in the face of every conceivable calamity. At the other extreme were members of the Charity Organization Society and others who feared that payments as of right would destroy the character and self-reliance of the poor, and therefore opposed them.[62]

Beside the opponents on principle, there were also the vested interests including trade unions and Friendly Societies, doctors and the 'industrial' insurance companies disagreeing about means as well as about principles, and the two could not be separated. The resulting Act was a compromise.

Both parts of the National Insurance Act had in common tripartite contributions, by employee, employer and the State, but otherwise there were great differences between them. Part II, dealing with unemployment insurance, included in the scheme seven industries only, mainly those considered most liable to cyclical fluctuation, with about $2\frac{1}{4}$ million workers in 1911, or one-sixth

[60] W. C. Mallalieu, 'Joseph Chamberlain and Workmen's Compensation', *J. Econ. Hist.*, 10/1, 1950.
[61] Quoted in Gertrude Williams, *op. cit.*, p. 145.
[62] Beatrice Webb, *Our Partnership* (1948), pp. 341–2, 383, 418, 482.

of the total industrial labour force. The benefit was 7s. a week, payable for up to 15 weeks in a year only.[63]

Part I, dealing with health insurance, by contrast, was well-nigh universal, affecting about 13 million workers. It was based on the German model, but was modified by the claims of the existing entrenched institutions, which became 'approved societies'[64] under the Act. Both schemes were thus run nominally on insurance principles, with accrued benefits as of right, and both paid out their first benefits in January 1913.[65]

The two Acts of 1908 and 1911 were flanked by other measures conceived in the same spirit. Thus the belief that much of the existing unemployment was 'frictional' led to an Act authorizing the establishment of Labour Exchanges in 1909. Under the Trade Boards Act of 1909, four Trade Boards were to be set up in the sweated trades of ready-made tailoring, paper-box making, lace making and chain making, and there were powers to make orders establishing Boards for other industries. Each Board had powers to lay down minimum time and piece wages, which were then enforceable at law. In 1913, when four more trades were added, altogether half a million workers were covered by this minimum wages legislation.[66] It represented a remarkable break with the past, and was followed quickly by the minimum wage legislation for coal miners in 1912.

Balfour's Education Act of 1902, which made a beginning with the provision of secondary eduction, was not only an important measure of social reform[67] in itself, but was also used as a basis for public health and other reforms. Thus school medical inspection, made permissive in 1902, became obligatory on local authorities in 1907 and in 1906 school meals for needy children were permitted. At about the same time, in 1908, a Children's Act made various acts of cruelty to children illegal, and in 1914 the Government undertook to subsidize milk depots, local welfare centres and other similar institutions of progressive local authorities.[68] An Act of 1902 provided for the training of midwives and the exclusion of the unqualified.

Medical interests secured two further sets of measures of far-reaching social significance. The first was a provision of the Factory and Workshops Act of 1891 under which the Home Secretary was empowered to enforce safety regulations for occupations he considered dangerous: by 1910, elaborate precautions had been enforced in 22 industries, and certain dangerous occupations prohibited altogether.[69] The other was the Housing and Town Planning Act of

[63] W. H. Beveridge, *Power and Influence* (1953); Sir Frank Tillyard and F. N. Ball, *Unemployed Insurance 1911–48* (Leigh-on-Sea, 1949), chapters 1 and 2.

[64] The 'Approved societies' were made up as follows in 1912: industrial life offices, 41·5%, friendly societies without branches, 22·8%, friendly societies with branches, 23·7%, trade unions, 11·5%, and employers' provident funds, 0·5%, of the membership of 12,390,000. Sir William Beveridge, *Social Insurance and Allied Services* (Beveridge Report) (1942. Cmd. 6404), para. 53.

[65] H. N. Bunbury (ed.), *Lloyd George's Ambulance Wagon* (1957); R. W. Harris, *National Health Insurance in Great Britain, 1911–1946* (1946), chapters 2–4; M. Bruce, *The Coming of the Welfare State* (1961), pp. 156–89.

[66] *Report of Committee on Trade Board Acts* (1922. Cmd. 1645); Stephen Gwynn and G. M. Tuckwell, *Life of Dilke*, vol. 2 (1917), chapter 52.

[67] G. A. N. Lowndes, *The Silent Social Revolution* (1937).

[68] W. M. Frazer, *History of English Public Health, 1834–1939* (1950), Part III and Part IV, sections 1 and 2; J. M. Mackintosh, *Trends of Opinion about the Public Health, 1901–1951* (1953), sections 1 and 2.

[69] H. A. Mess, *Factory Legislation and its Administration, 1891–1924* (1926), chapters 2–9.

1909, representing for the first time a positive, rather than a restrictive, approach to the building of towns and cities.[70]

Hours of work were regulated by Shop Acts in 1904 and 1911, and in the mines by the Miners' Eight Hours Act of 1908.[71] Lastly, the previously ineffective legislation to provide for small holdings for agricultural workers and others was replaced by the Small Holdings and Allotments Act of 1907, which enabled the Board of Agriculture to induce County Councils to use their compulsory powers to acquire land for small holdings. By 1914, 14,000 small holdings had come into existence under the Act.[72]

Views on the new social legislation did not as a rule differ along party lines: the political battle was fought out over the raising of the necessary finance. From 1908 onward, the Liberals attempted to use the growing tax burden itself as a weapon to redistribute income in favour of the poorer classes, but it was the budget for 1909/10, the first to be presented by Lloyd George, that was the basis of the most bitter party strife, and of a major constitutional crisis, two General Elections and the Parliament Act of 1911. The most controversial issue in this 'People's Budget' was the imposition of the 'land taxes', designed to tax part of the 'unearned increment' in land values – a stock proposal of Radical reformers for decades, but bitterly opposed by the 'landlords' House of Lords which attempted for the last time to throw out a money bill. It was not until 1911 that normal budgeting was resumed.[73]

These and other budgetary reforms represented a not insignificant transfer of purchasing power from the rich to the poor. Direct taxation, as a proportion of revenue, was raised steadily from about 50% in the years 1901–1905 to 57·5% in 1912/13, at a time when the working classes were virtually excluded from its incidence. The stormy last years of peace saw not only the foundations laid for the present Welfare State, but also the faint beginnings of the use of the budget, not merely to provide the means of the Government's expenditure, but also as an instrument of social policy.

4 Economic Control and the Effects of War on British Industry

When Britain declared war on Germany and her allies in August 1914, it was almost a century since a major war had been fought by this country and its lessons had long since been forgotten. In spite of some relevant parallels in the Boer War,[74] there was no experience of the economic stresses and the industrial efforts involved in a modern full-scale struggle. Moreover, there was the belief, common at the outbreak of all wars, that it would be short.

In so far as the economic problems were considered, they were thought of as specific, not general. It was recognized, for example, that recruitment for the army would have to be greatly expanded, that the Government would have to be prepared to borrow heavily and that foreign trade and the foreign exchanges

[70] W. Ashworth, *The Genesis of Modern British Town Planning* (1954), chapter 7.

[71] B. McCormick and J. E. Williams, 'The Miners and the Eight-Hour Day, 1863–1910', *Ec. Hist. Rev.*, N. S., 12/2, 1959.

[72] Hermann Levy, *Large and Small Holdings* (Cambridge, 1911), chapter 8; W. Hasbach, *History of the English Agricultural Labourer* (1908), chapters 5 and 6.

[73] J. F. Rees, *A Short Fiscal and Financial History of England, 1815–1918* (1921), chapter 7.

[74] Clive Trebilcock, 'War and the Failure of Industrial Mobilisation: 1899 and 1914', in J. M. Winter (ed.), *War and Economic Development* (Cambridge, 1975).

were likely to be affected. But apart from these and a few minor actions of a specific nature there would be 'business as usual'.[75]

In practice, until Lloyd George's Ministry of December 1916, which formed a watershed in the conduct of the war, the apparatus of Government control was limited almost entirely to such specific examples of intervention, though they were more extensive than had at first been assumed. Thus early measures of control had to be taken over the railways, over much shipping, and over sugar (drawn largely from the Central Powers in peace-time) and over wheat supplies, while the War Office, in order to secure its own supplies at, reasonable prices, of meat, jute (for sandbags), flax, wool (for blankets) and Indian kips (for boots), had to assume responsibility for competing civilian supplies also. But in general, 'it was thought preferable to rely on private enterprise and the laws of supply and demand'; 'a prosperous state of trade, regular employment at good wages and high profits for the Revenue to tax and the Treasury to borrow, were regarded with good reason as essential conditions for the successful prosecution of the war'.[76]

This attitude failed to reckon with the sheer magnitude of the military demand in an all-out war against a European power under modern conditions, and with the distortions that this would impart to the civilian part of the economy. What appeared at first as a specific need or shortage often quickly became a symptom of a much wider alteration in supply and demand relationships. Some relatively minor control, to deal with an immediate issue, often had repercussions which required Government intervention further and further back, until the State found itself directing a major part of the country's industries, and controlling or licensing most of the remainder. Thus a sudden demand for blankets would set up an immediate rise in the price and lead to the hoarding of wool tops, which would affect other sectors of the woollen and worsted industries; and this, in turn, might affect British agriculture or imports from Australia, and so on in unending progression. This lesson was learnt slowly, because it was learnt reluctantly. It was driven home, first of all, in the 'munitions' industry, the industry most immediately affected.

'Munitions' included arms and ammunition, transport of all kinds, including aircraft, and optical instruments used by the Forces. Deficiencies in their supply appeared with the very first recruiting drive of the war, but all that was done to meet the sudden flow of demand was to give the Service Departments virtually unlimited spending power, and it was hoped that by offering sufficiently high prices, the supplies would be forthcoming. In the circumstances, the price mechanism was quite unable to bring about the switch in resources of the required vast magnitude. The need for physical controls was all the more easily accepted in this field, since the main shortage, that of shells, was causing serious losses at the front and was turned into a major political issue as the 'Great Shell Scandal'.[77]

Greater powers given to the Government under the Defence of the Realm Act (DORA) in March 1915 to take over any existing factory or workshop

[75] Samuel J. Hurwitz, *State Intervention in Great Britain, A Study of Economic Control and Social Response, 1914–1919* (New York, 1949), chapter 2.
[76] E. M. H. Lloyd, *Experiments in State Control* (Oxford, 1924), pp. 22, 23, 261.
[77] D. Lloyd George, *War Memoirs*, vol. 1 (1933); *History of the Ministry of Munitions*, vol. 1 (1922).

making munitions failed to speed the supply of shells. By May 1915, the new Ministry of Munitions under Loyd George found that it had to cast its net of control and direction very wide indeed. One of the first necessities was an expansion of the labour force in the industry. This was done, first by blocking the enlistment of skilled engineering and metal workers, and next by organizing a large-scale recruiting drive of workers from outside the industry to provide for expansion.

For this, the consent of the trade unions concerned had first to be obtained. In the Treasury Agreement of March 1915, the unions were to permit 'dilution', i.e. the substitution of skilled labour by unskilled or semi-skilled men and women and to suspend other cherished trade union practices including the right to strike, and accept arbitration instead, for the duration of the war. In return, the trade unions obtained a guarantee that their practices would be restored at the end of the war, that the concessions would apply to munitions firms only, and that profits in these 'controlled' firms would be limited to the pre-war level plus an excess of one-fifth. By September 1915, 715 of the main engineering establishments were thus 'controlled'.

The Munitions Act incorporating all this, formed the beginning of a system of Government-directed production of the weapons of war, which quickly included Government-owned shell factories, the purchase and control of the supply and distribution of certain metals and chemicals, and a whole network of regulations stretching back to the raw material supply.[78] From a beginning of 20 clerks in the Army Contracts Department in August 1914, the Ministry of Munitions had grown to employ a staff of 65,000 by November 1918; it controlled the employment of 2 million workers directly, and 3·4 million all told; it managed 250 Government factories, quarries and mines and supervised operations in 20,000 'controlled' establishments; and between June 1915 and March 1919 it disbursed £2,000 million.

Munitions formed only one particular case of growing strains and stresses in the economy. By the end of 1916 it had become abundantly clear that the free price mechanism had failed to serve the country at war since it could also serve to divert resources to private luxury consumption.[79] Price rises led to profiteering, but did not bring forth increased supplies. What was required was a comprehensive system of control, using all available means together.[80]

The apparatus of control, as perfected in 1917 and 1918, used many different methods. There was direct control of productive capacity; there was State purchase of raw materials, especially abroad; there were restrictions of dealings, especially of imports and exports, by licensing and other means, and similar restrictions of capital expenditure. There was also price fixing; control of distribution, both of consumer goods and of raw materials; and control of labour, including military conscription, first undertaken with selected groups in March 1916. By the end of the war, the Government had direct charge of shipping, railways and canal transport; it purchased about 90% of all the imports and marketed over 80% of the food consumed at home, besides controlling most of

[78] J. Hurstfield, 'The Control of British Raw Material Supplies, 1919–1939', *Ec. Hist. Rev.*, 14/1–2, 1944, p. 2.

[79] E. Crammond, 'The Cost of the War', *J. R. Stat. S.*, 78/3, 1915, p. 399.

[80] The best concise discussion will be found in E. V. Morgan, *Studies in British Financial Policy, 1914–25* (1952), chapter 2.

the prices. Direct or indirect control over industry and agriculture was virtually all-pervasive. It may be illustrated by two examples: shipping and food consumption.

At the outbreak of hostilities, Britain possessed about 42% of the world's ocean-going steamer tonnage, much of which was unemployed. There therefore, appeared to be little cause to fear a shortage of shipping.

Some 4 million tons were at once requisitioned out of the total sea-going tonnage of 19 million gross tons in 1914, and by 1916 the requisitioned vessels, for British and Allied Governments, rose to 37% of the total. Four million tons of shipping were immobilized in enemy ports and elsewhere; mercantile launchings were down to one third of normal; enemy submarines had sunk 1·7 million tons and, on longer routes, loss of manpower and congestion in the ports had slowed traffic. On the other hand, as compensating factors, measures were taken to speed turnround in the ports, shipping space was controlled and rationed, and much enemy tonnage had been captured or impounded. Altogether, until about August 1916 these two tendencies roughly cancelled out, and the supply and demand for tonnage were not seriously out of step.

Nevertheless, because of the piecemeal or specific form of Government control in its requisitioning and re-directing of an ever larger share of the tonnage, the Government had so depleted the 'free' shipping available that in a market of notoriously inelastic demand, freights rocketed in some cases to four or five times their peace-time level. To the outcry caused by this profiteering was added a real major shipping crisis, as with unrestricted U-boat warfare from 1 February 1917, annual sinkings reached 3,730,000 gross tons of British shipping alone. Neutral shipping was driven away from British ports; convoy sailings and other precautions reduced the efficiency of the remaining fleet; and the failure of the North American harvest in 1916 forced Britain to divert ships to the longer Australian run for the home wheat supply.

Under the new Shipping Controller in the spring of 1917 all available liners were put on the North Atlantic track to collect grain, the whole of the liner tonnage was requisitioned, imports were restricted by licence, and in January 1918 coastal vessels came under much closer direct control. These vigorous measures kept the supply lines to Britain open, even though the tonnage 'deficit' had risen to 3 million tons by February 1918, while a further 20% was tied up in direct military service. The total losses were 7¾ million tons (38% of the tonnage under the British flag in 1914), and the tonnage available at the armistice was 18% less than at the declaration of war.[81]

Among the most complex schemes of control relating to foodstuffs was that evolved for meat, since it had to cover both imports and home-grown meat for both military and civilian use. Shortages began to appear early in 1917. The first measure taken was a price control on retail butchers, who, it was hoped, would be forced to lower their own bids for meat and thus reduce prices all down the line to the farmer or stockbreeder. This policy worked for a time, but towards the end of 1917, the Government had to step in by ordering heavy slaughtering and purchasing all meat from the farm from December–January 1917–18 onwards. All the firms engaged in slaughtering and wholesaling were

[81] C. E. Fayle, *The War and the Shipping Industry* (1927), and *History of the Great War: Seaborne Trade*, 3 vols. (1920, 1923, 1924); Sir Arthur Salter, *Allied Shipping Control* (1921).

turned into agents of the Government by April 1918 and finally meat was rationed to consumers.[82]

Food control in general was largely seen in terms of its effects on industrial unrest. The conjunction of shortages of supply, unwarranted price increases ('profiteering') and maldistribution was liable to touch on a peculiarly sensitive spot in the morale of the working population,[83] since 50–60% of the typical working-class household budget was still being spent on food and drink, and it was the workers whose consumption was reduced first when shortages pushed up prices. In July 1917, the prices of wheat, sugar and meat were fixed. Within the next six months, a food crisis of major proportions had enlarged the scope of the Ministry beyond all expectation.

Britain was at no time in actual danger of starvation or even malnutrition. The food crisis of November 1917 to February 1918 was, in fact, largely psychological: fear of shortages set up a tendency to hoard and created the conditions of highly inelastic demand in which a slight shortfall was translated into a substantial price rise. By November 1917 all the main categories of food were price-controlled, control reaching back in some cases through several earlier stages of production, and the bread subsidy began on 1 September. The first commodity to be rationed was sugar, the supply of which began to decline seriously. Some 2,000 local Food Control Committes were appointed to deal with sugar rationing, and the system adopted was essentially one of 'registration' with certain shops. By December 1917 shortages appeared in meat, butter, margarine, tea, bacon and cheese. The solution adopted was to ration sales locally, not nationally as in the case of sugar.

Food rationing proved difficult to abolish immediately after the war: the milk control scheme only *began* in the winter of 1918–19. The Ministry of Food was not wound up until March 1921,[84] but few other war-time controls which survived long into the early disturbed post-war years. '"Back to 1914" became a common cry',[85] and by the middle of 1922 virtually the whole machinery of Government control was dismantled.

As far as British industry in general was concerned, its total output had hardly declined at all in the years of war, in spite of the mobilization of 5,700,000 men in the fighting services, of shortages of materials and of losses at sea.[86] These results were achieved largely by longer hours of labour and more intensive work, by better organization, better equipment and better management. Even those who had been most critical of Britain's competitive position before 1914 had to admit that the stimulus of war had infused a fresh spirit of enterprise into British industry.[87]

[82] E. M. H. Lloyd, *Experiments in State Control* (Oxford, 1924).
[83] E. Cannan, 'Industrial Unrest', *Econ. J.*, 27/108, 1917, p. 456.
[84] W. H. Beveridge, *British Food Control* (1928).
[85] R. H. Tawney, 'The Abolition of Economic Controls, 1918–21', *Ec. Hist. Rev.*, 13/1–2, 1943, p. 14; S. M. H. Armitage, *The Politics of Decontrol of Industry: Britain and the United States* (1969); A. T. Lauterbach, 'Economic Demobilization in Britain after the First World War', *Political Science Quarterly* 57, 1942; A. C. Pigou, 'Government Control in War and Peace', *Econ. J.*, 28/112, 1918, p. 363; also *Aspects of British Economic History, 1918–1925* (1948 ed.), Part IV.
[86] W. G. Hoffmann, *British Industry, 1700–1950* (Oxford, 1955), Table 54; T. M. Ridley, 'Industrial Production in the UK, 1900–1953', *Economica*, 22/85, 1955.
[87] E.g. the articles in the *Economic Journal*, reprinted in J. W. Lea, *Britain's Decline* (Birmingham, 1922).

Scientific research, for example, unduly neglected by British industrialists, was stimulated by the Government which set up in July 1915 a department to promote science research in industry. In 1916 it became the Department of Scientific and Industrial Research, sponsoring research not only directly in universities and elsewhere, but also encouraging industry to set up its own research associations.[88]

Some industries had hardly existed at all in this country before the war and had to be established in war-time to maintain supplies formerly drawn from Germany. They included the making of scientific instruments, of ball bearings, of chemical and laboratory glassware, of tungsten and of chemical products including benzol, toluol and ammonia liquor.[89] Others, again, had been in infancy in 1914 and grew to manhood only because of military demands, the most important being the aircraft industry.

In general, the 'practical application (of control) to munitions and non-munitions industries, aided by the control of materials and the operation of the priority principle, resulted in an enormous increase in output, more efficient industries, and great economies in production'.[90] Again, the need to provide figures for cost-plus contracts, as well as for Excess Profits Duty, introduced up-to-date accounting practices into many firms. In its turn, the Government was obliged to collect new sets of statistics which could be of assistance to industrial management.[91]

Further, the controls and allocation and rationing schemes 'stimulated organization, advertised rationalization'; and broke 'down trade jealousies and secrecies'.[92] Among major industries, engineering was changed most. 'It would probably be true to say that no country in the world could show such a high level of workmanship, or so much out-of-date machinery.'[93] Under the stress of the voracious demands for arms, ammunition, motor vehicles and machinery for other war-important industries, the Government was soon forced to impose rationalization.

Much of the war-time capacity in engineering could be scrapped after the war with little hardship on capital or labour. What remained was new methods such as automatic welding, or the use of limit gauges by unskilled labour, as well as new techniques of management.

Shipbuilding was less fortunate. The heavy sinkings beginning at the end of 1916 had forced an enlargement of the mercantile building programme, while the USA and some neutral countries also enlarged their building capacity. When the transport difficulties and dislocations of 1919 simulated a world shipping shortage,[94] world output reached almost $5\frac{1}{2}$ million tons in 1919, 7 million in

[88] R. S. Sayers, 'The Springs of Technical Progress in Britain, 1919–1939', *Econ. J.*, 60/238, 1950, pp. 279–80; R. S. Edwards, *Co-operative Industrial Research* (1950), chapter 4; Sir Harry Melville, *The Department of Scientific and Industrial Research* (1962), chapter 2.

[89] E.g. C. M. Whittaker, 'The British Coal-Tar Colour Industry and its Difficulties in Times of War', *J. Royal Soc. of Arts*, 65/8 Dec. 1916; Roy and Kay MacLeod, 'Government and the Optical Industry in Britain, 1914–18', in J. M. Winter (ed.), *War and Economic Development* (Cambridge, 1975); H. and S. Rose, *Science and Society* (1969), chapter 3.

[90] *History of the Ministry of Munitions* (1922), vol. 7, Part 1, p. 87.

[91] E. M. H. Lloyd, *Experiments in State Control* (Oxford, 1924), pp. 389–92.

[92] R. H. Tawney, 'Abolition of Economic Controls, 1918–21', *Ec. Hist. Rev.*, 13/1–2, 1943, p. 8; *Ministry of Munitions*, vol. 7, Part 1, p. 102.

[93] *Ministry of Munitions*, vol. 7, Part 1, p. 94.

[94] Fayle, *The War and the Shipping Industry*, chapters 21, 25; p. 17 above.

1920 and nearly 6 million in 1921 and afterwards collapsed. Thus the main legacy of the war was a greatly inflated building capacity, which had to compete against an even more inflated capacity elsewhere.

Owing to the war-time demand for armaments and ships, the steelmaking capacity of the country was enlarged by 50%, though much of this was completed only in the years 1919–20. Capacity in the rest of the world was also greatly and permanently enlarged in war-time. The subsequent decline in world demand and in output was less steep than in shipbuilding, but it was still sufficient to make over-capacity a permanent feature of the inter-war years.[95]

In this period of Government-stimulated growth, some major technical changes were taken in hand. By far the most important was the long-overdue expansion of basic open-hearth capacity to make use of the extensive ore fields of the East Midlands in place of the high-grade ore from overseas. This change to open-hearth furnaces also allowed steelmakers to use more scrap and waste, and during the war years the steel scrap ratio was raised from 15% to 50%. The new works were more efficient than much of the existing capacity in other respects also.

War conditions gave the industry 'a taste of collective research'.[96] New alloys for aircraft and tanks were developed; metallurgists were learning to improve the tensile strength of steel, were perfecting manufacturing methods of cupro-nickel, were learning to build up worn mechanical parts by electro-deposit methods, and were introducing extrusion processes for brass rod and copper tubing.[97] However, the expansion of capacity during the war largely took the form of extensions to existing works: this prevented a major shift in favour of the areas with the lowest costs.

Beside the munitions industry and the metallurgical and chemical industries associated with it, the sectors of the economy most affected by the war were agriculture, coal mining and rail transport. At the outbreak of war, Britain imported from abroad four-fifths of the cereals consumed, two-fifths of the meat, three-quarters of the fruit, besides all the sugar and colonial products and substantial proportions of other foodstuffs. Yet no special attention was paid to the food supply of the country in the first two years of the war. By 1916 shipping losses and a poor harvest in North America forced Britain to expand her home supply by ploughing up pasture land for potatoes and, above all, grain.[98] For the harvest year of 1917 about one million acres were added to tillage and, for 1918, some 3 million acres more than in 1916 were ploughed up. Compared with the average harvests of 1904–13, the wheat production increased from 1·56 million to 2.58 million tons, oats from 3·04 to 4·46 million, barley from 1·52 to 1·56 and potatoes from 6·59 to 9·22 million tons in 1918.[99] This was achieved at the cost of reducing the grassland by $3\frac{1}{2}$ million acres and decreasing the home output of milk and meat.[100]

[95] T. H. Burnham and G. O. Hoskins, *Iron and Steel in Britain, 1870–1930* (1943); M. S. Birkett, 'The Iron and Steel Trades during the War', *J. R. Stat. S.*, 83/3, 1920.

[96] D. L. Burn, *The Economic History of Steelmaking, 1867–1939* (Cambridge, 1940), pp. 350, 369.

[97] *Ministry of Munitions*, vol. 7, Part 1, chapter 6, and vol. 7, Part 2.

[98] G. P. Jones and A. G. Pool, *A Hundred Years of Economic Development* (1959 ed.), chapter 16; A. S. Milward, *The Economic Effects of the two World Wars on Britain* (1984), p. 29.

[99] T. H. Middleton, *Food Production in War* (Oxford, 1923), pp. 112, 154, 192, 241.

[100] E.g., Sir R. Henry Rew, 'The Progress of British Agriculture', Pres. Address, *J. R. Stat. S.*, 85/1, 1922.

To help the British farmer in these efforts, the Food Production Department of the Board of Agriculture distributed and allocated scarce fertilizer and equipment; it supplied 22,000 men, including prisoners of war, 300,000 part-time women workers and a women's land army which at its maximum numbered 16,000. Above all, it sent out several thousand tractors to open up a new era in British farming. The tractor remained a permanent feature of British agriculture, but the distribution of land between pasture and the different crops reverted quickly to the pre-war proportions and the crops of 1924–8 (excluding the Irish Free State) bore a striking resemblance to the crops grown in 1909–13.[101]

In coal mining, after a decline of 11% of output, and a loss of a quarter of a million men in the first year of war, there was built up a most complex system of control, beginning with price control and export licensing in 1915 and ending, in 1918, with a state of virtual nationalization of the mines. During the period of control, the State determined capital investment, it 'zoned' all coal supplies to save transport, and it allocated scarce resources, in particular pit props, by central direction. The reason for the close official control of the coal mines was only in part the need to maintain the supply of a basic fuel and raw material; in large measure it sprang from the desire to keep down the price of coal to consumers while permitting miners' wages to rise in line with other wages and the cost of living. Wages were subsidized out of the very high prices secured by that part of the coal output that was exported. As soon as the post-war boom collapsed – export prices fell from 80s. to 40s. a ton in one month, December 1920 – and industrial relations deteriorated into bitter hostility, the Government withdrew and handed the mines over to the former owners in March 1921. The legacies of the war were, therefore, a capacity larger than normal peace-time exports could warrant, and a bitter hostility between employers and workers.[102]

The British railway companies were taken over by the Government on the outbreak of war, and administered as a single unit by a Railway Executive Committee. The ending of competition permitted many economies to be introduced, such as the closing of duplicated services over rival lines and the pooling of rolling stock. Rates and fares, like coal prices, were held down in order to stabilize the cost of living. After the War, the Railway Act of 1921 forced all existing lines, apart from some suburban and some light railways, into four companies, to be privately owned and run for profit.[103]

In contrast with the industries enumerated so far, cotton may be taken as an example of an industry which was not considered of importance to the war, and in which recruitment for the Forces proceeded apace, unhindered by badges or starred lists, though much of the labour force was female and remained at home. A Cotton Control Board was set up by the Board of Trade in June 1917 with the objective of rationing out the limited supplies of American cotton. Restriction of output was achieved by limiting the proportions of spindles and looms that could be worked, and collecting a levy on those worked in excess.

[101] A. W. Flux, 'Our Food Supply Before and After the War', Pres. Addres, *J. R. Stat. S.*, 93/4, 1930.

[102] R. A. S. Redmayne, *The British Coal Mining Industry During the War* (Oxford, 1923); W. H. B. Court, 'Problems of the British Coal Industry Between the Wars', *Ec. Hist. Rev.*, 15/1–2, 1945; M. W. Kirby, *The British Coalmining Industry 1870–1946* (1977), chapters 2 and 3.

[103] E. A. Pratt, *British Railways and the Great War*, 2 vols. (1921), esp. chapters 8, 9, 11, 47, 48, 49, 74; C. E. R. Sherrington, *The Economics of Rail Transport in Britain*, vol. 1 (1928), chapter 12.

The workers, most of whom agreed to be stood off a week at a time on a 'rota' system, received unemployment benefit out of the levies so collected.[104] The temporary success of the scheme was largely due to the fact that the reduction was in the supply of the raw material, not in the demand, so that its costs could be borne by the public who were charged higher prices.

Thus the war taught British industry collaboration and organization: trade associations for raw material allocation, common research projects, for price control or other purposes were formed in many industries for the first time.[105] The war also taught the country to look at its national equipment in a new light, not as private property alone, but as the capital helping to provide the national income. This was particularly so in industries administered nationally, like shipping, the railways or the coal mines, and it was no accident that it was under the influence of war that the compulsory amalgamation of collieries and nationalization of coal royalties, as well as a national electricity grid were first seriously considered,[106] or that protection of 'key' industries found general favour.

5 Finance and Trade During the War

At the outbreak of war it was assumed that the task of the Chancellor of the Exchequer would simply be the collection of sufficient funds, both by taxation and by borrowing, to allow the Government to bid in the open market, in competition with others, for such commodities and services as it required. By early 1917 it had become clear that there was a further objective in the removal of funds from private hands in which they would have helped to raise prices and divert resources to inessential uses.[107] 'In the face of extravagance and inflation', wrote the *Economist*,[108] 'the only cure was surely taxation or compulsory borrowing which alone could have taken out of the hands of thoughtless and ignorant people the power to warp the economic energy of the country from the war work on which it should be concentrated.'

Faced with the need to enlarge revenue at once, the first reaction of the Chancellor of the Exchequer was to increase the burden evenly over all the different groups of taxpayers. Thus in November 1914, the income tax and supertax rates were doubled, at the same time as the rates of duty on beer and tea were raised.[109] In the long run, however, it was clear that the taxes on consumption, falling mainly on the poor, would merely lead to demands for higher wages. Thus the main additional burden of taxation had to fall on the direct taxes. The 'normal' rate of income tax was raised, by steps, from 1s. 2d. in the pound in 1913–14 to 6s. in the two years 1918–19 and 1919–20, while the exemption limit was lowered from £160 to £130 in 1915.[110] Supertax rates were similarly raised. To these direct taxes was added the Excess Profits Duty,

[104] H. D. Henderson, *The Cotton Control Board* (Oxford, 1922).

[105] K. Middlemas, *Politics in Industrial Society* (1979), chapters 3 and 4; J. M. Rees, *Trusts in British Industry, 1914–21* (1922), p. 27.

[106] R. H. Tawney, 'Abolition', p. 11; Redmayne, *op. cit.*, pp. 81–2; *Ministry of Munitions*, vol. 8, Part 3, chapter 4.

[107] E.g. Hartley Withers, *Our Money and the State* (1917); A. W. Kirkaldy (ed.), *Industry and Finance* (1917), Preface; cf. also A. C. Pigou, *The Economy and Finance of the War* (1916).

[108] *The Economist*, 5 May 1917.

[109] D. Lloyd George, *War Memoirs*, vol. 1 (1933), pp. 116–19.

[110] Sir Bernard Mallet and C. Oswald George, *British Budgets (Second Series), 1913–14 to 1920–21* (1929), pp. 324–5; T. J. Kiernan, *British War Finance and the Consequences* (1920).

beginning with the second budget of 1915. Like the Munitions Levy, which preceded it, EPD was designed in part to meet the popular complaints of profiteering. It was subject to much evasion, delay and fraudulent practices. Yet it yielded, until its repeal in 1921, £1,154 million, or one-quarter of the total tax revenue in this period.[111]

By these means, as well as the simple effect of the inflation, the yield from direct taxes was raised from £94 million in 1913–14 to £508 million in 1917–18 and £721 million in 1919–20, or as a proportion of total tax revenue, from 57·5% in 1913–14 to about 80% in the last two years of war, to fall again to 68·2% in 1920–1. Indirect taxes, therefore, increased relatively much less. They included the entertainments duty, easy to collect and acceptable as taxing a 'luxury', and the so-called 'McKenna Duties' introduced in 1915. These were a tax of 33⅓% *ad valorem* on such luxuries as motor cars and cycles, watches and clocks and musical instruments, and a specific duty on film. The strong concentration of the additional taxation on direct taxes tended to increase somewhat the redistributive effect of the tax system, at least in the higher ranges.[112] This shift towards greater equality was mainly based on the belief that there was little additional taxable capacity left among the poor, so that all the additions had to come from the pockets of the rich.

By these means, revenue was increased fourfold to 1918–19 and sevenfold to 1920–1, the peak year; in real terms, it was more than doubled. Expenditure, however, grew at a vastly greater rate, as shown in Table 1·1.

Table 1·1:   Revenue and expenditure, United Kingdom

Financial year	Revenue £m.	Expenditure £m.	Surplus or déficit	
1913–14	198·2	197·5	+0·7	—
1914–15	226·7	560·5	—	−333·8
1915–16	336·8	1,559·2	—	−1,222·4
1916–17	573·4	2,198·1	—	−1,624·7
1917–18	707·2	2,696·2	—	−1,989·0
1918–19	889·0	2,579·3	—	−1,690·3
1919–20	1,339·6	1,665·8	—	−326·2
1920–21	1,426·0	1,195·4	+230·6	—

It will be noted that revenue did not fully meet expenditure until almost two years after the armistice. Further, it is evident that had taxation been as vigorous in the early years as it became later in the war, borrowing could have been kept down to more manageable proportions, especially before 1917.[113]

It was a mixture of motives which induced successive Chancellors to be gentle with taxpayers in the first three years of the war. At first, the duration, the cost, and the price rises of the war were greatly underestimated, nor would the public have been ready for higher taxation in the early years. Moreover, the

   [111] J. R. Hicks, U. K. Hicks and L. Rostas, *The Taxation of War Wealth* (Oxford, 1941); A. W. Kirkaldy (ed.), *British Finance, During and After the War, 1914–21* (1921), chapter 7.
   [112] Rt Hon Herbert Samuel, 'The Taxation of the Various Classes of the People', Pres. Address, *J. R. Stat. S.*, 82/2, 1919; Mallet and George, *op. cit.*, Table XXI.
   [113] J. M. Keynes, *A Treatise on Money* (1930), vol. 2, pp. 170–6; W. Ashworth, *An Economic History of England, 1870–1939* (1960), pp. 270–3.

Government was not, apparently, averse in principle to raising most of its war expenditure by borrowing as long as the sums raised in taxation were sufficient to meet the interest and the sinking fund for repayments on the debts outstanding, besides the normal peace-time expenditure.

Contemporaries were much preoccupied with the 'burden' of the vast national debt created during the war which, by modern measurement, increased from 0.258 of national income in 1913 to 1.569 by 1919. By 1917–19, much of the borrowing was made in depreciated pounds and at high rates. The average interest on the war debt was 4·65%, but several loans had been issued at less than par. Had the Government taken firmer measures to discourage other forms of investment, it could have secured far more favourable rates.[114] This large deadweight debt, together with a floating debt which rose from £16 million at the outbreak of war to a maximum of £1,570 million in June 1919, created most serious problems for the Treasury in the post-war years.

More important, perhaps, was the question how far the fiscal policy of successive Chancellors succeeded in diverting the necessary resources to the Government's war effort with the greatest possible efficiency and the least possible disturbance.[115] With private capital issues still running at an average of £52 million per annum in the years 1915–18, Government borrowings in 1914–17 were at about three times the pre-war level of savings,[116] and the deficit alone amounted to one-third of the national income in 1915–16 and to 40% of the national income in 1917–18. Budget policy was clearly the major factor in the war-time rise of prices. The ever-increasing stream of credit made necessary by it was ultimately fed by an unlimited issue of currency notes.[117]

In place of the pre-war bank notes backed by a highly sensitive gold reserve, there were now 'currency notes' in circulation, created by the Treasury early in August 1914, in denominations of £1 and 10s. as Britain came off the Gold Standard. The Treasury issued these notes freely to the public *via* the Bank of England and the joint-stock banks. The Bank was obliged to open a 'Currency Note Redemption Account', which became, in effect, a lender to the Government and a means of creating credit.

The direct inflationary effect of these notes was, however, small. High-powered money increased from £237 million in 1913 to £531 million in 1918 and to a peak of £658·8 million in 1920. The M3 multiplier, however, which included bank deposits, remained steady at about 3·9[118]. The share of the financial system in the price rise during the war was thus largely the creation of sufficient liquidity to allow the inflationary budgeting to proceed unchecked. The only decline was registered in the quantity of gold in the hands of the public.[119] Most of the gold was absorbed by the Bank of England, the holdings of which rose from about £30 million before the war to £87 million at the end of 1914, £107 million in 1918 and a peak of £155 million in 1920.

In addition, there occurred a real cost inflation from the middle of 1915 to

---

[114] Frank L. McVey, *The Financial History of Great Britain, 1914–1918* (New York, 1918).

[115] The best account will be found in E. V. Morgan, *Studies*, pp. 99 ff.

[116] Morgan, *op. cit.*, pp. 41–2, 264.

[117] Committee on Currency and Foreign Exchanges after the War, *First Interim Report* (1918), para. 10, reprinted in T. E. Gregory, *Banking Statutes and Reports*, vol. 2.

[118] Cf. also Mallet and George, *op. cit.*, p. 374.

[119] Forrest Capie and Alan Webber, *A Monetary History of the United Kingdom 1870–1982*, vol. I (1985), pp. 52–3, 76–7.

the middle of 1917, aided by such outside factors as shortage of materials and labour, losses at sea and consequent rises in freight and insurance costs, and rising costs of imports. From June 1917 until the middle of 1919, price control kept rises in the cost of living again to a minimum.[120]

If the consumer was considered only very belatedly, the financial institutions of this country were protected by a large number of comprehensive measures from the very beginning. At the outbreak of war, London was a long-term and probably also a short-term creditor to the rest of the world,[121] besides being its main foreign exchange market. There was thus no question of a foreign exchange crisis, or a gold drain, in London itself: on the contrary, in the critical days of late July and early August 1914, the world was engaged in attempting to make payments to London.

What strain there was, was internal. The joint-stock banks, in anticipation of demands for accommodation by the acceptance houses, called in their loans, and tried to strengthen their own position with the Bank of England. As a result, between 22 July and 1 August, the Bank of England's reserve fell from £29.3 million to £10 million.

On 1 August, the Bank raised its discount rate to the panic level of 10%, but in the then state of the City, this was not considered sufficient. A Bank Holiday was declared to Thursday, 6 August inclusive, in order to give five clear days for emergency measures. On 1 August, the Government authorized an increase in the fiduciary issue if necessary; in the next few days the decision to issue £1 and 10s. Treasury notes, mentioned earlier, was taken. Other early measures to steady the money market included a general debt moratorium on 6 August, and a scheme, announced on 31 October, to help those who held shares on margins and might be hit by the expected price falls. Altogether, the Government guaranteed about £500 million of securities, many of them enemy securities.[122]

These elaborate and costly defences of the financial system at a time when the greatest sacrifices were demanded from the rest of the nation, turned out to have been largely unnecessary. There was no sign of a run on banks, no drain of gold abroad; most of the internal drain seems to have been to the coffers of the joint-stock banks.

But careful measures of protection continued, and the financial institutions survived the war with few outward changes. The most important was the virtual completion of the process of amalgamation among the large banks. By 1920, there were only 20 independent banks left in England and Wales, having 7,257 branches between them, but of these, the five largest companies controlled 83% of the deposits.[123]

Public disquiet about the elimination of competition let to the appointment of a Treasury Committee which reported in 1918.[124] It considered further

---

[120] Morgan, *op. cit.*, pp. 291 ff.; S. E. Harris, *Monetary Problems of the British Empire* (New York, 1941), Part II, Book 4.

[121] Arthur I. Bloomfield, *Short-Term Capital Movements under the Pre-War Gold Standard* (Princeton, N.J. 1963).

[122] This account, as much else in this section, is based on Morgan, *op cit.* Also A. W. Kirkaldy (ed.), *British Finance, 1914–21*, chapters 1 and 2, and *Credit, Industry and the War* (1915), p. 197; R. G. Hawtrey, *A Century of Bank Rate* (1938), p. 125; R. S. Sayers, *Central Banking After Bagehot* (1957), p. 67; D. Lloyd George, *War Memoirs*, vol 1 (1933), pp. 101 ff.

[123] T. E. Gregory, *The Westminster Bank Through a Century*, vol. 2 (1936), p. 10.

[124] The Report is reprinted in Gregory, *Statutes and Reports*, vol. 2.

amalgamations to be undesirable and the banks agreed to follow the recommendations of the Committee. Thus banking in this country has remained an
oligopoly, yet strongly competitive in some respects.

In its external relationships the British economy had entered the war in a
strong position; even against the USA the annual claims of interest, dividends
and service charges brought in a sum approaching $400 million in dollar
exchange. Elsewhere, as country after country closed its Exchange and declared
a moratorium, and only New York remained open, the debtors of several
continents turned to it to use their dollar securities and holdings as means of
payment to London. American houses, obliged to make these remittances to
London, could not offset them because of the moratoria, 'so that New York, as
the centre of American finance, was called to pay one side of a running account
for the whole world'.[125]

By early 1915, however, as British productive capacity was switched from
exports to war production, and as exports of merchandise, as well as of shipping
and financial services, consequently began to fall off, while imports held up to
supply the booming war factories, the balance of payments began to turn heavily
against Britain. The USA, in particular, became a source of imports of all kinds
for which no equivalent goods or services could be exported, directly or *via*
another country. Gold was transferred to America by the Bank of England and
from Ottawa, and some dollar securities were sold, but the exchanges kept
falling from $4·86 in January to $4·76$\frac{1}{4}$ in July, $4·55$\frac{1}{2}$ in September and $4·49
in October. It became clear that the British deficits on current account with the
USA were of an order of magnitude which was beyond the power of the gold
reserve to sustain.

The monetary reserves, which in 1914 amounted to $165 million in central
gold reserves and $600 million other monetary gold for all purposes, could be
supplemented by British-held dollar securities worth $2,600 million.[126] At first,
it was intended that they should be used as collateral for loans only,[127] but
ultimately some £207 million were sold in 1915–19, plus perhaps another £54
million of sterling and other securities.[128] By a judicious use of loans, gold
payments, high interest rates, direct operation on the sensitive exchange markets,
and American loans, obtained at a high cost of lost independence[129] the Government successfully held the dollar exchange at between $4·76 and $4·77 from
January 1916 to February 1919, while at the same time financing large and
growing purchases from the USA and acting as an exceedingly generous lender
to her Allies. From the outbreak of war until the end of the financial year
1918/19, Britain had lent some £1,741 million, including £171 million to countries
within the Empire, £434$\frac{1}{2}$ million to France, £568 million to Russia and £412$\frac{1}{2}$
million to Italy. As against this, she had, in turn, received loans to the amount of
£1,365 million, of which £1,027 million came from the USA, £135 million
from Canada and the remainder mostly from neutral countries. British loans,
therefore, exceeded British borrowings by some £350 million, and American
loans had, in a sense, been transmitted to other Allies, the British Government

[125] F. L. McVey, *The Financial History of Great Britain, 1914–1918* (New York, 1918), p. 62.
[126] US Federal Reserve, *Bulletin*.
[127] Kirkaldy, *British Finance, 1914–21*, pp. 183 ff.
[128] Morgan, *Studies*, pp. 327 ff.
[129] Kathleen Burk, *Britain, America and the Sinews of War 1914–1918* (1985).

acting, as London finance houses had often done before, as intermediaries. The position may be made clear by Table 1·2.[130]

Britain will be seen to have fought the war out of her own resources, the sale of foreign securites (Column F) roughly balancing the net loans to the Allies (Columns G + H).

This conclusion emphasizes the comfortable balance of payments position of Britain, in spite of the buoyant demand for imports in the war years at a time

Table 1·2: Estimated balance of payments of the UK, 1914–19 (£m.)

Year	Deficit on merchandise account	Government payments abroad	Credit on invisible items	Miscellaneous*	Balance before Government loans, etc. (A+B+ C+D)	Sale of foreign investments	Government borrowing abroad	Government lending abroad
	A	B	C	D	E	F	G	H
1914	−170	−20	+315	−125	0	0	0	0
1915	−368	−50	+395	+225	+202	+43	+53	−298
1916	−345	−50	+520	−24	+101	+110	+319	−530
1917	−467	−80	+575	−57	−29	+60	+532	−563
1918	−784	—	+580	+97	−107	+23	+381	−297
1919	−663	—	+605	+109	+51	+29	+57	−139

* Short-term loans, gold movements, etc.

of severe cuts in exports. In values, exports (including re-exports) remained fairly stable, the average for 1914–18 being £547 million, compared with £578 million in 1911–12. Retained imports, however, rose roughly in proportion with prices, from £601 million in 1914 to £1,285 million in 1918. To some extent, the British position was eased by an improvement in the terms of trade, by the growth of 'invisible exports' and by reducing overseas long-term investment to a mere trickle, an average of some £20 million annually in 1915–18.

6 Labour and the War

By 1914, the working men's main defence organization, the trade union, was rapidly, if erratically, achieving official recognition. In the few employments in which trade unions were not 'recognized', the railways and the Shipping Federation being the outstanding examples, industrial disputes before the war largely took the form of attempts to enforce such recognition. Trade union membership, reaching over 4·1 million in 1913–14, covered perhaps 30% of the eligible working force, but, as always, this average hid a very high percentage of membership in a few sectors, such as the skilled grades in engineering, printing, textiles, transport and the mines, and an almost complete absence of organization elsewhere, as in agriculture and among shop-assistants.

The adverse legal decision of the House of Lords in the Taff Vale Case of 1901, which cost the Railway Servants' union £23,000 in damages and a similar

[130] Based on Morgan, *op. cit.*, p. 341.

sum in other costs, had appeared to trade unionists to shatter at one blow their power of striking, and thereby their bargaining power, built up over a long period.[131] It was restored by the Trade Disputes Act of 1906, passed without serious opposition, which freed the trade unions from liability for civil actions in respect of any wrongful act committed by or on behalf of the union.

The immediate pre-war years saw a series of extensive and often violent industrial disputes. Possibly universal education since 1870, which had created the first generation of fully literate wage-earners, had contributed to a feeling of discontent and to industrial tension.[132] There may have been special factors in certain industries to cause unrest, and it was noticeable that the main disputes took place within only a handful of industries.[133] The stagnation of real wages added to the rebelliousness and it was noticeable that there were many unofficial strikes. By 1911–13 some 20 million working days were lost every year in disputes.

The main industries affected were the railways, the docks and coalmining. Although there were major strikes and lock-outs also in other industries, as for example in the Lancashire cotton industry in 1910 and 1911, among the London builders in 1914, among woollen and worsted workers in 1911, and among the boilermakers in 1908 and 1910, the unions in the railways, transport and mining did, in a sense, act as pacemakers for the others, and in 1914 they combined in a 'Triple Alliance'. Originally intended to ensure that all their contracts were terminated, and all their claims made, at the same time it was quickly looked upon as an undertaking to call sympathetic strikes by the other two if any one of them was under attack.[134] There was clearly a powerful threat to the economy, and thus in the last resort to the Government, implied in an alliance of the workers in these three basic industries.

This movement received some impetus from a new outlook called 'Syndicalism'. The syndicalists believed in 'direct action', the political strike, using the trade unions to capture political power and administer the new society, especially its industries, and they distrusted any class collaboration as a stratagem designed to keep labour in subjection. Under Tom Mann, the most influential Syndicalist leader, the Transport Workers' Federation had been formed in 1910. The Miners' Federation of 1908 and the railwaymen's union in 1913 were other approaches to industrial unionism. In South Wales, an official committee had issued *The Miners' Next Step* in 1912, in which the new policy was preached, and in 1913, Larkin, the Irish leader, raised large audiences for other 'forward policies'.[135] There was, however, one other relic of the disturbed

---

[131] S. and B. Webb, *The History of Trade Unionism, 1666–1920* (1920 ed.), chapters 9–11; G. D. H. Cole and R. Postgate, *The Common People 1746–1938* (1938), chapters 38, 39; Pauline Gregg, *A Social and Economic History of Britain, 1760–1950* (1950), chapter 19.

[132] This is the argument strongly put forward by E. H. Phelps-Brown, *Growth of British Industrial Relations* (1959).

[133] R. V. Sires, 'Labour Unrest in England, 1910–1914', *J. Econ. Hist*, 15/3, 1955.

[134] G. A. Phillips, 'The Triple Industrial Alliance in 1914', *Ec. Hist. Rev.*, 24/1, 1971; Henry Pelling, 'The Labour Unrest, 1911–14', in *Popular Politics and Society in Late Victorian Britain* (1968).

[135] For information on the trade union development in this period, see the works quoted above by E. H. Phelps-Brown, S. and B. Webb, Pauline Gregg (chapter 19) and Cole and Postgate. Also George Dangerfield, *The Strange Death of Liberal England* (1936), Part II, chapter 4; Kenneth D. Brown, *Labour and Unemployment, 1900–1914* (1971); E. H. Hunt, *British Labour History 1815–1914* (1981); John Lovell, *British Trade Unions 1875–1933* (1977), chapter 4.

industrial scene of 1910–14 which was destined to grow into major importance. This was the 'machinery' for settling disputes and for conciliation and arbitration, strongly supported by the Labour Department of the Board of Trade and its Chief Industrial Commissioner, Sir George R. (later Lord) Askwith. At the time it was of particular importance in enabling employers and men to meet round the table on a basis of equality.[136]

The war began with unemployment, mainly caused by uncertainty and the collapse of certain specific markets,[137] but this quickly gave way to a labour shortage which continued to intensify as the war progressed. The voracious demands both of the army and of the munitions industries for manpower soon denuded the rest of industry and created an overriding shortage which dominated the history of labour in the war.

Within twelve months, the workers in all war-important skilled crafts were exempt from recruitment, but complex problems for staffing the home industries remained. These were not always solved smoothly and, at the worst time, after the beginning of compulsory military service in 1916, some men found themselves shuttled backwards and forwards between industry and the front. Again, the German spring offensive of 1918 caused a temporary panic in which military commanders disrupted the careful plans of attaching key workers to such vital industries as coal mining, agriculture and even engineering, in order to fill the depleted battalions with the last reserves of able-bodied men.

In general, after the initial pool of unemployment men had been used up in the early weeks of 1915, the only substantial reserve of labour was to be found among the women who could be induced to enter industry for the first time. There was some substitution of female labour for male everwhere, and in the munitions industry there was, in addition, substitution of unskilled labour for skilled, known as 'dilution', because of the impossibility of training skilled men requiring several years' apprenticeship fast enough to fill the rapidly expanding munitions works. In the end, the extent of the transfer carried through was remarkable. Several occupations in which women had begun to replace men to a slight extent before 1914, were turned permanently into female preserves. These included work in shops and offices, in hotels, theatres and cinemas, and to some extent on public transport. Elsewhere, in the course of 1919, much of the female labour had it left industry again.

One by-product of this shift in employment was a revolutionary advance in the economic position of women, whose new-found economic independence was rewarded with the vote after the war with virtually no opposition. Another important by-product was a greater concern for workers' welfare in industrial work, including the provision of works canteens and enquiries into fatigue,[138] hours and conditions of factory work. By November 1918, about 1,000 women supervisors had been appointed to observe and regulate the conditions of work of women, at a time when some 1,600,000 were employed, directly or indirectly, by the Government.[139]

[136] G. R. Askwith, *Industrial Problems and Disputes* (1920).

[137] G. D. H. Cole, *Labour in War Time* (1915).

[138] E.g. *Memorandum* No. 12 (1916. Cd. 8344), and *Industrial Efficiency and Fatigue* (1917. Cd. 8511); also, Henry Carter, *The Control of the Drink Trade* (1918).

[139] D. Lloyd George, *War Memoirs* (1933), vol. 1, pp. 292, 341 ff.; Asa Briggs, *Social Thought and Social Action* (1961), chapter 5.

Total female employment in industry, transport, commerce and the professions increased from 3,280,000 in July 1914 to 4,950,000 in November 1918, or by over 1½ million. This compared with a loss of 2½ million men in the same occupations in this period, but in the munitions industry, including the metals and chemical industries and the Government industrial establishments, the number of men employed rose from 1,869,000 to 2,309,000, and of women from 212,000 to 945,000, a total net increase of nearly 1,200,000 workers.[140] It was there that the chief labour problems of the war were bound to occur.

The general scarcity of labour might have been expected to push up wages; instead, workers seemed content to allow the value of their real wages to be whittled away by the creeping inflation of 1915–17. Most money wages were raised slightly in the course of these years, but not nearly as much as prices, until by July 1917 real wages had dropped by one-fifth compared with their immediate pre-war level: Bowley's wage index of those in full-time employment stood then at 135–140, with the cost of living at 160–180 (July 1914 = 100); according to Kuczynski, real wages had dropped from 97 to 74 (1900 = 100), and according to Layton and Crowther, from 174 to 142 (1850 = 100).[141]

There were several causes of this paradoxical behaviour of wage-earners. First, trade unions never fight as hard against a drop in real wages caused by rising prices as against a cut in money wage rates. Secondly, in the early months the war was generally expected to be of short duration, and the loss in real wages was felt to be an appropriate sacrifice on the part of those who stayed behind, to match that of the volunteers. Thirdly, the replacement of men by women (paid at 50–60% of men's rates even when doing a man's job) greatly reduced the pressure on the labour market. Fourthly, the trade unions were hamstrung by the Treasury Agreement of March 1915, later incorporated in the first Munitions of War Act. But above all, the decline was in real wage *rates* only; earnings, with secure full employment, overtime, night work, and bonus or piece payments, roughly kept in step with the rises in the cost of living. According to Feinstein's recent estimates, earnings for 1918 stood at 209 (1914 = 100) while the cost of living, July to July, stood at 210. The total wages bill, including forces' pay, stood at 250.[142]

There were some signs of dissatisfaction from an early date, but it was in the course of 1917 that all the factors which had kept wage claims within narrow limits seemed to break down at once. The impotence of the official trade union leadership was neutralized by the shop stewards on the one hand, and a more complete system of arbitration on the other. New members flocked into the trade unions, whose membership was doubled in the course of the war, from 3,959,000 in 1913 to 8,023,000 in 1919. Feelings of patriotism and self-sacrifice were giving way to disillusionment at the sight of the uninhibited profiteering and luxury spending of the rich, when it contrasted with the food shortages and

[140] A. W. Kirkaldy (ed.), *Industry and Finance* (1920), p. 96; A. S. Milward, *The Economic Effects of the Two World Wars on Britain* (1984), p. 36.

[141] J. Kuczynski, *A Short History of Labour Conditions in Great Britain, 1750 to the Present Day* (1946 ed.), p. 120; A. L. Bowley, *Prices and Wages in the United Kingdom, 1914–1920* (Oxford, 1921), p. 106.

[142] J. M. Winter, *The Great War and The British People* (1985), pp. 214 ff.; J. A. Dowie, '1919–20 is in Need of Attention', *Ec. Hist. Rev.*, 28/3, 1975, pp. 442, 449; C. H. Feinstein, *National Income and Expenditure*, T. 55.

queues in the working-class quarters. Also, prices were getting out of hand.[143] Other grievances noted by the Commissions on Industrial Unrest and the Select Committee on National Expenditure were the inability of workers in some industries and of some skilled workers to make up earnings by piecework and overtime, the restrictions on liberty, expecially the licensing laws affecting the sale of alcohol, the powers of employers over the mobility of their workers by the withholding of the leaving certificates, and compulsory arbitration.[144]

There set in a serious decline in morale, particularly in the centres of the munitions industry, the Clyde, Sheffield, Barrow and Coventry, which may be taken to epitomize the difficulties of adaptation to the war conditions, and the critical importance of morale. Here the key section was the engineering industry, where 550,000 men were organized in trade unions, about one-third of the work force, and of these 161,000 were in the Amalgamated Society of Engineers (ASE).[145]

The engineering industry had been in the throes of some painful changes and readjustments at the time of the outbreak of war. Superimposed on these was a series of wage claims and disputes, based on the rising prices since 1908, and a movement for an 8-hour day.[146]

The Treasury Agreement of March 1915, and the Munitions Act which incorporated it, had obliged the unions to give up precisely the main points of contention of peace-time. It is true that there was a Government promise that all the pre-war conditions would be restored at the end of the war, but few men believed that the march of history could be reversed in this way. At the centre of the agreement stood the division of jobs so as to allow 'dilution', the substitution of semi-skilled and unskilled workers in jobs hitherto regarded as skilled, and their upgrading.

Dilution itself proceeded by several stages. By the last stage, begun in the summer of 1917, when even skilled men began to be called up, there was no limit to substitution and upgrading.[147]

These changes occurred while new sets of payments by results and bonus rates had to be negotiated shop by shop, including minimum wages for women, and while extension of premises, or moves to newly established works, brought fresh problems. Before the war, employers had negotiated separately with representatives of the various craft and other unions in their shops. Now, the union leaders had largely abdicated their role, or had become irrelevant, and in their place there arose the shop stewards as the representatives and leaders of the men in the engineering shops, shipyards and arsenals irrespective of which union they belonged to or, indeed, of whether they belonged to a union at all. All of them forming their factory works committees, with chief shop stewards or conveners at their head, came to be taken, by employers and Government alike, as the accredited spokesmen of the munition workers.[148] In large munitions

[143] W. H. Beveridge, *British Food Control* (1928), pp. 322–3.

[144] *Select Committee of HoC on National Expenditure*, 167 (1917); E. Cannan, 'Industrial Unrest', *Econ. J.*, 27/108, 1917; Cole and Postgate, *The Common People* (1938), chapter 41; M. B. Hammond, *British Labor Conditions and Legislation during the War* (New York, 1919), chapter 9.

[145] Branko Pribićević, *The Shop Stewards' Movement and Workers' Control 1910–1922* (Oxford, 1959), p. 27.

[146] J. B. Jefferys, *The Story of the Engineers, 1800–1945* (1945), chapter 7 and 8.

[147] G. D. H. Cole, *Trade Unions and Munitions* (Oxford, 1923).

[148] G. D. H. Cole, *Workshop Organization* (Oxford, 1923).

centres representatives from all works formed a district Workers' Council, as in Coventry or Sheffield. Many of the leading shop stewards had a background of Syndicalism, and it was evident that some of the outrage of the craftsmen who invariably took the lead in this movement arose from the violation of their craft exclusiveness.[149] The power of the shop stewards' movement waned as soon as the war was over; the National Workers' Committee Movement, established with a new constitution in 1921, represented their last flicker of independent life.[150]

Meanwhile, however, the shop stewards' organizations bore the brunt of the war-time disputes. The Clyde Workers' Committee was the first, being formed out of the strike of February 1915. In November of that year the Glasgow 'rent strike', persuaded the Government to take the momentous decision of keeping rents down to near their pre-war level by the Rent Restriction Act. A renewed strike flared up on the Clyde in March 1916. Later in that year, as a result of a strike of munition workers in Sheffield, organized by the local shop stewards' committee, the 'trade card' scheme of exemption for skilled men was instituted by the Government. The scheme, in effect, handed over completely to the trade unions the task of certifying who were the skilled men who should be exempt from military service. It was badly organized and had, indeed, little to recommend it. But the proposal to extend dilution to private work caused the most widespread engineering strike of the war in May 1917, exclusively organized by the shop stewards. The first reaction of the Government was to arrest the strike leaders, but the men ultimately won their point. The dilution clause was withdrawn, and the 'leaving certificate', the most resented aspect of earlier Munitions Acts, was also abolished. The trade card scheme, however, was replaced by a 'schedule of protected occupations', under which wholesale recruitment of skilled men in April–December 1917 was carried through in spite of bitter opposition on the part of the engineering workers.

Perhaps the most important result of the labour unrest in 1917–18 was the belated upward revision of wage scales. In the munitions industry, wage awards were made by the Court of Arbitration under the Wages (Temporary Regulation) Act of 1918. In 1919 it became the Industrial Court under the Industrial Courts Act of that year. The system of changing wages uniformly over the whole country and the whole industry by arbitration continued into 1920.

One of the most striking changes wrought by the war of 1914–18 was the relative rise in the wage of the unskilled, as compared with that of the skilled men. Thus in the engineering and shipbuilding trades, representative wage rates moved as shown in Table 1·3:[151]

Table 1·3: Movement of wage rates in engineering and shipbuilding trades (July 1914 = 100)

	Skilled fitter and turner	Skilled plater	Unskilled labourer
July 1917	134	130	154
July 1918	173	169	213
July 1920	231	223	309

[149] James Hinton, *The First Shop Stewards' Movement* (1973).
[150] Pribićević, *passim.*
[151] Bowley, *Prices and Wages*, p. 131.

This difference may, to some extent, be ascribed to the simple effect of granting flat-rate increases, but it also represented the underlying reality in most industries of the declining importance of manual skill of the old type, and the growing predominance of semi-skilled or virtually unskilled machine-minders.

Given that skilled engineers were often on time rates, while the dilutees worked on piece rates and bonus work which might give them earnings in excess of those of the skilled men, and that the lucrative, repetitive jobs often went to the unskilled dilutees, while the skilled men were permanently on the intricate and difficult jobs, it is not surprising that a series of strikes in the munitions industry between October and December 1917 originated from those grievances.

The practice of industry-wide, in the place of local, collective bargaining, which first emerged in 1914–18,[152] was destined to spread to other trades in the inter-war years, while the Trade Board Act of 1918, extending the original Boards in the sweated trades to wherever 'no adequate machinery exists for the effective regulation of wages throughout the trade', further emphasized the trend towards national wage bargaining. Lastly, the war-time shop stewards' movement furnished much of the drive behind the giant amalgamation of the early 1920s, of which the Amalgamated Engineering Union, created out of the ASE and nine other societies, was the earliest.[153]

7 'Reconstruction' and Post-War Planning

As early as December 1914 the Board of Trade considered that there was an 'urgent need' to discuss the problem of unemployment after the war.[154] The later phrase of 'homes fit for heroes' expressed a general hope that out of the horrors and deprivations of the war there should emerge a society more worthy of the sacrifices it had demanded in its defence. 'Government emphasis on reconstruction grew out of the sufferings and the low spirit of the citizens during the three bitter years beginning in 1914.'[155]

The Government did not remain unaware of this mood, and it was also conscious of the post-war problems that were likely to arise out of the violently changed trading and financial conditions.[156] It set up a Reconstruction Committee in 1916 which was turned, in July 1917, into the Ministry of Reconstruction under Dr Addison.[157] The Ministry did its work through committees. The careful plans of the committee on demobilization were thwarted after November 1918 as soldiers refused to wait their turn and made their own way home, but their re-absorption into civilian posts caused much less trouble than expected. After a short rise of unemployment in January–February 1919, the able-bodied men found employment very quickly.

---

[152] S. and B. Webb, *History of Trade Unionism* (1920 ed.), chapter 9; B. C. Roberts, *The Trades Union Congress, 1868–1921* (1948), chapter 8.

[153] Jefferys, *op. cit.*, pp. 189 ff.

[154] W. H. Beveridge, *Power and Influence* (1953), p. 136.

[155] S. J. Hurwitz, *State Intervention in Britain. A Study of Economic Control and Social Response, 1914–1919* (New York, 1949), pp. 286–7; Arthur Marwick, *The Deluge* (Harmondsworth, 1967), pp. 296 ff.

[156] W. H. Dawson (ed.), *After-War Problems* (1917).

[157] Ch. Addison, *Politics From Within, 1911–1918*, 2 vols. (1924), vol. 2, chapters 14, 15, 18.

Labour questions were discussed by a committee under J. H. Whitley, later Speaker of the House of Commons. Its first report in 1917, the 'Whitley Report', proposed standing joint industrial councils, made up of representatives of employers and workers, on national, district and works level, as a peaceful means of resolving differences on labour questions and others. These proposals, although by no means new,[158] excited much attention in view of the existing labour unrest, but turned out to be of little practical significance; their only really successful application came to be in the Government service.

In the immediate post-war years there was a rash of new departments and authorities: the Ministry of Transport (1919), the Ministry of Health (1919), the Ministry of Pensions (1917), the Forestry Commission (1919), the Medical Research Council (1920) and the Electricity Commissioners (1919), though not all of these derived from a spirit of 'reconstruction'. The willingness to carry through significant reforms derived largely from the fear of a revolt from below,[159] just as the failure to hold on to many of the war-time gains, and the indecent haste with which most controls were abolished, owed something to the weakness of Labour in the centres of power that really counted.[160]

The Labour Party had been given a new constitution in 1918[161] which allowed individual membership and also accepted a Socialist programme, but it was badly defeated in the General Election immediately following the war. The question of reconstruction was however still open in 1919-21. Labour's policy of nationalization and the Socialist demands for a widely planned economy[162] had much widespread support because of the war time experience. The main battle was fought over coal, especially since the miners themselves were insistent that it be nationalized.

There is a view that the immediate postwar years, with their frequent strikes and the examples of continental revolutions before people's eyes, held the danger of revolution, and that it was Lloyd George's skilful delaying tactics, especially calling the Industrial Conference and appointing the Sankey Coal Commission, waiting until the appetite for nationalization had evaporated, which preserved the free enterprise system in this country.[163] Though the danger was actually small, the delaying tactics were undoubtedly effective. It has now been shown that a damaging coal strike was averted in March 1919 only on the promise that there would be some form of nationalization of the coal mines.[164] That promise

---

[158] E.g. A. W. Kirkaldy (ed.), *Labour, Finance and the War* (1916), pp. 42 ff., and *Industry and Finance* (1917), pp. 160 ff.; M. B. Hammond, *British Labor Conditions and Legislation during the War* (New York, 1919), pp. 272–9.

[159] E.g. Paul Barton Johnson, *Land Fit for Heroes. The Planning of British Reconstruction 1916–1919* (Chicago, 1968), pp. 301, 374, 403. Also see P. Abrams, 'The Failure of Social Reform, 1918–1920', *Past and Present*, 24, 1963.

[160] S. and B. Webb, *History of Trade Unionism* (1920 ed.), chapter 11.

[161] R. H. Tawney, 'The Abolition of Economic Controls 1918–21', *Ec. Hist. Rev.*, 13/1–2, 1943; P. Abrams, 'The Failure'; Albert T. Lauterbach, 'Economic Demobilization in Great Britain After the First World War', *Political Science Quarterly*, 57, 1942, Arthur Marwick, 'The Impact of the First World War on British Society', *Journal of Contemporary History*, 3 (1968), p. 61.

[162] E.g. Sir Leo Chiozza Money, *The Triumph of Nationalization* (1920).

[163] Charles Loch Mowat, *Britain Between the Wars, 1918–1940* (1956 ed.), chapter 1, sect. 9; G. D. H. Cole and R. Postgate, *The Common People 1746–1938* (1938), pp. 535 ff.

[164] S. M. H. Armitage, *The Politics of Decontrol of Industry: Britain and the United States* (1969), p. 120.

was broken, but meanwhile the Sankey Commission of 1919 produced a report which kept the parties talking and thus prevented a change in ownership of the coal mines. At the same time, the inflationary price rises of 1918–20, which forced the unions to spend most of their energies on raising wages, did as much as any deliberate action to divert interests from grand schemes of nationalization.

Something remained of the high hopes and militant actions of the years 1917–21. The Industrial Courts Act of 1919, one of the results of the Whitley Report, extended the Ministry of Labour's power of conciliation and inquiry, without power of compulsory arbitration.[165]There was progressive legislation in many fields, such as the Housing and Town Planning Act of 1919, and the extension of insurance by the Unemployment Insurance Act of 1920. The number of Trade Boards was multiplied. Less widely noted was the general reduction in working hours in 1919, a result of post-war trade union power as well as of studies in industrial fatigue. In virtually every industry, the working day was reduced from 9 hours[166] to about 8, and $46\frac{1}{2}$–48 hours became the standard working week, at no loss of wages; even in the steel works, when two shifts of 12 hours average had been worked, the change was to three 8-hour shifts.[167] This reduction in hours of work became firmly established, and remained perhaps the most valuable permanent gain from all the high hopes of post-war 'reconstruction'.

[165] R. Charles, *The Development of Industrial Relations in Britain 1911–1939* (1973). i Rodney Lowe, 'The Failure of Consensus in Britain: the National Industrial Conference, 1919–1921', *Historical Journal*, 21 (1978).

[166] In contemporary terminology, a 9-hour day meant a 54-hour week, usually $9\frac{1}{2}$ hours on weekdays, $6\frac{1}{2}$ on Saturdays.

[167] A. L. Bowley, *Prices and Wages*, Appx. III.

2

British Industry and Transport between the Wars

1 Production and Productivity

The inter-war years bear a dual character in the minds of those who lived through them, and this is reflected in much of the historical writing about them. On the one hand, there were to be found growing wealth, greatly improved amenities, a widening of horizons and a downward spread to new social groups of many benefits of civilization which had been available hitherto to only a small minority. On the other there existed prolonged and at times massive unemployment combined with privation, social stagnation and the personal hopelessness associated with it. 'Poverty in the midst of plenty', and the 'two nations' were concepts that were frequently used to describe these apparently contradictory trends. This chapter and the following two will explore these two themes further, as well as the relationship between them.

Statistics of the Gross Domestic Product (GDP) and of industrial and manufacturing output show at once the ambivalent nature of British economic progress. Peak to peak, there were satisfactory rates of growth that compared well with earlier periods, even if deflated for rising population. Thus GDP grew by an annual 1·9% between the peaks of 1920 and 1929, and 1·8% in 1929–39; manufacturing output rose by 2·8% and 3·3% a year in 1920–9 and 1928–37 respectively[1] the increase being spread among all major sections (see Table 2.2). Against this, the increase in Total Factor Productivity, at 0·2% a year, was historically low.[2]

Yet at the same time the losses of output between those peak years, not to mention the sharp drops from 1919 and after 1937, give an indication of the waste incurred by idle capital and idle manpower, quite apart from the immeasurable psychological costs borne by men and women without work. Industrial production was at least 22% below its former peak in 1921 and 11% below in 1931, and the losses were larger still when measured against the rising trend line.

The figures in Table 2·1 show clearly two distinct cycles after the post-war disturbances to 1920: they have high points in 1929 and 1937, and troughs in 1922 and 1931–2. Most statistics support the further conclusion that of these cycles, the second showed a more satisfactory and consistent growth than the first. This contrast between the decades is heightened by the comparison with other major countries: in fact, both in manufacturing production and

---

[1] D. H. Aldcroft, 'Economic Growth in Britain in the Inter-war Years: A Re-assessment', *Ec. Hist. Rev.*, 20/2, 1967: A. Maddison, 'Output, Employment and Productivity in British Manufacturing in the Last Half-Century', *Bull. Oxf. Inst. Stat.*, 17/4, 1955.

[2] S. N. Broadberry, *The British Economy Between the Wars* (Oxford, 1986) pp. 8–9.

Table 2·1: GDP and industrial production, 1919–1939* (Index: 1913 = 100)

Year	GDP at constant factor cost	Industrial production	Manufacturing
(1919)	(100·9)	(89·8)	(92·2)
(1920)	(94·8)	(99·8)	(101·5)
1920	91·3	97·9	99·7
1921	83·9	79·7	77·6
1922	88·2	92·2	90·3
1923	91·0	97·6	96·7
1924	94·8	108·4	106·5
1925	99·4	112·7	109·8
1926	95·7	106·6	106·3
1927	103·4	122·8	117·5
1928	104·7	119·5	117·2
1929	107·8	125·5	122·0
1930	107·0	120·1	116·8
1931	101·5	112·3	108·8
1932	102·3	111·9	109·4
1933	105·3	119·3	117·5
1934	112·2	131·3	128·2
1935	116·5	141·2	138·8
1936	121·8	153·9	152·8
1937	126·1	163·1	162·1
1938	127·6	158·7	157·4
1939	128·9	–	–

* C. H. Feinstein, *National Income, Expenditure and Output of the United Kingdom 1855–1965* (Cambridge, 1972), T. 19 and T. 112. Items in brackets include Southern Ireland. Also see K. S. Lomax 'Growth and Productivity in the United Kingdom', *Productivity Measurement Review*, 38, 1964.

Table 2·2: Output in manufacturing in 1935 (1907 = 100)

	Total manufacturing output	Manufacturing output per employee year	Manufacturing output per employee hour
Iron and steel	147·9	139·6	154
Engineering, shipbuilding, vehicles	271·5	177·6	196
Non-ferrous metals	135·2	121·0	131
Chemicals	222·6	157·7	174
Textiles	109·1	134·6	155
Clothing	125·3	125·3	146
Leather	131·8	120·9	136
Food, drink, tobacco	129·6	96·8	108
Timber	176·0	132·0	147
Paper, printing, publishing	262·6	192.7	208
Clay and building materials	213.3	160.3	180
Miscellaneous	362·0	207·8	228
Total Manufacturing	176·6	151·9	171

productivity, the USA and Germany performed far worse in the 1930s than the British economy.[3] Any explanation of the causes of the British growth and the British trade cycle will have to bear those differences in mind.

It is possible to see the whole period as essentially one of steady and even expansion.[4] Taking for purposes of comparison the three peak years 1924, 1929 and 1937 which had similar rates of unemployment (10·3%, 10·4% and 10·8%), this even rate of growth is seen in rates of change of input as well as output (see Table 2·3):

Table 2·3:   Annual rates of growth:

	1924–9	1929–37
Total output	2·2%	2·3%
Total employment	1·3	1·3
Total capital stock	1·6	1·7
Population	0·34	0·43

Overall, a considerable part of the growth, around an average annual increase of 0·9% of GDP, was due not to additional inputs of labour and capital, but to rising productivity, sometimes known as the 'residual'.[5]

However, if measured by capacity utilization, 1924, at 94·8%, is not comparable with 1929 and 1937, both of which may be put at 100%,[6] so that what emerges is a much faster growth of capacity in the second cycle than the first. This would support the view that, after a poor performance in the 1920s, the 1930s saw a genuine breakthrough not only in the quality of output but also in the structuring of British industry towards the growth-oriented sectors in the second phase;[7] at last, it seemed, Britain was beginning to catch up on the more advanced countries after years of falling behind.

Other observers have tended to differentiate between the declining old staple and the expanding 'new' industries, and the gradually growing weight of the latter over the former in the economy.[8] However, the distinction between 'new' and 'old' industries and their performance, attractive though it seems at first sight, is not always a clear one, and various measurements have shown that the

[3] L. Rostas, 'Industrial Production, Productivity and Distribution in Britain, Germany and the United States', *Econ. J.*, 53, 1943, p. 49.

[4] Aldcroft, *loc.cit.*, and *idem*, 'Economic Progress in Britain in the 1920s', *Scot. J. Pol. Econ.*, 13, 1960, and *The Inter-War Economy, Britain 1919–1939* (1970).

[5] J. A. Dowie, 'Growth in the Inter-War Period: Some More Arithmetic', *Ec. Hist. Rev.*, 21, 1968, p. 100; D. H. Aldcroft, *The Inter-War Economy: Britain, 1919–1939* (1970) p. 114; E. H. Phelps-Brown and B. Weber, 'Accumulation, Productivity and Distribution in the British Economy, 1870–1938', *Econ. J.*, 63/256, 1953; R. C. O. Matthews, 'Some Aspects of Post-War Growth in the British Economy in Relation to the Historical Experience', *Transactions of the Manchester Statistical Society*, 1964–5, pp. 14, 20.

[6] Neil K. Buxton, Introduction to Neil K. Buxton and Derek H. Aldcroft (eds.), *British Industry Between the Wars. Instability and Economic Development 1919–1939* (1979), p. 13.

[7] H. W. Richardson, 'The Basis of Recovery in the 1930s': A Review and a New Interpretation', *Ec. Hist. Rev.*, 15/2, 1962; *idem, Economic Recovery in Britain 1932–9* (1967); N. K. Buxton, 'Economic Progress in the 1920s: A Reappraisal', *Scot. J. Pol. Econ.*, 13, 1960.

[8] H. W. Richardson, 'Over-Commitment in Britain Before 1930' *Oxf. Econ. P.* 17, 1965; *idem*, 'The New Industries Between the Wars', *ibid.* 13, 1961; B. W. E. Alford, *Depression or Recovery? British Economic Growth 1918–1939* (1972).

growth rates were not very different and that overall growth was due much more to improvements within all industries than to a shift between them.[9] One is on safer ground with the assertion (though it has little explanatory value) that there were some industries which grew faster than the rest, while others stagnated and even declined, and that it was the former which carried the expansionary drive of the British economy.[10]

Despite these ambiguities in the concept as well as the role of the 'new' and 'old staple' industries, there is some value in the distinction. Thus the new industries showed a much higher rate of investment and, in terms of net output, they showed persistently better results in both decades though the exact rates depend on the base year chosen for comparison (see Table 2·4).[11]

Table 2·4:   Rates of change of net domestic fixed capital formation (% per annum at 1930 prices)

	'New' industries	Old staple industries	Other manufactures
1924–29	+5·9	−15·3	+7·9
1929–32	+4·0	−18·3	+15·3
1932–37	+7·1	−14·1	+18.7

Contribution to the value of total net output (in % of net output of all Census of Production trades)

	'New' industries	Old staple industries
1924	14·1	37·0
1930	15·9	29·6
1935	21·0	27·8

Indices of the output of the major new industries compared are shown in Table 2·5.

If the replacement of one set of industries by another is a normal aspect of economic progress,[13] why, in this period, was it associated with persistent mass unemployment? Why did the new industries not absorb more rapidly the resources, especially the labour, released by the declining staple trades? In part,

[9] B. W. E. Alford, 'New Industries for Old? British Industries Between the Wars', in Roderick Floud and Donald McCloskey (eds.), *The Economic History of Britain Since 1700*, vol. 2 (Cambridge, 1981), pp. 316–7; N. K. Buxton, 'The Role of the New Industries in Britain During the 1930s: A Reinterpretation', *Bus. Hist. Rev.* 49 (1975); Broadberry, *op. cit.* p. 9; Dowie, *op. cit.*; G. von Tunzelmann, 'Structural Change and Leading Sectors in British Manufacturing 1907–68', in C. P. Kindleberger and Guido di Tella' (eds.), *Economics in the Long View* (New York, 3 vols. 1982), Vol. III, pp. 1–49.

[10] J. A. Dowie, op. cit., p. 105.

[11] Neil K. Buxton, 'Role of the New Industries', p. 221; Aldcroft, 'Economic Growth', p. 320; S. N. Broadberry and N. F. R. Crafts, 'The Impact of the Depression of the 1930's on Productive Potential in the United Kingdom', *European Economic Review* 34 (1990).

[12] In 1907, it had been 6·5%.

[13] Simon Kuznets, *Six Lectures on Economic Growth* (Illinois, 1959), p. 33.

Table 2·5: Indices of the output of major new industries

	1924	1930	1935
Electrical goods	55	67	100
Electricity supply	45	71	100
Automobiles and cycles	42	61	100
Aircraft	23	65	100
Silk and rayon	20	47	100
Hosiery	70	69	100
Chemical and allied goods	67	69	100
Share of above, plus scientific instruments[12]	12·5%	16·3%	19·0%

the explanation lies in an overall failure of demand beyond the structural misallocation at the beginning of the period; in particular, the new industries were unable to capture the export markets lost by the old staples. It was the tragedy of British industry that the shift had to be made too quickly, and had to be carried out in the midst of a world depression, in conditions made more difficult by a change in the terms of trade, a restrictive monetary policy until 1931 and an open home market to the same date, in the midst of rampant protectionism abroad. Secondly many of the new industries were less labour-intensive than the old. Finally, the labour made redundant in the older industries, frequently consisting of men brought up to certain skills or to hard physical labour, could not be integrated in the new industries calling for different skills and located in the different parts of the country.[14] These points will be discussed further in later sections of this and the next chapter.

However, the shifts that did occur were not insignificant (see Table 2·6)[15].

Table 2·6: Numbers employed in the United Kingdom (000)

	Average 1920–1	Average 1937–8	Change
Agriculture, forestry, fishing	1,112	762	−350
Mining and quarrying	1,204	791	−413
Manufacture	6,668	6,539	−129
Building and contracting	840	1,159	+319
Gas, water, electricity	185	291	+106
Transport and communication	1,482	1,513	+31
Distribution, insurance, banking	2,120	2,897	+777
National, local government	1,381	1,222	−159
Professional services	721	950	+229
Miscellaneous services	2,025	2,755	+730
Grand Total	17,738	18,879	+1,141
Salaried workers	3,758	4,810	+1,052

[14] Aldcroft, 'Economic Growth', pp. 324–5; W. Ashworth, *An Economic History of England, 1879–1939* (1960), p. 321 also pp. 331–5, 414–16.

[15] Agatha L. Chapman and Rose Knight, *Wages and Salaries in the United Kingdom, 1920–1938* (Cambridge, 1953), p. 18; cf. also Mark Abrams, *The Condition of the British People, 1911–1945* (1945), p. 63; Sir William Beveridge, *Full Employment in a Free Society* (1945 ed.). pp. 316–20; Phyllis Deane and W. A. Cole, *British Economic Growth 1688–1959* (Cambridge, 1962), chapters 4, 5 and 9, sec. 3.

To this economic recovery, exports contributed but little. Investments fluctuated widely and in total rose from an average of £305 m. to £450 m. and £588 m. in those years, at constant (1938) market prices, or from 8·5% to 10·35% and 11·5% of GNP.[16] Most of the inter-war expansion was, however, associated with a growth in domestic consumer demand. According to one calculation, 46·7% of the increase in GDP between 1932 and 1937 was accounted for by the rise in consumers' expenditure, against 14.1% by public authorities' current expenditure, 20·1% by gross domestic investment and 19·1% by exports.[17]

One aspect of the economic growth, as we have seen, was the value of the 'residual', that part of the extra output not due to extra input of labour and capital. It largely represents improved technology, and better industrial organization and distribution. While the rate of technical progress is difficult to measure, it seems safe to say that in the inter-war years the consumer was offered more new products, and the industrialist more new machinery and materials, than at any comparable earlier period in history.

There was still a considerable time lag between invention and application. The new industries of 1919–39[18] were all based on inventions or discoveries made in the generation before 1914, if not earlier, just as the major discoveries of the inter-war years (e.g. television, penicillin, the jet engine and nylon) were turned to practical use only after 1939. Yet it would be true to say that it was in this period that at least some part of British industry became interested for the first time in technological discovery itself. It was significant that in a country which had so long maintained an industrial superiority by the skill of its artisans, and in which industrialists (not to mention dons) were content to rest in ignorance of the natural sciences,[19] this consciousness for the need of scientific training and research arose first because of military needs.

With the aid of the Department of Scientific and Industrial Research, set up in 1916 to provide Government support for scientific research with possible industrial applications, much research work was carried out by independent institutions, such as Universities, and in the following years successful grant-aided co-operative research associations for whole industries were established.[20] The Medical Research Council (1920), the Agricultural Research Council (1931) and several research stations, of which the National Physical Laboratory (1900) was the earliest, also received Government funds.

Apart from Government sponsorship, which declined in importance after the early 1920s, private industry was itself turning increasingly to research and systematic control techniques to improve its methods and products and discover new ones. The efforts were most uneven, and well below those of comparable

[16] Feinstein, *op. cit.*, T. 11, 15–16, 38–9, 48–9; T. Barna, 'Investment in Industry – Has Britain Lagged?', *The Banker*, April 1957, pp. 226–9 and see chapter 3, section 2 below.

[17] Sean Glyn and John Oxborrow, *Interwar Britain: a Social and Economic History* (1976), p. 30; K. G. P. Mathews, *The Inter-War Economy. An Equilibrium Analysis* (Aldershot, 1986), pp. 9–10.

[18] Including electrical engineering, chemicals, rayon, radio, motion pictures, aircraft and motor engineering.

[19] E.g. R. F. Harrod, *The Prof.* (1959), pp. 17–27, 53.

[20] Sir H. Frank Heath and A. L. Hetherington, *Industrial Research and Development in the United Kingdom* (1964), chapter 32 and Appx. II.

firms in the USA and Germany[21]: yet, compared with the pre-war years, progress had been rapid.[22] Partly with official sanction, a quiet revolution in the relative status of scientific and technical education was beginning,[23] and technical colleges and research laboratories in firms increased steadily and unobstrusively in number and standing.[24] Interest in the technical marvels of the new age, such as radio, aircraft, photography and film, more powerful telescopes and faster means of land transport, helped to popularize science from the 1920s onwards among wide sections of the population.[25]

Even in the industries most tenaciously clinging to 'practical experience' as distinct from scientific training, in coal, iron and steel, engineering and shipbuilding, it could be said at the end of the 1920s that 'scientific research is now regarded with respect by even the most conservative of our industrial leaders'.[26]

In some key industries later to be known as 'science-based', research came to be undertaken on a large scale, involving the collaboration of scientists of various disciplines, a measure of planning and co-ordination, and the much more costly work of 'development.[27] Beside the spectacular brainwaves, it was the gradual adaptation and improvement, often of only humble parts of machines or materials; the linked development of one new process waiting for improvements in others before it could be applied; and the constant pressure on the average firm to reach the level of the best which contributed to industrial growth. Examples were such new techniques as the extension of welding to many aspects of shipbuilding, new alloy metallurgy, precision control[28] and cellulose spray painting.

Last, but by no means least, science and research invaded the very citadel of entrepreneurship itself. The management of men, the layout of plant, the grouping, selecting, training of staff, work study and study of fatigue, besides many others, became aspects of 'scientific management' which were being introduced from across the Atlantic in at least a few large and progressive firms, and developed to fit the native soil.[29]

2 New and Growing Industries

One of the most critically important of the new industries was electrical engineering, together with the supply of electricity. It could be taken as the symbol of the new industrial Britain, freeing other industries from dependence on the

[21] Committee on Industry and Trade (Balfour Committee), *Survey of Industries*, vol. I (1927), pp. 318–20.

[22] D. E. H. Edgerton, 'Science and Technology in British Business History', *Business History* 29/4 (1987).

[23] *Natural Science in Education* (1918. Cd. 9011); IAAM and SMA, *The Teaching of Science in Secondary Schools* (1958 ed.) pp. 8 9.

[24] Balfour Committee, *Report*, vol. 1, pp. 178 ff.

[25] C. L. Mowat, *Britain between the Wars* (1956 ed.), pp. 219–22.

[26] Lord Aberconway, *The Basic Industries of Great Britain* (1927), pp. 353–4.

[27] C. F. Carter and B. R. Williams, *Investment in Innovation* (1958), p. 138.

[28] R. S. Sayers, 'The Springs of Technical Progress in Britain, 1919–1939', *Econ. J.*, 60/238, 1950.

[29] L. Urwick and E. F. L. Brech, *The Marketing of Scientific Management* (1957 ed.), esp. vol. 2; E. F. L. Brech (ed.), *The Principles and Practice of Management* (1958 ed.), pp. 56–64.

coalfields of the north and west and setting in motion a vast migration to the Midlands and the southeast. Backward technically until 1918, and behind other countries in consumption per head in the 1920s, by the late 1930s the industry, helped by the new national 'grid', was close, if not equal, to its foreign rivals.[30]

The early haphazard and scattered development had led to much technical inefficiency in an industry such as electricity generation. In 1925 there was still a bewildering variety of voltages and, in the case of AC, of cycles in use. Although larger stations were much more economical than smaller ones, in 1925 28 stations generated 50% of the power between them, and another 88 generated 39%, but the remaining 11% was shared between 322 suppliers.[31] The Electricity (Supply) Act of 1919 which attempted to encourage amalgamations remained a dead letter, but following the Weir Committee Report of the Ministry of Transport in 1925, the Electricity (Supply) Act of 1926 introduced more effective changes. A Central Electricity Board was set up and given the right to monopolize all the wholesaling of electricity. It successfully pursued a policy of concentrating all output in a small number of base load stations and new super-stations (144 by 1935), while closing down large numbers of the smaller, inefficient ones. The whole system was connected by means of a national 'grid' of high-tension transmission cables which incidentally employed about 100,000 people at the bottom of the slump, and total output rose from 6,600 million units in 1925 to 26,400 million units in 1939.[32]

As electricity became cheaper, it came within the reach of new classes of the community. There were 730,000 electricity consumers in 1920, 2,844,000 in 1929 and 8,920,000 in 1938; in the late 1930s, consumers were being added at a rate of 700,000–800,000 a year.[33] New electrical consumer durables like cookers, radios, refrigerators, washing machines, vacuum cleaners and electric irons as well as electric street lighting, and the conversion of some railway traction added important sources of demand. Thus, with falling marginal costs and an elastic demand a virtuous circle was set up.

These conditions offered great opportunities for electrical engineering. Employment rose particularly fast in the 1930s, and the number of insured workers grew from 173,600 in 1924 to 367,000 in 1937. Their contribution to the value of gross output rose from 1·9% in 1924 to 3·0% in 1935, and of net output of all manufacturing, from 3·9% to 4·8%. The export record of the industry was good, and although there were large imports of various electrical goods from Germany and of lamps and valves from Holland, the British industry kept control of its home market, aided as it was by protective measures in 1921

---

[30] *Committee on the Position of the Electrical Trades after the War, Report* (1918. Cd. 9072); M. E. Dimock, *British Public Utilities* (1933), p. 197; R. A. S. Hennessy, *The Electrical Revolution* (Newcastle, 1972), pp. 19 ff.

[31] H. H. Ballin, *The Organization of Electricity Supply in Great Britain* (1946), chapter 8.

[32] J. G. Crowther, *Discoveries and Inventions of the 20th Century* (1955 ed.), pp. 95–8; Sir Henry Self and Miss Elizabeth Watson, *Electricity Supply in Great Britain* (1952), chapter 4; Lincoln Gordon, *The Public Corporation in Britain* (1938), chapter 3; Leslie Hannah, *Electricity Before Nationalisation. A Study of the Development of the Electricity Supply Industry in Britain to 1948* (1979), pp. 95 ff.

[33] British Association, *Britain in Recovery* (1938), p. 265; Richard Stone, *Measurement of Consumers' Expenditure in the United Kingdom, 1920–1938* (Cambridge, 1954), p. 418; Alfred Plummer, *New British Industries in the Twentieth Century* (1937), chapters 2/1.

and 1926.[34] There were several innovations that originated in Great Britain.[35]

As in other countries, the industry came to be dominated by a few large firms. Further, in an industry so dependent on constant inventions and patents[36] it was perhaps not surprising that restrictive associations of producers were particularly rampant. Most of these, including, for example, the Electric Lamp Manufacturers' Association,[37] had international links, and so had some of the leading firms, such as EMI (Electrical and Musical Industries), a combine formed in 1931.

Comparable in importance with electricity in the inter-war years was the motor industry. The motor car changed people's habits of living, shopping, travelling and holidaying; it affected the layout of towns and suburbs; it created the first true conveyor-belt factories and stimulated innumerable ancillary industries, some of them of major importance in their own right, including oil refining, rubber, electrical goods, glass, metallurgy, both ferrous and non-ferrous, and mechanical engineering.

Before the war, motor vehicles had been made singly or at best in batches; 34,000 motor vehicles of all kinds were built in 1913, but among the cars alone there had been 198 different models.[38] During the war, motor engineers benefited greatly by the experience of building military trucks and engines, though the output of luxury cars had to be suspended. The war also left the McKenna duty of $33\frac{1}{3}$ *ad valorem* on imported cars.

After 1918 the industry grew quickly out of its pre-war methods. By 1922 Austin had started on the production of his first 'mass car', the Austin 7, and in 1924 had introduced 'continuous flow production'; by 1925 Morris, who had also introduced a production line, made 41% of the total output of British cars in his class. However, full 'Fordism' with its extreme division of work using unskilled labour was not adopted.[39] Omitting motor cycles, the annual output of motor vehicles rose from 95,000 in 1923 to a peak of 511,000 in 1937; employment rose more slowly, from 220,000 insured workers in 1924 to 380,000 in 1939 (including aircraft); and the average factory value of private cars made in Great Britain fell from £308 per car in 1912 to £259 in 1924 and £130 in 1935 6.[40] Falling costs and an elastic market thus went together as in the case

[34] Balfour Committee, *Survey of Industries*, vol. 4, chapter 3; Plummer, *op. cit.*, chapter 2/II; Lord Aberconway, *The Basic Industries* (1927), pp. 317 ff.; A. E. Kahn, *Great Britain in the World Economy* (1946), pp. 43–120; R. E. Catterall, 'Electrical Engineering', in Buxton and Aldcroft, *British Industry*, p. 241.

[35] Crowther, *op. cit.*, p. 372; S. G. Sturmey, *The Economic Development of Radio* (1948), p. 179.

[36] Thomas Wilson, 'The Electronics Industry', in Duncan Burn, *The Structure of British Industry*, vol. 2 (Cambridge, 1958), pp. 132–49.

[37] Monopolies Commission, *Report on the Supply of Electric Lamps* (1951. 287), esp. chapter 2; cf. also *Report on the Supply of Insulated Electric Wires and Cables* (1952. 209), chapter 4; *Report on the Supply of Electric Valves and Cathode Ray Tubes* (1956. 16), chapters 2–4; *Report on the Supply and Export of Electrical and Allied Machinery and Plant* (1957. 42), chapter 1.

[38] PEP, *Engineering Reports II: Motor Vehicles* (1950), p. 5.

[39] P. W. S. Andrews and Elizabeth Brunner, *The Life of Lord Nuffield* (Oxford, 1955), p. 112; Roy Church, *Herbert Austin. The British Motor Car Industry to 1941* (1979), pp. 73, 98; R. J. Overy, *William Morris, Lord Nuffield* (1976), pp. 29 ff.; M. Miller and R. A. Church, 'Motor Manufacturing', in Buxton and Aldcroft, p. 180; Kenneth Richardson, *The Motor Industry 1896–1939* (1977), pp. 83–88: Wayne Lewchuk, *American Technology and the British Vehicle Industry* (Cambridge 1987).

[40] G. C. Allen, *British Industries and their Organizations* (1959 ed.), p. 204; Plummer, *op. cit.*, p. 87.

of electricity, and by the early 1930s were beginning to tap an extremely elastic section of the market. Exports and imports were not of much importance, but the motor-cycle industry, which had exported over 40% of its output in the 1920s, suffered serious contraction when the foreign demand declined in the 1930s.[41] In this period, the number of car makers fell from 96 in 1922 to 20 in 1939. By then, much of the market was shared among the 'Big Six'.[42] Several small motor firms survived by catering for narrowly specialized markets in the luxury car and small sports car range.

Closely linked with the development of the motor car engine was the development of aircraft production. From 1930 onwards the needs of the RAF provided a backbone of orders as well as research, and in the early 1930s some 30,000 people were employed in aircraft manufacturing. Rearmament, the erection of 'shadow' factories from 1936 onward, and the installation of American machine tools, laid the foundation for the later war-time expansion of output.[43]

Some new industries were based on advances in the science of chemistry and in chemical engineering. One of the most significant of them was the man-made fibre industry, limited, before 1939, almost entirely to rayon and rayon staple, based on cellulose derived from wood-pulp or cotton linters. In 1913, the output had been something over 6 million lb. of rayon filament. By 1927 Britain produced 53 m. lb. of filament and 2 m. lb. of staple, the figures rising to 115 m. lb. and 58 m. lb. respectively by 1939, representing 7·7% of the world output, but even in 1939 all man-made fibres together only accounted for 8–9% of the fibres used in the world's textile industries.

In the 1920s, improvements made possible the production of mixed fabrics, and even the substitution for cotton and finally for wool and linen: high-tenacity types of viscose rayon could be used in the industrial field, e.g. for tyre cords. Nevertheless, the chief successes were scored in replacing silk and in opening wider markets for goods formely made of silk, helped by the marked decline in its costs and prices. By 1936, the total number employed in the rayon industry was about 100,000.[44]

The industry was from the beginning dominated by a small number of large firms. Before 1914, Courtauld's, an old-established silk-throwing firm had acquired the various British patents and factories in 1904. While its issued capital in 1939 was £32 million, and that of British Celanese £13·5 million, that of the other nine firms combined only came to £5·2 million.[45] The hegemony of the two leading firms was assisted by price agreements in the 1930s, by disguised protection since 1925, by international links with the main producers abroad,

[41] G. Maxcy and A. Silberston, *The Motor Industry* (1959), chapter 1; L. F. Duval, 'The Motor Industry', in *Britain in Recovery*, Part II, chapter 7.

[42] G. Maxcy, 'The Motor Industry', in P. L. Cook (ed.), *Effects of Mergers* (1958).

[43] Peter Fearon, 'The British Airframe Industry and the State, 1918–35', *Ec. Hist. Rev.*, 22/2, 1974, and discussion in *ibid.*, 28/4, 1975, pp. 648–662; *idem*, 'Airframe Manufacturing', in Buxton and Aldcroft, *op. cit.*; Corelli Barnett, *The Audit of War* (1986), pp. 125 ff.

[44] R. Robson, *The Man-made Fibres Industry* (1958), pp. 19–29; D. C. Hague, *The Economics of Man-made Fibres* (1957), p. 86; Plummer, *New Industries*, chapter 4/II, 'Rayon'; D. C. Coleman, *Courtaulds. An Economic and Social History*, 3 vols., vol 2 (Oxford, 1969), pp. 245–50, 319–20.

[45] Hague, *op. cit.*, p. 78. Courtauld's and British Celanese, the main producers of acetate yarn, merged in 1957. G. C. Allen, *British Industries*, p. 288; J. Harrop, 'The Growth of the Rayon Industry in the Inter-War Years', *Yorkshire Bulletin*, 20/2, 1968; *idem*, 'Rayon', in Buxton and Aldcroft; D. C. Coleman, *Courtaulds*.

and by maintaining a high rate of technical improvement.[46]

At the centre of the 'chemical industry' proper stood Imperial Chemical Industries Ltd., formed in 1926 by a merger of four companies. One of these, British Dyestuffs Corporation Ltd, had been set up in 1918 largely with Government financial support and protection by licensing (for synthetic dyestuffs) and by a $33\frac{1}{3}$% duty (for other organic chemicals). The other constituent firms were Brunner-Mond Ltd, a combine that had put up the first large-scale British plant for fixing nitrogen from the air at Billingham, Stockton-on-Tees, in 1923; United Alkali; and Nobel Industries, dominating the explosives industry. The company had an initial capital of £65 million. Several other chemical firms were absorbed soon after,[47] and the company joined international cartel and exchange of information agreements with foreign firms.[48]

The soap industry was dominated by the vast Lever combine, which joined with its chief Dutch rivals, Jurgens' and Van den Bergh (the Margarine Union of 1927), in 1929 and had interests in other industries also.[49] Oil refining was another related industry, dominated from the beginning in this country by large firms. Thermal cracking began in 1913, and catalytic cracking plants were developed just before the Second World War. In the 1930s, however, an increasing proportion of motor spirit was imported, while the output of British refineries actually fell from 604 m. gallons in 1929 to 455 m. gallons in 1938.[50]

Another industry which showed remarkable technical progress and came to be dominated by a single large firm was glass making. Between the wars, sheet glass making was revolutionized by Pilkinton's adaptation of the Slingluff process of the Pittsburgh Plate Glass Co. in 1930. Plate glass making, in turn, was changed into a continuous flow process between rollers; continuous polishing and grinding was also perfected at Pilkington's. During the First World War, the formerly neglected production of optical glass and chemical and heat-resisting glassware had been established, and in the inter-war years laminated and armour plate or toughened glass were developed from a pre-war British discovery.[51] Flat glass making, including plate and window glass, came to be dominated by the same firm.[52]

[46] Balfour Committee, *Survey of Industries*, vol. 3, chapter 3, 'The Artificial Silk Industry'; II. A. Silverman, 'The Artificial Textile Industry', in *Studies in Industrial Organization* (1946), ed. H. A. Silverman, pp. 307 ff., 334.

[47] W. B. Reddaway, 'The Chemical Industry', in Duncan Burn (ed.), *The Structure of British Industry*, vol. 1 (Cambridge 1958), pp. 233 ff.; Stephen Miall, *History of the British Chemical Industry* (1931), pp. 61–2; A. F. Lucas, *Industrial Reconstruction* (1937), pp. 178–90.

[48] Plummer, chapter 6/1, 'Synthetic Dyestuffs'; W. J. Reader, 'Chemical Industry', in Buxton and Aldcroft, *op. cit.*; *idem, Imperial Chemical Industries: A History*, vol. 2; *The First Quarter Century 1926–1952* (Oxford, 1975); L. F. Haber, *Chemical Industry 1900–1930* (Oxford, 1971), esp. chapter 10.

[49] Charles Wilson, *The History of Unilever*, 2 vols. (1954); Ruth Cohen, 'The Soap Industry', in P. L. Cook (ed.), *Effects of Mergers* (1958).

[50] Duncan Burn, 'The Oil Industry', in *Structure of British Industry*, vol. 1; PEP, *The British Fuel and Power Industries* (1947), pp. 199–209.

[51] Heath and Hetherington, chapter 10; L. M. Angus-Butterworth, *The Manufacture of Glass* (1948), chapters 16–19.

[52] Working Party Reports, *Hand-blown Domestic Glassware* (1947); T. C. Barker, *Pilkington Brothers and the Glass Industry* (1960); P. L. Cook, 'The Flat-Glass industry', in P. L. Cook (ed.), *Effects of Mergers* (1958); T. C. Barker, 'A Family Firm becomes a Public Company: Changes at Pilkington Brothers Limited in the Interwar Years', in L. Hannah (ed.), *Management Strategy and Business Development* (1976).

If glass making was typical of the old industries which were being revolutionized by new techniques, the working of aluminium, rubber and plastic typified the new industries based on new materials. British production of virgin aluminium increased from 10,000 to 25,000 metric tons between 1913 and 1939, and consumption from 16,000 metric tons in 1925 to 90,000 metric tons in 1939. Economies of scale led to an early concentration in large firms: in 1923 an international cartel agreement protected the European market, and after 1929 it was extended also to America and Canada.[53]

Rubber was used for rainwear and other purposes in the nineteenth century, but the rubber industry became of importance only with the motor vehicle of the twentieth. By 1937, two-thirds of the world's rubber supplies were used for motor tyres and tubes.[54] Rubber tyre making in Britain was dominated by the largest firm, Dunlop's,[55] and there were price agreements and far-reaching international links among the leading firms, particularly after a $33\frac{1}{3}$% tariff in 1927. Rubber footwear was similarly organized.[56] Among other consumer goods industries which showed steady increases in productivity without any spectacular technical changes were boots and shoes, and hosiery. Both had lost exports, but could more than make up for it by the buoyant home demand.[57]

The enormous technical advantages of size in flour-milling led to domination by a handful of firms, and at the end of 1938, Rank's, Spiller's and the Co-operative Wholesale Societies between them controlled 65–70% of the industry's capacity. Under the leadership of the former two the industry was 'rationalized' in 1929, by the purchase and removal of much redundant capacity by the 'Purchase Finance Co. Ltd', owned by the seven largest firms. Prices and profits were then effectively maintained by a quota system, organized by the 'Millers' Mutual Aid Association'.[58]

The canning of food, in contrast to flour-milling, faced a rapidly expanding market in the inter-war years. The consumption of canned vegetables is estimated to have risen from an average of 24,000 tons p.a. in 1920–2 to 193,000 tons in 1937–8, and the home production of canned and bottled fruit from 30,000 cwt to 180,000 cwt in the same years. The Board of Trade index of production of grain-milling, food, drink and tobacco showed a rise to 133 in 1939 (with 1924 = 100). The Metal Box Co., a firm with international links established in 1921, controlled 90% of the British output of cans, but imports, especially of canned fruit and vegetables, still acounted for the bulk of consumption.[59]

[53] Plummer, *New Industries,* chapter 4/1; J. D. Edwards, F. C. Frary and Z. Jeffries, *The Aluminium Industry* (New York, 1930), vol. 1, pp. 43–7.

[54] G. Rae, 'The Statistics of the Rubber Industry,' *J. R. Stat. S.,* 101/2, 1938, p. 340; Audrey G. Donnithorne, *British Rubber Manufacturing* (1958), chapter 3.

[55] In 1951–2, the company accounted for 47% of British sales. Pre-war figures are not available, but were similar. Monopolies Commission, *Supply and Export of Pneumatic Tyres* (1955. 133), p. 82.

[56] Monopolies Commission, *Rubber Footwear* (1956. 328).

[57] Working Party Reports, *Boots and Shoes* (1946), section 5; H. A. Silverman, 'The Boot and Shoe Industry', in *Studies in Industrial Organization* (1946), ed. Silverman; H. A. Silverman, 'The Hosiery Industry', in *ibid.*; F. A. Wells, 'The Hosiery Trade', in *Britain in Depression* (1935); Working Party Reports, *Hosiery* (1946), esp. chapters 2, 7, 8.

[58] H. V. Edwards, 'Flour Milling', in *Further Studies in Industrial Organization* (1948), ed. M. P. Fogarty.

[59] Richard Stone, *The Measurement of Consumers' Expenditure* (Cambridge, 1954), Tables 36, 40; Plummer, *New Industries,* chapter 5, 'Canning of Foodstuffs'; Forrest Capie and Michael Collins,

Building was considered non-essential during the First World War and the labour force had fallen from 920,000 in July 1914 to 438,000 at the time of the armistice and by July 1920 had recovered only to 796,000.[60] From then on a series of public programmes and favourable conditions for private building kept the industry booming throughout the inter-war years, except for a brief interval in 1928–30. The housing boom of the early 1930s was widely believed to have helped to pull the country out of the slump.[61] There was little rise in productivity, so that most of the increased output was achieved by increased employment. There were few large firms, and these were mostly in civil engineering. By contrast, the suppliers of many building materials, following in the footsteps of the Portland Cement industry before the war, became strongly cartellized in this period.[62]

The new or growing industries were thus of several types. Some were directly replacing an old industry, including artificial silk, motor cars, aluminium and canned food. Others represented genuinely new products or services: among them were radio, aircraft and electrical goods. Others still were long-established industries for which the home market was growing: these included building, boots and shoes, and hosiery. With some exceptions, such as electrical and motor engineering, they were based essentially on a buoyant home market. Similarly, most of the prosperous industries were 'sheltered' from the competition of foreign makers, by costs of transport, tariffs or by the nature of their supply. Many of the new industries depended on State support, encouragement or sponsorship; many required a high degree of scientific knowledge, and a surprisingly large number of them were dominated by a single large firm, or a few firms strongly cartellized, often with international links.[63]

Few of the new and growing industries were tied to the coalfields or even to the ports. In consequence, many settled in the Midlands, others in the new industrial suburbs to the north and west of London.[64] The geographical shift was distinctly away from the centres of the old staple industries in certain regions in the north and west.

3 The Old and Declining Industries

Coal had been the symbol of the old industrial Britain. It had driven her industries and it determed their location since the days of the Industrial Revolution. The decline in the output of coal after the peak of 1913 was equally symbolic. The coal industry was buffeted by all the storms which drove the other old staple trades before them in this period.

Prior to 1914, the traditions and organization of this industry had been geared to a steadily expanding market, and excess demand continued to 1919–20.

The Inter-War British Economy: A Statistical Abstract (Manchester 1983) p. 26; W. E. Minchinton, *The British Tinplate Industry* (Oxford, 1957), pp. 178–80.

[60] Quoted in G. C. Allen, *British Industries*, p. 304.

[61] pp. 120–1 below.

[62] Alfred C. Bossom, 'The Building Industry since the War', in *Britain in Depression;* Sir Harold Bellman, 'The Building Trades', in *Britain in Recovery*; Monopolies Commission Reports, *Cast Iron Rain Water Goods* (1951. 136); P. L. Cook, 'The Cement Industry', in P. L. Cook (ed.), *Effects of Mergers* (1958).

[63] Plummer, *op. cit.*, chapters 1, 6 and 7; H. Clay, *The Post-War Unemployment Problem* (1929), p. 108.

[64] D. H. Smith, *The Industries of Greater London* (1933), pp. 131, 154.

Thereafter a series of fortuitous events helped to prolong the illusion of a continuing sellers' market in coal, including the strike of April-July 1921, the American coal strike of 1922, and the French invasion of the Ruhr in 1923. Up to the end of 1924, in fact, unemployment in coal was below the national average.[65] It was not until 1925 that the industry was brought up against a sharp fall in demand, and it took some years longer before it recognized that the reduction in the aggregate demand for coal was permanent.

That part of the demand for coal which came from the home market ceased to grow for the first time in centuries: home consumption, including coastwise bunkers, was estimated at 183·8 million tons in 1913 and at 185 m.t. in 1937–8.[66] Exports, which were at a level of about 100 m.t. in 1913 and again in 1923 because of freak market conditions, generally reached only about 50 m.t. even in the relatively good years of 1937–8. The shortfall of demand as against capacity was thus of the order of 40–50 m.t. yearly.

Technically, the British industry fell behind its foreign competitors after 1918. Output per man-shift rose only by 10% between 1913 and 1936, much less than in other European countries.[67] There was some progress: in 1913 8% of the coal was cut by machine, in 1929 28%, in 1934 47% and in 1939 61%, while mechanical conveyance was used on 12% of the coal in 1928, 37% in 1934 and 54% in 1938.[68] Improvements were concentrated in the large modern pits sunk in the eastward extensions of the coalfield in Yorkshire, Nottinghamshire and Scotland.[69] The organization of the industry made it hard for it to put its house in order. The typical British colliery was too small to be efficient[70] and there were too many independent and competing firms to form effective voluntary associations.

The Sankey Commission of 1919 was the first of a series of official bodies which attempted to deal with the problem of organization in the coal industry in this period. Composed of owners' and miners' representatives in equal numbers with a judge as chairman, an agreed set of recommendations was most unlikely to emerge. In the event, the chairman appeared to use his casting vote in favour of nationalization, mainly on technical grounds, and virtually all members agreed on a recommendation to nationalize the coal royalties. Both suggestions were ignored by the Government, and the only permanent result was the miners' Welfare Fund financed by a levy of 1*d*. per ton of coal. In March 1921, when prices and profits were tumbling, the Government handed the industry and its problems back to its private owners.

[65] Cf. J. M. Keynes, *The Economic Consequences of the Peace* (New York, 1920), p. 93; W. H. B. Court, 'Problems of the British Coal Industry between the Wars', *Ec. Hist. Rev.*, 15/1–2, 1945, p. 8; Henry Clay, *The Post-War Unemployment Problem* (1929), p. 41.

[66] R. Stone, *Measurement of Consumers' Expenditure* (Cambridge, 1954), p. 235; A. M. Neumann, *Economic Organization of the British Coal Industry* (1934), p. 98.

[67] A. Beacham, 'Efficiency and Organization of the British Coal Industry', *Econ. J.*, 55/218–19, 1945, p. 207.

[68] P. E. P., *Report on the British Coal Industry* (1936), p. 2; G. C. Allen, *British Industries* (1959 ed.), p. 70; E. C. Rhodes, 'Labour and Output in the Coal Mining Industry in Great Britain', *J. R. Stat. S.*, 94/4, 1931. Cf. also Balfour Commission, *Survey of Industries*, vol. 4, chapter 5; Neil K. Buxton, 'Coalmining', in Buxton and Aldcroft, pp. 56–61.

[69] E. C. Rhodes, 'Output, Labour and Machines in the Coal Mining Industry of Great Britain', *Economica*, NS, 12/46, 1945.

[70] For a discussion, see Neil K. Buxton, 'Entrepreneurial Efficiency in the British Coal Industry between the Wars', *Ec. Hist. Rev.*, 23/3, 1970, and debate in *ibid.*, 25/4, 1972, pp. 655–73.

The newly found 'freedom' was ushered in by one of the most costly and bitter strikes in the history of coal mining,[71] ended by a complex agreement on the division of the surplus profits and wages, on a regional basis, but this broke down as soon as over-production and heavy unemployment began to affect the industry in 1925–6. A temporary Government subsidy of £23 million enabled the owners to cut prices while keeping up wages in 1925–6, but in the end they insisted on cutting wages, increasing hours from 7 to 8 and making regional in place of national wage agreements. The miners resisted in a seven-month strike, ushered in by a General Strike called in sympathy by the TUC, but ultimately had to give in.

Meanwhile, following the Samuel Commission of 1925, the Mining Industry Act of 1926 attempted to encourage colliery amalgamation schemes, but since the initiative had still to come from the industry, the Act had negligible results.[72] Of regional cartel schemes, the most effective was the Midland scheme which embraced Lancashire, Yorkshire, Nottinghamshire and Derbyshire and had a large and secure home market as base.[73]

The Coal Mines Act of 1930, the most important measure affecting the industry in the inter-war years, attempted to apply the lessons of the 1920s. Part I of the Act set up a compulsory cartel scheme. It failed to end price competition completely, but it did help to reduce output and keep up prices and profits, and since quotas were transferable, it led to some concentration of production.[74] While these cartel powers were designed to raise the price of coal temporarily, Part II of the Act was to effect a permanent cure. It set up the Coal Mines Reorganization Commission, charged with the task of reorganizing the industry mainly by amalgamations and concentration of production. In the face of the determined opposition of the industry, however, the Commission was unable to carry out its task.[75] Its powers were transferred to the Coal Commission by the Coal Act of 1938, which also authorized the nationalization of coal royalties, ultimately completed in 1942 at a cost of £66½ million.

The history of the coal industry has been described at some length since it illustrates better than any other the fundamental problems of the declining staple industries in the inter-war years. Largely because of the fall in exports, there was a drop in output from an annual average of 268 million tons in 1907–14 to 228 million tons in 1934–8. Even these figures were only achieved by drastic price cuts. In 1929, perhaps the best inter-war year, it was estimated that one-quarter of the German industry, one-quarter to one-third of the British, and one-half of the Polish were surplus to requirements. Employment fell drastically from 1,226,000 in 1920 to 702,000 in 1938. After 1925, unemployment

[71] A. R. Redmayne, *Coalmining During the War* (Oxford, 1923), chapters 14–16.
[72] Neumann, *op. cit.*, pp. 152 ff.; Lord Aberconway, *The Basic Industries of Great Britain* (1927), p. 22.
[73] Barry Supple, *The History of the British Coal Industry* vol. 4: *1913–1946: The Political Economy of Decline* (Oxford 1987), n. 180 f., 446–7; J. H. Jones, G. Cartwright and P. H. Guénault, *The Coal-mining Industry* (1939), chapter 6; W. M. Kirby, *The British Coalmining Industry 1870–1946* (1977), chapter 6. But see: Neil K. Buxton, 'Entrepreneurial Efficiency and the British Coal Industry between the Wars', *Ec. Hist. Rev.* 23/3, 1970; Ben Fine, *The Coal Question* (1990), chapter 2.
[74] J. H. Jones *et al.*, *Coal-mining Industry*, pp. 127–33.
[75] Supple, *Political Economy*, chapter 8i Ivor Thomas, 'The Coal Mines Reorganization Commission', in W. A. Robson (ed.), *Public Enterprise* (1937); M. W. Kirby, 'The Control of Competition in the British Coalmining Industry in the Thirties', *Ec. Hist. Rev.*, 26/2, 1973.

was seldom under 20% and generally well above this figure, while at least 200,000 miners drifted out of the industry.[76]

The iron and steel industry was another of the basic staple trades which suffered a decline in exports. Moreover, the war had created a large surplus capacity and the post-war boom of 1919–20 burdened it with much watered capital, and this hung like a millstone round its neck until the re-armament of the late 1930s. After a period of decline, steel output rose from the earlier peak of $9\frac{1}{2}$ m.t. in 1917–18 to 13 m.t. in 1937.[77] These figures may be compared with a capacity of 12 m.t. after the war.[78] There was thus, throughout, much redundant capacity and a high level of unemployment, generally fluctuating around the 20% level.

The British industry lost much of its competitive edge in the 1920s. While tariffs abroad and foreign cartels reduced exports, the home market was flooded with cheap foreign steel. The world output of steel had risen from 75 m.t. in 1913 to 118 m.t. in 1929, but the British output had increased by only 2 m.t.[79] In the post-war period Britain's capacity was still geared too much towards puddled bar iron and acid steel instead of basic steel, and, besides, her steelworks were antiquated, the furnaces too small, mechanical aids insufficient, and the layout of works dictated by history rather than technical needs. Blast furnaces were particularly backward and inefficient.[80] Some improvements did take place.

There was a geographical shift towards the Lincolnshire and East Midland ore fields, which produced 18·7% of the pig iron in 1920 and 37·4% in 1932. In North Lincolnshire, large integrated works were set up on the ore field, about 20 miles from the coal, but there was much expansion also in Sheffield, badly sited from almost every point of view, but containing 80% of the British electric furnace capacity, as well as in Consett and the Lancashire Steel Corporation, both away from the coast and the ore.[81] Amalgamations in the industry in the 1920s included South Durham and Cargo Fleet, Dorman Long and Bolckow-Vaughan, Cammell-Laird and Vickers, Guest, Keen & Nettlefold and Baldwin, Colville and Beardmore, the Lancashire Steel Corporation and the United Steel Companies.

The world depression hit the iron and steel industry with particular force because of its dependence on capital goods. The production of pig iron dropped by 53% between 1929 and 1932, and of steel by 45%. A large part of the industry's capital had to be written off, £42 million being thus wiped off among

[76] G. C. Allen, *British Industries,* chapter 3; J. H. Jones, G. Cartwright, and W. Prest, 'The Coal Industry', in *Britain in Depression*; J. H. Jones, 'The Colamining Industry', in *Britain in Recovery*; PEP, *Report on the British Coal Industry* (1936), pp. 23–5.

[77] H. G. Roepke, *Movements of the British Iron and Steel Industry, 1720–1951* (Urbana, Ill., 1956), p. 111.

[78] E. D. McCallum, 'The Iron and Steel Industry', in *Britain in Depression*.

[79] T. H. Burnham and G. O. Hoskins, *Iron and Steel in Britain, 1870–1930* (1943), Tables 91, 93; M. S. Birkett, 'The Iron and Steel Industry since the War', *J. R. Stat. S.,* 93/3, 1930, p. 373.

[80] E.g. Burnham and Hoskins, pp. 190–3; D. L. Burn, *The Economic History of Steelmaking, 1867–1939* (Cambridge, 1940), pp. 362–70, 408–13, 427; J. C. Carr and Walter Taplin, *History of the British Steel Industry* (Oxford, 1962), parts 4 and 5; Balfour Committee, *Survey of Industries,* IV, pp. 21–32; K. Warren, 'Iron and Steel', in Buxton and Aldcroft; Neil K. Buxton, 'Efficiency and Organization in Scotland's Iron and Steel Industry during the Interwar Period', *Ec. Hist. Rev.,* 29/1, 1976.

[81] Roepke, pp. 115–16; IDAC (May Committee): *Report on the ... Iron and Steel Industry* (1936. Cmd. 5507), p. 61.

37 firms in 1927–36.[82] The subsequent recovery was equally remarkable, assisted by a 33½% tariff in 1932, which however raised costs to consumers like the motor industry.[83] By 1934 output returned to the level of 1929, and continued to expand. If iron and steel did worse in Britain than in the rest of the world in the 1920s, it did better in the 1930s: the country's share of the world's steel output rose from 7·6% in 1931 to 9·7% in 1937.

Like Part I of the Coal Mines Act of 1930, the tariff on iron and steel in 1932 was granted on the understanding that reorganization was to follow. Accordingly, the British Iron and Steel Federation was formed in April 1934, and was given fairly strong powers. In 1935–6 it took over the price-fixing functions of earlier sectional associations, and it negotiated with foreign cartels to impose quantitative restrictions on imports, after establishing a position of strength by getting the tariff on steel raised temporarily from 33⅓% to 50%; it bought foreign scrap and pig iron for the industry as a whole and sold them cheaply to home producers, financing the transaction with a levy. BISF's planning, however, tended to be restrictive, and the location of new plants, such as the Richard Thomas works ultimately sited at Ebbw Vale, was bedevilled by political wire-pulling.[84]

Under pressure from the banks, there were further mergers and schemes of 'rationalization' and integration after 1928. In 1932, 10 vertical combines had 47% of the pig-iron capacity and 60% of the steel capacity between them.[85] These mergers and the officially supported cartel policy certainly kept up prices and profits but it is not certain that they contributed greatly to economic efficiency. In the boom beginning in 1935, and the rearmament which followed, the output of steel rose from 5·2 million tons in 1931, to 9·85 m.t. in 1935, 13·0 m.t. in 1937 and, after a relapse in 1938, to 13·2 m.t. in 1939.[86]

Shipbuilding suffered even more than steelmaking in the depression from the declining demand for capital goods. The combined result of the war and the post-war boom was that in 1919–20 the world shipbuilding capacity was more than doubled, while the world's shipping tonnage, and thus the potential demand for ships, hardly increased at all. From 1920 onwards the tonnage under construction fell, and in the slump, with millions of tons of shipping laid up, the building of new tonnage virtually came to a standstill: in 1933 the launchings from British yards fell to 7% of the pre-war figure.

Launchings for foreign owners continued to form a substantial proportion of the output.[87] Britain was slow in adopting some newer types of ship: thus in 1927–30 British yards built 65% of the world's tonnage of steamships, but only 41% of motor vessels.[88] Yards were older, sites often restricted, steel prices and labour costs higher here than elsewhere, but the problem of the industry was not so much its relatively high costs – it held its own quite well with other

---

[82] P. W. S. Andrews and F. Brunner, *Capital Development in Steel* (Oxford, 1951), p. 85.

[83] B. W. E. Alford, 'New Industries for Old?', in Roderick Floud and Donald McCloskey (eds.), *The Economic History of Britain Since 1700*, vol. 2 (Cambridge, 1981), p. 311.

[84] Roepke, chapter 6; Burn, pp. 461–4.

[85] G. C. Allen, *British Industries*, p. 115.

[86] E. D. McCallum, 'The Iron and Steel Industry', in *Britain in Recovery*.

[87] Leslie Jones, *Shipbuilding in Britain* (Cardiff, 1957), p. 64; J. R. Parkinson, 'Shipbuilding', in Buxton and Aldcroft, p. 95.

[88] G. R. Henning and Keith Trace, 'Britain and the Motor Ship: A Case of the Delayed Adoption of New Technology', *J. Econ. His.*, 35, 1975.

countries – as the low level of the world's needs compared with the available capacity. Surplus ships, laid up after 1920, but capable of being brought into use again, and estimated at 11 million tons in 1922 and 6 million in 1925–6, kept down freight rates and orders for new tonnage, except for new types of ships, such as motor vessels and oil tankers. In Britain, a capacity estimated at between 3 m.t. and 4 m.t. p.a. in the 1920s,[89] compared with an output which fluctuated between 640,000 and 1,540,000 tons.

There was a heavy decline of the labour attached to the industry, and the rate of unemployment was among the highest in the country. Some firms went out of business, others saved themselves by mergers, like Harland & Wolff of Belfast and the Clyde, Palmer's and the Northumberland Shipbuilding Co. on the Tyne, Hawthorne – Leslie and Vickers-Armstrong.[90] When the disastrous collapse of markets in 1929–33 threatened to obliterate much of the industry altogether, 'National Shipbuilders' Security Ltd.' was formed in 1930 with the support of nearly the whole of the industry, and aided by the 'Bankers' Industrial Development Co.', an organization set up by the Bank of England and the clearing banks to scrap capacity. By 1937, 28 firms with a capacity of over 1 million tons out of a total of perhaps $3\frac{1}{2}$ m.t. had been bought up and destroyed, while a number of others, less fortunate, had been forced into liquidation.

There was also the so-called 'scrap and build' scheme of Part II of the British Shipping (Assistance) Act of 1935, to help the builders of cargo tramp vessels. In return for an undertaking to scrap 2 tons of existing tonnage for every ton newly built, the Treasury offered loans on favourable terms to owners. Tramp ship owners availed themselves of this offer only to a limited extent, however, not least because of Part I of the same Act which gave them subsidies on sailings and thus discouraged the scrapping of tonnage. In the face of foreign subsidies and protection some British owners began to place their orders abroad,[91] deriving some indirect benefits from foreign subsidy payments.

Engineering in the widest sense had expanded faster than any other occupation during the war: the Census figures showed an increase in employment from 1,779,000 in 1911 to 2,491,000 in 1921, and the insurance figures, calculated on a different basis, registered an increase from 1,028,000 in 1913–14 to 1,647,000 in 1919–20.[92] The necessary reductions were less painful than they might have been because of the large numbers of women workers involved, but in some sectors male workers were affected also. According to the Census of Production, engineering output in 1924 was only slightly higher than in 1907. It then rose to 121 in 1929 (1924 = 100), dropped heavily in the depression, then rose quickly after 1933. By 1937, it was perhaps 60% above the 1924 level, employing 30% more workers, the increases being largely due to motor and electrical engineering, while general engineering and other sections showed substantial reductions in employment.[93]

Though there were some large specialist firms in the industry, e.g. Babcock & Wilcox, boilermakers, or Platt Bros. Ltd, textile machinery makers, most

[89] Balfour Committee, *Survey of Industries*, vol. 4, chapter 4; Jones, *op. cit.* p. 124.
[90] H. M. Hallsworth, 'The Shipbuilding Industry', in *Britain in Depression*, pp. 255–6, and 'The Shipbuilding Industry', in *Britain in Recovery*, p. 358.
[91] G. C. Allen, *British Industries*, p. 155.
[92] Balfour Committee, *Survey of Industries*, vol. 4, pp. 132–3; H. Clay, *Unemployment*, pp. 84–6.
[93] E. Allen, 'Engineering', in *Britain in Depression*.

firms in general engineering were of small or medium size.[94] It was not at all certain that large size necessarily promoted efficiency, which depended largely on technical innovation; good progress was being made particularly in mass-production and in accepting standard specifications for components, in association with the British Standards Institution which had arisen out of the British Engineering Standards Association. Direct comparisons of efficiency with other countries can only be made separately for each subsection of the engineering industry, if at all. Until 1929, world trade in engineering products was growing so fast that even British exports were increasing in absolute terms, though they declined as a proportion of world exports. This picture changed radically in the 1930s, when export markets collapsed. The industry then came to rely increasingly on the home market, largely protected by the tariff of 1932 and increasingly prosperous after 1933.

In 1909–13, Britain's share in the international trade of cotton yarns and piece goods had been 65%[95]. During the war the output of cotton textiles had been curtailed. As a result of the pent-up demand created thereby, prices rose excessively in the boom years 1919–20, and many cotton firms were lured into over-capitalization by bonus issues of shares at inflated values.[96] When the bubble was pricked, the highly competitive spinning and weaving sections suffered a disproportionate fall in prices, since the monopolistic finishing sections succeeded in maintaining their margins fairly well.

Table 2·7: The decline in the cotton industry

	Yarn (million lb.)		Piece goods (million sq. yds.)		Machinery		
	Pro-duction	Exports	Pro-duction	Exports	Spindles (m. mule equiva-lent)	Looms (000)	Labour in spinning, doubling, weaving (000)
1912	1,982	244	8,050	6,913	61·4	786	621·5
1930	1,047	137	3,500	2,472	63·2	700	564·1
1938	1,070	123	3,126	1,494	42·1	495	393·0

The decline in the cotton industry which followed, especially in the case of piece goods, was wholly due to the fall in exports; home sales, in fact, were rising.[97]

The fall in exports was due to the rise of newly established competitors abroad.

[94] PEP, *Agricultural Machinery* (1949), p. 10; T. R. Gourvish, 'Mechanical Engineering', in Buxton and Aldcroft, pp. 146–7.

[95] G. C. Allen, *British Industries*, p. 217.

[96] Balfour Committee, *Survey of Industries*, vol. 3, pp. 36–8, 123–7; G. W. Daniels and J. Jewkes, 'The Post-War Depression in the Lancashire Cotton Industry', *J. R. Stat. S.*, 91/2, 1928, pp. 170–80.

[97] Working Party Reports, *Cotton* (1946), p. 6; R. Robson, *The Cotton Industry in Britain* (1957), Appendix. The piece goods figures for 1912 are in millions of linear yards, but the difference is negligible: in millions of linear yards, the export figure for 1930 would have been 2,490 instead of 2,472. The figures for 1930 and 1938 include small quantities of spun rayon and mixtures. Imports

Lancashire was inclined to blame this loss entirely on the cheap labour of the East, but other Western countries showed that it was possible, by operating with high wages and first-class equipment, to stand up to low wages competition. The British industry remained technically backward[98] and was unable to reorganize at a time when markets, prices and profits were falling away. Output per man-hour rose very slowly compared with such countries as Japan or the USA.[99] Its proportion of the world's mill consumption of cotton fell from 20% in 1910–13 to 9% in 1936–8, and its share of the world's cotton goods exports, from 58% to 28%.

Up to 1930, some attempts were made to improve efficiency in the industry, but after that the world depression turned the emphasis away from technical improvements to a panic reduction in capacity. Both required reorganization in the industry[100] but most firms remained small and agreement was difficult to reach among the hundreds of independent producers. With the help of the Bankers' Industrial Development Corporation, the Lancashire Cotton Corporation was set up in 1929 for the American section of the industry. It quickly acquired 9 million spindles, which it reduced to $4\frac{1}{2}$ million by 1939, at the same time modernizing the property it retained. In the smaller Egyptian section, the banks set up the Combined Egyptian Mills Ltd. in 1929, which bought up 3 million spindles capacity. The Quilt Manufacturers' Association was formed in the same year. These 'voluntary' actions were reinforced by the Act of 1936, which set up the Spindles Board, with powers to raise a compulsory levy, used to acquire and scrap, by 1939, 6 million spindles out of the $13\frac{1}{2}$ million still thought to be redundant. The Cotton Industry (Reorganization) Act of 1939 created machinery for fixing compulsory minimum prices by setting up a Statutory Cotton Industry Board.[101] The State, having ensured the reduction of capacity, thus created a compulsory cartel to raise prices. The outbreak of war prevented the functioning of the Cotton Board as originally intended, and its powers were modified by an Act of 1940.

Structurally, the woollen and worsted industry was not dissimilar from the cotton industry. It consisted of large numbers of small firms, though in the woollen section vertical integration was common and most firms engaged in both spinning and weaving. Since it had always relied less on exports and more on the home market than cotton, it suffered less by the general decline in the former and benefited more by the buoyancy of the latter in the 1930s. Moreover, the British woollen and worsted industry did not lose its share of world exports, but suffered only from the decline in total world trade, caused by crippling tariffs in some countries and growing self-sufficiency in others. As far as the mechanical equipment was concerned, however, too much of it was antiquated,

---

were negligible, except in 1930, when they reached 10% of home consumption. Cf. also A. C. Pigou, *Aspects of British Economic History 1918–1925* (1948 ed.), Part III, chapter 4.

[98] William Lazonick, 'Industrial Organization and Technical Change: The Decline of the British Cotton Industry', *Bus. Hist. Rev.*, 1982; Lars G. Sandberg, *Lancashire in Decline* (Columbus, Ohio, 1974); J. H. Porter, 'Cotton and Wool Textiles', in Buxton and Aldcroft, pp. 35–6.

[99] Working Party Reports, *Cotton*, pp. 8–9, 50, chapter 6; L. Rostas, 'Productivity of Labour in the Cotton Industry', *Econ. J.*, 55/218–19, 1945, p. 199; A. J. Brown, *Applied Economics* (1947), chapter V/3.

[100] *Report of the Committee on the Cotton Industry* (1930. Cmd. 3615).

[101] H. G. Hughes and C. T. Saunders, 'The Cotton Industry', in *Britain in Recovery*, pp. 448–9.

and output per man-hour or per spindle was only a fraction of the American figure.[102]

After 1929, the more serious drop in exports was not fully made up by the growing home market of the 1930s, though the tariff of 1932 had reduced imports at once from 50 million to 7 million square yards of cloth. Employment declined steadily in the inter-war period, and unemployment was above the average, reaching 36·4% in 1931, the worst year. Schemes of control were being considered more seriously in the 1930s,[103] mainly with a view to ending price cutting in the home market, but were not implemented.

The pottery industry was smaller than those considered so far, yet it has occupied an important place in British industrial production and exports since the Industrial Revolution, and like the other old staples, it is highly localized so as to form the main livelihood of a substantial region of the country, the 'Potteries'. In some sectors of the industry, notably electrical porcelain accessories, there was growth rather than decline, but the industry as a whole, especially domestic pottery, suffered from falling sales at home, while tariffs abroad reduced export sales by half between 1924 and 1935.[104] Among technical innovations were the tunnel kilns, perfected in 1910, which spread in the inter-war years, replacing the beehive kilns, and firing by gas or electricity became more common. The production of tiles and electric fittings was mechanized in the 1920s.[105] These improvements reduced employment, and the industry had a high level of unemployment in the inter-war period, reaching 38·8% in 1931 and about 45% in 1932.

The staple industries which were in a state of depression or in absolute decline in the 1920s and 1930s were thus, to a large extent, victims of the same set of circumstances. There was, first, the contraction of vital foreign markets, largely because of self-sufficiency or tariffs abroad. Secondly, the British share of world trade was shrinking, as the British industries appeared antiquated, yet in a period of low profits unable to modernize their equipment, preferring, instead, restrictive and monopolistic schemes. Thirdly, the staple export industries on which Britain had concentrated in the past were no longer the growth sectors in world demand.[106] Fourthly, after 1925 the relative loss of markets was aggravated by the over-valuation of the pound discussed in chapter 3, section 5 below.

In addition, there were often specific causes for the depression in particular industries. Thus steel, shipbuilding and engineering suffered from the unhealthy over-expansion during the war; coal from being replaced, in part, by oil and hydro-electric power; and cotton from the ease with which backward low-wage countries could instal up-to-date machinery.[107] Finally, some industrial 'blocs' pulled each other down: thus the collapse of the shipyards reduced the markets for both steel and coal.

---

[102] Working Party Reports, *Wool* (1947), pp. 66–7, chapter 8.
[103] A. N. Shimmin, 'The Wool Textile Industry', in *Britain in Recovery*, p. 467.
[104] Working Party Reports, *Pottery* (1946), pp. 1, 36–7.
[105] John Thomas, 'The Pottery Industry', in *Britain in Depression*, p. 413.
[106] A. E. Kahn, *Great Britain in the World Economy* (1946), p. 74.
[107] W. A. Lewis, *Economic Survey 1919–1939* (1949), pp. 42, 87.

4 The Changing Location of Industry

One of the consequences of the interaction between the declining staple industries and the new and expanding trades was a decisive shift in the geographical location of British industry and population between 1920 and 1939.

Some of the declining industries including railways, shipping and agriculture were widely scattered geographically, but mostly they were highly concentrated in small and clearly defined areas. Some of these held concentrations of two or three of these old basic industries and were utterly dependent on their prosperity. These original locations had been determined largely by easily accessible coal and iron deposits, by water power available from mountain streams, and by other materials, such as salt in Cheshire, fireclay near Stourbridge, and grindstones near Sheffield. Once established, an industry would call into being others of an ancillary or complementary nature, as well as a large labour force, a canal and railway network, and these would in turn attract yet other industries by a snowball effect, the whole depending ultimately on steam power based on coal. Thus, by 1914, much of Britain's basic staple industry was to be found in a few areas in South Wales, Lancashire and the West Riding, the industrial West Midlands, the northeast coast and Clydeside.

The effects of the decline and depression of the old staple industries on employment and prosperity generally were naturally felt with particular force in these narrowly limited areas, and they were not compensated by a parallel establishment of the new industries there. In general, these settled in new areas, mainly in the Midlands and the south. This is illustrated in Tables 2·8a and 2·8b.

In June 1923, the four southern Divisions of the Ministry of Labour (London, South-East, South-West and the Midlands) contained 46·6% of the insured population, and the rest of the United Kingdom (including Northern Ireland) the remaining 53·4%: in June 1938 these figures had been almost exactly reversed, the south now having 53·9% and the north 46·1% of the insured population. There was a still larger shift when measured by net industrial output.

This shift was not so much the result of a southward 'migration' of industry, as of the fact that it was the south and east, sometimes also known as 'inner Britain', which contained mainly industries which were destined to expand,

Table 2·8a: Percentage of net output of industry in regions, 1924–35[108]

	1924	1930	1935
Old industrial regions*	49·6	42·4	37·6
New industrial regions**	28·7	33·4	37·1
Rest of Great Britain	21·7	24·2	25·3
Total Great Britain	100	100	100

* Lancashire and Cheshire, West Riding, Northumberland and Durham, South Wales and Monmouthshire and West Central Scotland Regions of the Census of Production.
** Greater London, Warwickshire etc. Regions of the Census of Production.

[108] PEP, *Report on the Location of Industry in Great Britain* (1939), p. 44.

Table 2·8b: Percentage of total population and insured population in regions, 1921–37[109]

	Total population		Insured population	
	1921	1937	1923	1937
Old industrial areas*	37·9	35·9	45·9	40·8
New industrial areas**	33·0	35·4	33·6	37·7
Rest of Great Britain	29·1	28·7	20·5	21·5
Total Great Britain	100	100	100	100

* Lancashire, West Riding, Notts, Derby, Northumberland, Durham, Mid-Scotland, Glamorgan, Monmouth.
** London, Home Counties, Industrial Midland Counties, except Notts and Derbyshire.

while the typical industries of the north and west or 'outer Britain' were declining. The extent of that factor is illustrated in Table 2·9, which should be compared with Table 2·8b.[110]

Table 2·9: Change of employment in regions, 1923–37

	Percent of insured workers in each region employed in:					Hypothetical change if employment in 21 industries had changed alike in all regions
	16 expanding industries		5 declining industries		Total change in employ-ment, %	
	1923	1937	1923	1937		
1 Lancashire	9	16	36	24	+8	+11
2 West Riding, Notts, Derby	9	14	43	32	‖15	+9
3 Northumberland, Durham	6	9	49	33	+5	+4
4 Mid-Scotland	10	13	24	15	+10	+18
5 Glamorgan and Monmouth	4	6	59	41	−4	+1
6 London and Home Counties	21	25	1	1	+43	+40
7 Midland Counties	26	30	12	7	+28	+29
Great Britain	14	19	23	14	+22	+22

To some extent, however, every industry showed rather better results in the expanding areas than in the declining ones,[111] the multiplier effect of local prosperity being particularly evident in 'local', as distinct from 'basic', industries, such as local transport, distribution, hotels and entertainment services and above all, building.[112]

[109] *Report of the Royal Commission on the Distribution of the Industrial Population* (Barlow Commission) (1940. Cmd. 6153). Based on the Ministry of Labour Regions. Cf. also Mark Abrams, *The Condition of the British People, 1911–1945* (1945), p. 22.

[110] M. P. Fogarty, *Prospects of the Industrial Areas of Great Britain* (1945), p. 16.

[111] R. C. Tress, 'Unemployment and the Diversification of Industry', *Manchester School*, 9/2, 1938; D. G. Champernowne, 'The Uneven Distribution of Unemployment in the United Kingdom, 1929–36', *Rev. Econ. Studies*, 6/2, 1938; A. M. Carr-Saunders and D. Caradog Jones, *A Survey of the Social Structure of England and Wales* (Oxford, 2nd ed., 1937), p. 43.

[112] S. R. Dennison, *The Location of Industry and the Depressed Areas* (1939), pp. 40–1, 158; J. H. Jones, in Appx. II to Barlow Commission, *Report*, pp. 274–6.

There was substantial migration involved in this geographical shift, as shown by the following *annual* gains and losses by migration in the years 1931–6:[113]

Table 2·10:   Migration of labour, 1931–6

London and Home Counties	+ 71,600	North West	− 6,900
South East	+ 18,300	Wales	− 22,100
South West	+ 11,400	North East	− 24,200
Midlands	+ 5,500		
Scotland	+ 1,300		

The pull of higher wages was relatively unimportant here: it was the comparative levels of unemployment – as well as the distance – which were the most powerful factors affecting the decision to migrate.[114] Yet at the end of our period, the northern and Welsh unemployment figures remained obstinately at double the southern rates, migration having been quite insufficient to level them out. The July proportions of the insured population unemployed in the eight years 1929–36 averaged 11·0% in the four regions of South Britain, and 22·8% in North Britain and Wales. The difference was even more marked in the case of protracted unemployment, of 12 months or over: in June 1936, for example, this ranged from 9% in London and the southeast to 37% in Wales. In December of that year, 'Inner Britain' of the South-East, the South-West and the Midlands had 51·6% of the insured workers, 40·7% of the recipients of insurance benefits, and 19·2% of those on unemployment assistance, the dole.[115] Moreover, the declining parts of the country had more underemployment and a markedly smaller percentage of the population seeking employment: where most of the men were out of work, women, youths and old men did not even trouble to sign on at the Labour Exchange.[116] Lastly, for a man on the unemployment register, the chances of reabsorption into industry were much higher in the prosperous than in the depressed areas.[117]

The new industries of the southern half of Britain differed from the old staples not only by the fact that they were growing instead of declining. They were also industries of a different character. Mostly they were no longer, as were many of the older staples, tied to any particular area by bulky fuel or raw material needs. Electricity was now available everywhere, especially after the completion of the grid. Secondly, in place of skilled or brawny male labour, most of the new industries required adaptable but essentially unskilled labour, much of it female. In place of the capital goods and foreign markets of the old staples, the new industries were largely mass-producing consumer goods for the home market.

[113] H. W. Richardson, *Economic Recovery in Britain, 1932–9* (1967), pp. 279–82.

[114] H. Makower, J. Marschak and H. W. Robinson, 'Studies in Mobility of Labour', *Oxf. Econ. P.*, 1/1, 1938.

[115] Stephen V. Ward, *The Geography of Interwar Britain* (1988), p. 142; H. W. Robinson, 'Employment and Unemployment', in *Britain in Recovery* (1938), p. 97.

[116] J. H. Jones, in Appx. II to Barlow Commission, *Report*, pp. 264–5; S. R. Dennison, 'The Effects of Recovery on the Various Regions', in *Britain in Recovery*, p. 109; Board of Trade and Scottish Office, *Distribution of Industry* (1948). Cmd. 7540), p. 7.

[117] H. W. Singer, 'Regional Labour Markets and the Process of Unemployment', *Rev. Econ. Studies*, 7, 1939–40.

Proximity to the market often became the decisive consideration, and the relaxation of the old localizing restrictions permitted industry to follow it.[118] As a result, London, forming the largest concentration of home consumers, became the main location for new industries: in 1932–7, it accounted for five-sixths of the net increase in the number of factories, two-fifths of employment in new factories and one-third of all factory extensions undertaken, even though it had only one-fifth of the population. Birmingham and its conurbation formed another large market attracting the new industries. Even in the depressed parts of the country, the large cities were exempt from the worst effects of industrial decline. In following the market as the main factor in location, industry was concerned not so much with transport costs as with speed and regularity of supplies, and immediate knowledge of changes in markets, tastes and fashions.

However, in preferring the south to the north, industrialists moved into areas of higher rents and higher wages[119]; they left areas with well developed public utilities and plentiful labour for districts in which good roads and other services had still to be laid out, and where labour was scarce and untrained. Nor was it true that trade unions were more restrictive in the north;[120] in fact, the only clear-cut case in this period of an industry driven out by high wages and trade union power was the printing industry, which migrated out of Central London to such places as St Albans, Cheltenham and Ipswich. Constricted space, high rents and traffic jams forced other industries also to move out of London into the suburbs, to make the outer ring of London the fastest growing area in the country: between 1901 and 1938, the population of the County of London declined by 150,000, but that of Greater London grew by 1,600,000.[121] There may have been a few industrialists who consciously preferred the climate or the amenities of the south, and there may have been a few others who worked out comparative costs in some detail. But largely, industry moved south because the south was expanding and prosperous.[122]

This left the north with a double burden. As the staple industries contracted, local multiplier effects also hit ancillary trades and finally local service trades, and as the most energetic workers left, the areas affected became caught up in a vicious circle of depression and decline. In the depression of the early 1930s, in some areas, up to 80% of the insured population was out of work: even after recovery had begun, in May 1934, 74·1% of the insured males were unemployed in Brynmawr, 73·4% in Dowlais, 69·1% in Merthyr and 65·7% in Ferndale.[123]

Regional surveys in 1931–2[124] showed that with the collapse of export markets

[118] P. G. Hall, *The Industries of London since 1861* (1962).

[119] G. D. H. Cole, *Building and Planning* (1945), p. 23.

[120] *First Report of Commissioner for the Special Areas (England and Wales)* (1935. Cmd. 4957), pp. 14–16.

[121] PEP, *Location of Industry*, p. 47, map on p. 171; D. H. Smith, *The Industries of Greater London* (1933); Fogarty, *Prospects*, chapters 14, 15; Mowat, *Britain between the Wars*, p. 225; Brinley Thomas, 'The Influx of Labour into London and the South-East, 1920–36', *Economica*, NS, 4/15, 1937.

[122] PEP, *Location of Industry*, chapter 3; Dennison, *Location of Industry*, pp. 30–2; Carol E. Heim, Industrial Organisation and Regional Development in Interwar Britain, *J. Econ. Hist.* 43/4, 1983; R. C. on the Geographical Distribution of the Industrial Population (Barlow Commission), *Minutes of Evidence* (1937), *passim*.

[123] Ministry of Labour, *Reports of Investigations into the Industrial Conditions in Certain Depressed Areas* (1934. Cmd. 4728), p. 136.

[124] *Industrial Surveys* of: *South Wales* (University College of South Wales and Monmouth, 1932);

and, in some areas, the exhaustion of the coal or other mineral deposits, there was little hope of rehabilitating the local staple industries which had formed the mainstay of employment in those districts. After further reports, published in November 1934, four of these areas were officially designated 'depressed', quickly renamed 'special areas', by the Special Areas (Development and Improvement) Act, 1934.

Under the Act, two Commissioners were appointed, one for the Scottish Special Area, and one for England and Wales, responsible for the other three Special Areas of South Wales and Monmouth, West Cumberland and Tyneside with part of Durham. At first their powers were very seriously limited and though nearly £17 million had been spent on grants by September 1938, the benefits were negligible. Two further Acts followed, the Special Areas Reconstruction (Agreements) Act of 1936, and the Special Areas (Amendment) Act of 1937. Additional help was given by the Finance Act of 1937, which permitted the Treasury to remit the defence contribution of firms in the Special Areas.

Under the Act of 1936, Special Area Reconstruction Associations were set up, with a Treasury guarantee, to finance firms settling in those areas. This financial aid was supplemented in 1936 by the Nuffield Trust, and by the outbreak of war £$\frac{3}{4}$ million had been spent by SARAs and £2·2 million by the Trust. The Act of 1937 gave the Treasury authority to provide direct assistance to firms, and £1·1 million had been loaned under this part of the Act by 1939. The Commissioners, at the same time, were permitted to make contributions towards the rent, rate and tax payments of firms settling there, and to provide factories for letting. They laid out trading estates on this basis in the Special Areas at Hillington, Treforest and Team Valley, providing by the outbreak of war employment for 1,600, 2,500 and 3,300 respectively, though they were still largely in the building stage. There were also minor schemes at Pallion (Sunderland), St Helens Auckland, Larkhall and Cyfarthfa, and employment for a total of 12,000 had been found by 1939. Given an appropriate multiplier, a total of up to 40,000 jobs may have been created in 1934–8.[125]

These results, while gratifying, could scarcely be said to have made a major impact on a surplus population in the Special Areas, variously estimated at between 200,000 and 400,000 insured workers with their families. Similarly, the transfer (assisted migration) scheme of the Ministry of Labour, and the preference in placing Government orders, or the compulsory diversion of firms set up by foreigners, made only a negligible difference. In 1938, the gap in the unemployment percentages between them and the rest of the country was, if anything, wider than in 1934. It was only the re-armament boom of 1938–9 which brought new employment opportunities for the older centres of industry.

Lancashire Area, excluding Merseyside (University of Manchester, 1932); *Merseyside* (University of Liverpool, 1932); *North East Coast Area* (Armstrong College, 1932); *South West of Scotland* (University of Glasgow, 1932); J. Jewkes and A. Winterbottom, *An Industrial Survey of West Cumberland* (1933); also see Neil K. Buxton, 'Economic Growth in Scotland Between the Wars: the Role of Production Structure and Rationalisation', *Ec. Hist. Rev.* 33/4, 1980.

[125] M. E. F. Jones, 'Regional Employment Multipliers, Regional Policy, and Structural Change in Interwar Britain', *Expl. Econ. Hist.* 22, 1985.

5 Agriculture

In the war years, agriculturists had found themselves in a sellers' market, and when unrestricted U-boat warfare began to threaten the food supply of these islands, the depleted labour force on the land was stretched to the utmost to produce the largest quantity of foodstuffs that the soil would yield. The Corn Production Act of 1917 gave farmers and farm workers the necessary security of prices and wages beyond the war years,[126] and the policy of deliberate encouragement of a high level of corn production was continued, largely for strategic reasons, by the Agriculture Act of 1920. This aided the farmers by guaranteeing minimum prices for wheat and oats, and the tenants by greater security of tenure, and spread some benefits to farm workers also by continuing the machinery of fixing agricultural wages.

No sooner was the Agriculture Act on the statute book, however, than world grain prices began to crash down from their inflated post-war height. The emergency which the Act was designed to meet had arrived much sooner than expected. The wheat harvest sold at an average of 86s 4d. a quarter in 1920, 49s. in 1921 and 40s. 9d. in 1922,[127] and it was estimated that the State would have to meet a bill of some £20 million under the guarantee laid down by the Act.[128] At this the Government took fright, and within a few months of their enactment, the price guarantees were repealed by the Corn Production (Repeal) Act of 1921. Wage fixing by the Agricultural Wages Board was also abolished and wage levels were reduced at once.

As world prices of foodstuffs continued to fall, British agriculture reverted to its pre-war trends. More and more farmers gave up their arable farming and concentrated on the products in which their proximity to the home markets outweighed the disadvantages of high rents and small fields: fruit, dairy produce and meat. With a rising standard of living, the consumption of these foods was rising,[129] and represented a considerable growth potential for British farming, but falling costs abroad and more efficient methods of packing, grading and preserving ensured that these former strongholds were now also under attack. The proportion of imported meat, dairy produce and vegetables was growing,[130] and agriculture again turned into a declining, and generally depressed, industry.

There were some scattered Government aid in the 1920s. After the heavy war fellings, the Forestry Commission was set up as early as 1919 to speed afforestation, and by 1939 about 1 million acres had been acquired, including 120,000 acres of Crown land.[131] The pre-war encouragement of small holdings was continued, first by the Land Settlement (Facilities) Act of 1919, under which 17,000 ex-servicemen were settled on small farms, and then by the Small

[126] R. J. Hammond, 'British Food Supplies 1914–1939', *Econ. Hist. Rev.,* 16/1, 1946, p. 2. Cf. p. 22 above.

[127] Jones and Pool, *A Hundred Years of Economic Development* (1959 ed.,) pp. 327–8.

[128] W. Philip Jeffcock, *Agricultural Politics* (Ipswich, 1937), p. 6; C. S. Orwin, *A History of English Farming* (1949), p. 84.

[129] Richard Stone, *Measurement of Consumers' Expenditure* (Cambridge, 1954); Viscount Astor and B. Seebohm Rowntree, *British Agriculture* (1938), p. 3.

[130] A. W. Flux, 'Our Food Supply Before and After the War', *J. R. Stat. S.,* 93/4, 1930, p. 541; E. M. Ojala, *Agriculture and Economic Progress* (1952), pp. 203, 209.

[131] E. P. Stebbing, 'The Forestry Commission in Great Britain', *Quarterly Review,* 256/508, 1931; Sir R. G. Stapledon, *The Land Today and Tomorrow* (1944 ed.), chapter 7; John Parker, 'The Forestry Commission', in W. A. Robson (ed.), *Public Enterprise* (1937).

Holdings and Allotment Act of 1926 and the Agricultural Land (Utilization) Act of 1931.

In 1928 agricultural land and buildings were relieved of local rate burdens. More generous credits were made available under the Agricultural Credit Act of 1928 and a separate Act for Scotland in 1929, though the credits made available under them were not of any great significance. Lastly, the Agricultural Holdings Act of 1923 gave the tenant freedom of cropping and greater security of tenure, though it permitted his eviction for bad husbandry.[132]

The most significant Government gesture of the 1920s in aid of agriculture was the creation of a beet sugar industry. By the British Sugar Subsidy Act of 1925 a tapering subsidy for ten years was granted, which brought the acreage under sugar beet from virtually nothing to well over 350,000 over most of the 1930s,[133] while the crop provided employment for an additional 32,000 men in agriculture, beside others in the factories, and became a valuable source of cash to many farmers in the depression.

The costs, however, were substantial. The subsidies in the original ten years' period of 1925–34 amounted to £30 million, to which has to be added the sum of £10 million in abatement of excise duty; on renewal, the annual cost of the subsidy was about £3¼ million. To justify this, the Government amalgamated the existing 18 factories into the British Sugar Corporation Ltd in 1936, run by Government nominees and limited in its profits. There was also a Sugar Commission appointed, to supervise research, education and other matters.[134]

Compared with this Government-sponsored development, the voluntary schemes organized by the farmers remained singularly ineffective or, like the hop growers', collapsed after only a short period.[135] Agricultural co-operation also made very little headway in Great Britain.[136] By 1935 there were, apart from small holding and allotment societies, about 230 co-operative societies in England, 81 in Wales and 88 in Scotland, with total sales of £12·6 million. Most of them were purchasing societies. Many of the remainder were organized to pack and sell co-operatively their members' produce, mainly eggs, dairy produce and meat.[137]

As the world depression spread in the early 1930s, most of the world's food, produced by farmers and peasants in conditions of inelastic supply, fell drastically in price and huge stocks accumulated in the food exporting countries. The index of wheat prices in Britain, taking 1911–13 as 100, fell from 130 in 1929 to 76 in 1931, that of barley from 125 in 1929 to 96 in 1932, and of oats from 125 in 1929 to 80 in 1933.[138]

In 1931 the Government abandoned free trade. Agriculture was turned into a highly protected, organized and subsidized sector of the economy, mainly by the Wheat Act of 1932, the Import Duties Act of 1932 and the Agricultural Marketing Acts of 1931 and 1933.

The Wheat Act provided the most direct subsidy. Producers were assured of

[132] Aston and Rowntree, *op. cit.,* pp. 378 ff.
[133] Noel Deerr, *The History of Sugar,* vol. 2 (1950), pp. 481, 497.
[134] Heath and Hetherington, chapter 8; Plummer, *New Industries,* chapter 6/II.
[135] C. S. Orwin, 'Agriculture: Grain and other Crops', in *Britain in Depression,* pp. 100–1.
[136] C. R. Fay, *Co-operation at Home and Abroad,* vol. 2 (2nd ed., 1948), chapter 13.
[137] M. Digby, *Producers and Consumers* (1938), chapters 6–8; Horace Plunckett Foundation, *Agricultural Co-operation in England* (1930).
[138] Royal Institute of International Affairs, *World Agriculture* (1932).

the 'standard guaranteed price' of 10s. a cwt, equivalent to 45s. a quarter, and if the market price fell below it the Government made up the difference to the growers in the form of a subsidy, up to a maximum of 27 m. cwt. When wheat prices gradually began to rise from their slump levels after 1933, the deficit payments to British farmers declined sharply. The hope of limiting the acreage under wheat was not, however, fulfilled; it rose from 1·2 million acres to over 1·7 million in 1934 and the limit of 27 m. cwt was exceeded nearly every year; the Agriculture Act of 1937, in fact, raised the limit of the subsidized crop to 36 m. cwt.

Import duties under the Act of 1932 and under a special Act were at first applied to horticultural produce only, but were soon extended to oats and barley also. In view of the prosperous home market on his doorstep, protection was a particular boon to the farmer, and in 1937 it was supplemented by subsidies to growers.

The Agricultural Marketing Act of 1931 enabled two-thirds of the producers of any agricultural commodity to prepare a scheme for organized marketing, and with Parliamentary approval, this became compulsory on all. The only price control scheme set up under this Act was that of the Hop Marketing Board. The Agricultural Marketing Act of 1933 added two new sets of powers. The organized producers were now authorized to control output as well as prices of their commodities, while the Government could add protection to any scheme that required it. On the basis of this formidable battery of powers, several schemes were organized with some differences of detail, but on the same basic principles.

The Potato Marketing Board was set up early in 1934, the Milk Marketing Boards, for England and Wales and for Scotland respectively, were formed at the end of 1933[139] and the Bacon and Pig Marketing Boards in 1933. This latter had virtually broken down by 1936. Marketing schemes for other livestock proved to be even more difficult to execute and had to be abandoned. Instead, severe and diminishing quota restrictions were imposed on imports of meat from non-Empire countries, and by the Cattle Industry (Emergency Provisions) Act of 1934 large subsidy payments were made to home producers. In the three years 1934–7 £11·4 million was paid out under this head.[140]

The massive State intervention in agriculture in the 1930s sketched here reversed a policy of *laissez-faire* which was nearly a century old. The annual costs of agricultural subsidies and protection in the 1930s were variously estimated at between £32 and £41 million;[141] including the additional costs of raising food at home which could more cheaply have been bought abroad, it might well have been £100 million. Even then, prices barely rose to levels at which British farmers could make a profit: the index of agricultural prices, taking 1927–9 as 100, fell as low as 77 in 1933, but even by 1937–9 had only crept back to 90–90$\frac{1}{2}$.[142] At the same time, it was evident that Britain could not simultaneously hope to

[139] A. W. Ashby, 'The Milk Industry', in *Britain in Depression*, and 'The Milk Industry', in *Britain in Recovery*; C. R. Fay, *Co-operation at Home and Abroad*, vol. 2 (2nd ed., 1948), chapter 14. See, in general, H. T. Williams, *Principles for British Agricultural Policy* (1960), chapter 2.

[140] A. W. Ashby, 'The Livestock and Meat Industry', in *Britain in Depression*, and 'The Livestock and Meat Trade', in *Britain in Recovery*.

[141] R. J. Thompson, 'State Expenditure on Agriculture in Great Britain in 1938–9', *J. R. Stat. S.*, 101/4, 1938, p. 737; Sir A. Daniel Hall, *Reconstruction and the Land* (1942), pp. 41–2.

[142] R. J. Thompson, 'The Future of Agriculture', *J. R. Stat. S.*, 106/1, 1943.

benefit her home farmers and the Empire growers whom she was pledged to support under the Ottawa Agreement of 1932.[143] In fact, these measures, did not change the general downward trend in British farming since the 1870s. The flight from the land continued: employment in agriculture and forestry in the United Kingdom fell from an average of 1,004,000 in 1920–2 to an average of 735,000 in 1937–8, or from 6·3% to 3·9% of total employment, parallel with the decline of the contribution of agriculture to the national income from 6·1% to 3·5%.[144] The exodus of the young men was particularly marked: the number of young male workers under 21 declined by 44% between 1921–4 and 1938.[145] By contrast, the number of farmers and members of their families working on their own farms declined but little.

The drift from the land had various causes. Low wages formed one of them. In spite of the Agricultural Wages (Regulation) Act introduced by the Labour Government in 1924 agricultural wages remained far below the industrial. In Scotland, statutory minimum wages had to wait until the Agricultural Wages (Regulation) (Scotland) Act of 1937.[146] In addition to low wages, agricultural workers complained of long and irregular hours of work, poor opportunities for advancement, poor housing, the system of tied cottages, poor schools and few amenities. As late as 1939 there were at least 5,186 parishes without a sewage system.[147]

Since gross agricultural output was stable or rising[148] the shrinking labour force implied rising labour productivity: the output per person engaged in agriculture over the country as a whole was estimated to have risen by 20% between 1921 and 1941, or 1% per annum.[149] Partly these results were achieved by mechanization, such as the employment of combine harvesters, milking machines and tractors: there were 55,000 of the latter on British farms by 1939 – and 549,000 horses.[150] Agricultural research, starting with the Development Fund of £2 million in 1910, was greatly expanded.[151] Yields, pest control and farm management generally were greatly improved, though crop yield per acre (as distinct from output per worker) in England and Wales rose but little between the 10-year periods 1886–95 and 1926–35 while much marginal land had gone out of production in the interim. In Scotland, progress was more marked.[152]

[143] Cf. esp. Astor and Rowntree, *passim*; R. J. Hammond, *op. cit.*, pp. 4–10.

[144] Agatha L. Chapman and Rose Knight, *Wages and Salaries in the United Kingdom, 1920–1938* (Cambridge, 1953), pp. 18, 20; C. H. Feinstein, *National Income, Expenditure and Output of the United Kingdom, 1855–1965* (Cambridge, 1972), T. 26–7.

[145] *Report of the Committee on Land Utilization in Rural Areas* (*Scott Report*) (1942. Cmd. 6378), p. 16; Edgar Thomas, *Introduction to Agricultural Economics* (1949), p. 65.

[146] Astor and Rowntree, p. 313; Thomas, pp. 91–4.

[147] *Scott Report*, pp. 16–19.

[148] Astor and Rowntree, p. 53; C. H. Feinstein, T. 24–5; Leo Drescher, 'The Development of Agricultural Production in Great Britain and Ireland from the Early Nineteenth Century', and T. W. Fletcher, 'Drescher's Index, a Comment', in *Manchester School*, 23/2, 1955; E. M. Ojala, *Agriculture and Economic Progress* (1952), pp. 208–9.

[149] R. M. Carslaw and P. E. Graves, 'The Changing Organization of Arable Farms', in *Econ. J.*, 47/187, 1937; Thomas *op. cit.*, pp. 86–7.

[150] Jonathan Brown, *Agriculture in England: A Survey of Farming, 1870–1947* (Manchester, 1987), p. 102; PEP, *Agricultural Machinery* (1949), p. 6.

[151] PEP, *Report on Agricultural Research in Great Britain* (1938).

[152] Hall, *op. cit.*, p. 93.

The trend in the size of holdings was downward, and the yield per acre was much higher on the smaller holdings.[153]

As noted above, the decline of arable land continued after the interruption of the war years. For Great Britain as a whole, it fell from 14·44 million acres in 1921–5 to 11·86 million in 1938, while permanent grass increased from 16·2 to 17·4 million acres and rough grazing, etc., from 14·5 to 16·1 million acres.[154] Livestock and livestock products remained by far the most important products of farming in Britain, accounting in 1937–8 for 70·5% of the value of output, with farm crops valued at 16·1% and horticultural products at 13·4%.[155] There was a considerable increase in market garden produce in the inter-war period, but even at the end of the period there were scarcely more than ¼ million acres under green vegetables.

There was one important respect in which a pre-war trend was reversed. The number of owner-occupied holdings rose substantially, from 10% in 1914 to over 20% in 1921 and 37% in 1927 in England and Wales, and there was a corresponding change in Scotland. The reasons included tax changes in war-time which favoured owner-occupancy compared with tenancy, a buying spree in 1919–20, and, after a lull in sales, renewed transfers to tenants in 1924–5, when a slight improvement in agricultural prices persuaded tenants that now was the time to buy, and landlords that now was the time to sell.[156] After 1925 the buying of land by tenants ceased. This was one of the most significant symptoms of decline, and of the deep depression which even the Government apparatus of protection and support of the 1930s could not fully stem.

6 Transport and Communications

The Railway Act of 1921 was a political compromise. Denying the clamour for nationalization after the war, it was designed to preserve the unified rates and charges over the whole country. The four main lines which emerged as a result of the Act were grouped partly with the aim of ensuring that each had its due share of revenue-earning and losing lines. The existing capital, including the compensation payable for neglected repairs and replacement, fixed at £60 million, was all converted into the new railway stock.

The four systems, the London and North Eastern Railway, the London Midland and Scottish Railway, the Great Western Railway and the Southern Railway, each covered a large region within which all competition ceased. To prevent the exploitation of this monopoly by the main lines, the Act laid it down, in the second place, that the railways were to provide reasonable service and that rates were to be fixed so as to secure to the companies a net revenue equivalent to the earnings of their constituent lines in 1913, plus an allowance for the capital invested since: the total sum thus arrived at was about £51 million per annum, allocated in fixed proportions among the companies. A Railway Rates Tribunal was set up to control rates on the new principle of securing this

---

[153] R. L. Cohen, *The Economics of Agriculture* (1940), chapter 4; A. W. M. Kitchin, 'Small Holdings and the Agricultural Structure', *Econ. J.*, 44/176, 1934.

[154] L. Dudley Stamp and S. H. Beaver, *The British Isles* (1937 ed.), p. 153.

[155] Thomas, *op. cit.*, p. 11.

[156] S. G. Sturmey, 'Owner-Farming in England and Wales, 1900–1950' *Manchester School*, 23/3, 1955.

agreed total net revenue,[157] as well as keeping to the former principles of equity as between traders.

In the third place, the Act established a permanent system of negotiation and conciliation with all grades of staff, in notable contrast with the pre-war refusal of the companies even to recognize the unions.[158] The system broke down in 1933, however, over a demand by the companies for a 10% reduction in pay, and new machinery was set up in 1935.

Lastly, the amalgamation of lines was expected to lead to great economies in running, and the Minister of Transport was authorized by Part II of the Act to require the companies to standardize their equipment and collaborate by common working, common use of rolling stock and similar means in the interest of economy. Estimates of possible economies varied from £4 million a year to £45 million.[159]

In sum, the Act of 1921, which dominated the history of railways in Britain until the outbreak of the Second World War, marked the end of an epoch. After almost a century of legislation to prevent the exploitation of their monopoly on the part of the railways, if was ironic that at the very moment when the long campaign for railway amalgamation and monopoly had at last been won, it should turn into a hollow victory by the rise of the motor vehicle and the decline of the industries providing the heavy mineral traffic, a vital component of railway receipts.

As a result, much of the Act became pointless if not directly harmful. The new system of fixing actual rates proved far too rigid in a period of falling costs and prices. Before long, 'exceptional' rates became the rule. The 'standard net revenue' of £51 million, beyond which the public was to share the benefits, was in fact never reached between the wars. Though there was no labour unemployment, the railways became a seriously depressed industry. In 1932, £260 million of their capital went without any dividend.[160]

Technical advance was slow and investment was low[161], perhaps still inhibited by the traditional monopoly thinking, though it was by no means negligible. Containers were introduced, easing the transport of fragile goods; railhead facilities were greatly improved; door-to-door services inaugurated. Electrification speeded up suburban services in the Manchester, Newcastle, Liverpool and London areas. The Southern Railway electrified its main line to Brighton and Worthing in 1933 and to Portsmouth, Reading, Maidstone and Chatham later in the 1930s. Diesel engines were put on shunting services and some passenger railcars were used by the GWR. From 1935 onward the main

---

[157] Sir Hubert Llewellyn Smith, *The Board of Trade* (1928), p. 142; C. I. Savage, *An Economic History of Transport* (1959), pp. 98–114; E. A. Pratt, *British Railways and the Great War* (1921), chapters 47, 48; C. E. R. Sherrington, *The Economics of Rail Transport in Great Britain*, vol. 1 (1928), pp. 251 ff.; Derek H. Aldcroft, *Studies in British Transport History 1870–1970* (Newton Abbot, 1974), pp. 125 ff.

[158] Sir W. M. Acworth, 'Grouping under the Railways Act, 1921', *Econ. J.*, 33/129, 1923, p. 19.

[159] Acworth, *loc. cit.,* p. 35; M. E. Dimock, *British Public Utilities and National Development* (1933), p. 80; H. J. Dyos and D. H. Aldcroft, *British Transport. An Economic Survey from the Seventeenth Century to the Twentieth* (Leicester, 1971), pp. 293–7, 308.

[160] H. M. Hallsworth, 'Rail Transport', in *Britain in Depression,* p. 193, and *Britain in Recovery,* pp. 286, 292; Savage, *op. cit.,* p. 114; Philip S. Bagwell, *The Transport Revolution from 1770* (1988), p. 255.

[161] D. H. Aldcroft, *British Railways in Transition* (1968), pp. 32 f.; Royal Commission on Transport, *Final Report: The Co-ordination and Development of Transport* (1931. Cmd. 3751), pp. 37–8.

line companies began to introduce faster non-stop long-distance services, often with specially named trains: by 1938 there were 107 daily trains with average speeds of over 60 m.p.h., compared with 25 in 1934 and 4 in 1914.[162] All this in spite of the difficulty of raising capital for a declining industry from the market or its own surpluses, leading to actual disinvestment on the railways in the inter-war years.[163]

The falling off in mineral traffic, caused by the decline in the production of coal, iron and steel, was bound to hit the railways more than any other means of traffic.[164] Basically, however, the railways were in decline because of the rise of road motor transport, growing particularly fast from about 1926 onward: indeed, much of the traffic lost in the strike of that year was lost permanently. By 1933–5, the main lines had lost an estimated one half of their traffic to the roads.[165] Among the railways' weaknesses imposed by law was a rigid and publicized rate structure: their competitors' rates were neither, and when in competition, could always be reduced just below the railway rates. As a result both for passengers and goods the roads skimmed off the cream and the railways were left with the less desirable traffic. Further, they had to run services between the less populous centres, and they had to accept all traffic, while the road haulier, knowing the railway rate, could overcharge for any load he did not want to carry.

As difficulties increased, the railways were relieved of some of their handicaps. In 1928, they were given powers to run road passenger vehicles, and within two years had invested £9½ million, mostly in joint omnibus undertakings with road companies. In 1934 they absorbed Carter Paterson and Pickford's, the leading road cartage contractors. The derating of railway property to the extent of 75% provided the companies with a freight rebates fund. In 1930 and 1933, the competing road vehicles were also restricted by legislation; and finally, in 1939 the railways were promised the repeal of many of their rate restrictions.[166] In spite of the triumphant advance of road transport, the railways were still by far the most important conveyers of goods and merchandise, in 1939, they carried 265 million tons of freight, compared with 100 m.t. by road and under 50 m.t. by canal and coastal shipping; and though the 4,526 million passengers carried by road greatly outnumbered the 1,237 million carried by rail, they were carried over shorter distances.[167]

The motor vehicle, however, was as a goods vehicle, more flexible in door to door deliveries and in supplying the distributive trade. In the case of public passenger service, motor vehicles rapidly replaced all other forms of the town omnibus, and were also turned into 'express carriages', i.e. long-distance coaches, and 'contract carriages', or coaches hired as a whole. Meanwhile, the private motor car and motor cycle diverted traffic from both trams and buses, as well as creating much new traffic. All these had been in their infancy in 1914;

[162] Hallsworth, in *Britain in Recovery*, pp. 294–5; Jones and Pool, *A Hundred Years of Economic Development*, p. 354.

[163] The disinvestment has been estimated at £125 million in the 19 years 1920–38. Bagwell, *Transport Revolution*, p. 255.

[164] Gilbert Walker, *Road and Rail* (1947 ed.), p. 20.

[165] *Ibid.*, p. 128.

[166] Gilbert Walker, *op. cit.*, p. 233; M. R. Bonavia, *The Economics of Transport* (1954 ed.), pp. 200–1.

[167] Savage, *op. cit.*, p. 175.

they appeared to sweep all before them in the inter-war years.

In 1914, the total number of motor vehicles licensed was 389,000. By 1939 there were over 3 million motor vehicles on the road, of which 2 million were private cars.[168] The motor car had become the normal means of transport for the middle classes, just as the motor goods vehicle had become indispensable to many businesses. Both vehicles and their fuel became large-scale sources of taxation: direct taxation yielded £1½ million in 1920 and £34½ million in 1937, while net fuel tax and import duty receipts rose from £5 million to £46½ million in the same period. Expenditure on the roads rose from £26½ million in 1920 to £65½ million in 1930. The number of motor vehicles per mile of road rose from 0·8 in 1909 to 7·5 in 1924 and to 16·4 in 1937.[169]

Legislation to cope with this kind of traffic increase limped behind in the 1920s. The three main statutes affecting road traffic were passed in the 1930s. The Road Traffic Act of 1930 included the abolition of general speed limits for private cars and compulsory insurance against third party risks. The Road Traffic Act of 1934 introduced provisions for a 30 m.p.h. limit in built-up areas, a driving test, and powers to establish pedestrian crossings, also amending the Act of 1933.

The remainder of the Act of 1930 dealt with the regulation of road passenger transport, largely on the lines laid down by the second report of the Royal Commission on Transport.[170] Up to that time, the bus and coach services outside London had grown up virtually without control. Buses were run by small one-man companies, by large combines, by the railways and by some municipalities.[171] In 1929–32, there were almost 4,000 motor transport undertakings in Britain.

The Act of 1930 introduced a strict system of control of public service vehicles with the dual objective of providing full and co-ordinated public regular services, and of protecting existing operators against competition by newcomers. The newly established Traffic Commissioners had powers to grant licences to bus operators and to regulate conditions of service, including the fares to be charged. In addition, vehicles had to meet various safety and other requirements before receiving a licence. In the event, the Commissioners interpreted their duties rigidly, giving preference to the 'prior' service and strongly discouraging new services. As a result, broadly speaking, the general structure and even the fare system of road passenger transport were frozen in the position they had reached in 1930, except that amalgamations still remained possible.[172] The Act also laid down conditions of service for drivers and conductors, including a system of licensing of drivers, maximum hours of work, and a 'fair wages clause'.

The other important measure relating to road transport was the Road and Rail Traffic Act of 1933, which regulated the carrying of goods on the road, and attempted to co-ordinate road and rail traffic. Part I established a licensing system for goods vehicles, operated by the existing Traffic Commissioners. The

[168] Savage, *op. cit.*, pp. 96, 142; L. F. Duval, 'The Motor Industry', in *Britain in Recovery*, p. 317.

[169] Duval, *loc. cit.*, pp. 312–15; K. G. Fenelon, 'The Road Transport Industry', in *Britain in Depression*, p. 213.

[170] R. C. on Transport, *Second Report, The Licensing and Regulation of Public Service Vehicles* (1929. Cmd. 3416).

[171] Bagwell, *Transport Revolution*, p. 214; Savage, *op. cit.*, chapter 6.

[172] D. N. Chester, *Public Control of Road Passenger Transport* (Manchester, 1936), pp. 50, 87; Aldcroft, *British Transport History*, pp. 187–207.

granting of 'A' and 'B' licenses (for carriers wholly or partly for reward) favoured existing operators and the number of vehicles on 'A' and 'B' licences actually fell in the years following the Act. 'C' licences for firms carrying their own goods continued to increase very rapidly. There were also regulations as to speed limits and the condition of vehicles, and there were clauses relating to the hours of work of drivers and to their wages. Ultimately, the Minister of Labour was given power to determine wages by order under the Road Haulage Wages Act of 1938. Part II of the Act referred to railway rates.[173] Unlike the public service companies, firms in the road haulage industry remained small: even in 1938, the average number of vehicles among 'A' licence holders was three, and 85% of operators had fewer than five.[174]

The only thoroughgoing scheme of co-ordination was that applied to the passenger transport of the Metropolis. In addition to main line and suburban railways, Metropolitan and underground railways, and trams, London was served in 1924 by nearly 500 independent buses besides those of the London General,[175] while outlying districts were left without any service at all.

The London Traffic Act of 1924, following a strike of tramwaymen and omnibus workers, created a powerful apparatus of control by the Minister and the licensing authority over London buses. As a result, most of the independent bus proprietors combined and in 1927 formed the London Public Omnibus Company, which quickly came to an agreement with the dominant firm, the London General. Lord Ashfield, the forceful chairman of the Underground Group, itself an amalgamation which included the London General Omnibus Co., pointed to the need for the extension of the electric and underground systems to the suburbs, but before these were built, demanded an assurance that no duplicate lines would be permitted. In 1928 the Underground, the Metropolitan and the main line railways decided to pool their London revenues, and complete unification followed the Act of 1933.

Under it, the London Passenger Transport Board took over the property of 5 railway companies (excluding the main lines), 17 tramway undertakings (including 14 municipally owned) and 66 bus companies, plus parts of 69 other companies, to run them as a unified service and as a monopoly in London and a region about 30 miles from Charing Cross, except for the four main line railway companies, with which all the Metropolitan revenues were pooled. The members of the Board were appointed by a panel of trustees of public standing, its stock amounted to £109 million on inception, and in 1936 it employed some 72,000 persons.[176]

British shipping suffered from the shortage of world demand in relation to supply. Freights tumbled from an index of 374 in 1920 to 166 in 1921, falling further to 115 in 1929. Tramp freights fell even faster, from 602 in March 1920 to 141 in 1921 and 106 in 1929.[177] In the slump, British tonnage laid up rose

[173] J. R. Sargent, *British Transport Policy* (Oxford, 1958), p. 43.

[174] Savage, *op. cit.*, p. 136; Alfred Plummer, *New British Industries in the Twentieth Century* (1937), chapter 3/I.

[175] London Transport (publ.), *London General – The Story of the London Bus, 1856–1956* (1956).

[176] T. C. Barker and Michael Robbins, *A History of London Transport*, vol. 2, *The Twentieth Century* (1974), chapter 15.

[177] C. E. Fayle, *The War and the Shipping Industry* (1927), chapter 25 and Table 2, p. 415; L. Isserlis, 'Shipping', in *Britain in Depression*, p. 239; Dyos and Aldcroft, *British Transport*, pp. 376–96.

from 630,000 g.t. in 1929 to 3,610,000 g.t. in 1932, and large fleets were sold to foreign flags, presumably to compete with the remaining British tonnage either with the aid of subsidies, or lower wage costs, or both. Tramp freight rates suffered particularly heavily, falling in 1933–5 to somewhere below three-quarters of the already low level of 1929.[178] As a counter-measure, the British Government introduced subsidies to tramp vessels in Part I of the British Shipping (Assistance) Act of 1935. A Tramp Shipping Subsidy Committee was successful to the extent of aiding the setting up of minimum freight schemes, including foreign tonnage, for the grain trade from Australia, Canada and the Argentine to Europe. The 'scrap and build' subsidy under Part II of the Act was noted above.[179]

Liner companies with their large resources, and the regular incoming payments of mail and other contracts, as well as their well organized 'rings' to keep up freights, found it easier than tramps to withstand the slump; nevertheless, several groups only survived by amalgamation. About one-quarter of the British tonnage, i.e. one-half of the liner tonnage, came under the control of the 'Big Five' – the P & O, Royal Mail, Cunard, Ellerman and Furness-Withy groups.[180] Of these, the Royal Mail group, an £80 million concern controlling the largest merchant fleet in the world, collapsed early in 1931, the whole of the ordinary capital of the company being lost.[181] Only the Cunard Company received a subsidy, on condition that it amalgamated with the White Star line (which in 1927 had been acquired by the Royal Mail group). It took the form of a loan on very easy terms to finance the construction of two new giant liners for regular transatlantic service, the *Queen Mary,* on which work had begun and had been suspended, and the *Queen Elizabeth.*

From 1936 onward, as traffic recovered, freight rates began to rise. However, the lagging sales of coal forced British shipping to make outward journeys in ballast and deprived it of one of its main competitive advantages.[182]

The heavier-than-air craft had proved itself in military missions during the war, and in August 1919 two air services to Paris began in tiny ramshackle planes. Several other companies followed, but apart from providing the main airports and navigational aids under the Air Navigation Act of 1920, the British Government refused to subsidize these services. Unable to withstand the competition of the heavily subsidized foreign aircraft, the British companies folded one by one, and for a time, in 1921, there was not a single commercial airline left in this country. The strategic importance of civil aviation could not, however, be ignored for long, and there followed subsidies to ultimately four companies amalgamated into a single company, 'Imperial Airways', in 1924.[183] Starting with 13 small aircraft, it quickly proved technically successful, and opened up new routes to India, the Far East, South Africa and Australia, experimenting, in 1937–9, with transatlantic flights also. By 1939, it had a fleet

[178] L.Isserlis, 'Tramp Shipping Cargoes and Freights', *J. R. Stat. S.,* 101/1, 1938, pp. 78–9, 94.
[179] p. 54 above.
[180] C. E. Fayle, *A Short History of the World's Shipping Industry* (1933), p. 298.
[181] *Economist,* 7.2.1931, pp. 299–300.
[182] Peter Duff, *British Ships and Shipping* (1949), p. 21.
[183] A. J. Quin-Harkin, 'Imperial Airways, 1924–40', *J. Transport History,* 1/4, Nov. 1954; E. Birkhead, 'The Financial Failure of British Air Transport Companies 1919–24, *Ibid.,* 4/3, May 1960.

of 77 aircraft and a staff of 3,500, but financially it was still dependent on the Government.[184]

Services to Europe were neglected by Imperial Airways and by 1935, 19 private companies operated 76 services within the British Isles, though that number was later reduced.[185] In that year, British Airways, a merger of three companies, was also given a subsidy, together with a monopoly of services to Berlin and Scandinavia and a share in the lucrative London–Paris route. With rising subsidies both companies soon showed high profits, and the British Overseas Airways Act, passed in August 1939, bought out the former shareholders and nationalized the property. BOAC came into operation after the outbreak of war, in November.

Telephones had been slow to get off the ground in Britain compared with other countries. The number of subscribers reached 1 million at the beginning of 1922, 2 million in 1932 and $3\frac{1}{4}$ million in 1939. The only special effort made to extend the service was the offer of subsidized terms to rural subscribers, and these greatly encouraged the spread of the telephone into the countryside.[186] By contrast, the British Post Office letter service remained second to none and was enormously expanded in 1919–39. Among its technical innovations in this period were the special electric underground railway, authorized in 1913 but completed only in 1927, linking six sorting offices and two main line stations by $6\frac{1}{2}$ miles of line below some of London's busiest streets, and the air mail service: by 1935, 19 million letters were sent by air mail.[187]

The original commercial application of wireless telegraphy, following Marconi's first English radio patent of 1896, was to link ships with the shore and with each other. The Marconi International Marine Communication Co. Ltd, formed in 1900, dominated the field here by controlling most of the necessary patents.[188] There followed radio communication between fixed points and the contract to link up various parts of the Empire was also ultimately awarded to Marconi's in 1913, but no stations had been built by the outbreak of war.

The need of war called forth important technical improvements, and innumerable signallers were trained. In 1924 Marconi's announced a revolutionary discovery, the 'beam', or directed short wave transmission which facilitated intercontinental radio links. Marconi's received the Imperial contract and, by 1928, 'beam' links had been established with Canada, South Africa, India and Australia. At the same time, the Post Office opened its own valve transmitter at Rugby, then the most powerful in the world, for radio telephony.

The two separate services, the cable systems and the wireless stations, were amalgamated in 1928, and the Post Office was forced to lease to the resulting organization its own beam station, which it finally made over in 1938. Cable and Wireless had some of the attributes of a Public Corporation: its rates and services were scrutinized by an official Advisory Committee and its distribution of profits was limited in the public interest, but compared with other Public

[184] Sir Osborne Mance and J. E. Wheeler, *International Air Transport* (1944), pp. 45–6.

[185] Plummer, *New Industries,* chapter 3/II; Aldcroft, *British Transport History,* pp. 208–25.

[186] Sir Evelyn Murray, *The Post Office* (1927), chapter 8; Arthur Hazlewood, 'The Origin of the State Telephone System in Britain', *Oxf. Econ. P.,* NS, 5/1, 1953.

[187] Howard Robinson, *The British Post Office, a History* (Princeton, N J, 1948), chapter 30.

[188] S. G. Sturmey, *The Economic Development of Radio* (1958), chapter 3; H. E. Hancock, *Wireless at Sea* (1951).

Corporations formed at that time, the shareholders' interests were more powerfully represented, and the deals shaping its financial structure more doubtful.[189]

Wireless broadcasting, as distinct from point-to-point communication, was
entirely a post-war development. In view of the adverse American experience
made with unregulated competing stations, and the Post Office preference for
monopoly, the decision was made in 1922 to hand broadcasting to a monopoly
controlled in the public interest.[190] A consortium of the six principal wireless
equipment makers, united as the 'British Broadcasting Company', which other
manufacturers ultimately also joined, was given all the manufacturing patent
rights and its income was derived from the heavy royalties charged on each
receiving set sold and from a share of the receiving licences, issued by the Post
Office. The large manufacturers were additionally rewarded with the restriction
of receiving licences to British-made sets only, at a time when foreign-made sets
were generally both cheaper and better. The BB Co., using some of the existing
stations of the Marconi Co., which had begun regular broadcasting in 1922,
started its regular services in 1923. At the end of 1922 there had been 36,000
licences issued; at the end of 1924, there were 1,130,000; at the end of 1926,
when the BB Co.'s existence ended, the number had risen to 2,178,000.

From the first, the broadcasting company and its programmes were dominated
by the General Manager, J. C. W. (later Lord) Reith, who imposed on it a
distinct shape which also influenced the structure and objectives of other Public
Utility Corporations in this country. In Reith's view, the company was to be a
monopoly established under the auspices of the State, but not subject to day-
to-day public control; it was not to be run to make profits, but to provide a public
service, with a conscious social purpose. It held a stewardship to contribute
'constantly and cumulatively to the intellectual and moral well-being of the
community', with idealism playing a part, 'perhaps a determining part'.[191] When
the extended licence of the BB Co. expired at the end of 1926, the British
Broadcasting Corporation, formed according to this new conception of a Public
Corporation, took it over. Its Governors, though appointed by the Government,
were not responsible to it; and operating within a secure income of licence fees,
it was not in need of revenue from advertisers or others. 'Their interest was in
the intellectual and ethical welfare of the listeners'.[192]

By the end of 1929, there were almost 3 million licence holders in Britain and
at the end of 1938, nearly 9 million, or the large majority of homes in this country.
The Corporation ultimately broadcast two complete sets of programmes, one
national and one for the seven regions.[193]

Television was based on scientific discoveries made before 1900, especially
the reactions of the selenium cell and the cathode ray tube, but it was not until
the 1920s that television broadcasting was seriously considered as a commercial
proposition. The system ultimately adopted was based on the experiments made
with a cathode ray tube by V. K. Zworykin in America in 1931 and developed

[189] Sturmey, *op. cit.,* chapters 4–6; Dimock, *op. cit.,* chapter 4; H. F. Heath and A. L. Hetherington,
Industrial Research and Development in the United Kingdom (1946), pp. 209 ff.
[190] Lincoln Gordon, *The Public Corporation in Great Britain* (1938), chapter 4.
[191] M. E. Dimock, *Public Utilities,* p. 268; R. H. Coase, *British Broadcasting, a Study in Monopoly*
(1950), chapter 3.
[192] Coase, *op. cit.,* p. 118; Asa Briggs, *The History of Broadcasting in the United Kingdom,* vol. 1
(1961); J. C. W. Reith, *Into the Wind* (1949), Part 2.
[193] Sturmey, *op. cit.,* chapters 8, 9.

in Britain by the Marconi-EMI combine. The BBC turned to it in 1937, providing the only regular television broadcasts anywhere before the war, received by an estimated 20,000 sets by 1939.[194]

7 New Forms of Industrial Organization

The earlier sections of this chapter contain numerous references to new forms of business organization and to a greatly extended range of functions of the Government and other public authorities in industry, agriculture and transport. These developments were evidence of a new attitude towards economic policy.[195]

The paid-up capital of registered joint-stock companies with limited liability, the typical form of industrial enterprise, rose from £2½ billion in April 1914 to £4·1 billion at the end of 1921 and to over £6 billion in 1938.[196] The large increase between 1914 and 1921 reflected in part the share boom of 1919–20 in which capital was increased by watering, by the ploughing back of the results of war-time profiteering and by speculative promotion[197], but throughout the inter-war period the expansion of genuine joint-stock enterprise continued and many of the remaining individually owned firms and partnerships were converted to the joint-stock form of organization. By 1938 the partnership or the individual trading on his own had become rather exceptional in industry, though they still persisted in retail distribution, in agriculture, in the professions and in a few other sectors. The share of joint-stock enterprise in the economy is difficult to estimate: according to the tax returns, it obtained about 85% of the profits of manufacturing industry in the late 1930s.[198]

The number of public joint-stock companies on the register actually declined in this period, but at the same time there was a large increase in the number of private companies, the typical form of organization of the family firm. In 1938, while the private companies outnumbered the public companies by ten to one, they had an aggregate capital of only £1,900 million, compared with the £4,100 million of the latter.[199]

Public or non-profit-making organizations showed a significant growth in this period. Among the most important types were the co-operative societies, registered under the Industrial and Provident Societies Acts, and the building societies, registered under the Building Society Acts; enterprises administered by charitable, educational and similar bodies; local authorities, administering over one-third of the gas works, two-thirds of electricity supplies, four-fifths of water supplies and of tramway mileage, virtually all the trolley-bus systems as well as a large proportion of omnibus and other services. There were, further, *ad hoc* authorities such as dock and harbour boards, including those of London, Liverpool and Glasgow, and the Metropolitan Water Board, established in 1902; companies established by Act of Parliament, mainly in the public utility field, including the railways; enterprises administered directly by the State,

---

[194] Sturmey, *op. cit.*, chapter 10.

[195] W. Ashworth, *An Economic History of England, 1870–1939* (1960), chapter 15.

[196] Balfour Committee, *Survey of Industries*, vol. 1 (1927), p. 125; A. Beacham, *Economics of Industrial Organization* (3rd ed., 1955), p. 6.

[197] H. W. Macrosty, 'Inflation and Deflation in the United States and the United Kingdom, 1919–1923', *J. R. Stat. S.*, 90/1, 1927, pp. 70–2.

[198] P. Sargant Florence, *The Logic of British and American Industry* (1953), p. 170.

[199] A. B. Levy, *Private Corporations and their Control*, vol. 1 (1950), sections 18 and 20.

including the Post Office, the dockyards, and the Crown Lands; and the Public Corporations. In 1928 the Liberal Industrial Inquiry found that the capital administered by these authorities came to about £4 billion (including £1¼ billion for roads and £1·15 billion for railways) and was thus of the same order of magnitude as the aggregate capital of all joint-stock companies.[200]

The extension of the joint-stock type of organization was, from the beginning, associated with the need for large sums of capital, and it proceeded fastest in industries composed of large firms and using much capital per worker. Technical needs and market conditions favoured the large unit in this period, and as the size of firms grew, the family firm gave way to the registered company with its numerous and anonymous shareholders and its elected Board of Directors.

In most of the larger companies the proportion of the shares held by any single holder (or indeed by the Board) had become insignificant and there were thousands, and even tens of thousands of shareholders; large holders were often found to be not individuals but other companies. Thus a relatively small holding might dominate a company in view of the scattered nature of the rest of the holdings, and this might mean 'government by bloc-holder', but more commonly left control in the hands of a self-perpetuating Board of Directors who were administering an institution rather than their own property.[201] As Keynes noted,

> When this stage is reached, the general stability and reputation of the institution are more considered by the management than the maximum of profit for the shareholders.[202]

Moreover, as was noted in 1939,

> The increasing dominance of industry by combines and cartels has given a further twist to the meaning of ownership. It is becoming less a right to draw a share in the profits, and more a right to draw dividends in perpetuity – the factor of risk, the short-term risk at least, is declining.[203]

In Britain that development might have been slower than elsewhere[204], but even here an increasing proportion of workers was to be found in large firms. By 1935 there were three industries in which more than half the workers employed worked in *plants* employing 1,000 workers or more (electrical machinery, motor and cycle manufacturing and iron and steel rolling and smelting) and in a further four industries (silk and art silk, newspaper production, shipbuilding and sugar and sugar confectionery) over 40% did so. All told, of about 5·2 million workers in the industries enumerated by the Census of Production, 21·5% worked in *plants* employing 1,000 and over, and another 13·9% in plants

---

[200] Liberal Industrial Inquiry, *Britain's Industrial Future* (1928), chapter 6; Balfour Committee, *Survey of Industries,* vol. 2 (1928), chapter 8; H. Campion, *Public and Private Property in Great Britain* (1939), chapter 5.

[201] E.g. P. Sargant Florence, 'The Statistical Analysis of Joint-Stock Company Control', *J. R. Stat. S.,* 110/1, 1947; also his *Logic,* pp. 176 ff., and *Ownership, Control and Success of Large Companies* (1961).

[202] J. M. Keynes, 'The End of Laissez-Faire' (1924), in *Essays in Persuasion* (1931), pp. 314–15.

[203] M. Compton and E. H. Bott, *British Industry* (1940), p. 128.

[204] Alfred D. Chandler, 'The Growth of the Transnational Industrial Firm in the United States and the United Kingdom: A Comparative Analysis', *Ec. Hist. Rev.* 33/3, 1980, pp. 401–2, 408–9.

employing 500–999 workers. The proportion working in *firms* employing 1,000 and over was 31·2% in 1935; and those in firms employing 500–999, 13·3%, i.e. nearly half the labour force was to be found in firms employing 500 workers and over.[205]

Even this does not show fully the extent of industrial concentration, for many firms, while nominally independent, were being combined in complex ways. Holding companies or subsidiaries were the most common means of control, but there were also interlocking capital holdings, frequently unknown to the public, and interlocking directorates. In 1936 it was found that among a sample of 623 directors of large firms with capitals of over £500,000 each, only 25% held single directorships. No fewer than 81 (13%) held 10 or more.[206]

In their pioneer study[207] Leak and Maizels, using the Census of Production of 1935, found that 55% of all workers enumerated, or just under 4 million, worked in 'units' (i.e. industrial groups) employing 500 men or over. Among the most highly concentrated trade groups were mining and quarrying (89%), public utilities (78%), engineering, shipbuilding and vehicles (67%), iron and steel, chemicals (both 59%), food, drink and tobacco (50%) and textiles (49%). Sub-groups with specially high proportions of employees in units of 500 and over included blast furnaces (92%), aircraft (91%), coal mines (94%), tramways (94%), tobacco (88%), biscuits (82%), iron and steel rolling and melting (87%) and railways (100%). Nearly 1.7 million workers worked in the 135 largest units employing 5,000 each or over and producing 44.5% of the gross output. Equally telling was the share held by the three largest units in any one industry, as a measure of concentration: there were no fewer than 33 trades in which the largest three units accounted for 70% of the total employment or more.[208] According to a different calculation, the share of the largest 100 companies in manufacturing net output rose from 17% in 1919 to 23% in 1939.[209]

Some concentration of industry derived from the technical and economic advantages of size, aided also by the contemporary revolution in office equipment and administrative techniques. In part it was the new mass consumers' markets and efficient means of transport and distribution to supply them, which called forth mass production by single large firms. In a few cases, large multidivisional firms appeared, including I.C.I., Unilever and S.T.C.[210] In part, concentration was the result of the growing control of companies by financial interests which looked for extensions, or it was defensive, in which case the mergers frequently failed.[211]

[205] Florence, *Logic*, pp. 24, 34.

[206] Florence, 'Joint-Stock Company Control', p. 14, and *Ownership*, chapter 4; J. M. Rees, *Trusts in British Industry, 1914–1921* (1922), pp. 28, 31, 71 ff.; H. Levy, *The New Industrial System* (1936), § 20.

[207] H. Leak and A. Maizels, 'The Structure of British Industry', *J. R. Stat. S.*, 108/1–2, 1945.

[208] P. E. Hart and S. J. Prais, 'The Analysis of Business Concentration: A Statistical Approach', *J. R. Stat. S.*, 119/2, 1956.

[209] Leslie Hannah, *The Rise of the Corporate Economy* (1976), p. 216.

[210] Alan Sked, *Britain's Decline* (Oxford 1987), p. 25, Alfred D. Chandler, *Scale and Scope* (Cambridge, Mass., 1990); Hermann Levy, *New Industrial System, passim*; A. Plummer, *New Industries of the Twentieth Century* (1937), chapter 7; J. E. Vaizey, 'The Brewing Industry', in P. L. Cook (ed.), *Effects of Mergers* (1958), pp. 413–19; and *The Brewing Industry 1886–1951* (1960), pp. 25–45, 149–55.

[211] H. A. Marquand, *The Dynamics of Industrial Combination* (1931), chapters 7–11; Leslie Hannah, 'Managerial Innovation and the Rise of the Large-Scale Company in Interwar Britain', *Ec. Hist. Rev.* 27/2, 1974, pp. 267–8.

In the main, however, growing concentration was associated with restriction of competition and the creation of monopolistic markets. Several single large monopolistic firms dominating an industry by controlling, say, 70% or more of its capacity survived from the period before 1914;[212] among the new combines established to dominate their markets as monopolists or quasi-monopolists were those in chemicals (1926), whisky distilling (1925), soap and margarine (1929), matches (1927), glass bottles, yeast and seed crushing.[213] In almost every case, increased prices and profits were easier to find as a result of mergers, than increased efficiency.[214]

Apart from the single firm, the most widespread form of monopoly organization to arise in the inter-war years was the trade association. At the end of the war, the Committee on Trusts enumerated 93 associations in many different industries which had had dealings with the Ministry of Munitions; John Hilton, the Secretary of the Committee, estimated that over 500 associations were then in existence.[215] The Federation of British Industries had been formed in 1916 with 50 affiliated organizations and by 1918 it had 129, mostly of the trade association type, claiming a membership of 16,000 firms; the National Union of Manufacturers also evolved at the same time, in 1917, out of the British Manufacturers' Association of 1915.[216]

By the late 1930s there were probably 1,000–1,200 trade associations in existence in manufacturing alone, with a similar number to be found in distribution and other spheres.[217] Most of them were driven sooner or later to concern themselves with price fixing and control. Where the power of these associations was bolstered either by the power of a quasi-monopolistic firm acting as price leader, as in soap making, rayon, tyres or matches, or by patents, as in electric lamps, pharmaceutical products or shoe making machinery, the fixed price was virtually unchallengeable.[218]

Some trade associations went further by controlling not only prices, but also output quotas or capacity. They included the Sulphate of Ammonia Federation, the National Benzol Co., the Nitrate Producers' Association, and the Cable Makers' Association, and similar methods were in use among large building and civil engineering contractors. Government-sponsored Marketing Boards and the coal industry operated in a similar way in the 1930s. The Shipping Conferences continued to exclude competition by their well-tried methods of deferred rebates. Finally, some associations sponsored subsidiary companies which systematically bought up and destroyed excess capacity. This occurred in shipbuilding, grain milling, wool combing, and among licensed houses, as well as (with Government assistance) in cotton spinning.

[212] Cf. chapter 1, section 1 above.

[213] P. L. Cook (ed.), *Effects of Mergers*; H. Levy, *Monopolies, Trusts and Cartels in Britain Today* (1927 ed.), chapter 9.

[214] E.g. A. F. Lucas, *Industrial Reconstruction and the Control of Competition* (1937), chapter 8; G. C. Allen, 'An Aspect of "Industrial Reorganization"', *Econ. J.*, 55/218–19; 1945; Ernest Davies, *National Capitalism, The Government's Record as a Protector of Private Monopoly* (1939).

[215] Min. of Reconstruction, *Report of the Committee on Trusts* (1919. Cd. 9236).

[216] R. F. Holland, 'The Federation of British Industries and the International Economy, 1929–39, *Ec. Hist. Rev.* 34/2, 1981; Wyn Grant and David Marsh, *The Confederation of British Industry* (1977), pp. 19–20.

[217] PEP, *Industrial Trade Associations* (1957).

[218] Lucas, *op. cit.*, chapter 9.

Some cartels shared out international markets according to prearranged quotas, including the international rail cartel, revived in 1926, and the associations among makers of electric lamps, chemicals, minerals, tobacco and glass bottles, among others. The oil industry was dominated by a few competing giant international concerns with price agreements and understandings.[219] On the other hand, the international cartels of such raw materials as tin, rubber, coffee and sugar had only temporary effects at best.[220] Finally, some large multinational firms spread networks of agreements across many frontiers: among them were Courtauld's, Unilever, the Swedish Match Co., Dunlop, J. & P. Coats, Nestlé, the International Nickel Co., the Amalgamated Metals Corporation Ltd., EMI, ICI, Ford's, General Motors, the Singer Sewing Machine Co., and the (American) General Electric Co.[221] 'As a feature of industrial and commercial organization', wrote an observer in 1937, 'free competition has nearly disappeared from the British scene.'[222]

At least as striking as the extension of monopolistic market conditions was the reversal of the public attitude towards it. The Committee on Trusts, at the end of the war, took it for granted that monopoly was undesirable,[223] but a change in outlook began to appear around 1924 with the drive towards the 'rationalization' of industry, introduced into this country from Germany. It began as a movement to improve techniques, but it was soon mainly looking for savings by structural and economic, rather than technical, reorganization, 'the right arrangement of the relations of producers to each other'.[224] This often required the collaboration of firms to provide a full load for the more up-to-date plant while scrapping the less efficient. Such measures were more logically applied to the whole of an industry, and thus rationalization led directly to schemes of control and monopoly. The height of the 'rationalization' movement was passed in 1929, for the slump created the fear that 'over-rationalization' would lead to higher output and more unemployment,[225] and the problem became less that of reducing real costs than that of reducing total capacity. Thenceforward 'planning' became the favoured term. Meanwhile, however, the former attitude to competition and monopoly had been largely reversed.

In 1926 a Departmental Committee gave its blessing to the co-operative selling of coal in 1926.[226] More significant was the cautious support given to industrial control schemes by the influential Balfour Committee on Industry and Trade in its Final Report in 1929.[227] By 1931 the Macmillan Committee added its powerful

[219] Patrick Fitzgerald, *Industrial Combination in England* (1927), chapter 19.

[220] PEP, *Report on International Trade* (1937), pp. 102 ff., gives some details of 28 international cartels and mentions 28 others.

[221] Alfred Plummer, *International Combines in Modern Industry* (3rd ed., 1951); F. Hexner, *International Cartels* (1946).

[222] A. F. Lucas, *op. cit.*, p. 64; J. Hurstfield, 'The Control of British Raw Material Supplies, 1919–1939', *Ec. Hist. Rev.*, 14/1–2, 1944, p. 1.

[223] PEP, *Industrial Trade Associations* (1957), chapter 1; G. C. Allen, 'Monopoly and Competition in the United Kingdom', in E. H. Chamberlin (ed.), *Monopoly and Competition and their Regulation* (1954).

[224] D. H. MacGregor et al., 'Problems of Rationalisation', *Econ. J.*, 40/159, 1930, p. 352; cf. also L. Urwick, *The Meaning of Rationalisation* (1929), and Walter Meakin, *The New Industrial Revolution* (1928).

[225] T. E. Gregory, 'Rationalisation and Technological Unemployment', *Econ. J.*, 40/160, 1930.

[226] *Report of the D. C. on Co-operative Selling in the Coal Industry* (1926. Cmd. 2770).

[227] Balfour Committee, *Final Report* (1929), pp. 297, 304, 308.

voice to the clamour of industry for organization and association and expressed its 'strong opinion that sectional interests should not be allowed to stand in the way of reorganizations which are in the national interest'.[228] In the same year, the Greene Committee on Restraint of Trade (in retailing) was equally emphatic that monopolistic practices should be tolerated in the name of 'freedom of contract'.

The new Labour members of the Committee on Trusts had as early as 1919 emphasized their belief that evolution towards combination and monopoly was 'both inevitable and desirable',[229] as long as it was controlled in the public interest. Some Conservatives were by the early 1930s even prepared to go further, and plan industry as a whole.

> Such a policy [wrote Harold Macmillan in 1932][230] is impossible without the co-operation of industry. Production cannot be planned in relation to established demand while industries are organized on competitive lines. ... It is for this reason that I regard it as a matter of primary importance to produce an orderly structure in each of our national industries.

Even the Liberal Industrial Inquiry of 1928 was prepared to see free competition in industry displaced. In many industries, it reported, public enterprise had proved itself superior and there 'the *ad hoc* Public Board points to the right line of evolution'. Elsewhere, they were averse to restoring

> the old conditions of competition, which often involve waste and [? of] effort, the uneconomic duplication of plant or equipment, and the impossibility of adopting the full advantages of large-scale production. In modern conditions a tendency towards some degree of monopoly in an increasing number of industries is, in our opinion, inevitable and even, quite often, desirable in the interest of efficiency. It is, therefore, no longer useful to treat trusts, cartels, combinations, holding companies and trade associations as inexpedient abnormalities in the economic system to be prevented, checked, and harried. ... We believe that there is still room ... for large-scale enterprises of semi-monopolistic character which are run for private profit and controlled by individuals.

As for trade associations, if they

> can show that 75 per cent of those affected are in favour of a trade rule or instruction ... the Association shall have the right to apply for powers to issue an order enforcing the rule in question on all members of the trade or industry or of the appropriate section of it, whether within the Association or not.[231]

Even the *Economist* believed that 'a very wide measure of public control will be necessary if the badly needed work of rationalization is ever to make any real progress.'[232]

[228] *Report of the Committee on Finance and Industry* (Macmillan Report) (1931 Cmd. 3897), para. 385.

[229] *Report of the Committee on Trusts* (1919. Cd. 9236), p. 13.

[230] Harold Macmillan, *Reconstruction, A Plea for a National Policy* (1933), pp. 9–10. Also see R. Boothby *et al., Industry and the State* (1927), pp. 157–8.

[231] Liberal Industrial Inquiry, *Britain's Industrial Future* (1928), pp. 77, 93–4, 99.

[232] *Economist*, 21 July 1934, 25 Aug. 1934. Cf. also Arthur Salter, *Recovery* (1932); and *The Next Five Years, an Essay in Political Agreement* (1935), written by 152 professional people of all parties.

[233] PEP, *Industrial Trade Associations* (1957), p. 29.

The Government was acting in the same sense. The compulsory railway amalgamation of 1921 was the first specific step. In 1930 came the Coal Mines Act with its compulsory cartel scheme and Reorganization Commission, and in 1931–3 the Marketing Boards. In 1930 and 1933 competition in road transport was restricted by Traffic Commissioners, in 1934 a Herring Industry Board was set up, and in 1936 the Spindles Board was established to restrict competition in cotton spinning. Subsidies were made the occasion by the State to restrict or end competition in beet sugar production, civil aviation and transatlantic passenger shipping, and tariffs were used to restrict competition in iron and steel making, among others. In the Finance Act of 1935 the Government provided that 'if a scheme of organization covering the majority of an industry had been certified by the Board of Trade as being of assistance in reducing excess capacity, contributions to it might be deducted from income for tax purposes'.[233]

In the course of the 1930s, the State thus played an active part in the cartelization of industry and it intervened directly to provide a monopolistic framework where firms were too weak or too scattered, as in the old staples of coal, cotton, iron and steel, shipbuilding and agriculture. For a third type of industry, the public utility, the country groped its way through to a new and significant form of organization, the Public Corporation.

Public Corporations had been pioneered by Dock and Harbour Boards before 1914. Between the wars the most important new authorities were the Forestry Commission (1919), the Central Electricity Board (1926), the British Broadcasting Corporation (1926), the London Passenger Transport Board (1933) and the British Overseas Airways Corporation (1939). In addition the Post Office was modelled more closely on that of the Public Corporation.

The Public Corporation was a compromise, to avoid both the exploitation of the public by a private monopoly, and the day-to-day political interference to which ordinary Departments of State are normally subjected. The capital might be held by the State or by former owners, including private shareholders, but there was the most complete separation possible between ownership and control. Despite its decisive rejection by the Haldane Committee in 1918,[234] the Public Corporation enjoyed general support and roused widespread interest as a new administrative device.[235]

The manifold new developments of industrial organization described here implied a fundamental change in thought. The nineteenth-century belief in an unlimited extension of markets was shattered by the experience of declining export markets in the 1920s and world-wide deficiency of purchasing power in the 1930s. The main task now was not how to supply ever-extending markets at the lowest cost, but how to cater for a stagnant demand without an excess of unemployment. For the manufacturer, the limits and capacity of his own industry thus acquired a new significance as it had to be measured against a known static demand. This required concerted action[236] and it seemed as though the

[233] PEP, *Industrial Trade Associations* (1957), p. 29.

[234] *Reports of the Committee on the Machinery of Government* (1918. Cd. 9230).

[235] See esp. W. A. Robson (ed.), *Public Enterprise* (1937); T. H. O'Brien, *British Experiments in Public Ownership and Control* (1937); Lincoln Gordon, *The Public Corporation in Great Britain* (1938); J. F. Sleeman, *British Public Utilities* (1953); M. E. Dimock, *British Public Utilities and National Development* (1933); Balfour Committee, *Survey of Industries,* vol. 2, chapter 8 (2); Ernest Davies, *National Enterprise: The Development of the Public Corporation* (1946), chapters 2, 3, 9.

[236] Lucas, *Industrial Reconstruction*, p. 43.

country was moving inexorably into a corporate economic structure, the solution tried in several fascist countries.

In the event, the extremes were avoided. Large sectors of the economy still remained unorganized, dominated by small units, and there was enough flexibility to allow a considerable switch from old to new industries. In retrospect, it seems that much of the organizational, anti-competitive phase of history in 1919–39 was directly derived from the world economic depression within a long-term trend, making necessary ever larger agglomerations of capital for maximum productive efficiency, and providing at the same time the administrative, transport and distributive means to manage them. This trend was evident before 1914, as it had continued after 1939.

3

Commercial and Financial Developments

1 The Changing Pattern of Retail and Wholesale Trading

The main theme of the last chapter was industrial change; above all the decline of industries producing for export and the growth of production and services for domestic use. This trend was bound to reduce the relative volume of international trade. At the same time, the differences between the industrial history of the 1920s and the 1930s were at least in part due to the differences in financial policy. The history of these commercial and financial developments, and their interaction with the changing pattern of industry, will be the theme of this chapter.

Many of the new mass-production industries, providing a wide range of consumer goods from electrical goods to patent polishes and cleaning powders, from plastic containers to artificial silk stockings and photographic apparatus for a prosperous home market, particularly in the late 1930s, were an aspect of the opening of the era of mass-consumption. One of the sectors most immediately affected was retail distribution. It had begun to change slowly even before 1914, but after 1919 its changes were greatly accelerated. The old-established boundaries between retailers were being broken down. New goods called forth new retailing specialists, and some of these, like electrical goods suppliers, had to undertake the new function of after-sales services. In other cases the change was in the opposite direction, as manufacturers increasingly performed many of the traditional functions of the retailer, such as weighing, packing and pricing, in the factory, and then substituted their own reputation for that of the retailer in the eyes of the consumer, among other methods by advertising in new media such as mass-circulation newspapers, radio and film. By 1938, it was estimated that about £106 million a year was being spent on advertising. Press advertising alone, according to another calculation, had risen from £22 million in 1907 to £60 million in 1930.[1] Cosmetics, cigarettes and medicaments were still among the most heavily advertised, 20–50% of the retail price being accounted for by advertising costs; but other commodities, including alcoholic drinks, manufactured foods and fountain pens, had now joined this group of highly advertised commodities.[2]

Motor transport also exerted great influence on retail distribution. From the early 1920s onward, motor vans and lorries permitted direct delivery from manufacturer or importer, or from depots to multiple branches, and they also

---

[1] N. Kaldor and R. Silverman, *A Statistical Analysis of Advertising Expenditure and of the Revenue of the Press* (Cambridge, 1948), pp. 7 ff.; F. P. Bishop, *The Economics of Advertising* (1944), pp. 54–5; Ralph Harris and Arthur Seldon, *Advertising in a Free Society* (1959), pp. 5–11, 25, Appx. C.

[2] Kaldor and Silverman, *op. cit.*, Table 75, pp. 144–7.

replaced the errand-boy. At the same time the rural motor bus brought villagers regularly into the market towns and transformed their shopping centres, while possession of private motor cars furthered the growth of the residential suburb. Estates generally had their own shopping centres, and the creation of new housing estates was one of the most potent causes of the increasing number of shops in this period.

Lastly, there was the effect of the general rise in living standards. Broad groups of the population began to demand better shops, greater choice, style, and fashion, and other improvements, and a different collection of goods. The weighting of the official cost-of-living index bears eloquent witness to the changes in the consuming habits of the working classes, though the earlier figures may be based on false premises (see Table 3·1).

Table 3·1:   Working-class expenditure

Proportions spent on:	Budget of 1904 (1914 cost-of-living index)	Budget of 1937–8 (1947 cost-of-living index)
Food	60%	35%
Rent and rates	16	9
Clothing	12	9
Fuel and light	8	7
Other items in 1904 Budget	4	16
	100	76
Items not in 1904 Budget	—	24
	100	100

For the whole population of the United Kingdom, proportions of retail sales have been estimated as shown in Table 3·2.[3]

Table 3·2:   Proportions of retail sales, 1910–1939

	1910	1920	1939
Food	57·7%	50·7%	46·6%
Clothing	18·8	24·6	19·4
Reading, writing materials, confectionery, tobacco	8·8	9·3	14·4
Other goods	14·7	15·4	19·6
Totals, in £ million	892	2,863	2,302

One effect of all these influences was the growth of capital and employment in retail distribution. Few reliable statistics exist, but one estimate put the annual increase in the years 1924–32 at about 6%, at a time when the population increased by 0·55% per annum, though other estimates put the rate of increase rather lower.[4] Wherever official figures existed for licensing or other purposes,

[3] J. B. Jefferys, *Retail Trading in Britain, 1850–1950* (Cambridge, 1954), pp. 44–5.
[4] Henry Smith, *Retail Distribution* (2nd ed., 1948), pp. 35–7, 90–106; P. Ford, 'Competition and the Number of Retail Shops, 1901–31', *Econ. J.*, 45/179, 1935, and 'Decentralisation and Changes in the Number of Shops, 1901–1931', *ibid.*, 46/182, 1936; also P. Ford and G. V. White, 'Trends in Retail Distribution in Yorkshire (West Riding), 1901–1927', *Manchester School*, 7/2, 1936.

as among tobacconists or vendors of medicines,[5] they confirmed a rapid rise. Furniture, hardware, electrical goods and other 'non-essential' types of shops were growing even faster in numbers.

The number of workers engaged in distribution (including wholesaling) grew from an average of 1,661,000 in 1920–2 to 2,436,000 in 1937–8, or from 10·4% to 12·9% of total employment. There was an actual increase even in such areas as the four depressed counties of South Wales[6] which lost population in this period.[7] Including owner-managers and working proprietors, distribution employed about 3 million people in 1939, mostly in the retail field.

The increase in resources devoted to distribution was natural, in view of the larger throughput, while there were few improvements in the technical equipment of shops; moreover, distribution required personal services at a time when a rising standard of living implied that the cost of labour rose as compared to that of goods. However, it is likely that the main cause of the growth of the resources devoted to the distributive trades was the decline of price competition in ever wider fields of retailing, and its replacement by competition in ever more lavish services. Although difficult to measure, the increase in productivity was less than in manufacturing.[8] As in industry,[9] these 'imperfections' were fostered by monopolistic associations, and these, in turn, were related to the increase in the size of firms.

The proportions of trade held by different types of retailer changed as shown in Table 3·3.[10]

Table 3·3: Proportions of trade by types of retailer, 1915–1939

	1915	1939	Change
Co-operative societies	7½–9%	10–11½%	+2½%
Department stores	2–3	4½–5½	+2½
Multiple shops	7 8½	18–19½	+11
'Independents', owning 1–9 shops each, by difference	79½–83½	63½–67½	−16

The growth of the 'multiple' shops retailer, owning 10 or more shops, was the most outstanding of these developments. Between the wars, this type of organization spread to virtually every trade, and to all price and quality ranges.[11]

Among the multiple firms, in turn, the growth occurred largely among the larger chains. Between 1920 and 1939, the number of shops in firms with 200 branches or more grew from 10,942 to 21,283. Variety chain stores grew from 300 to 1,200 in the same period. Some of the growth was accounted for by mergers among the larger chains, but other firms grew rapidly without

[5] Hermann Levy, *The Shops of Britain* (1948), pp. 31–43, 50, 56, 71; Jefferys, *op. cit.*, p. 53.

[6] Henry Smith, *op. cit.*, p. 106; A. L. Chapman and Rose Knight, *Wages and Salaries in the United Kingdom, 1920–38* (Cambridge, 1953), p. 18.

[7] British National Committee, International Chamber of Commerce, *Trial Census of Distribution in Six Towns* (1937).

[8] Sir Arnold Plant, 'The distribution of Proprietary Articles', in *Some Modern Business Problems* (1937), p. 313; Robert Millward, 'Productivity in the UK Services Sector', *Oxf. Bull. Econ. Stat.*, 52/4, 1990.

[9] Cf. chapter 2, section 7 above.

[10] J. B. Jefferys, *The Distribution of Consumer Goods* (Cambridge, 1950), pp. 29, 73.

[11] Jefferys, *ibid.*, pp. 120–2.

amalgamations: thus Boots' had 200 branches in 1900 and 1,180 in 1938, while Marks & Spencer had 140 in 1927 and 230 in 1938. Many chains were linked with manufacturing or importing organizations, either by the forward integration of manufacturers, or the backward integration of the stores.[12] Some department stores also combined, and by 1939 there were four large groups, controlling 200 stores between them.

Co-operative retail societies spread in the inter-war period from their traditional strongholds in Lancashire and the West Riding, north-eastern England and Scotland, into the co-operative 'deserts' of the south.[13] Their trading pattern remained that of the basic needs of working-class households. About two-thirds of the societies' sales were still in groceries and other food. The growth in the total share of co-operative retailing is shown in Table 3·3. Membership increased much more rapidly, from 3 million in 1914 to 4½ million in 1920 and 8½ million in 1939, and the fall in the average sales per member was to some extent a reflection of the increase in the number, and fall in the size, of families.[14] In 1919, with 4·1 million members, co-operative societies held 10·7 million sugar registrations, while in 1940, with 8·5 million members, they only held 13·5 million registrations.

Among co-operative retail societies the large organization also made headway against the small. The average membership of all societies rose from 3,054 in 1914 to 8,643 in 1939: by 1935, 56½% of the members were in large societies of 20,000 members and over.[15]

In retail distribution, the decline of price competition, mainly by the spread of 'resale price maintenance', depended basically on the existence of branded, identical goods with a very wide, and preferably a national, market. Thus it was that price maintenance was first found in bookselling as early as the eighteenth century, and by the 1890s had begun to spread to groceries and proprietary medicines.[16] The 'Proprietary Articles Trade Association' (PATA), established in 1896, exerted great power: in 1938 it had 3,000 different articles on its protected list. Price maintenance itself covered about 3% of the domestic consumer's expenditure on goods in 1900; by 1938, this had grown to 30%.[17] Other methods of control included stop lists, boycotts, deferred rebates, distance limits, and licensing, as in the case of pharmacists and motor and cycle dealers. The official Committee on Restraint of Trade, reporting in 1931,[18] deplored the propping up of prices and the restrictions of entry practised by many associations, but it felt that there was no 'compelling reason' for intervention by the State.

The small shop managed to survive in large numbers, in part because advertising, packing, weighing and branding by manufacturers or wholesalers reduced the necessary skill of keeping many types of shop. Thus retail distribution

[12] Hermann Levy, *Retail Trade Associations* (1942), pp. 29–34; H. Compton and E. H. Bott, *British Industry* (1940), chapter 6.
[13] J. A. Hough, *Co-operative Retailing, 1914–1945* (1949); S. M. Bushell, 'The Relative Importance of Co-operative, Multiple and Other Retail Traders', *Economica*, 1/1, Jan. 1921, Table 1.
[14] G. D. H. Cole, *A Century of Co-operation* (Manchester, 1944), pp. 371–2.
[15] A. M. Carr-Saunders, P. Sargant Florence, Robert Peers et al., *Consumers' Co-operation in Great Britain* (1938), pp. 45–6.
[16] B. S. Yamey, *The Economics of Resale Price Maintenance* (1954), chapters 7 and 8.
[17] *Report of the Committee on Resale Price Maintenance* (Lloyd Jacob Committee) (1949. Cmd. 7696), p. 1; Jefferys, *Retail Trading*, pp. 53, 96–7.
[18] *Report of the Committee appointed … to Consider Certain Trade Practices* (1931).

became one of the last refuges of the small entrepreneur. By 1938, of an estimated 747,000 shops, all but 90,000 were still in the hands of small firms with 1–9 branches, the overwhelming majority being single shops managed by working proprietors.

As the packing, blending and breaking bulk, even selection and pricing, were increasingly carried out by the manufacturer, and manufacturers of branded and advertised goods began to send their travellers and delivery vans direct to retailers, the scope for the wholesaler was severely reduced. This was particularly so in commodities in which condition at the time of sale, or after-sale service and guarantee, were important, including biscuits, flour, meat, soap, books, electrical goods, photographic and sports goods and furniture. The large chains, at the same time, did their own wholesaling. By 1938, there were some 25,000–30,000 wholesaling firms left, and a further 20,000 wholesaler-retailers, handling about 40% of the consumer goods sold.[19]

The scope of the merchant firms trading overseas was reduced by similar factors as well as by the decline in Britain's international trade, and the artificial barriers put up by many countries against foreign imports.[20] Britain's entrepôt trade fell from £110 million in 1913 to £62 million in 1938, despite the rise in prices. British merchants also suffered from the direct competition of foreign firms abroad partly because of the Government aid given to their foreign competitors, and in part, it was said, because of their lack of enterprise and adaptability. In this, British manufacturers were not without blame, for in their packaging, style and language of instructions accompanying their goods they took less account of local wishes than competing manufacturers from other countries.[21]

The British merchant abroad was squeezed not only by foreign houses, but also by the large British manufacturers. For if he succeeded in opening a region to large sales, the manufacturer was tempted to send out his own representative and keep the merchanting profits for himself; tariff regulations might also force him to open branch factories. If, on the other hand, the merchant failed to sell the product, the manufacturer was equally tempted to by-pass him and try other channels. The shift from merchant to manufacturers' agent was detrimental to British trade as a whole, since the latter, unlike the former, had no interest in return cargoes. At the same time the British merchant, who had often acted as local banker and shipper was weakened by the decline in British overseas investment, or pushed out altogether by developing native or Government-sponsored firms, reducing further the demand for British financial and shipping services.[22] A long phase of the history of British overseas commerce was coming to a close in the inter-war years.

[19] Jefferys, *Retail Trading*, pp. 47–9, and *Distribution of Consumer Goods*, pp. 21–9, 46–8, 117–18; D. C. Braithwaite and S. P. Dobbs, *Distribution of Consumable Goods* (1932).

[20] J. Hurstfield, 'The Control of Raw Material Supplies, 1919–1939', *Ec. Hist. Rev.*, 14/1–2, 1944, pp. 19–20.

[21] PEP, *Report on International Trade* (1937), pp. 140–1; A. E. Kahn, *Great Britain in the World Economy* (1946), p. 79.

[22] PEP, *ibid.*, pp. 12–14, 131 ff.

2 The Course of Overseas Trade

The decline in the position of the British overseas merchant was linked to the fall of the share of British trade. World trade as a whole recovered remarkably quickly and soon began to grow beyond its pre-war level. In this growth the industrial progress and rising national incomes of the advanced countries played a major part, but the exports of primary producers were lagging.[23] These factors, together with the over-stimulation of the production of primary products during the war, caused a certain weakness in the world demand for them even in the 1920s. In the depression of the early 1930s it suffered a disastrous collapse and the primary producing countries, which were generally also international debtor countries, found it impossible to service their debts or pay for imports from the advanced countries. Here was one of the main causes of a vicious circle of shrinking world trade in the 1930s.[24]

Before 1914, Great Britain, by a free market for gold as well as for imported commodities, and by large overseas investment operations, had held the balance between the world's raw material and manufactured exports. After the war, this role should have fallen to the United States by virture of her economic strength and her emergence as the world's main lender. Long-term foreign investments had changed as shown in Table 3·4.[25] The USA, however, was unable to play her role in world trade quite as Britain had played it.

Table 3·4:   Long term foreign investment (in £ million)

	1914	1929
Great Britain	4,004	3,737
France	1,766	719
Germany	1,376	226
USA	513	3,018

There were several reasons for this. For one thing, the USA retained her high tariff and in any case had far less need of imports than had Britain, the 'dumping ground of foreign exporters',[26] before 1931 and the largest market even after that date, but now too weak to stand the financial strain which such a position involved.

Secondly, the USA had become the world's chief lender at a time when international capital movements and indebtedness were being bedevilled by war loan repayments and reparations of vast dimensions. As for Germany, her annual reparations instalments, even after they were scaled down by the Dawes Plan of 1924 and the Young Plan of 1929 were largely advanced by the USA.

---

[23] W. A. Lewis, *Economic Survey, 1919–1939* (1949), pp. 149 ff., 196, and 'World Production, Prices and Trade, 1870–1960', *Manchester School*, 20/2, May 1952. F. Benham, 'The Muddle of the Thirties', *Economica*, NS, 12/45, 1945.

[24] A. E. Kahn, *Great Britain in the World Economy* (1946), pp. 42–3, 63; A. J. Brown, *Industrialization and Trade* (1943), pp. 11, 56–71; D. C. Corner, 'Exports and the British Trade Cycle: 1929', *Manchester School*, 24, 1956.

[25] Colin Clark, *Conditions of Economic Progress* (1951 ed.), p. 514.

[26] PEP, *Report on International Trade* (1937), p. 63.

As far as the war loans among the Allies were concerned, moratoria and standstill agreements lightened the burdens of the weaker nations, but the USA insisted on *some* repayments, based on ability to pay, so that Britain actually repaid more to the USA than she could collect from the financially weaker allies whom she had helped during the war. These payments gained little for the creditors,[27] but caused much harm to the debtors and to the vanquished nations, they disrupted the flows of international payments, and they created a new phenomenon, the highly industrialized debtor nation, of which Germany, Japan and Italy were the leading examples.[28]

Thirdly, American lending differed greatly in character from the overseas investments of Britain before 1914. It arose out of the war rather than out of normal trade relations. Much of it, also, was politically directed, but without effective political control. Above all, for the American investment market foreign investment was marginal, and was easily jettisoned, as in 1928, when the boom in American home securities diverted all funds to Wall Street. Yet for the rest of the world, the reversal of the outflow of American investments to become an inflow appeared to be of staggering proportions.[29] Similarly, there was a flight of short-term funds into the USA from 1934 onwards, converting a net export of short-term capital into a net import.

Nor was this all, for with the onset of the American slump in 1929, imports into the USA fell off drastically and were further reduced by the tariff of 1930:[30] payments on merchandise import account fell from $4,399 million in 1929 to $1,323 million in 1932. The amount of dollars thus made available to the rest of the world by American lending and purchases together, fell from $7,400 million a year to $2,400 million in the course of three years, 1929–32, or by 68%, and if the fixed debt payments which had to be met out of these totals are deducted, the dollars available to foreigners for other purposes were cut by an even greater percentage margin.

A cut of such magnitude, caused by sudden reversals of the trade and lendings flows, created an overpowering dollar shortage.[31] It forced other countries to deflate and ultimately to go off the gold standard, while as part of the large-scale capital inflows, $10 billion of gold was sent to America in 1934–9 and duly re-interred there without being allowed to affect the value of the dollar. Thus, the United States, instead of acting as a buffer, and using its vast gold reserves to stabilize world trade when threatened by the dislocations of the slump, tended by its policy to make matters worse.

Currency and trade restrictions in other countries, Government-sponsored autarchy, bilateral and regional agreements, all tended to reduce still further the flow of goods across frontiers, already affected by the depression. In the recovery which followed, world trade expanded again, but it failed to reach the

---

[27] H. W. Arndt, *The Economic Lessons of the Nineteen-Thirties* (1944), p. 28.

[28] PEP, *International Trade*, pp. 19–20; Sir Arthur Salter, *Recovery* (1932), pp. 51 ff., also 100–7 and chapter 3.

[29] Hal B. Lary *et al.* (US Dept. of Commerce), *The United States in the World Economy* (Washington, 1943, London, 1944), pp. 89 ff., Appx., Tables I–III.

[30] J. K. Galbraith, *The Great Crash* (1955), pp. 162–3.

[31] A. J. Brown, 'Dollars and Crises', *Ec. Hist. Rev.*, 2nd S., 12/2, Dec. 1959; Donald MacDougall, *The World Dollar Problem* (1957), pp. 35–42, Appx. 1A; M. E. Falkus, 'United States Economic Policy and the "Dollar Gap" of the 1920s', *Ec. Hist. Rev.*, 24/4, 1971.

levels of 1929, and in 1938 there began a renewed cyclical downward turn in world trade which was interrupted by the outbreak of war.

In the 1920s, Britain's volume of imports was steadily increasing, and her exports steadily declining.[32] In the slump, Britain suffered rather less than many other countries. Her share of the world export trade in manufactured goods fell from 27·5% in 1911–13 to 23·8% in 1921–5 and 18·5% in 1931–8, and as a proportion of national income, overseas trade declined as shown in Table 3·5.[33]

Table 3·5:   Decline in overseas trade as a proportion of national income

Ratio of exports to national product		Ratio of imports to national income	
1907	33%	1913	31%
1924	27%	1929	25%
1938	15%	1938	16%

With a strongly rising volume of imports, and an equally marked fall in the volume of exports, Britain would have been faced with a rapidly widening unfavourable trade gap, if it had not been for a remarkably favourable trend of relative prices with a peak in 1933 (Table 3·6).[34]

Table 3·6:   Terms of trade, exports/imports, 1908–1937

	Quantum of trade		Terms of trade	
	Quantum of imports	Quantum of exports	Export prices import prices 1913 = 100*	Net terms of trade 1938 = 100**
1908–13	92	91	97	143
1921–9	104	79	127	115
1930–7	115	64	138	103

* Lewis, Appx., Table XV, p. 202.
** B. R. Mitchell and Phyllis Deane, *Abstract of British Historical Statistics* (Cambridge, 1962), p. 332.

It was this change in the terms of trade which permitted, and in part caused, the rising standard of living in Britain while condemning the export industries to unemployment and decline. In 1929 it was estimated that the unemployment in the six leading staple export trades caused by the fall in exports since 1913 alone amounted to 700,000–800,000 workers, or virtually the whole of the intractable core of the unemployed of the 1920s. By another calculation, employ-

[32] H. S. Booker, *The Problem of Britain's Overseas Trade* (1948), chapter 3; H. W. Macrosty, 'The Overseas Trade of the United Kingdom, 1924–31', *J. R. Stat. S.*, 95/4, 1932; G. D. H. Cole, *British Trade and Industry* (1932), chapter 9.

[33] W. A. Lewis, *op. cit.*, pp. 82, 85. For slightly different figures, see G. D. A. MacDougall, 'General Survey, 1929–37' in *Britain in Recovery* (1938), p. 13.

[34] Derek H. Aldcroft, *The Inter-War Economy in Britain 1919–1939* (1970), p. 258; Elliott Zupnick, *Britain's Postwar Dollar Problem* (New York, 1957), pp. 24–7.

ment in 'export-sensitive trades' fell from a peak of 1,439,000 in June 1929 (seasonally adjusted) to a low of 953,000 in December 1930.[35] Meanwhile the low prices of primary products on the world markets were ruining many of the primary producers who had been the chief customers of Britain.

In the 1930s the favourable trade required the transfer of resources,[36] and the nature of import demand also changed. After 1929, virtually the whole of the increase in imports was in the form of consumption goods, mainly food, drink and tobacco.[37]

Compared with pre-war trade the 1920s saw a growth in the trade with Commonwealth countries, and a corresponding decrease in the trade with Europe. The negative balance in trade with North America was aggravated by the fact that other European countries also had an unfavourable trade balance with the USA, covering it by American loans and investments, and by running a surplus with Britain which was in surplus with her colonies. A large quadrilateral world trade thus had to be kept in balance by the dollar earnings of the British overseas territories which were members of the sterling bloc.[38]

In the 1930s this complex system of trade virtually broke down. One limb, the dollar earnings of the colonies, shrank disastrously with the price fall of primary commodities and the decline in the American demand for industrial raw materials in the slump. A second limb, the European (and American) surplus with Britain, was reduced in size by Britain's new policies of protection, currency manipulation and more direct aids. In the same period, she allowed her sales and purchases with the Commonwealth and South America to decline and the deflationary effects of these tendencies further aggravated the two main problems, the unemployment in the British export industries and the low income of the overseas trading partners.

The favourable price trend was approximately of the right order of magnitude to counteract the unfavourable volume movements and keep the visible trade gap in the inter-war years on a fairly even keel. It averaged £225 million in 1921–4, rose to an average of £396 million in 1925–31, fell to £276 million in 1932–5 and then showed a strongly rising tendency again, increasing to well over £400 million by 1937.[39] To meet this adverse merchandise trade gap of £200–400 million a year, Great Britain relied largely on her income from overseas investments, and on the 'invisible' earnings from shipping, banking, insurance and similar services.

These invisible earnings, apart from the income from gilt-edged securities expressed in sterling, were all dependent on prosperity abroad and a high level of international trade. With the onset of the depression, there was a drastic fall

[35] Forrest Capie and Michael Collins, *The Inter-War British Economy: A Statistical Abstract* (Manchester, 1983), p. 66; E. V. Francis, *Britain's Economic Strategy* (1939), pp. 55–6.

[36] W. A. Lewis, p. 78; for a different tabulation for 1927–8 see F. H. Awad, 'The Structure of the World Export Trade, 1926–1953', *Yorkshire Bulletin*, 11/1, 1959, p. 35.

[37] G. N. Butterworth and H. Campion, 'Changes in British Import Trade' *Manchester School*, 8/1, 1937.

[38] A. E. Kahn, *op. cit.*, chapters 12 and 13; Forrest Capie, *Depression and Protectionism: Britain between the Wars* (1983), p. 19.

[39] Annual figures will be found in e.g., E. V. Morgan, *Studies in British Financial Policy, 1914–25* (1952), p. 341; A. E. Kahn, *Great Britain in the World Economy* (1946), p. 126, also chapters 9 and 10. Recently revised figures in R. G. Ware, 'The Balance of Payments in the Inter-War Period: Further Details', *B. of Eng. Qtly. Bull.*, 14/1, 1974, pp. 47–52.

in net invisible earnings which had accounted for about a third of the balance of payments in the 1920s. Shipping incomes dropped to a nadir of £65 million in 1933, investment income to £150 million in 1932, and commissions and miscellaneous incomes to a bare £40 million: a fall for these three items together by £200 million. The small regular surplus available for foreign investment disappeared in 1930, and in 1931 became a deficit, leading to a repatriation of capital on balance to the extent of £104 million. The drastic steps taken in that year, including protection and depreciation of the currency, reduced the unfavourable balance (including 'invisibles') to £51 million in 1932 and to much smaller amounts later, but throughout the 1930s repayments of capital slightly exceeded foreign lending[40] for the first time since the Industrial Revolution.

What little lending occurred in the 1930s was made almost entirely within the Empire. New capital issues indicate the trend.[41] (see Table 3·7)[41]. This switch was partly due to growing Treasury control of foreign lending from 1931 on.[42]

Table 3·7:   Trends in investment, 1911–36 (in £ million annual average)

	1911–12	1925–9	1932–6
Home investment	38	165	124
Overseas investment: Empire	67	67	28
Overseas investment: elsewhere	95	48	3
Totals	200	280	255

With these capital repayments and large-scale defaults, the nominal value of British overseas investments fell from £4,100 million in 1927 to £3,490 million in 1939;[43] the fall in the real value, in terms of earning power, was certainly greater, since over £1,900 million of this investment was in the form of equity and loan capital of companies.[44]

3   Great Britain Under Protection

One of the emergency measures taken by Britain in 1931 to rectify the unfavourable trade balance was the imposition of protective tariffs. This decision represented a complete reversal of traditional economic policy. Moreover, the electorate could scarcely be said to have given the 'National' Government a mandate for ending free trade and, as for economists and economic advisers, they were also all but united in opposing protection. Their views were summarized in the brilliantly argued *Tariffs: the Case Examined*,[45] which appeared in the year in which protection was finally to triumph.

[40] Sir Robert Kindersley, 'British Overseas Investments, 1938', *Econ. J.*, 49/196, 1939, p. 694. His main figures are summarized in A. E. Kahn, *op. cit.*, p. 187; Royal Institute of International Affairs, *The Problem of International Investment* (1937); Tse Chun Chang, 'The British Balance of Payments, 1924–1938', *Econ. J.*, 57/228, 1947. Also see S. N. Broadberry, *The British Economy between the Wars* (Oxford, 1986), pp. 58–9.

[41] J. H. Richardson, *British Economic Foreign Policy* (1936), p. 73 and chapter 3.

[42] For control before 1931 see John Atkin, 'Official Regulation of British Overseas Investment, 1914–1931', *Ec. Hist. Rev.*, 23/3, 1970.

[43] Bank of England figures; Kindersley's are slightly higher throughout.

[44] Series of articles by Sir Robert Kindersley in the *Economic Journal* in the 1930s.

[45] W. H. Beveridge *et al.*, *Tariffs: The Case Examined* (1931).

There had been many digressions from the narrow path of free trade even before 1931, but they could all be deemed to have been measures dealing with particular issues which still left the main principle intact. During the war, in 1915, the so-called 'McKenna duties' were imposed, consisting of a duty of $33\frac{1}{3}$% *ad valorem* on some imported luxury goods. Their original object was the saving of foreign exchange and of shipping space, but they were not repealed after the war, except briefly in 1924–5. They allowed such industries as motor manufacturing to grow to maturity behind a substantial tariff wall.[46]

In the later years of the war, the prohibition of imports, except under licence, was extended to a wide range of commodities until September 1919, and was kept on afterwards for the products of certain 'key industries', such as dyestuffs and other chemicals, scientific instruments, laboratory glassware and magnetos. The Dyestuffs (Import Regulation) Act, 1920, prohibited the import of dyestuffs for 10 years, except under licence, allowing a vigorous growth of the industry in Britain. The second measure, the Safeguarding of Industries Act of 1921, was more complex. It protected the other 'key industries' by a tariff of $33\frac{1}{3}$% *ad valorem*, but by Part II it also permitted the extension of such protection to other industries (which could make no claim on grounds of military importance), provided they could show that foreign products undersold them either by selling below costs of production or by the depreciation of a foreign currency. Under the currency depreciation clause, a few minor manufactures, including fabric gloves, glassware, hollow-ware and gas mantles, were protected by tariffs. The German Reparation (Recovery) Act of 1921 permitted the Treasury to impose duties of up to 50% *ad valorem* on German imports in part payment of reparations, and these duties were in fact protective, to the extent of 26% *ad valorem* on the average.[47] In 1925 the Safeguarding Act was extended to industries in which imports enjoyed unfair advantages by virtue not only of currency depreciation, but also of subsidies or bounties, or by inferior conditions of employment abroad.[48]

A special type of protection was extended to the film industry by means of a quota system. It was an undoubted success, and by 1936 the British film industry had by its own efforts exceeded the minimum quota at home, and had established a growing export market for its products.[49]

All these measures together did not constitute a protectionist policy. In 1930 only 17% of imports by value were dutiable, mostly by revenue duties only: protective duties did not affect more than 2–3% of imports. This was altered drastically in the economic blizzard of 1931. While protection was being debated, the 'National' Government,[50] passed a temporary Abnormal Importations (Customs Duties) Act at once, to stop the rushing in of imports in anticipation of later duties. The Act permitted *ad valorem* duties of up to 100%, though only 50% was generally imposed in practice on a wide range of manufactured goods.

[46] PEP, *Engineering Reports, II: Motor Vehicles* (1950), p. 75.
[47] Forrest Capie, *Depression and Protectionism: Britain between the Wars* (1983); E. B. McGuire, *The British Tariff System* (1939), chapter 17.
[48] G. P. Jones and A. G. Pool, *A Hundred Years of Economic Development in Great Britain* (1959), pp. 317–23; J. H. Richardson, 'Tariffs, Preferences and other Forms of Protection', in *Britain in Recovery* (1938), p. 126; Sir Hubert Llewellyn Smith, *The Board of Trade* (1928), pp. 185–8.
[49] Alfred Plummer, *New British Industries in the Twentieth Century* (1937), chapter 6/IV.
[50] C. L. Mowat, *Britain Between the Wars* (1956 ed.), pp. 409–12.

Another early protective measure was the Horticultural Products (Emergency Duties) Act, also passed before the end of the year.

In February 1932, the Import Duties Act inaugurated the protectionist era in Britain. The Act was not to apply to Empire goods for the time being, nor to the commodities covered by earlier protectionist legislation. There was also a specific free list, including wheat, meat and other foodstuffs, as well as all important industrial raw materials. On other commodities, a general tariff of 10% *ad valorem* was imposed and an Import Duties Advisory Committee (IDAC) was appointed, to suggest alterations in that general tariff. Following its report in April 1932,[51] duties on manufactured goods in general were increased by 10% to a total of 20% *ad valorem*, on luxury goods to 25% or 30%, on bicycles and some chemicals to $33\frac{1}{3}$% and on certain industrial raw materials and semi-manufactures to 15%. After the alterations agreed to at Ottawa later in the year, the total effect was to leave about one-quarter of imports duty free (many of them, however, restricted by other methods), one-half paying 10–20%, 8% paying new duties of over 20% and the remainder of imports paying the old McKenna and Safeguarding Duties.[52] Among later alterations, the most important was the duty of $33\frac{1}{3}$% imposed on steel imports on condition that the industry was reorganized, and the temporary raising of the steel tariff to 50% in 1935 in order to force the European steel cartel to grant better terms to the British industry.[53] The protectionist measures introduced in the 1930s relating to agricultural products have been noted in chapter 2, section 5 above.

An Imperial Economic Conference assembled in Ottawa in July–August 1932, hoping to expand trade among the members of the British Commonwealth in a world of shrinking commerce and rising trade barriers. These hopes were to be largely disappointed, for in fact neither Britain nor the Dominions had much room to manœuvre. For one thing, there was no hope of making the Empire economically self-sufficient, since Empire countries were heavily dependent on exports going to countries outside the Empire,[54] and the Empire countries could not replace these markets. If they depended on sales to outsiders, they must needs allow foreigners to import goods in return, and their exports could not be sold in preferential Empire markets at prices higher than the ruling world level.[55]

In the second place, the mercantilist conception of an industrialized mother country linked with primary producer colonies, had become grossly anachronistic by 1932. The Dominions had infant industries, which they were determined to protect while Great Britain had at last decided to protect her farmers. As a result, all that could be achieved, after weeks of bitter wrangling, was a series of bilateral treaties,[56] mainly giving preference by raising tariffs on imports from the rest of the world (Table 3·8).[57]

[51] (Cmd. 4066). Also see *Recommendations of the IDAC*, 45 pts., Parliamentary Papers, 1932–3, XVI.

[52] J. H. Richardson, in *Britain in Recovery*, p. 129. Also F. Benham, *Great Britain Under Protection* (New York, 1941), chapter 2.

[53] D. Abel, *A History of British Tariffs, 1923–1942* (1945).

[54] PEP, *Report on International Trade* (1937), p. 66.

[55] Benham, *op. cit.*, pp. 80–1.

[56] *Imperial Economic Conference at Ottawa, Summary of Proceedings and Copies of Trade Agreements* (1932. Cmd. 4174).

[57] Francis, *Britain's Economic Strategy* (1939), p. 203; J. H. Richardson, *British Economic Foreign Policy* (1936), p. 128.

Table 3·8:   British tariffs before and after the Ottawa agreements

	1930	1932 Before Ottawa	After Ottawa
% of imports free of duty	83·0	30·2	25·2
% of foreign imports subject to new duties at: { 10% —		32·9	28·3
11–20% —		15·3	21.8
over 20% —		4·6	7·7
	83·0	83·0	83·0

The network was completed by the imposition, in the months which followed, of imperial preference on the Colonies also.

The Imperial preference system was followed by a diversion of part of the trade formerly conducted with outside regions towards Empire regions,[58] but it is not certain how far Ottawa was responsible for it, since it was in line with a long-term trend, as well as being furthered by the exchange stability within the sterling bloc. As Table 3·9 shows, the rest of the Empire benefited more from Ottawa than the United Kingdom, but Britain had started in a more favourable position:[59]

Table 3·9:   UK trade with Empire countries (excluding Irish Free State)

	% of UK imports from Empire	% of UK exports to Empire
1913	25·0	32·9
1924–9 (average)	26.8	35.2
1931	24.5	32.6
1933	34·3	36·0
1937	37·3	39·7

The new tariffs and quotas also permitted Britain to offer concessions, or threaten retaliation, to other countries. Britain made 20 such agreements in 1933–8.[60] The most important was the trade agreement between Britain and the USA made in November 1938 but there was no opportunity of developing it before the outbreak of war; a treaty with Germany in 1939 was similarly thwarted.

There has been much controversy over the total effects of protection in the 1930s on Britain's trade and prosperity. Politicians at the time appeared to be looking for such direct effects as the salvaging of individual industries and the

[58] PEP, *International Trade*, pp. 66–74.
[59] Richardson, in *Britain in Recovery*, p. 138; F. C. Benham, *Great Britain*, pp. 256–7; Ian M. Drummond, *British Economic Policy and the Empire 1919–1939* (1972), pp. 102–4.
[60] Capie, *Depression*, pp. 129 f.; McGuire, chapter 19.

prevention of undercutting by ill-paid labour or by subsidized importers. Some hoped for rising prices as a possible trigger for a cyclical upswing, others wanted simply to stop the unfavourable trade balance by the crudest method available, or to raise revenue. The 'National Government' had a 'doctor's mandate' and prescribed protection as a nostrum for a variety of ills.

Modern views are more sophisticated, but equally varied. Using the concept of 'effective protection', it was found that such industries as cotton, which had little effect on recovery, had received a high degree of protection, while building, which was a main carrier of the upswing, was probably even harmed by negative protection, i.e. by having to pay more for its inputs without compensating advantages (as was shipbuilding) – though even that is disputed. Foreman-Peck and Eichengreen both calculate a benefit of 2·3% of GNP arising from protection, though they arrive at these figures by different routes, and it may be said to be fairly well established that the main benefit of protection was to relieve pressure on the pound, which allowed monetary policy to be eased, and it was that which benefited the upswing of the 1930s.[61]

There was, certainly, an immediate sharp reduction in imports, and in the sequel home production rose much faster than imports, pointing to a possible replacement of one by the other. At the same time, however, there was also an even larger fall in exports, and the fall in total foreign trade as a proportion of home production was part of a secular trend, and may well not have been caused by the tariff as such. Similarly, protection did not seem to have led to any noticeable rise in prices: these continued to fall to 1932–3, and then rose slowly as the cyclical upswing began, as might have been expected (see Table 3·10).[62]

Table 3·10:   Price indices 1919–39

	Consumers' goods and services (1913 = 100)	Total final output (1913 = 100)	Retail prices all items (1958 = 100)
1931	168·6	158·0	35
1932	164·3	153·3	34
1933	160·9	150·7	33
1937	168·6	162·1	36
1938	171·2	163·4	37
1939	182·1	172·1	38

In the last resort, protection in Britain was only one in a long chain of measures. Its imposition in 1932 was motivated at least as much by politics as by economics and its effects cannot be isolated from the effects of other simultaneous measures taken at the time.

[61] Forrest Capie, 'The British Tariff and Industrial Protection in the 1930s', *Ec. Hist. Rev.*, 31/3, 1978 and discussion in *ibid.*, 34/1, 1981, pp. 132–42; Barry J. Eichengreen, *Sterling and The Tariff, 1929–32* (Princeton, NJ, 1981); S. N. Broadberry, *The British Economy between the Wars* (Oxford, 1986), pp. 133–8; Derek H. Aldcroft, *The British Economy*, Vol. 1 (1986), pp. 70 f.

[62] C. H. Feinstein, *National Income, Expenditure and Output of the United Kingdom, 1855–1965* (Cambridge, 1972), T. 133; London and Cambridge Economic Service, *The British Economy, Key Statistics 1900–1966*, Table E; G. D. N. Worswick, 'The Sources of Recovery in the UK in the 1930s', *Nat. Inst. Econ. Rev.*, 110 (1984), p. 91.

4 The Changing Role of the Budget

The dislocation of the public finances caused by the war, as described in chapter 1, section 5 above, continued for a further two years;[63] the budget of 1920–1 was the first to achieve a surplus, and it may thus be considered to have been the first 'normal' peace-time budget.

However, there could be no simple return to the pre-war type of budget. On the expenditure side, the changes, in Morgan's 'adjusted' terms, were as shown in Table 3·11.[64]

Table 3·11:   Budgetary changes, 1913–45 (in £ million)

	1913–14	1920–1	1924–5
Consolidated fund services	37	378	394
Fighting services	86	354	138
Munitions	—	33	—
Revenue departments	30	76	64
Other civil departments	55	466	257
	208	1,306	853
Less appropriations in aid*	12	150	54
	196	1,156	799

* Sales by Departments to other Departments or to the private sector.

Bearing in mind the temporarily high prices, the budget of 1920–1 was, broadly, representative of the inter-war budgets which were to follow.

Among the changes since 1913–14, the striking increase in the 'consolidated fund services' stands out, representing mainly the national debt. In money terms, its burden increased tenfold, and annual interest payments, negligible before the war, rose to over 40% of the budget. As prices fell in the early 1920s, the real burden of this debt, as a payment from mainly the active part of the population to mainly the inactive, became distinctly heavier.

The total national debt was at its maximum in March 1920, when it stood at £7,830 million. Of this, only £315 million was funded, £1,230 being external, and the rest consisting of a 'floating' debt of some £1,250 million and of other unfunded debt of nearly £5,000 million with varying repayment dates and terms. The floating debt was tackled first, and within three years the Treasury Bills outstanding were reduced from over £1,100 million to little more than half this sum, while Ways and Means advances, standing at over £200 million in March 1920, were almost wiped out at the end of the decade.[65] The funding of this part of the floating debt was achieved only by raising the nominal value of

[63] E. V. Morgan, *Studies in British Financial Policy, 1914–25* (1952), p. 98. On Professor Morgan's 'adjusted' figures, showing the sums actually collected and spent in the economic, rather than the administrative sense of the official figures, there was, in fact, a surplus of £110 million in 1919/20, p. 104.

[64] *Ibid.*, p. 101.

[65] A. T. K. Grant, *A Study of the Capital Market in Post-War Britain* (1937), pp. 86 ff.; F. W. Paish, 'The Floating Debt, 1914–1939' in T. Balogh, *Studies in Financial Organization* (Cambridge, 1947).

long-term issues by £1,000 million and forcing up long-term interest rates.

As it was, most critics were agreed that the war debts had been contracted at too generous a rate.[66] Moreover, with £2,100 million of the unfunded debt in 1920 falling due for repayment in 1–7 years, and £2,900 million in 8–10 years from the date of issue, repayments and renewals followed each other so closely in the 1920s that the whole tended to coagulate into one single mass of war debt, to be dealt with together. Repayment brought the nominal total down to £7,530 million in 1931, and by 1935, of the £5,590 million of public debt held outside the Departments, £4,483 million was over 15 years or undated.[67] The burden on the economy, however, was still high. The debt service fluctuated round 7% of the national income and rose to $8\frac{1}{4}$% in 1932 with the fall of incomes in the depression. Relief came only with the great War Loan Conversion of 1932, and the associated fall in short-term rates. The debt service burden then fell to 5·45% of national income in 1933, 5·00% in 1934 and 4·65% in 1935.

Next to the increase in the Consolidated Fund Services, the most striking increases occurred in the expenditure on the social services (see Table 3·12), though part of these were derived from special contributions under the insurance schemes.[68]

Table 3·12:   Social services expenditure, 1913–34 (in £ million)

Payments made:	Area covered	1913–14	1921–2	1933–4
Poor relief	GB	$16\frac{1}{2}$	46	47
Health insurance	GB	$14\frac{1}{2}$	$24\frac{1}{2}$	32
Old-age pensions	GB	10	22	$58\frac{1}{2}$
Widows', etc., pensions	GB	—	—	$22\frac{1}{2}$
War pensions	UK	—	$88\frac{1}{2}$	44
Unemployment insurance	UK	$\frac{1}{2}$	53	$88\frac{1}{2}$
Totals		$41\frac{1}{2}$	234	$292\frac{1}{2}$
Contributions levied				
Health insurance	GB	17	25	26
Pensions	GB	—	—	23
Unemployment insurance	UK	2	$30\frac{1}{2}$	$39\frac{1}{2}$
Totals		19	$55\frac{1}{2}$	$88\frac{1}{2}$

Housing and education were other costly services, both of which also derived some share of their incomes from local authorities. As a result, the budgets of the local authorities were rising as rapidly as those of the Central Government[69] (see Table 3·13).

[66] Ursula K. Hicks, *The Finance of British Government, 1920–1936* (1938), p. 317; E. V. Morgan, *op. cit.*, p. 139, also 94–7, 115–51; A. W. Kirkaldy (ed.), *British Finance During and After the War, 1914–21* (1921), pp. 161–2.

[67] *Report of the Committee on the Working of the Monetary System* (Radcliffe Committee) (1959. Cmnd. 827), Table 26.

[68] G. D. H. and M. Cole, *The Condition of Britain* (1937), pp. 328–9; C. L. Mowat, *Britain Between the Wars*, p. 497.

[69] A. R. Prest, *Public Finance in Theory and Practice* (1960), pp. 181–2.

Table 3·13: Local Authorities expenditure and revenue (£m.)

Current expenditure (excl. trading)	1913–14	1938–9	Revenue	1913–14	1938–9
Education	36	118	Rates	82	215
Health	9	86	Current grants	27	164
Roads	23	68	Trading and other	12	19
Other	54	114			
Totals	122	386	Totals	121	398

Capital expenditure (incl. trading)		
Housing	0	67
Roads	4	16
Trading	5	37
Other	16	52
Totals	25	172

Measured as a proportion of national income, social expenditure by the public authorities, national and local, increased from 5·5% in 1913 to 10·3% in 1924 and 13·0% in 1938; in the depression, when national income declined while relief payments kept up, it had risen even further, to 15·8% in 1932. Total Government expenditure as a proportion of GNP rose from 12·4% in 1913 to a peacetime peak of 29·4% in 1921, then levelled off around 24%, but with peaks at 28·8% in 1931 and 30·0% in 1938.[70]

Changes occured also in the methods of raising revenue, summarized in Table 3·14.[71]

Table 3·14: Sources of revenue, 1913–39 (in £ million)

	1913–14	1924–5	1932–3	1938–9
Inland Revenue	88	419	411	520
(of which Income Tax)	(44)	(274)	(251)	(336)
Customs and Excise	75	234	288	341
Miscellaneous	10	64	45	66
Totals	173	717	744	927

Again, the main alterations occurred in the war years, the only important change after 1920 being the imposition of the tariff in 1932. Income tax, standing at 6s. in 1920–1, never fell below 4s. in the pound in the inter-war years. A differential in favour of earned incomes, suggested by the Royal Commission on the Income Tax in 1920,[72] was adopted. The war time Excess Profits Duty was abolished in 1921 and Corporation Profits Duty was repealed in 1924.

[70] Ursula K. Hicks, *Public Finance* (1947), p. 32. Also Alan T. Peacock and Jack Wiseman, *The Growth of Public Expenditure in the United Kingdom* (1967), p. 166.

[71] Prest, *op. cit.*, pp. 157–8; *Statistical Abstract of the UK*, Annual.

[72] *Royal Commission on Income Tax, Report* (1920. Cmd. 615), paras. 126–40.

Among indirect taxation, the duties on tobacco and alcoholic drinks were retained at a high level after the war, and to these the hydrocarbon oil taxes and motor duties were added. New sources of taxation needed from 1925, largely in order to finance the growing social programme, were, apart from entertainments duty and the abortive betting tax of 1926, derived largely from protection. The tariff, even in the depression, yielded £40 million a year, and artificially raised food prices caused by protection constituted a further large burden on the poor.

Before the war, 57·5% of the revenue had been in the form of direct taxes. This rose to a peak of 82·7% in 1917–18 and then settled at about 66% in the 1920s. It fell somewhat with the imposition of protective duties in 1932. The lowering of real wages by taxing the consumption of the working classes was, in fact, one of the aims of the protectionists.

The examples in Table 3·15 show the changing burden of total taxation, including the estimated shares of indirect taxes, etc., expressed as a percentage of income, on a family of two adults and three dependent children, living on earned income only, at different levels of income:[73]

Table 3·15: Taxation as a percentage of income, 1913–38

	Income of £100	£200	£500	£1,000	£10,000
1913–14	5·4	4·0	4·4	5·2	8·0
1918–19	9·9	7·9	10·2	16·9	42·5
1923–4	14·1	11·8	8·0	14·1	37·1
1925–6	11·9	10·2	6·2	11·0	31·2
1930–1	11·0	9·6	4·5	9·7	35·8
1937–8	10·4	8·4	5·6	11·8	39·1

It will be observed that medium incomes between £200 and £1,000 a year enjoyed the lowest percentage burden. The heaviest burdens on the poorer families were duties on tea, sugar, tobacco, alcohol and, latterly, taxes on production, such as wheat and coal.[74] On the other hand, death duties and profits taxes, which fell more heavily on the rich, are omitted from the table.

As far as the allocation of expenditure was concerned, it also worked in the direction of redistribution in this period. According to one estimate, while in 1913 the working classes received less in social services than they paid in taxes, by 1925 they contributed only 85% of the cost (receiving the excess of £45 million from other classes) and in 1935 they contributed but 79%, receiving an excess of £91 million.[75] For 1937 it was found that, on various assumptions, the sums redistributed to the poorer income groups (receiving under £125 a year) were in the range of £193–274 million. The total redistributed amounted to

[73] G. Findlay Shirras and L. Rostas, *The Burden of British Taxation* (Cambridge, 1942), p. 58; cf. also Sir Bernard Mallet and C. Oswald George, *British Budgets* (*Second Series*), *1913–14 to 1920–21* (1929), Appx. Table XXI.

[74] Shirras and Rostas, p. 37; Hicks, *Finance of British Government*, chapter 16.

[75] Mowat, *Britain Between the Wars*, p. 492; Colin Clark, *National Income and Outlay* (1937), pp. 145–8.

5–6% of the national income.[76] Other calculations put the amount of redistribution lower than this.

These figures may seem disappointingly small. There were several causes for it. In the first place, a large proportion of the welfare schemes was financed by the working classes themselves, this through the employees' weekly insurance payments, protective tariffs, and excise duties on tobacco (49·4%) and alcoholic drinks (37·8%), widely consumed by the poorer classes.[77]

Secondly, not all the benefits of social welfare provisions went to the poorer families. The housing subsidies, for example, benefited chiefly the better-off manual workers and the white-collar workers and lower middle classes. The benefits of public provision for education were greatest for families still higher on the income scale. One estimate puts the incidence of divisible benefits in 1937 at the annual rates *per capita* (£)[78] as follows:

Table 3·16: Social welfare benefits per capita (£) in 1937

Income class	Education	Public health	Health insurance	Assistance and unemployment insurance	Pensions	Housing
Under £125	2·1	1·2	0·7	4·2	5·1	0·4
£125 and under £250	3·1	1·2	0·4	0·8	1·1	0·7
£250 „ „ £500	3·7	1·3	—	—	0.3	—

Lastly, the large annual national debt payments added a further strong regressive element to the tax system.

In addition to meeting Government expenditure and providing for an element of re-distribution, inter-war budgets acquired a third objective: the support of official monetary policy, and above all the maintenance of the value of the currency. Before 1914 the value of the pound sterling had been maintained in terms of gold by the free convertibility at the Central Bank. However, since the abrogation of the gold standard, in practice in 1914 and legally in 1919, there had occurred a considerable measure of inflation, which could plausibly be blamed on the over-expansion of the currency by the Government. As the restoration of the pound to its pre-war parity with gold became an aim of policy from 1919 onward, the Government was bound to accept the responsibility of playing itself a major part in the necessary deflation, to be achieved by 'orthodox' finance, which consisted in balancing the budget. In turn, this affected the parallel attempts to prevent, or cure, industrial fluctuations leading to mass unemployment. These turned, after years of debate, into yet a fourth task of the budget.

This new aspect of economic policy had several roots. It derived from the proposals of the Swedish economists in the late 1920s, from the budding 'national income' approach of economists, and the doctrines on money, interest,

[76] T. Barna, *The Redistribution of Incomes through Public Finance in 1937* (Oxford, 1945), pp. 229–30.

[77] Prest, *Public Finance*, p. 360.

[78] U. K. Hicks, *Public Finance*, p. 298.

investment and saving propagated by J. M. Keynes.[79] The new doctrine asserted that in depressions it was the duty of the Government to expand its activities and to create additional incomes by programmes of public works and other inflationary actions,[80] as well as to encourage investment by low interest rates. This was in direct contrast to the current 'Treasury view', described by the then Chancellor, Winston Churchill, in the House of Commons in April 1929 as 'the orthodox Treasury doctrine which has steadfastly held that, whatever might be the political or social advantages, very little additional employment and no permanent additional employment can, in fact, and as a general rule, be created by State borrowing and State expenditure'.[81] It followed from the new doctrine, that British budgetary policy in the inter-war years was of a nature to aggravate the ill effects of the trade cycle.[82]

Much of the post-war literature was inclined to follow this Keynesian arguments about the attitude of the Treasury, but recent writing has looked more favourably on its policies in the 1930s, as well as judging that Keynes', or Lloyd George's, employment creating proposals of 1929 and after would not have pulled Britain out of the slump. Senior Treasury officials while not convinced by Keynes' theoretical arguments, which in any case were not comprehensively available until 1936, were prepared to support public works if they concentrated on the depressed regions or sectors and did not 'crowd out' other work. They manipulated the rearmament expenditure of the late 1930s so as to minimize its inflationary effects,[83] and in the most sophisticated version of the defence of the Treasury, its policy was said to have been based on the realization that the stickiness of wages prevented the normal adjustment to depression by lowering costs. In consequence, it picked on the only realistically available policy of a once-for-all rise in prices (in order to reduce real wages) by means of the tariff, by devaluation and by the encouragement of price-fixing agreements.[84]

In the financial year 1919–20, when all the Government's efforts should have been directed to restraining inflation, it added to it by a budget deficit. From 1920–1, by contrast, the Government determined to achieve a surplus and reduce

[79] J. M. Keynes, *A Treatise on Money*, 2 vols. (1930), and *The Means to Prosperity* (1933); also R. F. Kahn's fundamental contribution, 'The Relation of Home Investment to Employment', *Econ. J.*, 41/162, 1931.

[80] R. F. Bretherton, F. A. Burchardt, R. S. G. Rutherford, *Public Investment and the Trade Cycle* (1941), chapter 1.

[81] Quoted in S. H. Beer, *Treasury Control* (1956), pp. 1–2; also see U. K. Hicks, *Finance of British Government*, chapter 13; A. D. Gayer, *Monetary Policy and Economic Stabilisation* (1935), chapter 10; Richard W. Lyman, *The First Labour Government, 1924* (London, 1957), chapter 9; K. J. Hancock, 'The Reduction of Unemployment as a Problem of Public Policy, 1920–29', *Ec. Hist. Rev.*, 2nd S., 15/2, 1962, pp. 335–8.

[82] J. M. Keynes, *General Theory of Employment, Interest and Money* (1936); G. C. Peden, 'Sir Richard Hopkins and the "Keynesian Revolution" in Employment Policy 1929–1945', *Ec. Hist. Rev.*, 36/2, 1983; Peter Clarke, *The Keynesian Revolution in the Making 1924–1936* (Oxford, 1988); W. R. Garside, T. J. Hatton, Sean Glyn, Alan Booth, debate in *Ec. Hist. Rev.*, 38/1 (1985), pp. 83–94; Roger Middleton, *Towards the Managed Economy* (1985), pp. 4–5, 144 f.; Jim Tomlinson, *Employment Policy 1939–1955* (Oxford, 1987), pp. 18, 45 f.; Alan Booth, *British Economic Policy 1931–49: Was there a Keynesian Revolution?* (Hemel Hempstead, 1989), pp. 23–9.

[83] S. N. Broadberry and N. F. R. Crafts, *The Implications of British Macroeconomic Policy in the 1930's for Long Run Growth Performance* (1990).

[84] U. K. Hicks, *Public Finance*, chapter 17; H. W. Arndt, *The Economic Lessons of the Nineteen-Thirties* (1944), chapters 2 and 8. Also chapter 5 section 3, below.

the floating debt in order to regain control over the market and prepare the way for the ultimate return to gold at the old parity. The consequent immense deflationary pressure, applied from April 1920 onwards, when the boom began to sag, greatly aggravated the effects and extent of the slump. Budgetary policy was similarly ill-timed in the recurring crises and difficulties of the remainder of the inter-war years.[85]

Deflationary policies were maintained in all the budgets of the early 1920s, and throughout the decade it proved possible to devote regularly, year by year, a sum averaging £50 million for debt redemption. Meanwhile, however, the severe depression continued, and the accepted doctrine for a rigidly orthodox Chancellor in such a case was to reduce taxation, but only if he could impose equivalent cuts in expenditure. A committee of businessmen, headed by Sir Eric Geddes, was therefore set up to suggest economies, and in three reports[86] recommended cuts totalling £87 million, quickly dubbed the 'Geddes axe'. The most severe cuts were reserved for the social services, including education and tuberculosis, maternity and child welfare services, although these destructive proposals were not accepted in their entirety by the Chancellor; nevertheless, some of the social services, above all education, took over a decade to recover from the cuts imposed in 1922. As it turned out, there was a large surplus of over £100 million achieved in 1922–3, used for debt redemption. In the next year, revenue was down by £77 million, largely owing to cuts in income tax, profits tax and beer duties, but as expenditure was also down by £24 million, there was still a sizeable surplus.

Snowden's budget of 1924 represented a partial reversal of the trend to erode the egalitarian legacies of the war. The result was virtually to wipe out the surplus of earlier years and to end the era of surpluses of the early 1920s: henceforth budgets were more closely balanced, and over the rest of the inter-war years, surpluses and deficits measured in the traditional way roughly cancelled out.

Winston Churchill's budget of 1925 was the second important budget of the decade. Apart from the re-introduction of the gold standard, the budget speech was notable for reversing the previous deflationary emphasis. The new Widows', Orphans' and Old Age Contributory Pensions Act laid extra burden on the Exchequer, particularly in years to come. Churchill's budget of 1928 added further expenditure and so did Neville Chamberlain's Local Government Act of 1929, which, among other reforms, included a major measure of derating for agricultural land, industry and the railways. The Treasury was to make up the losses of rates to local authorities, estimated at £30 million, by 'block' grants, which, unlike earlier grants, favoured the authorities with the poorer incomes and higher costs.[87]

While expenditure was thus increased in 1925, income tax rates were cut. Inevitably, the year 1925–6 ended with a deficit and so did the next year, and Churchill balanced his budgets only by short-term manipulation. These inflationary budgets were introduced just at a time when the re-establishment of the gold standard forced deflationary policies on the monetary authorities.

[85] Cf. also sections 5, 6 and 7 of this chapter.
[86] *Committee on National Expenditure, Reports* (1922. Cmd. 1581, 1582, 1589).
[87] C. L. Mowat, *Britain Between the Wars*, pp. 199–200, 339–42; P. J. Grigg, *Prejudice and Judgment* (1948), pp. 194–209.

Snowden's budget of 1930 was introduced in an atmosphere of worsening trade and mounting unemployment. Forced to find additional revenue to meet the shortfall expected because of declining incomes and mounting pension and relief payments, the Chancellor added heavily to direct taxes, including 6*d.* on the income tax, while allowing a whole series of safeguarding duties to lapse. No important changes were made in the budget of 1931; the threatening deficits were to be met by raids, anticipations and transfers on Churchillian models. Proposals for reducing expenditure expected from a Committee presided over by Sir George May, however, had a large share in bringing down the second Labour Government and setting thereby the political course for the 1930s.

Technically, the May Report was concerned with the narrow problem of making an estimate of the budget deficit to be expected, and suggesting means of meeting it. By taking an extremely pessimistic view,[88] and ignoring the possibility of reductions in the national debt payments, then at close on £300 million a year, which were recommended by the Macmillan Committee reporting at about the same time,[89] and in the event were carried out without a hitch in the following year, it was possible for the May Committee to forecast a total budget deficit of £120 million a year. This the Committee proposed to meet by raising another £24 million in taxes and cutting expenditure by £96 million, of which two-thirds was to be accounted for by slashing unemployment pay.

Several members of the Cabinet were not prepared to see relief cut to the extent demanded, but after the Labour Government had split on this issue, and a 'National' Government formed in August 1931, many of the May Committee suggestions were adopted by Snowden in his autumn budget.[90] Direct and indirect taxes were heavily increased, and unemployment contributions raised. On the expenditure side, there were reductions in the appropriations to the sinking fund, in salaries of civil servants, police, teachers and others, and a 10% cut in unemployment benefit rates and other reductions in benefits.[91] In the event, the budget balanced almost exactly, at £851 million.

From 1932 onwards, Chancellors operated in a less restrictive environment, helped by the successful conversion of some £1,970 million of War Loan from 5% to 3½% in the course of 1932, the revenue from the newly imposed tariff and the easing of the balance of payments by going off gold. However, Britain was alone among major Western nations not to resort to budget deficits to promote recovery and, according to the more accurate constant employment budget balance calculations, it appears that the budgets of the 1930s until 1936 were even more restrictive and therefore more harmful than had once been thought.[92]

In 1934, expecting a surplus, Neville Chamberlain restored unemployment rates and half the cuts in Government salaries, the rest being made good in 1935–6; at the same time, the standard rate of income tax was reduced by 6*d.*, from 5*s.* to 4*s.* 6*d.* in the pound. The 1936 budget was the first in which defence expenditure rose significantly, by £50 million to £187 million. Like the budget of the following years, it was met in part by a rise in income tax rates. Even so,

[88] P. J. Grigg, *op. cit.*, p. 255.
[89] *Committee on Finance and Industry, Report* (1931. Cmd. 3897), Addendum, I, paras. 28–30.
[90] C. L. Mowat, *op. cit.*, pp. 379–412.
[91] U. K. Hicks, *Finance of British Government*, pp. 361–2.
[92] Roger Middleton, 'The Constant Employment Budget Balance and British Budgeting Policy, 1929–1939', *Ec. Hist. Rev.*, 34/2, 1981.

Table 3·17: Indications of Fiscal Stance, 1920–1940 (£ million)

Calendar year	Budget surplus	Tax year	Fiscal stance
1920	+89	1929–30	0·0
1921	+38	1930–1	+71·3
1922	+69	1931–2	+152·4
1923	+76	1932–3	+174·7
1924	+34	1933–4	+141·2
1925	+20	1934–5	+112·2
1926	−8	1935–6	+69·8
1927	+52	1936–7	+22·7
1928	+53	1937–8	+12·0
1929	+26	1938–9	+56·5
		1939–40	+45·2

the budget of 1938–9 made provision for borrowing £90 million, and the budget of 1939–40 £380 million for defence expenditure.

5 Economic and Financial Policy in the 1920s

The war ended with wholesale prices 140%, and the cost of living 120–125%, above the level of July 1914. Technically, deflation might have been possible in 1919, but politically it was unthinkable.[93] As demobilized soldiers returned to civilian employment by the million, the fear among members of the Government and their advisers was of widespread unemployment, not of runaway inflation. Instead of restricting credit, Britain went formally off gold in March 1919 (having been *de facto* off gold since the outbreak of war) and allowed the credit expansion of the war years to go on into 1920.

On this swelling stream of easy credit, employment picked up rapidly in the summer of 1919, the demand coming from the backlog of necessary consumer goods restricted during the war years, translated into demands for stocks and capital goods, also run down during the war. Prices rose sharply, a speculative element in the boom feeding on itself to keep inflation going. Thus the boom of 1919–20 was largely one of prices, not output: at no stage did industrial output approach, let alone exceed, that of 1913.[94] An important element here was the substantial reduction in working hours enforced in most industries after the war, which raised labour costs without raising real earnings.[95] However, wages and other costs, while rising, rose less than prices, and there was a shift in the distribution of incomes in favour of profits, and this in turn led to the over-capitalization which was to burden several major British industries with top-heavy capital structures for the next two decades.

Before long, the Government turned its attention to the inflation.[96] In April

[93] C. H. Feinstein, *National Income*, T. 31–2. J. M. Keynes, *A Treatise on Money* (1930), vol. 2, pp. 176–7, S. N. Broadberry, *The British Economy between the Wars* (Oxford, 1986), p. 151; Roger Middeton, *Towards the Managed Economy* (1985), pp. 97, 132 f.

[94] A. C. Pigou, *Aspects of British Economic History, 1918–1925* (1947), p. 62.

[95] J. A. Dowie, '1919–20 is in need of attention', *Ec. Hist. Rev.*, 28/3, 1975.

[96] Susan Howson, 'The Origins of Dear Money, 1919–20', *ibid.*, 27/1, 1974; *eadem*, 'A Dear Money Man?: Keynes on Monetary Policy, 1920', *Econ. J.*, 83, 1937; *eadem*, *Domestic Monetary Management in Britain 1919–1938* (Cambridge, 1975), p. 28.

1920, a deflationary budget and determined action to reduce the floating debt was accompanied by a rise in bank rate, and there followed one of the most precipitous declines in British industrial history, unemployment rising from 2% to 18%, and the index of industrial activity falling from 117·9 to 90.0 in the space of one year.[97] Unemployment was no longer a major preoccupation: the social peace was no longer threatened.[98]

Some months before this reversal of policy, in December 1919, the influential Cunliffe Committee on Currency and Foreign Exchanges after the War had reported to recommend the restoration of the gold standard at the former parity at the earliest possible opportunity.[99] The gold sovereigns of pre-war years were not to be brought back but, for large transactions, the cheque and the bank deposit system was to return to gold by restoring the power of the Central Bank to force the joint-stock banks to vary the aggregate of their deposits in accordance with the state of its gold reserve. However in 1919 Britain was still far from such equilibrium. In order to regain a 'currency upon a sound basis', a stringent financial policy was necessary. The budget would have to be balanced, foreign lending suspended, foreign trade brought into balance, and the large surplus of bank notes reduced.

This programme was accepted by the Government in principle and in detail.[100] The severe deflation induced from April 1920 onward became the first step in a consistent policy which had one over-riding aim: the restoration of the gold standard at the old parity at the earliest possible moment.[101] Neither the heavy unemployment, nor the obstinate inability of production or exports to return to their pre-war figures, was to divert the authorities from their course. The efficacy of the gold standard, once established, would, so it was thought, restore British trade, prosperity and prestige. It was happily convenient for City interests that their own prosperity, security and comfort was the only way to benefit the British economy as a whole.

A bank rate of near panic level, at 7%, was kept on for a year, until April 1921, at a time of disastrous unemployment, and even afterwards the rate was reduced but slowly. The 'Geddes axe' became a by-word for callous meanness. Agricultural price support, in spite of a statutory guarantee for four years, was overthrown with indecent haste as soon as it became operative.[102] But, within its limits, the policy began to work.

The budget was balanced, and a favourable foreign balance of payments restored. The short-term debt was greatly reduced. So was the note issue, and bank deposits fell from over £2,000 million in December 1920 to £1,800 million in June 1925.[103] Above all, prices came down almost as fast as they had climbed:

[97] W. H. Beveridge, *Full Employment in a Free Society* (1944), p.313.

[98] Rodney Lowe, 'The Erosion of State Intervention in Britain 1917–24', *Ec. Hist. Rev.*, 31/2, 1978.

[99] Reprinted in T. E. Gregory, *Select Statutes, Documents and Reports Relating to British Banking, 1832–1928* (Oxford, 1929), pp. 366 ff.

[100] Treasury Minute of 15 December 1919 (Cmd. 485), reprinted in Gregory, *loc. cit.*, p. 371.

[101] A. C. Pigou, *Aspects of British Economic History, 1918–1925* (1947 ed.), Part V, chapter 1; S. E. Harris, *Monetary Problems of the British Empire* (New York, 1931), Part II, Book 5; Lawrence Smith, 'England's Return to the Gold Standard in 1925', *J. Econ. and Business History*, 4, 1931–2, p. 230.

[102] Chapter 2, section 5 above.

[103] E. V. Morgan, *Studies in British Financial Policy, 1914–25* (1925), pp. 73, 155–6, 220–31. Also pp. 97–8 above.

wholesale prices, which had risen from about 210 in March 1919 (1913 = 100) to a peak of 310–340 in mid-1920, were down to 190–210 in March 1921 and 160–170 in February 1922. Wage rates, which did not reach their peak until early in 1921, proved very flexible also (quite a number had been tied to the cost-of-living index) and fell from 275 in the winter of 1920–1 (July 1914 = 100) to 173 in the winter of 1923–4, rising slowly to 181 in March 1925.[104] From 1922 onwards it was even possible to pursue more normal policies appropriate to a slump, and a slight recovery was nursed up in 1922–4, though the preparations of the authorities for the return to gold helped to hold it back well below the recovery of other countries.

Substantial as this deflation in prices and costs was, however, it had just not gone far enough to match American prices and permit an easy return to gold at pre-war parities. The dollar rate of exchange, which had fallen to below $3·50 in the autumn of 1920, rose to about $4·70, or near parity, in the winter of 1922–3,[105] and then fluctuated, not about a mean of the pre-war gold equivalent rate of $4·86, but about a rate around $4·40 or $4·50. Home prices, costs and wages, were stuck at a level about 10% too high in spite of the 'capitalist offensive' fought from 1921 on to bring them down.[106] Wages in the 'sheltered' home industries remained immune to pressure;[107] combinations of capital and cartel agreements made other prices increasingly sticky downwards.[108]

If the stickiness of home costs was one reason for making the return to gold difficult, the level of the gold reserve was another. It had stood at about £150 million when the Cunliffe Committee reported, and this became accepted, for no very sound reason, as the safe minimum, but it was no easy task to keep the reserve at that level. With a weakened balance of trade, and capital exports in spite of the unofficial embargo on foreign loans by the Bank of England,[109] there was a tendency for gold to flow out, avoided only by attracting short-term funds to London, sources of trouble later.

From the middle of 1924, the authorities began to push up the exchange rate of the pound to a level which would make free convertibility possible. London rates of interest were raised substantially above those ruling in New York, and funds began to flow in. The belief that an attempt would be made to restore the pound to its old parity in the course of 1925, before inconvertibility would lapse automatically at the end of the year, attracted further funds. By April 1925 the pound had virtually reached its pre-war parity with the dollar, and Mr Churchill, the Chancellor of the Exchequer, announced the return to gold. Britain could claim to have made a major contribution to the stabilization of the foreign exchanges after the stress of wars and revolutions.

Nevertheless, the decision to return to gold at the old parity was one of the most controversial of the period. It called forth a large volume of criticism, among the most intelligent and far-sighted of which was that associated with

---

[104] Morgan, pp. 73, 271–86.
[105] A. J. Youngson, *The British Economy, 1920–1957* (1960), p. 29.
[106] W. A. Lewis, *Economic Survey, 1919–1939* (1949), pp. 43–4.
[107] Henry Clay, *The Post-War Unemployment Problem* (1929), p. 93. Also chapter 4.
[108] E. Nevin, *The Mechanism of Cheap Money, a Study of British Monetary Policy, 1931–1939* (Cardiff, 1955), pp. 23, 32; A. D. Gayer, *Monetary Policy and Economic Stabilisation* (1935), chapter 3; J. M. Keynes, *A Treatise on Money* (1930), vol. 2, pp. 180 ff.
[109] Sir Henry Clay, *Lord Norman* (1957), pp. 144–5.

the name of J. M. Keynes.[110] Although Keynes had most of the orthodox economic opinion against him at the time, there would be few today who would deny that Keynes's misgivings were warranted.[111]

Keynes's criticism ran along two lines. The first was concerned to show that at the old parity the pound would be over-valued to the extent of about 10%, while several other countries, including France, Belgium and Germany, returned to gold at lower parities, thus making the competitive disability of British prices greater still. The decision to return had taken appalling risks with British industry. It was a City decision, emphatically not a decision of the industrialists: 'had their views been given as much weight as those of the City, it is unlikely that the change would ever have been made'.[112]

There has been much debate recently on the correctness of Keynes' 10% figure. While the differential was less in the case of wholesale prices, the consensus seems to be that in terms of retail prices, GNP deflators or bundles of European currencies, the over-valuation was greater than 10% while, to restore British competiveness, the exchange rate should have been set below par. As it was, exports were hampered and imports encouraged. According to one calculation, a return to gold at the correct parity would, in a 'normal' year like 1928, have reduced unemployment by more than half, from 1,290,000 to 561,000 and allowed the authorities freedom to carry out most of the rest of their policies.[113]

Instead, the Bank of England was forced to maintain high interest rates to prevent the loss of gold as a result of the weaker trade balance. These kept up the burdens of the national debt charge, and thus of taxation, and they depressed enterprise and employment. This high structure of interest rates in a period of depression was to be described later as 'putting on the brake when going uphill'.[114]

These issues were debated at length in the evidence and in the Report of the Macmillan Committee which sat in 1929–31;[115] most dramatically, they came up in the exchanges between Montagu Norman, Governor of the Bank of England throughout this period, and a key figure in the working of the gold standard, and his questioners, above all Keynes and Ernest Bevin. The Governor at first denied that the high bank rate he was forced to impose to maintain the gold standard was responsible for creating unemployment (Questions 3328,

[110] J. M. Keynes, *Tract on Monetary Reform* (1923) and *The Economic Consequences of Mr. Churchill* (1925). Cf. also André Siegfried, *England's Crisis* (1931), chapter 2, §1; K. J. Hancock, 'Unemployment and the Economists in the 1920s', *Economica*, NS, 27/108, 1960, pp. 308. 11; D. E. Moggridge, *British Monetary Policy 1924–1931. The Norman Conquest of $4·86* (Cambridge, 1972).

[111] For recent contrary views, see Youngson, *op. cit.*, chapter 7; K. G. P. Matthews, *The Inter-War Economy* (Aldershot, 1986), p. 77; also R. S. Sayers, 'The Return to Gold', in L. S. Pressnell (ed.), *Studies in the Industrial Revolution* (1960), and T. E. Gregory, *The First Year of the Gold Standard* (1926), and *The Gold Standard and its Future* (3rd ed., 1934), chapters 3 and 4.

[112] Alan Bullock, the *Life and Times of Ernest Bevin*, Vol. 1 (1960), p. 267, cf. also pp. 428–9, and F. E. Gannett and B. F. Catherwood, *Industrial and Labour Relations in Great Britain* (1939), p. 283; S. Pollard, Introduction to *The Gold Standard and Employment Policies between the Wars* (1970); N. H. Dimsdale, 'British Monetary Policy and the Exchange Rate 1920–1938', *Oxf. Econ. P.*, 33, 1981, Supplement, p. 315.

[113] Moggridge, *British Monetary Policy*, pp. 100–6, 249–50; and *The Return to Gold, 1925* (Cambridge 1969) pp. 94–6; John Redmond 'The Sterling Overvaluation in 1925: A Multilinear Approach', *Ec. Hist. Rev.*, 37/3 (1984); J. F. Wright, 'Britain's Inter-War Experience', *Oxf. Econ. P.*, 33, 1981, Supplement, p. 297.

[114] R. G. Hawtrey, *The Gold Standard in Theory and Practice* (5th ed., 1947), pp. 108, 119.

[115] *Report of the Committee on Finance and Industry* (1931. Cmd. 3897); *Minutes of Evidence*, 2 vols. (1931).

3334–8, 3343–51); he was then driven to concede that his high bank rate was designed directly to create unemployment (Qq. 3492–3). The burden of his evidence to the Macmillan Committee was that he was under such constant pressure to keep up rates to prevent a drain abroad that he could not, even had he wished, consider the effects on industry, but that until 1930, at least, he had not greatly troubled about them.[116]

In retrospect, it seems impossible to deny that the preparations and the return to gold at too high a rate contributed to the depressed conditions of British industry in 1925–9, at a time when the rest of the world enjoyed a prolific boom, just as the removal of the handicap in 1931 was responsible for the sudden spurt of British exports relatively to other countries.

Keynes's second line of criticism was that in post-war conditions the international gold standard would not be allowed to work as freely as the idealized pre-war standard was said to have done. The large gold hoarders, the Bank of France and the Federal Reserve Board of the USA, would not play the game according to the rules, but would 'manage' their currency in spite of compensating gold flows, thus rendering impossible the task of a country like Great Britain with a gold reserve of barely £150 million to maintain stability in the sterling area as well as among several minor currencies.[117] Britain could stabilize either price levels or exchange rates, but could not do both; and she would do better to concentrate on stabilizing prices.[118]

In Britain, too, because of structural changes there was no longer an automatic regulative function of the gold reserve of the Bank of England, described with such great confidence by the Cunliffe Committee.[119] By 1925, a high bank rate did not bring in any provincial funds, as in former periods, for there were none. Instead, it merely attracted short-term foreign funds, which left again the moment the London rate was reduced, without effect on the general price level. If, on the other hand, a high bank rate did succeed in compressing incomes and creating deflation in Britain, with the consequence of a rise in exports and an influx of gold or funds, this would, under existing conditions, merely spread deflation abroad and thus counteract the British deflation.[120] It was an essential part of the mechanism of the pre-war gold standard that there was a single credit centre, London, which could enforce its monetary policies on the rest of the world. After the war, there were two major centres, London and New York, and several minor ones, and the mechanism was, therefore, likely to show very different responses.[121]

Secondly, the large quantities of Treasury Bills still outstanding even after the conversion and funding of 1921–5 and a weekly issue of £40 million of Treasury Bills to be absorbed, nullified the former power of the Bank of England

---

[116] *Minutes of Evidence*, 18th Day. Also see A. Boyle, *Montagu Norman* (1967), p. 258; T. Gregory; 'Lord Norman: A New Interpretation', *Lloyds Bank Review*, 88 (1968), p. 38.

[117] For some of these external burdens on the sterling reserves, see L. S. Pressnell, '1925: The Burden on Sterling', *Ec. Hist. Rev.*, 31/1, 1978.

[118] A. D. Gayer, *Monetary Policy and Economic Stabilisation* (1935), chapter 2; W. A. Morton, *British Finance 1930–1940* (Madison, 1943), pp. 87, 97–101.

[119] *First Interim Report*, Cd. 9182 paras. 4–7.

[120] R. G. Hawtrey (5th ed., 1947), pp. 124–5; A. E. Kahn, *op. cit.*, pp. 20–1; Keynes, *Treatise on Money*, pp. 309–15; Gayer, p. 23.

[121] W. A. Brown, Jr, *The International Gold Standard Re-interpreted, 1914–34*, 2 vols. (New York, 1940).

to influence the lending policies of the joint-stock 'banks via the latter's credit with it'.[122] The Macmillan Committee failed to note this development, though it found that one-half of the short-term assets of the clearing banks consisted of Treasury Bills even in the 1920s,[123] but it was discussed by Lord Bradbury, in a dissenting Memorandum.[124] The official recognition of this mechanism had to wait for the Radcliffe Report of 1959,[125] which at last killed the concept, 'given an extra thirty years' lease of life by the Macmillan Report, that the effective basis of credit resides in the cash reserves of the banks'.[126]

Lastly, a true international gold standard assumes that changes in the foreign exchange position would be rectified by changes in home prices, but industry in Britain (and elsewhere) in the 1920s was too rigid to stand this flexible price system. The City, ill-informed as it was of industrial affairs, remained ignorant of this inflexibility, and thus 'fundamentally economic policy and structural conditions were out of phase with each other'.[127]

The gold standard, re-established at too high a parity by Britain, would have been difficult to work at the best of times; as it happened, it set out on its course in the most unfavourable circumstances. Some countries returned to gold on a 'gold exchange' basis, basing their convertibility on reserves held in the form of balances in London or New York which could be turned into gold, thus putting a dangerous burden on London, especially since the 'gold exchange' countries got their London balances, not by foreign trade surplus, but by short-term loans.[128] In the pre-war days the Bank of England had held sufficient net short-term claims by London on foreign centres to make the effects of a change in bank rate felt quickly in all parts of the globe; but in the 1920s, foreign short-term holdings in London greatly exceeded the sterling bills on foreign account and other similar assets by a margin estimated by the Macmillan Committee at £250–300 million.[129]

Moreover, several countries, including Japan, Poland and France, returned to gold at rates which under-valued their currencies, giving their exporters an additional advantage over those of Britain, while others including Italy, Belgium and France, stabilized their currency at high home price levels, allowing their industrialists to preserve their inflation gains of lower real wages and other fixed charges. The slow fall of world prices after 1925 made the task of the export industries more difficult still.[130]

[122] Hawtrey, *Century of Bank Rate*, pp. 136, 257.

[123] *Committee on Finance and Industry, Report* (1931. Cmd. 3897), paras. 22, 29, 72–87, Appx. I, Table 3, pp. 296–7; also see Keynes, *Treatise on Money*, chapters 2, 25, 32; T. Balogh, *Studies in Financial Organisation* (Cambridge, 1947), pp. 39–40, 56 ff.; Nevin, *Cheap Money*, pp. 118–20; *Radcliffe Report*, paras. 506–11.

[124] Cmd. 3897, *Memorandum of Dissent* by Lord Bradbury, paras. 19–22.

[125] *Report of the Committee on the Working of the Monetary System* (1959. Cmnd. 827).

[126] W. Manning Dicey, 'Treasury Bills and the Money Supply', *Lloyd's Bank Review*, NS, 55, 1960, p. 1, and *Money under Review* (1960), p. 11, also pp. 52–63; cf. also R. S. Sayers, *Central Banking after Bagehot* (1957), p. 21.

[127] David Williams, 'Montagu Norman and Banking Policy in the Nineteen-Twenties', *Yorkshire Bull.*, 11/1, 1959, p. 55. For a full-scale study see Sir Henry Clay, *Lord Norman* (1957).

[128] W. A. Lewis, *op. cit.*, p. 47.

[129] Cmd. 3897, paras. 92–3, 260, 347–9; I. Drummond, 'Britain and the World Economy', in Roderick Floud and Donald McCloskey, *The Economic History of Britain Since 1700*, vol. 2 (Cambridge, 1981), p. 296.

[130] Henry Clay, *The Post-War Unemployment Problem* (1929), p. 76; J. H. Jones, in *Britain in Depression* (1935), pp. 8–13; p. 138 above.

High rates to prevent gold drains dampened incipient economic expansion in the late 1920s. The burden of high interest rates and restrictive bank policies could not be eased as long as internal costs stayed up,[131] and it proved impossible to lower these. By the end of the decade the harmful effect of British monetary policy on industry and exports was widely understood.

6 The Years of Crisis: 1929–1931

Up to 1929, Britain had been labouring under the special difficulties of over-large export industries and an over-valued currency, but the rest of the world had witnessed something akin to the orthodox cyclical sequence. The crash that marked the beginning of the downswing actually occurred in New York, in October 1929.[132] It was, to begin with, a purely financial phenomenon, but soon transmitted itself to the productive sectors, and as production and incomes contracted in the USA, the supply of dollars to the rest of the world fell drastically, as described in section 2 above, and depression spread quickly to the rest of the world.

It proved to be far more severe and protracted than any previous slump. In the worst-affected countries, industrial output fell by one-half in three years. Prices and overseas trade also showed falls of unprecedented dimensions. By contrast, real wages and consumption stayed up with negative effects on the balance of trade.[133] The onset of the depression in 1929 was further distinguished by a series of severe financial and foreign exchange crises. The background to these crises, the war debt and reparations obligations, the calamitous fall of primary product prices, and the maladjustment of the currencies of the leading countries, have been noted in earlier sections of this chapter. There was also no single financial centre to play London's part of the nineteenth century, to act as buffer and smoothe the flow of international payments.[134] When, at the end of 1929, the cessation of American lending was followed by the abrupt fall in American purchases, triggering off a general decline in world trade, each country tried to reduce its imports and increase its exports[135] by means of tariffs, restrictions and currency barriers.

We may now turn to observe how these affected the United Kingdom in the crisis years. In London, bank rate was raised to $6\frac{1}{2}\%$ late in September 1929, though it was reduced again with the inflow of funds from New York after the collapse there. But by now the world depression, carrying unemployment to industrial countries and loss of incomes to primary producing countries, had

---

[131] E.g. L. Robbins, *The Great Depression* (1934), chapter 5.

[132] The best account is in J. K. Galbraith, *The Great Crash* (1955).

[133] S. N. Broadberry, *The British Economy Between the Wars* (Oxford, 1986), p. 46; N. H. Dimsdale, 'Employment and Real Wages in the Inter-War Period', *Nat. Inst. Econ. Rev.*, 110 (1984), pp. 95–7.

[134] C. P. Kindleberger, *The World in Depression 1929–39* (1986), pp. 295–300; *idem, Manias, Panics and Crashes. A History of Financial Crises* (1978), pp. 4–6; D. E. Moggridge, 'Financial Crises and Lenders of Last Resort: Policy in the Crises 1920 and 1929', *Journal of European Economic History* 10/1, 1981; Sean Glyn and John Oxborrow, *Interwar Britain: a Social and Economic History* (1976), pp. 62–3.

[135] A. J. Youngson, *The British Economy, 1920–1957* (1960), pp. 79–80; Herbert Heaton, *The British Way to Recovery* (Minneapolis, 1934), p. 7.

begun its inexorable march. Prices, employment and production all turned down sharply. The British figures are given in Table 3·18.

Table 3·18:   Prices, employment and production, 1929–33

	Wholesale prices	Registered unemployed (Ministry of Labour)		Index of industrial activity*
	(Board of Trade) 1929 = 100	%	Numbers (000)	
1929	100	10·4	1,249	118·7
1930	87·5	16·1	1,975	107·4
1931	76·8	21·3	2,698	86·8
1932	74·9	22·1	2,813	81·1
1933	75·0	19·9	2,221	89·3

* W. H. Beveridge, *Full Employment in a Free Society* (1944), p. 313.

Elsewhere, the reduction was far greater. While British industrial production (1929 = 100) fell to 84 in 1932, it fell to 72 in France, and 53 in Germany and the USA.[136]

In the course of 1930, a drain of gold to Berlin was added to an earlier drain to Paris. The Bank of England was further weakened by the fall of share prices on the London Stock Exchange at the end of 1929 and other pressures, and to make matters worse, Paris added £95 million and New York £64 million to their gold reserves in the course of the year.[137] In 1930 the Bank of England succeeded in withstanding the strain by drawing gold from South Africa and Australia, but in 1931 it had to raise its rate well above those of New York and Paris, attracting funds which were to add to the embarrassment of London when the European financial crisis set in.[138]

A series of banking crises in Central Europe, beginning with the Austrian Kredit-Anstalt in May 1931, led to the freezing of funds in Germany, including short-term loans from Britain, which added materially to the problems of London.[139] 'British short-term borrowing came to an abrupt end while its lending became indefinitely prolonged.'[140]

Since, unlike the pre-war days, London no longer had large commercial bill claims on the rest of the world to balance this withdrawal of foreign short-term funds the Bank's gold reserve had to stand most of the strain and quickly

[136] H. W. Richardson, 'The Economic Significance of the Depression in Britain', *Journal of Contemporary History*, 4, 1969.

[137] *Committee on Finance and Industry* (Cmd. 3897), paras. 163–6, 311; Hawtrey, *Gold Standard*, pp. 115–18; H. F. Fraser, *Great Britain and the Gold Standard* (1933); G. Cassel, *The Crisis in the World's Monetary System* (1932).

[138] *Committee on Finance and Industry*, para. 295; J. G. Smith and G. J. Walker, 'Currency and Banking', in *Britain in Depression* (1935).

[139] Sir Arthur Salter, *Recovery* (1932), pp. 43 ff.; Royal Institute of International Affairs, *Monetary Policy and the Depression* (1933), pp. 10–12; A. E. Kahn, *Great Britain in the World Economy* (1946), p. 38; W. A. Morton, *British Finance, 1930–1940* (Madison, 1943), pp. 30–7; Edward W. Bennett, *Germany and the Diplomacy of the Financial Crisis, 1931* (Cambridge, Mass., 1962), pp. 121 ff.

[140] U. K. Hicks, *Finance of the British Government, 1920–1936* (1938), p. 348.

dropped to £130 million. The level of unemployment inhibited the raising of the bank rate to panic heights; it would, in any case, at best only bring back some 'hot' money which would leave again at the first opportunity, and meanwhile scare off many fund holders.[141] The only alternative was to raise a loan of £50 million in New York and Paris.

The irony was that New York and Paris, bloated with gold, experienced no drain at all. It was only in centres suspected of weakness that withdrawals began which turned the dreaded weakness into reality.[142] In the summer of 1931, the holders of these mobile funds, mentioned several times already, the undesirable, but essential buttresses of sterling under an over-valued gold standard, began to attack London. In three weeks, continental holders withdrew £41 million, and over the whole period of crisis, some £200 million of this 'hot' money was withdrawn.

The belief of the financiers in the weakness of London, which originated in the increasingly unfavourable trade balance of the United Kingdom and the threat to the gold reserve of the Bank of England, was further strengthened by the fact that it was a Labour Government which held office; by the emphasis of the Macmillan Report, which appeared on 14 July, on the unhealthy dependence of London on short-term funds; and by the threatened budget deficit, highlighted by the 'highly coloured account of the national finances'[143] of the May Committee Report presented on the last day of July.[144] When the drain on London continued into August and the Treasury sought a further loan of £80 million in Paris and New York, the British Government was told bluntly that it must carry through at least some of the May Committee's recommendations, especially the severe cut in unemployment pay, before its application would be considered.[145] In significant contrast, in 1939, when it was war, not unemployment, that threatened, 'the authorities in America, France and Holland co-operated with the British in suppressing activities of the cosmopolitan speculator whose only concern is profit'.[146]

Faced by the ultimatum of the bankers over the £80 million loan in August 1931, the Labour Government split on the issue of how far to cut back unemployment relief at their behest, and several of its members, led by the Prime Minister, Ramsey Macdonald, joined by Conservative leaders and by some Liberals, formed a 'National' Government on 24 August to save the country from its financial perils.[147] The ousting of the Labour Government at once reduced the speculative pressure on sterling, even before the new Government had taken any action. Thus favoured, it obtained the foreign loan that had been

---

[141] H. V. Hodson, *Slump and Recovery, 1929–1937* (1938), p. 67; Nevin, *Cheap Money*, p. 16; D. Williams, 'London and the 1931 Financial Crisis', *Ec. Hist. Rev.*, 2nd S., 15/3, 1963; D. E. Moggridge, 'The 1931 Financial Crisis – a New View', *The Banker*, 120, April 1970.

[142] *Second Annual Report* of the Bank for International Settlements (Basle, 1932), quoted in Gayer, p. 27; cf. also N. F. Hall, *The Exchange Equalisation Account* (1935), p. 19.

[143] Smith and Walker, p. 36.

[144] P. 104 above.

[145] Cf. the excellent discussion on this point in C. L. Mowat, *Britain Between the Wars* (1956 ed.), chapter 7, section 6. A detailed partisan account will be found in R. Bassett, *Nineteen Thirty One, Political Crisis* (1958).

[146] L. Waight, *The History and Mechanism of the Exchange Equalisation Account* (Cambridge, 1939), p. 143.

[147] Philip Viscount Snowden, *An Autobiography* (1934), chapters 76–80; Ramsay Muir, *The Record of the National Government* (1936), chapters 3–9.

refused its predecessor, and, confirmed in office by an overwhelming vote in the snap election of October 1931 by voters who fondly hoped it intended to cure depression when it merely wished to cause more effective deflation, stumbled into all the disasters which the Labour Government was ousted to prevent. The trade balance remained highly unfavourable, the payments to the sinking funds for debt redemption were partly suspended and, above all, the pound was driven off gold. Even in its decision to come off gold, the Bank of England's 'chief concern was not to gain advantages for British export trade by exploiting the new situation, but to conserve the international utility of the London money market'.[148]

This action, taken on 20 September 1931, afforded instant relief. Within 10 days sterling had depreciated by 18% and at the end of the year it was down to $3·40.

A large number of other countries inside and outside the sterling bloc followed Britain off gold in the course of the next few months, but since the USA, Germany, France, Belgium, Holland, Italy and Poland, among others, remained on gold for the time being, sterling goods enjoyed a sudden price advantage, reversing directly the unfavourable position of 1925–31.[149] Most of the countries adversely affected reacted by raising tariffs against British goods, but since Britain also introduced protection, the favourable impact on the trade balance remained for a time.

There was also relief in other ways. Foreign borrowers found repayment in sterling easier. Home prices kept very steady, so that confidence in sterling was quickly restored and funds began to flow in again. The panic loans of £130 million from France and America were repaid with surprising ease.[150] The vast resources of the large joint-stock banks which had emerged from earlier amalgamations, ensured that Britain, unlike other countries, suffered no bank collapses or defaults.

By April 1932, with the pound stabilized, a balanced budget and effective protection, the financial crisis was over. Bank rate was steadily reduced, reaching 2% in June. The industrial depression was at its worst in the third quarter of 1932, but thenceforward all indices showed a strong upward trend, leading up to the boom of 1937.

7 Financial Policy and Institutions in the 1930s

The 'cheap money' policy of a 2% bank rate ushered in a period of stable prices, stable interest rates and stable exchange rates. Stability in the foreign exchanges was achieved by means of the Exchange Equalization Account, established in April 1932, and its supporting measures.[151] Originally launched with a sum of £175 million in Treasury Bills, it began operations at a period when sterling was

---

[148] W. A. Brown, Jr, *The International Gold Standard Re-interpreted, 1914–1934*, 2 vols. (New York, 1940), vol. 2, p. 1093. Also Robert Skidelsky, *Politicians and the Slump. The Labour Government of 1929–1931* (1967).

[149] W. A. Lewis, *Economic Survey, 1919–1939* (1949), pp. 63–5; H. W. Arndt, *The Economic Lessons of the Nineteen-Thirties* (1944), pp. 96–9.

[150] J. H. Richardson, *British Economic Foreign Policy* (1936), pp. 36 ff.

[151] J. G. Smith and G. J. Walker, 'Currency and Banking', in *Britain in Depression* (1935), p. 45; John Redmond, 'An Indicator of Effective Exchange Rate of the Pound in the Nineteen-Thirties', *Ec. Hist. Rev.*, 33/1, 1980.

very strong and it was thus able quickly to acquire a large quantity of foreign currency in exchange for its sterling bills. Its financial basis was enlarged by £200 million in May 1933, and a further sum of £200 million was added in 1937.

The duty of the fund was to counteract, by suitable purchases and sales, any temporary divergence from the stabilized exchange rates without affecting their long-term level.[152] In practice, the Account appeared deliberately to depress the value of the pound below its natural level in order to favour the British balance of payments and in spite of devaluations elsewhere it was not until 1936 that the British advantage of lower exchange rate was dissipated.[153] In the process it accumulated a large gold hoard, which stood it in good stead when a heavy drain to France set in in 1938.[154]

The USA, one of the worst sufferers in the depression, went off gold in April 1933, and the dollar was ultimately stabilized at 50% of the old gold parity. The resulting unemployment and outflow of capital forced France to devalue also in 1936.[155] The three main currencies, the pound, dollar and franc, were thus all off gold, but were tied to each other, in theory if not always in practice, by the Tripartite Agreement not to alter exchange rates without prior consultation.[156]

The currency areas covered by the Tripartite Agreement formed the only important region in which international trade in the old sense was still carried on, but even there it proved possible to isolate each country from changes occurring in the others. Thus the collapse of the American prosperity in 1937 had far less effect on the rest of the world than the crash of 1929.[157] The currency systems of Germany and the countries in its orbit were even more immune from the effects of alterations in world trade, gold movements or exchange rates.[158]

After the financial strains of 1931, Britain was thus able to sail into calmer waters of protection, a managed currency, a balanced budget and cheap money. Before following out the consequences of these policies, it will be advisable to trace the main changes of the financial institutions of the United Kingdom between 1913 and the 1930s.

At the centre, with bank rate left unaltered for seven years at 2%, the Bank of England could no longer operate an interest rate policy, and instead manipulated cash supplies and exercised 'quality control'. The cash supply could safely be expanded as long as the American cash base was enlarged still faster under the 'New Deal' policies.[159] The responsibility over the foreign exchanges was transferred to the Exchange Equalization Account.

Between 1922 and 1924, the number of joint-stock banks was further reduced

---

[152] W. Manning Dacey, 'The Technique of Insulation', *The Banker*, 48/153, Oct. 1938; L. Waight, *The History and Mechanism of the Exchange Equalisation Account* (Cambridge, 1939), p. 11; N. F. Hall, *The Exchange Equalisation Account* (1935).

[153] N. F. Hall, 'The Foreign Exchanges, 1932–1937', in *Britain in Recovery* (1938); A. E. Kahn, *Great Britain in the World Economy* (1946), pp. 202–3; Redmond, p. 89.

[154] A. E. Kahn, pp. 196–8; R. G. Hawtrey, *The Gold Standard in Theory and Practice* (5th ed., 1947), p. 221.

[155] H. V. Hodson, *Slump and Recovery, 1929–1937* (1938), chapters 6, 10, 11; R. G. Hawtrey, *Gold Standard*, pp. 161–73.

[156] Ian M. Drummond, *The Floating Pound and the Sterling Area 1931–1939* (1981), chapters 8 and 9; *idem, The Gold Standard and the International Monetary System 1900–1939* (1987), p. 52.

[157] W. A. Lewis, *Economic Survey, 1919 1939* (1949), pp. 67–72.

[158] Royal Institute of International Affairs, *Monetary Policy and the Depression* (1933) Appx. IV.

[159] R. S. Sayers, *Central Banking After Bagehot* (1957), pp. 29–31; G. D. H. Cole, *Money, Trade and Investment* (1954), p. 84.

by eight.[160] In 1927–8, the Liverpool-based Martin's Bank was established out of a merger of three firms, and in 1935 a similar merger created the District Bank, based on Manchester, as the eleventh member of the London Clearing House in 1936. At the end of 1938, there remained independent only four London clearing banks, four Scottish and three Irish banks, besides the 'Big Five'. The dominance of the latter, the Midland, Barclay's, Lloyd's, the National Provincial and the Westminster Banks, is shown by the following comparison of deposits, capital and reserves on 31 December 1938:[161]

'Big Five' banks	£2,299 m.
Other English banks	239
Scottish banks	248
Northern Irish banks	151

Fundamentally, the policy of British banks remained unchanged in this period. Their loans, as far as they were made to industry or agriculture, were intended to be self-liquidating or short-term, and direct investment in the share or loan capital of industry continued to be shunned.[162] Overseas investment was much reduced, and home investment was also at a low ebb. According to one estimate, gross investment fell from 25% to 16%, and net investment from 17% to 6–7% of national income between 1911 and 1938.[163]

It thus became more important than ever to improve the defective channel of funds[164] from the money market to industry. This problem was noted by the Balfour Committee, but it received its first important public recognition in the Report of the Macmillan Committee:

> British companies in the iron and steel, electrical and other industries [it reported] must meet in the gate their great American and German competitors who are generally financially powerful and closely supported by banking and financial groups, with whom they have continuous relationships. British Industry, without similar support, will undoubtedly be at a disadvantage. But such effective support cannot be obtained merely for a particular occasion. It can only be the result of intimate co-operation over years during which the financial interests get an insight into the problems and the requirements of the industry in question.[165]

There was also particular reference to medium-term finance extended over 1–5 years; to long-dated industrial capital; and to small and medium-sized firms, needing capital in sums of up to £200,000, for which the City made very

[160] Joseph Sykes, *The Amalgamation Movement in English Banking* (1926).

[161] T. Balogh, *Studies in Financial Organisation* (Cambridge, 1947), pp. 14–15, 114–18; H. Compton and E. H. Bott, *British Industry* (1940), p. 171; R. J. Truptil, *British Banks and the London Money Market* (1936), Part I, chapters 2 and 6.

[162] F. Lavington, *The English Capital Market* (1921), chapters 31–3.

[163] A. E. Kahn, pp. 137–8; T. Balogh, p. 277; Colin Clark, *National Income and Outlay* (1937), pp. 185, 250–3; W. H. Beveridge, *Full Employment in a Free Society* (1944), pp. 104–5; J. B. Jeffreys and Dorothy Walters, 'National Income and Expenditure of the UK 1870–1952', *Income and Wealth*, Series V, 1955, p. 17.

[164] A. B. Levy, *Private Corporations and Their Control* (1950), vol. 1, pp. 164–5; A. T. K. Grant, *A Study of the Capital Market in Post-War Britain* (1937), chapter 8.

[165] *Report of the Committee on Finance and Industry* (1931. Cmd. 3897), para. 384, also paras. 378–83, 386; R. F. Harrod, *John Maynard Keynes* (1951), pp. 413–16.

inadequate provision – the 'Macmillan gap'.[166] A greater concern for the long-term rate of interest, including presumably industrial investment, was also urged on the Bank of England.[167]

In practice, several banks had become reluctant holders of shares or bonds in various enterprises in the collapse of 1920–1, and others had taken an interest in restrictive control schemes. The Bank of England itself had formed a separate agency, Securities Management Trust, in 1929 to administer the large and varied industrial property which had fallen into its lap, and this was enlarged in 1930 into the Bankers Industrial Development Co.[168] That concern was launched with a capital of £6 million, of which the Bank of England provided one-quarter, other large banks providing the rest. It was instrumental in financing reconstruction schemes concerned with destroying surplus capacity, including National Shipbuilders Security Ltd and the Lancashire Cotton Corporation, and with providing loans for the steel industry. The Bank of England also took part in the flotation of the United Dominions Trust with its various subsidiaries one of which, Credit for Industry Ltd (1934), was specifically designed to help smaller firms with long-term loans.[169]

These developments, however, could scarcely be said to have met the recommendations of the Macmillan Committee in full. The 'Macmillan gap' remained unbridged in the 1930s.[170] The banks, far from increasing their participation in industry, found in the 1930s that their industrial holdings of the slump years were being wiped out as soon as the recovery began.[171] As a result, the banks, though willing to hold 55–60% of deposits in the form of 'advances' to industry, could seldom manage to place more than 40%, and were obliged to hold the rest in the form of 'investments', i.e. Government securities which the private sector was selling at high prices caused by the prevailing low interest rates and which rose from £264 million in February 1932 to £610 million in October 1936.[172] The banks, however, contributed indirectly to the necessary outside financing of growing firms in the recovery period by their participation in Investment Trusts, Finance Companies and Hire-Purchase Finance Firms.[173]

It was a reflection of the general rise in incomes that an increasing share of the national savings came from 'small' and institutional savers, mainly the Building Societies and the Insurance Companies. The insurance companies in particular began to place a larger share of their investments in debentures and even in equities of industry.[174]

These 'small' savings which had amounted to only £32 million a year, or 13·2% of net accumulation, in 1901–13, had risen to £110·3 million a year, or

[166] Cmd. 3897, paras. 392–404. Also see S. E. Thomas, *British Banks and the Finance of Industry* (1930), chapters 4–6; U. K. Hicks, *The Finance of the British Government, 1920–1936* (1938), p. 259.

[167] Cmd. 3897, para. 306 (iv).

[168] Sir Henry Clay, *Lord Norman* (1957), chapter 8; p. 54 above.

[169] T. Balogh, *op. cit.*, pp. 199–201; A. Beacham, *Economics of Industrial Organisation* (3rd ed., 1955), pp. 22–4; Grant, pp. 215–17.

[170] (Radcliffe) *Committee on the Working of the Monetary System* (1959. Cmnd. 827), paras. 229–34, 932.

[171] Sir Arthur Salter, *Recovery* (1932), pp. 90–1.

[172] Truptil, *op. cit.*, p. 306; also *Radcliffe Report*, paras. 139–40; K. G. P. Matthews, *The Inter-War Economy* (Aldershot, 1986), p. 16; T. Balogh, pp. 73–4.

[173] T. Balogh, pp. 158 ff., 256–9, 278–88.

[174] Nevin, *Cheap Money*, pp. 264–5; Sir Harold Bellman, *Bricks and Mortals* (1961), chapters 7–9.

over half the total net investment, in 1924–35. The typical working-class savings, however, represented by Post Office and Trustee Savings Banks remained small.[175] The distribution of total assets changed as shown in Table 3·19.[176]

Table 3·19:   Financial assets, 1920–1939

	Total £m.	% Shares held by:				
		Banks and discount companies	Life insurance companies	Building societies	P.O. and other savings banks	Other
1920	4,552	59·5	16·4	1·9	17·5	4·7
1929	5,553	48·2	22·5	5·6	17·1	6·2
1939	8,126	41·3	23·2	9·5	17·1	8·4

In contrast with the rising opportunities of these new institutions, the older types of financial houses, notably the Acceptance House (merchant bankers) and the Discount Houses, found many of their pre-war markets closed or shrinking,[177] the former because of the shrinkage in international trade and lending, and the latter because of the decline of the inland bill,[178] while the clearing banks had captured a large share of the foreign acceptance business.[179] Since the supply of Treasury Bills also showed signs of drying up, because of successful funding operations at a time of cheap money on the one hand, and large increases in the holdings of Government departments and of foreigners on the other,[180] there was a 'bill famine', which drove down the rate on Treasury Bills issued by tender from about 4–5% in the years 1925–32 to 0·6% from 1933 onward, i.e. nearly 1½% below bank rate. The decline in the quantity and the interest rate of both commercial and Treasury Bills severely restricted the scope of the traditional business of the discount market.

With these changes in the institutional framework in mind, we may now turn to the course of the cheap money policy itself. In the beginning, in 1932, the policy was not the result of deliberate decision: rates were pulled down by a 'tangled mass of forces'.[181] The advantages of cheap money, which led to its retention for 19 years, until 1951, became apparent and acceptable only gradually. Market rates had been falling, and the prices of Consols and other gilt-edged securities rising, from September 1931 onward, without official action, and this allowed the authorities, as soon as the foreign loans of £130 million, raised during the crisis, were paid off to begin to reduce the bank rate in March 1932[182] to reach 2% in June, where it remained. Around it, the structure of other

[175] John Hilton, *Rich Man, Poor Man* (1944, 3rd imp. 1947), chapter 2; Colin Clark, 'Determination of the Multiplier from National Income Statistics', *Econ. J.*, 48/191, 1938, p. 436.

[176] E. H. Phelps-Brown and Bernard Weber, 'Accumulation, Productivity and Distribution in the British Economy, 1870–1938', *Econ. J.*, 63/250, June 1953; T. Balogh, p. 96; David K. Sheppard, *The Growth and Role of UK Financial Institutions 1880–1962* (1971), p. 3.

[177] *Macmillan Report*, paras. 88–95; Truptil, *op. cit.*, chapters 3 and 4, pp. 307–9.

[178] T. Balogh, pp. 167, 177–182.

[179] J. Sykes, *op. cit.*, p. 171.

[180] A. J. Youngson, *The British Economy, 1920–1957* (1960), pp. 194–5; T. Balogh, pp. 61 ff., 133, and Appx. I to Part II by F. W. Paish; Nevin, *Cheap Money*, pp. 134–43, 179.

[181] Nevin, *Cheap Money*, pp. 107–8, also 57–8.

[182] E. Nevin, 'The Origins of Cheap Money', *Economica*, NS, 20/77, 1953.

rates also settled down to exceptionally low levels, bill rates, in particular, staying round $\frac{1}{2}$% until 1939, as noted above, and even long-term rates being distinctly lower than in the 1920s.

There were at least four major reasons which launched, and kept, the Government on its cheap money course. First, low rates in London would keep away foreign 'hot' money. This consideration may have weighed heavily in the early period of this policy. Secondly, low rates were a simple device for reducing Government expenditure without causing social unrest. This, also, was an early motive, and was triumphantly vindicated by the great conversion of 1932, although low market rates were not the only precondition of success.[183] Thirdly, there may have been the desire to favour by low interest rates the active as against the passive members of the community: a step in the direction of what Keynes came to call the 'euthanasia of the rentier'.

Lastly, the authorities also began to look on cheap money as a method of increasing the total level of activity in the economy. This motive became operative, at the earliest, in 1933, but was later responsible for the continuation of the policy in the face of many changing circumstances. Whether low rates actually stimulated the economy in the 1930s is in some doubt. The money supply did not increase, merely its velocity[184] but as noted above on p. 117 there were few industrial borrowers in the early 1930s in the face of willing lenders – a circumstance which helped to keep down rates. In the later 1930s the net effect of the Government's policy was in the opposite direction. The shortage of bills made the banks illiquid and unwilling to lend, and in the incipient boom of 1936–7 the authorities induced a distinct cash shortage, which went directly and deliberately, though only temporarily, against the overall expansionary effect of cheap money.

How far Government policy as a whole, including other measures, could be held responsible for the industrial recovery has been subject to much debate, but few would give it much weight today. Low rates might, according to Hawtrey, have had directly beneficial effects in 1931, but by 1932 it was too late, and the recovery had to wait for other, more general factors.[185] Home capital issues, which one would have expected to be among the first indices to show the benefits of cheap money, did not begin to rise until some 18 months after the beginning of the upswing. The investments by the public utilities were all timed to begin much too late to affect the recovery, except for the electricity grid which by sheer accident rose to the peak of its constructional work in the depression.[186] More positive was the contribution made by the tariff. It is possible to argue that, by reducing imports, it reduced the extent by which British incomes had to decline by virtue of the decline in exports, i.e. that the downward multiplier was cut off. Further, by taxing imports (as well as by banning foreign capital issues) the protectionist policy encouraged expenditure in such sectors

[183] U. K. Hicks, *Finance of the British Government*, pp. 364–9.

[184] J. F. Wright, 'Britain's Inter-War Experience', *Oxf. Econ. P.*, 33 (1981) Supplement, p. 337.

[185] Hawtrey, *Gold Standard*, pp. 149–52.

[186] U. K. Hicks, *Finance of the British Government*, pp. 280–95, 376–7; also E. Nevin, pp. 229 ff.; R. F. Bretherton, F. A. Burchardt, R. S. G. Rutherford, *Public Investment and the Trade Cycle in Great Britain* (1941), p. 407; Roger Middleton, 'The Constant Employment Budget Balance', *Ec. Hist. Rev.*, 34/2, 1981.

as building and the service trades at home, which were undoubtedly connected with the onset of the recovery.[187]

Basically, the claim that the Government's cheap money policy assisted the economic recovery must rest on the claim that it helped to bring about the building boom of the 1930s.[188] The building boom was at once the symbol and a main carrier of British industrial recovery from the Great Depression. It began largely as a boom in the building of private dwellings, as distinct from local authority building.[189] Starting from the relatively high level of building of the 1920s, when an average of 150,000 dwellings a year of all kinds was completed, output stayed around the 200,000 mark in 1930–3, and then taking off in February–March 1933 it rose rapidly to well over 350,000 dwellings a year. In those totals, the figure of dwellings completed by local authorities remained fairly constantly at about 75,000 a year. From 1934 on, the boom was further boosted by industrial and commercial building which showed the usual accelerator effects during the upswing of a trade cycle.[190]

Building employed only 6–7½% of all insured workers in the 1930s, but it accounted for 30% of the increase in employment and over 40% of the increase in investment in 1932–5 if the increase in the indigenous building materials industry is included. If to this are added the usual multiplier effects and the increased demand for furniture, as well as the fact that the building indices were leading the others in the upswing, it is clear that here was a critical mechanism for stimulating British recovery at work.[191]

The connection between the building boom and low interest rates was not clear-cut. Most of the building, and 75% of the dwelling houses, were financed by building societies, the phenomenal growth of which was one of the most striking aspects of the boom, their total balances out on mortgage rising from £316 million at the end of 1930 to £706 million at the end of 1939. But it took eight years for their mortgage rates to fall by 1%, from an average of 5·87% in 1931 to 4·80% in 1939;[192] the average reduction by 1933, when building was in full swing, was only 0.3%. Local authority building was affected by Government policy rather than by the falling mortgage rates of the 1930s.[193] In sum, the direct effect of cheap money could not have been large. On the other hand, the fact that building societies kept up their rates on shares and deposits while others dropped, diverted increasing funds to them. Moreover, a large proportion of building was for investment, and it was clear that it was low interest rates at

[187] A. E. Kahn, pp. 154–6, 262–4; W. A. Morton, *British Finance, 1930–1940* (Madison, 1943), p. 82, also chapters 14–17.

[188] H. W. Richardson, *Economic Recovery in Britain, 1932–9* (1967), pp. 142 ff.; R. M. MacIntosh, 'A Note on Cheap Money and the British Housing Boom, 1932–37', *Econ. J.*, 61, 1951.

[189] G. D. H. Cole, *Building and Planning* (1945), pp. 96–7.

[190] Figures in E. Nevin, *Cheap Money*, p. 269; Forrest Capie and Michael Collins, *The Inter-War British Economy: A Statistical Abstract* (Manchester, 1983), p. 50; cf. B. Weber and J. Parry Lewis, 'Industrial Building in Great Britain, 1923–38', *Scot. J. Pol. Econ.*, 8/1, Feb. 1961.

[191] G. D. A. MacDougall, 'General Survey, 1929–1937', in *Britain in Recovery* (1938), pp. 46–8, also Sir Harold Bellman, 'The Building Trades', in *ibid.*; W. A. Lewis, *Economic Survey, 1919–39* (1949), p. 87; A. P. Becker, 'Housing in England and Wales during the Business Depression of the 1930s', *Ec. Hist. Rev.*, 2nd S., 3/3, 1951, p. 325; H. W. Richardson and D. H. Aldcroft, *Building in the British Economy Between the Wars* (1968).

[192] Becker, p. 335.

[193] U. K. Hicks, *Finance of the British Government*, p. 131.

a time when rents showed no disposition to fall which made returns on housing investment so attractive.[194]

The other main factor at work on the supply side was the reduction in cost: a house costing £350 in 1931 fell to well below £300 in 1933–4,[195] and despite a rise in the general price level, its price did not increase again until 1937.[196]

Of at least equal importance were the changes on the demand side. As part of the well-known 'building cycle',[197] the shortage of houses, estimated at 600,000–1,000,000 in 1920, increased to an estimated peak of 1.2 to 2 million in 1930. This was accentuated by the migration of population to new regions and suburbs and by the decline in the size of families.[198] Rising standards of consumption and of housing by-laws which condemned many houses as unfit to live in, contributed to this further demand in the 1930s.[199]

Higher incomes also called forth substantial increases in many service trades, entertainments, and other 'sheltered' industries in which Government action, even cheap money, played a relatively minor part. The impetus came from a rising demand, which was based in the final analysis on the greatly improved terms of trade and on lowered real costs of production, and the main positive action of the Government consisted in channelling the additional demand into home-produced goods and services rather than imports.

The trade cycle began to turn down in 1937, long before it had reached full employment levels. However, rearmament took up the slack,[200] and with building still booming, the recession of 1938–9 was milder than that following 1929, and was short-lived. The needs of war soon led to the full employment of all available resources.

[194] Nevin, *Cheap Money*, pp. 272 ff.

[195] L. R. Connor, 'Urban Housing in England and Wales', *J. R. Stat. S.*, 99/1, 1936, p. 39.

[196] I. Bowen, 'Building Output and the Trade Cycle (UK, 1924–38)', *Oxf. Econ. P.*, 3, 1940, p. 116; R. L. Reiss, *Municipal and Private Enterprise Housing* (1945), pp. 24–6.

[197] W. A. Lewis, *Economic Survey*, p. 86.

[198] D. H. Aldcroft, *The British Economy*, vol. 1, *The Years of Turmoil 1920–1951* (1986), pp. 93, 139; J. B. Cullingworth, *Housing Needs and Planning Policy* (1960), chapter 2.

[199] Herbert W. Robinson, *The Economics of Building* (1939), pp. 119–22; W. F. Stolper, 'British Monetary Policy and the Housing Boom', *Quarterly Journal of Economics*, 56/1, Part II, Nov. 1941; Reiss, *passim*; C. L. Mowat, *Britain Between the Wars*, pp. 458/61.

[200] Mark Thomas, 'Rearmament and Economic Recovery in the Late 1930s', *Ec. Hist. Rev.*, 36/3, 1983; H. V. Hodson, *Slump and Recovery, 1929–1937* (1938), chapter 12.

4

Social Conditions between the Wars

1 The Age of Mass Unemployment

The shift of resources in Britain between the wars from the old to the new industries, from the export trades to the sheltered home industries had important consequences on the well-being of different sections of the population, and in particular, on the poverty and long-period unemployment of many of those in the declining sectors. Unemployment of men and of resources occupies a central place in the history of the inter-war years.

At the end of the war, some transitional unemployment was expected as soldiers and war-workers were being demobilized and fitted into their normal peace-time occupations, but the actual transfer from the forces to civilian occupations was accomplished with remarkable smoothness. A maximum of 1,093,000 men were paid out-of-work donation in April 1919,[1] but it is doubtful how many of them were truly unemployed; a year later there was an acute labour shortage in most areas.[2]

Then the boom collapsed, and by March 1921 unemployment in the insured trades reached 15%. The coal stoppage of April to June raised the figure to 22%, but even after the dispute was over, the proportion remained obstinately at 16–17%. Employment improved in 1924, and was at a high level again in 1927–9, but even in the best months, the official unemployment rate stood at 9–10%, or over a million unemployed. Before the war, the maximum rate over a period of 60 years or more had been 11%, and the average $4\frac{1}{2}$% (and the insurance scheme had been built on the actuarial assumption of such a rate). Now, fluctuations in unemployment similar to those of the pre-1914 era seemed to be superimposed on an irreducible 'hard core' of close on a million unemployed men.[3]

The 'Great Depression' of the early 1930s brought with it a level of unemployment that put even the 1920s in the shade. The official unemployment rate reached a peak of 23% or nearly one-quarter of the insured population in August 1932, and stayed above 20% for over two years. In terms of numbers, this meant a figure of nearly 3 million people without work, but there were in addition several important sections of the population outside the field of insurance, and therefore excluded from the official statistics. Among them were agricultural workers, domestic servants, self-employed persons, persons employed by members of their immediate family, and most salaried employees,

[1] A. C. Pigou, *Aspects of British Economic History, 1918–1925* (1947), pp. 36–40.
[2] E. V. Morgan, *Studies in British Financial Policy, 1914–25* (1952), pp. 70–2.
[3] Henry Clay, *The Post-War Unemployment Problem* (1929), pp. 24, 28.

besides civil servants, police, armed forces and railwaymen. For these groups, the proportions out of work were lower so that, if the total workforce were to be considered instead of the insured population, total unemployment rates would have to be considerably reduced, from an average of 14·2% for the inter-war period as a whole to 10·9%. Yet they added to the total numbers which they brought up to an estimated 3,289,000 in 1931 and 3,750,000 in the peak period of September 1932.[4]

Improvement set in in 1933, and while the numbers out of work fell to a minimum of 9% (1,400,000 on the official register) by September 1937, the numbers in employment rose faster still. Some 2 million persons were added to the employed population between 1933 and 1937, of whom fewer than 1½ million came from the ranks of the registered unemployed.[5] The position worsened in 1938–9, when 1,800,000–1,900,000 persons (12%) were on the official unemployment registers, in spite of re-armament, but this deterioration was interrupted by the outbreak of war in September 1939.

General unemployment percentages hide very great differences between industries, areas, workers of different skills, ages or sex. On the basis of their pre-war expansion, as late as 1919 it was assumed that industries such as coal and cotton would have so little unemployment compared with other occupations, that they would want to establish their own 'special' insurance schemes at more favourable rates.[6] In the event, it was the old industrial areas and the old staple export trade which suffered most. These were above all coal mining, but also cotton, wool, shipbuilding, tinplate, iron and steel and pottery.[7] By contrast, industries which were rapidly expanding, like electrical engineering or motor engineering, or which catered largely for the home market, like distribution or motor transport, had relatively low rates of unemployment.

In 1929–31 the effects of a general world economic depression were added to the special problems of the export industries, and there were further changes. The new industries and services continued to enjoy the lowest unemployment figures until 1931, but they failed to show the same rate of recovery as the rest of the country in the next few years. The reason was that as soon as trade improved, there was an influx from the declining sectors in such numbers as to overstrain their capacity of absorbing labour[8] (see Table 4·1). Some capital goods industries, which are usually subject to much greater cyclical fluctuations than those producing consumer goods, had a much more than normally rapid expansion in the 1930s.[9]

[4] Colin Clark, *National Income and Outlay* (1937), p. 31; Sean Glyn and Alan Booth, 'Unemployment in Interwar Britain: A Case for Learning the Lessons of the 1930s?', *Econ. Hist. Rev.* 36/3, 1983; Alan E. Booth and Sean Glyn, 'Unemployment in the Interwar Period: a Multiple Problem', *Journal of Contemporary History* 10/4, 1975; Mark Thomas, 'Labour Market Structure and the Nature of Unemployment', in B. Eichengreen and T. J. Hatton (eds.), *Interwar Unemployment in International Perspective* (Dordrecht, 1988), p. 99; H. W. Robinson, 'Employment and Unemployment', in *Britain in Recovery* (1938), p. 95.
[5] R. C. Davison, *British Unemployment Policy since 1930* (1938), p. 49.
[6] W. H. Beveridge, *Unemployment, a Problem of Industry* (1930), pp. 291, 405.
[7] Clay, *op. cit.*, pp. 27–8, 41–52, 81–4, 92–5, 108; Pigou, *op. cit.*, pp. 46–50.
[8] W. H. Beveridge, *Full Employment in a Free Society* (1944), pp. 49–59, 83, Table 33 (pp. 316–20), based on his series of three articles, 'An Analysis of Unemployment', *Economica*, NS 3 and 4, Nos. 12–14, 1936–7, esp. No. 12, Nov. 1936, p. 374.
[9] E. H. Phelps-Brown and G. L. S. Shackle, 'British Economic Fluctuations', *Oxf. Econ. P.*, No. 2, 1939.

Table 4·1:   Unemployed percentages in selected industries

		1932	1937
(A)	Expanding Industries:		
	Building	29·0	13·8
	Motor vehicles, etc.	20·0	4·3
	Electrical engineering	16·3	3.1
	Food industries	16·6	12·4
	Hotel, etc., service	17·3	14·2
	Distributive trades	12·2	8·8
(B)	Declining Industries:		
	Coal mining	33·9	14·7
	Woollen and worsted	20·7	10·2
	Cotton	28·5	11·5
	Shipbuilding	62·2	23·8
	Jute	42·2	26·8
	Pig-iron making	43·5	9·8

Within industry it was, as ever, the unskilled workers who bore the brunt of the unemployment, and the salaried employees and managers who suffered least.[10] If person temporarily stopped were included also, the differences between these groups would be greater still.

In view of the strong localization of most of the basic and staple industries, the incidence of high unemployment in them was reflected in high local rates of unemployment in certain areas. It was noticeable also that every industry showed higher unemployment rates in the high-unemployment areas.[11] As late as 1934, most of the industrial towns in the Welsh valleys, and many towns on the Tyne and in Durham, had unemployment rates of over 50%, and some well over 70% of the total workers insured. In West Cumberland there were towns like Frizington, where a bare 33 men were on unemployment insurance benefit, while 515 had been unemployed for so long that they had exhausted their insurance claims and were kept on 'Transitional Payments'.[12]

Unemployment of such extent and durations was a social, as well as an economic problem. The man who was on the dole for a long period lost some of his skill and his self-respect, and often also the will to work, and some permanent damage to his personality was only too likely.[13] Men became bitter, cynical and disillusioned, and less sure of their moral bearings when they were denied work and found themselves and their families in poverty in the midst of a rich society.

There were also special problem groups among them. There were boys and

[10] Colin Clark, *National Income and Outlay,* p. 46, and *The Conditions of Economic Progress* (1951 ed.), p. 470; Thomas, 'Labour Market'.

[11] T. J. Hatton, 'Structural Aspects of Unemployment Between the Wars', *Research in Economic History*, 10, 1986.

[12] Ministry of Labour, *Reports of Investigations into the Industrial Conditions of Certain Depressed Areas* (1934, Cmd. 4728), pp. 27, 106, 136. Also chapter 2, section 4 above.

[13] H. W. Singer, *Unemployment and the Unemployed* (1940), chapter 12. Cf. also M. Bruce, *The Coming of the Welfare State* (1961), pp. 228–40; H. L. Beales and R. S. Lambert (eds.), *Memoirs of the Unemployed* (1934).

girls who never secured a steady job at all, even for a time;[14] there were the older men who found it impossible, once they were dismissed, ever to gain new employment; and there were craftsmen, proud of their skill, who refused inferior jobs and failed to realize that their craft had become out-of-date. There were, further, often local or perhaps even national differences in attitude: the proud families of Crook Town, keeping up an outward appearance of serenity and respectability, contrasted with the gregarious families of the Welsh valleys, only too eager to exaggerate their distress and dramatize their ill-luck.[15]

Among applicants for benefit or allowances in 1929, only 4·7% had been unemployed twelve months or more. But the proportion rose to 16·4% in August 1932, 25·0% in August 1936 and (after a change in the classification) 22·6% in August 1939.[16] In some of the badly hit areas, the proportions were very much higher. In September 1936, while only 0·4% of the insured fell into this category in prosperous Deptford, the proportion was 18·8% in Crook and 28·1% in the Rhondda, in both these places forming over one-half of the unemployed population.[17] In depression years spells of work consisted often of a few days' or a few weeks' employment only, interrupting years of general unemployment, so that a high proportion of those nominally on the register for a short period only were in fact long-period cases.[18]

After years of such experiences, a certain fatalism made itself felt. Sir William (later Lord) Beveridge recognized three main groups in 1937: (*a*) short-period, frictional or seasonal unemployment, amounting to 6–8% of the insured population, or 800,000–1,000,000 people and accepted as inescapable; (*b*) long-period hard-core unemployed in contracting industries and regions or handicapped by old age, numbering 4%, or 500,000, who might be reduced in numbers in the long run; and (*c*) cyclical unemployment of workers temporarily thrown out of work of whom there might be up to 6%, or 800,000, at the bottom of a slump. The numbers referred to insured persons only; there would be others outside the insurance scheme.[19]

The pre-war insurance scheme in certain industries was extended in 1916 to cover some 4 million workers. In November 1918, when the Government was in fear of rebellion, a non-contributory Out-of-Work Donation scheme was started as a temporary measure. It carried the burden of the transitional months and allowed the more permanent Act of 1920 to be introduced at leisure. The civilian scheme ended in November 1919 and the service scheme in 1921, and

[14] W. R. Garside, 'Juvenile Unemployment and Public Policy between the Wars', *Ec. Hist. Rev.* 30/2, 1977, and discussion in *ibid.* 32/4, 1979, pp. 523–32.

[15] (Pilgrim Trust), *Men Without Work* (Cambridge, 1938) is a report of six typical urban areas in 1936, including Crook and the Rhondda. Cf. also A. J. Lush, *Disinherited Youth* (Edinburgh, 1943).

[16] Beveridge, *Full Employment,* Table 8, p. 64. Cf. also Clark, *National Income and Outlay,* p. 48.

[17] *Men Without Work, passim.* The Report deals largely with those unemployed for 12 months or more.

[18] H. W. Singer., *op. cit.,* chapter 1; Thomas, 'Labour Market', p. 104.

[19] Sir William Beveridge, 'An Analysis of Unemployment, III', *Economica,* NS, 4/14, 1937, pp. 180–2. Cf. also R. C. Davison, *The Unemployed, Old Policies and New* (1929), chapter 6; Susan Howson, 'Slump and Unemployment', in Roderick Floud and Donald McCloskey, *The Economic History of Britain since 1700,* vol. 2 (Cambridge, 1981), p. 270; Alan E. Booth and Sean Glyn, 'Unemployment in the Interwar Period: A Multiple Problem', *Journal of Contemporary History,* 10, 1975.

their total cost of £66 million[20] seemed a small price to pay for social peace at a critical time.

The Unemployment Insurance Act of 1920 contained all the main principles of the Act of 1911, but extended its scope to virtually all employments.[21] Eleven million workers were included, rising gradually over the period to 15·4 million in 1938,[22] and all official unemployment statistics were based on that category of insured persons. The Act had hardly been put into effect when the slump set in, raising unemployment rates to well over 10% for the decade instead of 4%. This soon wiped out the accumulated surplus of £22 million, and presented the Government in 1921 with the dilemma which was to dog all administrations for the next two decades: how to preserve the 'insurance' principle of the original scheme, while at the same time preventing the hundreds of thousands who had exhausted their benefit entitlement from being treated as paupers. It was to solve this that a third type of benefit was interposed, neither insurance nor charity, but with some of the characteristics of both, changing in detail several times in the inter-war years, but remaining in essentials the same. It was usually subject to some form of means or needs test.

These 'intermediate' schemes, being neither insurance nor Poor Law, were improvisations, and there were no fewer than 18 amending Acts to the Unemployment Insurance Act between 1920 and 1930 and more in the 1930s. At first the intermediate scheme, called 'uncovenanted benefit' in 1921–4, then 'extended benefit' in 1924–8 and 'transitional benefit' in 1928–31, was paid out of the Insurance Fund, but since this destroyed its solvency, its cost was transferred to the Treasury. By 1928 there were almost as many unemployed who had exhausted their benefit and were on the supplementary scheme as there were on the full insurance scheme. Another group, numbering 120,000–140,000 insured, and making with their dependants some half million persons, had slipped through the meshes of both and had to be looked after by the Poor Law Guardians.

In both the Poor Law and the supplementary schemes, relief was given according to needs, and local administration and interpretation differed widely. By 1926 three Poor Law Unions had gone bankrupt, having exhausted their borrowing powers, and were replaced by Ministry nominees. In general, 'the level of assistance has varied with the political complexion, the social theories, and the financial status of the individual relief authorities'.[23]

Following the Blanesburgh Departmental Committee on Unemployment Insurance, which reported in 1927, the Unemployment Act of 1927, operative in 1928, set out to abolish 'extended benefit' by granting drawing rights to all who had 8 contributions in the past two years, or 30 weeks' contributions at any time.[24] But this scheme went gravely astray in its actuarial estimate of

---

[20] Karl de Schweinitz, *England's Road to Social Security*, p. 218; E. M. Burns, *British Unemployment Programs, 1920–1938* (Washington, 1941), p. 7. Miss Burns's work, together with the works by Davison and Lord Beveridge quoted earlier in this section, form the main sources for the study of unemployment insurance and assistance in this period.

[21] The main groups exempted are listed on pp. 122–3 above.

[22] Alan T. Peacock, *The Economics of National Insurance* (1952), p. 15.

[23] E. M. Burns, p. 28.

[24] *Report of the Departmental Committee on Unemployment Insurance* (1927); G. P. Jones and A. G. Pool, *A Hundred Years of Economic Development in Great Britain* (1959 ed.), pp. 392–5.

financial burden and return. Being launched in what was probably the least depressed year of the 1920s, it assumed an average unemployment rate of 6%; in fact, the rate rose from 9% in 1927 to 19·6% in December 1930, and then stayed above 20% for over two years. The heavy outpayments which plunged the Fund deeper into nominal debt helped to precipitate the economic and political crisis of 1931, as described in chapter 3 above. It also forced the Government to consider anew the principles of unemployment insurance.

Meanwhile, the burden of unemployment was also undermining the old Poor Law. Throughout the 1920s a minimum of 350,000–450,000 persons out of work received out-door relief in Great Britain, and at times these numbers were very much higher: there were 1,244,000 persons in June 1922, for example, and over $1\frac{1}{2}$ million during the prolonged coal strike of 1926. The local system of Poor Law Guardians was not designed for and was unable to take such strains. A new law, the Local Government Act of 1929 (and a similar Act for Scotland), confirmed by the Poor Law Act of 1930, abolished the traditional Poor Law and the Guardians as from 1930, and transferred their work to Public Assistance Committees of County Councils and County Borough Councils. Perhaps the most significant change was the turning of the labour 'test' for the able-bodied from a deterrent into the 'primary objective ... to maintain the employability of those able and willing to work, so that when opportunity offers, these men may have no difficulty in resuming their places in industry'.[25] The 'genuinely seeking work' clause, dating from 1924, was also abolished, since the notion of 'voluntary unemployment' had become patently unhelpful in existing conditions.

Meanwhile, the deficits of the Unemployment Fund mounted to new heights in 1931, even though the Treasury had taken over the total current costs of the 'transitional' benefits. It led to drastic cuts in benefits and increases in contributions. The terms on which benefit was granted were tightened up to the extent of reducing by some 700,000 the numbers receiving insurance benefits, matched by a rise of only about 250,000 in the numbers receiving transitional payments. Within a year about 180,000 persons were removed from the register altogether.[26]

Once a person had exhausted his insurance benefit, now reduced to a maximum of 26 weeks, he was forced to turn to the intermediate scheme, now called 'transitional', with a searching needs test, and the widespread bitterness resulting from reductions in the 'dole' because of earnings of other members of the family, or some small property, dates mainly from those years. The local standards of needs tests differed widely in practice, while many deplored, with Sir Henry Betterton, the Minister of Labour the 'complete divorce between the responsibility of the central authority, which is providing the money, and that of the local authority which disburses it'.[27]

The Royal Commission on Unemployment Insurance had been appointed in 1930, and reported in 1932, and on its Reports[28] was based the new Unem-

---

[25] E. M. Burns, *op. cit.*, p. 26, quoting from a Ministry of Health circular of 1930.

[26] G. D. H. and Margaret Cole, *The Condition of Britain* (1937), chapter 4; Michael Beenstock and Associates, *Work, Welfare and Taxation* (1987), p. 82; Sean Glyn and John Oxborrow, *Interwar Britain: A Social and Economic History* (1976), p. 256.

[27] HoC, 30.11.1933.

[28] *Interim Report of the Royal Commission on Unemployment Insurance* (1931. Cmd. 3872), *Final Report* (1932. Cmd. 4185).

ployment Act of 1934, which was to put the unemployment scheme at last on a sound and permanent footing. It was in two parts, dealing with insurance and assistance respectively. The insurance scheme was to remain actuarially sound, and watched over by an Unemployment Insurance Statutory Committee. In the event, with better trade leading up to the boom of 1937, and rates of unemployment much below the calculated break-even rate of $16\frac{3}{4}\%$ (the rate of 1934), the Fund succeeded not only in staying solvent, but could also afford to raise benefits and lower contributions, while paying off much of the accumulated debt. In 1936 agricultural workers were catered for by a new parallel scheme, and in 1937 several other groups formerly excluded were brought in.

For those whose spell out of work exceeded the limit of 26 weeks, and for many of those outside the insurable classes altogether, the transitional benefits were to be replaced by a new scheme, administered by a central Unemployment Assistance Board, with its own staff of full-time officers, in place of the local Committees. It was to pitch its benefits high enough to avoid any need for supplementation. In this way it was hoped to reduce the burden on the Poor Law, now administered by the Public Assistance Committees of the local authorities. In the event, its rates turned out to be too low, and it was not until the 'second appointed day', 1 April 1937, that the Board took over about 100,000 Poor Law cases, mostly able-bodied persons, and began everywhere to pay its own rates.

Public authorities also originated other measures of relief, besides direct benefit payments. Local schemes to help the depressed areas have been noted in chapter 2, section 4, above,[29] and the aid to land settlement was noted in the same chapter, section 5. Industrial Transfer Boards, established in 1928, helped individuals and whole families in their removal in search of work, though in practice voluntary migration achieved much more than assisted transfer. Until 1929 there were also substantial sums expended in assisting migration overseas.[30] The establishment of Government Training Centres, of residential Instructional Centres, and other means of training[31] were of some help to young persons and to those returning from the armed services after the war.

In recent years, a considerable debate has taken place on the question of whether the unemployment and other relief payments made available were themselves responsible for the high unemployment level of the inter-war years. The argument has much current relevance because of the widespread monetarist assumption that there is a direct connection between the wage rate and the rate of unemployment; the rates of relief paid, it is alleged, put a floor to wages, and prevent their downward adjustment, while often also providing a higher income than could be earned by the breadwinner concerned. The more extreme statements of this view[32] have been refuted on many points of detail both in method and in the data base[33] but the existence of a 'wage trap' for the lower-paid could

---

[29] A brief list will be found in the *Report of the Royal Commission on the Distribution of the Industrial Population* (Barlow Report) (1940). Cmd. 6153), pp. 146 ff.

[30] pp. 144–5 below.

[31] R. C. Davison, *Unemployment Policy,* chapter 6, and *The Unemployed,* chapter 7.

[32] Daniel K. Benjamin and Lewis A. Kohin, 'Searching for an Explanation of Unemployment in Interwar Britain', *Journal of Political Economy,* 87, 1979; K. G. P. Matthews, *The Inter-War Economy. An Equilibrium Analysis* (Aldershot, 1986), pp. 34 f.

[33] Barry Eichengreen, 'Unemployment in Interwar Britain: Dole or Doldrums?' *Oxf. Econ. P.*

not be denied. The rise of wages in the 1930s in spite of the large stock of the unemployed would also remain a puzzle if there were a strong link between wages and the rate of unemployment, but may be at least in part explained by the existence of a dual labour market, in 'Inner' and 'Outer' Britain, labour shortages in the former not being filled by the reserves in the latter.[34]

There was little help from public works as measures of relief. From 1921 on, local authorities undertook construction schemes, and there were some Government grants for the maintenance of public buildings and for afforestation, partly with the unemployed in mind. But the Central Government's contribution to road building in the 1920s came largely out of the Road Fund, and the important trunk road programme and five years' programme of 1929 were cut in 1931, for reasons of economy, when they might have been of the greatest use. The Unemployed Grants Committee itself spent £69·5 million between December 1920 and January 1932 assisting local authorities with public works, but this compared with the £600 million paid out in the same period in benefit and relief. A maximum of 60,000 men worked on these schemes in 1931, when total unemployment was over $2\frac{1}{2}$ million. Even this grudging aid was suspended in 1931, and though public opinion became more favourable towards public works from 1935 on,[35] little was done before the war.

2 Housing, Health and Other Welfare Provisions

The nineteenth century believed that the housing of ordinary families could safely be left to the forces of unfettered demand and supply. The sorry results of this policy of *laissez-faire* in house building are with us still.[36] But before 1914 the public provision of housing for the poorer classes was little more than experimental, and was limited to some slum-clearance schemes of a few progressive town councils.

The war completely revolutionized the market for houses for letting. Rent control, imposed as a result of protests by Glasgow munition workers in 1915 to keep down the cost of living, reduced the real level of rents in a period of rising prices, though ultimately an increase of 40–50% on pre-war rents was permitted. After the war, the housing shortage caused by the interruption of building would have raised rents so much beyond the pre-war figures as to cause widespread hardship and unrest. Hence rent control was kept on after 1918 and was, in fact, extended to more expensive property in 1919 and 1920.

In view of rising expectations of civilized minima for working-class houses, well expressed by the recommendations of the Tudor Walters Committee of the Ministry of Reconstruction in 1917–18, the rising costs of new houses would drive their economic rents far above the level of the old controlled rents. As a result of these developments, three interrelated conditions came to determine the housing market from 1919 onward. First, there remained an intractable shortage of working-class dwellings to let at current (controlled) rents; secondly, the level of rents of a large proportion of dwellings was artificial, being either

---

39/4, 1987; Sean Glyn and Alan Booth, 'Unemployment'; S. N. Broadberry, 'Unemployment in Interwar Britain: a Disequilibrium Approach', *Oxf. Econ. P.* 35.1983.
[34] Booth and Glyn, 'Unemployment'.
[35] See chapter 3, section 4 above.
[36] W. Ashworth, *The Genesis of Modern Town Planning* (1954).

controlled below its market level or subsidized; and thirdly, a gap had opened between the weekly rent which wage-earners were prepared to pay, and the costs of the sort of accommodation which they (and society) as a whole were coming to expect as a minimum. The shortage of houses in 1919 has been variously computed at between 600,000 and 1 million,[37] mostly in the cheaper range of houses. Since private investment in houses built for letting had been made unprofitable, it was decided to encourage it by a Government subsidy, believed in the face of the evidence[38] to be temporary only. In the event, housing needs grew faster than new dwellings and subsidized housing became one of the cornerstones of public welfare provision.

Under the first measure, the Housing and Town Planning Act of 1919 (the 'Addison Act') the building of houses was made obligatory on the local authorities rather than permissive, and they were to receive a subsidy to the extent of the entire loss beyond the proceeds of a penny rate. The Ministry of Health had certain powers over the building and the rents charged, and this ensured that subsidized houses were indeed built for those in most urgent need, irrespective of the rent they could afford. But since there was pressure to proceed quickly and the Act gave no incentive to local authorities, who were in immediate charge of the building, to practise economy, the building under the Addison Act was completed on the most extravagant terms. In March 1921, tenders for a non-parlour type of house reached £838 per unit, compared with £371 in January 1923. Building under the Addison Act was suspended in 1922 as part of the economy campaign of that year. By March 1923, the houses built in England and Wales under the legislation of 1919 totalled 155,000 by local authorities, 44,000 by private enterprise with subsidy, and 54,000 without. The additional need since 1919, because of the net increase in the number of families, was estimated at 460,000 in the same period, so that the shortage had increased by some 200,000 dwellings, in spite of the extravagant spending.[39]

New principles of subsidizing building were introduced by the ('Chamberlain') Housing Act of 1923. Local economies were encouraged by limiting the subsidy for each house to £6 a year for 20 years, all the remainder of the loss to be borne by the local authority. This method ensured local economy in housing management; but the Act failed to encourage the building of working-class housing. On the other hand, the Act was used by private enterprise builders, and nearly 400,000 of their houses ultimately claimed and received subsidies under it, mostly built for sale to the middle classes.

The tendency of the Chamberlain Act to use the taxpayers' money to subsidize the housing of those who needed it least, while leaving the large working-class demand unfulfilled, was redressed to some extent by the Labour Government in the following year. Its ('Wheatley') Housing (Financial Provisions) Act of 1924 raised the subsidy per house to £9 a year for 40 years, provided that the house was built for letting and that the rent did not exceed the 'appropriate

---

[37] p. 121 above; W. F. Stolper, 'British Monetary Policy and the Housing Boom', *QJE*, 56/1, part II, Nov. 1941, p. 90; Seymour J. Price, *Building Societies, Their Origin and History* (1958), pp. 292–3.

[38] *Royal Commission on Housing of the Industrial Population in Scotland* (1917, Cd. 8731).

[39] R. L. Reiss, *Municipal and Private Enterprise Housing* (1945), pp. 32 ff.; Marian Bowley, *Housing and the State* (1945), chapter 2; C. L. Mowat, *Britain Between the Wars* (1956 ed.), p. 44.

normal rent' of the district.[40] Local authorities were stimulated thereby to provide large numbers of houses for the better-off artisan classes, while private enterprise preferred to continue on the Chamberlain scheme, the two schemes continuing side by side. In 1927 the rates of subsidies on both were drastically reduced, and in 1929 the Chamberlain Act subsidies were ended, the Wheatley subsidies being abolished by the Housing Act of 1933.

The total number of houses built under the two schemes in England and Wales was nearly 960,000, of which 580,000 were provided by local authorities (358,000 of them by 1930) and 378,000 by private enterprise, nearly all of them by 1930. Including some 536,000 houses built since the end of the war without subsidy, the total of new houses built in England and Wales by the end of 1930 was almost $1\frac{1}{2}$ million, and from 1926 onwards the rate of construction had been 200,000 dwellings a year. Official opinion began to believe that the basic housing needs were now being met, and the general subsidy schemes began to be wound up, the subsidies of the 1930s being designed for particular purposes, such as slum clearance and the abolition of overcrowding.

In fact the housing shortage was by no means over for the poorer classes of the community,[41] though the demand for the more expensive accommodation was now being met. A private-enterprise housing boom developed in the 1930s[42] which provided almost 3 million new houses, virtually all for better-off owners and tenants. Those who occupied the cheaper houses could, in theory, find accommodation by 'filtering up' into dwellings thus vacated,[43] but mobility was low, partly as a result of rent control, and by the end of the 1930s there developed strong signs of an over-supply of expensive houses, while the shortage of cheap accommodation was as acute as ever.

The legislation of the 1930s dealt with special cases only. The first of the new Acts, the ('Greenwood') Housing Act of 1930, offered Government subsidies to local authorities for slum clearance schemes.[44] Up to then, it was estimated that only 11,000 slum houses in England and Wales had been pulled down and replaced, largely because of the absolute shortage of dwellings, but the new Act started from the assumption that the shortage was beginning to wane, and that replacement of slum property could begin. With the repeal of the existing general subsidies in 1933, it became the main effective subsidy scheme.

The Greenwood Act had the novel feature that subsidies varied, not with the number of houses, but with the number of people displaced and rehoused. The local authorities thus had a strong incentive to tackle the most populous areas first, and to provide new houses as fast as the old slums were pulled down. Further, all authorities with populations of over 20,000 were required to prepare five-year schemes for slum clearance, and continue them until all slums had been removed. Actual plans envisaged the scrapping of only 250,000 houses (out of at least 750,000 unfit), the building of 285,000 and the re-housing of $1\frac{1}{4}$ million people.

In 1935 a further Act extended subsidies to building designed to abate over-

---

[40] Richard W. Lyman, *The First Labour Government, 1924* (1957), chapter 8.

[41] G. D. H. and M. I. Cole, *The Condition of Britain* (1937), chapter 3.

[42] pp. 120–1 above.

[43] A. P. Becker, 'Housing in England and Wales during the Business Depression of the 1930s', *Ec. Hist. Rev.*, 2nd S., 3/3, 1951, p. 323.

[44] E. D. (Lord) Simon, *The Anti-Slum Campaign* (1933), esp. chapter 13.

crowding, especially if high-cost flats were required. By then, according to the Report on Overcrowding in England and Wales, published by the Ministry of Health in 1936,[45] only 3·8% of dwellings were judged to be 'overcrowded', but this figure hid large regional concentrations, especially on Tyneside, where working-class flats were still typical, and in Scotland (not covered by this Report) where 22·6% of working-class dwellings were overcrowded in 1935. In any case, 'overcrowding' depends on the standards adopted, and a slightly more rigorous standard produced an average of 9·5%.[46] The total number of houses built in England and Wales under the legislation of the 1930s was 289,000 by local authorities and 8,000 by private enterprise.

By 1939 much of the overcrowding of 1936 had been abolished. Of the 1¼ million persons to be rehoused, only 239,000 were left in their old quarters, nearly half of them in five cities – London, Leeds, Liverpool, Manchester and Sheffield. In many areas the five-year plans had been completed, and in others they were all but complete on the outbreak of war. But elsewhere slums were newly developing: in 1939, some 550,000 dwellings were still left which were fit for destruction under the slum clearance Acts, and 350,000 'marginal' dwellings, likely to become slums in a few years' time.

In Scotland, where housing needs were greater and conditions far worse, more houses were built by local authorities and fewer by private enterprise than in England and Wales. The total number of dwellings completed between the wars in Great Britain compared as shown in Table 4·2.[47]

Table 4·2:   Dwellings completed between the wars (in 000)

	England and Wales	Scotland	Great Britain
By local authorities	1,163	230	1,393
By private enterprise with subsidy	433	43	476
By private enterprise without subsidy	2,596	63	2,659
	4,192	336	4,528

New building thus amounted to 4½ million *dwellings*, of which over two-thirds were built by private enterprise. Virtually all of these, except for 48,000 built by Housing Associations, were for letting to middle-class tenants or for sale to owner-occupiers, again for the middle classes and the top group of artisans. Many of the remainder, built by local authorities, were also let at rents which could be afforded by the better-off workers only.

Bearing in mind that about 700,000 dwellings were pulled down or converted, the net addition was of the order of 3·8 million.[48] Since the number of families was estimated to have risen by 3·3 million, the gap was closed, mainly in the late 1930s, to the extent of half a million dwellings since 1919, or not quite

[45] Ministry of Health, *Report of Overcrowding Survey of England and Wales* (1936).

[46] Mowat, p. 507; G. D. H. Cole, *Building and Planning* (1945), pp. 102–3.

[47] Reiss, p. 15; Miss Bowley's figures vary slightly from these, *op. cit.*, Table 2, p. 271, and Appx. I.

[48] Richard Stone, *The Measurement of Consumers' Expenditure and Behaviour in the United Kingdom, 1920–1938*, vol. 1 (Cambridge, 1954), Table 92 and chapter 15.

enough to meet the estimated shortage of 1919. Between 1914 and 1939, while the share of housing privately rented had fallen from 80% to 46% of the total, local authority rented housing had risen from 1% to 14% and owner-occupied from 6% to 31%.[49] There was still a considerable shortage of cheap accommodation in 1938, besides the slum property condemned and waiting to be cleared and replaced.[50]

Nevertheless, there had been substantial improvements: 'the majority of those who benefited by the increase in the national income and by the more equal distribution of this income, tended to enjoy the bulk of their gains in terms of better housing conditions'.[51] Housing, like public health and education, was increasingly recognized to be an important public service.

Health insurance had a wide coverage from its beginnings in 1911. By 1921, over 15 million persons were included, and by 1938 the numbers insured had increased to nearly 20 million. Only the numbers of those insured under the Widows', Orphans' and Old-Age Pensions scheme exceeded those insured by the health scheme (by about 1 million) in 1938.[52]

There was little attempt made to integrate the insurance scheme with the public health legislation, in spite of the establishment of the Ministry of Health in 1919, responsible for both, but there were other changes.[53] The abolition of the Poor Law Unions, and the transfer of their duties and property (including the hospitals) to County and County Borough Councils were accomplished by Chamberlain's Local Government Act of 1929.[54] Despite much public criticism, the voluntary hospitals were persuaded only after the Council (ex-Poor Law) hospitals in 1930 provided some direct competitive spur in the 1930s to raise their standards, and after some collaboration between the local authority hospitals and the voluntary hospitals in their regions was established. Hospital contributory schemes increased greatly, and by 1937 there were at least 5 million voluntary contributors, paying for at least 10 million persons.[55]

Infectious diseases had been the responsibility of the local health authorities since the nineteenth century, and many of them maintained extensive isolation hospitals, tuberculosis sanatoria and similar institutions. In 1918, the Maternity and Child Welfare Act gave local authorities greater power to extend their facilities in this field, including the provision of clinics, and the Midwives Act of 1936 required them to provide trained midwives. In a little over 20 years, the number of Infant Welfare Centres had risen from a handful to 3,580 in 1938, and the number of ante-natal clinics to 1,795 in England and Wales.[56] The Venereal Diseases Act of 1917 and the Mental Treatment Act of 1930 opened

---

[49] Sean Glyn and John Oxborrow, *Interwar Britain: A Social and Economic History* (1976) p. 221.

[50] M. J. Elsas, *Housing Before the War and After* (1942).

[51] Mark Abrams, *The Condition of the British People, 1911–1945* (1945), p. 44.

[52] Alan T. Peacock, *The Economics of National Insurance* (1952), p. 15; D. C. Marsh, *National Insurance and Assistance in Great Britain* (1950), chapter 3; PEP, *Report on the British Social Services* (1937), p. 123.

[53] Sir George Newman, *The Building of a Nation's Health* (1939), chapter 4.

[54] Hermann Levy, *National Health Insurance* (Cambridge, 1944), chapters 3, 5; J. S. Ross, *The National Health Service in Great Britain* (1952), pp. 41–56.

[55] Levy, pp. 167–71; W. M. Frazer, *A History of English Public Health, 1834–1939* (1950), pp. 390–3; PEP, *The British Health Services* (1937), p. 16; Harry Eckstein, *The English Health Service* (Cambridge, Mass., 1959), chapter 5.

[56] R. M. Titmuss, *Birth, Poverty and Health* (1943), p. 33.

up news fields in the public health services. The Blind Persons Act of 1920 made Counties and County Boroughs responsible for the welfare of the blind, and granted them non-contributory pensions at the age of 50, lowered to 40 in 1938. Meanwhile, the Nurses Registration Act of 1919 gave an enhanced status to the nursing profession.

Thus at the end of the 1930s, there had been substantial progress made in many separate fields, without bringing the different aspects of public health administrations any closer together, except, perhaps, in the hands of the Local Medical Officer of Health. The insurance scheme covered only about half the adult population; it excluded some 15 million wives of insured persons except when they were child-bearing, and it failed to provide most types of specialist and hospital treatment even for those it covered. Youths of 14–16 years of age were brought in only in 1938, and children between one and five not at all.

The local authorities were entirely separate from those administering the insurance scheme, yet they gave medical and dental inspection, but not always treatment, to schoolchildren.[57] They were also responsible for medical services such as the treatment of infectious diseases, venereal diseases and insanity, as well as for more general legislation as to building, sewage, slaughter houses, food adulteration, and so forth. The Acts relating to most of these functions were consolidated by the Public Health Act of 1936, extended by the Food and Drugs Act of 1938 which adopted clauses found useful in local Acts. Since taking over the functions of the Poor Law Guardians in 1930, the Public Assistance Committees of the larger local authorities also controlled many hospitals, and were responsible for all medical assistance required by paupers. The other public hospitals, including the teaching hospitals, continued to be managed by yet a third set of authorities, the voluntary committees. Of the 3,029 hospitals in existence in Great Britain, 1,013 were voluntary, 116 were general public hospitals, 523 were Poor Law hospitals, and the rest was made up of special hospitals and sanatoria managed by the local authorities.[58] Efforts to unify these various services were, however, becoming more numerous. In 1930 the BMA and in 1937 the authors of a most comprehensive report on the British Health Services, published by PEP, favoured major reorganization,[59] while the Cathcart Committee on Scottish Health Services, which sat from 1933 to 1936[60] demanded an extension of insurance benefits and a comprehensive national health policy.

The third pre-1914 benefit scheme, the non-contributory old-age pension, was not changed in principle in this period, but payments were raised to 10s. a week and the income limits (above which no payments were made) were raised periodically also. Superimposed on this scheme were the new contributory pensions which would, in due course, be paid out as a right and without a needs test, and begin at the age of 65 instead of 70. They were linked with several other benefits in the comprehensive Widows', Orphans' and Old Age Contributory Pensions Act of 1925. In addition to old-age pensions for insured men (at 10s. a week), there were to be pensions for widows, children's allowances for widows,

[57] H. and M. Wickwar, *The Social Services, an Historical Survey* (2nd ed., 1949), p. 120.

[58] C. L. Mowat, *Britain Between the Wars* (1956 ed.), p. 497.

[59] PEP, *op. cit.*, p. 25.

[60] *Report of the Committee on the Scottish Health Services* (1936. Cmd. 5204).

and payments for orphans of insured persons. An Act of 1937 opened this scheme, on a voluntary basis, to independent workers of small means.[61]

In the field of public education, the Fisher Education Act of 1918 gave the Board of Education, and the Counties and County Boroughs, as local education authorities, strong encouragement and greater power to develop a comprehensive system of education from the nursery school to the evening class. The Board's financial aid to the local authorities was increased to at least 50% of expenditure. Full-time education to the age of 14 was made compulsory by revoking all concessions to part-timers and early leavers. Local authorities were permitted to raise the school-leaving age to 15, or, in default, to provide day continuation schools for youths aged 14 to 16 for one day a week. Finally, the noble aspiration was written into the Act, that 'adequate provision shall be made in order to secure that children and young persons shall not be debarred from receiving the benefits of any form of education by which they are capable of profiting through inability to pay fees'.

The hopes which had inspired the Act were largely disappointed. The Geddes axe and the general spirit of economy after 1921 killed all continuation schools except the one at Rugby. The school-leaving age remained at 14, and measures to tackle the overcrowding, the poor equipment, the lack of staff in so many of the ordinary Council Schools were deferred for yet another decade. Yet some impetus remained from the Fisher Act, particularly in the field of secondary education. The Hadow Report,[62] the work of a committee appointed by the Labour Government in 1924, proposed the ending of 'elementary' education at 11, and the provision of separate curricula beyond that age to children of differing abilities. In addition to the existing grammar schools and the junior technical and trade schools with their strong vocational bias, there should also be so-called 'modern' schools, selective and non-selective, which should combine practical teaching with a liberal approach, and should thus fill a gap between the other two types, while claiming staff and equipment comparable with those of grammar schools.

The Report was adopted, and reorganization proceeded throughout the rest of the inter-war period, though progress was slow in rural areas and among the 'voluntary schools' controlled by the churches.[63] By 1938, 63·5% of all children over 11 were in reorganized ('modern') schools.[64] The influential Spens Committee, appointed in 1933 and reporting in 1938,[65] further elaborated the idea of a type of school having parity of esteem with the grammar school, but giving a more practical education in place of the stress on classics and the preparation for a university: the 'Technical High Schools'.[66]

The extension of schooling to 15, planned by the Labour Government for 1931, was thwarted largely by the opposition of the churches, but was re-enacted

[61] Marsh, *op. cit.*, chapter 6; Charles E. Clarke, *Social Insurance in Britain* (Cambridge, 1950), pp. 7–9.

[62] Board of Education Consultative Committee, *Report on the Education of the Adolescent* (1927).

[63] H. and M. Wickwar, *The Social Services*, pp. 73–82; G. A. N. Lowndes, *The Silent Social Revolution* (1937), p. 101.

[64] A. M. Carr-Saunders and D. Caradog Jones, *A Survey of the Social Structure of England and Wales* (Oxford, 2nd ed. 1937), chapter 11.

[65] Board of Education Consultative Committee, *Report on Secondary Education* (1938).

[66] John Graves, *Policy and Progress in Secondary Education, 1902–1942* (1943), chapters 16–22.

in 1936, when the churches were appeased by large grants. Timed to come into effect in September 1939, it was again held up, this time by the war. Throughout the period, education expenditure rose as a proportion of net national income, from 1·2% in 1920 to 2·4% in 1935 for the public sector, plus a rise of from 0·15% to 0·21% for the private sector.[67] Children from poorer homes, however continued in practice to be denied the opportunity of higher education in all but the most exceptional circumstances.[68] Higher education was still mainly for the rich.

Taken all in all, the more generous impulses and the more ambitious social demands of the war years had not been entirely rendered nugatory by the reaction of the early 1920s. There was a considerable expansion of the public services into new fields; there was, at the same time, a gradual abandonment of comprehensive poor relief based on destitution, and its replacement by contractual insurance benefits. Administratively, also, there was a distinct movement away from *ad hoc* bodies, and the transfer of functions to the normal local authority, supported by Exchequer grants. The last years before the war saw numerous proposals, made by official and unofficial bodies of influence, to proceed farther in the same direction.

3 The Trade Unions and the Politics of Poverty

The war had brought about a remarkable increase in the power, status and size of trade unions. The peak of their membership was reached in 1920, when it stood at 8·3 million; after that it declined to 4·4 million in 1933, to recover again to 6·3 million in 1939. The membership of the unions affiliated to the Trades Union Congress in these years was 6·5 million, 3·5 million and 4·7 million respectively.[69] The unions' success in raising wages and improving conditions, the growth of the community spirit, and the knowledge of common hardships, helped to claim adherence and loyalty to the unions in the war. Conversely, the inability of the unions to hold their high money wage level after 1920, the mass unemployment, the disillusionment with the political impotence of Labour, and the return of the spirit of individualistic self-seeking were not without influence on the decline of trade-union membership after 1920.

The Trade Union (Amalgamation) Act of 1917 made amalgamation easier, and the widespread support for industrial unionism given by many of the shop stewards' committees during the war[70] worked in the same direction. The outcome was a series of major amalgamations establishing the very large unions which have dominated the union world to the present day. Among them was the amalgamation of the ASE with nine smaller societies in 1920 to form the Amalgamated Engineering Union, the National Union of Foundry Workers formed in the same year, the NU of General and Municipal Workers in 1924, the Transport and General Workers' Union in 1922, the Amalgamated Union of Building Trade Workers in 1921, the Amalgamated Society of Woodworkers

[67] John Vaizey and John Sheehan, *Resources for Education. An Economic Study of Education in the United Kingdom, 1920–1945* (1968), p. 139.

[68] K. Lindsay, *Social Progress and Educational Waste* (1926); R. M. Titmuss, *op. cit.,* pp. 63–4.

[69] N. Barou, *British Trade Unions* (1947), Appx. XIV.

[70] Branko Pribićević, *The Shop Stewards' Movement and Workers' Control, 1910–1922* (Oxford, 1959).

in 1921, and the Iron and Steel Trades Confederation in 1917.[71] Other amalgamations formed in the years 1920–2 led to the formation of the NU of Textile Workers, the NU of Distributive and Allied Workers, the NU of Printing, Bookbinding and Paper Workers, the Union of Post Office Workers, the Tailors' and Garment Workers' Union, the Civil Service Clerical Association, the NU of Sheet Metal Workers and the NU of Blastfurnacemen.

These amalgamations and others like them gave an appearance of greater strength to the unions concerned. But quite apart from the inevitable teething troubles, size was not necessarily an advantage even in the longer run. There developed a large full-time bureaucracy, while the power of the local branch diminished, and apathy grew. This tendency to settle down to respectable and responsible trade union policies became more evident after 1926, the year of the General Strike. By contrast, before about 1906 a policy of caution had been obligatory on many unions because of their weakness. The years in between, forming an interlude of stationary real wages in the secular upward movement of working-class living standards,[72] and interrupted by the war which gave its own strong impetus to trade union militancy, formed a unique period in which trade unions were both strong enough, and militant enough, to challenge their employers repeatedly and persistently, both in narrow skirmishes and on a broad front.

There were four main issues in the strikes of this watershed of trade union history: first, the recognition of trade unions by employers; secondly, increases in wages in the era of rising prices up to 1920, and resistance to wage cuts afterwards; thirdly, the integration of new types of skilled or semi-skilled work, from machine minding to bus driving, into the old-established categories of skilled, apprenticed crafts; and fourthly, the permanent retention of some of the gains in working conditions achieved in the period of labour shortage, 1915–20.[73] In addition, there were the political demands: 'Labour is challenging the whole structure of capitalist industry as it now exists', wrote one group of moderate leaders in 1919; 'it demands a system of industrial control which shall be truly democratic in character.'[74]

The earliest of the important post-war strikes took place on the Clyde, the storm centre of the war years, and in Belfast, where the engineers, led by their shop stewards, came out for a 40 and 44-hour week respectively in January and February 1919. Perhaps more significant for the unsettled conditions of the times was the police strike, in July 1919, following a successful action a year earlier, but ending in the defeat of the strikers and legislation outlawing the union.[75] The miners' threat to strike for the nationalization of coal in February

[71] J. B. Jeffreys, *The Story of the Engineers, 1800–1945* (1945), pp. 191–4; H. J. Fyrth and Henry Collins, *The Foundry Workers, a Trade Union History* (1959), pp. 151–8; II. A. Clegg, *General Union* (Oxford, 1954), Part I; V. L. Allen, *Trade Union Leadership* (1957), chapter 3 and Appendices; Alan Bullock, *The Life and Times of Ernest Bevin*, vol. 1 (1960), pp. 153 ff.; (Arthur Pugh) *Men of Steel* (1951), chapter 13; R. W. Postgate, *The Builders' History* (1923), chapter 18; S. Higgenbottam, *Our Society's History* (1939); G. D. H. Cole, *Organised Labour* (1924), Part 4; PEP, *British Trade Unionism* (1948), pp. 97, 103–4.

[72] E. H. Phelps-Brown, *The Growth of British Industrial Relations* (1959), p. 354.

[73] See pp. 35–6 above, also J. A. Dowie, '1919–1920 is in need of attention', *Econ. Hist. Rev.* 28/3, 1975.

[74] D. F. MacDonald, *The State and the Trade Unions* (1960), p. 98.

[75] V. L. Allen, 'The National Union of Police and Prison Officers', *Ec. Hist. Rev.*, 2nd S., 11/1, 1958.

1919 had been staved off by the appointment of the Sankey Commission, and by its report in favour of nationalization, but in June there was a strike of cotton workers, and in July of Yorkshire miners. The national railway strike of September–October 1919, to enforce a wage settlement, was important for being, in effect, conducted against the Government which was then still administering the railways.[76]

There were other disputes, concerned mainly with purely industrial questions. In 1920 a Special Court of Inquiry was set up under the Industrial Courts Act to hear the case of the Transport Workers' Federation for higher wages and decasualization in the docks. The union's case was brilliantly presented by Ernest Bevin, who earned the title the 'Dockers' KC' by his advocacy, and the court awarded a national minimum wage as well as proposing a scheme for regulating the labour market at the docks, though this latter was ignored by the employers. The largest of the post-war disputes outside the coal mining industry began in March 1922, when the engineering employers locked out all members of the AEU and of 47 other unions in their industry in order to enforce unlimited overtime working at the discretion of the employers. The struggle went on until June when the men, having exhausted their funds, returned to work on the employers' terms.

The high incidence of strikes in the post-war years is brought out in Table 4·3.[77]

The industrial unrest illustrated by these strike statistics was combined with

Table 4·3:   Incidence of strikes, 1911–39

Average of years	No. of strikes beginning in year	Workers involved in strikes beginning in year (million)	Working days lost by strikes during the year (million)
1911–14	1,034	0·88	17·9
1915–18	775	0·68	4·2
1919–21	1,241	2·11	49.1
1922–26*	568	0·63	38·8**
1927–39	570	0·31	3·1

* Excluding the General Strike.
** Average 1922–5; 11·7 million

much political activity on the part of labour, not least because of the Bolshevik Revolution.[78] The high point of activity, perhaps, occurred in August 1920, when a 'Council of Action' was set up by the Labour Party and the TUC to stop the sending of military aid by the British Government to the armies trying to destroy the young Soviet Union. This campaign was successful, and in the

[76] G. D. H. Cole, *A Short History of the British Working-Class Movement, 1789–1947* (1952 ed.), pp. 392–3; G. W. Alcock, *Fifty Years of Railway Trade Unionism* (1922).
[77] K. G. J. C. Knowles, *Strikes – A Study in Industrial Conflict* (Oxford, 1952), Appx. Table 1.
[78] Alan Bullock, *The Life and Times of Ernest Bevin*, vol. 1 (1960), p. 99.

same year a Communist Party was formed, but was refused affiliation to the Labour Party.

In 1920–1 the organization of the TUC was overhauled, and the Parliamentary Committee replaced by a 'General Council', more fully representative of all important sections of workers and with far wider industrial powers and duties. In 1924, further steps in the same direction were taken when Congress voted in favour of the 'Industrial Workers Charter', proposing to form one single union for each industry, with the object of maximizing its power. Congress also demanded the nationalization of the key industries, and the General Council was strengthened.[79]

The militancy of both the political and the industrial wings of the Labour Movement was met by the Government by some temporary expedients, like the Wages (Temporary Regulations) Act of November 1918, and some permanent reforms. The scheme of joint industrial councils based on the reports of the Whitley Committee of the Ministry of Reconstruction[80] was, after its initial widespread acceptance, not as successful as had been hoped. The high point of the movement was reached at the end of 1920, when there were 75 JICs, covering $3\frac{1}{2}$ million workers, and 33 'Interim Industrial Reconstruction Committees' but little of this survived except what was established in the Civil Service and by statutory authority elsewhere, as on the railways under the Railway Act of 1921 and in agriculture under the Agricultural Wages (Regulation) Act of 1924.[81]

The scope of Trade Boards was extended by an Amending Act in 1918 and between 1919 and 1921, 33 new boards were set up. After 1922, when the immediate need to pacify Labour had passed, and until 1939 only about 10 new industries were added, apart from 18 in Northern Ireland. The total number of workers covered was about $1\frac{1}{2}$ million.[82]

The third organization to emerge from the recommendations of the Whitley Committee was the Industrial Court, set up under the Industrial Courts Act of 1919. Composed of members drawn from three sections, employers, employed and 'independents', its decisions were not binding, but out of 1,700 awards in the 19 years to 1939, only four were questioned by one or the other party to the dispute.[83] In 1936 the Civil Service Arbitration Tribunal, working to much the same rules, was set up to deal with all Civil Service cases. The Industrial Court was also given additional jurisdiction from time to time. The Road Haulage Wages Act of 1938 included the unusual principle, first introduced by the Cotton Manufacturing Industry (Temporary Provisions) Act of 1934, of giving statutory sanction to wages arrived at by collective bargaining, and making them applicable to all firms.

[79] W. Milne-Bailey, *Trade Union Documents* (1929), No. 83. Also see Rodger Charles, *The Development of Industrial Relations in Britain 1911–1939* (1973), Part III.

[80] Cd.8606 (1917), Cd. 9001, 9002, 9099, 9153 (1918). Also chapter 1, section 7 above.

[81] J. B. Seymour, *The Whitley Councils Scheme* (1932); J. H. Richardson, *Industrial Relations in Great Britain* (Geneva, 1933), chapter 4.

[82] J. J. Mallon, 'Trade Boards', in G. D. H. Cole, *British Trade Unions To-day* (1939); Dorothy Sells, *The British Trade Boards System* (1923); Milne-Bailey, Nos. 116–18; Paul Barton Johnson, *Land Fit For Heroes. The Planning of British Reconstruction 1916–1919* (Chicago, 1968), pp. 459 ff.

[83] F. E. Gannett and B. F. Catherwood, *Industrial and Labour Relations in Great Britain* (1939), p. 18; G. P. Jones and A. G. Pool, *A Hundred Years of Economic Development in Great Britain* (1959 ed.), pp. 386–9.

In the period of the post-war unrest, the cockpit of the industrial struggles was the coal industry.[84] Among all the groups of workers demanding the nationalization of their industry after the war, the miners were the most insistent, and enjoyed the most widespread support. In view of the great coal shortage in Europe, and the ugly temper in many mining districts, the Government felt constrained to appoint the Sankey Commission early in 1919 to stave off a threatened miners' strike on this question. Its disregard of the recommendation of Lord Sankey for nationalization persuaded the miners that they had been tricked into calling off their strike when it stood the greatest chance of success, in February 1919, in order to enter into a period of procrastination in which their industrial power would steadily diminish. To the distrust of the coal owners, dating from pre-war years, there was added distrust of the Government.[85]

Meanwhile, in 1920, when the industry was still riding the high wave of prosperity the miners struck for higher wages in October, and achieved a partial victory after a three weeks' strike. A wage increase was granted, but made conditional upon increased output, the so-called 'datum line'. Meanwhile the threat of the Triple Alliance had led the Government to introduce the Emergency Powers Act of 1920, which empowered the Government to declare a 'state of emergency' and govern by decree, on threat of any action 'of such a nature and on so extensive a scale as to be calculated, by interfering with the supply and distribution of food, water, fuel, or light, or with the means of locomotion, to deprive the community, or any substantial portion of the community, of the essentials of life'.[86] It was put into force and used with some effect in the mining disputes of 1921 and 1926.

Before the new permanent rate of mining wages could be worked out, a sharp slump of coal export prices induced the Government to hand the industry back to the owners on 31 March 1921. The owners at once determined on drastic wage reductions and locked out the miners while the Government declared a State of Emergency. There followed a series of manœuvres and negotiations behind the scenes in which the Triple Alliance first appeared to be willing to back the miners, but later, on 15 April, 'Black Friday', withdrew their support. Whether betrayed, as sometimes alleged, or unable to agree where the decision-making power in the Triple Alliance should lie, the Alliance broke up, in effect, in 1921.[87]

Left in the lurch by their allies, the miners suffered a crushing defeat and had to return to work on the owners' terms in June 1921, when their funds were exhausted. They had to submit not only to a wage cut, but also swallow the bitter pill of a return from the national wage agreements of war-time to the earlier district agreements.[88] There followed large-scale wage reductions and a mass defection of membership in many industries. The bargaining positions in the labour market had radically changed with the change in the economic climate, from boom to slump.

The first Labour Government did not, in its short span of office in 1924, alter

[84] Knowles, *Strikes*, p. 203.
[85] A Hutt, *The Post-War History of the British Working Class* (1937), chapter 1, and *British Trade Unionism* (1952 ed.), chapter 7; also p. 50 above.
[86] Emergency Powers Act, 1920, 10 & 11 Geo. V, ch. 55, sec. 1.
[87] Francis Williams, *Magnificent Journey* (1954), chapter 21.
[88] J. W. F. Rowe, *Wages in the Coal Industry* (1923); J. R. Raynes, *Coal and its Conflicts* (1928).

the framework of the labour market.[89] Instead, it became clear that the post-war settlement of the labour question, the more permanent equilibrium of forces after the disorientation of the war years, would be decided in the industrial field, not the political. Again it was the coal mining industry which became the scene of battle.

In the summer of 1925, coal prices and sales had begun a further rapid and permanent decline, and the owners demanded, not only a return to the wages of 1921–4, but also the repeal of the Seven Hours Act of 1919 and its replacement by eight-hour shifts. The miners felt unable to resist these demands unaided, and turned for help to the General Council of the TUC, recently provided with authority which seemed to fit the new situation. In July 1925, the Trades Union Congress pledged its full support to the miners, to the extent of being prepared to call a general sympathetic strike.

Faced with this threat, the Government (which collaborated with the mine owners throughout this dispute) climbed down on 'Red Friday'. It decided to offer a temporary subsidy to enable the mine owners to continue to pay existing wage rates, and to appoint a Royal Commission. The Report of the Commission, presided over by Sir Herbert Samuel, the fourth official body to inquire into the industry since 1918, was subsequently ignored, but the subsidy had given a breathing space of nine months. This the Government used to prepare for an all-out struggle with the miners' union.

When the subsidy expired at the end of April 1926, the miners were locked out, and the General Council called a 'general strike' in support of the miners' case for midnight, Monday, 3 May. The 'first line' of trades, including transport, iron and steel, printing, building and electricity and gas workers, was called out at once, and the 'second line' of engineers and shipbuilders was called out on 11 May.

Despite the lack of preparation, the response of the rank and file exceeded all expectations. The strike, in the trades called out, was virtually complete. It brought forth much capacity for organization, enthusiasm and solidarity of the ordinary membership, but these were wholly nullified by the attitude of its leaders. 'For the rank and file the strike was a triumph: for most of its national leaders a humiliation.'[90] The General Council itself virtually disintegrated as a directing organ. Whatever positive directive was given from the centre, was due to individuals, above all Ernest Bevin, though most of the initiative seemed to come from below.

The members of the General Council, unwilling to win, and unable to enforce a compromise, used the pretext that a compromise formula suggested by Sir Herbert Samuel might be adopted and called off the strike on 12 May, after nine days, without any conditions or promises on the part of Government or owners. The miners' leaders had scarcely been consulted, and they stayed out, but after nearly eight months, the men were starved into submission, and

[89] G. D. H. Cole, *History of the Labour Party Since 1914* (1948); Richard W. Lyman, *The First Labour Government, 1924* (1957).

[90] C. L. Mowat, *Britain Between the Wars* (1956 ed.), p. 313. Other good accounts of the General Strike will be found in: Julian Symons, *The General Strike* (1957); W. H. Crook, *The General Strike* (1931); A. J. Cook, *The Nine Days* (1972); Hamilton Fyfe, *Behind the Scenes of the Great Strike* (1926); Alan Bullock, *op. cit.*, pp. 299–344; Milne-Bailey Nos. 141–52; G. A. Phillips, *The General Strike* (1976); John Lovell, *British Trade Unions 1875–1933* (1977), pp. 56–8.

agreements were made district by district, in each case involving major reductions in wages and increases in hours to $7\frac{1}{2}$ or 8 per shift.[91]

The immediate cost of the coal strike was the loss of 28 million tons of coal for export; the total losses, including losses of wages, have been put at £175–270 million. Among trade union leaders, the main consequence was the determination to avoid at all costs a repetition of the head-on clash with the Government.[92] The years beginning in 1927 were among the most peaceful in recorded history, as trade union leaders showed signs of 'exhaustion, disillusionment and recognition of the futility of industrial stoppages following the disastrous experiences of 1926'.[93]

The leading trade unionists turned to collaboration with the owners and managers of their own industries. They were met more than half-way by those employers who were coming to look for a solution to the grave industrial problems of the age in rationalization, association or a corporate form of industrial organization in which the workers' representatives would play a part.[94] They initiated the so-called 'Mond-Turner' conversations, with the full official support of the General Council of the TUC which told the 1928 Congress that it was

> for the trade union movement to say boldly that not only is it concerned with the prosperity of industry, but that it is going to have a voice in the way industry is carried on . . . the unions can use their power to promote and guide the scientific reorganization of industry.[95]

Although the conversations were never officially supported by any employers' organization, they helped to give trade unions a breathing space after their defeat of 1926, and to allow industry to reap the benefit of the boom of 1927–9 without being subject to claims for increased wages.

The General Strike also closed an epoch which began in 1907, in which unions relied on putting pressure on the public at large in order to induce the Government to mediate and enforce some concessions on the employers. Henceforward also the numbers of those favouring gradual reform would swamp trade unionists who were in favour of Syndicalism State Socialism or Guild Socialism. Finally, the fiasco of the General Strike destroyed the 'myth' of the efficacy of this ultimate weapon in the armoury of the working classes, which had haunted them since the days of Syndicalism before 1914.

The strike also left its mark on the Statute Book: the employers' victory was embodied in the Trade Disputes and Trade Union Act of 1927. This made general strikes illegal, mainly by outlawing all sympathy strikes which were held by the Courts to be designed to coerce the Government either directly or by

[91] R. Page Arnot, *The Miners: Years of Struggle* (1953), chapters 12–14; D. H. Robertson, 'A Narrative of the Coal Strike', *Econ. J.*, 36/143, 1926.

[92] Knowles, pp. 155–7; H. A. Clegg and R. Adams, *The Employers' Challenge* (Oxford, 1957), chapter 1; G. D. H. Cole, *An Introduction to Trade Unionism* (1953), chapter X/1.

[93] J. H. Richardson, 'Industrial Relations', in *Britain in Depression* (1935), pp. 59–60; also his 'Industrial Relations' in *Britain in Recovery* (1938), pp. 115–17.

[94] E.g. Sir Alfred Mond, *Industry and Politics* (1927); Bullock, *op. cit.*, chapter 15.

[95] Quoted in A. Hutt, *Post-War History of the British Working Class*, p. 178. Also Ben Turner, *About Myself* (1930); G. W. McDonald and H. F. Gospel, 'The Mond-Turner Talks 1927–1933', *Historical Journal* 16/4, 1973; Rodger Charles, *Industrial Relations*, Part IV.

inflicting hardship on the public. It forbade State employees to belong to societies or federations not consisting wholly of State employees. Further, it restricted picketing and gave the Government the power, by injunction, to attack trade union funds, the worst aspect of these sections of the Act being the vagueness and consequent uncertainty. Finally, it substituted 'contracting in' for 'contracting out' of the political levy, and thus at once reduced sharply the trade union contributions to Labour Party funds.

This measure, widely deplored as a needless act of vengeance, contributed to the General Election result of 1929, which returned Labour as the largest party in the House. Labour took office again but split over measures to deal with the effects of the great depression and worsening unemployment and, following an ignominious defeat at the polls at the end of 1931, the party was decimated in the House. The trade unions, with some significant exceptions, maintained their character of solidarity, and formed a steadying, conservative influence on the Labour Party itself.

4 Changes in Population and Social Structure

The population increase which had accompanied the industrialization of this country continued between the wars, the United Kingdom figures rising from 43·74 million in the middle of 1920 to 47·49 million in the middle of 1938,[96] but the rate of increase had begun to decline sharply in the second decade of the twentieth century. It contracted further in the 1920s and 1930s at such a headlong rate that fears began to be expressed about the ultimate decline of the population of the United Kingdom.[97]

In absolute terms, the natural increase of population in Great Britain was at its highest in 1901–11, when births exceeded deaths by nearly 4.6 million and despite heavy emigration, the net increase in the home population was 3·8 million in 1901–11.[98] In the following decade, 1911–21, the natural increase fell to 2·8 million (net, 1·9 million) and there were further drops after the war, the increase for 1921–31 being only 2·6 million (2·0 million) and in 1931–41 1·2 million, though there was a net increase of 1·8 million then, because of some net immigration. As the total population was rising throughout this period, the proportionate decline in the rate of increase was faster than these figures suggest; and since the death rate was falling it follows that the fall in the birth rate was precipitate.

The population increase between the wars was associated with a geographical shift, closely associated with the changing location of industry (see Table 4·4).[99]

The growth of the inter-war period was also accompanied by further urbanization, and it was still largely the rural areas that acted as population reservoirs for the growing towns. The main growth occurred in the smaller towns with

[96] Richard Stone, *Measurement of Consumers' Expenditure and Behaviour in the United Kingdom, 1920–1938* (Cambridge, 1954), Table 116, p. 414.
[97] E.g. D. V. Glass, *The Struggle for Population* (1936).
[98] *Report of the Royal Commission on Population* (1948. Cmd. 7695), Table IV, p. 9; most of this section is based on this report.
[99] Chapter 2, section 4 above. Also Mark Abrams, *The Condition of the British People, 1911–1945* (1945), p. 22. Cf. also A. Beacham, *Structure of British Industry* (1955 ed.), p. 150.

Table 4·4:   Distribution of the population in Great Britain

Regional distribution (R = largely rural)	Population in 1938 (million)	% Change 1921–38	Multiplication of population 1801–1921
Southeast	14.49	+18·1	5
Midlands	7·21	+11·6	4
West Riding	3·46	+6·0	5½
Eastern counties (R)	1·85	+3·7	2
Lancashire and Cheshire	6·16	+3·5	7
Southwest (R)	2·08	+3·3	2
Northern rural belt (R)	1·29	+3·1	3
Scotland	4·99	+2·1	3
Northumberland and Durham	2·20	−1·0	7
North and Central Wales (R)	0·68	−4·8	2
South Wales	1·78	−8·1	9
Great Britain	46·20	+8·0	4

growing industries (e.g. Oxford, York, Leicester and Norwich) and in the expanding coal and iron ore fields of the east Midlands.[100] The conurbations remained stationary or declined in population, with the exception of London and Birmingham,[101] whose unrestricted sprawl created some of the main social and transport problems of the age.

There was some emigration in the first post-war decade, mainly to Empire countries, but it was at an average rate of about 130,000 a year, or a mere 40% of the immediate pre-war rate,[102] and even then it had to be officially supported to a much larger extent than before 1914. It was not only that there were fewer potential emigrants: most receiving countries had reversed their attitude, and among the causes of the new restrictiveness were unemployment in the towns and the weakness of primary product prices. Even Britain became less liberal: the Aliens Act of 1914 and 1919 led to the Aliens Order of 1920, under which immigrants were admitted only if they could prove their ability to maintain themselves and their families.

The Dominions at first formed an exception, for they were eager to have British immigrants, even though in part at least this was due to their anxiety to avoid having to admit others. In 1919 the Government's free passage scheme for ex-service men and their families assisted 86,000 persons to emigrate within three years. When it became clear that there would be very little unaided migration on the pre-war scale, the Imperial Conference of 1921 proposed further assistance, and the Empire Settlement Act of 1922 authorized an expenditure of up to £3 million a year, provided the receiving Governments matched it by at least equal sums. 400,000 migrants in the next nine years benefited from aid under this Act, but most of them only by small sums, and it is doubtful how far these actually contributed to their decision to emigrate. Special schemes of

[100] PEP, *Report on the Location of Industry in Great Britain* (1939), p. 197, map on p. 171 and Appx. III, pp. 294–9.
[101] David C. Marsh, *The Changing Social Structure of England and Wales, 1871–1951* (1958), chapter 4; Mark Abrams, *op. cit.,* p. 35.
[102] W. A. Carrothers, *Emigration from the British Isles* (1929), Appx. I and IV.

settlement, as for example one designed to open up new land in Western Australia, failed dismally. In 1925, a more ambitious agreement made with Australia to settle 450,000 immigrants from Britain in 10 years, was also a failure and was terminated in 1932 after £4·3 million had been spent.[103] An official report in May 1938 pronounced against any further programmes of this kind.[104]

Long before this, however, the conditions relating to migration had changed. As the Great Depression began to affect overseas countries, the doors of even the Dominions were closed almost completely. Meanwhile the wish to emigrate had evaporated even faster than the official encouragement. There was, in fact, in the 1930s for the first time since figures were recorded a *net* annual immigration at a rate of 35,000 a year in 1931–4, and 13,000 a year in 1935–8,[105] though it should be noted that the net increase was confined to England. Scotland and Wales continued to lose population.

Not only migration, but the birth rate and the death rate too, were greatly influenced by economic and social conditions. The death rate had been falling steadily for over a century, and the fall had been particularly marked since the 1890s.[106] The 'standardized' death rate for England and Wales had fallen from 13·5 per thousand in 1911–14 to 9·3 in 1937, though it was still 13·3 in Scotland in that year.[107] The expectation of life for men increased from 43·7 years in 1881 to 61·8 years in 1938, and for women from 47·2 to 65·8 for the corresponding years.[108]

More significant as a measure of social conditions was the fall in the maternity and the infantile death rate. 'Infantile mortality is the most sensitive index we possess of social welfare and of sanitary administration, especially under urban conditions.'[109] While the infantile death rate (deaths in the first year of life per 1,000 live births) fell from 110 in 1911–15 to 58 in 1937 in England and Wales (but standing at 80 in Scotland in the latter year), the differences between classes and between regions hardly diminished (see Table 4·5).[110]

Table 4·5: Infant mortality per 1,000 legitimate live births (by social class of father)

Social Class	1920 2	1930–2	1939
Class V (unskilled labour)	97·0	77·0	60·1
Class I (upper and middle)	38·4	32·7	26·9
Excess	58·6	44·3	33·2
Excess, in %	152·6	135·5	123·4

[103] N. H. Carrier and J. R. Jeffery, *External Migration, a Study of the Available Statistics, 1815–1950* (1953).

[104] *Report of the British Overseas Settlement Board* (1938. Cmd. 5766).

[105] Julius Isaac, *Economics of Migration* (1947), Table 6, p. 64.

[106] *Report of the Royal Commission on Population*, pp. 18–20.

[107] C. L. Mowat, *Britain Between the Wars* (1956 ed.), pp. 513–14.

[108] Eva M. Hubback, *The Population of Britain* (1947), p. 23.

[109] Sir Arthur Newsholme, quoted in R. M. Titmuss, *Birth, Poverty and Wealth, a Study of Infant Mortality* (1943), p. 12. Cf. also N. L. Tranter, *Population and Society 1750–1940* (1985), p. 81; Fred Grundy, *The New Public Health* (1957), pp. 136–45.

[110] J. M. Winter, 'The Decline of Mortality in Britain 1870–1950'; in Theo Barker and Michael Drake (eds.), *Population and Society in Britain 1850–1980* (New York, 1982), p. 107, also p. 115.

The labourer's infant mortality rate was still well over double the best rate in 1939; where they could be isolated more exactly than in this crude general tabulation, the class differences were greater still.

The differences between regions were equally startling. Thus in 1935, the infant mortality rate was 57 for England and Wales and 77 for Scotland, but it was 32 in Coulsdon and Purley and 114 in Jarrow. There were similar differences in child mortality and maternal mortality, as shown in Table 4·6.[111] Comparisons between smaller areas, such as towns or urban districts, showed still greater

Table 4·6:   Child mortality and maternal mortality, 1935

	Deaths at ages		Maternal mortality per 1,000 births, 1936
	1–2	2–5	
	(per 1,000 living, 1931–4)		
North 1 (Durham and Northumberland)	22·05	6·57	5·29
Wales 1 (4 Southern Counties)	15·44	5·34	4·78
Southeast England	10·94	3·80	2·57
Greater London	12·55	4·25	2·16

differences, and more detailed analysis pointed to the conclusion that it was poverty and unemployment which thwarted the better sanitary conditions, better nutrition and better care that benefited the better-off.[112]

If the death rate was falling, the birth rate was falling faster still. The crude birth rate declined from 23·6 per thousand in England and Wales in 1911–15 (25·4 in Scotland) to 15·1 (17·7) in 1938. The annual number of births fell from about 1 million before 1914 to a minimum of 580,000 in 1932 and hovered around 700,000 for most of the 1930s, in spite of a larger total population. The excess of births over deaths fell to about $2\frac{1}{2}$ per thousand, or a mere 110,000 a year,[113] but on the basis of the 'net reproduction rate' of the number of girls born and likely to survive to child-bearing age to replace the existing female population of the same age group,[114] England and Wales failed to reach a rate of 1 (i.e. a long-run stationary population) from 1922 onward; in 1933 the rate fell to 0·75.

The causes for the fall in the birth rate were complex.[115] In part they lay in

---

[111] Richard M. Titmuss, *Poverty and Population* (1938), pp. 80, 102–3, 144.

[112] E.g. A. Hutt, *The Condition of the Working Class in Britain* (1933), pp. 41–2, 164; Charles Webster, 'Healthy or Hungry Thirties?', *History Workshop*, 13, 1982.

[113] A. M. Carr-Saunders, D. Caradog Jones and C. A. Moser, *A Survey of Social Conditions in England and Wales* (Oxford, 1958), chapter 2.

[114] Hubback, pp. 18–25.

[115] The best brief discussion will be found in *Royal Commission on Population. Report* (1949), chapters 4 and 5. Cf. also Hubback, *op. cit.*, Part II; Sean Glyn and John Oxborrow, *Interwar Britain: a Social and Economic History* (1976), pp. 193–204.

improved technical means and wider knowledge of methods of birth control, and in the relaxation of obedience to religious prohibition of their use; in part they were to be found in the improved status of women; in part they were the effects of the 'social example' of the upper classes which throughout this period had, on average, smaller families than the lower, and were thus ahead of them in the downward march. Some causes were economic: on the one hand, the Education Acts ensured that children had ceased to be a source of income to their families until they were near marriageable age; on the other, rising incomes made the alternatives that were available if the family size was kept down relatively more attractive.

The economic effects of these population changes worked mainly through the declining size of families, and the changed age structure of the population. The average number of live births per married woman born in 1841–5 was 5·71, and in 1861–5 it was 4·66; women married in 1900–9 had only an average of 3·37 live births, and those married in 1925–9 on 2·19.[116] As the span of life lengthened at the same time, the proportion of the lifetime spent with the children living at home was falling also, and the average family household size was falling even faster than the birth figures would indicate. Thus between 1911 and 1939, the number of families consisting of 1 or 2 persons almost doubled, from 1·9 million to 3·7 million, while the number of large families, of 5 persons or more, actually fell from 3·7 to 3·1 million.[117] As before, however, the size of family increased as one descended the social scale.

Each of this increasing number of families, demanded its separate household and thus contributed to the housing shortage and the building boom. For every adult wage-earner there was a smaller number of dependants – a potent cause of the improvement in living standards. With smaller families, married women found it easier to go out to work and could do so for a larger proportion of their married lives. The working housewife and the relative decline in the number of domestic servants for households of equivalent standing were, in turn, contributing factors to the great increase in the production of tinned foods, household gadgets, ready-made clothes, and other mass-produced consumption goods, as well as of services like laundries and restaurants.

There was a growing proportion of older people in the population, but there were ever fewer children, so that the population of working age could increase from 63·9% to 67·7% of the total population, or in absolute numbers, from 26·1 to 32·3 million. This contributed materially to the rising standard of income per head.[118] Meanwhile, among the consequences of the changing age structure were the growing burden of old-age pensions and, because of rising standards and expectation of life, the growth of private and company pension schemes, as well as the increasing rigidity which this ageing process of a whole society imposed on the economy.

These changes in population were inextricably interwoven with changes in the social structure of Britain. The decline in the birth rate, in particular, was closely connected with the relative growth in numbers of the professional and lower middle classes who tended to have smaller families than the manual

[116] *Royal Commission on Population*, Tables 15, 16 and 17.
[117] Mark Abrams, *op. cit.*, p. 41; Marsh, chapter 3.
[118] p. 150 below.

working classes. One of the major social changes in this period was, in fact, the growth of the 'white-collar' workers. This change, in turn, was a compound of two closely connected factors, the growth of the 'salariat' in industry and elsewhere, and the growth of the kind of occupations, like retail distribution, local government and entertainments, which employed a very high proportion of salaried persons.

The growth of the salaried personnel in industry is difficult to measure. One estimate puts the increase of salaried personnel in private industry between the Census years 1911 and 1931 at 1,170,000 (from 1·04 million to 2·21 million), and in public administration (including teaching) at 200,000 (from 489,000 to 687,000), or a total increase of nearly 1·4 million persons, of whom 650,000 were women.[119]

There are more reliable estimates available for the growth in the service industries and in tertiary industries generally. Table 4·7 reproduces some of the best estimates.

Table 4·7:   Industrial distribution of the working population, 1920–39

	Changes in numbers employed (000)			Average employment		
				(Chapman & Knight)††		
	1921–31 (Marsh)*	1931–9 (Frankel)**	Total change 1921–39†	1920–2	1937–8	Change 1920–2 to 1937–8
Primary industries	−466	−419	−855	2,135	1,586	−549
Secondary industries	−491	+1,050	+559	8,099	9,448	+1,349
Tertiary industries	+873	+1,210	+2,083	5,301	7,336	+2,035
All employment	−74	+1,841	+1,767	15,535	18,370	+2,835

* Marsh, *op. cit.*, p. 105; excludes defence and 'Miscellaneous'.
** H. Frankel, 'The Industrial Distribution of the Population of Great Britain in July 1939', *J. R. Stat. S.*, 108/3–4, 1945, pp. 420–1.
† A combination of the previous two columns; as they are not drawn up strictly on the same basis, this total should be taken as approximate only.
†† Agatha L. Chapman and Rose Knight, *Wages and Salaries in the United Kingdom, 1920–1938* (Cambridge, 1953), p. 18. Excludes armed forces. Cf. also Colin Clark, *National Income and Outlay* (1937), p. 38, Table 13, and *The Conditions of Economic Progress* (2nd ed., 1951), pp. 316–25; G. D. H. and M. I. Cole, *The Condition of Britain* (1937), pp. 45–9; C. W. McMahon and G. D. N. Worswick, 'The Growth of Services in the Economy 1', *District Bank Review*, No. 136, Dec. 1960.

This tendency of the growth of the service industries, and of the growth of the 'salariat' within each industry,[120] was common to all advanced countries. It

[119] J. G. Marley and H. Campion, 'Changes in Salaries in Great Britain, 1924–1939', in A. L. Bowley, *Studies in the National Income, 1924–1938* (Cambridge, 1942), p. 86; also P. S. Florence, *The Logic of British and American Industry* (1953), Table IVA, p. 139; L. Rostas, 'Industrial Production, Productivity and Distribution in Britain, Germany and the United States', *Econ. J.*, 53/20, 1943, p. 51.

[120] E. H. Phelps-Brown, *Growth of British Industrial Relations*, (1959) p. 61; also C. H. Lee, *British*

contributed a certain factor of stability to incomes, since their rate of unemployment was much lower than that of manual workers and their salaries also kept up better in the depressions (though they rose slower in the recovery, also),[121] and without it the depression would have been even worse. Moreover the growing salaried and professional groups also added to the social stability of the country, for with a birth rate below the average, they invariably largely recruited from below, offering opportunities for advancement to many ambitious and capable working-class children who might have otherwise joined the most rebellious ranks of Labour.[122]

5 The Rise in the Standard of Living

It is time to draw together the many strands of information available and weave out of them a picture of the country's economic progress. The statistics of national income have been widely used as the most general measuring rod of economic welfare since the pioneer work by Bowley, Stamp and Colin Clark. A. R. Prest's and C. H. Feinstein's more recent figures are summarized in Table 4·8.[123]

Table 4·8:   National income statistics, 1912–38

Average of years	Net national income of the UK at factor cost, £m.	Index of national income at constant (1900) prices, 1900 = 100		Net national product at 1938 factor cost 1921–4 = 100	
		National income	Income per head	Total	Per head
1912–14	2,301	118·4	106·6	(117·0)*	113·9*
1919–20	5,562	124·7	113·8	(109·4)*	104·3*
1921–4	4,020	110·6	102·4	100	100
1925–6	3,947	117·9	107·5	108·9	107·3
1927–9	4,159	130·1	117·5	116·6	113·9
1930–2	3,730	129·7	115·8	114·5	110·5
1933–5	4,006	143·1	126·1	126·5	120·5
1936–8	4,558	155·1	134·9	135·3	127·3

* Including Southern Ireland.

Regional Employment Statistics 1841–1971 (Cambridge, 1979); David Lockwood, *The Blackcoated Worker* (1958), p. 36; D. Caradog Jones, 'Some Notes on the Census of Occupations for England and Wales', *J. R. Stat. S.*, 1915, 78/1; Elie Halevy, *A History of the English People* (1926), vol. 6/1, pp. 262–5.

[121] Marley and Campion, *loc. cit.*, pp. 92–4.

[122] Lockwood, *passim*, esp. chapter 4; F. D. Klingender, *Clerical Labour in Britain* (1935).

[123] A. R. Prest, 'National Income of the United Kingdom 1870–1946', *Econ. J.*, 58/229, 1948; A. L. Bowley, *Studies in the National Income, 1924–1938* (Cambridge, 1942), esp. Table IX, p. 81; Colin Clark, *The Conditions of Economic Progress* (1951 ed.), esp. p. 63; A. L. Bowley and J. C. Stamp, *The National Income, 1924* (1927); Colin Clark, *National Income and Outlay* (1937), Table 37, p. 88, also pp. 267–9; J. B. Jeffery and D. Walters, 'National Income and Expenditure of the UK, 1870–1952', *Income and Wealth*, Series V, p. 19, Table VIII; C. H. Feinstein, *National Income,*

In spite of some apparent increases in the post-war boom, real national income (as well as income per head) had barely reached the pre-war level by 1924. Total output probably exceeded the best of the years before 1914, but it was neutralized by the loss of income from abroad owing to the sale of assets during the war. From 1925 onward a remarkable and sustained rise set in, barely held back by the depression. From the beginning of the recovery onward the rate of increase was speeded up, the late 1930s showing as much increase as the whole of the period between 1913 and the mid-1930s. This was true both of total national income, and of income per head, in real terms.

Within these totals of all incomes, real wages also rose substantially, though their rise was more evenly spread between the 1920s and the 1930s. The main changes are summarized in Table 4·9 (1930 = 100).[124]

Table 4·9:   Rise in real income of wage-earners, 1920–38

	Cost-of-living index	Index of intra-industry real earnings of wage-earners	Net real wages per full-time week (Kuczynski)	Real wage rates
1920	157·6	90·9	97·1	94·7
1924	110·8	92·3	88·3	91·9
1929	103·8	97·2	93·2	96·7
1932	91·1	105·9	102·9	106·1
1937	97·5	105·9	101·0	105·2
1938	98·7	108·7	103·9	107·0

It should be noted that these figures of real earnings depend heavily on the cost-of-living index, which was itself the subject of much debate. After stagnation in the early 1920s,[125] real wages rose by about 10% to 1930 and continued to rise in the depression years, remaining almost stationary for the rest of the 1930s.

This picture would be strongly modified by the incidence of unemployment. It is, in particular, to a large extent the improved employment position which caused the national income to rise in the late 1930s while real wages per head of employed worker remained constant. Further, if the earnings of the men in work were spread over the whole of the working class, including those out of work, the date at which the high wages of 1913 were being earned again would be postponed from 1927 to 1930, and would put the post-war peak of 1937 at a bare 5%, instead of 13%, above the 1913 real wage rate.[126] Some observers,

Expenditure and Output of the United Kingdom, 1855–1965 (Cambridge, 1972), T. 15–16, 121; H. W. Richardson, *Economic Recovery in Britain, 1932–9* (1967), pp. 36 ff.

[124] A. L. Chapman and Rose Knight, *Wages and Salaries in the United Kingdom, 1920–1938* (Cambridge, 1953), Tables 11, 14, pp. 30–3; J. Kuczynski, *A Short History of Labour Conditions in Great Britain, 1750 to the Present Day* (1946 ed.), p. 120; last column based on E. C. Ramsbottom. 'The Course of Wage Rates in the United Kingdom, 1921–1934', *J. R. Stat. S.*, 98/4, 1935, 'Wage Rates in the United Kingdom, 1934–1937', *ibid.*, 101/1, 1938, and 'Wage Rates in the United Kingdom in 1938', *ibid.*, 102/2, 1939.

[125] E. V. Morgan, *Studies in British Financial Policy, 1914–25* (1952), pp. 284–6.

[126] J. Kuczynski, *Labour Conditions*, p. 120; cf. also G. D. H. Cole and R. Postgate, *The Common People, 1746–1938* (1938), chapter 49.

however, expressed the more optimistic view that 'the British (working-class) consumer, in fact, has for several years been getting the best of both worlds. From 1929 to 1932 the fall in prices outweighed to his advantage the fall in employment. And from 1933 to 1937 the rise in employment outweighed to his advantage the rise in prices.'[127] Most estimates put the increase in real weekly wages between the pre-war years and 1937–8 at between 20% and 33%, while the working day was shorter by about one hour.[128]

The rise in living standards, and especially in real incomes of the working classes, was the outcome of several factors, some of which have been discussed already. Among them was the increase in output per man-hour,[129] the improvement in the terms of trade,[130] and an increase in the proportion of the national product consumed.[131] Other relevant factors were a change in the age structure,[132] an increase in the proportion of salaried, i.e. higher-paid, employees, and a slight tendency towards greater equality in incomes. The main factor working in the opposite direction, and cancelling a large part of these advantages, was the heavy increase in unemployment.[133]

Before the war, a large part, perhaps one-half, of the long-term increase in real wages had been due simply to a shift of wage-earners into better jobs, but in the inter-war years this effect was negligible.[134] Instead, there was a marked shift into salaried occupations, and in spite of their low remuneration in some cases,[135] this shift normally meant an increase in weekly pay.

Lastly, real wages may have risen because of a redistribution of income in favour of wage-earners. If the often observed constancy of the wage bill as a proportion of total national income around the 40% mark is compared with the steadily falling proportion of wage earners in the total occupied population, from 74·1% in 1913 to 71·4% in 1938, according to Phelps-Brown and Hart, there must have been a relative rise in their income. Against this, Atkinson noted the relative fall of skilled wages (incomes of all groups = 100) from 131 in 1913/14 to 121 in 1935/6, and of semi-skilled from 85 to 83, only the unskilled rising slightly from 78 to 80. The fastest rising groups were managers and administrators (247 to 272) and foremen (152 to 169).[136]

As far as the distribution of property was concerned, however, heavy progressive death duties and direct taxation did little more than counteract the

---

[127] *Economist*, 1.1.1938, p. 14; also in G. D. A. MacDougall, 'General Survey, 1929–1937', in *Britain in Recovery* (1938), pp. 26–7.

[128] E. H. Phelps-Brown, *The Growth of British Industrial Relations* (1959), p. 345; W. A. Lewis, *Economic Survey, 1919 1939* (1949), p. 139; J. A. Dowie, '1919–20 is in Need of Attention', *Ec. Hist. Rev.*, 28/3, 1975.

[129] p. 38 above.

[130] p. 90 above.

[131] p. 116 above.

[132] p. 147 above.

[133] Section 1 of this chapter. Cf. also A. E. Kahn, *Great Britain in the World Economy* (New York, 1946), p. 265.

[134] A. L. Bowley, *Wages and Incomes in the UK since 1860* (Cambridge, 1937), Appx. C; Chapman and Knight, *op. cit.*, pp. 33–4.

[135] A. Hutt, *The Condition of the Working Class in Britain* (1933), chapter 8.

[136] E. H. Phelps-Brown and P. E. Hart, 'The Share of Wages in the National Income', *Econ. J.*, 62/246, 1952. pp. 276–7; A. B. Atkinson, *The Economics of Inequality* (Oxford, 1983), p. 97; Clark, *National Income*, pp. 94, 100–1, 125; Bowley, *Studies in the National Income*, pp. 56–8; Chapman and Knight, pp. 18–23; Feinstein, *National Income*, T. 45.

tendency of the economic system to work in favour of those owning capital. According to estate duty returns, in 1911–13, 96·9% of persons owning property owned under £1,000 each, and in 1936–8 the figure was still 93·0%. At the other end of the scale, 0·4% of property owners owned 55·6% of the total capital in 1911–13, and in 1936–8, 0·95% of owners owned 55·68% of the capital. By another calculation, the share of the wealth of the top 1% of owners (England and Wales) fell from 61% to 55% between 1923 and 1938, and of the top 10%, from 82% to 77%.[137]

In sum, there was in this period an appreciable rise in the standards of comfort and welfare of working-class families, particularly those in which the wage-earners were in regular employment. This conclusion is supported by the increase in small savings: accounts in Trustee Savings Banks increased from 1·9 million in 1914 to 2·48 million in 1939, and in the Post Office Savings from 9·2 million to 11·6 million, perhaps three-quarters of these being held by members of the working class.[138] It is also supported by the significant change in the pattern of working-class expenditure, as shown in the budgets used by the Ministry of Labour, after large-scale sample inquiries, for its cost-of-living index.[139] Moreover, statistics fail to take full account of the difference made by electricity instead of candles, and gas cookers instead of coal or coke ranges, as standard equipment in working-class homes; of improved housing, including indoor water and sanitation; or of radio, the cinema and newspapers within almost everybody's reach. A most significant pointer was the adoption, in 1938, of one week's paid holiday as standard practice, after the report of Lord Amulree's Committee on Holidays with Pay,[140] in all the industries in which conditions were governed by Trade Boards or Agricultural Wage Boards. Up to 1937, paid holidays were granted to around 4 millions out of the 18½ millions earning £250 a year or less; in 1939 it was 11 millions, or the large majority, though few of these had the resources or experience as yet to spend their holidays away from home.[141]

Within the basic food bill itself, there was a decline in the consumption of the cheap filler and substitute foods, while the consumption of foodstuffs of which the demand was highly elastic with respect to income, or which were considered semi-luxuries, increased rapidly. The consumption of wheat, for example, fell from 4·28 lb. per head per week in 1910–14 to 4·05 lb. in 1924 and 3·77 lb. in 1938. Other foods are shown in Table 4·10.[142]

[137] H. Campion, *Public and Private Property in Great Britain* (1939); Atkinson, *Economics*, p. 168; Kathleen M. Langley, 'The Distribution of Capital in Private Hands, 1936–1938 and 1946–1947', *Bull. Oxf. Inst. Stat.*, 12/12, 1950. Table on p. 355 and 13/2, 1951, pp. 45–7; G. W. Daniels and H. Campion, *The Distribution of the National Capital* (Manchester, 1936); G. D. H. and M. I. Cole, *The Condition of Britain* (1937), p. 75; C. L. Mowat, *Britain Between the Wars* (1956 ed.), p. 494.

[138] pp. 117–8 above, also Paul Johnson, 'Credit and Thrift in the British Working Class, 1870–1939', in Jay Winter, *The Working Class in Modern British History* (Cambridge, 1983), pp. 165–7; G. D. H. Cole, *Money, Trade and Investment* (1954), pp. 220–1; Esme Preston, 'Personal Savings Through Institutional Channels (1937–1949)', *Bull. Oxf. Inst. Stat.*, 12/9, 1950, Table 7, p. 252; Henry Durant and J. Goldmann, 'The Distribution of Working-Class Savings', *ibid.*, 7/1, 1945.

[139] Table 3·1 above.

[140] Cmd. 5724 (1938).

[141] C. L. Mowat, *Britain Between the Wars* (1956 ed.), pp. 500–1; Phelps-Brown, *op. cit.*, pp. 347–8; Elizabeth Brunner, *Holiday Making and Holiday Trades* (1945), pp. 9, 13–15; J. A. R. Pimlott, *The Englishman's Holiday* (1947), pp. 214–15.

[142] Stone, *Consumers' Expenditure*, Tables 10, 21, 35, 45, 53, 109, 116; H. V. Edwards, 'Flour Milling', in *Further Studies in Industrial Organisation* (1948), ed. M. P. Forgarty, p. 77.

Table 4·10:   Changes in food consumption, 1920–38

	Annual consumption	
	1920–2	1937–8
Potatoes (tons per head)	0·083	0·074
Fresh milk (mn. gall.)	848	1,000
Cream (mn. gall.)	3·22	9·19
Eggs (mn.)	3,915	9,385
Soft drinks (mn. gall.)	1·72	5·79
Sugar, chocolate, confectionery (mn. tons)	1·06	1.53

The improvement in the general standard of nutrition is shown in the increase in the consumption of calories per head from 3,057 a day in 1901–13 to 3,139 in 1924–8 and 3,398 in 1937–8. Other indices are shown in Table 4·11.[143]

Table 4·11:   Nutrients available per head per day in the UK

	Average 1920–2	Average 1937–8
Protein (g.)	87·2	90·55
Fat (g.)	127·1	152·9
Carbohydrates (g.)	413·0	414·95
Calcium (mg.)	754	815
Vitamin A (i.u.)	3,616	4,749
„ B_1 (mg.)	1·31	1·375
„ C (Mg.)	118 0	135 5
Riboflavin (mg.)	1·71	1·90

Yet, in the face of all this indubitable progress, there were still enormous areas of poverty left, much preventible misery and illness and many premature deaths. In part, it was the greatly enlarged and more detailed knowledge of the poor and their problems which brought these tasks more urgently before the public eye. Apart from the official statistics, the best-known social surveys in this period were those for London, Merseyside, Southampton, York, Tyneside, Becontree and Dagenham, Brynmawr, Bristol and Sheffield.[144] The inquiries in York and London could be directly compared with the pre-war surveys, and this was also the case in the less ambitious survey made by A. L. Bowley in five Midland towns.[145]

'Primary poverty', poverty so great that the lack of the necessary food and

[143] Stone, *op. cit.*, Table 61; John Boyd Orr, *Food, Health and Income* (2nd ed., 1937), pp. 24–5.

[144] H. A. Mess, *Industrial Tyneside: a Social Survey* (1928); Sir H. Llewellyn Smith (Director), *The New Survey of London Life and Labour* (9 vols., 1930–5); P. Ford, *Work and Wealth in a Modern Port: an Economic Survey of Southampton* (1934); B. Seebohm Rowntree, *Poverty and Progress* (1941); D. Caradog Jones, *Social Survey of Merseyside* (3 vols. Liverpool, 1934); Terence Young, *Becontree and Dagenham* (1934); Hilda Jennings, *Brynmawr: A Study of a Distressed Area* (1934); Herbert Tout, *Standard of Living in Bristol* (Bristol, 1938); A. D. K. Owen, *Housing Problem in Sheffield* (Sheffield, 1931), *Unemployment in Sheffield* (Sheffield, 1932), *Juvenile Employment and Welfare in Sheffield* and *Standard of Living in Sheffield* (Sheffield, 1933); and, in general, A. F. Wells, *The Local Social Survey in Great Britain* (1935).

[145] A. L. Bowley and A. R. Burnett-Hurst, *Livelihood and Poverty* (1915), and A. L. Bowley and M. H. Hoggs, *Has Poverty Diminished?* (1925).

shelter actually impaired health and efficiency, occurred in York, in 1899, among 15·46% of the working classes, and in 1936 among 6·8%. In practice, human psychological needs would demand more than this bare physical minimum,[146] and a realistic standard would require a rather higher income level to meet some non-necessities as well as the minimum physical needs – the 'poverty line'. In York in 1936, 31·1% of working-class families (or 17·7% of the total population) fell below this line, and in Bristol in 1937 (a boom year), 10·7% of working-class families fell below it. In the other surveys, the 'poverty standard' differed. The London Survey used a lower figure, according to which 9·8% of the London working-class families lived in poverty in 1928, another good year. On the same standard, the proportion of Merseyside (1929), was 17·3%, in Liverpool (1929) 16·1% and in Southampton (1931) 20·0%. On the Rowntree standard, the Merseyside proportion would have been about 30%. On a different, even more rigorous physical needs standard, the Pilgrim Trust found 30% of the long-term unemployed to be in poverty, and another 14% just above it.[147]

A different study in this field was made by John (Lord) Boyd Orr in 1936,[148] who showed that as much as half the population was bound to have diets deficient in some respects even in the most prosperous years of the 1930s: the food consumption of the lower-income groups would have to rise by 12–25% before it became sufficient for maintaining perfect health.[149]

Tragically, the families with large numbers of children suffered most. 'The incidence of poverty', stated the Report to the Pilgrim Trust,[150] 'is progressively greater according to the number of children under working age in the family concerned.' In York, Rowntree found that while only 31·1% of the working-class population lived below the poverty line, 52·5% of the children under one and 49·7% of the children from one to five did so. It was out of considerations of this kind that a strong movement, led by Eleanor Rathbone, demanded family allowances for all.[151]

The causes of poverty were essentially the same as before 1914: the interruption of the earning power of the main breadwinner owing to illness, to casual type of work, or, above all, to unemployment; an inadequate wage; and a large family of dependants. Several of these causes could be present at the same time. There had been progress, but there was still much poverty. It was not the least of the consequences of the Second World War that the hopes and dreams of the small minority with the most sensitive social conscience in the 1930s became acceptable as social legislation to the large majority after 1945.

[146] G. D. H. and M. I. Cole, *Conditions of Britain*, pp. 134–8.
[147] Pilgrim Trust *Men Without Work* (Cambridge, 1938), p. 109.
[148] J. Boyd Orr, *Food, Health and Income* (1936, 2nd ed. 1937); also Sir George Newman, *The Building of a Nation's Health* (1939), pp. 352–9.
[149] *Op. cit.*, p. 11.
[150] Mark Abrams, *The Condition of the British People, 1911–1945* (1945), pp. 99 ff.
[151] See esp. E. F. Rathbone, *The Disinherited Family* (1924, new ed. 1949), and Mary Stocks, *Eleanor Rathbone* (1949), chapter 8.

5

The British Economy in Total War, 1939–1945

1 The War Economy and Economic Planning

The outbreak of the Second World War in September 1939 found the British Government prepared to a much greater extent for the policies of economic control than it had been in 1914. From the early 1930s on, several Government departments had been engaged in preparing elaborate war plans, and some of the necessary legislation was passed within a few days of the declaration of war. Some of the very officials chosen to implement economic war policy in 1939–40 were the same persons who had administered the controls of 1917–18. As a result many of the earlier errors were avoided.

Thus it was understood in 1939 that the apparatus of control would have to reach back far beyond the munitions industry.[1] Again, the authorities were aware that they had to enlist the voluntary support of labour, particularly in the munitions and other essential industries. Other lessons of value carried over from the first war to the second included the methods of civilian food rationing, and the Schedule of Reserved Occupations evolved in the 1930s, on the basis of the Schedule of Protected Occupations of the earlier war, to prevent the call-up of key workers.[2]

Nevertheless, it seems in retrospect that many lessons that ought to have been learnt had been forgotten, or were applied too late after great and unnecessary cost. The control of civilian trade and consumption, the control over the foreign exchanges and capital movements, the control over labour demand and supply, rationing of food and the expansion of munition-making and machine tool capacity all appeared as belated measures forced on the Government by the march of events rather than as orderly stages of the creation of a war economy. Even some specific errors of the First World War were repeated, including a rash over-recruitment from the mines, resulting in a fuel shortage later, an agricultural expansion programme neglecting the importance of saving the bulkiest imports, and an over-optimistic assessment of shipping needs and resources which seriously endangered military operations and civilian supplies at several critical points during the war.

There was a certain basic similarity between the two World Wars, as far as

---

[1] E.g. I. Bowen and G. D. N. Worswick, 'The Controls and War Finance' (1940), in Oxford Institute of Statistics, *Studies in War Economics* (Oxford, 1947).

[2] W. K. Hancock and M. M. Gowing, *British War Economy* (1949), pp. 48 ff. The present section is based largely on that work, which forms the central volume in the Official History of the Second World War, United Kingdom Civil Series (HSWW), as well as on the other volumes in that series. An excellent summary of Hancock and Gowing will be found in the form of chapter 5 of A. J. Youngson, *The British Economy, 1920–1957* (1960).

British economic strategy was concerned. Both wars were fought against a well-prepared Germany at the head of a continental coalition, while Britain and her Allies, entering the war far less prepared, depended on their command of the world's resources outside Europe to build up gradually a power superior to Germany's with which to crush her after weakening her by means of an economic blockade. But here the similarity ends, for not only were there technical changes, such as the vulnerability of Britain to serious air attacks, but whereas in the First World War the position of the chief belligerents in the west was never seriously threatened, the Second World War, besides the much greater part played in it by non-European battlefields, witnessed several startling reverses of fortune, including the fall of France and the successive entry of Soviet Russia, the USA and Japan into the war. Each of these imposed major changes of economic policy, so that the economic history of this period is best treated in the light of the needs of these successive phases of the war, rather than as a gradually emergent controlled economy, as in 1914–18.

Four main phases of the war may be distinguished. The first period, the 'phoney war', was essentially a period of waiting and preparation by the Allies, apparently secure behind the Channel and the Maginot line. It was shattered by the German invasion and occupation of Norway, Denmark, Holland, Belgium and part of France, and the period ended with the evacuation of the British Expeditionary Force from Dunkirk. The second period ran from the summer of 1940 to the Japanese attack on Pearl Harbor in December 1941. It began with the air 'Battle of Britain' which thwarted a German invasion of these shores, and continued as a war of attrition by air attacks and attacks on British merchant shipping. Germany also consolidated her power in the Mediterranean and seriously threatened the British positions in the Middle East. This was the period when Britain virtually stood alone and prospects seemed bleakest. Even the German attack in the east in the summer of 1941, which was ultimately to prove so disastrous to the Axis powers, gave no immediate relief to Britain who, on the contrary, made some of her scarce resources available to her new Russian ally.

With the entry of the USA into the war in December 1941 ultimate victory for the Allies seemed again a reasonable hope, but meanwhile the third phase of the war, which lasted until the invasion of Normandy in June 1944, had opened disastrously with the sinkings at Pearl Harbor, withdrawals in the Middle East, the loss of much of South-Eastern Asia to the Japanese and severe shipping losses in the Atlantic. Further, in the first year the entry of America increased rather than relieved the pressure on the British economy, for American Lend-Lease shipments were reduced in favour of American mobilization, and much valuable British tonnage was diverted to the use of the American services. It took some time for the vast productive potential of the USA to be converted into actual munitions, but when these began to come off the production lines, North Africa was invaded and cleared of the enemy, and Allied landings in Italy were paralleled by the Russian counter-offensives in the east and victorious American actions in the Pacific.

The fourth phase was ushered in by the invasion of Normandy by British and American forces after the Allies had established superiority at sea and in the air. Despite the successful establishment of a bridgehead in the west, and the advance of the Red Army in the east, the war against Germany, contrary to expectations, dragged on until May 1945, causing great strain on the Allied transport system. By contrast, the fighting against Japan, estimated to take 12–18 months after 'VE-day', was over in a few weeks, thanks largely to the grim destruction wrought by the atom bombs on Hiroshima and Nagasaki.

In the late 1930s the only significant concrete action by Britain was the possibly decisive expansion of aircraft building capacity under the programmes of 1936 and after.[3] Even the eleventh-hour suggestion by Sir Arthur Salter of stockpiling certain strategic raw materials was made too late to bring tangible results before the declaration of war on 3 September 1939.[4]

This declaration, it is true, was accompanied by a formidable array of legislation, prepared beforehand. The Emergency Powers (Defence) Act, 1939, had been passed on 24 August and gave the most far-reaching powers to the Government; in addition, some 60 other statutes were passed in the early weeks of the war. By 1 September several new Ministries had been created, including the Ministries of Supply, of Economic Warfare, of Home Security, of Information, of Food and of Shipping, united in May 1941 with Transport to become the Ministry of War Transport. Recruitment was added to the duties of the Ministry of Labour, which thus became the Ministry of Labour and National Service and as such played one of the central parts in the combined economic and military strategy of the war. There were also innumerable co-ordinating, planning and emergency committees and boards established at an early date.

The crucial role of converting industry to a war footing was intended for the Ministry of Supply. In the event, since the Admiralty hung on to its control over shipbuilding[5] and the RAF over aircraft, the Ministry of Supply was restricted to supplying the Army, and a limited range of arms and stores to the other two Services. In 1940 the Ministry of Aircraft Production was set up, occupying the centre of the stage in the critical summer months of 1940, and continuing as the third supply department thereafter.[6]

There was thus a great deal of administrative activity, but there was as yet little to show for it. Government expenditure ran at £20 million a week at the outbreak of war and was still only £33½ million weekly in the sixth month, and much of that increase was due to price rises. The production of munitions was nowhere near the limits of physical capacity. Control over foreign exchange was still lax, and there was still freedom of payments within the Sterling Area until May 1940.[7]

The numbers in the Services had risen from 480,000 in June 1939 to 1,850,000 at the end of March 1940, but there were still 1 million unemployed in April 1940, and little consideration was as yet given to a planned allocation of manpower. Similarly, there was no serious rationing of shipping space, and the

[3] P. W. S. Andrews and E. Brunner, *Life of Lord Nuffield* (Oxford, 1955), Part IV, chapter 6; PEP, *Engineering Reports II: Motor Vehicles* (1950), pp. 39–40.

[4] J. Hurstfield, *The Control of Raw Materials* (HSWW, 1953), p. 79, Appx. I, pp. 427–30, also his 'Control of Raw Material Supplies, 1919–1939', *Ec. Hist. Rev.*, 14/1–2, 1944, pp. 25–6.

[5] J. D. Scott and Richard Hughes, *The Administration of War Production* (HSWW, 1955), pp. 140–7, 213–16.

[6] Scott and Hughes, Part IV.

[7] T. Balogh, 'The Drift Towards a Rational Foreign Exchange Policy', *Economica*, NS, 7/27, 1940, and 'Foreign Exchange and Export Trade Policy', *Econ. J.*, 50/197, 1940; R. F. Harrod, *The Life of John Maynard Keynes* (1951), pp. 494 ff.

production of many inessentials continued unhindered.[8] Since so many resources were still not fully employed, there appeared to be as yet no need of general economic planning, and departments pursued their own policies, even competing for the same scarce resources without co-ordination with their neighbours. Only the pace of mobilization was co-ordinated: soldiers were conscripted only at the leisurely rate at which they could be equipped.[9] 'Reflecting upon this first period of the war, the historian finds himself oppressed by a feeling of lost opportunity.'[10]

One main preoccupation of the Government at this stage was the rise in the cost of living, but since in the official index, certain foods were heavily over-weighted, it was possible by food subsidies on some of these items to make a considerable impact on keeping down the cost-of-living *index*.[11] From this beginning was gradually built up a consistent policy of large-scale subsidy for items within the working-class cost-of-living index, and of heavy taxation of goods outside it.

By April–May 1940 the growing impact of mobilization was beginning to affect the economy at several points at once. The engineering industry, as the basis of the munitions industry, began to feel a shortage of skilled workers as well as of machine tools, a large proportion of which had to be imported; there was a drain on the foreign exchange reserves and a consequent need to divert resources to exports; there was need to build up stocks, in the face of a growing shipping shortage. These and other pressures were on the point of enforcing their own logic of a more thorough-going system of economic control, when the German offensive, ending in the collapse of France, completely shattered the long-term timetable to which the British war economy had been geared.

The debacle in the west led to the replacement of Chamberlain's Conservative Ministry by a Coalition Government led by Winston Churchill, which could pursue and enforce policies of a harshness which its predecessor would not have dared to contemplate. The British people as a whole had been shocked into a willingness to work and to bear privations inconceivable before May 1940. The isolation of Britain in Europe brought the realities of the war home also to the American people to a sufficient extent to permit President Roosevelt to authorize aid culminating in Lend-Lease in March 1941.[12] At the same time, Britain benefited by the end of the need to supply France with scarce coal, and the addition to shipping tonnage under British control as Norwegian, Dutch and other masters sought refuge in ports in Allied hands.

All these, however, were minor advantages compared with the strategic and economic problems posed by the devastating military reverse. Britain lay open to German bombing by air, especially of communications and war industries. The dangers to shipping were immeasurably increased, and the east coast ports had to be closed to the larger vessels, blocking up still further the bottlenecks at the west coast ports. The supply of several important raw materials, including high-grade iron ore, was cut off. The hope of strangling Germany by blockade

[8] E. L. Hargreaves and M. M. Gowing, *Civil Industry and Trade* (HSWW, 1952), pp. 16–18.
[9] M. M. Postan, *British War Production* (HSWW, 1952), p. 102.
[10] Hancock and Gowing, p. 149.
[11] H. M. D. Parker, *Manpower, a Study of War-Time Policy and Administration* (HSWW, 1957), p. 82; R. S. Sayers, *Financial Policy, 1939–1945* (HSWW, 1956), pp. 63–4.
[12] R. D. Hall, *North American Supply* (HSWW, 1955), p. 127.

was converted into an immediate danger of a blockade of this country, carried out by U-boats, mines and aircraft.[13] Meanwhile, contrary to Britain's tradition, she had for the first time to build up a large army, while strengthening the equipment of the other two Services also. The hastily improvised economic controls made necessary by these calamities were only slowly built up into an integrated system in the following years.

In the midst of the air Battle of Britain, the building of aircraft became number one priority and, by the orders of the new Minister of Aircraft Production, Lord Beaverbrook, in view of the threatening invasion, the projects that could be completed quickly had overriding priority claims to all resources. The air battle was won by such means, but only at the expense of disrupting long-term mobilization plans. From the autumn of 1940 onward, however, great strides were made in techniques of planning as well as in methods of financial control. By 1941, the economy as a whole began to be planned, rationed and allocated, and integrated with the flow of money payments by the new statistical analysis contained in the first white paper on national income and expenditure.[14]

Economists and statisticians in favour of the national income approach were employed in increasing numbers in key departmental posts. Keynes himself had become economic adviser to the Treasury in 1940.[15] One of the earliest lessons they taught was the interchangeable nature of scarce resources. Thus, for example, food could be brought in from North America, a short trip using little tonnage, but costly in hard currency, or it could be brought in from Australia, using only sterling currency, but much more costly in tonnage. Scarce shipping and scarce foreign exchange were thus substitutes for one another up to a point, and since both could be saved by employing more labour in home agriculture to raise British home output, scarce labour could be used as a substitute for both.

A second principle was also established as a result of the experience of the aircraft programme of the summer of 1940. 'Priorities' as a method of control had proved utterly unsuitable, except for the occasional crash programme, for often the higher-priority product was produced only at great cost in terms of another product, only slightly less essential. Instead, a system of allocation was evolved, which ensured to each department, and each manufacturer, a designated quantum of supplies, the total allocation being equivalent to the total quantity available.[16] The necessary knowledge and authority to make such a system work[17] led to the evolution of many new statistical services and methods, while the Production Executive, a Committee of the War Cabinet under the Lord President of the Council, emerged as the main arbiter on planning.[18] In February 1942, the Ministry of Production was created as a further co-ordinating agency.

[13] W. N. Medlicott, *The Economic Blockade,* vol. 1 (HSWW, 1952), chapter 12.

[14] Hancock and Gowing, p. 152. See pp. 172–5 below.

[15] U. K. Hicks, *Public Finance* (1947), p. 41; Harrod, *Life of Keynes,* pp. 501–3; D. N. Chester, 'The Central Machinery for Economic Policy', in *Lessons of the British War Economy* (Cambridge, 1951).

[16] Hurstfield, *op. cit.,* pp. 89 ff; Postan, pp. 159–61.

[17] Hargreaves and Gowing, chapter 13.

[18] Postan, pp. 142 ff., 248 ff., Scott and Hughes, Part 5; also Gilbert Walker, *Economic Planning by Programme and Control in Great Britain* (1957), chapter 3; E. A. G. Robinson, 'The Overall Allocation of Resources', E. Devons, 'The Problem of Co-ordination in Aircraft Production', R. Pares, 'The Work of a Departmental Priority Office', in *Lessons of the British War Economy.*

There was, in all this, little direct control of industry, though powers existed for it. Apart from the State-owned Royal Ordnance factories, which at their peak employed 300,000 workers,[19] the dockyards and the 170 'agency' factories, the Government did not own any enterprises itself. It had immediate direction of some basic industries and services, such as the railways or the ports, and it gave some detailed directives elsewhere, as in the 'concentration' schemes for less essential industries, organized by the Board of Trade in 1941.[20] But by and large private managements were left in control of their firms, being made to conform to central plans indirectly, by allocations of raw materials[21] and labour, by licensing of capital equipment and maintenance, by controlled prices and by taxes.

Similarly, in spite of the unrestricted powers of conscription of workers, and in spite of the fact that the manpower budget and allocation became the central planning tool, labour was not normally individually conscripted, the selective coalmining scheme of August 1943, yielding 22,000 as 'Bevin boys' to the mines, being perhaps the most spectacular exception. Under the Essential Works Order and the Registration for Employment Order, SR & O (1941), Nos. 302 and 368, workers could be sent to, or kept in, essential industries or occupations but generally kept the freedom to choose their employer.

Moreover, there were no full and self-consistent economic plans made for each period *ab initio*: instead, the system was to 'allocate upon the user basis for preceding periods, modified where necessary by changes in the requirements or supply situations'.[22] Some sectors, retail distribution being perhaps the most important, could not be controlled at all for the purpose of yielding up resources (other than labour) for the war effort.[23]

Nevertheless, the mechanism evolved was capable of mobilizing the British economy to an extent unmatched by any other belligerent.[24] As far as manpower was concerned, for example, Britain mobilized between mid-1939 and the peak period of September 1943, no fewer than $8\frac{1}{2}$ million insured persons (18% of the total population) for the Forces, the auxiliary Forces, and the munitions industries, beside some 400,000 workers past insurable age, 160,000 from Ireland (North and South), many thousands of other immigrants and refugees, and ultimately 224,000 prisoners of war. $4\frac{3}{4}$ million were drawn from civilian industries, $1\frac{1}{4}$ million from among the unemployed, and $2\frac{1}{2}$ million from formerly non-industrial classes, mainly housewives and domestic workers.[25] These shifts, in

[19] William Hornby, *Factories and Plant* (HSWW, 1958), p. 89; P. Inman, *Labour in the Munitions Industries* (HSWW, 1957), p. 180.

[20] Board of Trade, *Concentration of Production* (1941. Cmd. 6258); Hargreaves and Gowing, chapter 10; G. D. N. Worswick, 'Concentration in the Leicester Hosiery Industry', *Bull. Oxf. Inst. Stat.*, 3/6, 1941, and 'Concentration, Success or Failure?' *ibid.*, 3/16, 1941; G. C. Allen, 'The Concentration of Production Policy', in D. N. Chester (ed.), *Lessons of the British War Economy*.

[21] W. Ashworth, *Contracts and Finance* (HSWW, 1953), pp. 41 ff.

[22] Hurstfield, *op. cit.*, p. 95.

[23] Henry Smith, *Retail Distribution* (2nd ed., 1948), p. 145, chapter 6; J. B. Jefferys, *Retail Trading in Britain, 1850–1950* (Cambridge, 1954), chapter 3; H. Levy, *Retail Trade Associations* (1942), chapter 19; Board of Trade, *Reports of the Retail Trade Committee* (1941–2).

[24] C. T. Saunders, 'Manpower Distribution 1939–1945: Some International Comparisons', *Manchester School*, 14/2, 1946, p. 19; Scott Newton and Dilwyn Porter, *Modernization Frustrated* (1988), chapter 4; A. J. Brown, *Applied Economics* (1947), p. 23.

[25] Ministry of Labour and National Service, *Report for the Years 1939–1946* (1947. Cmd. 7225), pp. 4, 54–7; Sir Godfrey Ince, 'The Mobilisation of Manpower in Great Britain for the Second

turn, caused other complex shifts and replacements, from jobs of lesser war importance to jobs of greater importance. There were also the special schemes of allocating scarce craftsmen, the geographical transfer of factories from scarce labour areas to areas of surplus labour, the dilution of skills and re-designing of jobs, and many other adjustments.[26]

Similarly, with a shipping tonnage scarcely above the pre-war level,[27] and far less effective because of the convoy system and congestion at the ports, Britain succeeded in supplying the booming munitions and other industries with raw materials, in transporting and supplying troops to distant theatres of war, in sending convoys to Russia, in transporting American troops and their supplies to this country, and in launching the sea-borne invasions of North Africa, Italy, Southern France and, finally, Normandy, while feeding the home population better in many respects than it had been fed before the war.[28]

Again, rationing required a major planning effort in itself, and extended to food and clothing, as well as furniture and furnishing,[29] the total calculated not to exceed available supplies. It was supported by agricultural planning on the one hand, and by the unique British 'utility' scheme for clothing and furniture on the other, the latter begun under SR & O (1941), No. 1281, and quickly spreading, to permit control of standards, of prices and of supplies of materials to the producers.[30]

The entry of America into the war in its third phase did not permit any relaxation of the tight control over the British economy but required complex schemes of co-ordination and mutual aid.[31] By 1943–4, the USA supplied about one-quarter of the munitions need of the Empire, the United Kingdom still supplying well over 60%,[32] but nevertheless this co-ordination was not without its own difficulties for Britain. The method of Lend-Lease put Britain in a position where she could not order, merely request, and her requests were subjected to disconcerting amendment as a result of simultaneous demands by the American Services. As far as shipping was concerned, while in 1942 the losses were sustained by the British mercantile marine, the additions were made to the American, and the summer months of 1942 saw the most serious shipping crisis of the war.

From the autumn of 1943 onward, in the last phase of the war, the Allied output of aircraft, ships, tanks, vehicles and guns had become so vastly greater

---

World War', *Manchester School*, 14/1, 1946; M. Kalecki, 'Labour in the War Industries of Britain and the USA' (1943), in Oxford Inst. of Statistics, *Studies in War Economics*; Alan Bullock, *The Life and Times of Ernest Bevin II: Minister of Labour 1940–1945* (1967).

[26] P. Inman, *Labour in the Munitions Industries; Statistics Relating to the War Effort of the United Kingdom* (1944, Cmd. 6564), section 1.

[27] E.g. Central Statistical Office, *Statistical Digest of the War* (HSWW, 1951), Table 70.

[28] C. B. A. Behrens, *Merchant Shipping and the Demands of War* (HSWW, 1955), chapters 12–17.

[29] L. Robbins, *The Economic Problem in Peace and War* (1947), pp. 7–8; W. B. Reddaway, 'Rationing', in *Lessons of the British War Economy*, p. 191.

[30] H. E. Wadsworth, 'Utility Cloth and Clothing Scheme', *Rev. Econ. Studies*, 16(2)/40, 1949–50; E. L. Hargreaves, 'Price Control of (Non-food) Consumer Goods', *Oxf. Econ. P.*, No. 8, 1947; M. Kalecki, 'Rationing and Price Control', *Bull. Oxf. Inst. Stat.*, 6/2, 1944 (also in *Studies in War Economics*); P. Ady, 'Utility Goods', *ibid.*, 4/15, 1942; H. A. Silverman, 'The Boot and Shoe Industry', in *Studies in Industrial Organisation* (1946), p. 230.

[31] H. D. Hall and C. C. Wrigley, *Studies of Overseas Supply* (HSWW, 1956), chapters 4–6.

[32] R. G. D. Allen, 'Mutual Aid Between the US and the British Empire, 1941–5', *J. R. Stat. S.*, 109/3, 1946, p. 268.

than that of the Axis powers, that production had ceased to be a problem, and the main problem was to come to grips with the enemy to make the superiority effective. In Britain there could still be no relaxation, however. Manpower began to be transferred from industry to the Forces, and production and strategic allocations were afoot to deal with Japan, as well as with the reconstruction and export needs of the first years of peace. The manpower budget for the first year after Victory in Europe, for example, calculated that there would be an estimated shortfall of 800,000 workers.

2 Industry in the War Years

Britain being within easy reach of German aircraft and missiles, there was much direct damage to industry caused by bombing, and indirect damage caused by the necessary air raid precautions and salvaging operations. But beyond these, and in the long run more decisive, was the enforced consumption of capital by the enforced neglect of replacement and upkeep.

According to official estimates, annual net non-war capital formation in the United Kingdom fell from £214 million in 1938 to about £ − 1,000 million (capital consumption) in 1940–5, or from 5% of net national income to − 12%.[33] This in spite of the enormous increase in the stock of capital in certain key industries, especially the sums invested by the Government which contributed to the fact that by 1947 the stock of plant and machinery was equal to, or higher than, before the war (see Table 5·1).[34]

Table 5·1:   Plant and machinery in 1947, (£million in constant 1948 prices)

	Gross		Net	
	End 1938	End 1947	End 1938	End 1947
All plant and machinery	6964	7404	3759	3737
Manufacturing and distribution only	4141	4346	2127	2234

The losses were incurred elsewhere and were to be found, beside the housing sector, in the neglect of railway maintenance, the over-felling of timber or the selective working of the easiest coal seams. The lack of opportunity of industrial training among the men and women drafted into the Forces must be reckoned an additional capital loss.

War caused a violent twist to the allocation of resources, affecting different industries very differently. Those which catered mainly for civilian demands were cut down drastically and those which were considered unnecessary even for civilian morale, like furs or carpets,[35] lost an even larger percentage of their labour force. Shortages of materials or skilled labour led necessarily to simpler styles and plainer finishes. Official 'utility' schemes introduced methods of

[33] *National Income and Expenditure of the UK, 1938–1945* (1946, Cmd. 6784), Table 4.
[34] C. H. Feinstein, *National Income, Expenditure and Output in the United Kingdom, 1855–1965* (Cambridge, 1972), T. 89; T. Barna, 'Investment in Industry – Has Britain Lagged?', *The Banker*, April 1957, pp. 219–23; Philip Redfern, 'Net Investment in Fixed Assets in the United Kingdom, 1938–1953', *J. R. Stat. S.*, Series A, 118, 1955, pp. 159, 160.
[35] Board of Trade, *Working Party Reports; Carpets* (1947), p. 4.

mass-production and quality control for clothing and furniture, but elsewhere standards often lapsed haphazardly, without any corresponding benefits. Consumers and producers came to accept the second best and the general attitude of the sellers' market.

Other problems, as they affected the post-war position of many non-munitions industries, are aptly summed up in the following references to building. It should be noted that they were coloured by the need to explain the poor performance of the building industry even several years after the end of the war.[36]

> During the war, the industry lost a large part of its experienced labour force, and for six years the normal process of recruitment and training was interrupted. Many young craftsmen and apprentices were conscripted for national service before they had gained experience in industry. Other men who left the industry during the war had lost much of their skill by the time they returned while those who remained in the industry throughout the war were employed on work which usually differed markedly from that of peace time. ... Similar causes affected the efficiency of management. ... Directing and supervising staff had then to adapt themselves to a situation in which emphasis was no longer laid on speed of construction rather than on costs ... the Essential Work (Building and Civil Engineering) Order which was in force between 1941 and 1947 left its mark on the industry in the form of relaxed discipline.

The poor performance of industries such as building was, however, counterbalanced by the advances made in others. Between the Census of Production years 1935 and 1948, output *per employee hour* changed as shown in Table 5·2.[37]

Table 5·2: Output per employee hour, 1935–48 (1907 = 100)

	1935	1948
Iron and steel	154	176
Engineering, shipbuilding, vehicles	196	224
Non-ferrous metals	131	190
Chemicals	174	206
Clay and building materials	180	247
Paper, printing and publishing	208	221
Food, drink and tobacco	108	142
Textiles	155	198
Clothing	146	136
Leather	136	141
Miscellaneous	228	278
All manufacturing	171	203

In fact, against the direct damage, the lack of investment, and the loss of skill must be set certain distinctly favourable effects of the war. Among the most important were the scientific and technological advances induced by military and industrial demands, and the direct stimulus to a few industries of great

[36] Working Party Report, *Building* (1950), pp. 12–13; also Ministry of Labour and National Service, *Report for the Years 1939–1946* (1947. Cmd. 7225), pp. 87–91; I. Bowen, 'The Control of Building', in D. N. Chester, *Lessons of the British War Economy* (Cambridge, 1951).

[37] Colin Clark, *The Conditions of Economic Progress* (2nd ed., 1951), p. 270.

strategic importance, in particular engineering in the widest sense, including vehicles and aircraft, iron and steel and other metals, chemicals and agriculture.

The scientific discoveries of the war years, and those applied on a large scale for the first time during the war, are legion. Among the best known are magnetron valves, centimetric radar and other devices built on them, jet engines and other revolutionary aircraft developments, nuclear fission, electronic computing and control systems, antibiotics, DDT and other insecticides, and, on the Axis side, ballistic missiles, several of these being developments of a whole series of interdependent discoveries.[38]

The war also fostered a new attitude to science, and the practice of a massive deployment of scientists and technologists of many specialisms on a broad front, to solve given problems. To the scientists were given not only traditional, 'laboratory' tasks such as the development of a new apparatus or chemical, but also the solution of such logistic problems as the right order and balance of the loading of ships for D-day, an exercise in computation which has since, in principle, been followed in the internal organization of some large firms.

'When one compares the freedom and authority enjoyed by the civilian scientists and technicians', noted two historians of the war,[39] 'both at headquarters and in the establishments, in the period 1943–5 with the isolation and subjection of pre-war days, the change is among the most striking features of the organization of British war production.' Even at the very top, Winston Churchill leaned heavily on Lord Cherwell and a brilliant and unorthodox team of scientists.[40] This enhanced the role of the scientist, and his employment in large teams and with elaborate equipment has since been adopted by many of the major firms.

Aircraft, electrical and general engineering, chemicals as well as agriculture received the main benefits of expansion and modernization during the war. For example, in one of the most backward British sectors, the machine tool industry, tooling-up for rearmament led to an expansion of production by British makers from 20,000 machine tools in 1935 to 35,000 in 1939 and 100,000 in 1942, and employment in the industry rose from 21,000 in 1935 to a maximum of 68,600 in March 1943; at the same time, imports of American machine tools were expanded from 8,000 in 1939 to a maximum of 33,000 in 1940. The output of small tools, fine measuring tools and measuring instruments and industrial electrical equipment increased likewise.[41]

Much of the expanded munitions industry had a direct peace-time value, especially the works producing motor vehicles and aircraft. Of the 3·3 million people employed in armaments, excluding chemicals, explosives and iron

[38] E.g. D. E. H. Edgerton, 'Science and Technology in British Business History', *Business History* 29/4, 1987; W. H. G. Armytage, *A Social History of Engineering* (1961), pp. 310 ff.

[39] J. D. Scott and Richard Hughes, *The Administration of War Production* (1955), p. 288, also pp. 327–8.

[40] M. M. Postan, *British War Production* (1952), p. 144; J. D. Scott, 'Scientific Collaboration between the United Kingdom and North America', in H. D. Hall and C. C. Wrigley, *Studies of Overseas Supply* (HSWW, 1956), chapter 8; G. D. A. MacDougall, 'The Prime Minister's Statistical Section,' in Chester (ed.), *Lessons of the War Economy*; but see C. P. Snow, *Science and Government* (1961).

[41] Postan, pp. 206–7; Wm. Hornby, *Factories and Plant* (1958), chapters 10–13. For a critical view, see Correlli Barnett, *The Audit of War* (1986).

and steel, at the peak of 1943, 2·2 million were in industries with a civilian base.[42]

The output of aircraft increased from 2,800 in 1938 to nearly 8,000 in 1939, 20,000 in 1941 and over 26,000 in 1943 and 1944. Because of their growing complexity and the growing proportion of heavier aircraft, the structural weight increased even faster, from 9·8 million lb. to 28·9, 87·2 and about 200 million lb. in the same years. The aircraft repaired and engines delivered and repaired rose in the same proportion, and required an industrial effort almost as large as the new building. The capacity of the motor trade was also expanded, and in shipbuilding the output of mercantile tonnage rose to an average of well over 1·1 million g.t annually in 1941–4, while the launchings of naval and landing craft increased from 94,000 dw. tons in 1939 to 260,000 dw.t. in 1940 and 600,000 dw.t. in 1943.[43] Each of these trades, in turn, depended on large numbers of outside suppliers for materials and components. In the radio, electrical and electronics industry, for example, the output of radio valves rose from under 12 million a year in 1940 to over 35 million in 1944.

The enlargement of the vital engineering and chemical industries during the war is illustrated in Table 5·3.[44]

Table 5·3:   Growth in chemical and engineering industries, 1939–46

	Insured persons (000)		
	June 1939	November 1946	% Increase
Non-ferrous metal manufacture	55·9	87·8	57·1
Shipbuilding and repair	144·7	219·8	51·9
Constructional engineering	49·0	66·5	35·7
Electric cable, apparatus	195·9	265·5	35·5
Explosives, chemicals	174·3	235·5	35·1
Scientific instruments	48·3	65·0	34·6
Marine engineering	52·2	70·2	34·5
General engineering	704·7	944·3	34·0

The change was not merely one of size. The necessities of war taught new methods of mass-production, of industrial control and management, of design and quality control, and spread this knowledge among a host of sub-contractors. War-time training schemes increased the numbers of key workers, such as draughtsmen and tool-room operators. The capital equipment was greatly enlarged, the Government alone, according to one calculation, investing in 1936–45 over £1,000 million in fixed capital, spread over both Government-owned and agency factories, and capital subsidies to contractors.[45] At the end

[42] Hornby, pp. 28–30.

[43] Central Statistical Office, *Statistical Digest of the War* (1951), Tables 111, 130–1; R.J. Overy, *The Air War 1939–1945* (1980), pp. 156, 171; H.F. Heath and A.L. Hetherington, *Industrial Research and Development in the United Kingdom* (1946), pp. 200 ff.; Asa Briggs, *The History of Broadcasting in the United Kingdom,* 4 vols., vol. 3 (1970) p. 67.

[44] Postan, p. 385 also C.E.V. Leser, 'Changes in Level and Diversity of Employment in Regions of Great Britain, 1939–47', *Econ. J.,* 59/235, 1949, Table 4.

[45] Postan, p. 448, Hornby, *op. cit.,* chapter 14, puts the Government expenditure in the same years

of the war, machine tools alone worth £100 million were sold from Government factories to private industry, the normal pre-war intake being about £5 million a year.[46] To this have to be added private contractors' investments, which were particularly high in some public utilities, such as electricity generation.

The iron and steel industry was another important sector to be enlarged and modernized. The bulk steel capacity raised to 13 m.t. a year by the schemes of the 1930s proved sufficient for the needs of war, but to meet the sudden increase in the demand for alloy steel, capacity was increased from 500,000 tons (200,000 tons of which from electric furnaces) before the war to $1\frac{3}{4}$ m.t. (half of it in electric furnaces) by 1942. At the same time, the ingot capacity for aluminium, a vital structural material for aircraft, was raised to 31,000 tons in 1939 and increased further to 54,000 tons by 1943; the demand, by that time, had risen to 300,000 tons, of which 100,000 tons were provided from scrap by new plant set up during the war, and the remainder from imports.[47]

The other sector to emerge very much strengthened by the war was agriculture. In the late 1930s about 70% of the country's consumption of calories was supplied from abroad, but the proportion was 84% in the case of sugar, oils and fats, 88% of wheat and flour and 91% of butter.[48] As in 1914–18, shipping space for such bulky commodities as grain, and foreign exchange to pay for it, were among the most critical shortages, and agricultural policy was accordingly designed to reduce the dependence on imported food. It succeeded to the extent of saving about half the food imports, while keeping the home population well fed. Measured net of imported feeding stuffs, which were drastically reduced to save shipping space, home output increased from 14·7 billion calories in 1938–9 to 20·0 billion in 1941–2 and 28·1 billion in 1943–4, or by 36% and 91% respectively. Total home food production, by value, rose from 42% to 52% of consumption between 1938 and 1946.[49]

The basic feature of the Government's agricultural policy was the ploughing-up campaign, which raised the area under arable cultivation from just under 12 million to just under 18 million acres.[50] This increase was obtained at the cost of a corresponding decline in the acreage under permanent grass (the rough grazing remaining constant) and thereby involved a marked shift from animal husbandry to arable: between 1939 and 1945, the number of sheep and lambs, for example, in Great Britain fell from 26 million to $19\frac{1}{2}$ million, pigs from 3·8 million to 1·9 million, and poultry from 64 million head to 45 million. Only cattle were encouraged, and their numbers grew from about 8 million to 8·7 million head, in order to increase the home supply of milk. Imports could thus be converted from bulky cattle feeding stuffs to the more concentrated food

at £425·6 million for aircraft production, and £460·4 million for War Office and Supply. See also p. 162 above.
    [46] W. K. Hancock and M. M. Gowing, *British War Economy* (1949), pp. 551–2.
    [47] J. Hurstfield, *The Control of Raw Materials* (1953), pp. 335–48; J. Roepke, *Movements of the British Iron and Steel Industry, 1720–1951* (Urbana, Ill., 1956), chapter 7; P. Inman, *Labour in the Munitions Industries* (1957), p. 158; Duncan Burn, *The Steel Industry 1939–1959* (Cambridge, 1961), chapters 1 and 2.
    [48] R. J. Hammond, *Food.*, Vol. 1 (HSWW, 1951), Table V, p. 394.
    [49] E. F. Nash, 'War-Time Control of Food and Agricultural Prices', in D. N. Chester (ed.), *Lessons of the War Economy*.
    [50] *Statistical Digest of the War*, Table 55, p. 57; H. T. Williams, *Principles for British Agricultural Policy* (1960), chapter 5.

values contained in meat, eggs, etc., while British soil was converted to maintain the largest number of people per acre. Up to 1941, the prices of imports were a major consideration. Lend-lease arrangements removed this limitation, and imports were determined thereafter largely on the basis of their use of scarce shipping space.

The increase in the arable acreage was accompanied by remarkable increases in yields per acre. Thus the yield of wheat rose from 17·7 cwt in 1936–8 to 19·7 cwt in 1942–5, of barley from 16·4 to 18·5 cwt and of oats from 15·7 to 16·7 cwt, despite the likelihood that much of the newly ploughed land was marginal. This was achieved by an increase in the labour force in terms of man years from 99 in 1939–40 (1937 = 100) to a mere 109 in 1944–5, working an acreage increased by 50%.[51] The increase in home food production was, in fact, achieved by large-scale mechanization and increased use of fertilizers.

Between 1938–9 and 1945–6 the quantity of fertilizers used on United Kingdom farms (in terms of 1,000 tons) increased as follows: nitrogen, from 60 to 165; phosphate, from 170 to 359; potash, from 75 to 101; and lime, from 1,300 to 2,000. Similarly, between 1939 and 1946 total mechanical horse power on British farms rose from just under 2 million to just under 5 million.[52] Tractors increased from 56,000 to 203,000 in this period, and the increase of their equipment was as shown in Table 5·4.[53]

Table 5·4:   Increase in farming equipment, 1942–46 (in 000)

	May 1942	April 1944	June 1946
Disc harrows	33·8	58·9	65·2
Cultivators (grubbers)	161·7	191·4	247·8
Binders	131·6	144·0	149·5
Combine harvesters	1·0	2·5	3·8
Milking machines	29·5	37·8	48·3

This transformation was brought about by Government direction, to which was added a whole battery of financial inducements. The Government encouraged capital investment by subsidies for ditching, draining and water supplies, and by grants of between 25% and 75% for approved land reclamation schemes. For current costs, the 50% lime subsidy was continued with subsidies for hill sheep and cattle, and for wheat and potatoes. Meanwhile agricultural prices rose much faster than costs (see Table 5·5).

The widening gap between farm prices and the prices paid by consumers involved the State in ever-increasing food subsidies, quite apart from the direct subsidies and grants rising to £37 million a year in 1943–5, and their results were mainly to raise *net* farm receipts much faster than any other type of

---

[51] K. A. H. Murray, *Agriculture* (HSWW, 1955), pp. 85, 273.

[52] D. K. Britton and I. F. Keith, 'A Note on the Statistics of Farm Power Supplies in Great Britain', *The Farm Economist*, 6/6, 1950; Hancock and Gowing, p. 550.

[53] Murray, p. 276; *Statistical Digest of the War*, Table 64; cf. also PEP, *Agricultural Machinery* (1949), p. 95.

Table 5·5:   Agricultural prices 1939–45 (1936–8 = 100)

	Official cost of living	Retail food prices	Agricultural prices
1939	104	103	103
1941	130	123	172
1943	130	121	186
1945	133	125	196

incomes,[54] while increased security of tenancy was granted in 1941.[55] Thus agriculture emerged from the war in a healthier and more prosperous state than it had enjoyed for 70 years.

Not all primary production at home was equally fortunate. Elsewhere, the pressure to obtain the largest possible immediate return could lead to a long-run weakening of the industry by the running down of its capital. This may be illustrated by the timber and coal industries.

The shortage of timber was felt only after the Continent became closed to British shipping; then timber became one of the scarcest of materials. The country went to inordinate lengths to reduce its consumption and to find substitutes, often of other scarce materials such as steel, but at least part of the gap had to be filled by increased home plantings. They rose from an average of 150,000 tons in 1935–8 to a maximum of 1,251,000 tons in 1943 in the case of hardwood, from 180,000 tons to 861,000 tons (1942) in the case of softwood, and from 120,000 tons to 1,765,000 tons (1943) in the case of pitwood.[56] The cost of these fellings to the long-term forestry supply of the country was prodigious:

> By the end of 1945 some 60 per cent of Great Britain's softwoods had been taken, and some 40 per cent of the hardwoods. ... Moreover, the heavy cuttings in the 30–60 year classes has further jeopardized the future prospect. The distribution of age classes ... is completely out of joint.[57]

The problems of coal mining during the war were more complex. After 15 years of overproduction and unemployment, it was difficult to believe that the coal supply would fall short of needs. The fall of France and the closure of virtually all other export markets in the summer of 1940 reduced prospective consumption to about 40% *below* prospective output. There was unemployment in the export districts, and the recruitment of miners into the Forces was encouraged. The coal shortage in the winter of 1940–1 was due to transport difficulties, not shortage of supply.[58]

---

[54] Murray, *op. cit.*, chapter 11; E. F. Nash, 'War-Time Control of Food and Agricultural Prices', in *Lessons of the British War Economy*.

[55] S. G. Sturmey, 'Owner-Farming in England and Wales, 1900–1950', *Manchester School*, 23/3, 1955, p. 264.

[56] Postan, *op. cit.*, pp. 156, 216; P. Ford, 'The Allocation of Timber', in *Lessons of British War Economy*.

[57] Russell Meiggs, *Home Timber Production* (1949), p. 43.

[58] Hancock and Gowing, chapter XVI (ii).

Output, however, was falling. The quantity of total saleable coal had been 231 million tons in 1939, and 224 m.t. in 1940. It fell steadily to 175 m.t. by 1945. Up to 1941, the fall was simply due to the fall in the number of wage-earners on the colliery books, from 766,000 in 1939 to 698,000 in 1941. From then onwards, the numbers remained constant while output per manshift fell, largely because of the ageing of the work force, the deterioration of the fixed equipment, the long-term working out of the best seams, faulty planning and, not least, because of poor morale and absenteeism in the pits. When, in 1942, booming heavy industries and others began to push up the demand for coal there developed a major fuel crisis.

In order not to permit nationalization by the back door, war-time coal control had been left completely decentralized, the owners' District Executive Boards still determining output and pit-head prices under the cartel scheme. As the coal crisis developed in 1942, this chaotic structure could not stand the strain. A new policy for the mines became urgent, and in June 1942 a new department, the Ministry of Fuel and Power, was created to administer it,[59] and to raise the output of coal.

The most urgent problems related to labour. Though miners' wages and earnings had risen faster than most since the start of the war, they were still, in absolute terms, below the earnings of workers in the munitions industries and in other heavy, unpleasant trades. On the advice of a Board of Investigation under Lord Greene (the 'Greene Committee'),[60] a substantial wage advance of 2s. 6d. per shift and a national minimum wage were applied at once in 1942. The industry also adopted the National Conciliation Scheme drafted by the Greene Committee, but unrest in the mines was not abated, and in 1943–4 the bad industrial relations in the industry were the nearest approach to the rebellious spirit in the later years of the 1914–18 war.

The capital position of the industry gave equal grounds for concern. As the coal crisis developed, some of the country's scarce engineering capacity was turned over to mining engineering, and with the aid of Government finance, the provision of equipment was greatly increased. The proportion of coal cut by machinery rose from 61% in 1939 to 72% in 1945, and of coal conveyed mechanically from 58% to 71%,[61] but output, both absolute and per man-shift, continued to fall year by year. If it had not been for opencast coal, rising from 1·3 million tons in 1942 to 8·5 m.t. in 1944, it would have fallen more rapidly still. As it was, stocks were down to dangerous levels in the winter of 1944–5. With its equipment run down, and its manpower depleted and in an unco-operative mood, that unhappy industry, after nearly 20 years of sagging demand and excess capacity, emerged from the war with an almost limitless demand, but an utter inability to meet it.

If coal had its own special problems, the running down of capital was nowhere more marked than in inland transport. Ports and railway centres became special targets for enemy bomb attacks, while the public transport system had to carry a load in 1939–45 well above its normal peace-time weight, because of the virtual

[59] W. H. B. Court, *Coal* (HSWW, 1951), chapters 9 and 10.
[60] *Report of the Board of Investigation into the Immediate Wage Issue in the Coal-Mining Industry* (1942).
[61] Court, p. 279.

suspension of private motoring, the enforced residence of millions of people away from home, the military movements, and the disruption or lengthening of the normal supply routes of goods traffic. The increased load on the railways is evident from the figures in Table 5·6:[62]

Table 5·6:   Increase in railway traffic, 1938–44

Railways		1938	1942	1944
Net ton-miles (m. tons)	coal	8,104	9,951	9,267
	other	8,162	13,871	15,177
Wagons miles (m.)	loaded	3,003	3,983	4,064
	empty	1,492	1.412	1,427
Passenger miles, main line companies, billion		19*	—	32

* September 1938–August 1939 inclusive.

Apart from the greatly increased traffic, this tabulation shows an increasingly effective control over wagon loads, as full wagon mileage was raised by one-third without any increase in the empty wagon mileage.

In the later years of the war, the Central Transport Committee, set up in 1941, reduced the burdens on the railways to some extent by allocating an increasing quantity of goods to canals and coastal shipping. The traffic on the roads, by contrast, began to be curtailed from 1941 onward, owing to severe shortages of rubber and petrol.[63] Private cars lost their petrol ration completely in March 1942, *C* licence vehicles were severely restricted by zoning and other schemes, and *A* and *B* licence vehicles were gradually diverted from long-distance traffic, which was to be the responsibility of the railways, to short-distance goods traffic. By 1943 a special Road Haulage organization was set up under the Ministry of War Transport which came to control 388 large organizations, and all long-distance vehicles, a total of 34,000 goods vehicles.[64] Road passenger vehicles were left under the control of the Regional Transport Commissioners.

As in the First World War, the railways had been placed at once under Government control, the proprietors receiving a guaranteed income, settled at the end of 1940 at £43 million, Government and railways to share war damage costs equally. In view of the greatly increased traffic and the virtual suspension of maintenance, actual net receipts soon exceeded this figure and in 1943, the peak year, reached the total of £105½ million. But this left the railways near breakdown at the end of the hostilities, and it was to take years to restore them to good working order.[65]

The war, it may be concluded, had left the different branches of manufacturing industry, agriculture, transport and the public utilities, in very different positions. Some important sectors were forced to contract, losing skill, connections and capital equipment; others were forced to expand on a shrinking capital base;

[62] Hancock and Gowing, p. 481.
[63] C. I. Savage, *Inland Transport* (HSWW, 1957).
[64] Gilbert Walker, *Road and Rail* (2nd ed., 1947), p. 230.
[65] Savage, *Inland Transport*, pp. 634, 638–9.

but the effects of war were not wholly unfavourable to all. Some industries, notably engineering, metals and chemicals as well as agriculture, expanded and profited greatly.

3 Fiscal and Financial Policy during the War

The mobilization of the British industrial potential for the war required also fiscal and financial weapons. Further, Britain's dependence on imports made it necessary to husband the limited foreign exchange reserves. Finally, it was one of the objectives of the fiscal system to distribute the necessary burden fairly between classes and between individuals.[66]

Finance, then, though it had ceased to be the arbiter of military policy, was still one of its major instruments. Provided the physical resources were there, it was a criterion of the efficiency of the financial instruments that they should not stand in the way of their use. 'In the sense that financial obstacles were never allowed to obstruct the war effort, British policy in the Second World War was undoubtedly successful.'[67]

The subordination of finance to strategy was achieved virtually from the start. For this, the experience of the First World War, in which finance had too long and disastrously claimed prime consideration, was as much responsible as the fact that the country's re-armament effort was still small and therefore not too hard to bear. In those early months of 'phoney war', fiscal and financial policy had two main closely interrelated objectives: the prevention of inflationary price rises, which might lead to labour unrest, and the meeting of the costs of the war as far as possible out of increased taxation rather than by borrowing.

In the first weeks of the war there occurred an inevitable rise in the costs of certain materials in short supply, and of some wages, notably those of miners, accompanied by a corresponding rise in the price of coal. These increases pushed up the cost of living figure by some 10%, but there was clearly as yet no general inflationary pressure in the economy when the Government, as noted above,[68] was stampeded into subsidizing certain foods to keep down the official index. By January 1940 the Chancellor announced the continuation of subsidies on a broad front,[69] and within six months they had become an integral component of war policy. The budget of April 1941 laid it down that the cost-of-living index would be stabilized in the range of 25–30% above the immediate pre-war level. Later in the war, even some necessities outside the official index were held down in price, though others were deliberately allowed to rise to great heights.

The rising costs of the 'trading' losses incurred by absorbing higher import prices while keeping home prices steady, and for subsidizing home farmers, were borne by the Treasury. Another item, rent, was held down equally easily by rent control, and the Government also had powers to keep down the price to the consumer of several other goods and services, such as coal and railway fares. In the case of clothing, and what little furniture and other household durables came on the market after 1941, the 'utility' scheme was combined with price

---

[66] W. K. Hancock and M. M. Gowing, *British War Economy* (1949), pp. 48 ff.

[67] R. S. Sayers, *Financial Policy, 1939–45* (HSWW, 1956), p. 21. Also M. M. Postan, *British War Production* (1952), p. 82.

[68] p. 158 above.

[69] *HoC Debates*, vol. 356, cols. 1154–9, 31 January, 1940.

control. There were also some general provisions, such as the Goods and Services (Price Control) Act of July 1941, though price control was never quite complete.[70] By contrast, the Government could afford to levy a large part of its revenue by steeply increasing duties on tobacco and alcohol, since their weight in the official index was minute, and even the purchase tax, by careful discrimination, was gradually developed so as to raise the maximum of revenue with the minimum disturbance to the cost-of-living index.

The success of the retail price policy in its objective of limiting the war-time inflation and insulating the home consumer from world price changes may be judged by the statistics given in Table 5·7.[71]

Table 5·7:   Wartime price index (first half 1939 = 100)

	Wholesale prices:			Cost of living	Subsidies (£ million)
	Board of trade	Economist	Statist		
1940	140	139	144	121	72
1941	157	151	159	129	138
1942	164	160	169	130	164
1943	167	164	172	129	177
1944	171	168	177	131	215
1945	174	172	182	132	250

Subsidies for retail commodity prices could only deal with the symptoms of the inflationary problem. Its essence was the fact that the Government was attempting to absorb a much larger share of the national resources than individuals and firms were willing to forgo; and this underlying cause of inflation could ultimately be combated only by a conscious withdrawal of purchasing power from the public by a high level of taxation.

To begin with, borrowing was to be kept to a minimum. The autumn war budget in September 1939 actually over-estimated the total expenditure for the financial year 1939–40 by £116 million. Defence expenditure amounted to only £1,000 million, compared with £382 million in 1938–9. The budget proposals in April 1940 were equally timid, and of the limited sums required, about one-half was raised by taxation, and half by borrowing.

By this time budgetary policy had come under sharp criticism. The critics were led, once again, by J. M. Keynes. In correspondence to *The Times* in November 1939, published as a pamphlet early in 1940,[72] he condemned the traditional assessment of revenue according to the principle of what the taxpayer would bear, which turned out to be about half the required expenditure. By starting at the other end, and calculating the national income and its main

---

[70] E. L. Hargreaves and M. M. Gowing, *Civil Industry and Trade* (1952), p. 122; Hancock and Gowing, pp. 501–4.

[71] G. D. H. Cole, *Money, Trade and Investment* (1954), p. 95; subsidy figures from white paper on *National Income and Expenditure of the United Kingdom 1938 to 1946* (1947. Cmd. 7099), Table 19: these *exclude* housing subsidies.

[72] J. M. Keynes, *How to Pay for the War* (1940); cf. also R. F. Harrod, *The Life of John Maynard Keynes* (1951), pp. 489 ff.

components first, it would be possible at once to determine the capacity of war-making available, and the level of taxation necessary to transfer that part of the national income to the Government without creating an inflation. At existing levels of incomes and taxation, for example, he calculated that there was an inflationary 'gap', which could most usefully be viewed as the difference between the proposed Government expenditure and the total of taxes plus savings plus any income or dissaving available from abroad. He therefore proposed increased taxes, sweetened by promises to repay part of them after the war as 'deferred pay' (the later 'post-war credits').

He was swimming with the tide. In April 1940 the *Economist* pointed out that even after its great increase, the British war budget was still well below that of Germany, though it had several years' start to make up.[73] The Chancellor of the Exchequer was becoming impatient with the inability of his Treasury officials to suggest means of stopping the inflation, and in March a war loan of a mere £300 million had been a failure. Above all, it was the shock of the defeats of the summer of 1940 and the change of Government which precipitated the change-over to Keynesian policies.

The new, more vigorous, tax policies allowed war expenditure in the current year to be raised from a prospective £2,000 to £2,800 million. The income tax was increased, purchase tax was imposed on a broad front, and the Excess Profits Tax was raised from 60% to 100% (i.e. taxing the total increase in profits over a standard pre-war period) though it was later softened by various concessions, including a 20% post-war credit on the tax paid.[74] With Keynes and other leading economists installed at the Treasury by the end of 1940, and others in the Cabinet Office, the transformation was complete though the Treasury was far from being intellectually convinced by Keynes.[75]

Kingsley Wood's budget of April 1941 marked the turning point.[76] It was conceived in national income terms, and to symbolize the new approach, was accompanied by a white paper setting out the official estimates of the national income and expenditure,[77] the first of the series which has become, together with other tools developed in war-time, the indispensable guide to economic policy since. According to the official estimates, the 'gap' at existing rates of income and taxation would be of the order of £500 million, of which £200–300 million would be found by increased personal savings, and £250 million by additional taxation, over and above the estimated revenue of £1,636 million. This was to take the form of raising the standard rate of income tax by 1*s*. 6*d*. to 10*s*. in the pound, and other rates in proportion.

[73] 'A Budget of Delusions', *Economist*, 27 April 1940, pp. 759–60.

[74] J. R. Hicks, U. K. Hicks and L. Rostas, *The Taxation of War Wealth* (Oxford, 2nd ed., 1942), chapters 11 and 12; A. J. Youngson, *The British Economy 1920–1957* (1960), pp. 150–1; Hancock and Gowing, pp. 327–30.

[75] Alan Booth, *British Economic Policy, 1931–49* (Hemel Hempstead, 1989), pp. 69 f., and 'The "Keynesian Revolution" in Economic Policy Making', *Econ. Hist. Rev.* 36/1, 1983.

[76] Jim Tomlinson, *Employment Policy 1939–1955* (Oxford, 1987) p. 24; G. C. Peden, 'Sir Richard Hopkins and the "Keynesian Revolution" in Employment Policy, 1929–1945', *Econ. Hist. Rev.* 36/2, 1983; S. H. Beer, *Treasury Control* (Oxford, 1956), p. 66.

[77] *The Sources of War Finance. An Analysis and an Estimate of the National Income and Expenditure in 1938 and 1940* (1941. Cmd. 6261). Cf. also J. E. Meade and R. Stone, *National Income and Expenditure* (1944 ed.); R. Stone, 'The Use and Development of National Income and Expenditure Estimates', in *Lessons of the British War Economy*; E. F. Jackson, 'The Recent Use of Social Accounting in the United Kingdom', *Income and Wealth*, Series I (1950).

　　The actual figures underlying the budget of 1941 might have been unreliable, as some critics alleged;[78] certainly, the queues at the shops continued, and widespread rationing and price control had to be introduced, after all. But the principle was sound, and the remaining war budgets, 1942–5, showed little change in their mode of calculation or their method of presentation. The only major innovations were 'Pay As You Earn', introduced in September 1943 and applying to about 16 million earners, of whom 12 million were taxable, and the development of the purchase tax as a weapon not only for the raising of revenue, but also to restrict and generally influence consumption.[79] Up to 1942, direct and indirect taxation had roughly increased in step, the former by 177% over 1939, and the latter by 145%. By 1945 the revenue from direct taxes had increased by 300%, while that from indirect taxes had risen by only 160%.

　　The success of fiscal policy during the war has to be judged against the size of the problem: at the height of the war, about half the current consumption was diverted to the Government, while civilian consumption, in real terms, had to be reduced to something like 80% of the pre-war level[80] (see Table 5·8).

Table 5·8:　Comparison of net national product: % distribution

	Personal and Government consumption A	War B	Personal consumption C	Total Government consumption civil and war D	Net non-war capital formation E	Real personal consumption* F
1938	88	7	78	17	5	100
1939	83	15	73½	24½	2	100
1940	72	44	64	52	−16	90
1941	63	54	56	61	−17	83
1942	60	52	52	60	−12	82
1943	56	56	49	63	−12	79
1944	58	54	51	61	−12	83
1945	61	49	54	56	−10	86

* Index, 1938 prices.

　　In this table, the totals of columns A and B are equal to the totals of C and D. Either pair, together with column E, totals 100, i.e. the Net National Product. According to the A and B columns, it will be seen that at the peak of the war effort, in 1943, armament alone equalled the rest of national consumption. The other division (columns C and D) which forms a more realistic indicator of budgetary policy, shows that the Government share exceeded private consumption for the whole of the period 1941–45 inclusive. Table 5·8 also illustrates the gradual increase of mobilization to its high point in 1943, and the important

[78] M. Kalecki, 'The Budget and Inflation', *Bull. Oxf. Inst. Stat.*, 3/6, 1941.

[79] Sayers, *op. cit.*, chapter 4.

[80] Statistics based on *National Income and Expenditure of the United Kingdom, 1938–1945* (1946. Cmd. 6784), Tables 4 and 5. Some of the figures have been slightly revised since. Cf. also *Statistics Relating to the War Effort of the United Kingdom* (1944, Cmd. 6564).

contribution made by capital consumption to the total war effort.[81]

Government expenditure at such a rate could not conceivably be met entirely out of current revenue. Government borrowing covered, for the whole period 1939–45, about half the expenditure, but significantly its proportion fell progressively in the course of the war[82] (see Table 5·9). Virtually all of that was met by borrowing at home, and with the exception of some £770 million raised by the printing press, i.e. by increasing the fiduciary bank note issue,[83] was derived from savings.

Table 5·9: Government revenue and borrowing

	Total tax revenue (£m.) A	Total income, incl. income from property after paying National Debt interest (£m.) B	Total deficit on current account (£m.) C	Of which raised by public borrowing at home (£m.) D	Ratio A:D E
1939	980	771	490	352	—
1940	1,382	1,158	2,115	1,550	0·89
1941	2,143	1,905	2,828	2,553	0·84
1942	2,563	2,314	2,909	2,576	1·00
1943	3,052	2,759	2,826	2,972*	1·03
1944	3,262	2,897	2,672	2,792*	1·17
1945	3,265	2,806	2,131	2,442*	1·34

* There was some net lending abroad in these years.

Savings were channelled into the hands of the Government partly by what might be called direct controls, and partly by making attractive offers for them. Among the direct controls were the suspension of opportunities for investment, and pressure on the clearing banks to turn all their available resources over to the Government and to restrict bank advances intended to be used for capital construction.

The methods of raising Government loans showed a degree of subtlety far superior to that of the First World War.[84] Their essence was the exploitation of a discriminating monopoly, i.e. the offer of separate terms to each sector of the market. Expectations of interest rates, after seven years of Bank Rate at the 2% level, were low. It was raised to 4% on 24 August 1939, but in view of the pointlessness of this gesture, it was lowered again to 3%, and the authorities were able to conduct a '3% war'.

For the small saver, the 'National Savings' movement, which had survived from the First World War, was again made the vehicle of strong patriotic appeals, and savers were offered, besides the Post Office and the Trustee Savings

[81] Cf. also U. K. Hicks, *Public Finance* (1947), pp. 110–11; J. Hurstfield, *The Control of Raw Materials* (1953), pp. 106, 126.
[82] Sayers, Appx. I, Tables 4 and 5.
[83] Sayers, p. 223.
[84] The following paragraphs are largely based on Sayers, *op. cit.*, chapter 7.

Banks and similar holdings, a series of National Savings Certificates and Defence Bonds. For the larger savers, National War Bonds as $2\frac{1}{2}$% were provided on tap, i.e. as a continuous supply on application, and 3% Savings Bonds were also on offer. At the end of 1941 yet another type of security began to be issued, the Tax Reserve Certificate, to take advantage of the idle funds held by prudent firms in readiness for their tax liability.

Any funds not invested in any of these alternative loans would normally find their way into the banks, and the Government accordingly developed a whole battery of methods to absorb all 'idle' bank balances, including Ways and Means Advances, Treasury Bills and Treasury Deposit Receipts. The main weight fell on Treasury Bills. These were at first held mainly by the Departments and later became popular with the general public, being negotiable at the Bank of England; the clearing banks' share of assets held in that form fell from 30–40% in the 1930s to 10% in 1944–5.[85]

The banks were obliged to make their contribution to the floating debt by means of a new security issued in the perilous days of July 1940, the Treasury Deposit Receipt. It was rather less liquid than the Treasury Bill, having a currency of six months and being non-negotiable, though it could be repaid in full for bonds for either the banks or their customers, but its rate, delicately fixed at $1\frac{1}{8}$%, was just above the Bill rate which then stood at a shade over 1%. This meticulous mopping-up of bank liquid reserves was driven to such lengths that occasionally the cash reserves of the clearing banks were actually reduced below the safety level.

At the same time, in view of the restrictions placed on individual spending and on business investment, businesses and individuals had little option but to accumulate their funds in the banks, unless, indeed, they invested them directly in Government paper. For this reason, as well as because of the general inflation, total bank deposits rose from £2,730 million in 1939 to £5,551 million in 1945 (or by 103%), while total bank clearings, indicating the velocity of circulation, only rose from £36·6 billion to £66·9 billion, or by 83%. Business deposits held in the London clearing banks had risen during the war by over £1,500 million,[86] representing one aspect of the 'forced saving' which consisted of denying firms the real resources for investment in the private sector. Commercial advances, as a proportion of deposits declined dramatically from 44·1% in 1939 to a bare 16·1% in 1945, being smaller even in absolute terms than before the war, and bills discounted fell from 11·3% to 4·0%. Against this, TDRs rose from nil to 38·6%, while 'investments' kept a constant share of the total. In August 1945, Government paper and cash amounted to 83·3% of the deposits of the London clearing banks. They had thus become principally agents for the absorption of funds from the public for the use of the Government. Other financial institutions, for much the same reasons, had their investment portfolios similarly filled with Government paper.

[85] Edward Nevin and E. W. Davis, *The London Clearing Banks* (1970), pp. 152–3.
[86] Ashworth, *op. cit.*, pp. 234–5, Appx. I, Table L, p. 260.

4 The Problem of the Foreign Balance of Payments

Whereas the last years of peace before 1914 had seen large annual surpluses on current account, the balance of payments in the late 1930s had left no margin; and whereas the immediate panic in August 1914 led to a world shortage of sterling, the crisis of the spring of 1938 had led to a *withdrawal* of foreign funds to the extent of £150 million. An actual declaration of war could be expected to lead to a large-scale flight from sterling,[87] while the gold reserve, not least because of American pressure, had been dangerously reduced.[88]

Given expected high imports and reduced exports and 'invisible exports' in wartime, the trade balance was likely to become particularly adverse with dollar countries. The gold and dollar reserve, estimated at £450 million at the outbreak of war, and planned to be rationed out to last for three years at £150 million a year, was soon being depleted at a much greater rate.[89] Hence a major export drive, particularly to 'hard currency' countries, was undertaken in February 1940, and by April–May it contributed in no small measure to the growing shortage of resources. It had hardly got into its stride, however, before the military collapse in the west and the consequent need for war production at all costs forced the country to sacrifice its exports and its gold and dollar reserve. By late 1940, the hope of meeting all foreign payments necessary to maintain the much enlarged armament programme at home had plainly become illusory. The dollar import problem was solved by 'Lend-Lease', and it became possible to switch exports to areas that provided the most vital strategic materials. In the process, Britain lost many of her traditional markets, which were forced to turn to the USA instead,[90] and the volume of her exports fell to less than one-third of the pre-war figure. At the end of the war, less than 2% of the labour force was engaged on exports, compared with 9·5% before the war.

To the huge adverse balance on visible trade account, shown in Table 5·10,

Table 5·10:   The visible trade balance

	Exports (£m.)	Imports (£m.)	Visible adverse balance (£m.)	Volume index	
				Exports	Imports
1938	471	858	387	100	100
1939	440	840	400	94	97
1941	365	1,132	767	56	82
1943	234	1,228	994	29	77
1945	399	1,053	654	46	62

[87] R. S. Sayers, *Central Banking After Bagehot* (1957), p. 65.

[88] R. A. C. Parker, 'The Pound Sterling, the American Treasury and British Preparations for War, 1938–1939', *English Historical Review* 98/387, 1983.

[89] W. K. Hancock and M. M. Gowing, *British War Economy* (1949), pp. 112–17; J. Hurstfield, *The Control of Raw Materials* (1953), pp. 108–13; M. M. Postan, *British War Production* (1952), pp. 82–3.

[90] E. L. Hargreaves and M. M. Gowing, *Civil Industry and Trade* (1952), pp. 44 ff., chapters 7–9.

have to be added the expenditure by British troops overseas, and the free deliveries from the dollar area.[91]

Taking those additional items into account, over the war period as a whole (September 1939 to December 1945 inclusive) total British current debits amounted to £16,900 million, of which visible imports accounted for £12,200 million. Of this sum, only £6,900 million, or about 40%, was requited by goods and services by the United Kingdom; the rest was financed by sales of capital (£1,200 million), running up debts with other countries (£3,500 million) and *net* grants, mainly from the USA and Canada (£5,400m million).[92]

To keep the pound at a fixed value, settled at $4.03 (some 20% below the old gold parity), under conditions of such strain, two major weapons were used: import controls and financial controls. Britain lost £50 million in foreign exchange in needlessly increased prices,[93] before all imports of food were transferred to the Ministry in March 1940, and private importers were virtually squeezed out. Formal general import control was not imposed until June 1940.

Direct financial controls also took time to evolve. Dealings in gold and foreign exchange, payments abroad and purchases of foreign assets were put under Treasury control at once, but these early controls, like those of imports, left several major loopholes. For one thing, payments within the 'Sterling Area' were left free, and in some parts of it leakages occurred easily; the 'Sterling Area' in its modern sense with its single pool of gold and dollar resources evolved under the lead of the United Kingdom only in 1939–41.[94] Above all, foreign holders of sterling balances could still exchange them for dollars or other 'hard' currency, which then escaped control. The loss of these precious balances in the early months was estimated at $737 million,[95] but was considered necessary in order not to alienate American holders of sterling. Only in May 1940 were foreign-held securities blocked, the balances having by then become negligible, and all further leaks were then stopped by bilateral trade treaties.

By the war's end the 'Sterling Balances', i.e. the credits of other countries held in London in blocked accounts, were owed largely, though not wholly, within the 'Sterling Area'. The largest holder was India, whose credit in London rose to well over £1 billion even after more than £300 million of capital assets had been sold off by Britain. Other large sums were held by Egypt, Palestine and the Sudan mostly on account of the supply and expenditure of Empire troops in their area. Substantial balance also accrued to other Colonial areas, and to South Africa, Australia and New Zealand.[96] Outside the Empire, the western hemisphere held over £300 million; and several of the Western European Governments-in-Exile had also accumulated substantial sterling claims, either

[91] Re-exports and corresponding imports omitted. Central Statistical Office, *Statistical Digest of the War* (1951), Table 142.

[92] R. S. Sayers, *Financial Policy, 1939–45* (1956), Appx. I, Table 10, p. 499.

[93] T. Balogh, 'The Drift Towards a Rational Foreign Exchange Policy' (1940), in Oxford Institute of Statistics, *Studies in War Economics* (1947), p. 66.

[94] *Report of the Committee on the Working of the Monetary System* (Radcliffe Report) (1959. Cmnd. 827), paras. 647, 723 ff.; A. R. Conan, *The Sterling Area* (1952), p. 52; D. F. McCurrach, 'Britain's US Dollar Problem, 1939–45', *Econ. J.*, 58/231, 1948, p. 356.

[95] H. Duncan Hall, *North American Supply* (HSWW, 1955), p. 270.

[96] H. A. Shannon, 'The Sterling Balances of the Sterling Area 1939–1949', *Econ. J.*, 60/239, 1950, p. 540; H. D. Hall and C. C. Wrigley, *Studies of Overseas Supply* (HSWW, 1956), chapter 9; Sir Dennis H. Robertson, *Britain in the World Economy* (1954), p. 40.

by transferring their gold to the United Kingdom, or by the active trade balance of their colonies.

The total indebtedness grew at a steady rate of £600 million a year throughout the later war years, and by mid-1945 had reached the amounts shown in Table 5·11.[97]

Table 5·11:   British overseas debts in 1945

Australia, NZ, S. Africa, Eire	384
India, Burma, Middle East	1,732
Colonies and other Sterling Area	607
Total Sterling area	2,723
South and North America	303
European States and Dependencies	267
Rest of the world	62
Grand total	3,355

The sterling balances thus had many origins and many types of owners. Some were owned by populations overseas much poorer than the British; others by European Governments-in-Exile who could claim that their countries, at the end of the war, were in far greater need of rehabilitation than was Britain, and were therefore in no position to provide loans for the latter. While they accumulated, they allowed Britain to fight the war with resources greater than her own without damage to the international value of the pound sterling. At the end of the war, however, they represented a large financial burden, even when not subject to demands of withdrawal. The annual interest and service charge payable abroad, a striking reversal of the old role of Britain as international lender, was hard to bear in the early post-war years; while the need to hold credit balances against them was to lead to serious misunderstandings with the Americans.

By means of external borrowing, and by the sale of capital assets, the United Kingdom obtained from the non-dollar world a total of some £4 billion in 1939–45,[98] a sum of the same order of magnitude as the total British foreign investment at the outbreak of war. Yet it was put in the shade by the contribution of the dollar world (the USA and Canada), which provided £7·5 billion (£6·2 billion net) by gifts and over £1 billion against sales of investments, gold and by accumulating liabilities.

The Canadian contribution, large as it was in relation to the resources of the Dominion, was made with the minimum of friction. Having used up its liquid Canadian resources, the United Kingdom was granted an interest-free loan of $700 million in 1942, and when that was exhausted, the Canadians voted their magnificent 'billion-dollar gift' in 1943. It was followed by two 'mutual aid'

[97] Sayers, *Financial Policy*, p. 439; cf. also chapters 9, 10, 14; T. Balogh, 'The International Aspect', in G. D. N. Worswick and P. H. Ady, *The British Economy, 1945–1950* (Oxford, 1952), pp. 480–3.

[98] R. F. Harrod, *Life of John Maynard Keynes* (1951), p. 606; Alan S. Milward, *The Economic Effects of the Two World Wars on Britain* (1984), p. 67.

appropriations, without strings, totalling £1,800 million in 1943–4, and further credits lasted until 1946. Total gifts and free aids came to $3,468 million, and total supplies and services to the United Kingdom (including those paid for) to $7,441 million, or nearly £2 billion.[99]

Very different were the relations with the United States, bedevilled as they were by widespread suspicions of Britain's motives. The Johnson Act of 1934 had prohibited loans to foreign Governments which had defaulted on their First World War loans, including the United Kingdom Government, so that all purchases had to be paid for in cash. Apart from machine tools, the principal British need was for aircraft, and in the early months of the war they formed the most important military item ordered in the USA (as well as in Canada). After the fall of France, Britain took over the French orders placed there, which alone committed her to an ultimate expenditure of $612 million.[100]

Other British orders both for immediate use and for long-term supply were also stepped up enormously in the second half of 1940, but neither led to any tangible results. The immediate orders failed to materialize because of the sheer inability of American industry, increasingly drawn upon by the American forces also, to meet them quickly enough. It was estimated that at least $200 million of precious British reserves had gone by March 1941, not into buying arms, but into building factories in the USA and in Canada. For all her vast outlay and large future commitments, the United Kingdom had as yet, in the critical months to the end of 1940, received only the minimal actual supplies. Aircraft, for example, from the USA, perhaps the most critical item, only numbered 700 in 1939 and 2,000 for the whole of 1940 (compared with a British home production of 8,000 and 15,000 respectively).[101] Supplies of food, raw materials and other peace-time goods were, however, much more satisfactory and only in 1943 did munitions supply begin to exceed the imports of non-war goods.[102]

More disturbing than the short-term delay was the long-term prospect. Though the gold and dollar reserves had been enlarged by current earnings of $2,000 million between September 1939 and December 1940 ($345 by United Kingdom earnings, $670 by Empire commodities and $965 by Dominion gold),[103] the total liquid reserves, including saleable capital assets in the dollar area, were only just sufficient to pay for orders already placed. There was nothing left even to begin to pay the very much enlarged programme for 1941.

There had been some piecemeal expansion of American aid, as far as her position as a neutral and her Congress and public opinion allowed. The 50 destroyers, for example, handed over in September 1940 in return for British bases, were a welcome immediate contribution,[104] while the United States co-operated in denying some crucial war materials, such as molybdenum, to Germany and to neutrals within her control.[105] The crisis looming in December

[99] Sayers, *Financial Policy,* chapter 11; Hall, *op. cit.,* chapters 1, 2, pp. 483–7; Hall and Wrigley, pp. 46–65.

[100] M. Jean Monnet of the French Commission was taken on the British staff after the fall of France. Cf. also Parker, 'Pound Sterling'.

[101] Hall and Wrigley, p. 30.

[102] J. Hurstfield, *Control of Raw Materials,* p. 98.

[103] McCurrach, *loc. cit.,* pp. 358 ff.; Hall, *North American Supplies,* pp. 269–70.

[104] W. S. Churchill, *The Second World War, vol. II. Their Finest Hour* (1949), chapter 20.

[105] Hall, *North American Supplies,* chapters 3–6.

1940 was met by President Roosevelt announcing the provision of 'Lend-Lease'.

Lend-lease meant the supply, free of charge, for the duration of the war, of all goods and services needed by Britain and available in the USA; it was granted on the same terms to the other Allies, including Soviet Russia and China. Though lend-lease supplies were, until 1943–4 at least, only marginal to the United Kingdom's war effort, they solved the problem set by the running out of reserves and allowed Britain to dovetail her production with America. Its vast bulk, some $27 billion being made available to the United Kingdom, and $6 billion by the United Kingdom to the USA in 'reciprocal aid' or 'reverse lend-lease', dominated British economic warfare, and its conditions dominated British economic relations with the USA and the rest of the world.[106]

The Lend-Lease Act, though called the 'most unsordid act' in history, had to pass through Congress while America was still neutral and it had to run an annual gauntlet of renewal; and in this process several onerous conditions were exacted. To begin with, Britain had to strip herself bare of dollars and all capital assets in the USA, and great pressure was brought to bear on her to sell even those which could be sold only at a large loss. This reserve gone, the accumulation of a new one, even if desperately required as backing for the 'sterling balances', was viewed with hostility and suspicion.

Secondly, many months were to elapse before the first substantial lend-lease deliveries actually arrived in Britain, and over two years were to elapse before they exceeded the deliveries paid for in cash. In the interim Britain would, in fact, have been bankrupt if it had not been for a loan of $425 million extended by the Reconstruction Finance Corporation, an American Government agency, against the collateral of British-held American assets valued at $700 million.

Thirdly, lend-lease supplies were, in form, deliveries 'for the defence of the USA', so that, in the last resort, they depended on the wishes of the American Government. Thus, deliveries were liable to sudden cancellation in favour of the American Services.

Fourthly, there were the 'strings' deliberately put in, above all the demand for a prohibition of all British exports containing any raw materials which were also supplied through lend-lease, so that American exporters should not have to compete with the British who were subsidized by the American taxpayer. Somewhat toned down later, the British Government decided to accept this voluntarily in the Export White Paper of 19 September 1941,[107] before the American entry into the war. By the other main condition, the famous Article VII of the Mutual Aid Agreement of 1942,[108] Britain had to subscribe to the pronouncement against 'discrimination' in international trade after the war, generally understood to be an attack on Imperial preference.

This treatment continued even after Pearl Harbor, when America became a belligerent ally, and after Britain and the Empire granted 'reverse lend-lease' without any strings, representing, though it was much smaller in amount, as

[106] For the history of 'lend-lease', see Edward R. Stettinius, Jr., *Lend-Lease* (New York, 1944); Sayers, *Financial Policy*, chapters 13, 15; Hall, *North American Supplies*, chapters 8–11; Hancock and Gowing, chapter 9; Hall and Wrigley, chapter 3; Hurstfield, chapter 19; A. J. Youngson, *British Economy, 1920–1957* (1960), pp. 152–6.

[107] Cmd. 6311.

[108] *Treaty Series No. 7* (1942). Cmd. 6391 and Cmd. 6341.

high a proportion of the donor's national income, and a greater sacrifice,[109] and provided British scientific knowledge supplied free for such projects as radar, jet engines and nuclear fission.[110] Lastly, the American insistence on unilateral treatment made it impossible for Britain to propose pooling arrangements among her other Allies, so that lend-lease was, in a sense, responsible for the extent of the burdensome Sterling Balances at the end of the war.

When, in the later years of the war, American expenditure in Britain and elsewhere in the Sterling Area began to raise the dollar reserve, which the American president, unknown to the British, had determined should not exceed $1,000 million, there began a further series of restrictions to reduce it to that level. This was just as the American troops were leaving Allied soil and the dollar reserve began to fall again, and it was made clear that after the defeat of Germany, lend-lease supplies would be sent only for troops actually fighting the Japanese.

Keynes secured some concessions at the Washington Conference in October 1944 from this intransigent position, but the relief was short-lived. VE day, in June, was followed quickly by the surrender of Japan on 14 August. A week later, lend-lease was abruptly stopped, and Britain was faced with the immediate necessity of paying in dollars for goods already in the country or 'in the pipeline' to the tune of $650 million, as well as for continuation orders, if she was not to be starved of necessary food and raw materials.

With her capital equipment run down, more resources devoted to war and needing reconversion to a larger extent than any other Ally, her overseas earnings cut by the loss of one-quarter of her shipping and almost half her investments, Britain was quite unable to earn the necessary dollars, even if the standard of consumption were cut further. The rest of the world, much of it devastated and disorganized, was in no position to supply the needs hitherto filled from dollar sources, and was itself in need of dollar aid. The only possible course for Britain was to obtain an American loan of the type which she had succeeded in avoiding throughout the war, and at the end of the war Keynes was sent to Washington once again to negotiate it.

5 Work and Welfare in the War Years

There were several reasons why the costly strikes and the class hatred of the First World War were not repeated in the second. For one thing, the unions and their leaders enjoyed from the outset much greater official recognition, and when, in May 1940, Labour entered the Coalition Government, the outstanding trade unionist of the day, Ernest Bevin, was in charge of policy relating to manpower as Minister of Labour and National Service. Secondly, Labour was politically much more in sympathy with this war and its declared war aims than with the first. Thirdly, the Government made greater efforts to ensure a fair distribution of food and other necessities, and to enlarge social welfare schemes. Finally, unlike the years before 1914, the 1930s had seen very few large strikes, so that, perhaps, it was not surprising that apart from the coal mines, some

---

[109] R. G. D. Allen, 'Mutual Aid between the USA and the British Empire 1941–5', *J. R. Stat. S.*, 109/3, 1946; Hancock and Gowing, p. 353, Table 3(c).
[110] Hall and Wrigley, chapter 8.

engineers' strikes in 1940 and a boilermakers' strike in 1944, the war-time strikes were short, small and unofficial.[111]

Wages policy was more circumspect, and the Government itself allowed the very first major wage claim, that of the miners in October 1939, at the cost of raising the price of coal.[112] Under the Coalition Government, with Mr Bevin at the Ministry of Labour, manpower policy relied as far as possible on the voluntary co-operation of the unions and the use of peace-time machinery. As far as collective bargaining was concerned, the basic provision, the Conditions of Employment and National Arbitration Order SR & O (1940), No. 1305, preserved all the existing negotiating machinery, including arbitration and the powers of the Industrial Court. It was only for issues in which agreement could not be reached by existing methods that it established a new National Arbitration Tribunal. Strikes and lockouts were prohibited, unless the Ministry of Labour failed to act; normally the Ministry would refer a dispute either to the National Arbitration Tribunal or to any of the other existing arbitration bodies, and in that case their awards were to have legal force.[113] Altogether, in 1939–45, 816 decisions were handed down by the NAT, 692 by other arbitrators, and there were about 2,150 conciliation settlements. Strikes could not entirely be prevented and against large-scale strikes the Government was as helpless as in 1914–18.

Powers over the direction of labour were used sparingly for fear of industrial troubles such as accompanied the comb-outs after 1915. Dilution also relied heavily on the experience of 1915–18, and in the engineering industry was negotiated as early as August 1939. Between mid-1939 and mid-1943 the proportion of women workers in engineering was raised from 10·5% to 31·2%.[114]

Where labour was virtually conscripted into 'controlled' establishments, 'the Minister of Labour was convinced that he could not expect men to give up the right to free choice of employment without guaranteeing them certain conditions of work, including a guaranteed week and the restriction of the employers' right to dismiss them'.[115] This conviction moved him to provide for the expansion of welfare facilities,[116] the strengthening of the 'fair wages' clause in Government contracts, and the extension of statutory wage determination to trades hitherto poorly organized.

These last received much attention during the war years. In addition to road haulage covered just before the outbreak of war, joint councils for the distributive and the catering trades were set up. The Central Agricultural Wages Board was given powers in 1940 to fix national minimum wage rates for adult male workers. Lastly, in coal mining, owners and miners agreed to a national conciliation scheme, including a National Reference Tribunal of three neutral members. These developments culminated in the Wages Council Act of 1945

[111] Allan Flanders, *Trade Unions* (1952), p. 100; K. G. J. C. Knowles, *Strikes, A Study in Industrial Conflict* (Oxford, 1952), pp. 162–3; Keith Middlemas, *Power, Competition and the State*. Vol. I: *Britain in Search of Balance, 1940–61* (Stanford, 1986), p. 20; Central Statistical Office, *Statistical Digest of the War* (1951), Table 36; A. L. Bowley, 'Labour Disputes in Wartime', *London & Cambridge Economic Service*, No. 103 (1945), p. 8.

[112] W. K. Hancock and M. M. Gowing, *British War Economy* (1949), pp. 164–5.

[113] N, Barou, *British Trade Unions* (1947), pp. 153–4; H. M. D. Parker, *Manpower, a Study in War-Time Policy and Administration* (HSWW, 1957), chapter 25.

[114] P. Inman, *Labour in the Munition Industries* (HSWW, 1957), p. 80.

[115] Inman, p. 103.

[116] pp. 186–7 below.

which converted the existing Trade Boards and the Road Haulage Wages Board into Wage Councils, gave them additional powers over earnings and conditions, and fostered their extension into other industries. Elsewhere, 56 joint industrial councils were established or re-established in the war years.[117] Mr Bevin's greatest personal triumph was perhaps the decasualization of dock labour, which began in 1941.[118]

As in 1914–18, the trade unions grew greatly in stature and power during the war years. Membership rose from $6\frac{1}{4}$ million in 1939 to nearly 8 million in 1945. Trade union leaders were increasingly drawn into the machinery of Government. Joint consultation, originated in engineering in 1942, spread to many other industries, and Joint Production Committees, beginning spontaneously in Woolwich in 1940, covered $3\frac{1}{2}$ million workers by the end of 1944.[119]

The trade unions, unlike, for example, the farmers,[120] refrained from exerting their power to the full, and real wage *rates* rose more slowly than the cost of living, though faster than the official cost-of-living index, which had its components selectively held down in price (compare columns B and C in Table 5·12).

Table 5·12:   Wage rates, earnings and cost-of-living index

	Wage rates* Sept. 1939 = 100	Official cost-of-living index	Wage-earners' true cost-of-living index 1938 = 100	Weekly earnings Oct. 1938 = 100**
	A	B	C	D
1939	104	104	$102\frac{1}{2}$	—
1940	113–14	121	120	130
1941	122	128	135	142
1942	131–2	129	143	160
1943	136–7	129	148	176
1944	143–4	130	150	$181\frac{1}{2}$
1945	150–1	$133\frac{1}{2}$	—	$180\frac{1}{2}$

* July figures.   ** Current weights.

At the same time, overtime, night shifts and week-end work, together with much piecework and up-grading of workers, raised actual *earnings* a good deal more than wage rates.[121]

[117] D. F. MacDonald, *The State and the Trade Unions* (1960), chapter 9; PEP, *British Trade Unionism* (1948), pp. 39–54; Min. of Labour and Nat. Service, *Report for 1939–46*, pp. 269–94; Allan Flanders, 'Industrial Relations', in G. D. N. Worswick and P. H. Ady, *The British Economy 1945–1950* (Oxford, 1952), pp. 112–15.

[118] Hancock and Gowing, p. 240.

[119] Industrial Welfare Society, *Works Councils and Committees* (1943); Middlemas, *Power*; N. Barou, p. 170.

[120] Above.

[121] Ministry of Labour, *Report 1939–46*, pp. 304–5; Parker, *Manpower*, p. 433, pp. 167–8, J. L. Nicholson, 'Employment and National Income during the War', *Bull. Oxf. Inst. Stat.*, 7/14, 1945, Table 6, and 'Earnings and Hours of Labour', *ibid.*, 8/5, 1946, Table 2; Hancock and Gowing, p. 152.

Of the total increase in money earnings of 81%, it was estimated that 32% was due to a rise in wage rates, 9% to changes as between industries, 6% to increases in the hours of work, −1% to changes in the proportion of men, women, boys and girls employed, and 20% to all remaining factors, including overtime and piecework.[122]

Average wages, as always, hide many divergent movements in different industries. In conditions of full employment there was pressure to raise the wages of the low-paid unskilled and agricultural workers, of those who had dropped behind, such as miners and railwaymen and for workers in industries which had to attract much new labour quickly, such as engineering and aircraft. The Government accepted several of these grounds in its white paper on *Price Stabilization and Industrial Policy* of July 1941.[123] Altogether women's rates rose more than men's, and unskilled rates crept up from about 70% to about 80% of skilled rates in the course of the war.

In view of the profit limitations in force, the freezing of house rents by the Rent and Mortgage Interest Restriction Act of 1939, and the heavy burden of taxation on the rich, rising real wage earnings implied for the second World War, as it did in the first, a substantial redistribution of incomes in favour of wage-earners. While wage incomes (at constant, 1947 prices and after taxation) rose by 18% between 1938 and 1947, and 'social incomes' by 57%, incomes from property fell by 15% and salaries by 21%.[124] The following comparison exaggerates slightly the redistribution, since it omits the income from property represented by undistributed profits and capital appreciation[125] (see Table 5·13).

Table 5·13: Redistribution of income

	Post-tax real average Incomes in 1949. Index 1938 = 100	Percentage share in post-tax personal incomes at constant (1938) prices	
		1938	1949
Wages	122	37	47
Salaries	83	23	22
Forces' pay	82	2	3
Total work income	—	62	71
Farming income	191		
Professional earnings	89 }	12	10
Sole traders' profit	82		
Distributed property income	—	20	10
Social income	—	6	9
		100	100

[122] Nicholson, 'Earnings and Hours'; N. Barou, pp. 159–60.

[123] Cmd. 6294. Cf. also B. C. Roberts, *National Wages Policy in War and Peace* (1958), chapter 2.

[124] J. L. Nicholson, 'Employment and National Income', *loc. cit.,* Table 8; *National Income and Expenditure of the United Kingdom, 1938–1945* (1946. Cmd. 6784), Table 9; Dudley Seers, *Changes in the Cost-of-Living and the Distribution of Income since 1938* (Oxford, 1949), p. 64.

[125] Dudley Seers, 'The Levelling of Incomes', *Bull. Oxf. Inst. Stat.,* 12/10 (1950), pp. 278–9.

The war also saw a redistribution of property, though it was less marked than that in incomes. For example, the capital owned by owners of £100,000 and over fell from 22% in 1936–8 to 16·1% of the total in 1946–7, and that held by owners of £1,000–£10,000 rose from 29·3% to 32·8%.[126]

Control over consumption saw to it that while food consumption as a whole was cut by one-sixth in value,[127] the supplies of many basic foods were maintained at their peace-time levels, and others were even increased. These included liquid milk, flour and other cereals (partly by a higher extraction rate), potatoes, and fats other than butter. The basic foods were rationed in 1940 and consumption per head of meat, of sugar and of tea was cut substantially in the following years.[128] At the end of 1941 there followed the 'points system' rationing for other foods, as well as clothes rationing, and in 1942 'personal points' for sweets. Bread was not rationed at all during the war.[129] Among other goods, the consumption of tobacco and beer, as well as travel, increased most; consumption of fuel and light remained fairly constant; but consumption of clothing was down to less than one-half, and of household goods to less than 40% of pre-war. Private motoring was suspended and (unrationed) restaurant meals limited to 5s. Supplies of luxuries and non-necessities consumed by the rich were reduced most drastically. In general, it would be broadly true to state that personal consumption was stabilized at the pre-war skilled artisan level, and that of other classes cut down to approach it.[130]

There was also positive welfare provision, usually on grounds of national efficiency, but also out of the new feeling of common citizenship. For example, school meals were instituted, and they were served to all children, rich and poor alike. In the same way, nurseries were established for working mothers and for others. The cheap milk scheme for young children and expectant mothers began in 1940 and there followed the provision for orange juice, cod liver oil, a special egg allocation and vitamin tablets.[131] By these means there was achieved, after a slight deterioration in 1940 and 1941, a substantial improvement in the health of the country, especially in that of children, in spite of air raids, food shortages, overcrowding, the strain on medical services and other adverse factors. The infant mortality rate, perhaps the most sensitive index, declined substantially

[126] Kathleen M. Langley, 'The Distribution of Capital in Private Hands in 1936–8 and 1946–7, Part II', *Bull. Oxf. Inst. Stat.*, 13/2, 1951.

[127] *National Income and Expenditure of the United Kingdom, 1938–1945* (1946, Cmd. 6784), Table 9.

[128] *Statistical Digest of the War*, Tables 67, 70; *Food Consumption Levels in the United Kingdom* (1947. Cmd. 7203).

[129] A. S. MacNalty, *The Civilian Health and Medical Services*, vol. 1 (HSWW, 1953), chapter 5; Hargreaves and Gowing, *Civil Industry*, chapter 14; W. B. Reddaway, 'Rationing', in *Lessons of the British War Economy*; R. J. Hammond, *Food*, vol. 1 (1951), esp. chapters 8, 14, 15, 22, 23; vol. 2 (1956), Part C.

[130] J. Hurstfield, *The Control of Raw Materials* (1953), Appx. 15, Tables 1–3, Appx. 16; Hancock and Gowing, pp. 324, 492–5.

[131] Sheila Ferguson and Hilde Fitzgerald, *Studies in the Social Services* (HSWW, 1954), chapters 5, 6 and 7; D. J. Oddy, 'The Health of the People', in Theo Barker and Michael Drake (eds.) *Population and Society in Britain 1850–1980* (New York, 1982), pp. 132–3; MacNalty, *op. cit.*, chapter 4.

from 56 per 1,000 live births in England (77 in Scotland) in 1936–8 to 45 (58) in 1944–6.[132]

Munition workers and those employed in essential industries received special attention. Sometimes it was demanded in the interests of efficiency, in other cases it was necessary in order to attract and keep workers in factories inconveniently sited. There was humanity as well as an intelligent search for efficiency behind the increase from 35 whole-time and 70 part-time factory doctors in the whole country at the outbreak of war to 181 and 890 by 1944, and the increase from 1,500 industrial nurses to 8,000 in 1943. From November 1940 on, factory inspectors had power to make canteens compulsory in the large works, and in these they increased threefold, to 5,000, while in the smaller firms, not subject to the Order of 1940, they grew from 1,400 to 6,800, besides docks' canteens and seamen's welfare centres. The factory inspectorate was also given powers, by an earlier Order of July 1940, to insist on the appointment of welfare officers in large factories of 250 workers and over; their number rose from 1,500 to 5,378 in January 1944.[133]

Even outside the factories 'it would, in any relative sense, be true to say that by the end of the Second World War the Government had, through the agency of newly established or existing services, assumed and developed a measure of direct concern for the health and well-being of the population which, by contrast with the role of the Government in the 1930s, was little short of remarkable.'[134] Factory canteens were matched for the general public by the local authorities' 'British Restaurants'.[135]

As a result, the association of public welfare with charity and degradation was beginning to fade. Unemployment had virtually disappeared from the middle of 1941 on, but there were still many persons in need, and for them public aid was made more humane. The transfer, in 1940, of pensions, relief of war distress and allowances to families of men in the Forces to the renamed 'Assistance Board' did much also to change the attitude of that institution, and improved the treatment of old-age pensioners who drew supplementary relief under the Act of 1940,[136] and of other paupers.

It was part of the same trend that the committee of officials, set up in June 1941 under the chairmanship of Sir William Beveridge to report on social insurance and allied services after the war, should have been drawn towards one single comprehensive scheme, with similar benefit rates for all kinds of need, available to all as of right. Its report, issued (since its proposals were controversial) under Beveridge's name alone in November 1942, had an immediate and startling popular appeal as the 'Beveridge Report'[137] and became one of the pillars of the country's post-war plans.

---

[132] R. M. Titmuss, *Problems of Social Policy* (HSWW, 1950), p. 521, also pp. 509 ff.

[133] Inman, chapter 9; Parker, chapter 23; Ministry of Labour, *Report 1939–46*, p. 113.

[134] R. M. Titmuss, p. 506. Cf. also Alan T. Peacock and Jack Wiseman, *The Growth of Public Expenditure in the United Kingdom* (1961).

[135] R. J. Hammond, *Food*, vol. 2, chapters 23–25.

[136] W. H. Beveridge, *Full Employment in a Free Society* (1945 ed.), Part III; D. C. Marsh, *National Insurance and Assistance in Great Britain* (1950), pp. 51–2.

[137] Sir William Beveridge, *Social Insurance and Allied Services* (1942. Cmd. 6404).

6 Plans for Post-war Reconstruction

In response to 'the strong impulse to fuse the will to victory with aspirations for a better world after victory',[138] Churchill's Coalition Government set up a War Aims Committee of the War Cabinet in August 1940, although it was only in 1943 that a Minister of Reconstruction was appointed. A Minister without Portfolio had been assigned the duty of post-war planning since 1940, and it was as such that Mr Arthur Greenwood invited Sir William Beveridge to report on the insurance services.

The immediate occasion of the appointment of the Beveridge Committee was the protest by the trade unions at the suspension of the work of the Royal Commission on Workmen's Compensation in 1940.[139] The Committee's Report appeared in November 1942. Its main points were embodied in its six 'principles'.[140] The first was its comprehensiveness. It covered all the known causes of the 'giant', Want, by providing for unemployment benefit, sickness benefit, disability benefit, workmen's compensation, old age, widows' and orphans' pensions and benefits, funeral grants and maternity benefit. In addition to these financial provisions, the Report was also based on the assumption that a comprehensive health and rehabilitation service was to be established, and it made the further proposal that children's allowances should be paid to all. These two suggestions, translated into the National Health Service and Family Allowances, became as vital to the fabric of the Welfare State as social insurance itself. Lastly, a system of 'National Assistance' was to be maintained to cover those who despite all forethought did not fit into any of the categories of beneficiaries and those for whom the benefits paid were insufficient. The scheme was to be comprehensive also in the sense of covering the whole population, whether employed, occupied or unoccupied.

The second principle was that of unification of administrative responsibility. Instead of the nine different Government departments, and the multitude of local authorities and 'approved societies'[141] there was to be a single scheme, a single Ministry, and a single weekly stamp to be paid by the insured person and his employer to cover all the insurance provisions.

Thirdly, there was classification. The whole population was grouped from the outset in six main classes, and their contribution rates and benefit rights laid down from the beginning. The classes were: wage and salary earners, others gainfully occupied, housewives, others of working age, those below working age and retired persons above working age.

The fourth principle was that of adequate benefits. After careful study, the minimum needs were established and (subject to variations of the cost of living) were to be the standard basis of payment for all types of benefit, in place of the illogical differences of the rates under existing schemes. Only two exceptions were to be made, a lower rate for old-age pensioners in the early years of the scheme, because of their lower contributions in the course of their working life,

[138] W. K. Hancock and M. M. Gowing, *British War Economy* (1949), p. 534.

[139] For other Trade-Union action, see Keith Middlemas, *Power, Competition and the State ... 1940–61* (Stanford, 1986), p. 64; N. Barou, *British Trade Unions* (1947), pp. 184–5, chapter 16; PEP, *British Trade Unionism* (1948), p. 147; D. F. MacDonald, *The State and the Trade Unions* (1960), p. 134.

[140] Sir William Beveridge, *Social Insurance and Allied Services* (1942. Cmd. 6404), Paras. 303–9.

[141] W. A. Robson (ed.), *Social Security* (3rd ed., 1948), Introduction, p. 35.

and a higher rate in some cases of prolonged incapacity and industrial injury, the former 'workmen's compensation'.

The fifth principle, closely allied to the fourth, was that of flat-rate benefits, according to the size of the family, and irrespective of normal earnings or length of benefit. Corresponding to it was the sixth principle, flat-rate contribution. Of the tripartite income of the Insurance Fund, the Exchequer and local authorities were to contribute about 50%, insured persons (including the self-employed) about 30%, and employers about 20%. The scheme as a whole implied a considerable increase in social security payments.[142]

Though radical in the changes it proposed, the Beveridge Plan was not revolutionary. It resembled the British educational system in providing a national minimum by the State while allowing those who could afford it to buy better provisions, in the field of superannuation, for example, and, as it turned out, in the medical service also. Moreover, it was the natural culmination of the development of the 1930s and this perhaps explains the remarkable support it received. Its popular appeal was immense, 250,000 copies of the full report and 350,000 of an official abridgement being sold within a few months.[143]

The Treasury, however, was less than happy with it, in spite of Beveridge's 'deal' with Keynes representing the Treasury, whereby the additional burdens on the Treasury in the early years were limited to £100 million per annum, largely by postponing the full benefits for old-age pensioners. The Government's own proposals, set forth in two white papers in September 1944,[144] fell short of Beveridge's proposals, especially in respect of the principle of 'adequacy', but in many other respects followed them closely. The two parallel proposals for a complete and comprehensive health service after the war and for family allowances respectively, were, however, adopted by the Coalition Government during the war, the latter being enacted in June 1945.

The Beveridge Report had assumed a parallel employment policy with unemployment at no less than $8\frac{1}{2}$%, but Beveridge, with the help of a brilliant team of economists, prepared a second, unofficial report, proposing means of reducing the post-war unemployment rate to 3%.[145] Even before its appearance in November 1944, the Government had brought out its own white paper on Employment Policy[146] in May. This, in its way, was to have even more influence on post-war policies of British Governments. Though very carefully, on Treasury insistence, omitting any reference to budget deficits, or to a cyclical employment policy such as had been prepared by James Meade as early as 1941[147], and

---

[142] R. W. B. Clarke, 'The Beveridge Report and After', and 'Social Security Housekeeping', in *Social Security*; D. C. Marsh, *National Insurance and Assistance in Great Britain* (1950), pp. 65–9; Karl de Schweinitz, *England's Road to Social Security* (1943), pp. 228–44; Sir W. H. Beveridge, *Pillars of Security* (1942).

[143] Lord Beveridge, *Power and Influence* (1953), chapters 14, 15. For a critical view, see J. W. Nisbet and others, *The Beveridge Plan* (1943).

[144] *Social Insurance*, Part I (1944. Cmd. 6550) and Part II (1944. Cmd. 6551). W. H. Beveridge, 'Epilogue', in *Social Security*, pp. 412–17.

[145] W. H. Beveridge, *Full Employment in a Free Society* (1944), pp. 21, 126–8.

[146] Cmd. 6527.

[147] PRO CAB 87/54. 1EP(42) 21; Roger Middleton, *Towards the Managed Economy* (1985), p. 88; Alec Cairncross, *Years of Recovery. British Economic Policy 1945–51* (1985), p. 19; Jim Tomlinson, *Employment Policy 1939–1955* (Oxford, 1987), p. 80; Alan Booth, 'The "Keynesian Revolution" in Economic Policy Making', *Econ. Hist. Rev.* 36/1, 1983; G. C. Peden, 'Sir Richard Hopkins and the "Keynesian Revolution" in Employment Policy, 1929–1945', *ibid.* 36/2, 1983.

still hedged with qualifications[148] the white paper marks a decisive turning point in the Government's acceptance 'as one of their primary aims and responsibilities ... the maintenance of a high and stable level of employment after the war'.

The Government also prepared other social reconstruction plans. The policy for education was outlined in a white paper[149] and incorporated in the Education Act of 1944. This raised the school age to 15 (postponed, in the event, to 1947), foreshadowed its extension to 16, and enacted free secondary education for all. The uses of land and town planning were discussed in three official reports and in a Government white paper in 1944,[150] and in 1943 an independent Ministry of Town and Country Planning was set up. There were also specific plans made for housing after the war,[151] and in 1944 there was a white paper on 'Scientific Research and Development'.[152]

These were long-term plans of reconstruction, but there were the immediate problems of demobilization also. 'The "run-down" of war industry had begun a long time before victory in Europe was in sight and continued long after it had been achieved.'[153] The labour force in the munition industry had begun to be reduced in 1943, permitting some increased recruitment to the Forces, as well as conversion to peacetime and export needs. From the autumn of 1944 on, war contracts were broken on a large scale.[154] When hostilities were actually at an end, a vast controlled demobilization programme as well as tremendous shifts between industries, had to be carried out. Between the middle of 1945 and the end of 1946, for example, engineering lost half a million workers, mostly women, and building gained over half a million, nearly all men. Much of this transition had been planned well before the end of the war.[155]

Post-war planning also had to consider international economic relationships and policies. They had not been forgotten in wartime negotiations[156] and even before the end of the war, the Allies set out to determine the ground plans, not only for the political framework of the United Nations, but also for the operative conditions of post-war economic life.

Among the basic weaknesses in the 1930s, inhibiting international trade by a vicious circle of tariffs and restrictions, had been international illiquidity. An international bank, holding a generally acceptable currency, could provide the initial liquidity that could carry a much higher level of international trade on the basis of similar national resources. Plans to create such a world authority were first drafted in 1941 by Keynes in Britain and by Harry D. White in the

[148] U. K. Hicks, *Public Finance* (1947), pp. 325–9, chapter 18.
[149] *Educational Reconstruction* (1944. Cmd. 6548).
[150] *Royal Commission on the Distribution of the Industrial Population* (Barlow Report) (1939. Cmd. 6153); *Committee on Land Utilisation in Rural Areas* (Scott Report) (1942. Cmd. 6378); *Expert Committee on Compensation and Betterment* (Uthwatt Report) (1942. Cmd. 6386); *The Control of Land Use* (1944. Cmd. 6537).
[151] *Housing* (1945. Cmd. 6609).
[152] Cmd. 6514.
[153] M. M. Postan, *British War Production* (1952), p. 371.
[154] W. Ashworth, *Contracts and Finance* (1953), p. 64.
[155] E. L. Hargreaves and M. M. Gowing, *Civil Industry and Trade* (1952), pp. 618–27; H. M. D. Parker, *Manpower* (1957), chapter 16; Ministry of Labour and National Service, *Report 1939–1946*, pp. 73 ff., 194 ff. For a critical view, see Correlli Barnett, *The Audit of War* (1986), p. 263.
[156] Cf. p. 182 above.

USA, and as both tended to reflect the particular needs of their countries, they found their respective schemes championed by the two Governments. The economic strength of the United States ensured that her proposal was the one which was ultimately accepted.[157] The final scheme, as agreed to at the historic Bretton Woods Conference in July 1944,[158] was in two parts, one dealing with the problem of international liquidity by means of the 'International Monetary Fund', and the other establishing a 'Bank for Reconstruction and Development' for long-term loans.

For Britain, the Fund was of greater immediate interest. By the rules adopted by the IMF, each country paid a contribution to the Fund roughly according to its economic strength, and this was to be made partly in gold and largely in the member's own currency. These quota contributions were held by the Fund, to be available to any member state finding itself short of the currency of another, in exchange for its own, at fixed parity rates. It was clear to all the delegates that the IMF (as indeed the Bank) would in the first instance be used largely to make United States dollars available to the rest of the world, and their attitudes to the provisions of the Fund were largely coloured by that fact. Thus the United States insisted successfully on 'limited liability', i.e. a fixed quota, so that there was a clear limit to the total dollars to be contributed, as also on a penalty for being a persistent international borrower on short-term account. There was, however, the 'scarce currency' clause, which permitted other members to take protective measures against the country whose currency was in such demand that the Fund's holding of it was running down; in the circumstances, this was most likely to be the American dollar.

The Fund could not, and was not intended to, correct a fundamental and persistent disequilibrium; it was merely to act as a substantial buffer in the case of a temporary unbalance. Member states bound themselves not to devalue their currencies, except under certain conditions to 'correct a fundamental disequilibrium', not to discriminate against other member states and, after a transitional period, not to place restrictions on current international payments. There were, at the time, further negotiations in progress to lower tariffs and other trade restrictions and discriminations, and these ultimately led to the General Agreement on Tariffs and Trade (GATT) in 1947.

Other international obligations undertaken by Britain included the agreement to share in the costs of the United Nations Relief and Rehabilitation Administration (UNRRA),[159] the agency which prevented starvation and diseases from ravaging much of Europe, Asia and other parts of the world after the fighting; the Hot Springs Agreement, establishing the Food and Agriculture Organization

---

[157] R. F. Harrod, *Life of John Maynard Keynes* (1951), chapter 13; Richard N. Gardner, *Sterling–Dollar Diplomacy* (Oxford, 1956), chapter 5; J. H. Williams, *Post-War Monetary Plans* (New York, 1947), essays 8–11; Joan Robinson, 'The International Currency Proposals', in *The New Economics* (ed. Seymour E. Harris) (1949); R. Triffin, *Europe and the Money Muddle* (New Haven, 1957), chapter 3; Jacob Viner, 'Two Plans for International Monetary Stabilization', in *International Economics* (Glencoe, Ill., 1951); Brian Tew, *International Monetary Co-operation 1945–1952* (1952), chapters 6, 7; Alvin H. Hansen, *America's Role in the World Economy* (1945), chapters 4–7; A. J. Youngson, *The British Economy 1920–1957* (1960), pp. 155–6.

[158] *United Nations Monetary and Financial Conference, Final Act* (1944. Cmd. 6546).

[159] UNRRA, *Resolutions and Reports Adopted by the Council* (1943. Cmd. 6497).

(FAO);[160] and the International Labour Organization (ILO) surviving from the days of the League of Nations.[161]

Throughout all the discussions that were to shape the post-war world, Britain's vote tended to be cast for protection and discrimination. Having lost so many sources of her invisible earnings, Britain foresaw the most dire threat to the pound sterling and to her balance of payments if freedom of trade and exchange were to be allowed too quickly. From the viewpoint of mid-1945, before the war had yet ended, the British current balance for 1946, after the end of lend-lease, appeared as shown in Table 5·14.[162]

Table 5·14:   The British expected balance of payments, 1946

	1938	1946 estimate
Deficit on visible trade	−300	−650
Government expenditure abroad	− 16	−300
Net invisible income	+248	+120
Total unfavourable balance (including some other items)	—	−750

The Treasury experts making these forecasts could not then know that the war against Japan would barely outlast that in Europe, that lend-lease would be abolished at once at its end, and that several other unfavourable factors would combine to make Britain's post-war position far worse than they had dared to imagine in their most pessimistic moments.

[160] *Final Act of the United Nations Conference on Food and Agriculture* (1943. Cmd. 6451); *Documents relating to the Food and Agriculture Organisation of the United Nations* (1945. Cmd. 6590).

[161] Hansen, chapters 10–13; Sir Frederick Leggett, 'The Contribution of the ILO', in Ministry of Labour and National Service, *The Worker in Industry* (1952).

[162] Hancock and Gowing, p. 549.

6

Reconversion to Peace, 1945–1950

1 The Dollar Problem and the Sterling Crises

The gloomy forecasts about the British balance of payments, with which the last chapter ended, rested on two basic facts. The first was that Britain had for years lived beyond her means by consuming her capital, by borrowing and by gifts from abroad, and that these had to cease in the summer of 1945, leaving a large gap. The second was that the disruption and diversion of British productive capacity during the war had been so violent that, to fill that gap, several years would be needed before it could be restored to its full peace-time efficiency. The years of that restoration form the framework of this chapter.

The year chosen as the end of that period, 1950, is a somewhat arbitrary mark. In some respects 1949 would be a better date, seeing the end, for example, of the period of basic foreign exchange disequilibrium; if the political view is taken, 1951 was the year in which the Labour Government handed over to the Conservatives; and the economic repercussions of the Korean War did not give way to 'normalcy' until 1952 or 1953. In this chapter the artificial limit of the date chosen will be broken whenever events require it. But, broadly, 1950 may be taken as indicating the watershed when the worst of the effects of the war were over and when Britain had returned to a position comparable with that at the outbreak of war.

Of the fundamental economic problems left by the war the foreign balance appeared the most urgent. The economy desperately needed to import fuel, raw materials and food without having the means to pay for them. The only possible sources of supply in a war-ravaged world were in North America, and in order to tap them, Britain had to ask for an American loan.

In the negotiations over this loan, the causes of Britain's foreign trade weakness were put most succinctly.[1] Commodity exports had been reduced to little more than a third in the war, and the sources of invisible exports had also greatly diminished: total merchant shipping, for example, was down from 22·1 to 15·9 million dw. tons (ocean-going vessels of 1,600 tons and over), one-quarter of overseas investments, worth £1,118 million, had been sold off, while the overseas debt was increased by a rise in 'sterling balances' from £476 million to £3,355 million by June 1945 and £3,567 million by the end of the year. To meet this gap, exports would have to be raised by at least 50% in volume above pre-war; to meet at the same time the need of repaying the sterling debt, of building up a shrunken gold and dollar reserve, and of investments in the more

---

[1] *Statistical Material Presented During the Washington Negotiations* (December 1945. Cmd. 6707); cf. also H. S. Booker, *The Problem of Britain's Overseas Trade* (1948), chapters, 5, 9.

backward parts of the Empire, the volume of exports would have to be raised by 75%. Even that level was unduly optimistic, for it neglected the import content of increased export goods production (perhaps + 15% of imports) and the likely deterioration in the terms of trade.[2] It would take 3–5 years to reach that level of 175% of pre-war exports, and meanwhile an adverse balance of at least £1,250 million would have accumulated. This was the sum which the Americans were asked to cover by a loan.

From the American point of view, however, Britain was only one of many countries seeking aid, and among them she was the least to claim pity on grounds of poverty, and the most to be feared as a potential trade rival. Ultimately a 'line of credit', $3,750 million was granted to Britain, plus £650 million to pay the outstanding lend-lease debts, and to this the Canadians added a loan, on the same terms, of $1,250 million. The terms themselves were not ungenerous, interest being at 2%, to become payable, together with the capital repayments over 50 years, only in 1951. But there were 'strings'. One was the undertaking by Britain to reduce the sterling balances. Much more serious was the obligation to apply the Bretton Woods terms of making sterling convertible within a year of the actual granting of the loan, i.e. by July 1947.

This latter condition would inevitably endanger the 'dollar pool' of the sterling area. It would prevent Britain from using her strong importer position in bilateral trade treaties: with the 1930s in mind, Britain was particularly alarmed at being left defenceless against an expected American slump, which would aggravate the dollar payments problem.[3] There was widespread opposition to the acceptance of these onerous terms,[4] but the United Kingdom was not in a position to refuse.

Meanwhile, the high hopes placed on the international institutions designed to ensure a freer flow of trade were being generally disappointed. The International Trade Organization, proposed in December 1945,[5] was stillborn, and the more modest General Agreement on Tariffs and Trade[6] (the Havana Charter), designed to reduce tariffs, was being ratified very slowly and came into operation only in 1948. The International Monetary Fund was, perhaps, even less satisfactory. Its funds proved too small to carry the strain of the vast unbalance in world trade that was rapidly developing.[7] It had, in fact, been designed to deal with deflationary policies spreading from one country to another, not with persistent dollar shortages: with the problems, in other words, of the 1930s and

[2] PEP, *Britain and World Trade* (1947), pp. 61 ff.

[3] PEP, *op. cit.,* chapters 7, 9; O. Hoeffding, 'The US, and World Trade', in Mark Abrams (ed.), *Britain and Her Export Trade* (1946).

[4] *Financial Agreement Between the Governments of the United States and the United Kingdom* (1945. Cmd. 6708); Richard N. Gardner, *Sterling-Dollar Diplomacy* (Oxford, 1956), chapters 10, 11; R. D. Hall, *North American Supply* (1955), pp. 477–9; but see R. F. Harrod, *A Page of British Folly* (1946).

[5] *Proposals for Consideration by an International Conference on Trade and Employment* (1945. Cmd. 6709).

[6] 1947. Cmd. 7258.

[7] T. Balogh, 'The International Aspect', in G. D. N. Worswick and P. H. Ady, *The British Economy, 1945–1950* (Oxford, 1952), pp. 504–5; Gardner, Chapters 14–17; J. H. Williams, *Post-War Monetary Plans* (Oxford, 1949), essays 5–7; Brian Tew, *International Monetary Co-operation 1945–1952* (1952), chapters 7, 8; Sir Hubert D. Henderson, 'A Criticism of the Havana Charter', *Amer. Econ. Rev.,* 39/3, 1949; Donald B. Marsh, *World Trade and Investment* (New York, 1951), pp. 423–4, chapters 26–29, 32.

not of the late 1940s. It could, therefore, do little to cure the world's main economic ailment, which appeared in every country in turn as a dollar shortage or a dollar 'gap'.

The dollar shortage in the rest of the world, as in Britain, was caused by the desperate need for goods and services which could be obtained only in the dollar area – for dollars. In a sense, therefore, it was a transient phenomenon, until the war-shattered economies were re-built. Its very universality, however, induced the widespread belief that it would be permanent, and even that it had begun in the inter-war years.[8]

Europe's population was rising and its food production falling behind (see Table 6·1).[9]

Table 6·1 European population and food production

Average of years	Index of population	Index of output, 5 grains	Average of years	Index of output, 7 crops, weighted by value
1912–14	100	100	1909–13	100
1937–9	115	110	1934–8	113
1947–9	113	84	1949–50	103

In addition, many of the European raw materials were nearing exhaustion. The terms of trade were bound to turn against the industrialized countries,[10] and Western Europe was bound to lose her trade surplus even with the non-dollar primary producers. Since, further, American productivity was rising faster than that of the rest of the world, and the USA, unlike Britain in the days of her hegemony, neither allowed imports freely into the country, nor invested her surpluses freely abroad, but, on the contrary, went in for deflationary policies, the dollar gap was growing ever wider.[11] Keynes was almost alone in maintaining, in a posthumous article,[12] that the dollar shortage would be short-lived.

Britain achieved a fair degree of success in expanding exports, especially to dollar and other 'hard currency' areas, but the drain on the gold and dollar reserves continued. In July 1946, the dollars of the 'line of credit' became

---

[8] p. 89 above; also J. R. Sargent, 'Britain and Europe', in *The British Economy 1945–1950*, Elliott Zupnick, *Britain's Postwar Dollar Problem* (New York, 1957) chapters 5 and 6; G. Crowther, *Balances and Imbalances of Payments* (Boston, Mass., 1957), p. 34.

[9] Ingvar Svennilsen, *Growth and Stagnation in the European Economy* (UK, Geneva, 1954), pp. 236–7, 247, *passim*.

[10] C. P. Kindleberger, 'Industrial Europe's Terms of Trade on Current Account, 1870–1953', *Econ. J.*, 65/257, 1955.

[11] E.g. T. Balogh, *The Dollar Crisis, Cause and Cure* (Oxford, 1950), chapter 1, and 'The Dollar Crisis Revisited', *Oxf. Econ. P.*, NS, 6/2, 1954; J. H. Williams, *Economic Stability in the Modern World* (Oxford, 1952); A. J. Brown, 'Dollars and Crises', *Ec. Hist. Rev.*, 2nd S., 12/2, 1959, pp. 287–90; Seymour E. Harris, *The European Recovery Program* (Cambridge, Mass., 1948), pp. 96 ff.; R. G. Hawtrey, *The Balance of Payments and the Standard of Living* (1950), chapters 4 and 5; Donald MacDougall, *The World Dollar Problem* (1957), esp. chapter 15, Appx. IA and XVc.

[12] J. M. Keynes, 'The Balance of Payments of the United States', *Econ. J.*, 56/222, 1946; cf. also R. F. Harrod, *Life of John Maynard Keynes* (1951), p. 621; R. Triffin, *Gold and the Dollar Crisis* (New Haven, 1960), p. 5.

available, and it was intended that they should last until 1951, by which time equilibrium was to be restored, but it soon became clear that the loan was drawn on much more rapidly than was safe: in the year to 30 June 1947, purchases from hard currency areas totalled $1,540 million, sales to them on $340 million. A harsh winter was followed by a fuel crisis which held up production and transport and was estimated to have cost £200 million in exports; invisible earnings were disappointing; and the terms of trade turned sharply against the United Kingdom, adding £329 million to the import bill in 1947.[13]

It was in these unpropitious circumstances that the convertibility of sterling had to be permitted on 15 July, under the terms of the dollar loan. The run on the dollar pool was immediate, as almost every country with sterling earnings hurried to convert them into dollars.[14] The drain on the dollar reserve was so alarming that the restrictions had to be put on again after barely one month. The gold and dollar reserves fell in the course of 1947 by over $600 million, or one-quarter. On current balance of payments, there was a deficit of £545 million in the course of the year; with the dollar area alone, of £571 million.[15]

A similar dollar crisis hit the whole of Western Europe in 1947. Against the background of an emergent 'cold war' between East and West, General Marshall offered massive American aid to Europe in June 1947, provided Europe adopted a measure of economic co-operation. This was eagerly accepted by the governments of Western Europe, who met in September 1947 as the Committee of European Economic Co-operation (CEEC) of 16 nations and prepared a four-year 'plan'. Congress approved 'Marshall Aid' in April 1948, and in September 1948 Western Europe agreed on its distribution. The European Recovery Programme (ERP) provided over $6 billion in its first year (1948–9) and $3·8 billion in the next year, plus $700 million for military aid ('Mutual Defence Assistance'). Thereafter recovery aid tapered off, Britain declining Marshall Aid after the end of 1950, but the Marshall plan had fulfilled it main function of carrying Europe over its critical deficit years.[16] It had also induced closer co-operation among European nations, beginning with the first inter-European payments scheme in October 1948 and ending in the fully-fledged European Payments Union (EPU) of 1950, which encouraged European trade by creating a mutual clearing system.[17]

The United Kingdom drew its share of Marshall Aid, while its trade balance also improved impressively in 1948. But at the end of 1948 the relaxation of controls and the booming home demand again made inroads into the precarious balance of payments.[18] A sustained attack on sterling began in international

---

[13] A. J. Youngson, *The British Economy 1920–1957* (1960), pp. 164–8.

[14] Cf. Paul Bareau, 'The Position of Sterling in International Trade', in Institute of Bankers, *Banking and Foreign Trade* (1953).

[15] *UK Balance of Payments 1946–1950* (No. 2) (1951. Cmd. 8201).

[16] J. H. Williams, 'The Task of Economic Recovery', in *Post War Monetary Plans* (Oxford, 1949); H. B. Price, *The Marshall Plan and Its Meaning* (Ithaca, NY, 1955); Robert E. Summers (ed.), *Economic Aid to Europe: The Marshall Plan* (New York, 1948); OEEC, *9th Report. A Decade of Co-operation. Achievements and Perspectives* (Paris, 1958); Triffin, *Europe and the Money Muddle* (New Haven, 1957), chapters 3 and 4; Stanley Hoffmann and Charles Maier, *The Marshall Plan: A Retrospective* (Boulder, Col., 1984); T. Balogh, *Dollar Crisis*, chapter 2.

[17] R. Triffin, *Europe and the Money Muddle*, chapter 5; but see Per Jacobsson, 'Trade and Financial Relations between Countries – the Progress Towards Multilateralism', in Institute of Bankers, *Banking and Foreign Trade* (1953).

[18] Gilbert Walker, *Economic Planning* (1957), pp. 109–29; p. 205 below.

markets[19] and forced the Chancellor to devalue the pound sterling in September 1949, from $4·03 to $2·80.

The extent of the devaluation, 30·5%, was far larger than seemed warranted by internal purchasing power or by international markets. Apart from the Sterling Area itself, few of the other countries followed Britain's devaluation to that extreme, Italy, for example, devaluing by 8%, Belgium by 13% and Germany by 20% so that the devaluation against a trade-weighted bundle of other currencies amounted to only 9%.[20]

Further, the decision to devalue at all was questionable, nor did it improve Britain's international competitive position[21], for in the existing conditions of import control little could be hoped for from reduced imports, while exports had been held back, not so much by high costs as by sheer inability to produce. After the devaluation, more scarce resources would have to be devoted to exports to buy the identical quantum of imports, and higher import prices would boost inflation.[22]

The devaluation was a flagrant violation of the Bretton Woods Agreement, in spirit if not in letter (the Fund being forced to sanction it as a virtual *fait accompli*), and contributed no little to its weakness and to the general disillusionment with the post-war international institutions. With the ending of the speculative attack, the gold and dollar reserves rose again quickly, from $1,425 million at the end of September 1949 to $2,422 million in mid-1950, and by that time the rapidly rising volume of output and exports was beginning to restore the long-term trade balance. Though the Korean War and the stockpiling crisis associated with it in 1951 caused the third of what threatened to be regular economic crises in alternate years, British economic recovery was by then firmly set.

The main movements are illustrated by the following statistics (£m. except the last two columns)[23] (see Table 6·2).

The success of the export drive was quite outstanding, exports increasing even in real terms by 77% between 1946 and 1950. By 1948, the diminished annual dollar deficits were met largely by the net dollar earnings of the raw materials producers of the rest of the Sterling Area,[24] while, British trade with the rest of the Sterling Area also became increasingly favourable.[25]

What was at least as heartening as the 'phenomenal growth of British

[19] A. A. Rogow, *The Labour Government and British Industry 1945–1951* (Oxford, 1955), pp. 35–6, 121–2.

[20] Alec Cairncross and Barry Eichengreen, *Sterling in Decline* (Oxford 1983), p. 153.

[21] M. J. Flanders, 'The Effects of Devaluation on Exports, a Case Study: United Kingdom 1949–54', *Oxford University Institute of Statistics Bulletin*, 25/3, 1963; A. Cairncross. 'Caliban: The Devaluation of Sterling in 1949', in C. P. Kindleberger and Guido di Tella (eds.), *Economics in the Long Run* (3 vols., New York, 1982), pp. 121–54.

[22] Hawtrey, *op. cit.*, pp. 99–111; Triffin, *Money Muddle*, p. 75; R. F. Harrod, *Policy Against Inflation* (1958), pp. 132–51.

[23] *United Kingdom Balance of Payments, 1946–1954* (1954. Cmd. 9291); also *Committee on the Working of the Monetary System* (Radcliffe Report) (1959. Cmnd. 827), p. 234; Alec Cairncross, *Years of Recovery* (1985), pp. 212 f.; G. D. H. Cole, *The Post-War Condition of Britain* (1956), chapters 13, 14; *Annual Abstract of Statistics*.

[24] *Radcliffe Report*, paras, 649–56; D. H. Robertson, *Britain in the World Economy* (1954), p. 49; *United Kingdom Balance of Payments 1946–1953* (1953. Cmd. 8976).

[25] J. R. Sargent, 'Britain and the Sterling Area', in *The British Economy, 1945–1950*.

Table 6·2:   The British balance of trade

	Exports A	Balance of visible trade B	Total current balance of payments C	Change in sterling liabilities D	Inter-government transactions, + = receipts by UK − = payments by UK E	Other capital movements F	Changes in gold and dollar reserves G	Terms of trade Board of Trade, 1947=100 H	ECA mission,* 1938=100
1946	917	− 165	− 295	+ 43	+ 240	+ 99	+ 87	87**	108
1947	1,145	− 415	− 442	− 112	+ 639	− 301	− 216	100	117
1948	1,602	− 192	+ 7	− 346	+ 437	− 167	− 69	102	121
1949	1,841	− 137	+ 38	− 9	+ 160	− 207	− 18	101	122
1950	2,250	− 133	+ 297	+ 340	+ 127	− 81	+ 683	108	133
1951	2,748	− 733	− 419	+ 94	− 36	− 266	− 627	123	159†

* MSA Mission to the United Kingdom, *Economic Development in the United Kingdom, 1850–1950*, pp. 104–5.
** 1938.
† June 1951.

exports'[26] was their changed composition. Unlike her balance of the inter-war years, Britain was largely concentrating on the growth sectors of world trade:[27]

Table 6·3:   British export composition

Proportion of Exports in 1952–3	United Kingdom	World
Among expanding commodities	65·0%	53·6%
Among stable commodities	4·5	17·5
Among declining commodities	30·3	28·9

The improvement in the current balance of payments (Table 6·2, column C), except for the disastrous Korean War year of 1951, plus the proceeds from loans and aid (column E) were dissipated, not in strengthening the precarious reserves (column G), but in making foreign investments, probably under-estimated in the table;[28] and in paying off some of the sterling balances (columns F and D).[29] Thus the vulnerability of sterling at the beginning of the period was not yet cured at the end. With a reserve of barely £1,000 million, a swing of £200–300 million in any one year, relatively minute in comparison with the total trade of the Sterling Area of £10,000, would still cause a major crisis.

Critics were not wanting who attacked the order of priorities. Foreign investments at the rate of £1,650 million in six years 1945–51, were considered to be

[26] *Radcliffe Report*, para. 402.
[27] P. D. Henderson, 'Britain's International Position', in *The British Economy, 1945–1950*, p. 70; F. H. Awad, 'The Structure of the World Export Trade, 1926–1952', *Yorkshire Bulletin*, 11/1, 1959, p. 35; PEP, *Britain and World Trade* (1947), p. 117, also chapter 8.
[28] A. R. Conan, *Capital Imports into Sterling Countries* (1960), pp. 82–6; ECE, *Economic Survey of Europe in 1949* (Geneva, 1950), pp. 124–6.
[29] R. F. Harrod, *Policy Against Inflation* (1958), pp. 111 ff.

too high. Expenditure on maintaining troops abroad could also have been cut, and a strong case could be made for cutting imports rather than increasing exports, with the incidental merit of turning the terms of trade less sharply against Britain.[30]

The precarious foreign balance was not unconnected with the domestic problem of a rate of incomes and welfare schemes incommensurate with real output and thus a level of *ex-ante* plans of real consumption spending and investment which production did not warrant,[31] but which all classes considered to be their right as victors in a long and weary struggle. It was the same excess of incomes over output which created the foreign unbalance and the domestic inflationary pressure, and to understand the former fully, it is therefore necessary to turn to a consideration of domestic economic policy.

2 Full Employment Policies in Practice

Economic policy making by the post-war Government was dominated by its inheritance of a large measure of suppressed inflation, i.e. an excess of purchasing power over goods available at current prices, prevented from resulting in open inflation only by price controls and physical restrictions. In that sense the war-time Keynesian 'National Income' budgeting had not been harsh enough, for it had been unable to prevent the accumulation of potentially inflationary funds, ready to burst forth as soon as the control barriers were removed. The banks were in a state of over-liquidity which was potentially even more dangerous.[32]

The liquid assets of the personal sector had changed as shown in Table 6·4.[33]

Table 6·4:   The growth of liquid assets

	1938	£ million 1946	1951	% Change 1938–46
Net personal deposits in London Clearing Banks	c. 560	1,423	1,675	c. +154
Building Society deposits and shares	682	785	1,216	+15
Post Office savings bank deposits	495	1,910	1,902	+286
Trustee savings bank deposits	233	643	917	+176
Total liquid assets	c. 1,970	4,762	5,710	c. +142
Personal disposable income	4,675	7,569	10,389	+62
Liquid assets as % of incomes	42%	63%	55%	

[30] R. F. Harrod, *Are These Hardships Necessary?* (1947), and *Life of Keynes*, pp. 615–16; H. S. Booker, *op. cit.*, pp. 168–71; S. E. Harris, *European Recovery Program*, pp. 37–41.

[31] Triffin, *Money Muddle*, chapter 2.

[32] Cf., in general, G. D. N. Worswick, 'The British Economy 1945–50', in G. D. N. Worswick and P. H. Ady, *The British Economy 1945–1950* (Oxford, 1952); also R. F. Harrod, *Policy Against Inflation* (1958), pp. 93–106; Edward Nevin and E. W. Davis, *The London Clearing Banks* (1970), p. 149.

[33] *Committee on the Working of the Monetary System* (*Radcliffe Report*) (1959. Cmnd. 827), Table 22.

Similarly, 'tender' Treasury Bills had risen from £650 million before the war to £1,800 million, the banks held £1,800 million of TDRs, and total money supply as a proportion of national income which had been 52·4% in 1939 and 69·6% in 1945, rose to a peak of 79·2% in 1947. The M3 multiplier had risen from 3·969 in 1944 to beyond its pre-war level at 4·624 in 1950.[34] The total excess liquidity in the economy was of the order of magnitude of £3 billion, or a year's tax revenue.[35]

Opinion differed widely on the best methods of dealing with it. To follow the model of 1918–19 by removing the controls as quickly as possible was hardly practical politics. More realistic was the proposal of a tax on capital or savings, disguised, perhaps, as a currency 'reform'.[36] The methods used in several continental countries were ably canvassed here,[37] but the Labour Government at no time seriously considered any measure of confiscating capital, apart from the small 'special contribution' of the budget of April 1948. A third group of proposals, favoured by many economists, was for a deflationary policy, including high interest rates, in order to let 'the market', rather than the Government, decide where the necessary cuts were to be made,[38] but given the degree of liquidity, rates would have to be impossibly high to be effective.

In the policy which it eventually adopted, the Government had the advantage of possessing vastly greater economic powers than any peacetime Government had ever possessed before, and it disposed of a larger share of the national income, public revenue (including that of local authorities and the Insurance Funds) amounting to 37·7% of gross national product in 1946 and 34·9% in 1951, compared with 19·0% in 1938.[39] But it had also more objectives to be pursued simultaneously. These included full employment, high and rising productivity, the retention of the more equitable income distribution and the welfare scheme of the war years, a healthy foreign trade balance, the maintenance of the value of the pound, and a speedy dismantling of the more irksome of the war restrictions and controls, among others.[40]

The Labour Government placed the greatest weight on the first two.[41] In its concern to raise output as fast as possible, particularly of the basic and the export industries it was brought up against the shortage of capital. Though manufacturing industry was better equipped than pre-war, net written down values of fixed assets having actually risen from $9·0 billion (1950 prices) in

[34] W. Manning Dacey, *The British Banking Mechanism* (2nd Rev. ed., 1958), p. 176; *Radcliffe Report*, para. 46; Forrest Capie and Alan Webber, *A Monetary History of the United Kingdom, 1870–1982*, vol. 1 (1985), pp. 76–7.

[35] R. G. Hawtrey, *The Balance of Payments and the Standard of Living* (1950), pp. 34–45.

[36] *Radcliffe Report*, para. 45.

[37] E.g. F. W. Paish, 'Planning and the Price System', in *The Post-War Financial Problem and Other Essays* (1950). Cf. also Thomas Wilson, *Inflation* (Oxford, 1961), pp. 153 ff. Keynes, in his essay *How to Pay for the War*, had also suggested a capital levy after the war.

[38] J. E. Meade, *Planning and the Price Mechanism* (1948); John Jewkes, *Ordeal by Planning* (1948).

[39] J. C. R. Dow, 'Fiscal Policy and Monetary Policy as Instruments of Economic Control', *Westminster Bank Review*, Aug. 1960, p. 12.

[40] E.g. *Radcliffe Report*, paras. 53–71.

[41] Hugh Dalton, *High Tide and After, Memoirs 1945–1960* (1962).

1938 to $12·3 billion in 1948,[42] the needs were great to sustain rapid technological progress and substitute capital for imports. But savings were low and it was clear that much of the investment would have to be made by the Government itself. Further, a regular budget surplus to remove the threat of the suppressed inflation would require a high rate of taxation, diminishing thereby the source of private saving still further.[43] Accordingly, the Government was torn between opposite taxation policies. In its first budget, it reduced the standard rate of income tax by 1s. and made other concessions, but later the need for a budget surplus, disinflation and high revenue to carry through the welfare and investment programme required periodic upward revision of tax rates.

The results of these (and other) conflicting aims behind the budget are summarized in Table 6·5.

Table 6·5: Post-war budgets and incidence of taxation (£m.)

	Revenue	Expenditure Excl. transfer to capital account	Surplus	Transfer to capital account	Direct taxes on capital	Taxes on outlay	Subsidies	Taxes on outlay, less subsidies
1938	1,017	1,099	−82	9	78	410	32	378
1946	3,364	3,742	−378	552	143	1,282	360	932
1947	3,440	3,271	169	393	164	1,478	444	1,034
1948	3,985	3,323	662	219	215	1,703	542	1,161
1949	4,270	3,519	751	248	254	1,655	496	1,159
1950	4,323	3,513	810	160	190	1,722	455	1,267

A further conflict appeared to exist between the anti-inflationary budget and what became the most controversial of Dr Dalton's financial policies, the policy of 'cheap money'. Low and steady interest rates had been in operation since 1932 and were one of the accepted weapons to counteract a threatened depression. The post-war Chancellor, however, maintained them in a period of full employment and inflation, which meant, in effect, that the monetary weapon could not be used until 'cheap money' was ended in 1951.[44] The policy was not, however, entirely without justification.

To begin with, full employment could by no means be taken for granted. The white paper had assumed an average of 1½ million persons out of work, the insurance contributions were calculated on a basis of 8½% unemployment, and there was substantial unemployment in several continental countries at the time. A cheap money policy at least removed that danger. It was only after the fuel crisis in 1947 that scarcity, rather than surplus, was generally taken to be the

[42] F. W. Paish, 'Savings and Investment', *op. cit.*; cf. also C. A. R. Crosland, *Britain's Economic Problem* (1953), pp. 20–3; *Radcliffe Report*, paras. 31–41; F. W. Paish, 'The Post-War Financial Problem', *loc. cit.*; I. Bowen, *Britain's Industrial Survival* (1947), pp. 110 ff; T. Barna, 'Investment in Industry – Has Britain Lagged?', *The Banker*, April 1957, pp. 226, 229; also see p. 162 above.

[43] Findlay Weaver, 'Taxation and Redistribution in the United Kingdom', *Rev. of Econ. and Statistics*, 32/3, 1950.

[44] For the state of opinion on using monetary policy again at that time, see the discussion in *Bull. Oxf. Inst. Stat.*, vol. 14, Nos. 4, 5, 8, 1952.

main problem,[45] and only in 1951 that the Insurance Scheme officially used lower unemployment figures as the basis for its actuarial calculations.[46] It was in the emergency budget of 1947 that the Treasury first used Keynesian arguments on demand management, rather than traditional arguments, for balancing the budget.[47]

Secondly, low interest rates kept down the cost of borrowing, not only of the Government, but also of the local authorities, mainly for house building, and of some of the basic industries after their nationalization. They also kept down the sums payable abroad, as Britain was a net short-term borrower. Thirdly, the policy permitted the Government to preseve, for some years, the redistributive gains of the war years in favour of the lower incomes.[48]

Against this policy it was urged that it weakened and distorted economic incentives, that it was inflationary and that, therefore, thirdly, it made necessary the retention of many irksome and inhibiting controls.[49] As for the first of these, the weakened incentive was the concomitant of full employment, and while some of the critics were consistent enough to state that 'a moderate degree of unemployment would do a great deal of good – on the two conditions ... that it does not exceed 5 to 7 per cent ... and that the total does not contain many pockets of heavy or long-continued unemployment',[50] this was a policy which all the political parties were specifically pledged to avoid. The 'misdirection' of resources was a matter of opinion: many of the controls were specifically imposed to correct the undesirable allocations by market forces.[51]

The other two arguments, which were closely linked, had more substance. The lowering of the rate on Consols by $\frac{3}{8}$% to $2\frac{1}{2}$% in January 1947 involved a large-scale creation of new short-term debt and of additional liquidity: deposits of the 11 clearing banks rose by £900 million in this period, of which perhaps one-half was due to this operation. The serried ranks of Government paper, added to the balances and the outstanding short- and medium-terms loans of the war years, which had to be renewed at a rate of £600–£1,000 a year, made financial control of the Money Market by the Government (other than keeping the rates down) quite impossible.

Basically, the institutions of the Money Market had not changed during or after the war except that the Bank of England was nationalized in 1946. Investments of the clearing banks had fallen from the pre-war figure of 70% of deposits to 46·8% in 1948, the rest of the mounting deposits being covered largely by Government short-term paper. The total bill holdings of the London clearing banks increased from £369 million at the end of 1945 to £1,408 million at the end of 1950, or nearly four-fold, while the total of investments plus advances was allowed to rise only from £2,049 million to £3,175 million, or by 50%.[52] In

[45] Especially *Economic Survey* (1947. Cmd. 7046).

[46] A. T. Peacock, *The Economics of National Insurance* (1952), pp. 27, 119–20; *Report on Social Insurance and Allied Services* (*Beveridge Report*) (1942. Cmd. 6404), Appx. A., para. 14.

[47] Jim Tomlinson, *Employment Policy 1939–1955* (Oxford, 1987), pp. 102 ff.; Alan Booth, 'The "Keynesian Revolution" in Economic Policy Making', *Econ. Hist. Rev.* 36/1, 1983 and debate in *ibid.* 38/1, 1985.

[48] F. W. Paish, 'Cheap Money Policy', *loc. cit.*; W. Manning Dacey, pp. 116 ff.

[49] A. J. Youngson, *The British Economy, 1920–1957* (1960), pp. 159–61.

[50] *Economist*, 4 June 1949, p. 1026. In terms of numbers, 5–7% meant 1–1$\frac{1}{2}$ million unemployed.

[51] PEP, *Government and Industry* (1952), p. 41.

[52] W. Manning Dacey, chapter 8; C. N. Ward-Perkins, 'Banking Developments', in *The British Economy, 1945–1950*.

these conditions, the withdrawal of cash from the banks by the authorities was not pyramided into a substantial restriction of credit: it merely led to the reduction (or a refusal to take up more) of the banks' holdings of Treasury Bills and, up to 1952, TDRs. Nor was any other 'credit squeeze' likely to be effective when so much surplus liquidity was left in the system.[53]

Institutions, like Insurance Companies or pension funds, had dutifully absorbed much Government paper during the war and after; but the risk of capital losses (i.e. the risk that low rates could not be indefinitely maintained) was beginning to make them unwilling to absorb more and eager to increase their equity holdings instead, with prospects of capital gains in a period of inflation.[54]

Given the prevailing conviction that Government paper, rather than the availability of cash as such, was the source of liquidity, 'there has been no attempt in the post-war period to operate on the banking position by limiting the supply of cash: the banks have always been automatically provided with whatever was necessary,' and the fiduciary issue was raised accordingly.[55] Thus the inflationary pressures generated after 1945 ran up against no money barriers.

Hence 'the controls' had to stay, and in the prevailing boom conditions it seemed to each entrepreneur that only they stood between him and the opportunities for making much greater profits, even though he might, in reality, have been far worse off in the chaos of their removal. The pressure for their abolition may have come from a very small section of society only, but it forced the Government steadily and relentlessly to dismantle the apparatus of control inherited from the war.[56] The accusation against the cheap money policy was that it slowed down this process of dismantling.

The controls surviving after 1945 were many and various. Consumer rationing of clothing, furniture, petrol, soap and many foodstuffs was abolished by 1950, but the main foodstuffs were still rationed and coal still 'allocated', and there were still restrictions on tourists' expenditure and on hire-purchase agreements. Rationed foods (and others) were subsidized, and subsidies could be attacked as contributing to the high taxation which reduced incentives for the higher income earners. Sir Stafford Cripps drastically reduced food subsidies in 1949 from an estimated £568 million to a maximum limit of £465 million, and to £410 million in 1950.

In other sectors, price control of non-food goods, raw material allocation, including that of steel, control over labour (reimposed briefly and ineffectually in 1947) had all been repealed by 1950, timber only remaining to 1951; in October 1948, a veritable 'bonfire of controls' had been lit by the Board of

---

[53] Sir Oliver Franks, 'Bank Advances as an Object of Policy', *Lloyds Bank Review*, NS, No. 59, 1961, pp. 5–6.

[54] *Radcliffe Report*, paras. 145–8, 162 ff., 185 ff., 252 ff., also chapters 5, 9; G. Clayton, 'The Role of the British Life Assurance Companies in the Capital Market, *Econ. J.*, 61/241, 1951, pp. 91–2; G. Clayton and W. T. Osborn, 'Insurance Companies and the Finance of Industry', *Oxf. Econ. P.*, NS, 10/1, 1958.

[55] *Radcliffe Report*, para. 430; W. Manning Dacey, chapter 11.

[56] A. A. Rogow, *The Labour Government and British Industry 1945–1951* (Oxford, 1955), chapter 3, pp. 138–72; J. D. Stewart, *British Pressure Groups* (Oxford, 1958); S. E. Finer, *Anonymous Empire* (1958), pp. 8–10.

Trade, and by 1951 most of the 'utility specifications' had lost their bite.[57] Apart from exchange restrictions under the Exchange Control Act of 1947, and import restrictions, therefore, there was very little to restrain private enterprise.

Controls were much more persistent in the capital investment field.[58] Building licences were still tightly controlled and attempts were still made to put into practice the war-time blueprints for the planned use of land;[59] the vast profits realized by 'developers' since explain in part the bitter opposition to these controls. Other powers survived after 1951, including the Town and Country Planning Act. The six 'Development Areas', extensions of the former 'Special Areas', were aided under the Distribution of Industry Acts of 1945 and 1950 by Government funds for the construction of factories to be let to light industry at pre-war rents. It was the difficulty of obtaining labour, licences and facilities elsewhere that made the efforts to deal with the deep-set problems of these districts temporarily successful.[60]

Apart from the physical controls over building and siting, the Capital Issues Committee survived from the war years and its powers were extended by the Borrowing (Control and Guarantees) Act of 1946, which made Treasury sanction necessary for any new borrowing or raising capital by share issue of sums over £50,000, the CIC acting as adviser to the Treasury.[61] At the same time, banks were issued with memoranda of advice. Capital exports came under particularly severe scrutiny. To these negative measures was added positive aid. In 1946, the Industrial and Commercial Finance Corporation was set up by the Bank of England, the London clearing banks and the Scottish banks, in order to provide loans in the range of £5,000–£200,000, the 'Macmillan gap', while the Finance Corporation for Industry was established to finance larger schemes, particularly in rapidly expanding industries.[62] 'In the early post-war years the discount market played an important part in absorbing offerings of short-dated bonds sold by industrial companies to finance reconversion.'[63]

It was generally assumed that these various controls were the tools of an integrated Labour Party policy of economic 'planning'. In practice, the Government's policy of 'democratic planning' was to be eclectic, varied, and changing rapidly in its brief years of office.[64] The actual controls taken over from the Caretaker Government at the end of the war and continued by the Supplies and Services (Transitional Powers) Act of 1945 contained fiscal, financial and physical planning powers: 'the use of quantitative production

---

[57] Gilbert Walker, *Economic Planning by Programme and Control in Great Britain* (1957), p. 147; G. D. N. Worswick, 'Direct Controls', in *The British Economy, 1945–1950*.

[58] PEP, *Government and Industry*, chapter 2; Rogow, pp. 27 ff.

[59] See p. 190 above; also N. Rosenberg, *Economic Planning in the British Building Industry, 1945–1949* (1960).

[60] Michael P. Fogarty, 'The Location of Industry', in *The British Economy, 1945–1950*, pp. 266, 275; Christopher M. Law, *British Regional Development Since World War I* (1980), p. 47; *Distribution of Industry* (1948. Cmd. 7540), Parts II and III; *Town and Country Planning, 1943–1951* (1951. Cmd. 8204); Board of Trade, *The Development Areas Today* (1947); R. S. Edwards and H. Townsend, *Business Enterprise, its Growth and Organisation* (1959), chapter 16; also see p. 225 below.

[61] *Radcliffe Report*, paras. 272, 966, *passim; Memorandum of Guidance* (1945. Cmd. 6645).

[62] C. N. Ward-Perkins, 'Banking Developments', in *The British Economy 1945–1950*, pp. 218, 223; Raymond Frost, 'The Macmillan Gap 1931–53', *Oxf. Econ. P.*, NS, 6/2, 1954.

[63] Dacey, p. 65.

[64] The best account will be found in A. A. Rogow, *op. cit.*, esp. chapters 1 and 2.

programmes' has been called 'the outstanding feature of our war-time economic organization'.[65] They might have survived into the peace economy.

> The essence of planning and control by the State in relation to productive industry and commercial activity must be the same in war and peace [it was said in 1947],[66] ... the essential elements are plans consisting of decisions of policy quantitatively expressed in the form of programmes and such measures as ... may be necessary to ensure the performance of these programmes.

Such a policy appealed strongly to the Socialists among the Labour Government's supporters, but in fact it was not developed further.

Instead, with Germany and Japan out of the way as competitors, the dollar loans secured, and industrial output rising, Labour Ministers and officials were remarkably self-satisfied about their economic policy,[67] and many quantitative controls were allowed to lapse before the crises of early 1947 shocked the Government out of its complacency. Only in July 1947 were the membership and functions of the Economic Planning Board announced. In August, the exchange crisis occurred, but it was not until the end of the September that economic policy was taken seriously enough to cause the appointment of Sir Stafford Cripps, hitherto President of the Board of Trade, to the newly created post of Minister of Economic Affairs, with the Economic Planning Staff, the Economic Information Unit and the surviving Economic Section of the Cabinet Secretariat to assist him. The relationship of this new Department to the Treasury was, however, never clarified, for almost at once Dr Dalton resigned from his post as Chancellor of the Exchequer, and Sir Stafford became Chancellor, taking most of his department with him.

With this chance event in its favour, and the general opposition of the business world and even of some Labour opinion[68] against physical controls, the Treasury found it easy to reassert its former authority by concentrating all power in the financial and fiscal weapons of control. 'The *Economic Surveys* became annually less ambitious. The "targets" of 1947 and 1948 became the "estimates" of 1949; in 1950 and 1951 the estimates became less detailed and more cautious; by 1952 they had almost disappeared.'[69] In spite of much complaint over an allegedly bureaucracy-ridden, atrophied planned economy, the period 1945–50 was essentially one in which war-time controls were dismantled as fast as the highly vulnerable external position of the country and the need to preserve full employment would permit.

The evidence makes it equally difficult to sustain the charge that a misguided cheap money policy was responsible for continuing inflation. The inflation was world-wide and its progress in Britain not exceptional. In an economy in which prices and wages moved rigidly together,[70] rising import prices alone could fuel

---

[65] Sir Hubert Henderson, *The Uses and Abuses of Economic Planning* (Cambridge, 1947), p. 10.

[66] Sir Oliver Franks, *Central Planning and Control in War and Peace* (1947), p. 17.

[67] D. N. Chester, 'Machinery of Government and Planning', in *The British Economy, 1945–1950*, p. 341.

[68] E.g. W. A. Lewis, *The Principles of Economic Planning* (1949).

[69] A. J. Youngson, *op. cit.*, p. 264; Samuel H. Beer, *Treasury Control* (Oxford, 1956), pp. 79 ff.; Keith Middlemas, *Power, Competition and the State, vol. 1 ... 1940–61* (Stanford, 1986), pp. 137 f.; Gilbert Walker, *op. cit.*, chapters 4, 5.

[70] J. C. R. Dow, 'Analysis of the Generation of Price Inflation. A Study of Cost and Price Changes in the United Kingdom 1946–1954', *Oxf. Econ. P.*, NS, 8/3, 1956, pp. 252–301.

it in Britain. Significantly, the change to higher interest rates after 1951 did not end the inflation, despite the fact that the import prices were then falling. Further, the actual policy followed was not entirely unsuccessful in reducing the weight of the suppressed inflation.[71]

The price level had a relatively low priority in the Government programme. Its economic policy should mainly be judged by its chief objectives of maintaining full employment, a rising output, and a high and socially desirable allocation of investment. The employment policy was successful beyond all hope: apart from the fuel crisis in February–March 1947, unemployment was generally below 400,000 of insured workers (i.e. under 2%), many of whom were either unemployable or waiting between jobs. Capital investment was also at a rate higher than many had believed possible: by 1948–52, net domestic capital formation was running at 6·61% of net national product, compared with only 4·13% in 1934–8, while an additional 0·2% was made available for foreign investment (compared with −0·5%).[72] There might be disagreement as to detail at the time,[73] but its general aptness and right proportions are in restrospect hardly open to doubt.[74]

Production as well as productivity showed a rise, despite the reduction in the average (actual) working week,[75] which compared well with any previous period in British history. It was also bound to make the most effective contribution to the solution of the other major problems, including the foreign trade gap and the inflation. It is therefore not a little surprising that the period appears in much of the contemporary literature as a period of chaos and failure.

Much of this was no more than the normal bias of economic literature which regularly tends to portray periods of low profits as 'depressions' even though output and wage incomes are booming.[76] But something was also due to genuine causes. One was that higher production was not fairly matched by higher incomes. On a rough calculation, of the £2,050 million increase in national output between 1938 and 1950 (£2,000 million at constant 1948 prices), £700 million was 'lost' by changes in world prices, £400 million by the need to increase exports to cover loss of foreign income, £100 million by a higher rate of capital investment, and £350 million by higher Government spending. The consumers were left with only a quarter of the increase, £500 million,[77] to share between an additional 6% of the population. Another calculation shows the real output per head in the United Kingdom to have risen, between 1937 and 1950, by about 25%, while the real income per head only rose by 7%.[78]

[71] Cf. the figures on Table 6·5 above.

[72] Based on C. H. Feinstein, *National Income, Expenditure and Output of the United Kingdom 1855–1865* (Cambridge, 1972), T. 6 and 106. Also see J. B. Jefferys and Dorothy Walters, 'National Income and Expenditure of the UK 1870–1952', *Income and Wealth*, Series 5 (1955), p. 19, Table VIII; Alec Cairncross, *Years of Recovery. British Economic Policy 1945–51* (1985) pp. 448 f.

[73] E. Devons, 'The Progress of Reconversion', *Manchester School*, 15/1, 1947, pp. 12–17.

[74] Sir Dennis H. Robertson, *Britain in the World Economy* (1954), pp. 11–20; E. Nevin, 'Social Priorities and the Flow of Capital', *Three Banks' Review*, No. 19, 1953; Elliott Zupnick, *Britain's Postwar Dollar Problem* (New York, 1961), pp. 61–5.

[75] Dudley Seers, 'National Income, Production and Consumption', in *The British Economy, 1945–1950*, p. 38; figures on p. 208 below, Table 6·6.

[76] E.g. H. L. Beales, 'The "Great Depression" in Industry and Trade', *Ec. Hist. Rev.*, 5/1, 1934.

[77] Cairncross, *Recovery*, p. 27; Seers, *loc. cit.*, p. 46.

[78] C. F. Carter, 'The Real Product of the United Kingdom 1946–1950', *London and Cambridge Economic Service*, 29/3, 1951.

Secondly, there were the periodic crises and uncertainties, though it was external factors, particularly the erratic nature of American aid, that were largely responsible. However, 'if there is a lesson of the years 1945–50,' an observer summed up, 'it is that the recurrence of alternate periods of apparent austerity and apparent ease of supply is the price of stability of employment.'[79]

Lastly, there was the dissatisfaction with restrictions, with lack of choice, with continued shortages and high taxes. There was some substance in the complaints that there were too many resources devoted to manning the controls and to avoiding them, instead of to productive purposes. The gross unbalance of the late 1940s inevitably called for controls and austerity, but the solid foundations of reconstruction laid then could make an expansion possible which might well need greater freedom for enterprise, both public and private. If after decades of association, rationalization and control, British industry appeared to have lost the zest for enterprise,[80] this may have contributed to the weaknesses of the 1950s.

3 Industrial Reconstruction

The most encouraging aspects of the post-war economy were undoubtedly the maintenance of a high level of employment, and of a high and rising level of output. These were achieved even though there were raw material and fuel shortages, and in the face of the reduction of hours. The high rate of production increase was, in fact, maintained well into the 1950s, and was then slowed down only by deliberate Government policies of deflation and restriction.

For this progress, science and technology claimed a growing share of the credit. Never before had the resources devoted to science been greater, yet never had there been so much criticism of their inadequacy.[81] There was some truth in the complaint that the traditions of British industry were against the use of academic knowledge and in favour of skill and experience learnt on the job, even on the part of senior management,[82] but this was less true for the new and now expanding industries.

With a population increase of 3% between 1946–50, the rise in output per head was substantial[83] (see Table 6·6). Manufacturing industry expanded the

[79] G. D. N. Worswick, 'Direct Controls', p. 311.

[80] Economist Intelligence Unit, *Britain and Europe* (1957), p. 62.

[81] Sir F. H. Heath and A. L. Hetherington, *Industrial Research and Development in the United Kingdom* (1946), chapter 39; R. S. Edwards, *Co-operative Industrial Research* (1950); C. F. Carter and B. R. Williams, *Investment in Innovation* (1958), pp. 138–40, and *Industry and Technical Progress* (1957), chapters 1–3; R. L. Meier, 'The Role of Science in the British Economy', *Manchester School*, 18/2, 1950, pp. 101–2, 114–18; Duncan Burn, in *Structure of the British Economy*, vol. 2, pp. 436–40; Lord Hankey, 'Technical and Scientific Manpower', in Ministry of Labour and National Service, *The Worker in Industry* (1952).

[82] Stephen F. Cotgrove, *Technical Education and Social Change* (1958), chapter 7; *First Annual Report of the Advisory Council on Scientific Policy* (1948. Cmd. 7465), p. 15.

[83] C. H. Feinstein, *National Income, Expenditure and Output in the United Kingdom 1855–1965* (Cambridge, 1972), T. 16–17, 112–13. Also see *National Income and Expenditure, passim*, linked to pre-war figures according to A. R. Prest, 'National Income of the United Kingdom 1870–1946', *Econ. J.*, 58/229, 1948; N. H. Leyland, 'Productivity', in *The British Economy, 1945–1950*, p. 393; L. Rostas, 'Changes in the Productivity of British Industry, 1945–50', *Econ. J.*, 62/245, 1952.

Table 6·6:   The rise in industrial output

	Total production*	All industries**	Manufacturing industry only**
Average			
1936–8	86·0	97·5	95·6
1946	100	100	100
1947	97·8	105·4	105·8
1948	100·1	114·4	115·4
1949	103·9	121·0	122·7
1950	108·3	127·9	131·1

* At 1938 factor costs, recalculated to 1946 = 100. 1949 and 1950 recalculated from 1958 factor costs.
** 1946 = 100, recalculated from 1913 = 100.

fastest; transport and the services expanded the least, being pulled down by actual declines in railway transport and domestic service.

Within manufacturing, again, the progress was very uneven. It was greatest in metals, engineering, chemicals and related industries. Unlike the post-war period 25 years earlier, the heavy industries, including shipbuilding and coal, as well as agriculture, were encouraged to continue their war-time expansion, instead of suffering a painful contraction; while others, like paper, printing, textiles, distribution and building, which had had to contract in the war years, were also urged to expand.[84] In general, however, reconstruction was dominated by the capital goods and the export industries,[85] largely because of deliberate policies designed to save imports, especially from the dollar area, to increase exports, and re-equip British industry. There was also a marked shift from some of the older industries to some of the newer. The industries which showed the most consistent expansion throughout, showed also the largest increase in labour productivity.[86]

The course of industrial change may be summarized in the statistics of selected main industries shown in Table 6·7.[87]

Among the main industries, the progress of coal was the most disappointing. Output crept up from the nadir of 175 million tons in 1945 to 204 m.t. in 1950, but this increase was largely due to an opencast output of 12 m.t. and an increased labour force, output per man-shift reaching the pre-war figure only in 1950, in spite of heavy investment in new equipment. As a result, a shortage of fuel remained one of the most serious brakes on recovery, and it culminated in the crisis of February–March 1947 when several million workers were kept idle for lack of power and export markets were disappointed also.

Coal mining was the first industry to be nationalized, but it was not until

[84] For employment statistics, see A. Beacham, *Economics of Industrial Organisation* (3rd ed. 1955) pp. 155 *passim*, and D. C. Marsh, *The Changing Social Structure of England and Wales, 1871–1951* (1958), chapter 6.
[85] E. Devons, 'The Progress of Reconversion', *Manchester School*, 15/1, 1947.
[86] W. E. G. Salter, *Productivity and Technical Change* (Cambridge, 1960), pp. 109, 144, 177–83. This is based on a study of 28 selected industries in the period 1924–50; cf. also Rostas, 'Changes in Productivity', pp. 23–4.
[87] Lomax, pp. 192–3, 203.

Table 6·7: Production and productivity changes in selected industries

	Index of industrial production (1924 = 100)			Average rate of productivity increase (%)*	
	Average 1936–8	1946	1950	1935–49	1949–55
Metal manufacture	139	$157\frac{1}{2}$	$201\frac{1}{2}$	1·2	3·3
Engineering, shipbuilding, electrical engineering	141	179	256	1·0	3·3
Vehicles	215	245	339	4·0	3·9
Chemicals	143	210	289	2·7	6·2
Textiles	$118\frac{1}{2}$	$86\frac{1}{2}$	128	2·0	1·4
Clothing	130	85	110	0·3	2·0
Food, drink, tobacco	141	163	181	1·6	0·5
All manufacturing	148	154	207	2·0	3·1
Building, contracting	174	132	157	− 3·6	3·6
Gas, water, electricity	206	290	372	3·7	4·5
Mining and quarrying	92	71	80	− 0·4	− 0·1
All industry	146	149	195	1·3	3·2

* Output per operative hours.

1950 that the NCB published its long-term plan.[88] The tasks of the Board were indeed formidable, for the industry had much leeway in capital equipment to make up,[89] at a time when geological conditions tended to diminishing returns, and when the absolute coal shortage made the continuance of uneconomic pits essential.[90] The obligation on the NCB to charge less than market prices (except for exports) gave the rest of industry cheap coal, but stimulated demand artificially, and deprived the NCB of reserve funds, for investment or as buffer to offset future losses.[91]

The iron and steel industry also had much leeway to make up, but it found it easier to recruit additional labour, and it benefited more quickly from its capital investment. Its supervisory Board, appointed after the war, had on the request by the Government to prepare a five-year plan of expansion which was published in 1946.[92] The plan was criticized for 'patching' existing plants everywhere rather than proposing bold new construction in the low cost areas. After some scrapping of obsolete plant, it proposed to increase the total steel

[88] NCB, *Plan for Coal* (1950); also A. Beacham, 'Planned Investment in the Coal Industry', *Oxf. Econ. P.*, NS, 3/2, 1951.

[89] *Coal Mining, Report of the Technical Advisory Committee* (Reid Report) (1945. Cmd. 6610); A. Beacham, 'Efficiency and Organisation of the British Coal Industry', *Econ. J.*, 55/218–19, 1945.

[90] Sir Hubert Houldsworth, 'The National Coal Board', in Institute of Public Administration, *Efficiency in the Nationalised Industries* (1952); *Report of the Advisory Committee on Organisation* (*Fleck Report*) (1955).

[91] G. C. Allen, *British Industries and Their Organisation* (3rd ed., 1951). pp. 56–9, 77–83; cf. also 4th ed. (1959). These volumes will also be found useful for the other staple industries.

[92] *Report of the British Iron and Steel Federation and the Joint Iron Council on the Iron and Steel Industry* (1946. Cmd. 6811).

capacity only to 15–16 million tons and pig iron capacity to $8\frac{1}{2}$–9 m.t. In the event the targets were raised again in 1948, but capacity continued to lag behind demand, though the average productivity was raised easily by the replacement of inefficient old plants by new works:[93] The index of output per man-year (1938 = 100) rose to 115 in 1947 and 139 in 1950. There was a large expansion of the output of basic open-hearth furnaces and of electric furnaces, and a beginning was at last made in the building of a large integrated plate mill at Margam, as well as in the replacement of the old pack mills by modern continuous tinplate mills.[94]

In engineering the centre of the picture came to be held by the motor-car industry. The pre-war peak output of 526,000 units (cars, commercial vehicles and tractors) in 1937 was almost reached in 1947 and exceeded in 1948, when 626,000 units were produced, and further large expansion schemes brought the output in 1950 up to 903,000 units, excluding motor cycles. In view of the delayed recovery of Western European production and the inaccessibility of American cars because of the dollar shortage, export markets were wide open and limited only by productive capacity. Instead of using the sellers' market to rationalize, British makers wasted their opportunity by making too many models, by building for the needs of British rather than of foreign roads, and by neglecting the vital aspects of service and spare parts, especially overseas.[95] There was some concentration in the industry, the 'big six' (reduced to five by the formation of the BMC) producing 85% of the cars and commercial vehicles by number, and 60% by value, in 1948.[96]

The aircraft industry, heavily subsidized by the taxpayer, was untypical in maintaining its technical lead and international competitive power. The shipbuilders and marine engineers, by contrast, failed in 1945–50 to modernize the yards and works and were soon to be driven out of neutral markets by builders in Germany, Japan, Sweden, Holland and elsewhere. Their output rose only from 1,133,000 gross tons in 1946 to 1,315,000 in 1950.[97]

The machine tool industry, though still much inferior to the American in efficiency, maintained its high output of the war years: total production in the United Kingdom, by value, rose from £$6\frac{1}{2}$ million in 1935 to £47 million in 1951. Some of the most spectacular developments occurred in the electronics industry with the introduction of radar devices and of computers. The prewar output of radio receivers was reached in 1947, when over $\frac{1}{2}$ million television sets were produced also. Employment in the whole electronics industry fell from 98,000 in 1943–4 to about 80,000 in 1946–7, to reach 93,000 again in 1950, though it doubled afterwards in only five years. Like electrical engineering as a whole, it

[93] BISF, *Monthly Statistical Bulletin, passim*; Duncan Burn, *The Steel Industry 1939–1959* (Cambridge, 1961), chapters 3–5, and 'Steel', in *Structure of British Industry*, vol. 1; Anglo-American Council on Productivity, *Iron and Steel* (1952); H. G. Roepke, *Movements in the British Iron and Steel Industry, 1720–1951* (Urbana Ill., 1956), chapters 7 and 8; Cole, pp. 155–61.

[94] W. E. Minchinton, *The British Tinplate Industry* (Oxford, 1957), chapter 8.

[95] Peter J. S. Dunnett, *The Decline of the British Motor Industry* (1980), pp. 32–40; PEP, *Engineering Report II: Motor Vehicles* (1950), p. 25.

[96] Aubrey Silberston, 'The Motor Industry', in *The Structure of British Industry*, vol. 2.

[97] Ely Devons, 'The Aircraft Industry', and A. K. Cairncross and J. R. Parkinson, 'The Shipbuilding Industry', in *The Structure of British Industry*, vol. 2; L. Jones, *Shipbuilding in Britain* (Cardiff, 1957), chapter 9; Andrew Shonfield, *British Economic Policy Since the War* (Harmondsworth, 1958), pp. 41–8; *Economist*, 27.12.1952, pp. 901–2.

was dominated from the beginning by a few giant firms and agreements and associations between them.[98]

The chemicals and allied industries also continued to expand, even after the military stimulus was removed. The temporary eclipse of the main competitor, Germany, turned Britain from an importer into a large-scale exporter and permitted the industry to build up substantial markets abroad. At the same time, there occurred a phenomenal growth of demand for some of the industry's diverse products, notably plastics and pharmaceutical goods. Production of synthetic resin, for example, rose from 16,000 tons in 1941 to 25,000 in 1945 and 52,500 in 1950. The volume of output of the whole complex of chemical industries rose from an index number of 100 in 1946 to 120 in 1948 and 142 in 1950.[99] The industry remained dominated by a handful of very large firms.[100]

Particular mention must be made of oil refining, which Britain was driven to undertake in order to save dollars by substituting imports of crude Middle Eastern oil for refined American motor spirit. By large-scale projects, some of them built on virgin sites, rated capacity was increased seven-fold between 1938 and 1953. Oil refining formed one of the prime examples of the substitution of capital for imports after the war.[101]

Among investment industries only building lagged behind, having by 1950 scarcely recovered its pre-war position. The typical building firm was still small: by 1949, only 6·5% of the skilled operatives and 20·6% of the others worked for very large fims employing over 1,000 employees each. Repair and maintenance accounted for about half the output of the industry, new building being shared between domestic and industrial or commercial building in the ratio of 3 : 2. By the end of 1949, one million houses had been built or reconstructed, and the ratio of houses to population was beginning to exceed the pre-war ratio, but unfulfilled demand remained as high as ever, because of smaller families and rising expectations of living standards.[102]

In contrast with the industries noted so far, most consumption goods industries showed relatively modest increases in output, not least because for many, domestic demand was still held down by rationing. Textiles were, perhaps, the outstanding example. War conditions had greatly reduced the output and the labour force of the traditional textile industries, and even in the post-war period they enjoyed a low priority. Employment in the cotton industry dropped by

[98] M. E. Beesley and G. W. Troup, 'The Machine Tool Industry', in *The Structure of British Industry*, vol. 1; T. Wilson, 'The Electronics Industry', *ibid.*, vol. 2; S. G. Sturmey, *The Economic Development of Radio* (1958), pp. 181–5, 209–11.

[99] *Annual Abstract of Statistics.*

[100] W. B. Reddaway, 'The Chemical Industry', in *The Structure of British Industry*, vol. 1; C. J. Thomas, 'The Pharmaceutical Industry', *ibid.*, vol. 2; T. I. Williams, *The Chemical Industry* (1953), Part II; Association of British Chemical Manufacturers, *Report on the Chemical Industry, 1949* (1950) and *Supplement, 1953* (1954).

[101] Duncan Burn, 'The Oil Industry', in *The Structure of British Industry*, vol. 1; Richard Evely and I. M. D. Little, *Concentration in British Industry. An Empirical Study of the Structure of British Production 1935–51* (Cambridge, 1960), pp. 203–8; Institute of Petroleum, *The Post-War Expansion of the UK Petroleum Industry* (1954).

[102] Working Party Report, *Building* (1950); C. F. Carter, 'The Building Industry', and B. R. Williams, 'The Building Materials Industry', in *The Structure of British Industry*, vol. 1; Anglo-American Council on Productivity, Report on *Building* (1950).

42% between 1937 and 1945, and in the woollen and worsted industries it dropped by 37% between 1939 and 1945; much of the equipment was out of date and most firms were small.[103] After a brief post-war boom, exports of cotton goods were to slump again in 1952, though the woollen and worsted industries fared rather better, reaching by 1950 an output just below the pre-war level.[104] Man-made fibres on the other hand were being developed very rapidly. In 1952–3 nylon and rayon accounted for 80% of production of ladies' seamless hose, and for 90% of fully-fashioned ladies' hose. New fibres, such as 'Terylene', for which a pilot plant was set up in 1950, 'Orlon' and 'Ardil', which went into production in 1951, were also being developed for other uses. The proportion of employment accounted for by nylon and rayon spinning was still quite small, being 2·8% of all textile employment in July 1946 and 4·9% in 1950,[105] but its growth rate was significant. Among other consumer goods industries, paper and printing experienced a remarkable post-war expansion in spite of the severe restriction in the supply of wood pulp.

Agriculture was urged to advance even beyond its war-time output after the war, in order to help to economise on foreign currency. In 1946 bread had to be temporarily rationed – a measure which had not been necessary in either the First or the Second World War. The Agriculture Act of 1947 provided the framework for the official policy of 'stability and efficiency'. The former was to be achieved by annual price reviews and guaranteed markets for the most important farm products, which raised average farm incomes to six times their pre-war peak in 1949–50, and the latter by continued mechanization and the intelligent use of mixed farming techniques, encouraged by tax concessions.

The Government's 'plan' called for a 20% increase in output (to 150% of pre-war) in five years, especially of dollar-saving crops. By 1950–1 the quantum of output reached, in fact, 146% of the pre-war level.[106] Most food crops and farm animals shared in this increase, as illustrated in Table 6·8.

In sum, British industry proved to be more adaptable than many observers had believed possible.[107] Its flexibility contrasted strongly with the tendency towards restriction and rigidity between the wars, and nowhere was the contrast more marked than in the attitude to monopoly.[108]

---

[103] Working Party Reports: *Cotton* (1946), pp. 52 *passim, Wool* (1947), pp. 51 *passim*.

[104] G. W. Furness, 'The Cotton and Rayon Textile Industry', and G. F. Rainnie, 'The Woollen and Worsted Industry', in *The Structure of British Industry'*, vol. 2; J. F. Brothwell, 'The 1951 Depression in the British Wool Textile Industry', *Yorkshire Bull.*, 4/2, 1952, and 5/2, 1953.

[105] D. C. Hague, *The Economics of Man-made Fibres* (1957), p. 171, and 'The Man-made Fibres Industry', in *The Structure of British Industry*, vol. 2; G. C. Allen, *op. cit.*, 1951 ed., pp. 184–5; 1959 ed., pp. 208–10.

[106] A. J. Youngson, *op. cit.*, pp. 199–200; H. T. Williams, *Principles for British Agricultural Policy* (1960), pp. 44–58, 72 ff.; K. E. Hunt, *Changes in British Agriculture* (Oxford, dupl. 1952); PEP, *Agricultural Machinery* (1949), pp. 18–26, 95; H. C. Chew, 'Changes in Land Use and Stock over England and Wales, 1939 to 1951', *Geog. J.*, 122/4, 1956; John R. Raeburn, 'Agricultural Products and Marketing', in *The Structure of British Industry*, vol. 1; D. K. Britton, 'Agriculture', in *The British Economy, 1945–1950; Agriculture Bill: Explanatory Memorandum* (1946. Cmd. 6996); C. H. Blagburn, 'Import Replacement by British Agriculture', *Econ. J.*, 60/237, 1950.

[107] E.g. E. A. G. Robinson, 'The Changing Structure of the British Economy', *Econ. J.*, 64/255, 1954.

[108] S. R. Dennison, 'New Industrial Development and Exports', in University of London and Institute of Bankers, *The Industrial Future of Great Britain* (1948).

Table 6·8: Increase in agricultural output

	1938	1946	1950
Crops harvested in GB (m. tons):			
Grains	4·95	7·22	7·78
Potatoes	5·11	10·17	9·51
Fruit and vegetables	2·33	3·67	3·85
Animals on agricultural holdings in June (m.):			
Cattle	8·76	9·63	10·62
Sheep and lambs	26·77	20·36	20·43
Pigs	4·38	1·95	2·99
Poultry	74·25	67·12	96·11

In this period it was no longer certain whether the average size of plant was still growing. Between 1935 and 1948, it is true, average employment in all manufacturing plants rose from 107 to 124,[109] and there was evidence 'consistent with the operation of a process of amalgamation and the concentration of some production in larger and more efficient plants'.[110] Such comparisons, however, by their very nature excluded the new industries which arose after 1935, and which would reduce the overall degree of concentration.[111]

Irrespective of these trends, however, it was the full employment policies which demanded the release from monopolistic restrictions hinted at already in the white paper on Employment Policy in 1944.[112] The growing antirestrictionism found expression in the Monopolies Act of 1948, which set up a Monopolies and Restrictive Practices Commission, with powers to inquire and to recommend action. By 1951 only two small industries had been reported on, but ultimately, it produced several valuable reports on individual industries and one general report,[113] and in 1956 an Act was passed giving power to curb restrictions which were deemed to be against the public interest. A separate Committee reported on resale price maintenance in 1949.[114]

By contrast, associations which were in the public interest were encouraged by the Government. In particular, the attention of economic policy makers turned to productivity, and to the enormous margin by which American productivity exceeded the British.[115] An Anglo-American Council on Productivity was set up in August 1948. It sent many teams selected from trade associations,

[109] P. Sargant Florence, *The Logic of British and American Industry* (1953), p. 31; J. B. Jefferys, *Retail Trading in Britain, 1850–1950* (Cambridge, 1954), chapter 3.

[110] Richard Evely and I. M. D. Little, *Concentration in British Industry* (Cambridge, 1960), pp. 173–4, also chapter 12.

[111] P. E. Hart and S. J. Prais, 'The Analysis of Business Concentration: A Statistical Approach', *J. R. Stat. S.,* 119/2, 1956; PEP, *Government and Industry* (1952), p. 186.

[112] Cmd. 6527 (1944); I. Bowen, *Britain's Industrial Survival* (1947), pp. 63–4; S. R. Dennison, 'Restrictive Practices and the Act of 1956', *Lloyds Bank Review*, NS, No. 59, 1961, pp. 36–7; Margaret Hall, 'Monopoly Policy', in *The British Economy, 1945–1950*; Cole, *op. cit.*, chapter 19.

[113] Monopolies and Restrictive Practices Commission, *Report on Collective Discrimination* (1955. Cmd. 9504).

[114] *Report of the Committee on Resale Price Maintenance* (Lloyd Jacobs Report) (1949. Cmd. 7696).

[115] E.g. L. Rostas, *Comparative Productivity of British and American Industry* (Cambridge, 1948); E. Rothbarth, 'Causes of Superior Efficiency of American Industry', *Econ. J.,* 56/223, 1946.

trade unions and employers' federations to study American practices and publish their findings.

In the iron and steel industry a Board was set up in 1946 to steer the industry in the public interest. Elsewhere, it was decided in September 1945 to set up 'Working Parties' in inquire into individual industries and make recommendations. Seventeen were eventually appointed, and they reported in 1946–8, making many specific recommendations. One general result was the Industrial Organization and Development Act of 1947, which allowed the Government to set up Development Councils. However, in spite of the specific recommendation of most Working Parties for Councils of this kind, the results of the Act were disappointing: apart from the transformation of the existing Cotton Board into a Development Council, there were only three Councils formed and three other Orders made, for compulsory levies for research and exports.[116]

Much more significant than these schemes was the programme of nationalization, which formed one of the main platforms of the Labour Government. Apart from the minor measures which were little more than formalities, including the Bank of England Act, 1946, the Cable and Wireless Act, 1946, and the Civil Aviation Act, 1946, which set up British European Airways (BEA) and British South American Airways (the latter merged with BOAC in 1949), there were five major measures of nationalization: the Coal Industry Nationalization Act (1946), the Electricity Act (1947), the Transport Act (1947), the Gas Act (1948) and the Iron and Steel Act (1949). The Act nationalizing the steel industry was first held up by the House of Lords and its vesting date was further delayed until after the second post-war election, to 1951; by its provisions the firms were largely left intact and it was thus easy for the Conservative Governments to reverse the process of nationalization in the years after 1951. In the case of the other four major industries, the actual transfer took place in each case in the year following the passing of the Act.

This programme of nationalization was probably the most controversial part of the post-war Government's policy.[117] Socialists of many hues[118] hoped thereby to organize production for use, in place of production for profit, and to remove the power of the capital-owning classes, thus bringing about a peaceful social revolution.

In retrospect it is clear that there was never any danger of such a revolution,[119] and the heat and passion aroused by the controversy were largely misdirected. Industry was nationalized, the 'commanding heights' of the economy were occupied to the extent of 20%, not to dominate or transform the mainly profit-making industries composing the remaining 80% of the economy, but because it seemed a rational form of organization in each individual case, and to give the Government additional powers, besides those it already possessed in the

[116] N. H. Leyland, 'Productivity', in *The British Economy, 1945–1950*; P. D. Henderson, 'Development Councils: an Industrial Experiment', *ibid.*

[117] E.g. R. Kelf-Cohen, *Nationalisation in Britain. The End of a Dogma* (1959).

[118] Cole, *op. cit.*, chapter 9, also his *The Case for Industrial Partnership* (1957); H. A. Clegg, *A New Approach to Industrial Democracy* (1960), esp. chapters 1, 2, 4, 16; Austen Albu, 'The Organization of Nationalized Industries and Services', in W. A. Robson (ed.), *Problems of Nationalized Industry* (1952).

[119] Cf. H. A. Clegg and T. E. Chester, *The Future of Nationalization* (Oxford, 1955), chapter 1; G. D. H. Cole, *Socialist Economics* (1950).

fiscal, monetary and other spheres, to pursue its economic objectives. The measures of nationalization actually carried out are therefore best seen not as representing a revolutionary economic doctrine, but as lying well within a long tradition of the growth of Government responsibility, represented by the Employment white paper of 1944, on the one hand, and by the pre-war public corporations[120] on the other: 'British experience of nationalization shows once more how one control leads to another.[121] Some of the nationalized undertakings had, in fact, been public corporations (e.g. London Transport) or largely in the hands of local authorities (e.g. gas and electricity).

There was no 'pattern' of nationalization, the organization chosen for each industry having different characteristics. Thus the National Coal Board began as a single unit controlling its numerous properties by a classic line-and-staff form of organization. In the electricity industry, by contrast, generation and bulk supply came under the (national) British Electricity Authority, while distribution was the preserve of the fairly autonomous Area Boards. The Gas Industry was split up entirely among 12 Area Gas Boards with very little co-ordination between them, and transport had the most complex organization of all, a Transport Commission controlling six main 'Executives', one for each of the operational sectors.[122]

This diversity was dictated by the diversity of the industries concerned, their differences in needs, structure and size. Their size compared 1950 as shown in Table 6·9.

Table 6·9: Comparative size of nationalized industries, 1950

	Employees (000)	Fixed assets (less depreciation) (£m.)	Gross revenue (£m.)
Coal	765	288	481
Electricity	170	548	214
Gas	141	211	192
Inland transport	888	1,341	560
Air transport	23	35	33
Grand total	1,988	2,443	1,480

Even where some uniformity was desired, as in the principles of pricing,[123] different circumstances led to different results. The Coal Board could not hold down costs in line with the slow rise in selling prices permitted because of the rapid rise in miners' wages and the high proportion of wage costs to total costs.

[120] See p. 81 above.

[121] H. A. Clegg, 'Nationalized Industry', in *The British Economy, 1945–1950*, p. 246.

[122] Acton Society Trust, *Nationalised Industry. 9. Patterns of Organisation* (1951); D. N. Chester, *The Nationalised Industries* (2nd ed., 1951).

[123] A vast literature grew up on the theoretical principles of pricing (as well as other managerial decisions by nationalized industry), but it cannot be said to have had any effect on actual policy. J. Wiseman, 'The Theory of Public Utility Price – An Empty Box', *Oxf. Econ. P.*, NS, 9/1, 1957; D. N. Chester, 'Note on the Price Policy indicated by the Nationalization Acts', *ibid.*, NS 2/1, 1950; J. F. Sleeman, *British Public Utilities* (1953); D. H. Aldcroft, *British Railways in Transition. The Economic Problems of Britain's Railways since 1914* (1968), pp. 135–45.

Against this, in electricity generation, rapid technical advance and advantages of scale helped to absorb many of the cost increases.

In the absence of any real intention of changing the structure of society, each separate act of nationalization had to stand on its own merits. On such a basis, the nationalization of coal mining and the railways was justifiable not only by such evident savings as the avoidance of overlapping, but also by the necessity of raising the morale of the labour force and providing a source of finance for the very large capital schemes required after decades of neglect. The nationalization of gas and electricity supply, while partly justifiable as permitting economies of scale, and the opportunity to bring the average up to the best practice,[124] as well as providing much necessary finance, would stand or fall much more with the possibility of planning energy supply as a whole.[125]

Any hoped-for nationalization of inland transport was ended by the sale of part of the road transport fleet to private ownership in the 1950s,[126] Elsewhere, as physical planning gave way to steering by fiscal and monetary methods and by exhortation, the nationalized industries, far from acting as instruments of control for the rest of industry, were directed increasingly to become its servants, and to suffer worse buffetings than private industry in their long-term investment plans with every change of wind of Government policy. Forced increasingly to deny the principle which they were established to promote, the principle of public service, and to justify themselves on the same commercial grounds as privately owned firms, the Boards of the nationalized industries have come to be neither able to maintain consistent financial policies nor give adequate attention to consumers' interests, despite the safeguards of consumers' councils written into the Acts,[127] nor could they defend their industries from the kind of public attacks which would be unthinkable in the case of the owners or managers of private industry.

4 Incomes and Work

The transition to peace involved a reduction in the numbers in the forces by $4\frac{1}{2}$ million persons and in the war industries by $3\frac{1}{4}$ million by the end of 1946, and their absorption into civilian industry or back into domestic duties.[128] The remarkable smoothness and absence of transitional unemployment with which this huge transfer of labour was carried through was due in part to Government planning, but was largely the result of the pressure of unfilled demands pervading

[124] E. g. *Report on the Gas Industry* (Heyworth Report) (1945. Cmd. 6699); H. F. H. Jones, 'The Gas Industry', and Lord Citrine, 'Electricity Supply', in Institute of Public Administration, *Efficiency in the Nationalised Industries* (1952).

[125] Youngson, pp. 187–97; E. Stanley Tucker, 'Fuel and Power', in *The Industrial Future of Great Britain*.

[126] Gilbert Walker, *Road and Rail* (2nd ed., 1947), chapter 12.

[127] J. A. G. Griffith, 'The Voice of the Consumer', *Political Quarterly*, 21/2 1950; A. M. de Neumann, *Consumers' Representation in the Public Sector of Industry* (Cambridge, 1950); Frank Milligan, 'The Consumer's Interest', in Robson (ed.), *Nationalized Industry*; W. A. Robson, *Nationalized Industry and Public Ownership* (1960), chapter 10.

[128] Ministry of Labour and National Service, *Report for the Years 1939–1946*, pp. 131–2, 151, 199–202, 225; T. Wilson, 'Manpower', in G. D. N. Worswick and P. H. Ady, *The British Economy, 1945–1950* (Oxford, 1952).

all sectors of the economy.[129] By and large, labour was attracted to the expanding sectors by the offer of better wages and conditions, and this process contributed powerfully to the upward drive of wages.

Even without this additional element of 'bottleneck' wages, full employment was bound to raise the bargaining strength of the trade unions. They could count on a friendly Government which passed, as one of its first measures, the Trade Disputes and Trade Union Act of 1946, reversing the 1927 Act with its many cramping provisions. Their membership continued its upsurge of the war years, rising from 7,875,000 in 1945 to 9,243,000 in 1950, to embrace 43% of all employees (53% of the men, 23% of the women), including an increasing number of non-manual workers.[130] Trade union power was further increased by the extension of the Wages Council system under the Act of 1945,[131] which ensured that by 1950, 80% of employees were governed by statutory or voluntary forms of wage regulation; by the appointment of at least one former trade union officer to each of the Boards controlling the nationalized industries; by improved negotiating machinery in those industries; and by the continued Government consultation with trade union leaders on matters of economic policy, informally or formally through the National Joint Advisory Council, the Economic Planning Board, the Development Councils and elsewhere.[132]

The number of working days lost by disputes remained minute, averaging 2 million a year in 1945–50. The war-time Order No. 1305 which made arbitration compulsory and made strikes without resort to arbitration illegal,[133] was operative throughout this period, and since the wage awards under it allowed wages to rise parallel with prices, it satisfied the leaders of most unions, particularly the weaker ones. The order did not, however, prevent unofficial strikes, in spite of some prosecutions, and when in 1951 the Government failed to secure the conviction of some dockers, a new Industrial Disputes Order was brought in.[134]

On the question of the control over the nationalized industries, the trade union leadership (with few exceptions, of which the Union of Post Office Workers was the most conspicuous) agreed with the Labour Government view that the unions should have no direct representation on the Boards, but should be free to criticize and represent their members' views as independent bodies. But there were many grounds for disagreement over wages policy. One concept of a 'wages policy' was the determination of the total available for wage increases in any given period from the national income estimates, and its division among the different groups of workers according to agreed principles. Such proposals generally hoped to curb wage increases and thereby reduce the rate of inflation, as well as using the wage structure as an instrument of economic planning.[135] But trade union leaders were too suspicious of Governments, and too jealous of their own powers, to sanction this, while experience in other countries showed

[129] G. D. N. Worswick, 'Personal Income Policy', in *The British Economy, 1945–1950*, pp. 320–4.

[130] G. D. H. Cole, *The Post-War Condition of Britain* (1956), chapter 30.

[131] See pp. 183–4 above.

[132] Allan Flanders, *Trade Unions* (1952), p. 100; PEP, *British Trade Unions* (1948), pp. 50, 114.

[133] p. 183 above.

[134] D. F. MacDonald, *The State and the Trade Unions* (1960), pp. 177–8.

[135] E.g. Allan Flanders, 'Wages Policy and Full Employment in Britain', *Bull. Oxf. Inst. Stat.*, 12/7–8, 1950, pp. 235–42, and 'Can Britain have a Wage Policy?', *Scot. J. Pol. Econ.*, 5/2, 1958 (Symposium on Wages Policy); C. W. Guillebaud, 'Problems of Wages Policy', in Min. of Labour and National Service, *The Worker in Industry* (1952).

that, whatever else might be said for it, a 'wages policy' would not cure an inflation.[136] A resolution proposing it was heavily defeated at the TUC in 1951.

Instead, wages continued to be determined by free collective bargaining between unions and employers' organizations, and by statutory bodies such as Wages Councils, which tended, in so far as they had a consistent policy, to keep their awards in line with the wages of comparable trades arrived at by union bargaining.[137] Given the end of price control, rising prices, the labour shortage and union power began an upward push on wages which employers (including the nationalized industries) were unwilling to oppose, since they could easily recoup their higher costs by still higher prices. In these conditions, only trade union restraint could prevent accelerating inflation. 1946 was the only year in which increases in wage rates (and earnings) exceeded the rise in the cost-of-living index; the restraint in personal income claims from 1947 onward is reflected in the index figures given in Table 6·10.

Table 6·10:   Wage restraint and cost-of-living, 1945–50

	Average weekly earnings (M.o.Labour)	Wage rates (Bowley)	Cost of living (London and Cambridge Econ. S.)
1945 (1938=100)	180 (July)	154	148
1946 " "	190 (Oct.)	167	150
1946 (1946=100)	100 "	100	100
1947 " "	107 "	105	107
1948 " "	116 "	112½	115
1949 " "	120½ "	116	119
1950 " "	126 "	118	123
1950 (1938=100)	240 "	197	184

Wage *rates*, in fact, rose less than prices after 1946, and real incomes were kept up only by the inflation of earnings by overtime and piece-rate payments or by the upgrading of workers. It could even be argued that the trade unions kept wages down: 'the fact that the employers are willing to pay more than the negotiated wage rates in order to obtain the labour they require points to a situation where wages are lagging behind the levels that they would spontaneously reach as a result of market pressure'. Therefore, it could be said, 'it is in no small measure the employers who have undermined the standard rates and made further wages claims from the unions almost inevitable'.[138]

The official wage restraint policy between 1947 and 1951 had several distinct phases. In January 1947 the Government in its *Statement on the Economic*

[136] H. W. Singer, 'Wage Policy in Full Employment', *Econ. J.*, 57/228, 1947; E. H. Phelps-Brown and B. C. Roberts, 'Wages Policy in Great Britain,' *Lloyds Bank Review*, NS, No. 23, 1952; B. C. Roberts, *National Wages Policy in War and Peace* (1958); T. L. Johnstone, 'Wages Policies Abroad', *Scot. J. Pol. Econ.*, 5/2, 1958.

[137] Barbara Wootton, *The Social Foundations of Wage Policy* (1955).

[138] B. C. Roberts, *National Wages Policy*, p. 16; C. W. Guillebaud, *loc. cit.*, p. 46; also A. T. Peacock and W. J. L. Ryan, 'Wage Claims and the Pace of Inflation', *Econ. J.*, 63/250, 1953.

Considerations affecting Relations between Employers and Workers[139] a white paper issued with the endorsement of the National Joint Advisory Council, drew attention to the need to keep incomes and prices down in order to remain competitive in world markets. As its earlier exhortation had met only a limited response, the Government felt compelled to issue the much sharper *Statement on Personal Incomes, Costs and Prices* in February 1948.[140] This white paper, after referring to the anti-inflationary effects of the Government's policy of high taxation, demanded a total standstill of profits and rents at their present levels, and a qualified limitation of wage increases. These were to be granted only where justified by increased productivity or by the national interest, e.g. in order to attract labour to undermanned occupations, and there was to be no unofficial 'wage drift'. The Government took care to bring its views to the attention of Wages Councils and other negotiating bodies.

Not unlike the white paper of 1941 in tone and effect,[141] this document marked a turning point in wages policy. The General Council of the TUC fully endorsed the demand for wage restraint for the time being. A conference of trade union executives held in March 1948 also supported this, on condition that two further exceptions to the general wage standstill be granted. One was the proviso to raise wages if they were found to be below a reasonable absolute minimum, and the other, to maintain differentials. These four grounds for exception would, between them, exempt from wage restraint virtually all the trade unions which voted for it, the others, a sizeable minority, voting against, so that the Government might be said to have won but a hollow victory. Yet in practice the unions did observe restraint in a period of full employment.

After devaluation in September 1949, the General Council of the TUC again urged a wage standstill, until the end of 1950, provided the interim retail price index did not rise by more than 5%, and asked the trades whose wages were tied to sliding scales to forgo increases due to them. Put before another meeting of trade union executives in January 1950, these propositions could, however, muster such a narrow majority only (4,263,000 against 3,606,000) as to lose all their moral force.[142] The General Council itself abandoned its policy in June 1950 when it urged more 'flexibility' in wage negotiations. The impending crisis of 1951 led to a renewed attempt to peg wages with the help of enlarged subsidies, and Mr Gaitskell proposed a statutory dividend limitation, but the Labour Government fell before these measures could be given a trial.

Wages did not fall in the post-war years as a proportion of the national income, and as usual, in a period of industrial boom, the share of profits went up, though this was hidden by the widespread practice of heaping up undistributed profits in view of the penal rates of taxation and the powerful pressures to dividend restraint. In consequence, it was rents and salaries which had to bear the brunt of the necessary reductions.

Moreover, the proportion of wage-earners was falling: according to one calculation, wage-earners received 39·2% of the national income in 1938, when they formed 71·4% of the occupied population; in 1950 they received 41·9%,

[139] Cmd. 7018.
[140] Cmd. 7321.
[141] p. 185 above.
[142] B. C. Roberts, *National Wages Policy*, p. 60; cf. also D. F. MacDonald, *The State and the Trade Unions* (1960), pp. 151 ff.; Allan Flanders, *Trade Unions* (1952), pp. 110–12.

but then they only formed 66·2% of the occupied population.[143] Conversely, the rising share of salaries has to be set against a rising number of salary earners: the growth of the 'salariat' interrupted or reversed during the war, was resumed with undiminished vigour after it.[144] In industry, the proportion of administrative, clerical and technical employees to operatives rose from 13·5% in 1935 to 18·6% in 1948. The 'middle classes' of managerial, professional and white-collar workers, as well as proprietors, numbered 10·4 million, or over 20% of the population, in 1951; of these, 'proprietors and managerial' numbered 4·3 million.[145]

Statistics of pre-tax incomes like those in Table 6·11 should be read with all these provisos in mind:[146]

Table 6·11:   Composition of pre-tax income, 1938 and 1949

Proportion of Personal Incomes	1938	1949
Wages	37·8	41·9
Salaries	17·9	20·5
Other employment incomes	3·8	6·0
Self-employed	12·8	13·1
Rent, dividends, interest	22·3	11·4
Government transfers	5·4	7·1
	100	100

Whatever redistribution of incomes there had been, however, had largely occurred in the war period, not in the post-war years. Thus the share of rents, dividends and net interest in personal pre-tax incomes had fallen from 22·9% in 1938 to 14·4% in 1946 and 11·5% in 1950.[147] The inclusion of undistributed profits (including gains from stock appreciation) in the calculations does, however, confirm the general impression of the constancy of the main shares of personal incomes in the gross national product in the post-war years:[148]

Table 6·12:   Proportions of personal incomes in GNP, 1946 and 1950

Incomes of	1946	1950
Employees and Forces	57·2%	57·3%
Grants from public authorities	6·8	5·8
Self-employment	12·0	10·9
Property, including undistributed profits, additions to reserves	24·0	26·0

[143] The figures are not quite on the same base. E. H. Phelps-Brown and P. E. Hart, 'The Share of Wages in National Incomes', *Econ. J.*, 62/246, 1952, p. 277.

[144] pp. 149 above. D. C. Marsh, *The Changing Social Structure of England and Wales, 1871–1951* (1958), pp. 105, 145, 194, *passim*.

[145] PEP, *Government and Industry* (1952), p. 171; Ministry of Labour and National Service, *Annual Reports*; C. W. McMahon and G. D. N. Worswick, 'The Growth of Services in the Economy', *District Bank Review*, No. 136, 1960; Cole, *op. cit.*, chapter 3.

[146] H. F. Lydall, 'The Long-Term Trend in the Size Distribution of Income', *J. R. Stat. S.*, 122/2, 1959, p. 17, Table 9. Cf. also p. 186 above.

[147] C. H. Feinstein, *National Income, Expenditure and Production in the United Kingdom, 1855–1965* (Cambridge, 1972), T. 28.

[148] Based on *National Income and Expenditure, 1946–1952* (1953), Table 9, excluding incomes of

The statistics of savings showed again the concentration of 'small' savings in the hands of a minority of the working classes and in those of the middle classes; the building societies, attracting mainly middle-class savers, showed by far the largest increases.[149]

Government still continued to restrict luxury spending by rationing and restricting imports. Additionally, a large part of incomes from property was in the form of undistributed dividends, and was as yet only potential spending power. The two largest reductions of personal expenditure (at constant, 1948, prices) occurred in the categories limited to the wealthier classes: expenditure on domestic service fell from £265 million in 1938 to £80 million in 1946 and £85 million in 1950, and private motoring from £250 million to £140 million and £160 million.[150]

The relative fall in salaries, as compared with wages, tended to level out earned incomes as a whole,[151] but there also took place a certain measure of levelling of wages during the war which was maintained in the post-war years. The differential of skill remained at about 20% of the unskilled wage, and women's and youths' wages were rising relatively to those of men. Above all, a large part of the bottom slice of the income pyramid, the population living in absolute poverty, was removed.

The virtual abolition of primary poverty in post-war Britain was caused mainly by two developments: full employment on the one hand, and the State welfare provisions on the other. B. S. Rowntree, visiting York in 1950 to conduct his third social survey there,[152] found the proportion of the working-class population living in poverty to have dropped from 31·1% in 1936 to 2·8% in 1950; of those living below the poverty line, nearly one-third gave unemployment as the reason in 1936, while no one was found in 1950; in that year 68% attributed their poverty to old age. At the same time, Rowntree and Lavers calculated that if the welfare provisions (including subsidies) in 1950 had been only those of 1936, the proportion of working-class families living in poverty would have been, not 2·8%, but 22·2%. It seems reasonable to conclude that for the majority of the population, who before 1939 had never been quite beyond the danger of want, the most important single development after 1945 was the creation of the 'Welfare State'.

5 The Welfare State

The limits of the post-war 'Welfare State' which did so much to abolish poverty are not easy to draw. At the centre, without a doubt, stood the Social Insurance

---

public authorities and public corporations, and remittances abroad. Cf. also Worswick, 'Personal Income Policy', pp. 315–17.

[149] Kathleen M. Langley, 'The Distribution of Private Capital, 1950–1', *Bull. Oxf. Inst. Stat.*, 16/1, 1954; Esme Preston, 'Personal Savings through Institutional Channels (1937–1949)', *ibid.*, 1950.

[150] Dudley Seers, 'National Income, Production and Consumption', in *The British Economy, 1945–1950*, p. 47.

[151] David Lockwood, *The Black-Coated Workers* (1958), pp. 67–8.

[152] B. S. Rowntree and G. R. Lavers, *Poverty and the Welfare State* (1951), pp. 30–5.

scheme as proposed in the Beveridge Report,[153] and the National Health Service and the family allowances associated with it. The family allowances were enacted in 1945, providing 5s. a week for all children except the eldest; and in 1946 the National Insurance Act, the National Insurance (Industrial Injuries) Act and the National Health Service Act were passed, coming into operation together on the 'appointed day', 5 July 1948. In that year the National Assistance Act and the Children Act completed this group of reforms.

In its detailed provisions, the Beveridge Report was followed remarkably faithfully. There were only two major departures from its principles. The first was caused by the rise in prices unmatched by increases in benefit rates, so that the principle of sufficiency was violated, and the National Assistance scheme, intended only as a 'safety net' for a small minority, became a necessary standby for large numbers of insured persons. Thus by the end of 1950, 1,350,000 persons were receiving weekly allowances from the Assistance Board, of whom no fewer than 873,000 were persons who were in need because the benefits under the insurance scheme were too low; 650,000 of them were old-age pensioners.[154] The National Assistance Board had to apply a needs test, and this threatened to bring back the old Poor Law under a new guise.

The other important departure from the war-time recommendations was the decision to apply increased retirement pensions at once, instead of after an interval in which the beneficiaries might have accumulated sufficient credits by their in-payments; indeed, higher pensions were paid as from October 1946, instead of waiting for July 1948, and the full rates were to come in after only 10 years instead of 20.[155] The numbers involved were 3·3 million persons in 1946 and 3·5 million in 1948. This decision, made largely for political reasons, was all the more remarkable since even without it the growing number of retirement pensioners was certain to swallow a rapidly mounting share of the scheme's income. According to the available calculations, the number of people over 65 was expected to grow from 5 million in 1947 to around 8 million in the late 1970s. As a proportion of the total population, they would increase from 14% in 1951 to 18% in 1979. At the rates of the 1946 Act, the cost of the retirement pensions would then rise from £238 million in 1948 to £501 million in 1978, and the resulting deficit would fall entirely on the Exchequer, the contribution of which would grow quite disproportionately from £36 million to £338 million.[156]

In strict logic, this would take from the Insurance Fund the last vestiges of pretence of 'insurance'. Since the Treasury contributed a share of the normal income, adding sums at will or altering rates according to the short-term 'balance' of the Fund, as well as controlling the investment of the 'surplus' and finding most of the interest on it, the scheme was not run on insurance lines at all,

---

[153] pp. 188–90 above. Also, M. Bruce, *The Coming of the Welfare State* (1961), chapter 7.

[154] G. D. H. Cole, *The Post-War Condition of Britain* (1956), chapter 23; D. C. Marsh, *National Insurance and Assistance in Great Britain* (1950), chapter 12.

[155] *Report of the Ministry of National Insurance for the Period 17th November 1944 to 4th July 1949* (1950 Cmd. 7955), chapters 4, 12; Lord Beveridge, 'Epilogue', in W. A. Robson (ed.), *Social Security* (3rd ed., 1948).

[156] *Report of the Royal Commission on Population* (1949. CMd. 7695), pp. 112–17; *Report of the Committee on the Economic and Financial Provisions for Old Age* (Phillips Report) (1954. Cmd. 9333), esp. Table IV, paras. 117–22, and Section IV.

but was a system of redistribution of incomes financed by three sets of taxes: direct 'poll tax' on insured persons, an indirect tax in the form of the employer's contribution (which in the prevailing sellers' market he could be expected to pass on to consumers in higher prices) and the total tax base in the form of the Exchequer contributions.[157] Yet the pretence of an insurance scheme would bring to the members a feeling of security and would change the spirit in which they would claim its benefits.

In other respects, the national insurance scheme followed the earlier proposals. It was compulsory and universal, the population being 'classified' into several separate classes of contributors and beneficiaries. The single insurance stamp provided unemployment, sickness and disablement benefits, and payments for retired persons, widows and orphans; there were also maternity benefits, death benefits (from July 1949) and associated schemes of family allowances (paid out of the Exchequer) and industrial injuries benefits (paid out of a separate fund), while the Insurance Fund also made an annual contribution to the Health Service. The total numbers insured rose from about $15\frac{3}{4}$ million to $21\frac{1}{2}$ million for unemployment insurance and from $24\frac{1}{3}$ million to 25 million for other benefits.

A comparison of the *real* values of the new scheme in 1948 with those of the earlier schemes before the war[158] shows that both contributions and benefits of single men remained below the pre-war level, but the family allowances raised the real value of the benefits for family men considerably above it, while old-age pensioners enjoyed the largest rate of increase. The decline of mass unemployment reduced the share of the social insurance budget in the total Government budget:[159]

Table 6·13: The social insurance budget as a percentage of the total budget

	1938	1946	1950
Social Insurance contributions as % of total Government revenue	15·4	6·7	13·6
Social Insurance expenditure as % of total Government expenditure	13·6	3·9	11·3

The National Health Service, inaugurated on the same day, was also intended to be comprehensive, though a small proportion of the population elected to pay for private service.[160] It was to provide, free of charge, all medical services and needs, in so far as they could be met from existing resources, and it was to bring into a single organization the many different institutions that had grown up to form the existing variegated service.[161] At the inauguration, the service

[157] Alan T. Peacock, *The Economics of National Insurance* (1952); cf. Douglas Jay in *Hansard*, HoC, 26 April 1951, vol. 487, cols. 641–4; Walter Hagenbuch, *Social Economics* (Cambridge, 1958), pp. 265–7.
[158] E.g. D. C. Marsh, *op. cit.*, p. 116.
[159] Peacock, pp. 17–20.
[160] D. H. Hene, *The British Health Service* (1953), pp. 7–10.
[161] Harry Eckstein, *Pressure Group Politics* (1960), chapter 4.

had to overcome the handicap of much hostility on the part of the medical profession. It also inherited a severe shortage of hospitals, of equipment and of staff, and a geographical maldistribution of doctors, none of which could be remedied in the short run. Further, there was an unexpectedly large backlog of hidden demand, especially for dentures and glasses, which created long waiting lists and other early problems. The service also became quickly the victim of many ill-judged economy drives. In 1950 a ceiling on total expenditure of £400 million gross was imposed, leading to charges for spectacles and dentures, and capital expenditure on hospitals was cut to the derisory figure of one-third of the pre-war level.[162]

Nevertheless, the National Health Service became one of the most popular and successful measures of the post-war years.[163] The most sensitive public health index, the infant mortality rate, showed a welcome drop from 47·4 per 1,000 births in 1939 to 29·3 in 1949–50. The class differences still remained, however: in 1949–50, mortality ranged from 18·4 in the top (professional) class to 39·8 in the lowest (unskilled workers), while the differences in post-neo-natal deaths (at ages 4 weeks to 1 year), where environment counted for most, were greater still, ranging from 4·9 to 17·9.[164]

Housing standards had suffered perhaps more than any others from the war, both by the building backlog and the loss by enemy action of $\frac{1}{2}$ million houses. The total shortage, estimated officially at $1\frac{1}{4}$ million houses in 1945 would, together with other needs, require the construction of 3 million dwellings. Thus the annual needs of building, for the next 10 years, were set at a minimum of 300,000 houses,[165] compared with a maximum pre-war building rate of 350,000 dwellings, when, however, the building labour force had been double the post-war size.

In the event, some 55,000 permanent buildings were completed in Great Britain in 1946, rising to 140,000 in 1947 and well over 200,000 a year for the next three years. In 1946–8, there were also 148,000 'temporary' prefabricated houses erected, so that at the time of the Census of 1951, the number of occupied dwellings, 13·3 million, exceeded the 1931 figure by over 3 million. Yet the number of households had been growing even faster, and in the Census year there were nearly 14·5 million married households. The number of houses per 1,000 of the population was higher than pre-war, but the shortage was still calculated to lie between 1 and 2 million houses.

New houses and re-buildings for private owners amounted to only 158,000 in 1945–50 and most of the post-war houses were built by local authorities, subsidized by the Government under Bevan's 1946 Act, in order to ensure that the new houses went to those in greatest need. Rent restriction kept the rents of older houses at their 1939 levels, and was extended to about 1 million

---

[162] Brian Abel-Smith and R. M. Titmuss, *The Cost of the National Health Service in England and Wales* (Cambridge, 1956), pp. 137–8.

[163] Harry Eckstein, *The English Health Service* (Cambridge, Mass., 1959); J. S. Ross, *The National Health Service in Great Britain* (1952), Parts IV-VI.

[164] Cole. *op. cit.*, pp. 380–1.

[165] E.g. R. L. Reiss, *Municipal and Private Enterprise Housing* (1945), pp. 18–19; G. D. H. Cole, *Building and Planning* (1945), p. 150; Herbert Ashworth, *Housing in Great Britain* (1957), p. 43.

furnished houses by an Act of 1946 which set up Rent Tribunals. The Landlord and Tenant (Rent Control) Act of 1949 gave the Tribunals the additional powers to fix rents for unfurnished houses for the first time, but at no time did the price of houses come under control.[166] This legislation kept down rents for a large proportion of the population in the face of an acute housing shortage, at the price of making families immobile, but it could not cure the shortage[167] which fell, as ever, mainly on the poorer families.

The planning powers of the Town and Country Planning authorities, the Counties and County Boroughs, were greatly extended by the Act of 1947. A more ambitious approach to town planning was symbolized by the creation of 14 'New Towns', eight of them in the London region. These were to end the unco-ordinated urban sprawl of the inter-war years by creating complete self-contained and balanced communities, offering local employment as well as housing. The capital was provided by specially formed public corporations which were to act also as local authorities in the initial stages. Less successful was the nationalization of the 'development value' of land, following the Uthwatt Report,[168] with the object of transferring to the community the additional values created by the community rather than the individual. The scheme, however, was badly designed and was quickly modified out of existence by the Conservative Government.[169]

In education, also, the brave post-war plans were held up by the shortage of buildings and teachers, in spite of the imaginative post-war Emergency Teacher Training Scheme. The raising of the school-leaving age to 15 under the Butler Act of 1944 had to be postponed to April 1947, and its planned extension to 16 was postponed further.[170] Total expenditure on education, at constant prices, rose from an index of 76 in 1937–9 to 83 in 1946 and 122 in 1950 (1948 = 100), but as the birth rate 'bulge' loomed ahead, most of this was devoted to increasing quantity rather than quality.[171]

The most important educational innovation of the post-war period was the creation of a universal and free secondary education system for children aged 11–15 and upwards. In practice, most authorities divided the children into three streams, grammar, technical and modern (not necessarily in separate schools), selected in most areas by an aptitude test taken at about the age of 11, the 'eleven-plus'. Though open in practice to many objections,[172] this reorganization of secondary education did more than any other previous measure to make higher education available to capable children of all classes. It left untouched the privileged 'public school' system for those whose parents were able and willing to pay for it.

[166] F. W. Paish, 'The Economics of Rent Restriction,' in *The Post-War Financial Problem and Other Essays* (1950).

[167] Hagenbuch, *Social Economics*, p. 83; J. B. Cullingworth, *Housing Needs and Planning Policy* (1960), chapter 3.

[168] p. 190 above.

[169] G. D. H. Cole, *The Post-War Condition of Britain*, chapters 25, 26; Herbert Ashworth, chapters 17–19; Cullingworth, chapter 7; A. C. Duff, *Britain's New Towns* (1961).

[170] H. C. Dent, *Growth in English Education, 1946–1952* (1954), and *Secondary Education for All* (1949), chapter 4; Cole, *loc. cit.*, chapter 24.

[171] John Vaizey, *The Costs of Education* (1958), p. 70.

[172] E.g. Robin Pedley, *Comprehensive Education, A New Approach* (1956), also P. E. Vernon (ed.), *Secondary School Selection* (1957).

Besides social insurance, health, housing and education, there was also an expansion of many minor social services, for aged persons, for the blind, the mentally deficient, the problem families and others. In addition, there was still much scope for voluntary social work,[173] to fill the inevitable gaps left by national and local authorities. Finally, there were the provisions which involved no public expenditure, like Factory Acts, Food and Drug Acts, and rent control. Indeed, in its widest definition, the concept of the modern Welfare State was to focus much attention on intangible social improvements, such as the protection of personal rights including the prevention of neglect or cruelty to children, the fostering of the arts and recreational facilities, the abolition of ignorance and illiteracy, as well as of the grosser forms of inequality and privilege.[174]

Not all the welfare schemes necessarily favoured the poor at the expense of the rich, or the working classes at the expense of the middle classes. The public education system, for example, benefited the average child of middle-income families much more than it benefited the lower-income child.[175] The Health Service, likewise, was to benefit the middle classes more than the working classes, who were generally insured before 1948, though there was some justification for describing it as satisfying the quest for efficiency, always an important ingredient in Fabian and Labour Party doctrine, as much as the quest for social justice.[176] Whether the working classes as a whole gained from the social services, or whether the redistribution was merely 'horizontal', within classes, turned on definitions and assumptions.[177] Certainly, the major redistribution achieved by the social services was horizontal, e.g. from single and healthy men to large families, the sick, and the aged,[178] and this met with widespread approval, for, after all, the net contributor and the net beneficiary was commonly the same person at different stages of his or her career.

It is also worth emphasizing that few of the post-war schemes were entirely novel: most of them developed naturally out of the older existing schemes. In spite of a widespread belief to the contrary, Britain did not spend significantly more on the social services after 1948 than she did before 1939, apart from the retirement pensions. The outlay on many services, in real terms or as a proportion of national income, had actually fallen. Comparisons are difficult and estimates differ widely. In terms of calendar years, the post-war growth, excluding capital expenditure, was of the order of magnitude shown in Table 6·14.[179]

---

[173] G. Williams (ed.), *Voluntary Social Services since 1918* (1948); Lord Beveridge, *Voluntary Action* (1948); Hagenbuch, *op. cit.*, chapters 4, 7.

[174] W. A. Robson, *The Welfare State* (1957).

[175] Vaizey, *The Costs of Education*, p. 84.

[176] Eckstein, *The English Health Service*, esp. Introduction, and pp. 3 ff.

[177] Cf. p. 201 above. Findley Weaver, 'Taxation and Redistribution in the United Kingdom', *Rev. of Econ. and Statistics*, 32/3, 1950; A. T. Peacock and P. R. Browning, 'The Social Services in Great Britain and the Redistribution of Income', in Peacock (ed.), *Income Redistribution and Social Policy* (1954), esp. pp. 157–66; Asa Briggs, 'The Social Services', in G. D. N. Worswick and P. H. Ady, *The British Economy 1945–1950* (Oxford, 1952), p. 373.

[178] R. M. Titmuss, 'Social Administration in a Changing Society', *British Journal of Sociology*, 2/3, 1951.

[179] *National Income and Expenditure 1946–52* (1953), Tables 27, 30, 34, 35.

Table 6·14: Post-war growth in social services outlay (£m.)

	1946	1950
Subsidies (incl. local authorities)	387	475
Current grants to persons (incl. LAs)*	453	730
Net current Central Government expenditure on the Health Service	n.a.	401
Net current expenditure on social services by local authorities**	285	319
Totals	1,125	1,935

* Excluding Forces' allowances and pensions, grants for research and post-war credit payments.
** Incl. Northern Ireland.

A different classification omitting subsidies and some other transfers, and couched in terms of financial years, yields the figures given in Table 6·15:[180]

Table 6·15: Increase in social services expenditure (£m.)

	1938-9	1947-8	1949-50
Social security services	310·5	559·8	714·8
Education	111·8	222·8	228·5
Health	74·4	174·7	408·6
Housing	23·7	55·8	54·5
	520·4	1013·1	1406·4

Much of this increase was accounted for by rises in prices and by the Health Service.[181] In comparison with the pre-war years, the increases in the old-age pensions, the family allowances and the subsidies were counter-balanced in part by a reduction in unemployment benefits:[182]

Table 6·16: Proportional growth in social services expenditure.

	1937-8	1947-8	1950-1
Total expenditure on the social services as % of gross national income at market prices, plus transfers	9·8	14·8	16·9
Transfer payments, as % of personal incomes before tax, including transfers	5·4	5·4	5·7
Gross capital expenditure on the social services, as % of gross domestic capital formation	10·4	15·3	14·8

Most of these changes, planned in the last years of war, were forced through

[180] Based on the *Monthly Digest of Statistics*; also John Vaizey, *The Cost of the Social Services* (Fabian Research Series, No. 166) (1954).
[181] Cf. other figures in A. J. Youngson, *The British Economy 1920–1957* (1960), p. 216; A. T. Peacock, *The Economics of National Insurance*, p. 24; Peacock and Browning, pp. 144 5; Hagenbuch, p. 213.
[182] Peacock and Browning, p. 151.

in the early years of peace by the Labour Government, which could rightly claim to have been an administration of social reform, even if not, as its programme implied, of Socialism.

7

Production and Incomes 1950–1980

1 Industrial Growth and Decline

By 1950 the immediate after-effects of the war had been overcome, both in the United Kingdom and abroad, and the world could settle down to the peaceful creation of wealth which most of its citizens expected after the holocaust. The Korean War, it is true, was soon to shatter the precarious peace and to distort prices and production once again. Nevertheless, the economic disturbances caused by the war were not strong enough to interrupt the upward movement of output and productivity, which became perhaps the most striking of all aspects of post-war economic history among the advanced Western nations.

In the United Kingdom, as elsewhere in the West, the rate of saving, the level of investment in scientific research and development, and the rate of application of technical progress were very high in comparison with any earlier period of history and in consequence there was a faster rate of economic growth than perhaps in any previous age. Industrial output, the key factor, rose, according to one calculation, by 3·7% a year in 1948–60, compared with 3·1% in the inter-war years, and 1·6% in 1877–1913. In 1962–79, though losing in importance in the national income, it still rose by 2·2% a year. Physical output per head rose by 1·60% a year in 1924–50 and 1·84% in 1954–63; thereafter output per man-hour in manufacturing rose by as much as 3·1% a year in 1963–1979. There was, however, a slowing-down in the 1970s: manufacturing output per head, which had been growing at 3·5% a year in 1960–73, grew by only 0·9% in 1973–9, and output per person-hour in manufacturing, by 3·9% and 1·1% respectively. For total factor productivity over the economy as a whole, the figures were 2·5% and 0·8% in those years.[1]

Extended over the economy as a whole, including all other sectors, the standard measure is the Gross Domestic Product (GDP). GDP *per head* rose by 40% in 1950–66 against 29% in the similar pre-war period, 1920–36. Its growth until 1979 is shown in Table 7·1.[2]

---

[1] K. S. Lomax, 'Growth and Productivity in the United Kingdom', *Productivity Measurement Review*, 38 (1964), p. 6; W. B. Reddaway, in W. E. G. Salter *Productivity and Technical Change* (2nd ed., Cambridge, 1966), p. 198; Rudiger Dornbush and Richard Layard, *The Performance of the British Economy* (Oxford, 1987), pp. 168, 170; and calculations based on *National Institute Economic Review* (quarterly).

[2] Ministry of Labour, *National Statistics on Incomes, Prices, Employment and Production*; (London and Cambridge Economic Service), *The British Economy, Key Statistics 1900–1966*, Table C; Angus Maddison, *Economic Growth in the West* (1964), p. 37; *National Institute Economic Review* (quarterly). Also Phyllis Deane and W. E. Cole, *British Economic Growth, 1688–1959* (2nd ed., Cambridge, 1967), Appx. Table 90, and *National Income and Expenditure* (annual). Series spliced around indices based on 1958, 1970 and 1975.

Table 7·1:   GDP per head of the labour force, at constant prices

	1950	100·0
Average of years	1951–5	106·0
	1956–60	116·8
	1961–5	132·0
	1966–70	151·0
	1971–5	169·8
	1976–80	178·6

This amounted to an annual compound growth rate of **GDP** of 2·2% per head. Large as this was by historical standards, it was low by comparison with other contemporary economies, and is discussed further below.

Such an increase was necessarily accompanied by a substantial change in the industrial and geographical distribution of employment, by the introduction of new technology and new products, and by the replacement of some existing industries by others. On the whole, the changes in industrial structure followed, and in some cases completed, the structural transformation of the economy which had begun in the 1920s. Its main components were a relative and, in some cases, an absolute decline of the old 'staple' and export industries, including shipping; their replacement by others fulfilling the same functions; and the creation of altogether new industries, meeting new needs or using new materials and components. It was a significant feature of this transformation that improved technology and rising productivity were to be found both in the declining and in the expanding industries and occupations.[3]

Agriculture was a good case in point. Its output doubled from an index number of 88 in 1950 to 178 in 1980, while its employment declined sharply by about one-third.[4] This increase in output was spread over all the main products – grain, meat, dairy and market gardening. Land use, in fact, changed little over the period (see Table 7·2).[5]

Since land remained constant and labour declined, the output increase was achieved largely by better equipment and better techniques. The equipment included the further extension of mechanization: the number of agricultural tractors licensed increased from 313,000 in 1951 to 508,000 in 1979. The new techniques included intensive breeding and better pest control. The stock of plant and machinery in agriculture, valued in constant (1958) prices at replacement cost, increased from £0·5 billion in 1951 to £0·8 billion in 1965, and gross capital at 1975 replacement cost, increased from £7·4 billion in 1970 to £9·7

---

[3] G. N. von Tunzelmann, 'Structural Changes and Leading Sectors in British Manufacturing, 1907–68', in C. P. Kindleberger and Guido di Tella (eds.), *Economics in the Long View* (3 vols., New York, 1982), III, pp. 1–49.

[4] *Key Statistics*; National Income and Expenditure. On another base (1975 = 100) at constant factor cost, the output of agriculture, forestry and fishing moved as follows:

1950	60·8
1960	75·7
1970	95·5
1980	120·5

[5] *Agricultural Statistics* (annual).

Table 7·2: Land utilization, United Kingdom (million acres)

	1948	1965	1980
Tillage	13·2	12·0	12·4
Rotational grass	5·5	6·6	4·9
Arable	18·7	18·6	17·3
Permanent grass	12·4	12·1	12·7
Rough grazing	17·2	17·8	16·9
Total agricultural area	48·3	48·5	46·9

billion in 1980.[6] The approximate calculations of annual percentage changes in Table 7·3 summarize the components of the output and productivity rise in agriculture:[7]

Table 7·3: Agricultural output and productivity, annual growth rates

	1951 64	1965–80
Output	+2·6%	+2·1%
Labour	−2·4%	−1·7%
Capital	+1·5%	⎮3 0%
Labour productivity	+5·0%	+3·8%
Total factor productivity	+3·5%	+0·8%

This heavy programme of investment in an industry still made up of relatively small units[8] reflected the confidence of farmers in a continuing policy of agricultural support by the Government. After Britain joined the European Community in 1973, its common agricultural policy (CAP) strengthened the British farmer's feeling of security.

Agricultural policy, in fact, went through several phases. At first, under labour, the object was to secure higher production at all costs. This was continued up to the price review of 1952, when the saving of dollars was still stressed in a further expansion programme designed to raise output from 50% above pre-war, at which it stood then, to 60%. After this, policy changed sharply: the Government was no longer willing to 'plan' but would undertake only to attempt to let supply and demand meet at acceptable consumer price levels. The actual

[6] *National Income and Expenditure.* Also see S. G. Hooper, *The Finance of Farming in Great Britain* (1955); M. T. Stewart, 'Capital in Scottish Agriculture', *Scottish Agricultural Economics*, 15 (1965); and literature quoted in K. E. Hunt and K. R. Clark, *The State of British Agriculture*, 6, 1965–6 (Oxford, 1966), pp. 20–1.

[7] J. F. Wright, *Britain in the Age of Economic Management* (Oxford, 1979), p. 28; *Agricultural Statistics; National Income and Expenditure; Employment Gazette*; A. P. Power and S. A. Harris, *Agricultural Expansion in the United Kingdom with Declining Manual Labour Resources* (1973).

[8] In England and Wales, the average size of holdings increased from 66·4 acres in 1949 to 75·5 in 1964, and 188·4 in 1980, and the land in holdings of 500 acres and over, from 2,663,000 to 3,917,000 acres between 1949 and 1964, while the number of holdings over 500 acres rose from 5,747 in 1964 to over 9,000 in 1980. Hunt and Clark, p. 58; *Agricultural Statistics*.

mechanism of support was highly complex. Cereal and fatstock producers, who were in substantial competition with importers, were compensated by a set of 'deficiency payments' to meet the gap between the prices they obtained and the higher prices guaranteed by the annual review. From 1954, milk and potatoes, and from 1957, eggs, were sold by monopolistic official marketing boards which recovered and distributed the subsidies on behalf of the Government.[9] The system as a whole was designed to give the consumer the benefit of (lower) world food prices while keeping up efficiency incentives for farmers.

In the mid-1950s the post-war world food shortage gave way to an incipient surplus in Western markets and it was largely due to the striking improvement in productivity and reduction in real costs that the subsidies declined in this period from the £382 million paid over in 1950 to an annual figure of around £250–£300 in the mid-1960s to the early 1970s. They then rose about fivefold to a peak of £1,336 million in 1975, only to fall back again to £465 million in 1979 and £649 million in 1980 in current prices, or an index, in real terms, of 217 in 1975 and 81 in 1980 (1970 = 100). The Agriculture Act of 1957 attempted to allay the farmers' fears of drastic cuts in support by limiting the annual guaranteed price changes. In the 1965 annual price review, in a special white paper,[10] and in the National Plan for economic development of that year, the emphasis was again put on the increase in total output and on import savings.

The system has been criticized for giving greater support to the well-off farmer who needs it least, and less support to the farmer on poorer land or with less managerial ability; from the mid-1950s on, this was borne in mind when improvement grants were extended for capital investment under the Farm Improvement Scheme of 1957, and other direct grants to the small farmer under the Small Farm Scheme of 1959, the Horticulture Act of 1960 and the Agriculture and Horticulture Act of 1964. The system has also been criticized for attempting to achieve several, and partly contradictory aims:[11] the saving of foreign exchange, the improvement of home standards of nutrition, particularly milk consumption, and the provision of stable incomes and employment in agriculture. Certainly, over two-thirds of farmers' net income after the end of rationing has been provided by subsidies, which still left the average farmer's income at only £1,200 a year gross, or £900 net (i.e. after deducting interest on his capital), in 1960. Yet the gains were substantial. As a proportion of GNP, food imports fell from 8·9% in 1951 to 4·1% in 1976,[12] partly because of better terms of trade, partly because of the low income elasticity of food[13] and in part

[9] E.g. Report on *Agricultural Marketing Schemes for the Years 1938–55* (1957); *Guarantees for Home-Grown Cereals*, Cmd. 8947 (1953); J. G. S. and Frances Donaldson, *Farming in Britain Today* (1969), pp. 41–8.

[10] *Annual Review and Determination of Guarantees*, Cmnd. 2621 (1965), *The Development of Agriculture*, Cmnd. 2738 (1965).

[11] John R. Raeburn, 'Agricultural Production and Marketing', in Duncan Burn (ed.), *The Structure of British Industry* (2 vols., Cambridge, 1958), I, pp. 42–4; E. F. Nash, *Agricultural Policy in Britain: Selected Papers* (Cardiff, 1965).

[12] J. F. Wright, *Britain*, p. 10.

[13] It was calculated in 1968 that the income elasticities of demand for food in the United Kingdom were as follows:

Beef	0·71
Pigmeat	0·61
Mutton and lamb	− 0·10
Butter	0·60

by greater efficiency. The strongest justification for the support which agriculture has received lies in its high rate of increase in output and, above all, in productivity.[14]

The CAP which Britain had to accept on joining the European Community (EC) in 1973 had been inspired by similar objectives: rising efficiency, guaranteed regular supplies and stable markets with reasonable prices for consumers and fair incomes for the farming population. However, the latter formed a much larger proportion of the population than in Britain and was able to supply a much larger proportion of its food needs. Consequently, instead of holding prices down to world levels and paying subsidies to the farmers as in Britain, the CAP allowed prices to rise to 'target' levels, suited to their own high farming costs, and levied duties on imports at a rate to bring them up to those prices. 'Intervention' prices were set somewhat below the target prices, and if prices fell below them, the CAP intervened, usually by buying up the surpluses. The system including export subsidies was financed through the European Agricultural Guidance and Guaranteed Fund, which in turn received its income from the import levies and from direct Government payments.[15]

From the British point of view, the CAP had a large number of disadvantages. First, it had no incentive to efficiency. Secondly, it produced surpluses which had to be stored at great expense or sold at give-away prices to third countries. Thirdly, it led to high prices. Thus in 1972–3, at the time of the British entry, typical prices compared as shown in Table 7·4.[16]

Fourthly, the CAP blocked the sale of foreign low-cost producers and was

Table 7·4:   British and EEC agricultural prices, 1972–3

	EEC		UK
	Target	Basic Intervention	Guaranteed
Soft wheat, £ per ton	47·41	40·05	34·40
Barley, £ per ton	43·44	39·88	31·20
Pig meat, £ score dw.	—	3·10	2·81
Milk, p. per gallon	23·00	—	20·60 (pool)

Cheese	0·39
Margarine	−0·49
Bread	−0·76

T. E. Josling, 'The Future Demand for Food in Western Europe', in S. T. Rogers and B. H. Davey, *The Common Agricultural Policy and Britain* (Farnborough, 1973), p. 88.

[14] Peter Self and H. J. Storing, *The State and the Farmer* (1962), pp. 220 ff.; *Agriculture*, Cmnd. 1249 (1960); H. T. Williams, *Principles for British Agricultural Policy* (1960), pp. 64 ff., 167; Gavin McCrone, *The Economics of Subsidizing Agriculture. A Study of British Policy* (1962); OECD, *Agricultural Policies in 1966*.

[15] A. R. Prest and D. J. Coppock, *The UK Economy. A Manual of Applied Economics* (7th ed., 1978), pp. 175–8; T. Josling, 'Agricultural Policy' in Peter Coffey (ed.), *Economic Policies of the Common Market* (1979).

[16] B. H. Davey, 'Supplies, Incomes and Structural Change in UK Agriculture', in Rogers and Davey, p. 97. While the average consumer's loss due to the CAP was 0·41% of GNP for the 9 as a whole in 1978, the British loss was 0·86% of GNP. Francesco Giavazzi, 'The Impact of EEC Membership', in Dornbusch and Layard, *Performance*, p. 100.

protectionist, while the British system was free. Fifthly, there was no upper limit set to the necessary support. Sixthly, by throwing part of the burden of inefficient farming, especially in France and Italy, onto other countries, mainly Germany and Britain, it led to recurring annual recriminations. Lastly, because of the shift in the value of currencies to each other, artificial units of account (the 'green pound') had to be used in the CAP to preserve the target and intervention rates which diverged increasingly from real prices and encouraged large-scale smuggling, totally contrary to the spirit in which the Common Market was designed. For Britain, with her highly efficient farms and high import needs, the system was particularly harmful.

The CAP also made provision for grants and payments; the basis was the notion of 'viability', which related farm incomes to locally current wage rates. In 1972 it was calculated that of 4·2 million farmers in the community, 3·5 million were 'non-viable'.[17] Payments are made for capital and other improvements as formerly in Britain; but also for older people, aged over 55 and 60 respectively, to leave farming altogether – in direct contradiction to the bulk of the CAP which encourages them to stay.

The shifts within industry, and manufacturing in particular, are illustrated in Table 7·5 opposite, showing the changes from 1950 to 1980–81 in some major industrial sectors.[18]

Two developments stand out. One was the divergence in the output statistics, particularly between the old staples, which actually declined sharply even in absolute terms, and the 'new' industries and others which recorded rises in output. Motor vehicles, a leading growth sector of the 1930s, was now among the losers[19] and the sharp decline in iron and steel, compared with its relative stability in the inter-war period, may seem equally surprising.

The second notable development is the steep fall in employment in all manufacturing industries, even in those still supplying growing markets in real terms. That downward drift, which reverses the trend of at least two centuries began only in the early 1970s. Up to then, employment in manufacturing industry had been stable, with a peak in 1965–6, and in 1970 was actually 145,000 above the level of 1963. Since then, the decline has been steady and seemingly irreversible. Falling at a rate of 1·1% in 1966–74, it then accelerated to over 3% a year. The decline in manufacturing *output* as a proportion of GNP at constant prices began just a little later, the turning point being 1972.[20]

The causes of this decline are made up of three main components. The first is the shift, worldwide and evident since the beginning of this century, from the manufacturing (as well as the agrarian) sector to employment in the tertiary, service sector.[21] Thus, while employment in manufacturing fell by almost 30%

---

[17] J. van Lierde, 'Recent EEC Decisions in Price and Structural Policy', in Rogers and Davey, p. 53.

[18] *Employment Gazette*, and Central Statistical Office. The Index of Industrial Production splices the index of weight 1970 with that of 1975, and is therefore only approximately correct.

[19] See pp. 242–5 below.

[20] Ajit Singh, 'UK Industry and the World Economy: A Case of De-industrialisation?' *Cambridge Journal of Economics* 1, 1977, pp. 123–4.

[21] V. R. Fuchs, *The Service Economy* (New York, 1968); Colin Clark, *The Conditions of Economic Progress* (3rd ed., 1957).

Table 7·5: Production and employment in industry

	Index of industrial production, 1980 (1964=100)	Index, employees in employment		
		June 1950	June 1963	Sept.–Dec. 1981
Coal mining	59·7	136·2	100*	56·5*
Food, drink and tobacco	131·8	101·8	100	75·2
Coal and petroleum products	120·9	—	100**	57·0**
Chemicals and allied	190·4	92·9	100	75·5
Ferrous metals	49·6 }	92·5	100	52·4
Non-ferrous metals	55·8 }			
Mechanical engineering	115·3†	81·9	100*	59·0*
Electrical engineering	140·0	60·8	100*	71·1
Shipbuilding and marine engineering	72·3	150·1	100	66·3
Motor vehicles	75·7	111·1	100*	66·2*
Textiles	88·3	140·3	100	43·5
Clothing and footwear	111·4	129·3	100	53·8
Bricks, cement	92·1 }	73·9	100	59·9
Pottery, glass	139·6 }			
Timber, furniture	101·1	110·8	100	76·9
Paper, printing, publishing	115·6	83·5	100	77·7
All manufacturing	114·3	100·1	100	67·0
Construction	96·0	88·5	100	70·7
Gas, electricity, water	181·0	91·4	100	82·3
All industries other than construction	128·9	—	100	66·9
All industries	122·4	99·8	100	91·1††

* Base: March 1965 = 100
** Base: June 1970 = 100
† Mechanical and electrical engineering not separated out 1971–80.
†† All industries and services.

Table 7·6: Changes in employment in the service sector (1970=100)

	June 1950	Sept. 1981	Average annual change, %
Transport and communication	113·9	90·4	−0·7
Distributive trades	81·3	97·2	+0·6
Insurance, banking, finance, business services	46·0	127·9	+3·3
Professional and scientific services	51·7	125·3	+2·9
Miscellaneous services	95·6	130·0	+1·0
Public administration and defence	101·9	109·5	+0·2

between 1970 and the end of 1981, employment in the service sector rose, as shown in Table 7·6.[22]

[22] *Employment Gazette.*

In five of these services (excluding transport and communication) there worked, in September 1981, some 11·2 million employees, or 54% of all employed, and almost twice as many as in the workforce in manufacturing. These services have, therefore, in a real sense, become the determining sector in the labour market. These five services also accounted for the following shares in GDP:[23]

1950	35·1%
1960	36·3%
1970	40·6%
1980	49·5%

Inasfar as the switch to the services represents a necessary shift in the industrial structure, arising from differing demand elasticities for services, and from the success of mass production techniques in saving labour in the manufacturing sector, it has to be viewed as a desirable phenomenon within a growing and modernizing economy.

One aspect of this phenomenon has been the expansion of the public sector. After declining as a share of national income to around 1965, giving rise to the criticism of 'private affluence and public squalor', the public sector has grown substantially since then despite repeated efforts to halt that growth. This growth has been held responsible by some for the poor showing of British manufacturing. But apart from the fact that it was occurring in other countries too, it created competition for a different type of labour, mostly low-paid female labour in place of the skilled male labour displaced in manufacturing.[24] Nor can it be termed non-productive as is sometimes done: it is frequently only political tradition which decides whether, say, the telephone system, education or steel production should be profit-making or public. It may well be that growing incomes, and the growing complexities of production necessary to create them, demand an enlargement of just those sectors which tend to be public or non-market oriented.

The two other components in this significant decline in manufacturing employment are not unconnected with each other. One is the successful penetration of the British market by foreign manufacturers, without an equivalent success of British manufacturers abroad; and the other is the rising unemployment, evident from the mid-1970s, and concentrated heavily on the manufacturing sector. Both have given grounds for concern, and together they have raised the spectre of the de-industrialization of Britain.

The high and rising level of unemployment, as far as it is connected with British and world problems of monetary dislocations and economic policies, will be considered in section 3 of this chapter and in chapter 9; here we turn to the falling competitiveness of British manufacturers. This is shown above all by the falling share of British manufactured exports among the main suppliers of

---

[23] *National Income and Expenditure* (annual).
[24] Alec Cairncross, 'What is De-Industrialisation?' p. 8 and C. J. F. Brown and T. D. Sheriff, 'De-Industrialisation, a Background Paper', p. 253, in Frank Blackaby (ed.), *De-Industrialisation* (1979); Robert Bacon and Walter Eltis, *Britain's Economic Problem: Too Few Producers* (1976).

Table 7·7: The fall in British manufactured exports

Averages of years	British exports of manufactures as percentage share of world total
1951–3	21·4
1959–61	16·5
1969–71	10·9
1977–9	9·5

world markets, a fall which has been continuous since the war (see Table 7·7).[25]

This decline was not due, as in the 1920s, to a permanently overvalued currency. At current rates of exchange, Britain was increasingly becoming a low-wage country. Average hourly wages in manufacturing had by 1981 (based on calculations in Deutschmark), with Britain as 100, reached 171·6 in Sweden, 156·4 in Germany, 156·1 in the USA and even 102·0 in Japan.[26] Nor was the decline due to adversely changing patterns of trade. The problem was, rather, inability to deliver on time or at the appropriate quality, in other words, a supply problem.[27] In the same way, the significant observation that with rising incomes the United Kingdom had a very high elasticity of demand for imported manufactures, in many cases of a value of 2, while the world had a much lower income elasticity for British exports, in like cases a little over 1,[28] was related to the failure of British manufacturers, in competition with others, to produce adequately what the market wanted.

Of equal concern in that period was the rise in import penetration. This had been noticeable earlier, but became acute in the second half of the 1970s. The failure of British manufactures in the home market was particularly noticeable among some of the high-technology, high-growth industries, but also affected some of the older staples. Among the worst were those shown in Table 7·8.[29] Some industries held their own, and others even enlarged their share.

In the widespread debate about the relative decline of British manufacturing in an international comparison, many causes have been held responsible. Among the causes cited, apart from factors specific to particular industries, have been: a low rate of investment, Government interference and the expansion of the

[25] *National Institute Economic Review* (quarterly); Karel Williams, John Williams, Dennis Thomas, *Why are the British Bad at Manufacturing?* (1983), pp. 116–7. Also see Sir Alex Cairncross, J. A. Kay and A. Silberston, 'The Regeneration of Manufacturing Industry', *Midland Bank Review*, Autumn 1977, pp. 11–12.

[26] On unit labour costs, see p. 273 below.

[27] Brown and Sheriff, pp. 256–9; Michael Posner and Andrew Steer, 'Price Competitiveness and the Performance of Manufacturing Industry', p. 159, D. K. Stout, 'De-Industrialisation and Industrial Policy', pp. 176–7 and Thomas Balogh, 'Comment', pp. 178–9, in F. Blackaby, *De-Industrialisation*; Report in *Frankfurter Allgemeine Zeitung*, 19.6.1982; S. Pollard, *The Wasting of the British Economy* (1982), pp. 81–4; *Nat. Inst. Econ. Rev.*, 39, February 1967, p. 16.

[28] A. P. Thirlwall, 'The UK's Economic Problem: a Balance of Payments Constraint?' *National Westminster Bank Review*, February 1978, pp. 29–30, and 'The Balance of Payments Constraint as an Explanation of International Growth Rate Differences', *Banca Nazionale del Lavoro Quarterly Review*, 128, 1979, p. 51.

[29] *Annual Abstract of Statistics*; Williams et al., *Why are the British Bad ...?*, pp. 118–19.

Table 7·8:   Imports as a percentage of home demand

	1971	1980
All manufacturing	16	30
Vehicles	15	39
Electrical engineering	18	37
Instrument engineering	37	61
Clothes and footwear	14	30

Government sector, high taxes, trade-union obstruction, poor management including the 'cult of the amateur', structural survivals from the nineteenth century and an unhelpful banking sector, apart from Government policies themselves.[30] Some of these strictures have been of long standing. The remainder will be discussed in the following pages, and particularly in chapter 9, section 3 below.

We now turn to individual industries. Coal mining remained a problem, but the issues had changed since the inter-war years. In the early years of the National Coal Board, coal mining was slow to show any improvements in output per manshift. Long-term improvement began with the plan of 1950[31] which proposed major reconstructions, the closure of 350–400 pits then working, new sinkings and general re-equipment to meet the estimated demand for coal for the next 15 years, until 1965. However, all these efforts did little beyond counteracting the natural tendency of mining costs to rise with the age of the workings. Output per manshift refused obstinately to reach the magic figure of 25 cwt, and total saleable output similarly did not rise beyond the 210 m.t. level, while from 1953 onward the number of workers in the industry actually began to fall. Throughout this period, the supply of coal was well below the demand, the gap being variously estimated at between 15 and 20 million tons a year.[32] In one sense this 'gap' only existed because coal was seriously under-priced,[33] both in terms of costs and in terms of what the market would bear, and coal thus became a hidden means of subsidizing British industry, even to the extent of negative dumping, or selling at a higher price abroad than at home. But in fact, in the boom years of the 1950s, incredible as it might have seemed to another age, coal had to be imported, to the tune of 25 million tons all told, much of it from the dollar area.

In the recession of 1957–1959, a major change-over to oil, fostered by the coal shortage itself, was superimposed on the long-term decline in demand. Coal consumption in the United Kingdom fell from 214 million tons in 1956 to 187

[30] The best introductions to the debate will be found in David Coates and John Hillard, *The Economic Decline of Modern Britain* (Brighton, 1986); and Williams *et al., Why are the British . . .?*, pp. 14 f.

[31] National Coal Board, *Plan for Coal* (1950); the revised plans were published as *Investing in Coal* (1956) and *Revised Plan for Coal* (1959). Cf. also A. Beacham, 'Planned Investment in the Coal Industry', *Oxf. Econ. P.*, 3/2 (1951) and K. S. Lomax, 'The Demand for Coal in Great Britain', *ibid.*, 4/1 (1952).

[32] PEP, *Growth in the British Economy* (1960), pp. 99–103; Beacham, 'The Coal Industry', in Burn, *op. cit.*

[33] I. M. D. Little, *The Price of Fuel* (Oxford, 1953).

million tons in 1959, while oil consumption rose from 18 to 33 million tons (coal equivalent) and 0·5 m.t. equivalent was produced by nuclear energy. Coal stocks began to build up to 8·6 m.t. at the end of 1957, 19·7 m.t. in 1958, and 35·7 m.t. or about two months' output at the end of 1959. Ironically, it was precisely at this point that the investment and reorganization of earlier years began to bear fruit. Productivity increased, and over-production, as in the inter-war years, appeared on the horizon.[34] In the light of the apparent permanent fall in demand, the plans were changed in 1959 from the 1965 target of 240 m.t. to a target of 206 m.t., which was about the level of the actual 1959 production. This scaling down allowed the closing of high-cost pits to proceed even faster than had been intended, and the number of NCB mines in production in Great Britain fell from 901 at the beginning of 1951 to 438 in March, 1967. Output per manshift rose from 24·9 cwt in 1957 to 36·6 cwt in 1966–7, or by nearly one-half, and similarly output per man year stood at 293 t. in 1950 and 390 t. in 1966–7.

This striking success was reflected also in the accounts. In spite of the low-price policy, which deprived the National Coal Board of its own finance and forced it to increase its interest burden very heavily by outside borrowing, the rise in costs was kept below that of proceeds and in the mid-1960s it appeared that the Board might be permanently out of the red. The Board's chairman, Lord Robens, succeeded in reducing employment from a maximum of 711,000 in 1952 to 419,000 in 1967,[35] without arousing insuperable opposition from the men. The care with which local closures and transfers of labour were prepared compared very favourably with the methods of some other industries in similar circumstances.

In November 1967, a new white paper[36] announced a planned reduction of manpower to one-sixth, or a mere 65,000 by 1980 in the seven main regions, and an expected share of coal of only 120 m.t. out of a national total of 350 m.t. coal equivalent by 1975, a fall of 31% in output and 24% in the share of all fuels, giving way to oil, which turned out to be cheaper for all purposes and to natural gas from the mid-1960s onward. The output of the National Coal Board did indeed fall by −4·3% a year in 1960–75, and employment by −5·9%. Productivity rose by an annual +1·7%, achieved in part by continuing mechanization. While 92% of coal was already mechanically cut in 1960, power loading increased from 38% in 1960 to 93% in 1973, and coal from power-supplied faces, from 10% to 91%.[37]

An even greater fall in the demand for coal was prevented by the deliberate Government policy to keep coal-fired power stations going: these took 21·8% of coal supplies in 1957 and 62·9% in 1976. Meanwhile, however, the oil price rise of 1973–4 made coal competitive once more and transformed the industry's prospects. Re-expansion of output was planned, to add 42 million tons by 1980, and newly discovered fields were being developed at Selby in Yorkshire, and in Warwickshire. Output, having fallen from around 180 m.t. in the 1960s and

---

[34] E. S. Simpson, *Coal and the Power Industries in Post-war Britain* (1966), p. 16.

[35] National Coal Board, *Annual Report and Accounts*.

[36] *Fuel Policy*, Cmnd. 3438 (1967).

[37] National Economic Development Office, *A Study of the UK Nationalised Industries* (1976), p. 13; G. F. Ray and L. Uhlmann, *The Innovation Process in the Energy Industry* (Cambridge, 1979), p. 43.

135 m.t. in 1970, stabilized around 110 m.t. saleable coal in 1971–81, the share of coal in energy consumption staying around the 37% mark in 1973–1980, while the share of petroleum fell from 46·5% to 36·8% and the share of natural gas rose from 12·5% to 21·5%. The hoped-for increase in output per manshift (OMS) of 4% a year failed to materialise, OMS staying around 2·3 tons between 1972 and 1980.[38] The number of miners also stabilized, being 230,000 in 1980–1, and this has allowed the men to return to their former position near the top of the wages league from which the temporary eclipse of coal had dislodged them.

Until 1973, oil was the fastest grower in the energy sector. Refining in Britain was furthered for strategic reasons and to save imports, but a home-based oil refining industry also provided some flexibility in varying the proportions of the product according to home needs, and it created a base for the petro-chemical industry. Beginning with the Shell plant at Stanlow (1947) and the Esso refinery at Fawley (1951), capacity in Britain increased from 29 million tons in 1953 to 88 million tons at the end of 1966 and 133 million tons in 1980. At the latter date, all but 3% of the refining was carried out in plants of over 1 million tons capacity, and three plants were at, or above, the 10 million ton optimum: Fawley (Esso), Kent (BP) and Shell Haven (Shell).[39]

The industry is highly capital intensive, and the small labour force showed one of the fastest rises in productivity per man in British industry. Larger throughput led to lower costs, so that a refinery of a capacity of 10 million tons had little more than one-third of the unit cost of a refinery of a half million ton capacity. Oil is dominated by a handful of giants, British, American and Dutch, all with large international interests, forming one of the world's most powerful oligopolies.[40] Nevertheless, competition was fierce in certain areas and one form which it took after 1945, the buying up and tying in of the retail outlets, the petrol stations, was in striking parallel to the action of the brewers over half a century earlier. Opinion was divided on the value of this system to the customers, but the Monopolies Commission refused to condemn it outright.[41]

In the 1970s, two dramatic developments affected the oil industry. The first was the sudden price rise engineered by OPEC, the organization of the leading oil exporters, following the Arab-Israeli war of 1973. From a stable level of £7–8 per tonne, held over the whole period 1950–72[42] in the face of a general inflation of world prices, the price was quadrupled to £33 per tonne by 1974, rose to £50–60 in 1976–8 and was increasing substantially once more in 1979.

---

[38] Prest and Coppock, p. 179. Actual output was 122·4m. tonnes in 1979 and 130·1m. tonnes in 1980. Department of Energy, *Digest of United Kingdom Energy Statistics*, 1981; Department of Energy, *Coal Industry Examination: Interim Report* (1974); William Ashworth, *The History of the British Coal Industry*, vol. 5, *1946–1982: The Nationalized Industry* (Oxford, 1986), pp. 367, 377 f; NCB, *Plan for Coal* (1974).

[39] C. Pratten and R. M. Dean, *The Economics of Large-Scale Production in British Industry* (Cambridge, 1965), pp. 93, 97; Duncan Burn, 'The Oil Industry', in *Structure of British Industry*, I; E. S. Simpson, *op. cit.*, chapters 8 and 10; J. H. Dunning and C. J. Thomas, *British Industry, Change and Development in the Twentieth Century* (1961), pp. 89–92.

[40] Peter Odell, *Oil: The New Commanding Height* (Fabian Society, 1965), pp. 5–7.

[41] Monopolies Commission, *Petrol: A Report on the Supply of Petrol to Retailers in the United Kingdom* (1965); Harry Townsend, 'Exclusive Dealing in Petrol: Some Comments', *Economica*, 32/128 (1965).

[42] D. I. MacKay and G. A. Mackay, *The Political Economy of North Sea Oil* (1975), p. 5.

The drastic cutback in consumption and switch to other fuels, with which all countries, including the United Kingdom, reacted to this sea-change, together with the rapid development of new oil fields in many parts of the world, could mitigate but not remove its catastrophic effects. In Britain, oil consumption, which had been rising at a rate of 8% a year, actually dropped from a maximum of 113 m. tonnes in 1973 to stabilize around 90 m.t. from 1975 onward; for Western Europe as a whole, where consumption had been growing much faster, the fall was from 749 m.t. in 1973 to around 700 m.t. thereafter. But despite these savings, the quantities involved were large enough to create unprecedented balance of payments difficulties for all importing countries, which included the major western industrial nations, and an unmanageable surplus for the oil exporters, estimated at $66 billion in 1974 and $42 billion in 1975. The earlier switch to oil and other fuels was everywhere reversed, and the worldwide technological search for fuel economy was boosted.

Equally dramatic was the impact of the discovery of oil in the North Sea, first confirmed as commercially viable in 1971. In November 1975 oil from the Forties field reached British shores, by 1976, one-eighth of consumption was met by the home field, by 1978 it was five-ninths, and by 1981 North Sea output was larger than home needs and provided a small net export surplus.

The effects of this turn-round were felt in all sectors of the economy. The oil payments deficit, which had risen in the early 1970s to around £3·5 billion a year, was kept up at first by the need to import much of the necessary heavy equipment, such as drilling platforms and pipelines; their imports peaked at £1·2 billion in 1976 and 1977. In the heavy investment years, 1976–9, the annual capital formation in North Sea gas and oil exceeded £2 billion and amounted to one-quarter of all British industrial investment and one-tenth of total gross fixed capital formation. Between one-third and two-fifths of this came from British companies, and to the extent that it relied on bank finance, it represented 4·4% of all advances of UK banks to UK residents by August 1978.[43]

On the positive side, the oil bonanza created at once new wealth and new jobs: 19,000 in Scotland in 1974 alone. Aberdeen became the centre of a boom region and the builders of the oil rig platforms also found lucrative, if fluctuating, employment. On a national basis, the flow of oil likewise reversed the age-old balance of payments threat into an easy surplus and the pound sterling rose on the foreign exchanges. Lastly, as the concessions of the early years expired, a large and growing share of the oil revenue began to flow to the Government, in the form of royalties and petroleum revenue tax in addition to the normal corporation and profits taxes. The oil boom thus helped both to explain and to compensate for the decline of manufacturing industry in the later 1970s: in 1977–9 it added 0·7% to the annual growth rate of GDP.[44] In the 1970s the contribution of nuclear power stagnated at 12–14 m. tonnes coal equivalent, or 3–4% of British energy consumption.

Space does not permit a detailed treatment of each of the manufacturing industries. We must content ourselves with cursory accounts of some select

[43] L. P. Tempest, 'The Financing of North Sea Oil 1975–1980', *Bank of England Quarterly Bulletin*, 19, March 1979, pp. 31–4; L. P. Tempest and R. J. Walton, 'North Sea Oil and Gas in the UK Balance of Payments since 1970', *ibid.*, September 1979, pp. 283–9.

[44] *National Institute Economic Review*, February 1978. Also chapter 10 below.

examples, representing 'new' industries (motors, chemicals), mixed (steel) and the 'old staples' (cotton, shipbuilding).

The spread of car ownership among ever widening circles of the population was proof positive that the austerities and privations of the war years were over; car manufacturing was also a yardstick of the producing country's industrial power.

In the sellers' market of the post-war years which did not end until 1955 or even later,[45] all that could be made, could be sold. On the face of it, Britain appeared to have done well also thereafter, since her output rose 88% between 1955 and 1964 (or by 7·3% a year). But world production outside the USA rose from 4,331,000 to 12,762,0000 vehicles, or by no less than 195%[46]. By the late 1950s or early 1960s, the leading competitors had not merely recaptured their share, but had overtaken the United Kingdom in the productivity of their plant and the skill of their salesmanship and presentation.

By the 1970s, the British lag had become disastrous. Output of vehicles per employee year, adjusted for certain incomparabilities, changes as shown in Table 7·9.[47]

Table 7·9:   Output of vehicles per employee year

	1950	1955	1959	1965	1973	1976
USA	10·0	11·1	10·3	13·9	14·9	26·1
United Kingdom	3·3	4·2	5·2	5·8	5·1	5·5
France	3·2	3·6	5·7	6·1	6·8	—
West Germany	2·2	3·9	5·6	7·1	7·3	7·9
Italy	—	3·0	—	7·4	6·8	—
Japan	—	1·2	—	4·4	12·2	—

The differences were particularly striking in the case of identical cars assembled in similar plants (or where differences in plants could be allowed for). Thus in 1973, the British plant needed 67% more labour to produce a Ford Escort than the German, 87% more for the Cortina than the Belgians needed for the Taunus, and 132% more than the Belgians for a Mini.[48]

The absolute decline of what had not long ago been a growth industry, typified the decline of manufacturing. The shrinking employment is tabulated on Table 7·5 above. But even output fell off, as shown in Table 7·10.[49]

Yet registrations continued to increase, for private cars from 2½ million in 1951 to over 9½ million in 1966 and over 15 million in 1980, and for commercial vehicles and tractors, from 1·4 to 2·2 and 3·6 million. The gap between shrinking output and rising registrations was filled by imports. Imports took 5% of the

[45] G. Maxcy and A. Silberston, *The Motor Industry* (1959), pp. 18–19.

[46] A. Silberston, 'The Motor Industry 1955–1964', *Bull. Oxf. Inst. Stat.*, 27/4 (1965).

[47] *Ibid.*, p. 270; J. S. Dunnett, *The Decline of the British Motor Industry* (1980), p. 131; Central Policy Review Staff, (CPRS), *The Future of the British Car Industry* (1975), p. 80.

[48] *Economist*, 20 December 1975; Wayne Lewchuk, *American Technology and the British Vehicle Industry* (Cambridge, 1987), pp. 185 ff.

[49] Ministry of Transport. There was some re-classification, especially of estate cars for export, between 1952 and 1953.

Table 7·10: Output of motor vehicles

	Output, '000 vehicles				% Exported		
	1951	1966	1972	1980	1951	1966	1981
Passenger cars	476	1604	1921	924	77	34	24
Commercial vehicles	258	439	408	389	53	36	37
Agricultural tractors	137	214	134	103·5	82	63	—

British car market in 1965, 14% in 1970, 49% in 1978 and 58% in early 1982.[50] The major car manufacturers, it is true, have in recent years tended to distribute their components production over different countries, so that the meaning of an 'imported' or 'home'-produced car is no longer clear-cut.[51] Nevertheless, the figures give a fair indication of the catastrophic market losses.

Why had British makers failed to improve their productivity in line with the others? One answer was: too many makers and too many models. In the early post-war years, minimal costs might be reached by an output of half a million units a year; for the whole range, one million or more was needed in the 1970s.[52] No British model ever reached that figure even though the number of models in the cheaper classes was indeed reduced, and there also occurred a striking movement of amalgamation which turned the numerous firms of 1945 into little more than four large groups, of which one was British owned (Leyland-BMC), and the other three were subsidiaries of the three major US Companies, Ford, General Motors (Vauxhall) and Chrysler (Rootes). The last was sold, in turn, to Peugeot-Citroen in 1978. Between them, they controlled over 90% of car and commercial vehicle output, and those left outside were mostly specialist sports or high-class car makers. British Leyland had to be saved from bankruptcy in 1974 and was nationalized in 1975; British Chrysler also received large subsidies to keep it in being in 1975–9.[53]

Among the main landmarks were the mergers of Standard and Triumph (1945), Austin and Nuffield (1952), Rootes and Singer (1955), Jaguar and Daimler (1960), Leyland and Standard-Triumph (1961) and Leyland and BMC (1968).[54] In the 1950s, at a time when the steel industry was unable to supply sufficient sheet steel to the British car industry, there was also a general scramble to link up with the body manufacturers, including Ford-Briggs Motor Bodies (1953), BMC-Fisher & Ludlow (1953), BSA-Car Bodies (1954), Standard-Mulliners (1958), and BMC-Pressed Steel. Components manufacturing also became dominated by a few large firms which might secure even longer runs by standardizing output between rival car makers: Joseph Lucas for electrical

[50] See also Table 7·8 above and Stephen Wilks, *Industrial Policy and the Motor Industry* (Manchester, 1984), p. 70.

[51] George Maxcy, *The Multinational Motor Industry* (1981), p. 233.

[52] A. Silberston, 'The Motor Industry', in D. L. Burn, *op. cit.* II. p. 18; Krish Bhaskar, *The Future of the UK Motor Industry* (1979), pp. 25–6.

[53] Department of Industry, *The British Motor Vehicle Industry*, Cmnd. 6377 (1976).

[54] G. Maxcy, 'The Motor Industry', in P. Lesley Cook (ed.), *Effects of Mergers* (1958). In the BMC (or more correctly, BM Holdings) merger with Leyland, official support was forthcoming with an investment of £25 million by the Industrial Re-organization Corporation.

equipment, S. Smith and Sons for instruments. Champion for sparking plugs and other equipment and Dunlop for tyres.

Yet, having amalgamated, the companies were slow to undertake a thorough structural reorganization. British Leyland, for example, still operated on 60 different sites. In the 1970s Ford's rationalized by sharing their components manufacture among works in four countries (including Northern Ireland), and General Motors (Vauxhall) went even further, moving virtually all its car making to Germany, and its commercial vehicles to Britain.[55]

The Government contributed to the fateful dispersal of productive plant by forcing the industry to build its extensions, not next to the main works, but in regions lacking employment. In the early 1960s, in consequence, Rootes opened a plant in Linwood, Scotland, for the production of the 'Imp' model, Vauxhall developed a unit in Ellesmere Port, Standard-Triumph in Speke (Liverpool), Ford at Halewood (Merseyside) and BMC in Llanelly. This necessarily raised costs, and in the long run did nothing to help the regions.[56] Weakened by inefficiency, labour troubles or just bad luck, several of these plants have had to be closed again, throwing large numbers of workers on the dole just when alternative employment was also disappearing.

A further cause was the failure to bring the capital equipment up-to-date: or in other words, inadequate investment. This was particularly striking in the case of British Leyland before the Edwardes reorganization, but it was evident among other British firms also, just as, on an international basis, those countries and firms did best which provided the most modern plant for their workers.[57]

The causes of this low investment rate are complex, but one major influence was undoubtedly the Government's periodic, yet unpredictable switches to restraint and cutback, the reign of 'stop-go', which disoriented, destabilized and penalized precisely those industralists who had to make large lumps of costly investments. The motor industry was additionally harmed by the frightening frequency of further changes in purchase tax, VAT rates and HP regulations, each of which altered the market conditions for cars, threw all planning into confusion and was bound to create difficulties and to demoralize all those concerned with making and selling motor vehicles. There were no fewer than 18 such changes in 1961–74,[58] precisely the years when makers abroad moved unhindered into newly expanding mass markets.

Other failings which emerged clearly in international comparison were bad and slow workmanship; extremely poor maintenance work; antiquated layout and employment practices; and numerous labour disputes and strikes. In those years, the motor industry took over the lead from the miners in strike proneness,

[55] Maxcy, *Multinational*, pp. 145–6, 189; Derek F. Channon, *The Strategy and Structure of British Enterprise* (1973), pp. 107–8; Richard Pryke, *The Nationalised Industries: Policies and Performance since 1968* (Oxford, 1981), pp. 218 ff.

[56] C. Pratten, *Economies of Scale in Manufacturing Industry* (Cambridge, 1971), p. 132; Dunnett, *Decline*, pp. 77 f.; The Society of Motor Manufacturers and Traders (SMMT). *The British Motor Manufacturing Industry – A Students' Guide* (1979), pp. 2·2–2·3.

[57] For some striking figures, see CPRS, *Car Industry*, p. 54; Bhaskar, *Motor Industry*, p. 88.

[58] CPRS, *Car Industry*, pp. 123–5; SMMT, p. 6·1; Bhaskar, *Motor Industry*, pp. 15–16; NEDC, *Industrial Report by the Motor Manufacturing EDC: Economic Assessment to 1972* (1970), p. 37; *idem, The Effect of Government Economic Policy on the Motor Industry* (1968); Maxcy and Silberston, pp. 44–5; Dunnett, *Decline*; J. C. R. Dow, *The Management of the British Economy* (Cambridge, 1965), pp. 275–82.

particularly harmful in an assembly industry where holdups in one sector quickly affected the output of others.

All of this adds up to atrociously bad management. When Lord Stokes took over BMC in its merger with Leyland, he found its 'management . . . overmanned in practically every area, it was short of management skills in lots of areas, its model replacement programme was almost non-existent.' Instead of planning, 'BMC was still relying on a combination of hunch and whim to plan and price its products, which, in retrospect, appears naive and amateurish.'[59]

The motor industry may thus, by its early post-war rise in a sellers' market and its later failures, be taken as symbolic for much of British industry. It was, however, more than a symbol. Its own size, together with its impact on the suppliers of components, such as sheet steel, glass, tyres and electrical equipment, made it in itself a significant determinant of British industrial progress. Elsewhere, including Germany, Italy, Japan and even France, car manufacture became a 'leading industry', pulling others up, creating an export surplus, and encouraging modern techniques at several levels. By the same token, the decline of the British motor industry had wider effects; above all, it was among the most significant causes of the growing balance of payments weakness, which in turn led to repeated bouts of deflation.

Chemicals, the second among our examples of 'new' industries, combined rapid technical progress with the opportunity to displacing older industries as well as creating new markets. The limits of the industry are ill-defined, and on some counts oil refining itself might be subsumed under it. A rough division into heavy chemicals and fine chemicals, such as pharmaceutical products, is often used. Yet the processes used, if not commercial considerations also, impose much vertical and horizontal integration and the chemical industry, in Britain and elsewhere, remained in this period one of the most highly concentrated of modern industries. ICI alone employed about one-third of the labour force and there have been several mergers among the other giants.[60] The major take-over bid, by ICI, was, however, beaten off successfully by Courtaulds's, the intended victim, in a dramatic battle in 1961, in which ICI had obtained as much as 38% of the Courtauld shares.[61]

In this industry, also, technical progress compared badly with the achievements of other countries. Britain, for example, delayed too long to switch from coal-based to gas- or oil-based technology, and fell behind in the production of plastics. While the chemical industry was among the fastest growers, averaging 5·39% a year in 1957–77, it formed a smaller share of manufacturing output than in all other comparable countries.[62] In this, as in other faster than average growth industries heavily based on science and technology, like electronics and man-made fibres, for which reasons of space forbid more detailed treatment,[63]

[59] Jonathan Wood, *Wheels of Misfortune. The Rise and Fall of the British Motor Industry* (1988), pp. 172, 246; Lewchuk, *American Technology*.

[60] W. B. Reddaway, 'The Chemical Industry', in *Structure of British Industry*, I, and C. J. Thomas, 'The Pharmaceutical Industry', *ibid.*, II; Charles Wilson, *Unilever 1945–1965* (1968), pp. 149 ff.

[61] D. C. Coleman, *Courtaulds. An Economic and Social History*. vol. 3. *Crisis and Change 1940–1965* (Oxford, 1980), chapter 10.

[62] Prest and Coppock, pp. 172–3; Pratten, *Economies of Scale*, pp. 309, 319.

[63] E.g., Thomas Wilson, 'The Electronics Industry' and D. C. Hague, 'The Man-Made Fibres Industry', *Structure of British Industry II*.

we find the same story of inadequate investment in new capacity and tardy adoption of new technology, so that the windfall technical lead which was acquired during the war and still held in 1950 was lost and competitive power suffered.[64]

Among industries of near-average growth, the iron and steel industry was machines, ships, buildings, vehicles and bridges, as also for many of the durable consumer goods, on which so much of the newly increased income was expended. The first iron and steel nationalization was speedily reversed: the Iron and Steel Act of 1953 sold the industry back to private owners, but leaving 'an adequate measure of public supervision'[65] to be exercised by the Iron and Steel Board. A separate Iron and Steel Holding and Realization Agency was to dispose of the shares and by 1957 had sold 86%; after 1963 those of only one firm, Richard Thomas & Baldwin, were left, and were held by the State until the second nationalization act.[66]

By 1950 capacity had been raised to 16 million tons of steel. A second 'plan' in 1952 envisaged investment at around £60 million a year, to raise capacity to over 20 million tons, later revised to $22\frac{1}{2}$ million tons, by about 1957. This, however, was still well below national needs and forced Britain to spend foreign exchange on imports of sheet steel and other similar products in the 1950s.

A third development plan was published in 1957, envisaging an increase in capacity to 29 million tons by 1962, and it was under its provision that some of the most important new plants were built and others extended, including the continuous strip mills at Ravenscraig and in South Wales and the R.T.B. Spencer Works at Newport, while the Dorman-Long Lockerby plant, a universal beam mill, was opened in 1958. Conversions to electricity and to Oxygen processes, such as the LD or Kaldo furnaces, and extensions at Shotton, Appleby-Frodingham, Stocksbridge and elsewhere were also undertaken, though no complete new plant was put up. Fixed capital investment which had fluctuated around £60–80 million a year in 1947–55 (at constant, 1936 prices), rose to a peak of £207 million in 1961, only to drop back to *c.* £75 million by 1963–4.[67] A fourth plan, in April 1961, envisaged a further increase in capacity to 32 million tons in 1965, and a fifth plan, published under the shadow of nationalization in 1966, aimed at a capacity of 35·3 million tons in 1975, but meanwhile the sellers' market had collapsed and the plans were largely still-born. The annual growth rate of 2·7% in 1950–69 compared with 6·4% in the Common Market and 34·0% in Japan (1952–1969),[68] but at least there was still a net addition. In the following decade, crude steel production actually fell from 27·9 million tonnes in 1970 to a catastrophic 11·4 m.t. in 1980. With imports then at 6·1 m.t.

[64] The mid-1960s did, however, see some massive investments and the ICI issue of £50 million in 1965 was the largest such private operation since the war. S. J. Wells, *Trade Policies for Britain* (1966), pp. 92–3.

[65] Quoted in A. J. Youngson, *Britain's Economic Growth, 1920–1966* (1967), p. 217.

[66] Duncan Burn, 'Steel', in *Structure of British Industry*, I, pp. 298–300; G. W. Ross, *The Nationalization of Steel* (1965), pp. 153, *passim*.

[67] B. S. Keeling and A. E. G. Wright, *The Development of the Modern British Steel Industry* (1964), p. 169. See also J. C. Carr and W. Taplin, *History of the British Steel Industry* (Oxford, 1962).

[68] A. Cockerill, with A. Silberston, *The Steel Industry. International Comparisons of Industrial Structure and Performance* (Cambridge, 1974), pp. 9, 55; Department of Trade and Industry, *Steel*, Cmnd. 5226 (1973).

and exports 3·4 m.t., Britain had for the first time in modern times turned, between 1979 and 1980, into a net importer of steel.

To some extent, steel was a victim of the failure of the economy as a whole to grow as fast as expected; technological changes, steel 'economies' and displacement by other materials also played a part.[69] But the import surplus showed that British steel was falling behind in general competitive power. Average furnace capacity, a good measure of technical efficiency,[70] increased three-fold in 1950–66, but was still low by international standards, and plant size failed to grow as fast as abroad. Among the particular British handicaps were said to be: price controls, Government interference, especially on investment decisions, lack of working capital, delays in approval for closing high-cost plants, and endemic labour troubles. The British share of world output fell from 10% in 1950 to 5% in 1966 and 1·6% in 1980, and in 1967 crude steel output per man hour compared as follows:[71]

EEC, average	0·107 tons
USA	0·106
Japan	0·081
UK	0·037

By the Iron and Steel Act of 1967, the 14 major units of the industry were nationalized for the second time. After reorganization in 1970 into four major product divisions, general steels, special steels, strip mills and tubes, as well as constructional engineering and chemicals,[72] rationalization by concentration in certain plants was possible, and was aided by some support for redundancy by the European Coal and Steel Community (ECSC) to which Britain belonged by joining the EEC in 1973. Renewed efforts at modernization were made, and despite repeated stops imposed by Government in the interest of macroeconomic policies, gross capital formation rose, at 1975 prices, from £316 million in 1970 to a peak of £600 million in 1976. But thereafter it collapsed, amounting only to £155 million in 1980.[73]

Among the declining industries, cotton furnishes an important example. After a post-war boom in which all that could be made could be sold with ease at home and abroad,[74] the decline from 1951 onward was swift and would have been swifter still but for quotas and high protection including voluntary ceilings

[69] Keeling and Wright, pp. 95–7; British Iron and Steel Federation, *The Steel Industry, Stage I Report of the Development Co-ordinating Committee* (1966).

[70] The notional index of costs was as follows:

Blast furnace:

capacity of		Open hearth furnace size	
100,000 t.p.a.	131	75 t.	131
200,000 t.p.a.	100	150 t.	100
1,000,000 t.p.a.	58	400 t.	85
1,500,000 t.p.a.	52		

Pratten and Dean, pp. 67,70. Also see Cockerill, p. 82.

[71] Cockerill, pp. 32, 38, 94; D. L. Burn, *The Steel Industry 1939–1959* (Cambridge, 1961), p. 558; Wells, *op.cit.,* p. 99; L. Nabseth and G. F. Ray, *The Diffusion of New Industrial Processes. An International Study* (Cambridge, 1974), pp. 175–6, 193–5, 241, 247; Richard M. Duke *et al., The United States Steel Industry and its International Rivals* (Washington, 1977), pp. 353, 438, 442.

[72] British Steel Corporation, *Third Report on Organisation,* H. of C. 60 (1969–70).

[73] *National Income and Expenditure, 1981.* Figures deflated by the 'implied deflator' for gross domestic capital formation in the same volume.

[74] G. W. Furness, 'The Cotton and Rayon Textile Industry', in *Structure of British Industry,* II.

of exports to Britain from Commonwealth countries since 1958, and regulations for imports from low wage countries. After 1964, replacement by man-made fibres accelerated the downward trend in the cotton industry: Courtaulds had by then acquired one-third of Lancashire's spindles,[75] and they continued to convert more capacity towards artificial fibres in the following years, as did other firms, including ICI. In a period of good employment, labour moved out fairly smoothly; in 1963–74 alone, employment in cotton was halved, but over-capacity in capital equipment was less easily dealt with. It was estimated in 1959 to have reached 30% in spinning, 60% in doubling, and 25–40% in finishing. The cotton industry thus appeared to be in an exceptionally unfavourable position in an otherwise booming Britain and the Government, in two minds whether to make grants for scrapping old plant or for installing new, was pressurized into doing both. The Cotton Industry Act, 1959 provided for the payment of two-thirds of the compensation by the Government, and one-third by an industrial levy towards the scrapping of obsolete plant. The Government, in addition, was to make grants covering a quarter of the cost of any new machinery installed before 1962 and displaced labour was also to obtain compensation. The effectiveness of the Act was greater and speedier than had been anticipated. By the end of March 1960, the number of spindles had been cut by nearly half (12·4 million out of 25·3 million), and the number of looms by two-fifths (105,000 out of 259,000); 300 mills were closed completely in 1959–60 and a total of over £30 million was ultimately paid out for scrapping and for new plant.[76]

The result was a remarkable rise in productivity as total employment fell: it rose by 10% in 1956–61, and by 8% a year on average in 1963–74. Even so, this rise was much slower than the productivity rises abroad.[77]

While large firms dominated one sector of the industry, family controlled firms continued to cling to independence; in 1968, there were still over 1,000 of them.[78] Similar observations could be made in other declining or stagnant industries, as in wool and worsted spinning and weaving, in the clothing industry and in leather and furs.

Finally, among declining industries, shipbuilding deserves a special mention. Again, following the short-term post-war competitive advantage because of the destruction of shipyard capacity among other belligerents, and the inability of the rest of the world to buy tonnage launched in the dollar area, it is the relative British decline in competitiveness with the shipyards of other countries which is most striking. In the years 1949–51, the United Kingdom was still the leading producer for exports (i.e. foreign registration), selling 522,000 gross tons, or 38% of the world total; by 1956, she had become a poor third behind Japan and Germany, selling 435,000 g.t., or less than 14%; by 1967, sales were an

[75] William Lazonick, 'Industrial Organization and Technical Change: The Decline of the British Cotton Industry', *Bus. Hist. Rev.,* 1982; Franz Fabian, 'Der Konzentrationsprozess in der britischen Textilindustrie', in W. G. Hoffmann (ed.), *Textilwirtschaft im Strukturwandel* (Tübingen, 1966) pp. 81–120.

[76] P. D. Henderson, 'Government and Industry', in Worswick and Ady, *The British Economy in the Nineteen-Fifties* (1962), p. 351; *Reorganization of the Cotton Industry,* Cmnd 744 (1959); *Economist,* 2 April, 1960.

[77] Kenneth Keith, 'Finance and Structural Change in British Industry with Particular Reference to Cotton', *Moorgate and Wall Street* (Autumn, 1963), p. 26; Nabseth and Ray, p. 265.

[78] Pratten, *Economies of Scale,* p. 226.

exceptional 612,000 g.t. but in 1964–6 they averaged only 186,000 g.t. a year.[79] Similarly, total merchant tonnage launched in 1950 was 1,325,000 g.t., compared with a world total of 3,489,000 g.t., and in 1966 1,094,000 g.t. out of a world total of 14,307,000. In that year, Britain slipped to fourth place among the world's producing nations. In 1977, launching 1·0 m.g.t., she produced 4% of the world's output, and by 1980 had slipped to eighth place. By 1980, output had fallen dramatically once more to less than half, 431,000 g.t. Export orders were falling also, while imports approached 50% of British home demand.

In the 1950s the chief competitors had been other European producers, such as Sweden and Germany, using mass production techniques on standardized vessels or standardized components, and a highly efficient technology. After that, Japan came to dominate the international market, defeating opposition both on cost grounds and on technological ability by building super-tankers measuring hundreds of thousands of gross tons. Any growth of this magnitude attracts to itself the further advantages of mass production. Thereafter, even less likely low-wage countries came to the fore: Taiwan, South Korea, Brazil, Poland and Yugoslavia.

As always, the basis of the British decline was the failure to invest in efficient, high-productivity equipment while the market was in Britain's favour.[80] The Geddes report of 1966 found fault with out-of-date equipment, poor sites, divided trade union allegiance leading to costly demarcation disputes and relatively high costs of labour and raw materials in British yards. The proposed remedies included rationalization, standardization and amalgamation. Government support, totalling some £68 million in credit and compensation for losses, was to be made available to bring about the amalgamation of the 62 yards into three or four large combines, of which two were to be in the north-east and one or two on the Clyde. The 15 unions were similarly to amalgamate into five. In this way, the British share of the world market, which had fallen steadily to 10%, was to be raised to 12·5%.[81] Meanwhile, the Fairfield yard on the Clyde, one of the best equipped in the country, had to be rescued from bankruptcy by the Government, which reconstructed the firm in February 1966, a month before the Geddes Committee Report.

In the event, the industry remained racked by labour disputes, unable to deliver on time, technically backward. Without orders for oil rigs it would have fared worse still. As it was, it gained orders only by quoting at a loss, made up by heavy Government subsidies which caused resentment abroad. Finally, after an earlier amalgamation of Upper Clyde Shipbuilders and others into Govan Shipbuilders, the whole collection of some up-to-date but several ramshackle plants, some 27 companies, was taken over by the State under the Shipbuilding Industry Act of 1977, and several repair yards joined later. In the following year, 1978, 'British Shipbuilders' employed 86,000 and had sales of £548 million on which they made £108 million losses.[82] Closures and redundancies became the order of the day here also.

[79] A. K. Cairncross and J. R. Parkinson, 'The Shipbuilding Industry', in *Structure of British Industry*, II, p. 102; Lloyd's Register, *Annual Summary of Merchant Ships Launched*.

[80] Andrew Shonfield, *British Economic Policy Since the War* (1958), pp. 41–8; Williams *et al. Why are the British . . .?*, pp. 49–50.

[81] *Shipbuilding Inquiry Committee 1965–6, Report*, Cmnd. 2937 (1966).

[82] D. F. Channon, 'British Shipbuilders', in John M. Stopford, D. F. Channon, John Constable, *Cases in Strategic Management* (Chichester, 1980).

Lastly, the post-war years have also seen important changes in the provision of services. In transport, the outstanding development has been the progressive replacement of the railways and shipping by road and air transport, respectively. In consequence, the railways saw a yearly decline in the surplus out of which interest had to be paid; in 1956 they registered the first working deficit, i.e. before meeting central charges, and by 1958 the working deficit had rocketed to £48 million. As in the subsequent years the competitive position continued to deteriorate, all attempts to wipe out the deficit proved abortive, but meanwhile its existence led to a bewildering series of changes in policy,[83] which could only have increased the difficulties of those who had actually to manage the railway system.

The avalanche of conflicting advice which descended upon British Railways had two broad targets: organization, and technical equipment and control. On the first, the Transport Act of 1953, by abolishing the Railway Executive, left the British Transport Commission to supervise, rather than manage, a series of disparate enterprises, including a substantial proportion of road vehicles.[84] More usefully, many of the restrictive powers of the Transport Tribunal were abolished, giving greater pricing freedom to the railways. Following a white paper,[85] the Transport Act of 1962 carried decentralization further, by abolishing the BTC and creating separate boards for railways, for London Transport, the docks, inland waterways and a holding company for the auxiliary services, such as British Road Services, buses, hotels and Thomas Cook and Son. Meanwhile, the Transport Tribunal, which had on several occasions considerably increased the losses of the railways by withholding or delaying rate increases, was to be shorn of its power, except for London.[86]

As for re-equipment, there was the common post-war delay. At last, a plan of 1955 envisaged the investment of £1,200 million (at 1954 prices) in 15 years, divided about equally between maintenance and modernization of track, the introduction of diesel and electric drive, etc., and proposed the closing of unprofitable branch lines.[87] But investment was soon cut down for reasons of short-term Treasury policy and because long-term prospects deteriorated. Actual traffic returns were to change as shown in Table 7·11.[88]

In passenger traffic, the railways' share was to shrink to a fraction of its former size, but at least total numbers did not change very greatly. In goods traffic, the railways lost not only three-quarters of their share, but half their traffic. They were driven back essentially on to a small number of items which the roads could not or would not carry, such as coal or mail.

In the 1950s, this transformation was visible but dimly. Indeed, in 1959 the earlier investment plan was optimistically extended to a total of £1,500 million

---

[83] Derek H. Aldcroft, *British Railways in Transition: the Economic Problems of Britain's Railways Since 1914* (1968), pp. 135–45.

[84] *Transport Policy*, Cmnd. 8538 (1952); Gilbert Walker and C. I. Savage, 'Inland Carriage by Road and Rail', in *Structure of British Industry*, I.

[85] *Reorganization of the Nationalized Transport Undertakings*, Cmnd. 1248 (1960).

[86] Philip S. Bagwell, *The Transport Revolution from 1770* (1974), pp. 336–9; H. Pollins, *British Railways: An Industrial History* (Newton Abbot, 1971), pp. 175 ff.

[87] British Transport Commission, *Modernization and Re-equipment of British Railways* (1955), and *Proposals for the Railways*, Cmd. 9880 (1956); M. Beesley and A. A. Walters, 'Investment in British Railways', *Westminster Bank Review* (May 1955).

[88] *Annual Abstract of Statistics*.

Table 7·11:   Changes in the distribution of passenger and freight traffic

	Shares % 1952	1960	1970	1980	Absolute terms 1952	1980
Passengers:					Billion passenger-km	
Railways	21	15·6	8·7	6·9	38·8	36·0
Public road	45	27·7	13·7	9·8	80·6	51·0
Private road	34	56·4	77·1	82·8	61·0	433·0
Air	—	0·3	0·5	0·5	—	2·8
Freight:					Billion tonne-km	
Rail	54	38·0	24·0	14·6	36·0	17·6
Road	46	61·2	73·2	77·1	30·2	93·1
Inland waterways	—	0·4	0·1	0·1	—	0·1
Pipeline	—	0·4	2·6	8·2	—	9·9

(at 1958 prices), much of it to be spent in the next four years, when it was to run at £200 million a year,[89] and it was still hoped to turn the annual deficit into a surplus by these means. But 1959–60 proved to be a turning-point. There was to be a new policy not only in organization, but also in equipment. Investment was cut down to about £100 million p.a. in 1963–4. Dr Beeching, a leading industrialist, was called in in 1961 to advise, and while the 'Beeching Report',[90] which appeared in 1963, did not disagree fundamentally with the diagnosis of 1955, the remedy was now put on closures rather than on re-equipment. The only mention of the latter in the report was an estimate of new rolling-stock, liner trains, etc., of £250 million over an unspecified period. The main proposal was the closure of 5,000 miles of track, together with 2,363 out of 4,293 passenger stations. Against this, freight handling was to be rationalized and the trunk lines were to provide a faster and more efficient competitive service. Thus the reduction in the deficit was to be achieved largely but cutting costs, rather than by attracting new traffic, and the reduction in the labour force by 1966 was put at 70,000. These proposals were accepted in principle, and many of the closures were carried out quickly. Nevertheless, the deficits remained in 1963–8; only 1969 and 1970 showed small surpluses.

Preceded by a battery of white papers,[91] the Transport Act 1968 created a new National Freight Corporation, which included all the assets of the Transport Holding Corporation and all the road traffic assets. It was hoped to catch much of the developing container trade thereby, as also to co-ordinate road and rail traffic and limit long-distance heavy road traffic. Special funds were made available, as 'social service' grants, for keeping open unremunerative branch lines, and the capital burden on which interest was payable after 1969 was reduced to £300 million: £700 million of the original debt and £557 million of the commencing capital of 1962 were cancelled. Thereafter, however, no more

[89] British Transport Commission, *Reappraisal of the Plan for the Modernization and Re-equipment of British Railways*, Cmnd. 813 (1959).
[90] British Railways Board, *The Reshaping of British Railways* (1963); also D. L. Munby, 'The Reshaping of British Railways', *J. of Industrial Economics*, II/3 (1963).
[91] *British Waterways*, Cmnd. 3401; *Railway Policy*, Cmnd. 3439; *The Transport of Freight*, Cmnd. 3470; *Public Transport and Traffic*, Comnd. 3481.

Government capital was to be made available, and funds would have to be borrowed on commercial terms. Finally a National Bus Co. was created out of 93 companies and 21,000 vehicles, the Scottish group remaining separate. The Transport (London) Act of 1969 handed London transport over to the London Transport Executive, to be appointed by the Greater London Council, and another act of that year extinguished the LTB's debt, to allow London also a new start.[92]

In the 1970s, growing car ownership affected both bus and rail revenues adversely and made a co-ordinated policy more necessary than ever. A consultative document of 1976[93] also stressed the problems of rural areas without access to any public transport after the closure of both railways and bus services; it also noted environmental problems and the rising subsidies going to the railways. These had risen from £300m. in 1968 to £630 m. in 1975, while the railways had had £3 billion of debt written off in 20 years. Suggestions included subsidies for buses, as they were more likely to benefit poorer people, increases in railway fares, and higher taxation of heavy road vehicles. A 1977 white paper[94] foreshadowed reduced rail subsidies, and reduced expenditure on the roads, so that railway management has since then resolved itself into keeping the annual losses to a manageable size and persuading the unions to accept redundancies and more efficient working.

On roads, curiously, new investment also lagged until the mid-1950s, but thereafter the momentum of the increase has been supported by powerful pressure groups and has been maintained. Even here, however, investment in major trunk road schemes and motorways has been too erratic to get the full

Table 7·12:   Expenditure on roads and public lighting (£m. current)

Average of years	Current	Capital formation	Total
1950–1	87	12	99
1955–6	115	28	143
1960–1	152	106	258
1964–5	209	212	421
1969–70	257	401	658
1974–5	550	673	1223
1979–80	1154	825	1979

economies of contractors' teamwork. Official figures of public expenditure on the roads (see Table 7·12) show the slow start of new building (as against repair, etc.) and its sharp increase in the late 1950s.[95]

After a long delay from the mooting of the first plans in 1939 for the building of motorways[96] legislation in 1949 led to active preparation in 1955 and (apart from the short Preston by-pass in 1958) the opening of the first major stretch of motorway in 1959. Building continued apace thereafter, despite rising costs

[92] Bagwell, pp. 350 ff.
[93] Department of the Environment, *Consultative Document on Transport Policy* (1976).
[94] *Transport Policy*, Cmnd. 6836 (1977).
[95] *National Income and Expenditure*.
[96] Bagwell, pp. 367–72.

as the routes moved from rural stretches to costly suburban and urban properties. The length of all types of public road open to traffic increased as shown in Table 7·13.

Table 7·13: Lengths of roads (000 km)

	1962	1970	1980
Motorways	0·23	1·06	2·57
Trunk roads	13·4	13·4	12·5
Principal roads	31·8	32·5	34·2
Other roads	270·1	275·4	290·2
Totals	315·6	322·6	339·5

This cursory review of certain sectors of the economy cannot give a complete picture of the development of the productive equipment of the nation in 1950–80. It is intended merely as an illustration of some typical experiences of the primary, secondary and tertiary (service) industries in a period which began with much solid, if chequered expansion, but then saw the beginnings of a long-term decline of the manufacturing sector, while the service sector continued to expand.

The rise in output was essentially based on improved technology in its widest sense. This, by its nature, is likely to spread into most if not all fields. Where, however, new techniques were difficult to apply or were slow in appearance, e.g. in service trades like retail distribution, the rising real wages created by general productivity rises and transmitted by the pressures of the labour market and trade union power to the lagged sector, set up particularly strong incentives to save the now dearer labour by re-organization. The self-service revolution in retailing typifies this reaction. By 1971, it was estimated that 65% of food sales were in self-service shops (93% in the case of multiple traders) and that turnover per employee was on average 63% higher than in traditional shops.[97] Where, on the other hand, productivity rises were well above the average, then unless the industry was very small and in its early growth stages in this period, like oil refining, the general sluggishness of the growth of the economy as a whole held back the potential expansion, and inhibited massive investment in new methods of the kind which could be absorbed by faster-growing economies like those of Germany or Japan.

2 Changes in Business Organization and Structure

The pre-war trend towards greater concentration of firms continued strongly in this period, particularly in manufacturing industry.[98] While the Bolton Com-

---

[97] A. D. Smith and D. M. W. N. Hitchens, *Productivity in the Distributive Trades* (Cambridge, 1985), p. 73.

[98] Alan Armstrong and Aubrey Silberston, 'Size of Plant, Size of Enterprise and Concentration in British Manufacturing Industry, 1935–1958', *J. R. Stat. S.,* 128/3, Series A (1965); K. D. George, 'Changes in British Industrial Concentration 1951–1958', *J. of Industrial Economics*, 15/3 (1967); W. G. Shepherd, 'Changes in British Industrial Concentration, 1951–1958', *Oxf. Econ. P.*, 18/1 (1966).

mittee[99] found that 'small firms', defined as having 200 employees or less, had dropped in numbers from 136,000 in 1935 to 60,000 in 1963, and their share of manufacturing output from 35% to 16%; the fastest growth was at the other end of the scale, among the largest firms. Plants also became larger, though not as decisively.[100] Growth of firms occurred, in fact, largely by the acquisition or erection of additional plants, and only in part by the growth of the average individual plant. The 100 largest manufacturing companies had 27 plants per enterprise in 1958 and 72 in 1972, while the average employment of these enterprises rose from 20,300 to 31,180 in those years, and average plant size correspondingly diminished.[101]

The most detailed study of the largest 100 manufacturing firms showed that they were responsible for 21% of net manufacturing output in 1948, 38% in 1963 and 47% in 1976. In addition to more than doubling their share they were in this period also thoroughly transformed: whereas only 13% had a multidivisional structure in 1950, the proportion was 72% in 1970; and whereas 34% still made only a single product in 1950, this proportion had shrunk to 6% in 1970. Thus the large British firms followed, if somewhat belatedly, the American pattern of diversification, as they also advanced further along the road from family control to control by professional management. 54% of the 92 companies were still controlled by one family in 1950, but only 30% in 1970. On average, the boards of the 100 largest manufacturing firms held only 0·46% of the shares in 1972.[102] For individual industries, concentration showed itself in the growing share held by the top three firms in this period: the average share of the largest three firms in each industry rose from 29% in 1951 to 42% in 1973.[103]

The giant firm has thus become typical for manufacturing as a whole, and predominant in some sectors. Altogether, 45% of manufacturing employees worked in enterprises of 5,000 employees or over in 1972, compared with only 35% in enterprises employing 999 or under; and almost 60% worked in individual plants employing 500 or more. Even in building, perhaps the last stronghold of the small firm, large companies were increasing their share, while in the service industries, banks and insurance companies had been among the first to turn into giants. In retail distribution, the 'multiples' or organizations having 10 establishments or more, raised their share of the trade from 22% in 1950 to 39% in 1971, while the giants, with 100 establishments or over (omitting the co-ops), grew from 12·9% in 1950 to 28·3% in 1971. In the latter year, in fact, the firms with 1,000 shops each or over had 7·9% of private retail trade and employed 8·1% of the work force. Large retailers further increased their

[99] *Report of the Committee of Inquiry into Small Firms*, Cmnd. 4811 (1971).

[100] Leslie Hannah, *The Rise of the Corporate Economy* (1976), p. 175.

[101] S. J. Prais, *The Evolution of the Giant Firm in Britain* (Cambridge, 2nd ed., 1981), p. 62.

[102] Hannah, *Corporate Economy*, pp. 172–4, 216; Derek F. Channon, *The Strategy and Structure of British Enterprise*, pp. 52 ff.; Alfred F. Chandler, *Visible Hand: the Managerial Revolution in American Business* (Cambridge, Mass., 1977) and *idem*, 'The Growth of the Transnational Industrial Firm in the United States and the United Kingdom: A Comparative Analysis', *Ec. Hist. Rev.*, 33/3, 1980; M. A. Utton, *Diversification and Competition* (Cambridge, 1979), pp. 3, 79; Prais, *Giant Firm*, p. xv.

[103] P. E. Hart and R. Clarke, *Concentration in British Industry 1935–1975* (Cambridge, 1980), pp. 1, 37; P. E. Hart, M. A. Utton, G. Walshe, *Mergers and Concentration in British Industry* (Cambridge, 1973), p. 25; G. C. Allen, *The Structure of Industry in Britain* (1970), pp. 41–4.

share of the turnover to 54·2% in 1979 (including the co-ops), and grew by 81% between 1976 and 1980, compared with only 27% for small retailers. There were, by 1974, at least 12 retailing firms having over 25,000 employees each, the largest being Woolworth with 81,669.[104]

What was the cause of this remarkable drive towards concentration? Technical considerations seem to have played but little part. Economies of scale are, indeed, highly significant in many industries, but plant size, where such economies should occur, grew very little; the significant growth was in the size of firms. The cause of the drive for expansion has to be looked for in the market rather than on the factory floor. From a larger base, outside services such as transport or communications might be obtained more cheaply, buying and selling agreements more favourably concluded, advertising more effectively driven home. Expansion into other fields reduced risks, particularly if secular decline or stagnation threatend the main activity of an industry, like tobacco because of health legislation, or natural textile fibres because of competition from man-made substitutes; diversification might also use resources more fully or more efficiently.[105] At the same time, simple horizontal expansion into a growing share of sales would strengthen monopolistic powers over the market and monopsonistic powers over suppliers. There was also the possible hope of stronger leverage on Government, or within the employers' organizations, strengthened in 1965 by the formation of the Confederation of British Industry (CBI) out of the Federation of British Industries, the British Employers' Confederation and the National Association of British Manufacturers.[106] In expansion overseas, other motives, such as by-passing a tariff, access to cheap supplies or cheap labour might play a large part.[107]

Lastly, in companies in which ownership was wholly divorced from control, the purpose of directors and managers themselves might have been very different from the interests of their shareholders and might have included the elimination of troublesome competition, sheer personal aggrandizement or prestige. In more than a few mergers and battles for control the process of acquisition itself, rather than any long-term benefits at the end of it, seems to have been a major attraction among the contestants. Conversely, the incident of taxation, possible large investment needs in order to introduce new technology, and sheer failure of succession, contributed to the willingness of some family owners to sell their companies.

For, although internal growth was significant, between one-third and one-half of the rise in concentration since 1950 has been accounted for by mergers and absorptions.[108] Firms grew largely by absorbing other firms. Large firms, themselves the products of mergers, seem to have been particularly prone to repeat the experience.[109] Of the largest 100 manufacturing companies in 1948,

[104] A. R. Prest and D. J. Coppock, *The UK Economy* (7th ed., 1978), pp. 215–16; C. G. Powell, *The Economic History of the British Building Industry 1815–1979* (1980), p. 159; *Census of Distribution*, 1961 and 1971; Derek F. Channon, *The Service Industries: Strategy, Structure and Financial Performance* (1978), pp. 27–31, 58–31, 58–63, 163, 170 ff.

[105] Prais, *Giant Firms*, pp. 50–9, 66–80; Channon, *Strategy and Structure*, pp. 220–1.

[106] Stephen Blank, *Industry and Government in Britain. The Federation of British Industries in Politics, 1945–1965* (Farnborough, 1973); W. Grant and David Marsh, *The Confederation of British Industry* (1977).

[107] See p. 260 below.

[108] Prais, *Giant Firm*, p. xvii; Hart, Utton and Walshe, pp. 101, 135.

[109] But acquisitions did not seem to increase with size. S. Aaronovitch and M. C. Sawyer, 'Mergers, Growth and Concentration', *Oxf. Econ. P.*, 27/1, 1975.

48 had disappeared by 1968: 9 had been nationalized, 12 had fallen back to lower rankings, and no fewer than 27 had been acquired by other firms. After slowing down in the first post-war decade, compared with the pre-war years, merger activity was particularly intensive in the years 1959–73 (see Table 7·14).[110]

Table 7·14:   The scale of merger activity

	No. of firms disappeared by merger	Merger values as % total investment expenditure
1950–9	1,867	10
1960–9	5,635	28
1970–3	2,036	23

One particular technique which attracted much attention at that time was the 'takeover bid', in which one company was able to acquire control of another by offering to buy out its shareholders at prices much above market quotations, and was able to do so profitably because balance-sheet assets had been under-valued, or dividends had been kept unduly low in relation to earnings. Such a takeover represented a cashing in on hidden capital reserves and could be used to finance further acquisitions. Another method, particularly suitable in stores and offices, was to sell the premises or freehold, retaining a long lease, and use the capital thus freed to buy up similar property, to repeat the process in a snowballing series. Other entrepreneurs created holding companies in which their own limited holdings controlled large quantities of non-voting share capital. Some of the most spectacular post-war fortunes were made by these methods.[111] Additionally speculation in urban land and city centre 'development' proved to be most profitable activities in the expansion years of the 1950s and in the early 1970s.[112]

Battles and bids of this kind caused much comment, some of it adverse. Whether they contributed to social welfare by using fully hitherto under-used resources, or whether they were merely the actions of power-hungry men in boardrooms, was one of the issues debated. One way of testing the answer would be to see whether the earning performance of companies improved after their merger. Tests show that the large majority of mergers have been followed by falling profits and/or poorer returns than a similar group of internal-growth firms.[113] Whatever marketing or technical gain there was to be had, was more than swallowed up by the additional costs of large organizations. There were in

[110] Hannah, *Corporate Economy*, pp. 167, 214; Channon, *Service Industry, loc. cit.; idem, Strategy and Structure*, pp. 135, 161, 201; Graham Turner, *Business in Britain* (1969), pp. 84–8; G. Walshe, *Recent Trends in Monopoly in Great Britain* (Cambridge, 1974), pp. 25, 62; Hart, Utton and Walshe, p. 3; R. Evely and I. M. D. Little, *Concentration in British Industry* (1960); J. M. Samuels, 'Size and the Growth of Firms', *Rev. Econ. Studies*, 32/90 (1965).

[111] William Mennell, *Take-over: The Growth of Monopoly in Britain, 1951–1961* (1962); J. F. Wright, 'The Capital Market and the Finance of Industry', Worswick and Ady., *op. cit.*, pp. 464–73; *idem, Britain in the Age of Economic Management* (Oxford, 1979) pp. 71–2.

[112] See p. 328 below.

[113] The most consistent study in the United Kingdom is that of 78 firms between 1961 and 1970 by M. A. Utton, 'On Measuring the Effects of Industrial Mergers', *Scot. J. Pol. Econ.*, 21/1 (1974); also see Hart, Utton and Walshe, p. 2; A. Singh, *Take-overs: Their Relevance for the Stock Market*

those cases few signs of rationalization, at least in the short run, but much friction between old and new personnel. Mergers, and particularly takeover bids, were thus to be largely explained by the hopes of quick promotional gains, and the quest for power.

In the amalgamations of the giants the motives included the desire to occupy monopolistic positions. This was the case, for example, in the amalgamations and takeovers in the motor trade noted above, in the abortive bid by ICI for Courtauld's in 1961, in the acquisition by Courtauld's of the Lancashire Cotton Corporation in 1964 and the takeover of AEI by GEC in the electrical engineering field in 1967. In some cases the aim was near or total monopoly, as in the amalgamation of the aircraft industry into five units, of which two were to produce engines, two airframes, and one helicopters, all of which was engineered by the Government in 1959–60,[114] in the proposals of the Geddes Committee for the concentration of shipbuilding into three or four firms, or in the merger in 1968 of all British computer interests into a single combine, International Computer (Holdings) Limited, in which 10·5% was to be held by the Government.

Meanwhile, control in the public interest over restrictive practices was slowly being built up by the authorities. The Commission set up under the Monopolies and Restrictive Practices (Inquiry and Control) Act of 1948 produced in the early 1950s reports on individual industries which showed great variety in the methods used. It was not, however, always clear whether the public suffered, or whether, as in the report on electric cables and on insulin, the monopoly merely provided countervailing power against another monopoly, or, perhaps, used its large size and control over supplies to achieve greater technical efficiency.

Little positive action arose out of these detailed reports, but the general report, commissioned in December 1952 and published in May 1955, *Collective Discrimination: A Report on Exclusive Dealing, Collective Boycotts, Aggregate Rebates and other Discriminatory Trade Practices*,[115] was followed by legislation. The Restrictive Trade Practices Act of 1956 set up a Restrictive Trade Practices Court, of the status of a High Court, and inaugurated the change from inquiry to control.[116] All restrictive agreements were to be registered and a total of 2,430 were proffered voluntarily and about 100 others brought to light in other ways by 1963. About 100 of these were laid before the Court by the Registrar as contrary to the public interest under the Act and, while most were abandoned before the hearings were completed, most of the remainder were condemned as being against the public interest.[117] As a result of the early unfavourable judgements, over 1,500 agreements were abandoned or altered, and a further

and the Theory of the Firm (Cambridge, 1971), chapter 7; Channon, *Strategy and Structure*, pp. 224–5; Hannah, *Corporate Economy*, pp. 181–3.

[114] For a good account, see P. D. Henderson, in 'Government and Industry', pp. 361–9.

[115] Cmd. 9504 (1955).

[116] Catherine Brock, *The Control of Restrictive Practices from 1956* (1966); R. B. Stevens and B. S. Yamey, *The Restrictive Practices Court: The Judicial Process and Economic Policy* (1965); P. H. Guénault and J. M. Jackson, *The Control of Monopoly in the United Kingdom* (1960); Margaret Hall, 'The Consumer Sector', in Worswick and Ady, *op. cit.*, pp. 449–57; Alex Hunter, *Competitors and the Law* (1966); C. K. Rowley, *The British Monopoly Commission* (1966).

[117] In 29 cases and 42 issues decided in 1958–64, 29 Agreements were declared contrary to the public interest and 13 were not. A. Sutherland, 'Economics in the Restrictive Practices Court', *Oxf. Econ. P.*, 17/3 (1965), pp. 427 ff.

unknown number were abandoned in preference to registration.

In one respect, the Act allowed more restrictiveness than before: while prohibiting collective price fixing, it strengthened the power, hitherto very uncertain, of any individual firm to maintain the resale prices of its goods. This was shown to be contrary to the spirit of the rest of the legislation, and in 1964 the Resale Prices Act aligned resale price maintenance with the other restrictive practices.

Thus, on paper, the anti-monopoly legislation had scored some formidable successes and, in some areas, particularly in retail trading, an unwonted freedom had by the mid-1960s replaced the earlier rigid price structure. Yet it was found to be easier to legislate against restrictive practices than to prevent them. For one thing, unofficial and unwritten agreements proved often as effectual as formal compacts. But secondly, the authorities had come to the conclusion that mergers provided in certain critical cases the preconditions for rationalization and greater technical efficiency.

An attempt to discriminate between those restrictive actions that were in the public interest, and those which were not, was foreshadowed in a white paper in 1964;[118] in the event, the prosposals remained abortive. Meanwhile the Monopolies and Mergers Act of 1965 gave the Board of Trade (and later the Department of Trade and Industry) authority to refer to the Monopolies Commission any merger in which the assets acquired were valued at over £5 million, or which would give control over one-third of the market, reduced by the Fair Trading Act of 1973 to one quarter.

The new emphasis was thus on firms as criteria rather than on commodities or markets, but the effectiveness of this, as of the earlier legislation, depended on the strictness with which it was enforced. Altogether 833 mergers were considered in the first phase, 1965–73, by a Government panel, but only 20 of them were referred to the Monopolies Commission, and of those, seven were abandoned, seven were allowed and six were stopped, and while these included the merger of Barclays and Lloyds Banks, which might have created the largest banking combine in the world, and of Rank and De La Rue, the effects of the new Act were obviously circumscribed by the Government's hesitation to use it.[119] Of around 700 merger cases in the next phase, 1973–7, only 23 were referred. Similarly, the Restrictive Trade Practices Act 1968, which empowered the Board of Trade to enforce the registration of certain types of 'information agreements' was not likely to be very significant as long as knowledge of such agreements could effectively be kept from the Department.

The Act of 1973 extended to a moderate extent, and in several directions, the powers to curb market control. The market share test, reduced to one quarter, could now be applied to a local as well as a national market; uncompetitive practices adopted by firms as employers, restrictive labour practices, and uncompetitive practices by nationalized industries could also now be investigated; and legislation could be extended to services, and this was in fact implemented in 1976. By the end of 1977, 206 cases relating to the supply of services had been so registered.

Altogether, by then over 60 alleged monopolies had been investigated by the Commission, and several hundred merger cases screened. Twelve voluntary

---

[118] *Monopolies, Mergers and Restrictive Practices*, Cmnd. 2299 (1964).
[119] Hannah, *Corporate Economy*, pp. 175–6.

codes of practice to protect the consumer had been introduced, the Office of Fair Trading had exacted promises of good behaviour from numerous individual companies, and it had monitored the Consumer Act 1974 and carried out licensing under it. Well over 3,000 restricive practices had been registered, of which almost 90% had been abandoned. Many practices harmful to the private consumer had been reformed.[120]

Yet there were misgivings about the effectiveness of the whole bundle of policies. They led to an Inter-Departmental Committee in 1978, but this in turn could do no more than suggest certain modest reforms.[121] As before, the two main problems were the effectiveness of stopping secret or unofficial collusive action, and the point that while size might help to exploit the public, it might also aid efficiency and enable British firms to stand up to foreign competition.

The multinational (or transnational[122]) firm had existed in some form at least since the beginning of the century, but had grown particularly fast after the Second World War and had risen to prominence in the 1970s. The United Kingdom was still a net capital exporter, also in this 'direct', as well as in the more traditional 'portfolio' type of investment abroad, but foreign direct investments in Britain were growing apace (see Table 7·15).[123]

Table 7·15:   Stocks and flows of direct foreign investment

	Stocks ($ billion)		Flows (av. annual $ million)		
	UK assets abroad	Foreign assets in UK		Outflows	Inflows
1967	12·5	5·9	1967–9	−1027	631
1974	23·8	15·9	1970–2	−1600	965
(Market values)			1973–5	−3428	1590
(1960)	(12·0)		1976	−3379	1353
(1971)	(24·0)				
(1976)	(32·1)				

The foreign share of capital investment flows in the UK fluctuated in those years between two-ninths and one-third. The stock of manufacturing capacity held in the United Kingdom by subsidiaries of foreign firms was particularly high (50% or over) in the manufacture of computers and electronics, typewriters, razor blades and electric razors, photographic equipment, spark plugs, sewing machines and boot and shoe machines, soap, detergents and cosmetic prep-

---

[120] Prest and Coppock, pp. 198–202.

[121] *A Review of Monopolies and Mergers Policy*, Cmnd. 7198 (1978).

[122] There is no agreement on the definitions of these terms, though some authors do use them to distinguish different types. E.g. Thomas G. Parry, 'The International Firm and National Economic Policy: A Survey of Some Issues', *Econ. J.*, 83/332, 1973, p. 1201; Neil Hood and Stephen Young, *The Economics of Multinational Enterprise* (1979), pp. 3, 117; J. E. S. Parker, *The Economics of Innovation* (1974), p. 159.

[123] James W. Vaupel and Joan P. Curhan, *The World's Multinational Enterprises* (Boston, Mass., 1973), pp. 66, 74; United Nations, *Multinational Corporations in World Development* (N.Y., 1973), pp. 130, 146, 161, 173; idem, Economic and Social Council, Commission on Transnational Corporations, *Transnational Corporations in World Development: A Re-examination* (NY, 1978), pp. 238–40.

arations, breakfast cereals, custard powder, cake mixes, instant coffee, frozen food, tractors, tyres and refrigerators. Most of them fell neatly into two groups: high-technology, or heavily advertised articles. Conversely, 22·9% of British direct investment abroad in 1965 was in petroleum and 4·5% in mining.[124] In the rapid internationalization of services which occurred in the 1970s, Britain kept a positive balance, in the sense of an excess of exports over imports in banking and insurance services, but was less successful among the large advertising agencies, which were also crossing national frontiers.[125] About four-fifths of Britain's outward direct capital flows went to the advanced industrial countries, with a tendency for the link with the members of the EC to strengthen after 1973.[126]

It was the larger firms which were most likely to spawn subsidiaries abroad: of the 41 largest manufacturing companies in Britain in 1976, 15 had more than half their sales abroad, and only two sold less than 5% of their turnover overseas. Conversely, the average numbers employed by the 49 largest British multinationals in 1973 was 82,244, or a total of 4 million. In 1970, of the 200 largest non-American multinationals in the world 53 were British; the Japanese came next with 43.[127]

Apart from the obvious point that a local factory was an alternative to imports, thus affording work and income to British citizens and paying British taxes, foreign firms often introduced superior methods of management and technology. By 1970, sales per employee of multinationals in Britain were almost twice as high as among all firms, while the rapid rise of the share of patents granted to foreigners, from 40·1% in 1955 to 76·4% in 1972 largely reflected the technology transfer to Britain within the multinationals. There were numerous examples of foreign intruders who had forced British firms to modernize.[128] Moreover, this type of firm was most likely to foster an international division of labour and distribution of work among countries according to resources and relative factor prices.[129]

Yet there were misgivings. Foreign firms, particularly the American firms which formed the largest contingent, were likely to import from their headquarters or from other branches rather than buy in Britain;[130] they would be

[124] UN, *Multinational Corporations*, pp. 151, 166; Vaupel and Curhan, p. 50 and *passim*; Michael Hodges, *Multinational Corporations and National Government . . . 1964–1970* (Farnborough, 1974), p. 28.

[125] UN, *Transnational Corporations*, pp. 46–8, 215–19; D. F. Channon, *British Banking Strategy and the International Challenge* (1977).

[126] J. M. Stopford, 'Changing Perspectives on Investment by British Manufacturing Multinationals', *Journal of International Business Studies*, 7/2, 1976.

[127] UN, *Transnational Corporations*, pp. 212–13; Andrew Gamble, *Britain in Decline* (1985), p. 109; Hood and Young, pp. 17, 131.

[128] Thomas G. Parry, *The Multinational Enterprise. International Investment and Host-Country Impacts* (Greenwich, Conn., 1980) p. 111; Raymond Vernon, *Storm over the Multinationals. The Real Issue* (Cambridge, Mass., 1977), p. 8; Richard E. Caves, 'Industrial Organisation', and Edwin Mansfield, 'Technology and Technical Change', both in John H. Dunning, *Economic Analysis and the Multinational Enterprise* (1974).

[129] Hood and Young, pp. 60–2, 82–4, 149–50; John H. Dunning, *American Investment in British Manufacturing Industry* (1958), and 'Technology, United States Investment and European Economic Growth', in Charles P. Kindleberger (ed.), *The International Corporation* (Cambridge, Mass., 1970), p. 168.

[130] Curiously enough, British branches abroad did not. Thomas G. Parry, 'International Firm',

managed in the interests of foreign owners, and, on occasions, even to be put under duress by their home government to pursue the latter's political aims, by-passing the wishes of the British Government, as in the case of American sanctions against the Soviet Union in 1982. They could defeat taxation and pricing rules by internal price manipulation, and the trade unions feared their ability to escape abroad from excessive demands – though they were often also able to pay the highest wages. Others expressed unease that the multinationals would make Britain too dependent on foreign technology, and drive potential British winners out of the market.[131] The Industry Act 1975 included some provisions for restricting takeovers by non-residents, but otherwise Britain, unlike some other countries, placed few handicaps on British branches of foreign multinational companies.

The Government's attitude towards the task of providing a competitive environment for British industry was, in fact, vacillating and ambiguous. In spite of its elaborate provisions for 'fair trading' and against monopolies, it was at times itself enforcing or encouraging the monopolistic organization of industry, as in the case of British Leyland, the aircraft industry, shipbuilding, computer manufacture, cotton spinning and agricultural marketing noted above, not to mention the nationalized industries. Under the Labour government, the Industrial Reorganization Corporation of 1966–70 had been given the task of actually aiding and initiating mergers, including the spectacular creation of the GEC–AEI–English Electric combine[132] and British Leyland, all in the interest of efficiency and economy – while elsewhere mergers were blocked or treated with suspicion.

In the nationalized industries the problem of combining monopolistic powers with the obligation not to exploit them had been present from the start, but was aggravated in practice by the inability of many of them, including some of the largest, to operate at a profit, so that they required either regular or at least intermittent subsidies. The issue of the financial burden on the State was thus superimposed on such questions as the size of the industries, the level of invest-ment, and the criteria and the means of enforcement of economically efficient working. A further complication in these delicate decisions was the strength of unionization, and the particularly inflexible nature of the unions concerned, precisely in the least profitable industries of the nationalized sector. The earlier Socialist hopes that the nationalized industries would usher in a regime of better industrial relations, a motivation of unselfishness and a social purpose in industry, were soon disappointed.[133] Instead, there was an amalgam of social and commercial objectives.[134]

---

pp. 1208–10, quoting W. B. Reddaway, *et al.*, *Effects of UK Direct Investment Abroad, Interim and Final Reports* (Cambridge, 1967, 1968); John H. Dunning, *The Role of American Investment in the British Economy* (1969); Hood and Young, p. 314.

[131] Mansfield, 'Technology', p. 170; S. Hymer and R. Rowthorn, *Multinational Corporation and International Oligopoly* (New Haven, 1969); Vernon, *Storm*, pp. 103–28; UN, *Multinational Corporations*, pp. 35, 46, 67 and *Transnational Corporations*, pp. 95, 141; Hodges, *Multinational Corporations*, pp. 40, 51–2, 220; Dunning, 'Technology', pp. 160–2.

[132] Robert Jones and Oliver Marriott, *Anatomy of a Merger: A History of GEC, AEI and English Electric* (1970); P. J. Curwen and A. H. Fowler, *Economic Policy* (1976), pp. 24–5.

[133] Herbert Morrison, Foreword to Institute of Public Administration, *Efficiency in the Nationalized Industries* (1952); also W. A. Robson, *Nationalized Industry and Public Ownership* (1962 ed.) pp. 460 ff.

[134] Roy Jenkins, in Michael Shanks (ed.), *Lessons of Public Enterprise* (1963), p. 10.

The industries were put into impossible dilemmas. If they made large surpluses, they were accused of abusing their monopoly powers: if small profits or losses, of being inefficient. For years low coal prices and low railway freight rates were used as a deliberate subsidy to industry, and then the two industries were derided for failing to make ends meet and to supply their own capital needs. It needed an outside Court of Inquiry into a labour dispute on the railways to lay down the obvious, but at that time startling, principle that, in broad terms, the railwayman should receive a wage no lower than that of his colleague in a comparable industry.[135] The industries were not only attacked for ideological reasons by partisans of free enterprise, but also freely by press and public at large[136] in terms which, had they been used against a private firm, would have resulted in large damages against the libeller. Shortcomings were put down freely to the fact of nationalization, while comparable shortcomings elsewhere were never blamed on private enteprise as such, but on weaknesses of individual firms. In fact, far from becoming the spearhead of a Socialist economy, the nationalized industries remained anomalies in a private enterprise economy.

Most nationalized industries were exceptionally heavily capitalized. In 1977 they employed 7·6% of the labour force, produced 12·7% of GDP and were responsible for 16% of gross fixed capital formation.[137] In addition to the industries taken over in the years after the war and the steel industry (1967), the State also formed the British National Oil Corporation in 1976 and nationalized the aerospace and the shipbuilding firms in 1977. To these have to be added the individual firms taken over on behalf of the Government by the National Enterprise Board (NEB),[138] including Rolls Royce, Alfred Herbert, Ferranti and, in 1975–6, British Leyland. The list contains essentially two groups. One consists of some key sectors, especially in energy provision, transport and communications; the other is made up of lame ducks which could not be allowed, for various social reasons, to sink; and several fit both categories. It is not irrelevant to note that all comparable European countries have found it necessary to build up a similar list of socialized undertakings.

Neither the level of output, nor any long-term investment policy was at first laid down for these enterprises. They were merely required to break even, taking one year with another. Originally, their Boards had been given a great deal of autonomy, but political realities, including the power of the Minister to dismiss members of Boards of Public Corporations, led to a substantial degree of political control over the management. Members of the Boards were often picked from among the 'great and the good', with little competence for management and at salaries well below those of private firms. At the same time, according to one view, the Select Committee on Nationalized Industries had between 1957 and 1961 'documented the extent to which Whitehall has exercised power without responsibility, by exerting pressure on the Boards of these "independent" corporations, but in such a way as not to be accountable to the public, and so as

[135] *Interim Report*, Cmd. 9352 (1955), p. 6.

[136] Robson, pp. 409–10, 447–8.

[137] Richard Pryke, *The Nationalised Industries. Policies and Performance since 1968* (Oxford, 1981), pp. 1–2.

[138] See pp. 214–51 above and pp. 346–72 below.

to enable blame to be thrown onto the Boards. They have also documented the amateurishness and incompetence of the civil servants responsible for the major economic decisions.'[139] After 1955 this control was further tightened by obliging the Boards to borrow from the Treasury, instead of the market, even though Local Authorities were, at precisely the same time, given the directly opposite instructions to borrow outside.[140]

If, as it was widely thought, this development was inevitable,[141] many observers agreed with the Herbert Committee that the Ministers' ultimate power should be exercised openly and in specific cases only.[142] A white paper criticized the interference with long-term investment plans in the interests of short-term policy.[143] Further, it was seen to be incongruous that these industries received, not the capital they needed, but the capital which the Treasury could spare from year to year, and that the Treasury's naive aim of self-finance would lead to a wrong pricing policy.[144]

By the end of the decade, a new relationship began to crystallize. In 1961 a major white paper on the *Financial and Economic Obligations of the Nationalized Industries* laid down anew the divisions of power and the criteria of management. The Government, it stated, had the ultimate responsibility for seeing that the industries were administered economically and efficiently; further (in a passage begging all the main questions), 'although the industries have obligations of a national and non-economic kind, they are not, and ought not, to be regarded as social services absolved from economic and commercial justification'. More concretely, the industries were to accumulate adequate reserves, by depreciating at replacement, not historic cost; they were to plan to break even over five-year periods; and the rate of return expected from each of them was to be settled between the Minister and the Board and was to take account of any compulsory unprofitable activities. As a consequence, Electricity Boards agreed to aim at $12\frac{1}{2}\%$ on net assets, the Gas Board at $10\frac{1}{4}\%$, and the Coal Board, to break even, on certain assumptions.[145]

New guidelines on prices and investment decisions were introduced in 1967[146] 'Arms length rule', the freedom from direct interference by the politicians, was to be preserved, and the general instructions were to cover long-run marginal costs, a concept more familiar to economists than to people of practical

[139] Select Committee, First Report, *Ministerial Control of the Nationalized Industries* H.C. 371–I (1967–8); Keith Middlemas, *Power, Competition and the State*, vol. 1, *Britain in Search of Balance, 1940–61* (Stanford, 1986), p. 129; D. L. Munby, 'The Nationalized Industries', in G. D. N. Worswick and P. H. Ady, *The British Economy in the Nineteen-Fifties* (1962), p. 384.

[140] Harrod, *British Economy*, pp. 105–8.

[141] E.g., A. H. Hansen, *Parliament and Public Ownership* (1961), pp. 210 ff.

[142] *Report of the Committee of Inquiry into the Electricity Supply Industry*, Cmd. 9672 (1956).

[143] *Public Investment*, Cmnd. 1203 (1960); also *Report of the (Plowden) Committee on the Control of Public Expenditure*, Cmnd. 1432 (1961), para. 23. John Key and David Thompson, 'Policy for Industry', in Rudiger Dornbusch and Richard Layard (eds.), *The Performance of the British Economy* (Oxford, 1987), pp. 186–9.

[144] Michael Shanks, p. 61.

[145] Cmnd. 1337 (1961); Pauline Gregg, *The Welfare State. The Economic and Social History of Great Britain from 1945 to the Present Day* (1967), p. 126.

[146] Treasury, *Nationalized Industries. A Review of Economic and Financial Objectives*. Cmnd. 3437 (1967); Michael G. Webb, *Pricing Policies for Public Enterprises*, pp. 79–82, and *idem, The Economics of Nationalised Industries* (1973), chapter 11; Prest and Coppock, pp. 184–91.

experience,[147] which was quickly and mercifully forgotten. What remained was first, the obligation to meet costs in full together with a surplus to meet the financial targets, and secondly the principle that the consumer should pay 'the true costs of the goods and services he consumes in every case where these can be sensibly identified.'[148] The financial target consisted of a 'test discount rate' (TDR) of 8%, later raised to 10% in real terms and investment decisions were ordered to be governed by the net-present-value (NPV) principle.

The TDR was an attempt to align the nationalized industries with what was then thought to be the average rate earned in private industry, but it failed to have any rationing or allocation functions. The capital programmes continued to be justified as being simply necessary for expansion or replacement, or slashed to meet Government short-term panic demands. Some had the appearance of being little more than the results of Buggins's turn, or of the political muscle of the respective chairmen. The most that the TDR was called upon to do was to help to minimize costs of schemes already determined on.[149]

Whatever chance these policies might have had were lost by the industrial failures in the public sector. Of the nine major enterprises, four suffered declines in output and seven declines in employment between 1960 (1968 in the case of the British Steel Corporation) (BSC) and 1975, though gas, electricity, the airline, telecom and (after 1978) steel showed fast rates of productivity growth, mostly faster than in the decades before nationalization. Meanwhile they gobbled up capital, much of which was soon lost, and thwarted successive governments' plans to cut public spending (see Table 7·16):[150]

Table 7·16: Nationalized industries (£ billion)

	Capital needs	Total net impact on PSBR
Average of years		
1961–5	1·69	2·11
1966–70	3·48	3·19
1971–5	5·36	7·37

Some of the losses were caused by the obligation to keep prices down.[151] Nevertheless, the requests for ever more capital and current subsidies brought

---

[147] R. L. Meek, 'The New Bulk Supply Tariff for Electricity', *Econ. J.*, 78/1, 1868.

[148] Cmnd. 3437, para. 18.

[149] David Heald, 'The Economic and Financial Control of UK Nationalised Industries', *Econ. J.*, 90/2, 1980, pp. 243–6; R. Rees, *Public Enterprise Economics* (1976), pp. 18–19; National Economic Development Office, *A Study of UK Nationalised Industries. Their Role in the Economy and Control in the Future* (1976), pp. 9–10; Treasury (Working Paper No. 9), *The Test Discount Rate and the Required Rate of Return on Investment* (1979).

[150] *Nationalised Industries*, pp. 13, 19. PSBR = Public Sector Borrowing Requirement, for which see chapter 9 below.

[151] C. D. Foster, 'The Cost of Financing the Nationalized Industries', *Bull. Oxf. Inst. Stat.*, 22, 1960; R. Millward, 'Price Restraint, Anti-Inflation Policy and Public and Private Industry in the United Kingdom 1947–73', *Econ. J.*, 81/2, 1976; Graham Turner, p. 172; Richard M. Duke et al., *The United States Steel Industry and its International Rivals* (Washington, 1977), p. 353. The Price Commission was given authority in July 1977 to investigate most nationalized industry price increases.

in political and bureaucratic interference and repeated switches of policy, which in turn led to uncertainty and demoralization among the managements. In 1976, cash limits were introduced and gave the Government further means of control, since ministerial assent was required to exceed them. They encouraged self-finance or, as in the case of BSC in 1977–8, savage reductions in capital programmes.

Following two further white papers,[152] the rules were changed once more in 1978, concentrating on prices, as in 1961, rather than on investment criteria as in 1967. The new index was to be the Required Rate of Return (RRR) calculated on the whole of the new capital instead of, as the TDR, separately on each individual project. It was set initially at 5% before tax, again in alignment with private industry, the rate to be reviewed every three to five years. Individual prices and investment priorities were once more left to the industries themselves, subject to the requirement to relate the price structure to the cost structure. The existing capital was also made subject to financial targets, measured as a return on all assets after interest, but there was a different rate set for each industry,[153] and for persistent loss makers like British Rail the target might be set by the size of the subsidy. Industries which had some hopes of making a surplus or breaking even had in 1966 been given 'Public Dividend Capital' on which, as in private companies, no dividends need be paid in bad years, thus reducing the burden at critical times. This scheme was limited to British Airways, BSC, British Aerospace, British Shipbuilders and the Giro, and in 1978 it was decided not to extend it.[154] Instead, the 1980s were marked by a policy of privatization.

3 Incomes and their Distribution

The increases in output described in the first section of this chapter were reflected in increases in incomes over the same period, and consumers' expenditure showed a comparable rise (see Table 7·17).[155]

It will be seen that in 30 years, both real incomes and consumers' expenditure almost doubled, rising at rates around 2% a year. The variations in the growth rates between the decades depend to some extent on the terminal years and should therefore not be used to read off a sequence of phasing: the phases and cycles of this period will be discussed in chapter 9.

The distribution of incomes showed some clear trends over the years 1950–1980 (see Table 7·18). Incomes from employment remained remarkably stable as a share of total incomes, but within this total, employers' contributions to national insurance more than doubled in what seemed like an inexorable rise of the social welfare state, and freely disposable wages and salaries correspondingly fell. Incomes from self-employment showed a sharp fall until the mid-1960s and thereafter rose again slightly, but this relative stability likewise hid a significant internal shift among the three major categories (see Table 7·19).

---

[152] *Capital Investment Procedures*, Cmnd. 6106 (1975); *The Nationalized Industries*, Cmnd. 7131, (1978).

[153] E.g. Keith Hartley and Peter A. Watt, 'Profits, Regulation and the UK Aerospace Industry', *Journal of Industrial Economics*, 29/4, 1981, p. 418; Treasury, *Test Discount Rate*, pp. 12–13, 25.

[154] Cmnd. 7131, para. 88. Also Heald, pp. 247–62.

[155] Based on *National Income and Expenditure*. Index of 1958 = 100 has been spliced into the 1975 = 100 index.

Table 7·17:   Increases in income and expenditure

	Total domestic incomes			Consumers' expenditure		
	£ b.	Real domestic incomes per head		£ b.	Real consumers' expenditure per head	
		Index 1975=100	Av. annual growth %		Index 1975=100	Av. annual growth %
1950	12·0	57·8		9·5	61·7	
1955	17·0	64·6	2·0	13·1	67·4	2·0
1960	22·9	70·5		16·9	75·4	
1965	31·6	74·4	1·7 2·1	22·9	82·8	1·8 2·0
1970	45·1	83·5		31·8	90·0	
1975	99·1	100·0	2·6	64·7	100·0	2·1
1980	202·0	107·5		135·4	110·3	

Table 7·18:   Percentage shares of domestic incomes before tax

	1950	1955	1960	1965	1970	1975	1980
Wages and salaries	65·0	67·7	66·4	64·9	63·9	62·8	59·5
Employers' contrib. to Nat. Ins. etc.	4·1	4·3	4·9	5·6	6·4	8·3	8·7
Total incomes from employment	69·1	72·1	71·3	70·5	70·3	71·1	68·2
Incomes from self-employment	12·6	10·6	9·4	8·4	8·8	8·9	9·2
Rents, divid., net interest received by: Life Assurance and Superannuation schemes	1·3	1·6	2·1	2·7	3·1	2·8	3·5
Imputed rents from owner-occupied houses					3·0	3·5	3·8
Others	10·3	8·5	9·3	9·1	4·6	2·8	2·6
Nat. Insurance benefits etc.	6·9	7·1	7·8	9·2	10·0	10·7	12·7
Total personal incomes	100	100	100	100	100	100	100

Table 7·19:   Shares among incomes from self-employment*

	1950	1965	1980
Professional persons	16·0	17·3	18·2
Farmers	25·0	23·9	15·5
Other sole traders and partnerships	59·0	58·8	66·3
	100	100	100

* Before tax, and before providing for depreciation and stock appreciation.

There was a marked fall in the income of farmers, but it was compensated by the rise in the incomes of sole traders and partnerships. Similarly, the stability of the share of incomes from property hides a rise in the share of imputed rents, and a near trebling of the incomes of insurance companies and pension funds, implying consequently a sharp drop in the property incomes of individuals, particularly in the 1970s. Finally, the share of national insurance and social welfare benefits doubled, and may be considered to be a counterpart of the growth of contributions recorded in the second line of Table 7·18.

Some of the implications of these shifts will be discussed in the following paragraphs, but the limitations of these statistics should be borne in mind. Above all they cannot be taken as an indication of relative income changes because of parallel changes in the numbers concerned. Among these were the fall in the number of farmers and the wholesale conversion of small businesses into companies leading to the conversion of the incomes of their owners from 'profits' to 'salaries'. Moreover, the growing skill in tax avoidance among larger companies and richer individuals may also not have been without significance.[156]

A better measure of the distribution of incomes is the share of total incomes taken by the top 1% or top 10% of income earners, and of each following decile (or 10%). This shows a marked, if not overwhelmingly strong levelling of incomes in the post-war period, visible in incomes both before and after tax (see Tables 7.20 and 21).[157]

Table 7·20: Share of incomes before tax (UK)

	1949	1959	1976–7
Top 1%	—	8·4	5·6
Top 10%	33·1	29·4	26·0
Lowest 20%	5·4	5·3	6·2
Gini coefficient	—	39·8%	36·6%

Table 7·21: Share of incomes after tax (UK)

	1949	1964	1973 4	1976 7
Top 1%	4·6	5·3	4·5	3·5
Top 10%	27·1	25·9	23·6	22·4
2nd decile	14·5	16·1	15·5	15·9
9th and 10th deciles	—	6·5	7·5	7·8
Gini coefficient	35·5	36·6%	32·8%	31·5%
As % of median income:				
Top 1%	508	445	388	
Top decile	208	212	201	
Lower quartile	—	54	60	

Calculated in tax units rather than incomes, the Gini coefficient of the income distribution fell similarly from 36·5% in 1948 9, to 30·2% in 1949 50, 29·1% in 1959–60 and 27·5% in 1973–4.[158]

[156] S. Pollard and D. W. Crossley, *The Wealth of Britain*, 1086–1966 (1968), p. 263.
[157] Royal Commission on the Distribution of Income and Wealth, *Report No. 4, Second Report on the Standing Conference,* Cmnd. 6626 (1976) pp. 12, 101–2 and *Report No. 7,* Cmnd. 6999 (1979). Distribution is the more equitable the lower the Gini coefficient. Also Paolo Roberti, 'Income Distribution: A Time Series and a Cross-section Study', *Econ. J.,* 84/3, 1974, p. 635.
[158] Royal Commission, *Report no. 4,* p. 104.

For the top earners, the fall was more drastic. Thus the incomes of the highest-paid males, as a multiple of median incomes, dropped as shown in Table 7·22.[159]

Table 7·22:   Highest incomes as a multiply of median incomes

		Highest decimillile	Highest millile	Highest centile
Before tax:	1959/60	21	10	4
	1972/3	15	8	$3\frac{1}{2}$
After tax:	1959/60	11	7	3
	1972/3	7	5	3

It will be noted that the tax system continued its function of redistributing incomes from the rich to the poor, although that levelling effect tended to become weaker rather than stronger in our period as shown in Table 7·23.[160]

Table 7·23:   Effects of the tax system on redistribution

	Average taxes as % of incomes before tax			% of total taxes contributed		
	1959	1967	1974–5	1959	1967	1975–5
Top 1% incomes	43·2	43·3	47·1	34·5	23·3	15·8
Top 10%	23·5	24·5	29·1	64·9	50·0	42·2
Bottom 20%	0·1	0·8	1·0	—	0·4	0·3
All incomes	10·5	13·6	18·3	100	100	100

However, the influence of the State on income distribution reached further than the direct taxation system. In order to assess its full impact, indirect taxes, direct cash benefits and benefits in kind have to be calculated in as well, and some of these went to the credit of the rich as well as that of the lower-income groups.

For 1970, some percentage change effects on the Gini coefficient (negative values mean a move in the direction of greater equality, positive values tend towards greater inequality) have been calculated as shown in Table 7·24.[161]

Some benefits in kind, such as security and good government, cannot be allocated at all fairly. They have been omitted here. One estimate attempting to chart the redistribution resulting from State action in 1980 came to the results shown in Table 7·25 for the top two and the lowest two deciles of incomes.[162]

---

[159] Chris Pond, 'the High Paid and the Crisis of Living Standards', in Frank Field (ed.), *The Wealth Report* (1979).

[160] *Ibid.*, p. 58.

[161] J. L. Nicholson, 'The Distribution and Redistribution of Income in the United Kingdom', in Dorothy Wedderburn (ed.), *Poverty, Inequality and Class Structure* (Cambridge, 1974), p. 80.

[162] A. B. Atkinson, *The Economics of Inequality* (Oxford, 1983), p. 83; also see Royal Commission, *Report No. 4*, p. 27. The totals do not add up because the mathematical operations were not always performed on the same incomes.

Table 7·24: Percentage change effects on the Gini coefficient, 1970

Taxable pensions	−3·58
Income tax	−2·66
National health service	−1·57
Education	−0·63
Sickness benefit	−0·58
Supplementary benefit	−0·55
Housing subsidies	−0·22
Indirect duties on oil	+0·15
Direct duties on oil	+0·16
Local rates (net)	+0·23
Duties on beer	+0·26
Duties on tobacco	+0·83

Table 7·25: Household income distribution, taxes and benefits, 1980, UK (£ p.a.)

		Bottom 20%	Top 20%	All
Average	original income	170	14445	6350
"	direct cash benefits	+1970	+390	+950
"	benefits in kind	+960	+1270	+1120
"	direct taxes	−5	−3280	−1330
"	indirect taxes	−545	−2530	−1460
	final incomes	2550	10295	5630
% Change		+1400	−29	−11

The poorest 20% were largely dependent on income redistributed by the State by means of Social Insurance and the Social Services, but the losses suffered in the redistribution by the top earners were moderate. The middle groups including the better-paid wage earners largely covered their own needs supplied *via* the State.[163]

The taxes-cum-welfare system also tended to favour families and pensioners, at all levels of income. The effects in two not untypical income ranges worked out as shown in Table 7·26.[164]

Property or wealth, which was far more unevenly distributed than incomes, tended similarly towards greater equality in this period, but the levelling process slowed down in the 1960s. Definitions and valuations are even more difficult than in the case of incomes, and much depends on the assumptions made. Most, but not all, of the British estimates take the distribution revealed by the estate duty as their starting point and then make allowances for those dying without taxable estates and for other factors. Two sets of estimates, both derived from

[163] Dudley Jackson *et al., Do Trade Unions Cause Inflation?* (1972), pp. 66–7; Geoffrey Stephenson, 'Taxes, Benefits and the Redistribution of Incomes', in Cedric Sandford, Chris Pond, Robert Walker (eds.), *Taxation and Social Policy* (1980), pp. 18–20.

[164] J. L. Nicholson, 'Distribution', pp. 76–8.

Table 7·26: Net total state benefits received (+) less total taxes paid (−) for certain income ranges, 1971 (£ p.a.)

		Original income per annum (£)	
		816–986	987–1193
Non-retired households:	1 Adult	− 250	− 286
	2 Adults	− 18	− 139
	2 Adults, 1 Child	+ 45	− 122
	2 Adults, 2 Children	+ 99	+ 78
	2 Adults, 3 "	+ 456	+ 213
Retired households:	2 Adults	+ 218	+ 45

the 'estate' method, for the share of personal wealth held by the top 1% and the top 10% of wealth holders, are presented in Table 7·27.[165]

Table 7·27: Estimates of shares of personal wealth

	Royal Commission		Atkinson and Harrison		
	Top 1%	Top 10%	Top 1%	Top 5%	Top 10%
1936/8	56	88	54·6	77·2	85·3
1950	—	—	47·4	74·3	—
1954	43	79	45·3	71·8	—
1960	38·2	76·7	33·9	59·4	71·5
1970	29·0	70·1	29·7	53·6	68·7
1972	29·9	71·9	31·7	56·0	70·4
1975	23·2	62·4	—	—	—

Even if correctly evaluated, these comparisons would to some extent still be misleading, since the smaller wealth holdings consisted very largely of use values, such as dwellings, or of claims on insurance and pension funds, to be used up in later life, while among the very rich, property was a major or even the sole source of income. Thus in the wealth range of £10,000–£19,999 in 1974, 64% of assets were in the form of dwellings and household goods and $17\frac{1}{2}$% in the form of life policies, but these amounted to only 15% and $2\frac{1}{2}$% respectively in the case of the largest fortunes of over £200,000; against this, shares, other company securities and land figured at a negligible 3% of the small properties, but represented 64% of the larger. In line with the relative decline of the larger fortune, shares and other securities (but not land) fell sharply as a share of total assets in this period, whereas dwellings and life policies, the assets of the smaller fortunes, rose as rapidly (see Table 7.28).[166]

[165] A. R. Prest and D. J. Coppock, *The UK Economy* (1978), p. 238; A. B. Atkinson and A. J. Harrison, *Distribution of Personal Wealth in Britain* (Cambridge, 1978), p. 159; Louie Burghes, 'The Old Order', in Frank Field, *Wealth Report*, pp. 11, 20, 26; Peter Townsend, *Poverty in the United Kingdom* (Harmondsworth, 1979), p. 904. Atkinson, *Economics*, p. 168 gives the top 10% only 57% in 1972 for Great Britain, and 56% for England and Wales alone.

[166] Royal Commission, *Report No. 4*, Cmnd. 6626, pp. 52, 59; Thomas Stark, *The Distribution of Personal Incomes in the United Kingdom 1949–1963* (Cambridge, 1972), p. 72.

Table 7·28: Personal wealth, asset composition (GB)

	1960	1974
Dwellings	20·7%	42·7%
Land	2·1	4·5
Life policies	11·9	14·9
Listed ordinary shares	15·2	6·8
Other company securities	7·8	4·0
Other assets	50·7	37·2
Debts (liabilities)	−8·4	−10·1
	100	100

At the other end of the scale, abject poverty, such as was still to be found among substantial groups of people between the wars, has practically disappeared in the post-war years. Applying the standards of 1971, for example, it fell from one-fifth of the population in 1953 to one-fortieth in 1973.[167] Yet it is also legitimate to define poverty in relative terms, being deprived of what others conventionally deem necessities. Thus poverty might mean being among the poorest, say, 10% of the population: in that sense no society will ever be without poverty. Another, similar approach might be to take some arbitrary fraction of average or median income, say one half, and designate everything below it as 'poverty'. The problem is further complicated by differing basic needs of different-sized families, the question of 'equivalence'.[168]

In post-war Britain, the tendency has been to take the National Assistance, and after 1966 the 'Supplementary Benefit' payments level as the threshold standard of poverty. This used both family size and circumstances, such as rent payments, and, formally after 1959, a scale raised in line with the real wage level,[169] and it thus paid tribute to the proportional or conventional element.

The hopes of the Beveridge scheme of providing adequately by insurance for all conceivable causes of need were not fulfilled, and the gap between payments received as of right, and the minimal National Assistance/Supplementary Benefit scales was never closed. In the 1970s the numbers on National Assistance/ Supplementary Benefits rose substantially to 2 million families in 1979, of whom 1 million were pensioners, 440,000 were single people or couples without children, and 560,000 were family units with children, 170,000 of them with three or more children. The number of families of those normally in full-time work or self-employed, with incomes below the Supplementary Benefit level rose from 130,000 to 290,000 between 1974 and 1976, and the number of persons

[167] Prest and Coppock, p. 259; for other estimates see Stark, *Distribution*, pp. 48 *passim*.
[168] Peter Townsend, *Poverty*, pp. 262 ff; G. Fiegehen, P. Lansey, A. Smith, *Poverty and Progress in Britain 1953–73* (Cambridge, 1977), pp. 15–17; P. Townsend, 'Poverty as Relative Deprivation: Resources and Style of Living', in Dorothy Wedderburn (ed.), *Poverty, Inequality and Class Structure* (Cambridge, 1974), p. 15.
[169] Department of Health and Social Security, *Low Pay* (1977), p. 9; Sir John Walley, *Social Security: Another British Failure?* (1972).

involved, from 360,000 to 890,000.[170] Even those earning little above the minimal levels found themselves increasingly in a 'poverty trap' if they attempted to raise their earned incomes, as rising taxes and falling benefits then reduced the value of each additional pound earned to a few pence, and in certain critical ranges, even to a negative sum.

Among the causes of low pay continued to be handicaps such as repeated illnesses and frequent job changes, and undemanding, unskilled work. The old, the very young, and women were additionally likely to be found in low-pay occupations.[171] Women's earnings in manufacturing as a proportion of male remained remarkably stable from pre-war years until 1970. The Equal Pay Act of 1970, phased to come into full force in 1975, brought a dramatic change, and its momentum was continued by the Sex Discrimination Act of 1975 which prohibited nonpecuniary discrimination such as access to jobs or promotion. By 1975, women's wages had risen to $57\frac{1}{2}\%$ of men's and by 1978 to 61%. Average hourly earnings for women, which had always been relatively higher, at around 60%, also rose by 11%, to 71%, and for non-manual earnings, the gap was reduced in similar manner: between 1970 and 1980, men's wages rose by 303%, but women's by 368% while the participative rate of women in the paid labour force also increased.[172]

Average real weekly wage and salary earnings just failed to double in the 30 years 1950–80 (see Table 7·29): (Total domestic real incomes are added for comparison from Table 7·17 above.)

Table 7·29:   The rise in earnings

	Average real weekly earnings		Total domestic real incomes per head	
	Index 1970 = 100	Av. ann. growth rate	Index 1975 = 100	Average annual growth rate
1950	65·3 ⎫		57·8 ⎫	
1955	73·4 ⎭	2·5	64·6 ⎭	2·0
1960	83·8 ⎫		70·5 ⎫	
1965	94·6 ⎬	1·8	74·4 ⎭	1·7
1970	100·0 ⎭		83·5 ⎫	
1975	115·8 ⎫		100·0 ⎬	2·6
1980	122·4 ⎭	2·0	107·5 ⎭	

Again, not too much should be read into these figures for the purpose of phasing these changes.

Throughout this period, British wages rose considerably faster in relation to prices and to productivity than the wages in comparable countries abroad. The

[170] Frank Field, 'Poverty, Growth and the Redistribution of Income', in Wilfred Beckerman (ed.), *Slow Growth in Britain, Causes and Consequences* (Oxford, 1979), pp. 86–8, 95; Atkinson, *Economics*, pp. 241–2; Department of Health of Social Security, *Social Security Statistics*.

[171] National Board for Prices and Incomes, *Report* No. 169: *General Problems of Low Pay*, Cmnd. 4648 (1971) pp. 36–63, 123.

[172] *Department of Employment Gazette.*

result was a more rapid rise in unit labour costs, which in turn contributed to the loss of markets for British goods.[173]

Table 7·30: Changes in unit labour costs

	1950–62 (whole period)	1963–80 (% per annum)
United Kingdom	+70%	+10·4
Germany	+48	+3·1
France		+5·8
USA	+27	+3·7
Japan	+9	+4·7

Particularly rapid was the rise of additional costs per employee in the form of national insurance contributions, taxes, etc., even after employment subsidies were deducted. Those rose in a steady progression from £6.25 per employee, or 21% of net earnings, to no less than £19·29, or 47% of net earnings, between 1960 and 1980.[174] Some of the implications of these changes will be discussed in chapter 9 below.

The levelling up of the lower paid in relation to skilled wages that occurred in war time was very slightly reversed thereafter. By the mid-1960s, in a number of representative industries, the ratios of unskilled wage rates were around 85% of those of the skilled. In earnings the gap was wider, the unskilled rates averaging between 71% and 87% of skilled earnings. The income policies of the 1970s had a slight tendency to compress wages once more. More strongly in the same direction worked the inflation, in which, as on previous occasions, top incomes failed to keep pace with price rises.[175] In the later 1970s the trend was reversed again, however, and, taking the wage distribution in deciles, there was virtually no change over 1960–80.[176]

Salaries drifted down against wages in the 1950s, and in the following two decades their decline was dramatic. Thus, taking annual earnings of adult men between 1960 and 1977, with skilled wages as 100 in each year, the incomes of higher professionals (doctors, lawyers), fell from 255 to 164, those of managers from 232 to 147, those of foremen and supervisors from 127 to 104, and those of clerks from 86 to 84. Only lower professionals (teachers, librarians) succeeded in raising their differential, from 106 to 131.[177] In their way, changes of that magnitude amount to a minor social revolution.

[173] Calculated from *Nat. Inst. Econ. Rev.* Also G. F. Ray, 'Labour Costs in OECD Countries 1964–1975', *ibid.*, 75, February 1976, pp. 60–1; OECD, *Economic Outlook*; UN, *Statistical Yearbook*.
[174] *Nat. Inst. Econ. Rev.*, 98, November 1982, p. 11.
[175] William Brown, 'Incomes Policies and Pay Differentials', *Oxf. Bull. Econ. Stat.*, 38/1, 1976, pp. 44–5 and 'Engineering Wages and the Social Contract 1975–1977', *ibid.*, 41/1, 1979, pp. 51–2.
[176] L. C. Hunter and C. Mulvey, *Economics of Wages and Labour* (2nd ed., 1981), p. 76; *Annual Abstract of Statistics*; Christine Craig *et al.*, *Labour Market Structure, Industrial Organization and Low Pay* (Cambridge, 1982), Chapter 1.
[177] Hunter and Mulvey, p. 79; G. Routh, *Occupation and Pay in Great Britain 1906–60* (Cambridge, 1965), pp. 102–7, 150; A. R. Thatcher, 'The Distribution of Earnings of Employees in Great Britain', *J. R. Stat. S.*, 131/1 (1968); Atkinson, *Economics*, p. 97; R. C. O. Matthews, C. H. Feinstein, J. C. Odling-Smee, *British Economic Growth 1856–1973* (Oxford 1982), p. 167.

They were underlined by an equally dramatic collapse of the returns to capital over the same period. Crude measures of the rate of profit in quoted companies showed a fall from 25·2% in 1950–4 to 21% in 1960–4 and 12·1% in 1970. More accurate measures are available from 1960 on. Their precise meaning, however, is in dispute in view of the tax changes and the problems of inflation accounting and stock valuation. Several alternative measures to take account of this exist and have been revised from time to time. They all show, in their different ways, the same sharp downward trend. For industrial and commercial companies, excluding North Sea oil and gas, some typical rates of return are presented in Table 7·31.[178]

They show the most serious decline to have taken place between 1960 and the mid-1970s; following a slight recovery thereafter, there was a further collapse in 1979–80, which continued into the following year. It may be that these two downward phases had different causes.

The authors who first drew attention to the decline, associated it with the withdrawal of investment incentives by the Labour Government in the late 1960s.[179] Others, however, have pointed out that this fall was accompanied by a considerable rise in productive investment in those years which may by itself be expected to reduce its relative rates of return. Firms were then unable to compensate fully for their rises in costs by raising prices because of the militancy of the trade unions, the price freeze, and sharpening competition from abroad. Also, companies were slow, especially in the early 1970s, to realize that they had to set aside larger sums for stock appreciation in order to compensate for the rise in replacement costs if they wanted to stay solvent.[180] But it has also been argued that part of the rise in the costs of stocks might on certain assumptions be considered to be profit, and firms were aided further in this respect by the tax changes of 1974 (see Table 7·31). In those terms, it could be shown that while profits before tax were falling in this period, profits after tax were not.[181]

Rising incomes, and the marked levelling of incomes, were reflected in the patterns of consumption. The motor car, once a middle-class status symbol, now became a leveller, as ownership extended yearly to lower income groups, and it was closely paralleled by radio and television sets, by domestic electric and gas appliances, by furniture and furnishings in the home and even by clothes and fashion goods, particularly among the young. The ambitions and the tastes among the classes came much closer together, though there were still differences in the more common ambition by the middle classes to own, rather than rent, their home, and the desire to pay for private, privileged schooling and aim for

---

[178] J. S. Flemming, L. D. D. Price, D. H. A. Ingram, 'Trends in Company Profitability', *B. of Eng. Qtly. Bull.*, March 1976, pp. 36–7, 42; 'Profitability and Company Finance: A Supplementary Note', *ibid.* 19, June 1979, pp. 183–5; *ibid.* 17, June 1977, p. 156. *Nat. Inst. Econ. Rev.*, 99, Feb. 1982, p. 23; John Black, *The Economics of Modern Britain* (1980), p. 81; *National Income and Expenditure.*

[179] Andrew Glyn and Bob Sutcliffe, 'The Collapse of UK Profits', *New Left Review*, 66, March–April 1971.

[180] J. R. Sargent, 'Productivity and Profits in UK Manufacturing', *Midland Bank Review*, Autumn 1979, pp. 10–13; Flemming, Price and Ingram, pp. 43–4; *B. of Eng. Qtly. Bull.*, 17, June 1977, p. 156; J. F. Wright, *Britain in the Age of Economic Management* (Oxford, 1979), pp. 187–90.

[181] Mervyn A. King, 'United Kingdom Profits Crisis: Myth or Reality?' *Econ. J.*, 85/1, 1975; Frank Field, 'Private Capital's Blood Transfusion', in *idem, The Wealth Report*, pp. 98–101; M. Panić and R. E. Close, 'Profitability and British Manufacturing Industry' *Lloyds Bank Review*, April 1975.

Table 7·31: Rates of return for industrial and commercial companies

	1960	1965	1970	1974	1975	1976	1977	1978	1979	1980
Pre-tax historic cost returns	19·0	16·2	14·4	17·1	16·0	17·7	17·0	15·8	—	—
Pre-tax real rates of return, after revaluation of capital consumption and stock appreciation	13·4	11·2	8·1	5·4	4·6	4·9	6·0	5·9	4·1	0·2
Post-tax real rates of return:										
forward looking	9·7	6·6	3·4	4·7	3·3	2·9				
do., excl. tax relief on stocks				0·2	0·5	0·2				
backward looking	8·3	6·1	4·2	4·3	2·8	2·4				
do., excl. tax relief on stocks				0·1	0·7	0·3				
Profit margin: Net trading profits and rents,		21·1	16·9	13·5	11·4	12·4	15·2	14·9	10·9	5·8
All companies and financial institutions, as % net nat. product		10·6*	9·4	5·8	4·5	5·3	8·1	8·4	7·4	5·3

* 1968

a University education. Differences in expenditure patterns were now often larger between differently constituted families, e.g. those with many small children as compared with those with children who were earners themselves, than between social groups.[182]

The raising of incomes was reflected in the national consumption patterns. In terms of quantity, the small increase in food and clothing contrasts with the sharp increase in 'luxuries', in spite of the new-found freedom to spend when food rationing ended in 1954 and coal rationing in 1958.[183] Expenditure elasticity' in the 1950s was found to be as high as 2·48 for transport and 1·57 for clothing, but only 1·05 for household expenses, 0·74 for drink and tobacco and 0·26 for food.[184] In terms of actual expenditure, however, because of the incidence of purchase tax and excise duties, and the increasing returns in the mass-production goods industries, the shares changed rather less, except for motor vehicles, which had still been held back by rationing in 1950, and among which increases in quantity greatly outweighed the relative reductions in costs. (See Table 7·32)[185]

Table 7·32:   Consumers' expenditure, 1950–1980

	Volume of consumption (1950 = 100)		% of consumers' expenditure, current prices		
	1965	1980	1950	1965	1980
Food	125·7	138·9	29·1	26·0	17·2
Drink, tobacco	129·8	183·1	16·5	12·8	11·1
Clothing	135·4	202·3	11·5	9·1	7·3
Housing and maintenance	137·3	190·3	8·6	11·1	14·6
Furniture, household goods	142·4	177·3	5·0	4·1	5·1
Radio, electrical	281·4	726·3	1·9	2·4	2·4
Motor vehicles and fuel	694·1	1199·4	1·9	7·6	10·4
Population (1950 = 100)	(108·5)	(111·5)	—	—	—

The demand for food and for furniture was seen to have been largely sated by 1965, and rose but little with incomes thereafter; but drink, tobacco, clothing, housing, radio and electrical goods and motor vehicles proved highly income-elastic. Because of changing prices, however, the distribution of money expenditure shifted in a different way from the changes in volume. Thus housing, where real cost gains were low, rose disproportionately as a share of consumer expenditure; spending on radio and electrical goods, where cost reductions were particularly striking, rose hardly at all despite a sevenfold increase in the volume of sales between 1950 and 1980.

Further, with rising standards, there were 'luxury' elements even among

[182] Ministry of Labour and National Service, *Report of an Enquiry into Household Expenditure in 1953–4* (1957); Ministry of Labour, *Family Expenditure Survey for 1963.*

[183] Margaret Hall, 'The Consumer Sector', in Worswick and Ady, p. 439.

[184] I.e., the percentage increase in expenditure corresponding to an increase in income of 1%. W. Beckerman and Associates, *The British Economy in 1975* (Cambridge, 1965), p. 180.

[185] *National Income and Expenditure.*

nominal necessities. Thus there was a substantial replacement of 'inferior' foods by 'superior' ones after the war, though this trend was much weakened after 1965 (see Table 7·33):[186]

Table 7·33: Consumption per head, UK

	1944	1965	1980
Liquid milk (litres)	139·7	141·7	129·3
Meat (kg)	51·7	69·1	71·4
Eggs (no.)	78·4	250	231
Butter (kg)	3·6	8·8	6·1
Vegetables, fruit and nuts (kg)	87·1	106·4	108·9
Margarine (kg)	8·2	5·4	7·1
Potatoes (kg)	124·8	100·9	105·4
Wheat, flour and other cereals (kg)	114·8	75·8	69·2

Interestingly enough, milk reached its maximum consumption in 1975, eggs in 1970 and potatoes their minimum in 1976, after which the trends changed direction.

The move towards uniformity, both of commodities available to the consumer and of the shops in which they were sold, which had been evident between the wars, took further strides forward, aided by the economies of mass-production and by advertising. Advertising, indeed, became one of Britain's most successful growth industries, particularly after the establishment of Independent Television, and, after a temporary setback owing to the incidence of SET, resumed its growth in 1967–8. It rose from an estimated £102 million in 1950 to £2,562 million in 1980, the highest expenditure at constant prices being in 1973. It also called forth the consumers' countervailing power of self-protection by association and information. Consumer Co-operative Societies had performed this function in the nineteenth century, but they were essentially working-class organizations. In 1957 the Consumers' Association, a middle-class body, began to publish *Which?*, reporting objective tests on articles and services of widespread sale, and registered immediate and lasting success, with a membership of 400,000 at their tenth anniversary. *Shoppers' Guide*, also dating from 1957, a similar publication linked with the Consumer Advisory Council of the British Standards Institute, was less successful, but some of its work was transferred to a new magazine, *Focus*. Following the report of the Molony Committee,[187] official interest was also shown by the appointment of a national Consumer Council in 1963, and a tightening up of legislation protecting the consumer in the following years, culminating in the Trade Descriptions Act of 1968. Several cities, beginning with Sheffield, also appointed their own consumer protection officers. In one respect this movement simply made use of the possibilities provided by mass production and national chain stores to approach

---

[186] J.C. McKenzie, 'Past Dietary Trends as an Aid to Prediction', in T.C. Barker *et al.*, *Our Changing Fare* (1966), p. 136: *Annual Abstract of Statistics*.

[187] *Final Report of the Consumer Protection Committee*, Cmnd. 1781 (1962); T.R. Nevett, *Advertising in Britain, a History* (1982), pp. 177, 188.

these problems nationally; in another, it represented a new way of dealing with monopolistic traders and producers.

In the first 20 years of peace one major source of pre-war poverty had virtually disappeared. Unemployment averaged 1·8%, or around 400,000, well within the limits of what were considered to be justifiable numbers of those changing jobs and the temporarily or permanently unemployable. In the later 1960s the numbers rose to 600,000 and reached a brief peak of 950,000, or 3·8% in 1972 before the Barber boom, but did not fall below 500,000 thereafter. In 1975 there was a second swell rising to a new level of one million, or 4%, and it stayed between 5·6 and 6·1% in the next five years, or around 1½ million.

These trends were not dissimilar from those of other comparable economies (see Table 7·34)[188], and the deterioration of the 1970s must be brought into relation with the world economic recession released by the OPEC rise in oil prices. The particular causes responsible for the high level of unemployment in Britain after 1979 and its concentration on the manufacturing sector, are discussed elsewhere;[189] here we are concerned with the relationship of unemployment to incomes.

Table 7·34:   Standardized rates of unemployment, %, US definition

	1960	1970	1979
United Kingdom	2·2	3·1	5·8
U.S.A.	5·5	4·9	5·8
France	1·8	2·6	6·1
West Germany	1·1	0·8	3·0
Italy	3·8	3·1	3·9
Japan	1·7	1·2	2·1

Economists have not been wanting who have considered much of this unemployment to be voluntary, induced by over-generous State benefits. As a general statement this cannot be accepted, in view of the very low unemployment rates 1945–66 despite higher benefits than pre-war, and in view of the fact that British benefits as a proportion of incomes from employment were substantially below those of other countries. Thus the share of social expenditure in GDP was 13·9% in the United Kingdom in 1960 and 23·7% in 1981, compared with 13·7% and 24·8% for the seven leading industrial nations. The unemployment compensation share in this was 1·4% and 5·9% in these two years, compared with 3·8% and 4·9% for the seven; and the annual growth rate of social expenditure was 5·9% in 1960–75 and 1·8% in 1975–81, compared with the much higher rate of 8·3% and 4·3% for the seven.[190] But it is not impossible that small minorities of workers have been induced by particular provisions to fall back on State benefits.

[188] Constance Sorrentino, 'Unemployment in International Perspective', in Brian Showler and Adrian Sinfield, *The Workless State: Studies in Unemployment* (Oxford, 1981), p. 170; OECD, *Labour Force Statistics*. Problems of definition are discussed in G. D. N. Worswick (ed.), *The Concept and Measurement of Involuntary Unemployment* (1976), and *Unemployment Statistics. Report of an Interdepartmental Working Party*, Cmnd. 5157 (1972).

[189] Pp. 236–8 above and chapter 10 below.

[190] OECD, *Social Expenditure 1960–1990* (Paris, 1985), pp. 21, 24.

Two measures have mainly been held responsible. One was the Redundancy Payments Act 1965, which benefited older workers in particular, and it was indeed followed by a rise in the unemployment rates of older men; but in many cases, this had clear structural reasons. The other was the introduction of the Earnings Related Supplement (ERS), operating from 1966. Again, there appeared to be a not unreasonable mathematical relationship between the higher benefits and the higher numbers out of work: but in fact, only a small minority of the latter benefited from ERS. Thus in a comparison between 1965, before ERS, and 1972, while 467,000 additional men and 68,000 additional women were on unemployment benefit, only 129,000 of the former and 16,000 of the latter were on ERS and for some of them the benefits thus received were so low that they had to be made up by Supplementary Allowances. In May 1976, ERS recipients numbered 245,000, or one-sixth of the unemployed.[191] Combined tax and benefit changes actually reduced the so-called 'replacement ratio' of benefits to income from work, that is to say, the 'incentive' to live on benefit in the 1970s.

As in the inter-war period, there were strong regional variations in the incidence of unemployment, but while the early post-war years showed a distribution not unlike the pre-war one, in the 1970s the 'Central Regions' of Yorkshire and Humberside, the West Midlands and the northwest suffered more than proportionately – a reflection of the contraction in textiles, engineering and motor vehicle manufacture. While GDP for the country as a whole fell by 0·5% in 1974–81, in these regions it fell by 4·9%. Losses in manufacturing are shown in Table 7·35.[192] Particularly affected were also the young, the old, the unskilled and, as a newly emergent discriminated group, the coloured, who all had more than average rates of unemployment. For women the official figures of 'registered' unemployed are probably under-estimates, since many do not bother to register in adverse times. There was a sharp increase in the duration of unemployment for each individual out of work, rather than an increase in the numbers affected.[193] It was a signal that in depressions cyclical, structural

[191] A. B. Atkinson and J. S. Flemming, 'Unemployment, Social Security and Incentives', *Midland Bank Review*, Autumn 1978, p. 8; Malcolm A. Sawyer, 'The Effect of Unemployment Compensation on the Rate of Unemployment in Great Britain: an Account', *Oxf. Econ., P.*, 31/1, 1979, p. 143. Also Z. A. Spindler and Dennis Maki, 'The Effect of Unemployment Compensation on the Rate of Unemployment in Great Britain', *ibid.* 27/3, 1975, and *idem*, 'More on the Effect of Unemployment Compensation on the Rate of Unemployment in Great Britain', *ibid.*, 31/1, 1979; J. S. Cubbin and K. Foley, 'The Extent of Benefit-Induced Unemployment in Great Britain: Some New Evidence', *ibid.* 29/1, 1977; K. Holden and D. A. Peel, 'The "Shake-Out" Hypothesis: A Note', *Oxf. Bull. Econ. Stat.*, 1967; D. Gujarati, 'The Behaviour of Unemployment and Unfilled Vacancies, Great Britain 1968–71', *Econ. J.*, 82/1, 1972; D. I. McKay and G. L. Reid, 'Redundancy, Unemployment and Manpower Policy' *ibid.* 82/4, 1972; S. Nickell, 'The Effect of Unemployment and Related Benefits on the Duration of Unemployment', *ibid.* 89/1, 1979; Brian Showler, 'Political Economy and Unemployment', in Showler and Sinfield, esp. pp. 44–5; J. K. Bowers and D. Harkess, 'Duration of Unemployment by Age and Sex', *Economica*, 46, 1979, pp. 255–7. Frank A. Cowell, 'Income and Incentive for the Working Poor', *Three Banks Review*, 122 (June 1979), 32–48; Michael Beenstock and Associates, *Work, Welfare and Taxation* (1987); Jon Stern, 'Who Bears the Burden of Unemployment?' in W. Beckerman (ed.), *Slow Growth in Britain* (Oxford, 1979), pp. 70–82. Also see chapter 4, section 1 above.

[192] John Rhodes, 'Regional Dimensions of Industrial Decline', in Ron Martin and Bob Rowthorn, *The Geography of De-industrialisation* (1986), p. 149.

[193] Andrew Dean, 'The Labour Market in a Slow-Growing Economy', in Wilfred Beckerman (ed.), *Slow Growth in Britain*, pp. 45–7; Bowers and Harkess, pp. 239, 246; Showler and Sinfield,

and that novel phenomenon, 'capital-shortage' unemployment added more significantly to the total than frictional job-seeking:[194]

Table 7·35:   Share of manufacturing output by region, 1974–1981.

	Manufacturing output as share of GDP 1974 %	Decline in share of manufacturing 1974–81 %
West Midlands	41·4	−23·7
North-West	34·8	−13·8
East Midlands	33·3	−14·7
North	33·6	−17·6
Yorkshire and Humberside	32·3	−20·4
Wales	29·5	−21·4
Scotland	27·5	−20·4
Northern Ireland	27·5	−32·0
East Anglia	24·9	−10·0
South-West	23·5	−13·2
South-East	22·0	−14·1
UK	28·5	−17·9

4 Trade Unions and Industrial Relations

After the momentous accession of strength to the trade-union movement in the war years, total union membership grew only very slowly for some years after 1950, from 9·3 million to just over 10 million in 1967, or rather less than the rate of growth of the labour force. There then followed a considerable boost in numbers, possibly encouraged by favourable legislation and the militancy of the unions which also extended the closed shop principle to Labour-controlled councils and other new fields. By 1979 there were 13·5 million members, or a rise from about 45% to 58% of the labour force.

Meanwhile, there were some significant amalgamations following the Trade Union (Amalgamations) Act of 1964, including the Society of Graphical and Allied Trades in printing, ASTMS among management and scientific staff and the Amalgamated Engineering and Foundry Workers' union in engineering in 1967. There were nine unions with over a quarter of a million members each in 1968 and 11 such in 1979, and their membership rose from 5·5 to 8·4 millions or 62% of the total.[195] Great differences between them still remained: thus Donovan in 1968 counted a range of 1978 members (USDAW) to 6807 members (AEU) per full-time official. They were matched by over 10,000 personnel officers in firms.[196]

'Introduction, pp. 12–13; T. F. Cripps and R. J. Tarling, 'An Analysis of the Duration of Male Unemployment in Great Britain 1932–73', *Econ. J.*, 84/2, 1974, p. 306.

[194] OECD, *A. Medium-Term Strategy for Employment and Manpower Policies* (Paris, 1978), p. 126.

[195] H. A. Turner, 'British Trade Union Structure: A New Approach?' *British Journal of Industrial Relations*, 2/2 (1964). Also, TUC *Annual Report*, 1966, pp. 114 ff.; John Hughes, *Changes in the Trade Unions* (Fabian Society, 1964), pp. 14 ff.; Royal Commission on Trade Unions and Employers' Associations, *Report* (*Donovan Report*), Cmnd. 3623 (1968), p. 181.

[196] *Report*, pp. 25, 188.

With the nominal widening of the range of national negotiations among ever larger unions there had ensued the use of a second, and usually more effective, system of negotiations at lower levels:

Britain has two systems of industrial relations. The one is the formal system embodied in the official institutions. The other is the informal system, created by the actual behaviour of trade unions and employers' associations, of managers, shop stewards and workers.

This second, informal system, was said to have weakened the impact of national incomes and wages policies, since actual plant earnings could move differently from nationally fixed levels and were at times 100% above them.[197] It was also in the ambit of the 'labour process', the actual conditions in the workplace, that unions and even unorganized workers were said to have obstructed progress and change, and thus contributed to the poor British economic performance.[198] While Donovan undoubtedly exaggerated the significance of this dual system, being too prone to take conditions in some industries to be typical for all,[199] an enquiry some 10 years later showed that national or regional bargaining determined only one-quarter of money wages in 1977, while 'single-employer bargaining has become the important means of pay determination for two-thirds of manual workers'.[200] The wages-drift imparted an element of realism to the annual wage round.[201]

Donovan pronounced in favour of continuing voluntary bargaining, as well as of that peculiarly British institution, the 'closed shop'.[202] Affecting $3\frac{3}{4}$ million workers in 1962, equivalent to 39% of all trade unionists and of 51% of manual workers in the TUC, it rose to 4 million in 1974 and perhaps 7 million in 1975, after the legislation of 1975. Between 1962 and 1978 it had increased from 6% to 19% in clothing and footwear, 7% to 32% in chemicals and allied trades, 4% to 39% in food, drink and tobacco, and 44% to 67% in metals, vehicles, etc. In 1980 it was estimated that 44% of manual, and 9% of non-manual workers, were in closed shops.[203]

White-collar workers had largely held aloof from trade union organization before 1914 and even in the inter-war period had favoured them only in certain occupations. It was in the post-war decades that their trade unions increased by

[197] *Donovan Report*, pp. 12–16.

[198] Andrew Kilpatrick and Tony Lawson, 'On the Nature of Industrial Decline in the UK', *Cambridge Journal of Economics* 4/1, 1980; Karel Williams, John Williams, Dennis Thomas, *Why are the British Bad at Manufacturing?* (1987), pp. 34 ff. Also David Coates and John Hillard (eds.), *The Economic Decline of Modern Britain* (Brighton, 1986). pp. 99 ff.

[199] Kevin Hawkins, *Conflict and Change. Aspects of Industrial Relations* (1972), p. 88; Evans and Creight, pp. 10–11.

[200] William Brown (ed.), *The Changing System of British Industrial Relations. A Survey of Manufacturing Industry* (Oxford, 1981), p. 24.

[201] E. H. Phelps-Brown, 'New Wine in Old Bottles: Reflections on the Changed Working of Collective Bargaining in Great Britain', *British Journal of Industrial Relations*, 11, 1973, pp. 333 4.

[202] In most other countries it is outlawed, Stephen Milligan, *The New Barons. Union Power in the 1970s* (1976) p. 74.

[203] W. E. J. McCarthy, *The Closed Shop in Britain* (Oxford, 1964), pp. 28–35; John Burton, 'The Economics of the Closed Shop', in Lord Robbins *et al., Trade Unions*, p. 43; W. W. Daniel and Neil Millward, *Workplace Industrial Relations in Britain* (1983), p. 67; Brown, *Changing System*, pp. 54–6.

leaps and bounds and they were largely responsible for the growth in the total numbers organized. Between 1948 and 1960 the membership of manual unions rose by +0·6%, that of white-collar unions by +33·6%; density in 1960 was particularly high in local government (84% – up 16% from 1948) and in national government (83% – up 19% from 1948).[204]

There were two major causes for this expansion: the rapid growth in white-collar employment itself, and the relative loss in earnings and status vis-a-vis the manual workers which has accompanied this growth and has led to a radicalization of the attitudes of salaried personnel. It is significant that several of their organizations, which have in the past stood aloof from association with other unions, joined the TUC in these years, where they now form a large minority. Contrary to expectations they have not exercised a moderating influence there: postmen, civil and local govenment servants, teachers and health workers have been among the strikers of recent years.

British trade unions have in the post-war years acquired a reputation of being unusually strike prone. The statistics do not bear this out, but the impact of a disciplined strike in, for example, the US motor industry in which several hundred thousand men stay out for some weeks while the works, having had due warning, are subject to planned total closure, is quite different from the impact of the same number of working days lost by several hundred unofficial strikes, in which each group of strikers causes damage, hardship and lay-offs to groups several times their own size. British unions tended to specialize in the latter. In the period 1969–73, for example, 94·5% of the average annual of 2,723 strikes outside the coal industry, and 55·7% of the working days lost were in unofficial strikes. One calculation – very much disputed – put the direct costs of strikes in 1976 at £6 billion, or 6% of GNP, not counting the indirect costs such as the cutting off of growth potential.[205]

Simple statistics are given in Table 7·36.[206]

Table 7·36:   Strikes in British industry

| | Average of years: | | | |
	1961–74	1975–8	1979	1980
Number of stoppages	2,575	2,368	2,080	1,330
Workers involved, 000	1,465	930	4,584	834
Working days lost, 000:				
All industries and services	7,351	7,211	29,474	11,964
Mining and quarrying	1,507	108	128	156
Metals, engineering, shipbuilding,				
vehicles	3,373	4,507	20,389	10,224

The leading post-war role of coal miners among the strikers (70% of all strikes in 1952–7 were in coal) was coming to an end in the 1960s, particularly after

[204] G. S. Bain, *The Growth of White Collar Unionism* (Oxford, 1970), pp. 25, 28; Kevin Hawkins, *Conflict*, pp. 138 ff.

[205] J. W. Duncan, W. E. J. McCarthy, G. P. Redman, *Strikes in Post-War Britain* (1983), pp. 174, 192–3; Lord Robbins, *et al.*, *Trade unions: Public Goods or Public Bads?* (1978), pp. 50, 57.

[206] *Nat. Inst. Econ. Rev.*, 95, Feb. 1981, p. 12 and 97, August 1981, p. 28.

the National Power-Loading Agreement of 1966 and possibly also because of the decline in numbers and the end of the sellers' market in coal; instead, metal and especially car workers took on the mantle of strike leaders. By contrast, in 1971–3, very active strike years averaging 14·9 million working days lost, 95% of plants in manufacturing had no stoppage at all. Around 95% of all strikes were unofficial, but the official ones tended to be larger and last longer. Two years, 1979 and 1980, stand out as major strike years, having several large rather than more numerous strikes.[207]

The more generous benefits, including tax rebates to strikers, have been held responsible not only for the level of unemployment as noted in chapter 4 section 1 but also for the rising numbers of disputes from the 1960s on, and indeed, the concessions offered to British strikers on these two counts greatly exceeded those available in other countries. Yet the evidence is inconclusive,[208] and the influence of such factors, while real, is likely to be marginal.

In this period some Wages Councils were abolished when the need for them had gone, including the one for chainmaking, one of the first four of 1909, and by the consolidating Wages Councils Act of 1959 the Minister of Labour was given power to order independent inquiries into industry and abolish Wages Councils on his own initiative. By 1968, there were still 57 Wage Councils covering $3\frac{1}{2}$ million workers and these were reduced to 33, and 3 million workers, by 1980.

In 1959 the war-time method of compulsory arbitration was ended, but powers of conciliation and of originating Courts of Inquiry or Committees of Investigation remained and were used frequently. The latter were particularly important in cases in which relatively limited disputes might have widespread repercussions elsewhere, so that the public would clamour for intervention. There were many such in the 1950s and 1960s.[209] Industrial relations in the nationalized industries, in which it was quite often the Government's policy that was responsible for the employer's intransigence, were particularly fit subjects for official or semi-official inquiries. In this regard, Selwyn Lloyd's 'July measures' of 1961 formed a landmark, for they actually included a total standstill for wage increases (except for those already sanctioned) among all Government employees and employees of nationalized industries and a similar directive to the Wages Boards, backed by the power of the Ministry of Labour to refer back proposed increases. No such powers were available to use in private industry.

All collective bargaining, however, was in this period increasingly distorted and hampered by the Government in the interest of its own short-term policies. The justification, apart from the recurrent crises, was the inflationary framework in which, it was felt, employers were unable to provide a sufficient counterweight to trade union pressure and were likely, instead, to raise prices against the public after conceding higher wages to their workers.

[207] E. V. Evans and S. W. Creigh (eds.), *Industrial Conflict in Britain* (1977), esp. pp. 63–4, 80, 91–6, 127; Duncan, McCarthy, Redman, *Strikes*, p. 174; R. Elliott, 'Industrial Relations and Manpower Policy', in F. T. Blackaby (ed.), *British Economic Policy 1960–74* (Cambridge, 1978), pp. 566–8.

[208] See discussion in *British Journal of Industrial Relations*, 12, 1974, John Gennard and Roger Lasko, pp. 1–25, J. W. Duncan and W. E. J. McCarthy, pp. 26–47 and Laurence C. Hunter, pp. 438–44; and John Gennard, *Financing Strikes* (1977).

[209] J. W. Grove, *Government and Industry in Britain* (1962), chapters 8, 17; W. E. J. McCarthy and B. A. Clifford, 'The Work of Industrial Courts of Inquiry', *British Journal of Industrial Relations*, 4/1 (1966).

We have noted in the last chapter the beginnings of voluntary wage restraint and its mixed success in the late 1940s. Little was heard of it in the early years of the Conservative Government, but in 1956 it was tried again. Trade union opinion was hostile and, when the engineering employers took the Government's exhortations seriously and determined to fight against a wage claim early in 1957,

> the Government was forced to beat a hasty and humiliating retreat, conceding to the railwaymen a bigger wage increase than had been awarded to them by an independent arbitration tribunal and putting severe pressure on the engineering employers and their shipbuilding allies to come to terms with their own unions.[210]

The experience was repeated later in the year by the dock employers. This retreat was, not unnaturally, resented by private employers, and under their pressure the Government then went to the opposite extreme of attempting to prevent at all costs pending wage rises in the public sector. The result was to discredit temporarily the official conciliation and arbitration machinery, and in the next two years, Government intervention swung back again to the pole of leniency for the sake of industrial peace.

Meanwhile, in August 1957, the Council on Productivity, Prices and Incomes (the 'Three Wise Men') had been set up to advise the Government on the criteria by which wage claims should be judged, or, as the trade unions alleged, to find respectable reasons for refusing wage increases. When the Council's first Report in 1958 seemed to confirm the unions' suspicions, with the suggestion that a wage standstill was desirable,[211] and that an effective level of unemployment might achieve it, 'the TUC virtually boycotted the Council ever after'.[212] In 1959 and 1960 official policy was again expansionist, and the Council's pronouncements became less rigid. Its influence, however, had much waned by that time, and any chance of a more discriminating incomes policy was rudely shattered by the more severe pay freeze introduced in 1961. The Council was dissolved in 1962, together with the still-born Economic Planning Board proposed in 1961, on the formation of the NEDC. In the same year the National Incomes Commission was set up to advise the Government on income claims. In due course the restrictionist policy of 1960–61 gave way to the easier conditions of the 'guiding light' between March 1962 and November 1964. Beginning with the severe crisis of late 1964, however, there was a further tightening up.

The Declaration of Intent of December 1964 pledged the Government, the employers' organizations and the TUC, which was now once again amenable to steering by a Labour Government, to raise productivity, to keep income increases in line with output increases and hence to maintain a stable general price level. In February 1965 the agreement on the *Machinery for Prices and Incomes Policy* was published, which included the setting up of a National Board for Prices and Incomes (PIB), and an agreed white paper in April laid it down

[210] Michael Shanks, 'Public Policy and the Ministry of Labour', in B. C. Roberts (ed.), *Industrial Relations: Contemporary Problems and Perspectives* (1962), pp. 263–4.

[211] *Council on Prices, Productivity and Incomes, First Report* (1958), p. 52.

[212] K. G. J. C. Knowles, 'Wages and Productivity', in G. D. N. Worswick and P. Ady, *The British Economy in the Nineteen-Fifties* (Oxford, 1962), p. 511.

that all wage increases must be kept in line with the annual productivity rise, put somewhat optimistically at 3–3·5% p.a.[213]

The PIB, however, could look only at a few cases at a time, and neither the employers' organizations nor the unions were willing to operate a wide-compulsory scheme themselves. There was also no effective scheme to hold price increases. In November 1965 the Government, therefore, instituted a voluntary notification scheme, whereby all wage claims were to be notified to the TUC and the Ministry of Labour, and all price increases to the appropriate Ministry for the industry concerned, and neither was to be granted without the Ministry's or the PIB's consent.[214] In the sterling crisis of July 1966 a complete wage standstill for six months was decreed, followed by six months of severe restraint, and thereafter a return to something like the notification scheme, with the difference that the TUC operated on a 'norm' of nil instead of 3–3½%, and the Government had power to delay any settlement for up to seven months. The result of this elaborate and demoralizing machinery was derisory: in the 20 months before the 'freeze' (October 1964 to June 1966) earnings rose by 7½%, and in the 14 months from June 1966 to October 1967, which included the freeze, by just over 5½%.[215] Bearing in mind the rising unemployment and consequent short-term working in the second period, this reduction in the rate of increase can hardly be termed a success for the restrictive policies adopted.[216]

The Report of the Donovan Commission, a major investigation into collective bargaining, which had taken three years to complete, appeared in 1968. Its emphasis, as noted above, was on the localized and unofficial sources of most of the effective decisions on wages and conditions, and its tendency was therefore to question the wisdom of national policies and regulations. But drawing attention to the powers of the trade unions, it proposed, *inter alia*, a Commission for Industrial Relations (CIR) which should work for some orderliness on the shop floor, essentially by voluntary means. The CIR was set up in March 1969.

There was also general agreement on the need for trade-union reform. Barbara Castle, the responsible minister, whose Department had meanwhile been re-named from 'Ministry of Labour' to 'Department of Employment and Productivity' to emphasize the link between values created and incomes paid out, proposed her own set of reforms early in 1969 in a document, the title of which highlighted what troubled the legislators: *In Place of Strife*.[217]

In return for some additional legal privileges, including the power to force an employer to recognize a union, *In Place of Strife* proposed some curbs on the trade unions' freedom of action. They included compulsory ballots before a strike involving public interests or a serious threat to the economy; in the case of certain 'unconstitutional strikes', a conciliation pause of 28 days; the right of the Minister to impose a settlement in inter-union disputes; and financial pen-

[213] *Machinery for Prices and Incomes Policy*, Cmnd. 2577 (1965); *Prices and Incomes Policy*, Cmnd. 2639 (1965); R. B. McKersie and L. C. Hunter, *Pay, Productivity and Collective Bargaining* (1973).

[214] *Prices and Incomes Policy: An Early Warning System*, Cmnd. 2809 (1965); Allan Fels, *The British Prices and Incomes Board* (Cambridge, 1972); Campbell Balfour, *Incomes Policy and the Public Sector* (1972).

[215] F. Blackaby and M. Artis, 'On Incomes Policy', *District Bank Review*, 165 (March 1968).

[216] See in general, Samuel Brittan and Peter Lilley, *The Delusions of Incomes Policy* (1977).

[217] *In Place of Strife: A Policy for Industrial Relations*, Cmnd. 3888 (1969).

alties to back up these regulations. Though whittled down in the formal Industrial Relations Bill, its provisions still displeased the trade unions, and they used their power over MPs to have it defeated in cabinet despite the support for it by Harold Wilson as well as Barbara Castle.[218] Instead, the General Council of the TUC who were willing enough to see unofficial actions curbed as long as their own were not, composed a 'Programme for Action' in May 1969 to assume more power to intervene in 'unconstitutional strikes' and inter-union disputes and in June they signed with the Government a 'solemn and binding contract' to implement this programme, whereupon the Government withdrew its bill, though it must have known that no undertaking by the TUC has any operative value.[219]

This spill-over of trade-union power into the political sphere was to see its most remarkable demonstration in the following four years. Large-scale strikes in late 1969 drove up wages at unexpectedly fast rates[220] and, indeed, wage rises were to race ahead of price rises over the whole of the 1970s, except for the restrictionist period 1972–4. The newly elected Conservative Government abolished controls in 1970, but worked for lower pay settlements, and in the public sector set out what in effect was the 'n–1' policy, i.e. each year's wage settlement to be 1% below that of the previous year. Its Industrial Relations Act of 1971 was simultaneously to lower the pressure of wage demands by weakening the bargaining powers of the trade unions. Central was the requirement for unions to register in order to keep their privileges; there was also a version of the cooling-off period and the secret ballot, beside other restrictions. The National Industrial Relations Court (NIRC) and the CIR were to supervise these provisions. They were to lead to an immediate boycott by the TUC – it suspended 32 unions in 1972 and expelled 20 in 1973 for registering under the Act – and to a continuing battle until 1974.

Among its more spectacular episodes was the defiance of the NIRC by the dockers, who were rescued by the Court of Appeal; the failure of the cooling-off period in the railway dispute; the freeing from prison of five unrepentant dockers, on a legal technicality, by the previously inconspicuous Official Solicitor; and the solution of a deadlock over a fine on the engineering union (AEUW) by its payment by an anonymous donor.[221] The miners meanwhile won wage awards of 17–20% in 1972 after a national strike in January–February followed by the Wilbeforce Court of Enquiry.

By mid-1972, it was clear that the inflation was geting out of hand with settlements in excess of 20% and that the Government's belief in the free market tempered by anti-union legislation had failed, as had the trial of a voluntary prices and incomes policy agreed between the TUC and the CBI. The Government therefore returned to a direct incomes policy, beginning in November 1972 with a total wages and prices freeze. For March–autumn 1973, Stage II of the statutory policy envisaged a maximum of £1 a week plus 4%, with £250 a year as the upper limit. A 'Pay Board' and a 'Prices Commission' were set up, and there appeared to be widespread support for this policy, as elaborated in a green

---

[218] Peter Jenkins, *The Battle of Downing Street* (1970).

[219] Gerard A. Dorfman, *Government versus Trade Unionism in British Politics since 1968* (1979).

[220] Hugh Clegg, *How to Run an Incomes Policy and Why We Made Such a Mess of the Last One* (1971), pp. 60–1.

[221] For a brief account, see Peter Calvocoressi, *The British Experience 1945–75* (1978), pp. 76 ff.

paper.[222] Stage III relaxed conditions a little more, with a maximum of £7 a week or £350 a year, plus 1% flexibility allowance, plus additional pay for productivity rises and 'unsocial hours'.[223] While the latter allowed all the strong unions to ignore the limits set for the rest, a further provision of 40 p. per week for every 1% that prices rose over the threshold of 7% built in almost automatic inflationary settlements when the oil price explosion was added to domestic inflation. The miners, once more, refused to be bound by the general rules, though offered an award above the norm: their dispute led to a State of Emergency, a three-day week, power cuts and a general election early in 1974, lost by the Heath Government, before the Pay Board could find a face-saving formula to pay the miners more than the rest.

The new Labour Government, like the new Conservative one before it, began by abolishing the existing pay policy, and reimposed a new one shortly afterwards when prices and pay went through the roof: the 'Social Contract' of voluntary pay restraint had proved to be worth as little as all trade-union promises before, and between the second quarter of 1974 and the same period in 1975 average earnings were up by 28% and retail prices by 25%. The new policy limited pay increases to 6% or £10–12 a week (Stage 1), and in 1976 to £2.50 to £4 or 5% within those limits (Stage 2). However, because of wages drift, average earnings rose, not by 4·5% as they should have done, but by 9%. In 1977 (Stage 3) the limitation consisted merely of putting in a single claim a year, with the interesting innovation of promising tax concessions contingent on low wage increases, and there was a 14% wage rise against a 10% target. 1978 had a 5% target, but as in the end of the unions refused to collaborate, a series of disputes made 1978–9 a 'winter of discontent', at the end of which the Government were defeated at the polls.[224]

In 1979 the new Conservative Government once more abolished the restraint policies of its predecessor, and reintroduced the discipline of the market instead. Unheard-of rates of unemployment did indeed induce lower pay claims after an initial wage explosion, at least in firms threatened by bankruptcy, though workers in the public services unaffected by unemployment were as militant as ever.

The effectiveness of incomes policies has been subject to much debate. After the experience of the 1960s and 1970s it had few friends, though some were willing to admit that, as part of a larger package, incomes policy may have had at least a temporary impact. In any case, there were few alternatives in sight.[225]

The growth in union power and militancy, to the point of defying legislation and challenging the courts as in 1972–3, had several causes. One lay in the favourable legislation passed by successive Labour Governments which indirectly strengthened the hands of the employees and their unions. Among these must be reckoned, beside the Redundancy Payments Act 1965 mentioned

---

[222] Treasury, *Price and Pay Code, Consultative Document*, Cmnd. 5247 (1973).

[223] Treasury, *Pay and Price Code for Stage 3. A Consultative Document*, Cmnd. 5444 (1973).

[224] For a brief review see Dermot R. Glynn, 'The Last 14 Years of Incomes Policy – a CBI Perspective', *National Westminster Bank Quarterly Review*, November 1978. Also Leo Pliatzky, *Getting and Spending* (Oxford, 1982), pp. 172–5.

[225] J. J. Fallick and R. F. Eliot, *Incomes Policies, Inflation and Relative Pay* (1982); R. G. Lipsey and Michael Parkin, 'Incomes Policy: A Reappraisal', *Economica*, NS 37/146 (1970), 115–38; Samuel Brittan and Peter Lilley, *The Delusions of Incomes Policy* (1977).

above,[226] the Employment Protection Act, the Health and Safety at Work Act (1974) and the Industry Act of 1975. The Trade Union and Labour Relation Act of 1976 more directly put the unions into an even more favourable position than they had been in before 1971. Many of these provisions, including generous redundancy payments, were consolidated in the Employment Protection (Consolidation) Act of 1978.[227] A second cause of militancy lay in the industrial and economic experience of the age: mounting inflation, stagnating living standards, and the climb into higher tax rates. A third lay in the structural changes among the unions themselves: local or shop steward bargaining, productivity bargaining, sham or real,[228] the power of small groups to do intolerable damage to larger groups not concerned in the dispute,[229] all offered opportunities of driving up wages and earnings to well above prices or nationally settled rates. Finally, there was the frustration over the injustices implicit in the repeated policies of restraint themselves.[230]

Industrial relations were therefore played out inside a tightening net of restrictions and enforceable guidelines, which reflected the immanent incompatibility of free bargaining and anti-inflationary policies in the given conditions. Did trade unions in this period contribute directly to the inflation, and in this sense abuse their powers so as to call forth the very countermeasure to curb them once more?

Up to the mid-1960s most observers trusted to the explanatory power of the 'Phillips Curve': this was the assumption, based on a study of British wage rates for about a century, that wage changes depended on the state of aggregate demand, for which the level of unemployment was a good guide, however modified it might be by other influences, such as structural changes in the labour market or external trade.[231] Such a view gave unions, at best, only a transmission role in generating wage inflation. From 1964–5 on, however, wage rises were no longer held back by high unemployment: the presumed negative correlation between them had disappeared. A different explanation was needed, and interest returned once more to cost push and institutional factors, above all to trade union activity.[232]

A second explanation, once more based on the observation of several decades, but stressing supply rather than demand, was then offered in terms of union 'pushfulness', defined as membership growth and density. According to A. G. Hines, trade unions *did* influence wages. However, this relationship not only found many critics on theoretical grounds; it also failed to stand up to the test of British statistics in the period 1951–76.[233] Yet the role of the trade unions in

---

[226] P. 279 above.

[227] Patrick Minford, *Unemployment, Cause and Cure* (Oxford, 1985), pp. 178–83.

[228] S. Lerner and J. Marquand, 'Regional Variations in Earnings, Demand for Labour and Shop Stewards Combined Committees in the British Engineering Industry', *Manchester School*, 31, 1963; J. E. Mortimer, *Trade Unions and Technological Change* (1971), pp. 35 ff.

[229] Charles K. Rowley, 'The Economics and Politics of Extortion', in Robbins *et al.*, *Trade Unions* pp. 91 ff.

[230] A. B. Tylecote, 'The Effect of Monetary Policy on Wage Inflation', *Oxf. Econ. P.*, 27/2, 1975.

[231] A. W. Phillips, 'The Relation Between Unemployment and the Rate of Change of Money Wage Rates in the United Kingdom, 1861–1957', *Economica*, 25/4, 1958; Prest and Coppock, pp. 273–81. There is a large critical literature.

[232] Milligan, *New Barons*, pp. 33–9.

[233] A. G. Hines, 'Trade Unions and Wage Inflation in the UK 1893–1961', *Rev. Econ. Studies*,

the inflationary spiral was not thereby disproved, and pushfulness need not be reflected directly in membership figures.

Three linking mechanisms by which trade unions influence wages have been observed. There was, in the first place, the effect of a disjointed labour market, which meant that a rise in pay for any group of workers, no matter how justified, would, in the competitive world of union politics, be taken as a guideline and be followed by others even if they had no justification other than the success of the first group.[234] Secondly, rises could sometimes be enforced by a new organization or a newly organized group, and would then be propagated throughout the system.[235] Lastly, it appears that in years of pressure, union wages did rise faster than those of the unorganized;[236] more conspicuously, the excess pay demands of a well organized group of workers were punished, not by their own unemployment, but by the loss of jobs of weaker groups elsewhere, so that the market sanctions, believed to hold all wage claims in check, did not operate in the way presumed. The share of the trade unions and the industrial relations mechanism as a whole in causing the wage-price spiral and thus the destructive Government policies designed to stem it, is still obscure in part, but it cannot be written off altogether.

5 Economic Growth

In the years from 1950 to 1967 the population of the United Kingdom increased from 50·2 million to 55·4 million (mid-year figures), or by an average of around 270,000 a year. Thereafter the increase slowed down, and in 1973–80 the population remained virtually stationary at around 56 million, having fluctuated by less than 40,000 from one year to the next.

The growth, while it lasted, was based entirely on the excess of births over deaths. Annual births fluctuated around 800,000 in 1960–6, then rose in the second post-war baby boom to a peak of 1,015,000 in 1964, and declined thereafter to a low of 657,000 in 1977, with a slight upturn again in 1978–80. Deaths fluctuated much less and had a continuously rising tendency. Divided into 10-year periods, annual population changes averaged as shown in Table 7·37.

Migration, it will be seen, was a small and largely negative influence: only in the years 1951 and 1959–63 was there an actual net in-migration. Yet those relatively small net migration figures hide considerable losses, generally between 200–300,000 year by year by emigration, made up by somewhat smaller numbers of immigrants. While the emigrants went mostly to the white Commonwealth countries, Europe and the USA, there were important shifts among the immigrants. In addition to the Irish, arriving at a rate of 60–70,000 a year, the

31, 1964; D. Dogas and A. G. Hines, 'Trade Unions and Wage Inflation in the UK. A Critique of Purdy and Zis', *Applied Economics*, 7, 1975; D. L. Purdy and G. Zis, 'Trade Unions and Wage Inflation in the UK. A Reply to Dogas and Hines', *ibid.* 8, 1976; Wolfgang Fautz, 'Union Militancy, Excess Demand and Inflation in post-war United Kingdom, *ibid* 12, 1980.

[234] J. Tobin, 'Inflation and Unemployment', *Amer. Econ. Rev.,* 62/1, 1972; J. R. Hicks, *The Crisis in Keynesian Economics* (Oxford, 1974), pp. 71–2, 80.

[235] Brian Griffiths: 'Economics of Labour Power: Can Unions Raise Real Wages?', in Robbins *et al., Trade Unions*, p. 107; D. Metcalf, 'Unions, Incomes Policy and Relative Wages in Britain', *British Journal of Industrial Relations*, 15/2, 1977, p. 169.

[236] Ralph Turvey, 'Counter-Inflationary Policies', in Michael Posner (ed.), *Demand Management* (1978), p. 195.

Table 7·37:   Changes in UK population (annual averages) (000)

	Births	Deaths	Natural increase	Migration etc. (net)	Total change
1951–61	839	593	246	+ 6	+ 252
1961–71	962	638	324	− 44	+ 280
1971–81	745	678	67	− 29	+ 37

post-war wave from Europe, particularly into the service trades, continued in the 1950s but at a diminished rate. They were joined by Commonwealth immigrants from the West Indies, whose numbers rose to a peak of 30,000 in 1955–6, but then subsided because of the recession in Britain. The smaller numbers from India, Pakistan and Africa also declined in the later 1950s for the same reasons.

It was the threatened Commonwealth Immigrants Act, passed in 1962, which brought in a rush to beat the restrictions. In the 18 months from the beginning of 1961 to 30 June 1962, almost as many came (203,000) as had come in the six preceding years (219,000) from India, Pakistan and the Caribbean. Thereafter, only wives and children of those already in Britain were allowed in freely and the migration of men was strictly controlled: thus by December 1968, only 78,000 voucher holders from the New Commonwealth were admitted, compared with 257,000 dependants.

Estimates for 1966 put the total coloured population at 924,000 (or 1·7% of the resident population) of whom 213,000 were born in Britain and 711,000 overseas. The total foreign-born population in Great Britain was 2,600,000, or 5%; of these the 739,000 born in the Irish Republic formed much the largest contingent.[237]

Since then immigration has been continuously more restricted, particularly by the Commonwealth Immigrants Act of 1968, but the birth rate of coloured immigrants is high, and the issue has become highly controversial: even the numbers concerned (and the definition) are in dispute. What is clear is that immigrants tended not only to settle in particular districts, but that they were younger than the resident population, their work participation rate was higher and they tended to concentrate in certain occupations. Among the men, the Irish had in 1966 a particular interest in the building industry, their proportion in it being far above the norm (30·7%), and an unusually high proportion of unskilled, and few among white-collar workers. Those from the Caribbean were concentrated in building, transport, engineering and catering, also mostly as unskilled or semi-skilled labourers, but with a higher ratio of skilled workers and a lower ratio of non-manuals than the Irish. Indians were in transport and engineering, but had a higher ratio among professional and scientific workers even than the British; and Pakistanis were concentrated in semi-skilled and

---

[237] *Immigration from the Commonwealth*, Cmnd. 2739 (1965); E. J. B. Rose *et al., Coloured Citizenship. A Report on British Race Relations* (1969), pp. 68–72, 83–88; Stephen Castles, Godula Kosack, *Immigrant Workers and Class Structure in Western Europe* (1973) pp. 4–5; also R. B. Davison, *Commonwealth Immigrants* (1964) and *Black British* (1966); Arnold M. Rose, *Migrants in Europe* (Minneapolis, 1969), pp. 15–21.

unskilled jobs in textiles, metals and engineering. Among women, over half the Irish born were in services, especially hospitals, catering and distribution. Of those born in the West Indies, 30–35% were in professional and scientific services, including nursing. Of the Indian women, over 60% were in similar 'non-manual' jobs; but there were very few Pakistani women in paid employment.[238] None of the immigrant groups had their full share of employers or managers, and only the Indians exceeded the average for professional workers. It is clear that their main flow had been into undermanned industries and services, a tendency strengthened by the immigration provisions.

For the population as a whole, in a period of generally full employment the proportion of males at work remained consistently high, but there was a significant increase in the proportion of females at work. Of those of working age (15–64), employment rose from 40·5% in 1950 to 47·9% in 1965 and 57·8% in 1979, reflecting the high demand for labour as well as continuing a long-term trend. While the male labour force remained constant at around 15·9 million between 1951 and 1976, having risen to a peak of 16·2 million in between, and the number of unmarried women in the labour force fell from 4·3 million to 3·2 million, married women rose from 2·7 million to 6·7 million. The whole of the increase in the working population of 3 million between those two dates was therefore furnished by women. According to the Census of Great Britain, the proportion of women in jobs or looking for jobs rose from 21·7% in 1951 to 42·2% in 1971. Many of those were part-time workers, whose numbers consequently also rose in those years.

Partly as a cause, and in part no doubt as a consequence, the technical facilities available to make paid work by married women possible were greatly improved: gadgets in the home, pre-packed food, easy and quick shopping facilities near the place of work. Moreover, the smaller number of children per family reduced the years when women were tied to the home. It seems that against a background of rising incomes and rising relative pay for women, the attractions of additional purchasing power, and perhaps even the attractions of the independence and the interests provided by an outside job, exceeded the increase in leisure preference.[239]

Actual weekly working hours remained at over 46 in the early 1950s and were still 44·3 in 1966–8 despite the decline of the official working week from an average of 44·6 hours in 1951 to 40·5 hours in January 1968. By 1976, normal hours were 40·0 a week, and actual hours worked, 42·6. The typical holiday probably doubled in length in those years[240]. Overtime work for men and female

[238] Castles and Kosack, pp. 75–9; Rose, *Coloured Citizenship*, pp. 160 ff.; *Census of Population*, 1971.

[239] Roderick Floud and Donald McCloskey (eds.), *The Economic History of Britain since 1700*, vol. 2 (Cambridge, 1981), pp. 395–6; A. R. Prest and D. J. Coppock, *The UK Economy* (1978), pp. 225–30; I. F. Wright, *Britain in the Age of Economic Management* (Oxford, 1979), pp. 24, 92–3; A. R. Thatcher, 'Labour Supply and Employment Trends', in Frank Blackaby (ed.), *De-Industrialisation* (1978), pp. 27–9; R. McNabb, 'The Labour Force Participation of Married Women in Great Britain', *Manchester School*, 45/3, 1977; Christine Greenhalgh, 'Labour Supply Function of Married Women in Great Britain', *Economica*, 44/175, 1977.

[240] *Min. of Labour Gazette; Key Statistics*, Tables E and F; Beckerman, p. 83; *Statistics on Income, Prices, Employment and Production*, 24 (1968); E. G. Whybrew, *Overtime Working in Britain* (Research Paper No. 9 of the Royal Commission on Trade Unions and Employers' Associations) (1968); R. C. O. Matthews, 'Some Aspects of Post-War Growth in the British Economy in Relation to Historical Experience', *Transactions of the Manchester Statistical Society* 1964–5, p. 6.

employment were the most sensitive to changes in demand for labour, though employment never fluctuated as much as total demand.[241]

A second secular trend of the inter-war period, the growth of the proportion of white-collar workers as against manual workers, also continued with undiminished force into the post-war decades. This was associated both with technical changes within industry and the growth of the service trades at the expense of extractive and manufacturing industries. White-collar employees formed 30·9% of the occupied population in 1951 and 35·9% in 1961.[242] In manufacturing, white-collar employees grew further from 25·8% in 1968 to 30·0% in 1980. By 1971 the proportion had risen to 48·3% in all occupations measured in the same way, or 43·4% leaving out employers and proprietors. Among women the proportions had by then reached 54·1% (excluding employers), though most of these were in the lower-paid clerical, shop assistant and 'lower professions and technicians'' grades, including teaching, and fewer in the higher professions and managerial grades.

In recent years attempts have also been made to measure the degree to which capital has been fully used, or left unemployed. The exercise bristles with difficulties, and the series produced often show contradictory results, but some broad movements do appear, as they do in the case of unemployed labour. One index of 'capital utilization measure' in manufacturing (1973 = 100) shows the changes indicated in Table 7·38, and is compared with the unemployment rate:[243]

Table 7·38:   Capital utilization and unemployment

	Capital utilization index (1973 = 100)	Unemployment rate %
Averages of years:		
1960–2	86	1·6
1963–5	91	1·7
1966–8	93·3	2·1
1969–71	94·7	3·1
1972–4	96·7	3·0
1975–7	89·3	5·0
1978–80	85	6·0

Even if the measure could be relied on for accuracy, it shows only overall rates. As in the case of labour, local bottlenecks might inhibit output and growth even at times of under-use of resources; thus in October 1981, in the worst slump in

---

[241] L. C. Hunter, 'Cyclical Variation in the Labour Supply: British Experience, 1951–60', *Oxf. Econ. P.*, 15/2 (1963); R. R. Neild, *Pricing and Employment in the Trade Cycle* (Cambridge, 1963), chapter 3; Harrod, *Economic Policy*, pp. 15–18.

[242] Paul Galambos, 'The Growth of the Employment of Non-Manual Workers in the British Manufacturing Industries, 1948–1962', *Bull. Oxf. Inst. Stat.*, 26/3 (1964); G. S. Bain, 'The Growth of White-Collar Unionism in Great Britain', *British J. of Industrial Relations*, 4/3 (1966); K. Prandy, *Professional Employees: A Study of Scientists and Engineers* (1965); *Scientific and Technological Manpower in Great Britain 1963*, Cmnd. 2146 (1963); R. M. Blackburn, *Union Character and Social Class: White-Collar Unionism* (1967).

[243] *Nat. Inst. Econ. Rev.*, 98, Nov. 1981, p. 13. Compare with it the Wharton measure, *ibid.*, and also *ibid.*, 39, Feb. 1967, p. 16.

British experience for almost 50 years, 7% of CBI correspondents reported plant capacity, and 3% labour, as constraints on output.[244]

The rate of investment was much more amenable to steering by Government policy than was the labour supply. The effect of Government action was to depress it, and the low rates of investment achieved in Britain compared with other countries is generally held to have had some connection with the low rate of economic growth of the British economy in international comparison. The issue is a controversial one,[245] but we may briefly trace the consequences here.

Fixed capital formation, in absolute terms and as a proportion of GNP, changed as shown in Table 7·39 (absolute values in £ billion, at 1975 prices).[246]

Table 7·39: Fixed capital formation

	Gross fixed capital formation		Capital consumption	Net fixed investment	
	£ b.	% GNP	£ b.	£ b.	% GNP
1950–2	4·8	14·7	2·7	2·1	5·9
1953–6	5·9	16·3	3·1	2·8	7·3
1957–9	10·5	17·6	5·2	4·5	8·6
1960–2	12·9	19·3	5·9	6·9	10·4
1963–5	15·1	20·4	6·7	8·4	11·3
1966–8	17·8	20·1	9·0	8·8	10·0
1969–71	19·3	20·3	9·0	10·3	10·8
1972–4	20·5	19·5	10·2	10·2	9·8
1975–7	20·4	19·0	11·4	9·0	8·3
1978–80	20·7	19·0	13·0	7·7	7·1

Investment thus started at a very low level in the early post-war years, rose rapidly in the 1960s to reach near European proportions, and fell back again in the 1970s. Since capital consumption continued to rise in line with the growing stock of capital, the key variable of net fixed capital formation, the actual increase in the productive apparatus, actually declined quite sharply in that decade, back to the levels of the 1950s.

However, about one-fifth of fixed capital formation was in the form of dwellings and of transfer fees (see Table 7·42 on p. 294), being particularly high in the 1950s and in the mid-1970s. The rise of productive investment in the 1960s was thus rather steeper, and the drop in the later 1970s rather less, than the earlier table would imply.

It is time to pull together these various strands and to describe the overall growth in the economy in our period, as summarized by the rise in GDP together with the factorial components that went into this growth. The total figures are very similar to those for incomes;[247] that is to say, they just failed to double over

[244] CLARE Group, 'Problems of Industrial Recovery', *Midland Bank Review*, Spring 1982, p. 16.
[245] S. Pollard, *The Wasting of the British Economy* (1982), chapter 2: pp. 328–9 and chapter 9 (below).
[246] *National Income and Expenditure*. Price indices of base 1958 have been spliced with those of 1975.
[247] Pp. 265–6 above.

Table 7·40:   Share of dwellings, transfer fees etc. in gross fixed capital formation

1950	21·9%
1955	24·3
1960	19·6
1965	21·5
1970	20·2
1975	23·4
1980	18·8

the 30 years. The broad division into periods and factors is given in Table 7·41, with the inter-war years included for comparison:[248]

Table 7·41:   Annual growth rates, per cent

	GDP	Labour	Capital	Labour productivity	Weighted inputs	Weighted total factor productivity
1924–37	2·2	1·5	1·7	0·7	1·5	0·7
1951–64	2·9	0·0	2·8	2·9	0·7	2·2
1964–73	2·7	−0·5	4·0	3·2	0·7	2·0
1973–80	0·6	−0·1	2·9	0·7	0·5	0·1

Another calculation splits the period 1951–73 into five phases, and distinguished between a gross and a net capital input:[249]

Table 7·42:   Annual growth rate of total factor productivity

	Gross capital	Net capital
1951–55	1·8	1·6
1955–60	2·1	1·7
1960–4	2·5	2·3
1964–8	2·5	2·4
1968–73	2·2	2·2

These rates confirm the impression given by other indicators that, measured by earlier phases, even by the relatively expansionary inter-war period, the three decades 1950–80 were remarkably successful in achieving growth in the total domestic product. It was on this foundation that much of the improvement in economic welfare and social amelioration could be erected. Coupled with the fact of almost full employment, it should have given those years the character of an era of success, a golden age. To some extent it did; but widespread misgivings remained. They were largely connected with the fact that other, comparable economies achieved much faster growth and were able to provide

[248] Wright, *Britain*, p. 26; *National Income and Expenditure*.
[249] A. Matthews, Feinstein and Odling-Smee, p. 208.

more of the economic goods to their people than the British. Comparisons may be invidious, but looking at their example, the impression is strong that Britain could have done very much better than she did.

Whether measured as a growth rate per head, per worker or consumer, or a growth rate overall, the abysmal relative performance of the United Kingdom stands out from Table 7·43 (overleaf).[250] Other, smaller advanced countries of Europe showed rates similar to those of the larger economies listed here. There was, in fact no advanced country anywhere with a record as poor as the British, except for the American in some phases; or, putting it differently, a rate of economic growth similar to that of the rest of the advanced world would have almost doubled the standard of living that obtained in the UK in the 1970s and would have put Britain at the level of the richest countries in Europe, Sweden and Switzerland.

Failure of labour productivity to grow adequately is likely to be connected with inadequate provision of capital.

Physical investment in industry is a necessity of technical and even of social progress; new techniques of production, new commodities and changing tastes of consumers require new equipment. Hence it is difficult to achieve a high rate of technical advance without a high level of investment. Conversely, a high level of investment tends to stimulate technical progress since it gives rise to increased opportunities to introduce improved techniques and to experiment with new ideas. In short, a high level of investment and rapid technical progress go hand in hand and it is not practicable to answer the question what would happen to one in the absence of the other.

It is a more useful approach to regard technical progress and investment as different aspects of the same process, namely the application of new ideas to industry and the adaptation of industry to a changing environment.

All new methods require investment outlays before they can be utilized, irrespective of whether they are more mechanized or not. . . . The relevant concept is gross investment; all investment expenditures increase productivity, either by bringing the capital stock up to date or by increasing the degree of mechanization.[251]

Of course, there is no precise correlation between productivity increases and investment, for some investment may be misplaced; there are periods and industries in which a high incremental capital/output ratio must prevail, and some 'investment', like technical education, may not appear in any official statistics at all. Moreover, productivity increases come about partly by more intensive or more intelligent use of existing equipment, by smoother organization, by more rapid adaptations to market demands or the use of different raw material inputs. Yet, on the whole, it is only by investment that new methods of production can be introduced; and given a similar structure of industry and

[250] Floud and McCloskey, vol. 2, p. 376; *UN Monthly Bulletin of Statistics*; Matthews, Feinstein and Odling-Smee, p. 31.

[251] Tibor Barna, *Investment and Growth Policies in British Industrial Firms* (Cambridge, 1962), p. 1; W. E. G. Salter, *Productivity and Technical Change* (Cambridge, 1966), p. 145. For obvious technical reasons, there was no correlation *as between industries* between investment and speed of productivity growth. R. J. Nicholson, 'Capital Stock, Employment and Output in British Industry 1948–1964', *Yorkshire Bulletin*, 18/2 (1966), p. 83; also W. B. Reddaway and A. D. Smith, 'Progress in British Manufacturing Industries in the Period 1948–1954', *Econ. J.*, 70/277 (1960).

Table 7·43: Annual growth rates, percent

| | Real Domestic product | | | | | | | Output per person-hour in manufacturing | | | | GDP per man-year |
	1950–5	1955–60	1960–4	1964–9	1969–73	1970–80	1963–73	1973–76	1976–79		1951–73
UK	2·9	2·5	3·4	2·5	2·8	1·9	4·5	1·3	1·2		2·4
France	4·4	4·8	6·0	5·9	6·1	3·6	6·7	3·9	3·9		4·4
Germany	9·1	6·4	5·1	4·6	4·5	2·8	5·7	4·5	3·7		4·8
Italy	6·3*	5·4	5·5	5·6	4·1	3·0	7·0	2·3	3·0		5·5
Japan	7·1	9·0	11·7	10·9	9·3	4·9	11·2	2·0	7·7		7·9
USA	4·2	2·4	4·4	4·3	3·4	3·0	3·7	3·4	2·1		2·3

* 1952–55

a similar stage of technology, the country with a higher investment rate will cash in more on technical advance, while the country whose investment plans are brusquely cut by decisions originating outside industry, will find it particularly difficult to gain the full advantages of any new technology.[252]

The provision of capital, though difficult to measure, did indeed bear a strong correlation to annual growth in output. Japan, the fastest grower, did invest the highest proportion of her national income. Britain and the USA, the slowest, invested the least; and other countries ranged between these extremes.[253] (See Table 7.44.)

Table 7·44: Investment as a proportion of GNP

| | Gross domestic investment 1950–60, % GNP | Fixed capital less residential | | Gross domestic investment 1980, % GNP |
		1956–63 % GNP	Rate of growth of stock per man-hour 1950–76	
UK	15·4	6·9	4·2	18·3
France	19·1	12·1	5·7	21·8
Germany	24·0	14·7	6·4	22·4
Italy	20·8	13·7	(5·6)*	20·2
Japan	—	21·4	8·7	31·9
USA	—	9·7	3·4	16·8

* Gross Stocks only.

Absolute quantities of capital equipment per worker in manufacturing are equally clearly related to output and their growth is related to the growth of output.[254] (See Table 7.45.)

Table 7·45: Gross fixed capital formation per head of employed labour in manufacturing ($)

	1960	1965	1970	1975
UK	334	460	604	1006
France	—	905	1439	2682
Germany	—	—	—	1707 (1974)
Italy	332	367	751	1469 (1974)
Japan	492	760	1317	1768
USA	—	1675	2145	2947

[252] This phenomenon is also well known in historical instances, e.g. P. Temin, 'The Relative Decline of the British Steel Industry, 1880–1913', in H. Rosovsky (ed.), *Indusrialization in Two Systems: Essays in Honour of Alexander Gershenkron* (New York, 1966). Also Kenneth Hilton, review of Beckerman, in *Bankers Magazine*, 203/1 (1967); T. P. Hill, 'Growth and Investment in International Comparison', *Econ. J.,* 74/294 (1964); and the general tenor of Richard E. Caves and Associates, *Britain's Economic Prospects* (Washington, DC, 1968).

[253] Angus Maddison, *Economic Growth in the West*, pp. 76, 81; and 'The Long-Run Dynamics of Productivity Growth', in Wilfred Beckerman (ed.) *Slow Growth in Britain* (Oxford, 1979), p. 203; OECD, *National Accounts*; J. Carrington and G. Edwards, *Financing Industrial Investment* (1978), p. 72.

[254] Frank Blackaby (ed.), *De-Industrialisation* (1978), p. 247.

The United Kingdom showed both a slow growth and a low investment rate. In productive industry, the British capital equipment became particularly dangerously antiquated. By the end of 1961, it was calculated, 60% of the buildings and 38% of plant and machinery in manufacturing and construction dated from before 1948. In some industries the proportion was much higher: 50% of the plant and machinery of the metal-using industries, 39% in textiles and 43% in paper and printing was built in 1947 or earlier. Similarly, 32% of all fixed capital in mining and quarrying, 78% of railway capital, 87% of docks and harbours and 71% of the capital sunk in roads, dated from before 1948.[255]

Much ingenuity has been shown in recent economic literature, beginning with Solow's seminal essay,[256] in the exploration of the relationships between investment, technology and productivity changes in advanced economies. As far as concrete observation was concerned, two main phenomena have emerged in recent years in Britain and elsewhere.[257] The first is that the post-war increases in output were larger than the increases in the inputs of capital, labour and other factors. The second is that this 'extra' was the larger, the larger the addition to capital and the higher the growth rate, so that it grew more than proportionally with investment: 'there is ... clear evidence that the residual is correlated with the growth rate'.[258]

Neither of these observations should occasion much surprise. The first confirms that one kind of technological progress consists precisely in the creation of increased output per unit of capital-and-labour input. The second confirms that it is only by re-equipment and by investment in new methods, new organizations and new locations that this 'residual' can be created. Even with a similar technology, there are economies of scale in individual enterprises, which fast-growing economies reach more quickly.[259]

---

[255] G. A. Dean, 'The Stock of Fixed Capital in the United Kingdom in 1961', *J. R. Stat. S.*, 127/3, Series A (1964), pp. 338–9, 343.

[256] R. Solow, 'Technical Change and the Aggregate Production Function', *Rev. of Econ. and Statistics*, 39/3 (1957). Also see Solow, 'Investment and Technological Progress', *Mathematical Methods in Social Science 1959* (Stanford, 1960), and literature quoted in J. C. R. Dow, *The Management of the British Economy 1945–1960* (Cambridge, 1965), p. 394; B. R. Williams, 'Investment and Technology in Growth', *Manchester School*, 32/1 (1964); P. A. David and Th. van der Klundert, 'Biased Efficiency, Growth and Capital-Labour Substitution in the US, 1899–1960', *Amer. Econ. Rev.*, 55/3 (1965); National Bureau of Economic Research, *Output, Input and Productivity Measurement* (Princeton, 1961).

[257] B. Williams, 'Research, Development and Economic Growth in the United Kingdom', *International Social Science Journal*, 18/3 (1966); United Nations, Economic Commission for Europe, *Some Factors in Economic Growth in Europe during the 1950s* (Geneva, 1964).

[258] W. Beckerman and Associates, *The British Economy in 1975* (Cambridge, 1965), p. 42, and Table 1·12 on p. 41. Also pp. 256–7. Cf. also T. P. Hill, 'Growth and Investment According to International Comparison', *Econ. J.*, 74/294 (1964).

[259] One recent study of the comparative growth of Britain and Germany attributes more of the difference to economies of scale than to technology – but the latter ('advance in knowledge') is an artificial and quite arbitrary figure, derived from the experience of the USA, and is in this context quite indefensible.

Sources of Growth, Annual growth rates, %

	UK	W. Germany
Input of factors: Labour	0·35	0·94
Capital	0·80	1·57
Due to factor inputs	1·15	2·51

The close relationship between faster growth of output and faster growth of productivity applies essentially to manufacturing. In a comparison of the growth rates of different industries in Britain in 1924–63, Salter showed that the correlation coefficient of the rise of output with the rise of output per head was +0·81 for the years 1924–50 and +0·69 for 1954–63. The 'fit' was better for the faster than the slower growing industries.[260] This relationship, sometimes known as 'Verdoorn's Law', showed up less clearly in the more turbulent years after 1966, but by no means disappeared altogether.[261] It has no significance in non-manufacturing sectors, other than possibly agriculture, but there is widespread agreement that in economies like the British it is manufacturing that has to supply the mainspring of growth.

Beside inadequate investment, poor management and poor industrial skills have also been blamed for the low rate of British economic growth. In particular, the amateurism and lack of technical understanding of British directors and managers, their bias towards finance rather than production, their conservative attitude to practical training, to changing their firms, to risk taking and competition[262] have been held responsible for many of Britain's economic ills. No doubt, much of this criticism is justified, e.g. in the motor industry. Yet these alleged failings did not apparently prevent British industry from performing magnificently in wartime, nor did they prevent British banks and other service industries from maintaining their world lead, nor yet all British industry from being more productive, even if slower growing, than the Continent for many years after the war. It would be fairer to state that in view of the repeated discouragement and actual penalty received by enterprise and investment at the hands of Government economic policy since 1947, the caution of British industrialists is perhaps not entirely surprising.[263] Certainly, it is in the Civil service that scientists and technologists have been severely discriminated against.[264]

Labour, similarly, is said to have been too traditional in its training and the trade unions to have been more restrictive in relation to technical progress than those of other countries. Both are justifiable observations, and not even the

Other causes:	Advance of knowledge	0·76	0·76
	Contraction of agriculture and self-employment	0·09	0·66
	Economies of scale	0·43	1·25
	Other	0·16	0·21
Due to other causes		1·12	2·88
Total observed growth in National Income		2·27	5·39

Edward Dennison, *Why Growth Rates Differ* (1968).

[260] Salter, *Productivity*, pp. 82, 123, 206–7.

[261] P. J. Verdoorn, 'Verdoorn's Law in Retrospect: A Comment', *Econ. J.*, 90/2, 1980: A. P. Thirlwall, 'Another Interpretation of Verdoorn's Law, *ibid.*; Nicholas Kaldor, *Causes of the Slow Economic Growth of the United Kingdom* (Cambridge, 1966), p. 25; P. Stoneman, 'Kaldor's Law and British Economic Growth 1800–1970', *Warwick Economic Research Papers* No. 93 (1976).

[262] E.g. Richard E. Caves, 'Market Organization, Performance and Public Policy', in *idem, Britain's Economic Prospects* (1968), pp. 301–5; Roger Betts, 'Characteristics of British Company Directors', *Journal of Management Studies*, 4, 1967.

[263] Pollard, *Wasting*, pp. 102–6. But see Correlli Barnett, *Audit of War* (1986).

[264] Select Committee on Science and Technology, *2nd Report* (1969), pp. xxviii–xxxii, 263–5.

extensive efforts following the Industrial Training Act of 1973[265] could modernize some of the more antique apprenticeship schemes. Yet here, too, the experience under 30 years of Government economic policy may seem an adequate explanation for the stance of trade union leaders.[266]

[265] Ian Jones, 'The New Training Initiative – An Evolution' *Nat. Inst. Econ. Rev.,* 99, Feb. 1982, pp. 68–70; Treasury and Department of Industry, *An Approach to Industrial Strategy,* Cmnd. 6315 (1975), p. 5.

[266] Pollard, pp. 102–6.

8

Trade and Finance in Transformation

1 Trade and the Balance of Payments

The traditional British balance of payments, in which exports of manufactured goods and services, together with incomes from earlier foreign investments, were large enough to pay for all necessary imports of food and raw materials as well as manufactures, and even leave a margin for investment abroad, was disturbed, as we have seen, in the immediate post-war years 1945–50. In one sense, Britain never returned to a comfortable position of balancing her international accounts. Until the oil flow of the late 1970s dramatically reversed Britain's fortunes, the economy suffered from a persistent tendency to import more than could be paid for or, in other words, to run a balance of payments deficit.

In consequence, a large part of the Government's economic policies was devoted, year by year, to rectifying this apparent underlying unbalance and since, as we shall see,[1] its policy measures gravely damaged Britain's productive capacity, while it was the very failure in productivity which in turn lay behind the balance of payments deficit, a vicious circle was set up which was at the very heart of Britain's disappointing economic performance since the war. Foreign trade and payments thus occupied a key role in the fortunes of the British economy after 1950.

One of the outstanding characteristics of that period was the failure of Britain to maintain the share of her exports in world markets. Her share of manufactured exports fell dramatically from 25·4% in 1950 to 16·2% in 1961, 10·8% in 1970 and 8·8% in 1981.[2] Significantly, the expansion of foreign exports at the expense of the British was fastest in the boom; in the depressed 1970s, British exports hardly lost any ground at all.

Britain's poor export performance was not due, as it had been in the 1920s, to her concentration on stagnant, rather than on growth industries: on the contrary, her switch to new industries had been very successful, and in the post-war years Britain had a higher share of trade in the expanding industries than any of her leading competitors, except Germany.[3] Her area pattern, it is true, was slightly less favourable, since traditionally Britain was geared to supplying the underdeveloped areas of the world which grew more slowly in these years,

---

[1] Chapter 9 below.
[2] London and Cambridge Economic Service, *Key Statistics,* 1966, Table N; *Nat. Inst. Econ. Rev.*
[3] M. Panic and T. Seward, 'The Problem of UK Exports', *Bull. Oxf. Inst. Stat.,* 28/1 (1966), p. 26; also H. Tyszynski, 'World Trade in Manufactured Commodities, 1899–1950', *Manchester School,* 19/3 (1951); S. Spiegelglass, 'World Export of Manufactures, 1956 vs. 1937', *ibid* 27/2 (1959); PEP, *Growth in the British Economy* (1960), p. 166.

rather than the European market which grew fastest,[4] but against this it may be held that Japan, the most successful exporter, had an even less favourable area distribution from a growth point of view to begin with. Moreover, by the end of our period a significant switch in the direction of exports had taken place. The share of exports to the expanding EEC market jumped from 26·7% in 1968 to 35·6% in 1976 and 43·4% in 1980, and the share going to the oil producing nations from 5·7% to 12·4% and 10·1% in the same years. By contrast, the share going to the rest of the less developed world and the centrally planned economies fell from 22·6% to 16·6% and 15·5%.[5] What was significant was that Britain's exports did substantially less well than her competitors' in each main market separately. There may, perhaps, also have been a failure in salesmanship, though this is difficult to prove, and is in any case a part of economic efficiency.

The basic causes of the lag in exports are not in any doubt. There was, first, the inability to deliver at the right quality and on time.[6] Secondly, there was the change in prices. Compared with the price level of all world imports, UK export - prices rose, i.e. deteriorated competitively, by 14·5% in 1953–63; compared with total import prices into the Common Market, they rose 15.5% more; and compared with other imports into the USA, their excess was 22·9%. Only US export prices rose to the same extent as the British.[7]

The reason for both these factors was the same: exports were affected by the relative decline in British productivity, or the rise in real costs, relative to those of the chief competitors which tended to price British goods out of the competitive world markets. Nevertheless, the main lines of British Government policy were to have a succession of incomes restraints and devaluations, rather than efforts to raise productivity; in other words, they were attempts to make prices reflect the relative impoverishment of Britain, rather than to remedy the causes of that impoverishment, and they may thereby even have made matters worse, for there is some evidence of a 'positive feedback from growing product inferiority, through devaluation, to increased product inferiority'.[8] Also, in a weak economy, efforts to lower the exchange rate may get out of control, as in 1976.

In 1967 Britain devalued the pound sterling from $2·80 to $2·40 or by 14·3% after the Government had attempted to hold the pound to its parity, at increasing cost to the economy,[9] in the preceding years. The result, however, was not a

[4] S. J. Wells, *Trade Policies for Britain. A Study in Alternatives* (1966), p. 127.

[5] Peter Maunder (ed.), *The British Economy in the 1970's* (1980), p. 250; *United Kingdom; Balance of Payments;* K. Williams, J. Williams, D. Thomas, *Why are the British Bad at Manufacturing?* (1983), pp. 112 ff.

[6] E.g. Lawrence A. Krause, 'British Trade Performance', in Richard E. Caves (ed.), *Britain's Economic Prospects* (1968), pp. 218–26; D. K. Stout (NEDO), *International Price Competitiveness, Non-Price Factors and Export Performance* (1977); M. J. Brech and D. K. Stout, 'The Rate of Exchange and Non-Price Competitiveness', *Oxf. Econ. P.* 33, Supplement, 1981, pp. 268–81; Michael Posner and Andrew Steer, 'Price Competitiveness and the Performance of Manufacturing Industry', in Frank Blackaby (ed.), *De-Industrialisation* (1978); pp. 294–300 above.

[7] H. B. Junz and R. R. Rhomberg, 'Prices and Export Performance of Industrial Countries, 1953–1963', IMF *Staff Papers*, 12/2 (1965), pp. 235 *passim.*

[8] Brech and Stour, 'Rate of Exchange', pp. 278–9. Also, see pp. 366–7.

[9] W. Beckerman (ed.), *The Labour Government's Economic Record: 1964–1970* (1972), especially the introductory essay by Andrew Graham and Wilfred Beckerman; B. Gould, J. Mills and S. Stewart, *Monetarism or Prosperity?* (1981), pp. 85–7; H. Brandon, *In the Red: the Struggle for Sterling 64/66* (1966).

simple return to more competitive British export prices and thus to an improved payments balance. At first, exports declined not only in value terms, as might be expected: there was even a decline in volume and a lengthening of delivery dates to certain key foreign markets.[10] In due course, there was indeed a substantial improvement in the balance of payments in 1969–70, but significantly, it was much more marked among 'invisibles', that is to say in services, than among commodities.[11] As far as goods were concerned, in practice, exporters did not lower their foreign prices to the full amount of the devaluation but absorbed some of the gap in higher unit profits and lower sales, while importers, similarly, did not pass on all the price increases. Home prices then began at once to rise until they had returned to something like their former parity with prices abroad.[12]

After the collapse of the Bretton Woods system in 1971, sterling exchange rates were allowed to float from July 1972, and in those conditions the pound sterling drifted down steadily, more or less in line with British productivity and comparative prices, from 115·5% in 1967 (1975 = 100) to 66·1 in 1976. 'Export competitiveness' thus remained stable in 1968–77, fluctuating only gently between a maximum of 104·1 (1972) (at 1970 = 100) and a minimum of 94·3 (1976); thereafter relative export prices rose sharply, from 101·8 in 1977 (1975 = 100) to 134·6 in the last quarter of 1980.[13] It will be noticed that while there was no obvious association on a year-to-year basis between price 'competitiveness' and export performance, since quality, delivery and other non-price effects played an important part, in very broad outline they did agree: Britain's losses of markets *c*. 1950–70 coincided with loss of competitiveness, while in the 1970s both indices tended to stabilize, though unit values of exports of manufactures rose by 253% in the UK, but by only 193% in the six leading industrial nations, giving the other five, on average, a price advantage of 21% over the United Kingdom in 1980, compared with 1970.[14] The hardening of the pound after 1978 to reach an exchange rate value by the end of 1980 30% higher than in 1976 was made possible by the oil flow from the North Sea, which rose from almost nothing in 1975 to add *c*. £8·5 b. a year to the current balance in 1979–80.[15]

[10] R. L. Mayor, 'The Competitiveness of British Exports Since Devaluation', *Nat. Inst. Econ. Rev.*, 48 (1969), pp. 31–4.

[11] According to one estimate, of the £425m improvement in the balance of payments by 1970, £295m was due to the invisible balance and only £130m to visible trade. Nat. Inst. of Economic and Social Research, 'The Effects of the Devaluation of 1967 on the Balance of Payments', *Econ. J.*, 82, Special Issue (March 1972); G. D. N. Worswick, 'Trade and Payments', in Sir Alec Cairncross (ed.), *Britain's Economic Problems Reconsidered* (1971), p. 87. In services themselves, the British share of world transactions was also falling, but not as fast: J. R. Sargent, 'UK Performance in Services', and T. M. Rybczynski, 'Comment', in Blackaby, *De-Industrialisation*.

[12] W. Robinson, T. R. Webb and M. A. Townsend, 'The Influence of Exchange Rate Changes on Prices. A Study of 18 Industrial Countries', *Economica*, 46/181 (1979); J. Odling-Smee and Nicholas Hartley, *Some Effects of Exchange Rate Changes* (Government Economic Service Working Paper No. 2, 1978).

[13] Michael Posner (ed.), *Demand Management* (1978), pp. 88, 105; *Nat. Inst. Econ. Rev.*

[14] *Nat. Inst. Econ. Rev.*

[15] L. P. Tempest and R. J. Walton, 'North Sea Oil and Gas in the UK Balance of Payments since 1970', *B. of Eng. Qtly. Bull.*, 19 (1979), pp. 383–4; Graham Hacche and John Townend, 'Exchange Rate and Monetary Policy: Modelling Sterling's Effective Exchange Rate 1972–1980', *Oxf. Econ.* p. 33, Supplement (1981).

As in other countries, exports grew faster than output, so that the share of exports in final total expenditure continued to expand, rising in absolute volume (at 1975 prices) from £13·1 b. in 1960 to £33·3 b. in 1980, or by 154%, and as a proportion of total final expenditure exports increased from 14·9% in 1960 to 18·2% in 1970 and 22·5% in 1980. This did represent some measure of success of the export industries and services, but essentially these figures show the growing integration of the world economy, particularly among the advanced countries, since imports grew at a comparable pace. They rose from £15·8 b. to £34·1 b. at constant prices of 1975, or by 115% and as a proportion of total final expenditure, from 18·0% to 20·1% and 23·1% in the same years.

All advanced countries were in fact returning to the development pattern of the pre-1914 era, when their mutual trade had increased faster than their output. Trade among the developed nations formed a growing share of this expansion, and consisted increasingly of similar, mainly manufactured, goods crossing the frontier in both directions. This could be associated with the 'variety hypothesis', i.e. the assumption that with rising incomes, consumers were prepared to pay higher transport charges in order to have a wider variety of choice of commodities.[16] Among exports, engineering products and chemicals continued to increase while textiles, metals and basic materials declined, oil more than making up by 1980 the decline of coal among 'fuels' in 1955–75. In imports there was a more remarkable switch still, from food, beverages and tobacco to finished manufactures which increased their share from 5·1% to 35·6%.[17] The frightening import penetration, threatening some of Britain's key industries,[18] accelerated at the end of the period.

It is easy to see that given an income elasticity of demand of 2 or 3 and a marginal 'propensity to import' of 0·30 or over for manufactures, almost the whole of additional incomes will be spent on imports.[19] When combined with a low export elasticity for British goods, Britain faced an inevitably increasing adverse trade gap that no manipulation of exchange rates could cure, as soon as she went in for economic growth bringing rising incomes.[20] In those terms, Britain's balance of payments difficulties could be presented as being no one's fault, but the result of unfortunate 'elasticities'.

As a matter of fact, however, elasticities for British exports have been shown to have been much higher, around two, and thus neither dissimilar from the import elasticities, nor from the export elasticities of other countries.[21] But even if they were not, even if a high propensity to import were peculiarly adverse in Britain, this would be 'not so much an explanation as a reformulation of the

[16] T. Barker, 'A Priori Restrictions on Income and Price Elasticities' (1975), quoted by Jim Hibberd and Simon Wren-Lewis, *A Study of UK Imports of Manufactures* (Government Economic Service Working Paper No. 6, 1978), p. 10.

[17] A. R. Prest and D. J. Coppock, *The UK Economy* (1978), p. 127; *Overseas Trade Statistics.*

[18] Pp. 242–3 above.

[19] Hibberd and Wren-Lewis, p. 10; A. D. Morgan, 'Imports of Manufactures into the UK and other Industrial Countries, 1955–69', *Nat. Inst. Econ. Rev.*, 56 (1971).

[20] A. P. Thirlwall, 'The UK's Economic Problem: A Balance-of-Payments Constraint?', *National Westminster Bank Quarterly Review* (Feb. 1978), pp. 24–32; J. J. Hughes and A. P. Thirlwall, 'Trends and Cycles in Import Penetration in the UK', *Oxf. Bull. Econ. Stat.*, 39 (1977), pp. 301–17; C. J. F. Brown and T. D. Sheriff, 'Background Paper', in Blackaby, *De-Industrialisation*, p. 259.

[21] R. M. Stern, J. Francis, B. Schumacher, *Price Elasticities in International Trade* (1976); Gould, Mills and Stewart, p. 91.

problem'.[22] These elasticities were not God-given, but the result of real factors, above all the growing inability of Britain to produce competitively, particularly in booms.[23] The emphasis on elasticities instead of the real factors, illustrates the growing tendency of modern economics to objectify ratios that are by their nature tenuous, temporary and derived. Had Britain been able, say, to produce cars as cheaply and as well as Japan, she would have found her markets at home and abroad just as elastic as the Japanese car makers. In periods of restriction, with output at less than capacity, British costs were particularly adverse.[24]

The NEDC Inquiry of 1965 investigated in detail the general rise of imports in 1954–64, and the sharp rise in 1962–4, of eight groups of manufacturers. In three cases (chemicals, textiles, especially man-made fibres, and electrical household goods), shortage of capacity was given as the main reason; in three others, it was given as one of the main reasons (paper and board, iron and steel, building materials); and in the remaining two (engineering products, motor vehicles) performance and consumer preference were put to the fore.[25] Once again in the 1960s it was the shortage of machine-tool capacity which imperilled all hopes of faster growth, and its inadequacy was explained by the low and irregular demand it had met in the past.[26] Moreover, the progressive deterioration of British technical competitiveness meant that at each crisis, the dependence on imports increased and when the tide receded, left them at a higher level than before. This 'ratchet effect' was noted among all advanced countries, but in the United Kingdom it was particularly powerful in the case of machinery and other capital goods.

One method of dealing with the threat to home industry by foreign imports was the raising of tariff barriers. As early as October 1964, the Labour Government had attempted to correct the threatened adverse trade balance by a so-called 'import surcharge', a thinly disguised tariff of 15%; an export rebate, involving a refund of certain indirect taxes, amounting to about 2% on exports, also became operative from 1964. The former, if not both, were almost certainly in breach of the international GATT agreements and they were repealed in 1966 and 1968 respectively. They were followed by an 'import deposit' scheme in November 1968, penalizing importers by making them deposit with the Government for six months a sum equal to half the value of the imports. This scheme never had much effect, and after being gradually reduced in amount, was ended in December 1970.

From the mid-1970s on, protection was demanded also by economists such as the Cambridge Economic Policy Group. The cry to 'buy British' was taken up in various quarters, and attempts were made to negotiate limitations of

[22] Gould, Mills and Stewart, p. 91.

[23] W. A. Eltis, 'Economic Growth and the British Balance of Payments', in D. H. Aldcroft and Peter Fearon (eds.), *Economic Growth in Twentieth-Century Britain* (1969), pp. 197–9. See also Youngson, *Britain's Economic Growth 1920–1966* (1967), pp. 232–5; J. R. Parkinson, 'The Progress of United Kingdom Exports', *Scot. J. Pol. Econ.*, 13/1 (1966); M. FG. Scott, *A Study of United Kingdom Imports* (Cambridge, 1963); Lynden Moore, 'Factors Affecting Demand for British Exports', *Bull. Oxf. Inst. Stat.*, 26/4 (1964), p. 347.

[24] W. A. H. Godley and J. R. Shepherd, 'Long-Term Growth and Short-Term Policy', *Nat. Inst. Econ. Rev.*, 29 (1964).

[25] *Loc. cit.*, paras. 19, 26, 34, 48–50, 58, 61, 77–9, 82.

[26] E. W. Evans, 'Some Problems of Growth in the Machine Tool Industry', *Yorkshire Bulletin*, 18/1 (1966), pp. 43, 47–8.

imports such as Hongkong textiles and Japanese cars,[27] since international agreements inhibited direct protectionist policies. As the slump spread throughout the advanced world from 1979 on, the practices of hidden subsidies, as for steel, and disguised protection were taken up by one nation after another, an echo, albeit a very soft one, of the reactions to the slump of the 1930s.

The returns from property, etc., abroad showed an increasing trend in monetary terms, though they declined in real terms. The other 'invisibles', however, showed a sad decline from their former importance in Britain's balance of payments. Civil aviation showed a small surplus year by year, but shipping, once a very large net earner of foreign currency, was a net loser by the 1960s. Much of this was due to a negative balance on tankers, some of it also to the growing competition from Third World countries and to flags of convenience. The Merchant Shipping Act of 1974 permitted some retaliation against the latter and by 1980 the balance was positive again. Travel and private transfer were negative items in the 1960s, but after 1968 they became increasingly net earners, achieving a surplus of around £1,000 million a year in the late 1970s.

Only financial and other services, the work of the City of London, were positive throughout, and if it is borne in mind that the official statistics may slightly under-state the rise in these earnings,[28] these may have kept pace with prices and thus kept their real value. The growth of international banking services from the late 1950s onward, discussed in section 3 of this chapter, and in which London played a leading part, contributed to this buoyant increase. Overall, the earning power of invisibles held up well in international competition. Their net surplus could pay for 6–8% of total imports at the beginning of our period, and 8–10% at its end.

Criss-crossing the changes in relative prices caused by currency alterations, there were significant changes also in the terms of trade, i.e. the world prices of goods bought and sold by the UK. We have seen that an adverse movement in the terms of trade hampered the recovery in the years 1945–50, but thereafter their improvement aided the British balance of payments. It was partly the end of this favourable shift which made the devaluation of 1967 necessary, and by the late 1970s the terms were back at the low levels of the Korean War,[29] adding to the difficulties of that decade (see Table 8.1).

It is time now to consider the actual trade balance and some aspects of the balance of payments in the decades 1950–1980 (Table 8·2).[30] Two features stand out at once. One is the wide margin of fluctuations from year to year in the private series. The other is the basic stability in the relationships nonetheless, with commodity trade showing a substantial deficit in most years, invisibles showing a substantial surplus, and net Government transactions representing a large and increasing negative item. That stability is an *ex-post* result, having

[27] Peter Maunder, 'International Trade' in *idem, British Economy,* pp. 256–8.

[28] A. E. Holmans, 'Invisible Earnings', *Scot. J. Pol. Econ.,* 13/1 (1966), pp. 56–7. Also, British National Export Council (William M. Clarke, Director of the Study), *Britain's Invisible Earnings* (1967); F. N. Burton and P. Galambos, 'The Role of Invisible Trade in the United Kingdom's Balance of Payments, 1952–1966', *National Provincial Bank Review,* 82 (1968); Peter Maunder, 'International Trade', pp. 260–77; *The Times,* 4 August 1982.

[29] Sir Alec Cairncross, 'The Postwar Years 1945–77', in R. Floud and D. McCloskey (eds.), *The Economic History of Britain since 1700* (Cambridge, 1981), vol. 2, pp. 389–90; *Economic Trends,* Annual Supplement.

[30] *UK Balance of Payments; B. of Eng. Qtly, Bull.*

Table 8·1: Terms of trade (1970 = 100)

1938	98
1950	83
1955	82
1960	93
1965	98
1970	100
1975	81
1980	84

Table 8·2: United Kingdom current balance of payments 1950–80 (£m.)

	Private sector					Government sector		
	Exports f.o.b. £b.	Imports f.o.b. £b.	Visible balance of trade	Invisible balance	Total private balance	Services and transfers (net)	Interest profits divid's.	Total current government balance
1950	2·3	2·3	(51)	(+433)*		−136	*	
1951	2·7	3·4	(−689)	(+330)*		−150	*	
1952	2·8	3·0	−279	(+355)*		−61	*	
1953	2·7	2·9	−244	(+398)*		−66	*	
1954	2·8	3·0	−204	(+406)*		−131	*	
1955	3·1	3·4	−313	(+283)*		−138	*	
1956	3·4	3·3	+53	(+309)*		−175	*	
1957	3·5	3·5	−29	(+328)*		144	*	
1958	3·4	3·4	+29	(+285)*		−219	*	
1959	3·5	3·6	−118	(+190)*		−227	*	
1960	3·7	4·1	−408	(+59)*		−283	*	
1961	3·9	4·0	−153	+554	+401	−332	−164	−496
1962	4·0	4·1	−102	+730	+628	−360	−146	−506
1963	4·3	4·4	−80	+719	+639	−382	−133	−515
1964	4·5	5·0	−519	+688	+169	−432	−119	−551
1965	4·8	5·1	−223	+775	+552	−446	−132	−578
1966	5·2	5·3	−66	+783	+717	−470	−156	−626
1967	5·1	5·7	−557	+886	+329	−462	−168	−630
1968	6·3	6·9	−659	+1091	+418	−466	−230	−696
1969	7·1	7·2	−143	+1407	+1046	−467	−324	−791
1970	8·2	8·2	−34	+1612	+1578	−486	−269	−755
1971	9·0	8·9	+190	+1658	+1849	−520	−204	−724
1972	9·4	10·2	−748	+1698	+950	−561	−142	−703
1973	11·9	14·5	−2586	+2573	−13	−769	−199	−968
1974	16·4	21·5	−5351	+3272	−2079	−842	−352	−1194
1975	19·3	22·7	−3333	+3266	−67	−940	−541	−1454
1976	25·2	29·1	−3929	+5151	+1222	−1455	−648	−2103
1977	31·7	34·0	−2248	+4815	+2567	−1839	−733	−2572
1978	35·1	36·6	−1542	+5497	+3955	−2401	−615	−3016
1979	40·7	44·1	−3458	+6028	+2570	−2857	−576	−3433
1980	47·4	46·2	+1178	+5306	+6484	−2623	−655	−3278

* The invisible balance figures contain the negative element for the Government sector interest, profits and dividends which cannot be separated out. Without these, the private invisible balance would show larger positive figures.

been achieved only by dint of deliberate policies to maintain it, some of which were costly in growth and prosperity. The fluctuations underlying these policies will be discussed in chapter 9 below. But the main ratios are real enough. Private current transactions were adequate to keep Britain in balance and even leave a fairly regular surplus for foreign investment, as in former times; in many years the British surplus was as high, or higher, than those of the most successful exporting nations, Germany and Japan. Yet the country was in almost constant balance of payments difficulties. How can this be explained?

There have been two main causes for the pressure on the balance of payments. One has been the sum of overseas capital transactions, or net foreign investment. The other has been the sum of Government activities. Between them they have repeatedly imposed a burden on the British economy beyond its powers to bear. We shall examine them in turn.

The actual annual sums invested abroad may seem large (see Table 8·3)[31] but a substantial proportion of them were derived from retained earnings overseas. Although capital exports have come under attack from time to time as being greater than the economy could afford,[32] their economic case is a strong one. Given a surplus on current account which obtained throughout, and which was maintained until 1959 even when Government expenditure was included, it was in the interest of world trade and prosperity, particularly of less developed countries, to use Britain's trading surplus precisely in this traditional way. Moreover this expenditure was productive and contributed to the growing 'invisible' surpluses on current account.[33]

In concrete terms, many of these investments opened out and developed British markets and supply areas, mainly in the earlier years of the period. In the later years, they represented, in part, the necessary attempts of British firms to establish themselves behind tariff barriers. Private capital abroad, estimated at £3,300 million at the end of the war, rose to around £9,300 million in 1957 and to £11,800 million in 1961 according to one calculation.[34] Capital assets abroad are notoriously difficult to value, and official figures put private long-term investment abroad at £7,855 million at the end of 1962, at £9,600 million at the end of 1966 and at £48,300 million in 1980.[35]

In these totals, portfolio investments showed some increases, but the largest growth was registered in direct investment in non-financial companies, and particularly in oil. According to Revell, these two items grew from £6,080 million

---

[31] *UK Balance of Payments.*

[32] E.g. A. R. Conan, 'The Unsolved Balance of Payments Problem', *Westminster Bank Review* (Nov. 1963), p. 11; David Coates and John Hillard, *The Economic Decline of Modern Britain* (Brighton, 1986), p. 360; F. W. Paish, 'Britain's Foreign Investment: the Post-War Record' (1956), in *Studies in an Inflationary Economy. The United Kingdom 1948–1961* (1962), chapter 9.

[33] W. B. Reddaway *et al.*, *Effects of UK Direct Investment Overseas: Interim Report* (Cambridge, 1967) and *Final Report* (Cambridge, 1968).

[34] Jack Revell, *The Wealth of the Nation. The National Balance Sheet of the United Kingdom, 1957–1961* (Cambridge, 1967), Table 12·3, pp. 268–9, taking 'Private' and 'Direct Investments', less 'Cash and Short-Term Assets' and Bank 'Advances', which still overstates the long-term holdings.

[35] *UK Balance of Payments; B. of Eng. Qtly. Rev.* Also 'An Inventory of UK External Assets and Liabilities: end 1978', *ibid.* 19 (June 1979), pp. 160–5 and Alexander G. Kemp, 'Long Term Capital Movements', *Scot. J. Pol. Econ.*, 13/1 (1966), pp. 143–9.

Table 8·3: UK long-term private foreign investment (£m.)

Average of years	Foreign capital invested in the UK	UK capital invested abroad	Net investment
1958–61	+258	−342	−84
1962–4	+224	−320	−97
1965–7	+313	−376	−63
1968–70	+653	−745	−92
1971–3	+1095	−1341	−246
1974–6	+1935	−1595	+341
1977–9	+3538	−4508	−970
1980	+4646	−6891	−2245

in 1957 to £7,387 million in 1961, or by £325 million a year, and according to the official figures, direct investment rose from £3,755 million in 1962 to £6,880 million in 1970 and £31,700 million in 1980, and oil investment from £1,100 million in 1962 to £2,700 million in 1974 and £7,350 million in 1980. Even more striking was the change in direction. Before 1960 most of British overseas investment went to areas like Canada and Australia, but since then it was made increasingly in Western Europe, both in the Common Market and the EFTA countries as well as the USA. As the return on investment was scarcely higher abroad than at home (7·8% as against 7·6% by 1960–2),[36] it was likely that many of these investments were made to enlarge markets rather than to find profitable outlets for capital.

Within the Sterling Area[37] there were no limitations on foreign investment, apart from the closure of the 'Kuwait gap' in July 1957 through which sterling funds had escaped, but there were restrictions on raising new money in London; in 1966–72 investment in the white Commonwealth Sterling Area countries was however made subject to some restraints. To the outside world, foreign investment was strictly limited through exchange control until 1969, when there was some liberalization. After sterling was allowed to float in 1972 conditions were eased outside the Sterling Area. It is not clear that these restrictions ever had much effect, but it seems that after the liberalization, funds withdrawn from the Sterling Area in 1972–3 were invested outside.[38] Entry into the EEC brought further easements and in the course of 1979 all exchange controls limiting outward investments were removed.

The growth of real overseas long-term assets was in part matched by foreign investment in Britain. Inward investment grew from around 20% of outward capital flows in the early 1950s to 70–80% from the mid-1960s onwards, and in 1961 and 1967 as well as the years after the oil crisis of 1973 the balance was actually positive. The main component of capital imports, was direct investment, particularly by American firms, in subsidiaries to beat the British tariff or to

---

[36] J. H. Dunning, 'Does Foreign Investment Pay', *Moorgate and Wall Street* (Autumn 1964); Wells, pp. 59–60; W. Beckerman and Associates, *The British Economy in 1975* (Cambridge, 1965) pp. 116–19.

[37] See pp. 310–2 below.

[38] J. H. B. Tew, 'Policies Aimed at Improving the Balance of Payments', in F. T. Blackaby (ed.), *British Economic Policy 1960–74* (Cambridge, 1978), pp. 325–37.

form bases for covering British and European markets. American investment in Britain was estimated at $847 million in 1950 and $1,420 million in 1955, of which 80% was in oil and manufacturing; by 1967, it was estimated to have reached $7,000 m. Total private foreign-held capital was estimated at £3,150 million in 1957 and £5,750 million in 1961 by one calculation, and by another to have risen from £3,160 million in 1962 to £7,280 million in 1970 and by an enormous jump to £33,150 million in 1980. The inward investments of the 1970s were boosted by the billions of OPEC funds seeking investment opportunities abroad, by foreign investment in North Sea oil, and by the foreign borrowings of the nationalized industries. The net sum of private long-term capital investment in favour of Britain thus rose in money terms from £5·9 b. in 1962 to £15·1 b. in 1980; but in real terms this represented scarcely any change at all.[39]

American capital introduced into Britain the advantages of American systems of management, as in the building of the Esso Fawley refinery, or American technical know-how, as in the motor and other engineering firms, and the American-owned plants were often much concerned with exports or with import-saving.[40] In the long run, however, these investments burdened the economy with a flow of annual service charges to match the in-payments from British investments abroad.

These sums were swamped in the annual statistics by the growth in the overseas assets and liabilities of the banking and commercial sector, arising largely from the rise of the Euro-currency system, to be discussed below.[41] While these assets rose more than fifty fold from £2–3 bn. in 1962 to £158–60 bn. in 1980, they largely balanced out year by year.

In addition to these private capital transfers, there were also official investments, of which the 'sterling balances' were the most important in the early post-war years. Created first in wartime by the expenditure of British forces in such countries as India and Egypt, they had become almost as large as British investment overseas in the immediate post-war years. After 1950 the total never moved far from the £3,500 million mark: within this total, India, Pakistan, Ceylon and Egypt used up most of their holdings and those of Australia, New Zealand and South Africa also declined, while, by contrast the oil countries of the Middle East, and some Far Eastern areas like Malaysia and Hong Kong, the surplus economies of the sterling area, greatly increased their holdings in London.[42]

The concept of the 'Sterling Area' itself underwent considerable changes.[43] The level of the sterling balances proved that London was still favoured by many countries, mainly those in the Commonwealth, as a place to hold their

[39] *UK Balance of Payments*; Revell, *loc. cit.*; J. McMillan and Bernard Harris, *The American Take-Over of Britain* (1968); *B. of Eng. Qtly. Bull.*

[40] J. H. Dunning, *American Investment in British Manufacturing Industry* (1958), pp. 290–310, and 'US Manufacturing Subsidiaries and Britain's Trade Balance', *District Bank Review*, 115 (1955); and discussion on multinationals, pp. 259–61 above.

[41] P. 336 below.

[42] Beckerman, p. 113; Bank of England, *Quarterly Bulletin*; S. Strange, *The Sterling Problem and the Six* (PEP, European Series No. 4, 1967), Table 6, p. 68. Also see pp. 178–9 above.

[43] C. W. McMahon, *Sterling in the Sixties*; Symposium in *Bull. Oxf. Inst. Stat.*, 21/4 (1959); J. M. Livingstone, *Britain and the World Economy* (Pelican, 1966), chapter 2; David Williams, 'The Evolution of the Sterling System', in C. R. Whittlesley and J. S. G. Wilson (eds.), *Essays in Money and Banking in Honour of R. S. Sayers* (Oxford, 1968).

reserves, and the high and rising interest rates payable in London, a reflection of the increasing weakness of sterling, helped to continue them in their resolve.[44] Meanwhile, the attractions of other markets grew, as sterling's role as an international currency declined with British trade, British shipping and the importance of the London Money Market: by the mid 1960s, well under one-third of world transactions was left to be made in sterling.[45]

Yet even with this diminished responsibility, the burden on the British reserves was great. The sterling balances of almost £4,000 million in the mid-1960s were far larger than the reserves or the annual surplus or deficit of the payments balances, and hung there as a threat. They were a major reason for the costly postponement of devaluation, which nevertheless had to be submitted to in the end, in 1967. Here was a prime example of how the historical burden of Empire and of former economic strength led to particular policies which were bound severely to curtail British prosperity.[46]

The devaluation hit the remaining holders of sterling balances hard in 1967 by diminishing the value of their reserves. Not surprisingly, there followed in 1968 a massive withdrawal of funds from London by the overseas sterling countries in search of safety, which Britain, significantly, could stem only by internationalizing the burden. Under the Basle Group Agreement of that year, 12 central banks together with the Bank for International Settlements extended a credit of $2 billion to Britain, to allow her to meet the drain of these withdrawals and to guarantee the dollar value of a large proportion of the remaining official sterling holdings. In the event, the sterling balances, both official and other, increased again in the following years, and the Agreement was ended in 1974, not before having involved Britain in large compensation payments arising from the loss of value of sterling against the dollar in 1972–4. Thereafter, the sterling balances rose once more, in 1974–5, largely with OPEC funds, though by then the oil prices were expressed in dollars. But they remained a highly volatile element, as soon as the value of sterling was threatened, unless compensated by exceptionally high interest rates in London: thus in 1976 another Basle Agreement was negotiated, but did not have to be activated. Meanwhile the accession of Britain to the EEC increased the pressure on London to relinquish the role of sterling as a reserve currency, for which it no longer had the resources.

A glance at Table 8·2 will show that there was one burden on the external balance of the UK far larger than the two we have considered so far, foreign investment and the constraints imposed by the Sterling Balances: this was the overseas expenditure of the Central Government itself. Year by year, a large and increasing Government deficit wiped out the surpluses achieved by the rest of the economy and kept it in an almost continuous state of crisis. The deficit up to the devaluation of 1967 was, in fact, larger than appears from the table, since in addition to the current items shown here, a substantial and rapidly rising proportion of capital investment, amounting to a net £386 million for the

[44] G. D. A. MacDougall and R. Hutt, 'Imperial Preference: Quantitative Analysis', *Econ. J.*, 64/254 (1954); Wells, pp. 18 ff; G. Arnold, *Economic Cooperation in the Commonwealth* (1967), pp. 57–67.
[45] P. M. Oppenheimer, 'Monetary Movements and the International Position of Sterling', *Scot. J. Pol. Econ.*, 13/1 (1966).
[46] S. Strange, *Sterling and British Policy* (Oxford, 1971); Jim Tomlinson, *British Macroeconomic Policy Since 1940* (1985), pp. 52, 148.

four years 1963–6, was also on Government account. Even omitting these large sums, the net expenditure[47] of Government abroad rose eightfold in monetary terms in this period, and the purely military (net) expenditure within it rose even more sharply from £12 million in 1952 to £313 million in 1966. This item alone, therefore, was sufficient to wreck the delicate balance of payments of the United Kingdom since 1950, and to account for the worsening imbalances, in spite of the progressively improved trading accounts. Whether expenditure of this order of magnitude was wise or justifiable, or whether it contributed to the political strengthening of the United Kingdom, are political questions outside the purview of this book.[48] It may, however, be of interest to compare the Government foreign balances of payments and receipts of nine major countries in 1966[49] (see Table 8·4).

Table 8·4:   Net Governmental foreign balances of payments and receipts

	$ million
USA	− 6,385
UK	− 1,288
Belgium/Luxembourg	− 46
Sweden	− 45
Netherlands	− 42
Italy	− 9
France	− 1
Japan	+ 315
Germany	+ 339

With the exception of the USA, which at least achieved superpower status on the basis of her expenditure, Britain was clearly in a class of her own. Given the unwillingness to impose overseas trading and payments restrictions which might have permitted Britain to incur this kind of expenditure without repeated deflation at home, the real cost-benefit analysis of British foreign policy would have to count the cost of Government activities abroad not merely in the hundreds of millions annually spent, but in the billions annually lost in output and income because of the restrictions made necessary to maintain it.

The deficit on Government transactions continued to grow in money terms after 1967, though it declined in real terms with the reduction in military and other commitments 'East of Suez', but meanwhile Government overseas transactions were swamped by the need of the central monetary authorities to raise large credits, mainly from the IMF and from other central banks, to cover the periodic British balance of payments deficits. Britain became a regular debtor in need of aid on the world's money markets, subject to control and inspection by her foreign creditors, even though her own non-Governmental economic

[47] Gross expenditure rose less, it was the collapse of counterbalancing in-payments which caused the multiplication of the net figure.

[48] For other politically inspired burdens on the British economy, see R. N. Gardner, *Sterling-Dollar Diplomacy* (1956). Also Andrew Gamble, *Britain in Decline* (1985), pp. 110 ff.; Alan Sked, *Britain's Decline* (Oxford 1987), pp. 32–4.

[49] W. A. P. Manser. *Britain in Balance* (1971), p. 31.

transactions left her normally in healthy surplus, and her private citizens were still year by year investing heavily abroad. Even when there were temporary surpluses as in 1969–71, these could not be used fully to expand the economy, but had to be devoted to repaying the foreign loans.

An indication of the sums involved and the yearly fluctuations is provided by Table 8·5.

Table 8·5:   UK balance of payments – official financing, 1964–1980*

	Net transactions with overseas monetary authorities		Foreign currency borrowing		Alloc. of spec. drawing rights £m.	Gold subscr. to IMF £m.	Official reserves** £m.	Total official financing £m.	Out-standing official borrowing abroad end-year† $m.
	IMF £m.	Other £m.	By HM Gov't £m.	By other public bodies £m.					
1964	+357	+216					+122	+695	1,604
1965	+489	+110					−246	+353	3,282
1966	+15	+610††				−44	34	+547	3,542
1967	−339	+895††					+115	+671	4,356
1968	+506	+790					+114	+1410	7,464
1969	−30	−669		+56			−44	−687	5,803
1970	−134	−1100			+171	38	−126	−1287	3,406
1971	−554	−1263		+82	+125		−1636	−3146	1,447
1972	−415	+864			+124		+692	+1265	266
1973				+999			−228	+771	2,982
1974			+644	+1017			−105	+1646	7,092
1975			+423	+387			+655	+1465	8,921
1976	+1018	−34		+1791			+853	+3628	14,160
1977	+1113		+871	+242			−9588	−7302	18,042
1978	−1016		+191	−378			+2329	+1126	15,847
1979	−596			−250	+195		−1059	−1710	14,585
1980	−140		−629	−312	+180		−291	1192	11,991

* *UK Balance of Payments; Bank of Eng. Qtly. Bull.* Plus signs indicate borrowings, minus signs repayments.
** Plus signs mean drawings, minus additions.
† Short and medium term borrowings.
†† Includes transfer of dollar portfolio to reserves.

The British economy thus proceeded in its foreign transactions in heavy lurches and ever-deepening dependence on foreign credits, which in the 1970s involved even the nationalized industries. By 1980 also over £6 billion of UK Government stock was held abroad, almost £4 billion of it outside the central banks.[50] Nevertheless, there was no collapse as in the 1930s. The shocks to the British economy were caught and buffered by a smoothly functioning system of international credit provision created to deal with just such imbalances. To its creation and evolution we must now turn.

[50] *B. of Eng. Qtly. Bull.*, 21/2 (June 1981), pp. 203–5.

2 International Economic Co-operation

Among the institutions devised in the early post-war years to prevent a repetition of the economic warfare of the 1930s[51] was GATT, the General Agreement on Tariffs and Trade. It came into operation at the beginning of 1948, after the more ambitious Havana Charter of 1948 to set up an International Trade Organisation (ITO) had failed to get support, and it offered some hope of limiting obstacles to international trade. Its objective was the lowering of tariffs and other trade barriers and the elimination of discrimination, and one of its main instruments was to be the most-favoured-nation clause.

The great hopes set on it in the beginning were to be largely disappointed. After some initial reductions in tariffs on individual commodities which no country thought vital, it soon found its success diminishing when it attempted to tackle those which members held to be important. It therefore turned, instead, to across-the-board percentage cuts. Some of these were negotiated on a multilateral basis in the 'Kennedy Round' of 1964–7, but they were limited in extent. The 'Tokyo Round', lasting from 1973–9 was even less productive of direct cuts. It did, however, lead to some significant agreements on customs valuation, on the removal of technical barriers and of export subsidies and countervailing duties, all of which could make further concessions easier in the future. Even if not very effective in lowering barriers, GATT has been fairly successful in inhibiting member states from raising them too blatantly. As in the case of the British 'surcharge' of 1964, it lacked the enforcing power to hold its members to the spirit of the agreement when they felt themselves to be under pressure, but it still represented a considerable moral force in that direction. This had become more important in the late 1970s, when mounting unemployment led Britain as well as other major trading countries to 'manage' their foreign trade.[52]

The less developed countries of the world were mainly responsible for assembling the United Nations Conference on Trade and Development (UNCTAD) in 1964 for the purpose of obtaining particularly favourable terms, the right to impose unilateral restrictions, and aid from the richer nations. Some aid has flowed in their direction as a result, though Britain has never reached the target of 1% of its national income to be provided for the poorer countries, as recommended then, nor has any other advanced nation. However, the Integrated Programme for Commodities, agreed to by UNCTAD in 1976, led to the establishment of the first agreement, for natural rubber, in 1979 and in the same year Britain agreed to relieve 17 of the poorest countries of their debt repayments.

Much more significant than these attempts to foster trade on a world-wide basis were the regional agreements which sprang up in Europe. The European Economic Community, or Common Market, deriving from the earlier Coal, Iron and Steel Community among the 'Six' (Germany, France, Belgium, Holland, Italy and Luxemburg), was set up by the Treaty of Rome, signed in 1957. It came into operation in 1958 with a 12-year programme of gradual removal of all barriers to trade among the members and the erection of a unitary tariff to the outside world. In the event, not only were the customs union

---

[51] See chapter 5, section 6 above.
[52] S. A. B. Page, 'Management in International Trade', in R. Major (ed.), *Britain's Trade and Exchange Rate Policy* (1979).

provisions speeded up, but it proved possible to 'harmonize' many other economic activities, from social welfare provisions and agricultural protection to taxation, much faster than most observers had thought possible.[53]

The United Kingdom attempted to gain associate status at the foundation, offering an internal free-trade area without full economic integration, but this was turned down. In the event, the EEC countries made immense economic progress in the years after the signing of the Treaty, although it is open to doubt how far this was as a result of it or how far they merely continued their earlier fast growth.[54] The large and expanding market among the 'Six' not only stimulated trade among the members, but even offered a market to British exporters which, in spite of the increasing tariff discrimination implicit in the Treaty, grew faster and became more important than any other.[55] The temptation to apply for full membership proved irresistible in the United Kingdom, despite many misgivings expressed in various quarters, but two attempts to join, in 1961–3 and in 1966–7, were turned down by French veto.

Meanwhile, after refusing to sign the Rome Treaty, the United Kingdom proceeded with her own proposal of a free-trade area, involving the abolition of tariffs and trading restrictions among the members, but not the harmonization of their tariffs against others, or of any other economic or social policies. In 1959 she was instrumental in setting up the European Free Trade Area, the 'Seven', by the Stockholm Convention. The other members were the three Western Scandinavian countries, Switzerland and Austria, both of whom were reluctant to imperil their status of neutrality by joining the EEC, and, somewhat incongruously, Portugal.[56] Finland became associated with them in 1961. The political and geographical viability of EFTA was much less obvious than that of the EEC. The 15% surcharge on imports imposed by the United Kingdom in 1964 without prior consultation caused grave offence, and it was clear that the United Kingdom and some other members were prepared to jettison EFTA as soon as the British attempts to enter the EEC succeeded. Nevertheless, the internal tariff reductions were kept in line with those of the EEC to advance to full free trade by the end of 1966 instead of 1969, and, given the existence of one trading block, the members found clear advantages in belonging to another block with a population of nearly 100 million, a large proportion of whom enjoyed a very high standard of living.[57] There was some mutual adjustment of trade, some specialization and some investment among the members which possibly might not have come about without EFTA's existence. In the first 10 years 1959–69, intra-EFTA trade rose by 186% (exports f.o.b.) compared with a rise of 108% of imports and 111% of exports from and to non-EFTA countries. Britain's overall export figures, it has been estimated, were 2% higher than they would otherwise have been owing to EFTA.[58]

[53] M. Camps, *Britain and the European Community, 1955–1963* (1964) and *European Unification in the Sixties. From the Veto to the Crisis* (1967); U. Kitzinger, *The Politics and Economics of European Integration* (1962); J. F. Deniau, *The Common Market. Its Structure and Purpose* (1960); Sidney Dell, *Trade Blocs and Common Markets* (1963).

[54] A. Lamfalussy, 'Europe's Progress: Due to Common Market?' *Lloyds Bank Review*, 62 (1961).

[55] S. J. Wells, 'Trade with Europe', *Scot J. Pol. Econ.*, 13/1 (1966).

[56] F. V. Meyer, *The Seven* (1960); EFTA, *A Free Trade Area in Europe* (Geneva, 1966).

[57] *EFTA Trade 1959–1966* (Geneva, 1968); S. J. Wells, 'EFTA – The End of the Transition', *Lloyds Bank Review*, 82 (1966).

[58] M. A. G. van Meerhaege, *International Economic Institutions* (2nd ed., 1971), p. 355; EFTA Secretariat, *The Effects of EFTA on the Economies of the Member States* (Geneva, 1969), p. 162.

Nevertheless, and despite the two earlier rejections, Britain began in 1969 a renewed series of negotiations which ultimately led to her accession to the EEC as from 1 January 1973. With her also joined Denmark and the Irish Republic; Norway, which had also been accepted, withdraw as the result of an adverse referendum. The Six thus became the Nine while only a rump of EFTA remained in being, linked by special treaties in an industrial free-trade system with the EEC.[59] By the Treaty of Accession signed in 1972, Britain became simultaneously a party to EURATOM, and a decision of the Council of Ministers also made her a member of the European Coal and Steel Community.

In the midst of her negotiations for entry, the Community itself attempted to strengthen its bonds by a progressive harmonization of the one major economic sphere still left outside its purview, the monetary sphere. It agreed to a locking of the members' currencies to each other within a much narrower band of variation than had been fixed by the Smithsonian agreement of December 1971 (the 'snake in the tunnel', April 1972) with a view to a complete monetary union by 1980. Britain was unable to keep the weakened pound within the snake for more than a few weeks, and also stayed outside the renewed attempt at fixing the European exchange rates to each other, the European Monetary System (EMS) of 1979.[60] In trade matters, tariffs on industrial goods were progressively adjusted over four years, so that Britain obtained completely free trade with the EEC and a common tariff to the outside world by 1977; the agricultural policies were similarly progressively adjusted,[61] and by 1979 the full adjustment to the Community budget had been achieved.

The effects of joining the Common Market have been much disputed, not least because they are difficult to isolate from the effects of the other major simultaneous jolts suffered by the British economy since 1973. Linking up with the western European economies represented for Britain a major switch from the centuries-old position as the intermediary between the colonial and overseas world on the one hand, and the continent on the other. It meant an end to cheap food, drawn from the extensive agriculture of Australia, New Zealand and the Americas, in favour of dear food, produced by the European peasantry. It also meant a loss of old-established preferences overseas and in consequence a forced diversion of industrial exports and probably also capital exports from their wonted extra-European destinations into the bitterly competitive markets within the EEC. At the same time the highly efficient industries of Western Europe would obtain free access to the British home markets. The immediate effects of all this would undoubtedly be a decline in living standards, a deterioration of the current account balance and possibly also of the capital account balance, with various other associated adverse effects; but it was hoped that these would be more than counterbalanced in the longer run by the faster growth and the dynamic atmosphere of the EEC and the economies of scale which almost 200 million additional consumers would provide. Efficient firms would benefit,

[59] Victoria Curzon, *The Essentials of Economic Integration* (1974), pp. 226 *et seq.*

[60] R. Jenkins, 'European Monetary Union', *Lloyds Bank Review* (Jan. 1978); Michele Fratianni and Theo Peeters, *One Money for Europe* (1978); Dennis Swann, 'The European Community Dimension', in W. P. J. Maunder (ed.), *The British Economy in the 1970s* (1980), pp. 284 ff.

[61] See pp. 233–4 above.

inefficient ones would go to the wall, and this would jog many firms out of their current inefficiency.[62]

In the event, the diversion of trade was less than had been assumed: it seems that most of the adjustment effects had been exhausted by the Six before the British entry, by which time they had raised the share of their mutual trade from one-third in 1958 to one-half. Moreover, even before entry, trade with the EEC had been growing at the expense of trade within the Commonwealth. Nevertheless, while British exports to the EEC had been rising by an average of 12·5% a year in 1969–73 and imports thence by 17·7%, in the years of adjustment to full internal free trade they rose by 25·7% and 28·5% a year respectively. Also, European food prices were rising less fast than world prices, so that here, too, the effects were less than had been feared.[63]

Moreover, internal tariff-free trade within the Community did by no means mean the removal of all trade barriers, as the queues of trucks at all European frontier posts testified, and 'harmonization' was far from perfect.[64] Subsidies and other obstructions, including preferences in public tendering, more or less hidden, persisted. Official complaints about non-tariff barriers numbered 70 in 1970, 114 in 1974 and topped 300 by the end of the decade.[65] VAT rates remained different, and a complex 'destination system' had to be devised to eliminate distortions arising therefrom.[66] There was much illicit traffic across the intra-EEC frontiers to cash in on these anomalies. In some cases, industry erected its own barriers: possibly the best-known case was that of the motor manufacturers, who by the early 1980s were maintaining new car prices in Britain about one-third above prices elsewhere in the EEC.

On the other hand, there were plans to have the corporation tax system of the member countries aligned; the EC law on monopolies was given precedence over the legislation of individual countries, as was the legislation on labelling, design and composition; and in 1977–9 the UK abolished all restrictions on capital movements. As far as movement of labour across the frontiers was concerned, restrictions had been dismantled in the early years of the EEC so that there was no formal discrimination in access to jobs or social security benefits. Yet some disadvantages of the immigrant worker inevitably remained: access to subsidized housing depending on length of residence, knowledge of legal entitlement, the language barrier. Moreover, discrimination on grounds of public health, public order, or within the State service was permitted. By 1976

---

[62] *Britain and the European Communities: An Economic Assessment,* Cmnd. 4289 (1970); *The United Kingdom and the European Communities,* Cmnd. 4715 (1971); Robert L. Pfaltzgraff. Jr, *Britain Faces Europe* (Philadelphia, 1969), chapters 4, 7, 8; (Overseas Development Institute), *Britain, the EEC and the Third World* (New York, 1972); Douglas Evans (ed.), *Destiny or Delusion: Britain and the Common Market* (1971); A. D. Morgan, 'Commercial Policy', in F. T. Blackaby (ed.), *British Economic Policy 1960–74* (Cambridge, 1978).

[63] A. R. Prest and D. J. Coppock, *The UK Economy* (1978), pp. 156–7.

[64] C. C. Twitchett (ed.), *Harmonisation in the EEC* (1980).

[65] Fratianni and Peeters, p. 14; EEC Commission, *Programme of the Commission for 1977* (Brussels, 1977); Alexis P. Jacquemin, 'European Industrial Policy and Competition', in Peter Coffey (ed.), *Economic Policies of the Common Market* (1979); D. L. McLachlan and D. Swann, *Competition Policy in the European Community* (1967), chapters 3 and 4.

[66] Dennis Swann *loc. cit.,* p. 283; Alan R. Prest, 'Fiscal Policy', in Peter Coffey, *op. cit.,* pp. 69–97; A. E. Walsh and John Paxton, *The Structure and Development of the Common Market* (1968), chapter 6.

a start was made on easing the migration of the self-employed by recognizing professional qualifications gained abroad: thus doctors wholly trained within the EEC were allowed to practice anywhere within it from 1977, dentists from 1978 and nurses from 1980.[67]

The EEC had also taken common action on economic relations with the outside world, notably the USA, Japan and the former colonial possessions of its member states, and on political issues, such as the 1975 Helsinki Conference on Security and Co-operation in Europe and on the Arab-Israeli conflict.[68] The impact of this collaboration is difficult to quantify, though there can be no doubt that at least diplomatically, a unit comparable in size with the USA or the Soviet Union must carry more weight than the several member states would do individually.

In the public debate in Britain, however, what appears to have weighed most heavily was the effect of the EC budget, for here the figures are clear-cut and easily intelligible. Here, after an initial period of adjustment, the UK was to take her full share from 1979 onward. The income of the Community is made up of 90% of the proceeds of the common external tariff and of the levies on food imports (the remainder being held back as costs of collection), plus the equivalent of 1% of VAT receipts. Of the expenditure, Britain stood to gain by net inward payments from the Regional Fund, of the order of £60 million in 1975–7 (compared with £500 million spent out of home funds for the same purpose) and by net inward payments to the Social Fund, of a similar order of magnitude. There is also the Investment Bank which loaned Britain about £2 billion in 1973–81. These, and some minor items, were however wholly swamped by the EEC expenditure on agriculture. Ratios in 1978 were as follows:[69]

Agriculture	73·87%
Social sector	4·52%
Regional sector	4·25%

Agriculture had become the tail to wag the EEC dog and it was here, because of her high imports, and her small but efficient agriculture, that Britain stood to pay in much more, and get back far less than her 'fair' share.

As early as 1977, the Treasury had forecast *net* outpayments, by 1980, of £830 million; before long it was clear that, if uncorrected, they would be well over £1,000 million a year by then. The Dublin summit of 1975 had agreed to a 'corrective mechanism' to provide refunds to members paying in more than their share of the budget, but it was of a minor nature only. The main problem remained: only Germany and the UK made net in-payments, and the UK, as one of the poorest members of the Community, felt this imposition to be particularly unjust.

The overall effects of joining the EEC are thus made up of several separate

---

[67] C. C. Twitchett, 'The EEC and European Co-operation', in K. J. Twitchett (ed.), *European Co-operation Today* (1980), p. 67; Peter Coffey, 'Social Policy', in *idem, op. cit.* pp. 52–68.

[68] Kenneth J. Twitchett (ed.), *Europe and the World: the External Relations of the Common Market* (1976); Ph. P. Everts, *The European Community in the World* (Rotterdam, 1972).

[69] Peter Maunder, 'International Trade', in *idem, British Economy*, p. 275; C. C. Twitchett, 'EEC', p. 63.

components. By 1980, when some of the benefits had begun to operate, the regular impact had been diminished to small, if not negligible proportions. One calculation put the British loss due to the agricultural policy at -0.86% of GDP, and the overall loss to the economy at -0.4% of GDP. Another put the loss in 1972–80 at 1.53% of GNP or, less precisely, at somewhere in the range of 1–2% of GNP.[70]

The OEEC, having been formed to distribute the Marshall Plan funds, remained as a permanent organization of the Western, mainly industrialized nations. In its early days it helped to set up the EPU (see below) and to liberalize trade among the member states. Re-named Organization for Economic Co-operation and Development (OECD) in 1960, its economic functions remained limited to the co-ordination of information and the provision of a forum for discussion.[71]

More significant was the European co-operation in the monetary sphere. Bretton Woods had ushered in a long period of stable or fixed exchange rates, to be changed only rarely under great pressure,[72] as in the case of the sterling devaluations of 1949 and 1967, and had provided a buffer of international credit to maintain them. Its early days were dominated by a severe dollar shortage in Europe[73] which caused each country to hoard its 'hard' currencies and thus to restrict international monetary transactions even with countries whose currency was not in short supply. In 1950 the European Payments Union (EPU) was formed to get round this problem by setting up what was in effect a form of European clearing, in which all the debits and credits of each country with all the others were settled as a single monthly sum, in US dollars or 'credits' with the Bank for International Settlements. Trade between them could therefore expand irrespective of the general shortage of American or Canadian dollars.

Rapid recovery in Europe and the positive balances of payments of most OEEC countries soon made such limitation unnecessary. In 1958 the EPU was dissolved and foreign payments liberalized: the UK too, made non-resident sterling officially convertible into US dollars, and the regulations applying to hard and soft currency areas coalesced. But as the world boom developed in the 1950s and 1960s, as trade greatly expanded and prices rose, the ever mounting sum of monetary transactions had to be pyramided on what was basically a fixed metallic reserve, the gold in the IMF and in the banks of member countries, and the US dollar, also tied to gold. The strains which arose therefrom[74] were

[70] Francesco Giavazzi, 'The Impact of EEC Membership', in Rudiger Dornbush and Richard Layard (eds.), *The Performance of the British Economy* (Oxford 1987), p. 100; Earl L. Grinols, 'A Thorn in the Lion's Paw: Has Britain Paid Too Much for Common Market Membership?' *Journal of Industrial Economics* 16 (1984), 271–293.

[71] Meerhaege, pp. 203, 213; D. Mallet, 'The History and Structure of OEEC', *European Yearbook*, 1 (1955), pp. 62–70; A. S. Miller, 'The Organisation for Economic Co-operation and Development', *Yearbook of World Affairs*, 17 (1963), pp. 80–95; OECD, *OECD – History, Aims, Structure* (Paris, 1971); Henry G. Aubrey, *Atlantic Economic Co-operation: The Case of the OECD*, (New York, 1967); Michele Fratianni and John C. Pattinson, *The Economics of the OECD* (Amsterdam, New York, 1976), pp. 75–140.

[72] See pp. 190–1 above.

[73] Donald McDougall, 'A Lecture on the Dollar Problem', in *Studies in Political Economy*, vol. 2 (1975), pp. 81–98, and *The World Dollar Problem* (1975).

[74] There is a large literature. See, e.g. H. G. Grubel, *World Monetary Reform* (1964); R. Triffin, *The International Monetary System* (New York, 1968); *idem, Gold and the Dollar Crisis* (New Haven, 1960) and *The World Money Maze* (New Haven, 1966).

greatly aggravated by the fact that the system was designed, at best, to deal with temporary unbalances, but had in practice also to accommodate the payments problems of countries that were permanently or structurally out of balance, the United Kingdom being the leading example.

This world monetary reserve problem was solved, or at least held at bay, in two ways. The dollar shortage was eliminated by a continuous balance of payments deficit of the United States, caused by her vast military and 'political' expenditure to the point that, by the 1960s, not only dollars, but also the gold reserve began to leave America and be redistributed among the central banks of other countries. As the American holdings of gold fell from $20 billion in 1958 to $11·9 billion in 1969,[75] other countries could expand their gold holdings accordingly and increase the quantity of their own currency on the base of their added gold and dollar reserves, while the USA had no fewer dollars circulating than before. But since the dollar continued to be sought after as reserve currency (sterling having lost that role) and as a store of value, it kept up its worth, and the United States had to live with an increasingly overvalued currency, in spite of the ever larger quantities of dollars in the world's banking vaults. Ultimately, in the early 1970s, the gold-dollar system was to collapse. Until then, the falling value of the dollar against gold on the open markets forced the eight 'gold pool' countries to confine their action to hold the dollar to $35 per ounce to that part of the metal held by central banks; gold elsewhere was allowed to appreciate in what became in effect a two-tier system.[76]

The other remedy was the increasing willingness of the major states to come to the aid of deficit countries. In 1961 10 leading members of the IMF, the 'Group of Ten' (11 in 1963 with the addition of Switzerland) offered to make additional quotas of $6 billion available to the IMF for temporary credits in the General Agreement to Borrow (GAB). The IMF itself raised its quotas in 1959 and 1966, so that, with the aid of the quotas granted in the same period to new members, its total rose from $9·2 billion at the end of 1958 to $21·3 billion at the end of the 1960s. There was also the 'swap' agreement between the USA and 14 other countries to make available lines of credit to each other of up to $20 billion for up to three months. In 1969 the IMF devised its 'Special Drawing Right' (SDR) scheme to extend the credit facilities for deficit countries by $3·5 billion in 1970 and $3 billion each in 1970 and 1971, to be more readily available than the standard credits. Finally, by the Jamaica Rules of 1976, effective from 1978, there was a further increase of one-third in all IMF quotas. Within the EEC short-term as well as medium term credit facilities were developed in the early 1970s.

Yet none of this could help the ailing dollar, and in 1971 the Bretton Woods system finally collapsed. Following exceptional balance of payments deficits of the USA of $10 billion in 1970 and $30 billion in 1971,[77] and concomitant increases in official US liabilities to foreign holders of $8 billion and $27 billion

---

[75] Brian Tew, *The Evolution of the International Monetary System 1945–81* (1982), pp. 52, 104; US Department of Commerce, *Survey of Current Business* (Monthly).

[76] Robert Solomon, *The International Monetary System, 1945–1976: An Insider's View* (New York, 1977), pp. 114–19.

[77] Of this latter figure, the genuine deficit amounted to only $10 billion or so. The rest was caused by panicking speculators.

respectively,[78] America went off gold in August 1971 and the world was once more without a metallic standard. In order to avert the threat of uncontrolled fluctuations, the major countries concluded the 'Smithsonian Agreement' in Washington in December of that year to keep their currency fluctuations within a narrow band of each other after taking into account the fall of the dollar from $35 to $38 per ounce of gold, or by 8·6%. The EEC was more ambitious, narrowing the percentages within which its currencies could fluctuate even more, and thus, as noted above, aiming for what was picturesquely called the 'snake in the tunnel'.

Neither scheme held for very long. The dollar, once more under pressure in 1972, was further devalued in February 1973 from $38 to $42·2 per ounce (the commercial value being by then more like $100) and in a further crisis in the following month, all the major currencies floated away from it. The 'snake', which Denmark, Ireland and the UK had joined in May 1972, was left by the last only a month later, when sterling was allowed to float. The other weaker members also left and re-joined in bewildering sequence, so that at the start of the EMS in 1979[79] only Germany, Denmark, Norway and the Benelux countries were still in membership. The attempt by the 'Committee of Twenty' in 1972–4 to re-establish some kind of firm new monetary standard also failed.[80]

As the world's major currencies were thus afloat, held in some reasonable stability to each other only by the actions of individual monetary authorities, they were hit by the OPEC oil price increases which sent shock waves of hitherto unimaginable dimensions through the system. By a fourfold price rise in 1973–4 (2½-fold if measured against the soaring inflation of industrial goods prices) and a further doubling, measured against other prices, in 1979–80, the hitherto poor oil exporters acquired almost overnight far more financial resources than they could possibly absorb in imports of goods and services. Estimates of the quantities involved are given in Table 8·6.[81]

Table 8·6: Oil exporters, annual balances, $ billion

	Trade balance	Services and transfers	Current balance	Identified deployment of cash surplus			
				UK	USA	Other, incl. international organizations	Total
1973	19	−13	6				
1974	84	−17	67	21·0	11·7	20·5	53·2
1975	54	−25	29	4·3	9·6	21·3	35·2
1976	64	−29	35	4·5	12·1	19·2	35·8
1977	65	−38	27	3·8	7·3	20·6	31·7
1978	44	−45	−1	−1·8	0·9	15·5	14·6
1979	112	−40	66	17·2	6·8	36·6	60·6
1980	160	−54	106	17·6	14·5	54·4	86·5

[78] Tew, pp. 142–3.
[79] Above p. 316.
[80] John Williamson, *The Failure of World Monetary Reform, 1971–4* (Sunbury, 1977).
[81] Tew, pp. 177–9, based on Bank of England, *Quarterly Bulletin*.

Expressed in a different form, the price rise of 1974 was the equivalent of a tax of 2% of GNP of the whole of the OECD and exerted a deflationary pressure not unlike the inter-war reparations.[82] It will be seen that just when the world had, remarkably, learnt to absorb these vast deficits in 1978, it was floored once more by the increases of 1979–80.

In barely seven years, 1974–80, a total of over $300 billion in the hands of the oil producers had thus had to be absorbed or 'recycled'. Its distribution has been estimated as follows ($ billion):

Bank deposits	147
US and UK Government securities	28
Finance supplied to IMF and International Bank for Reconstruction and Development	14
Finance supplied to developing countries	47
Other capital flows	81
	317

Much of this formed an enormous volatile and inflationary mass, threatening by speculative attack any currency or any money market that showed any sign of weakness, and similarly boosting currencies considered 'safe', like the pound sterling as soon as the North Sea oil had begun to flow. That the world monetary system was capable of absorbing two such shocks shows a remarkable stability and willingness to collaborate among the individual monetary authorities, in sharp contrast to the inter-war experience. But they did it at a price: industrial decline and mass unemployment, especially after the second OPEC increase, on a scale not seen since the 1930s.

3 Finance and the Banking System

Thanks to the heroic efforts of the later 1940s, the immediate danger posed by the high post-war financial liquidity in the British economy had been overcome by the end of the decade. Clearing bank deposits, which had risen nearly tenfold from pre-war days to 1950, were then held steady for three years, and rose by only 50% to 1967, much less than prices and also much less than notes and coins in circulation. The ratio of net bank deposits to GDP, which had been around 50% in the late 1930s and had risen to a maximum of 65% in 1947, fell steadily to a mere 30% in 1966. Currency circulation was also held at the same level over 1945–50, and afterwards rose less than incomes, and although deposits with acceptance houses and overseas banks rose much faster, these were not large enough to affect appreciably the general liquidity position. It was only in the 1970s that the M3 multiplier was to rise sharply from around 4 to around 6.[83]

[82] Solomon, p. 292; Thomas Balogh and Andrew Graham, 'The Transfer Problem Revisited: Analogies between the Reparations Problem and the Problem of the OPEC Surplus', *Oxf. Bull. Econ. Stat.*, 41/3 (1979), 183–91.

[83] *Financial Statistics*; London and Cambridge Economic Service, *Key Statistics 1900–1966*, Table M; Forrest Capie and Alan Webber, *A Monetary History of the United Kingdom, vol. 1* (1985) Tables 1(2), 1(3) and 1(8); G. L. Bell and L. S. Berman, 'Changes in the Money Supply in the United Kingdom, 1954 to 1964', *Economica*, 33/130 (1966), p. 149.

One of the main factors which helped to reduce the inflationary pressure was the reduction in Government borrowing. On current account, the Government achieved annual surpluses averaging £450 million a year in the 1950s, and while this was more than counterbalanced by heavy Government capital formation, so that on combined revenue and capital account there was still an annual deficit, it was so small that over much of the period it could be covered by the growth in the net National Savings. The decline of the latter in the mid-1960s, when they increased by only £175 million in the three years to the end of 1967, was not enough to weaken the Government's monetary control, which in any case depended on many other factors. As for short-term borrowing, 'the value of tender Treasury bills outstanding in 1965 was less than the sum of tender bills and Treasury deposit receipts outstanding in 1948', so that there was no floating debt increase either, to weaken monetary control.[84]

It was this more 'normal' money supply situation which allowed the Conservative Government to re-introduce monetary policy, including the bank rate. After 20 years of a 2% Bank Rate, cheap money ended in 1951 and changes in the rate began to be used vigorously to support Government policies. As the long-term position of Britain worsened from 1956 on, the general tendency for the Bank Rate was upward. It never fell below 4% and the crisis rate of 7% was used with increasing frequency, but this medicine (like all the other dosages of restrictiveness) became ever less effective with increasing use.

The Radcliffe Committee Report,[85] one of the most thorough and intelligent examinations of the British Monetary System, was in this respect very much a document of the 1950s. The Committee totally failed to see both the slow erosion of the United Kingdom's positive balance of payments, and her failure to keep up competitively with production and productivity increases abroad. Instead, its attention (like that of Montagu Norman in the 1920s) was largely concentrated on protecting the reserve and on suppressing inflation, still thought to be the main danger. Their particular concern was the monetary mechanism by which these aims could be accomplished, particularly in the crisis years of high pressure. In this field they made one of their most valuable contributions by showing that the traditional braking mechanism, the reduction of the 'liquidity' of the banks which forced them, in turn, to restrict their credit, was no longer working efficiently.

A major reason for that was that even when the Government finances were in balance, the high level of the floating debt required periodic renewal, while the large sums to be borrowed for the capital programme of the nationalized industries could not be switched off at will when the authorities wished, on general grounds, to reduce the creation of credit. The banking system therefore could compensate for any reduction of liquidity engineered by the authorities by simply reducing its holdings of Government short-term debt, particularly Treasury Bills. Particularly clear cases of this process in the restrictions of 1955 and 1957 were very much in the forefront of the Committee's mind.[86]

[84] W. B. Reddaway, 'Rising Prices for Ever?' *Lloyds Bank Review*, 81 (1966), p. 3; Bell and Berman, p. 163.

[85] *Committee on the Working of the Monetary System*, Cmnd. 827 (1959).

[86] Charles Kennedy, 'Monetary Policy', in G. D. N. Worswick and P. H. Ady (eds.), *The British Economy in the Nineteen-Fifties* (1962), pp. 310–11; Edward Nevin and E. W. Davis, *The London Clearing Banks* (1970), pp. 261–2.

Put differently, since restricting the money supply could always be circumvented by substituting other forms of money, the Committee were concerned
to extend the concept of the 'supply of money', by which the authorities hoped
to regulate demand, beyond the cash and bank deposits to which it used to be
limited, to a much wider range of alternatives and to 'the state of liquidity of
the whole economy'.[87] The velocity of circulation was thus practically unlimited,
and there was no stable ratio between the quantity of money and the price
level.[88] The Committee were also concerned to evolve a mechanism which would
limit the effect on home activity of fluctuations caused by changes in the foreign
balance, and in general they were aiming for stability rather than, as in recent
years, for restriction. For all these reasons they recommended operating on
interest rates rather than on the money supply.[89] For a time the Committee's
ideas carried all before them.[90] A more passive monetary policy was pursued,
and interest rates remained at the centre of the picture for the time being.[91]
From the mid-1960s onward, the restrictive rather than the stabilizing element
in monetary policy began once again to become dominant. Moreover, while the
problems of 1964–7 were seen to be essentially those of balancing the foreign
balance of payments, in the 1970s the target became increasingly to hold back
the rate of inflation. The response of Government policy to this was twofold: a
gradual, but clearly marked turning away from Keynesian policies towards
monetarism, with the control (i.e. reduction in the rate of growth) of the quantity
of money as the main target, and linked with this, an emphasis on reducing the
Government's deficits, which were once more on the increase.[92]

The move toward monetarism was a world-wide phenomenon, not unconnected with the world-wide acceleration of inflation in the 1970s. Indeed, its
acceptance by Britain was speeded up by the monetarist obligations imposed
on the British Government by the IMF and other foreign bankers as the price
for their loans, and accepted as early as 1967 in the 'letter of intent' by the then
Chancellor of the Exchequer in which he promised that the growth of the money
supply in 1968 would not exceed its expected growth in 1967. The doctrine itself
had been propounded with great verve by the American economist Milton
Friedman, on the basis of the experience of the USA: in Britain even its
supporters had difficulty in finding proof without complex manipulation of its
central tenet, a relationship between the supply of money and the price level.[93]
However, a number of British economists embraced the new ideas with enthusi-

[87] *Radcliffe Committee,* para. 981.
[88] E. Victor Morgan, 'The Radcliffe Report in the Tradition of Official British Monetary Documents', in D. R. Croome and H. G. Johnson (eds.), *Money in Britain 1959–1969. The Radcliffe
Report Ten Years After* (1970), pp. 10–11; *Radcliffe Report,* Para. 391.
[89] *Nat. Inst. Econ. Rev.,* No. 99 (Feb. 1982), p. 62.
[90] E.g., W. Manning Dicey, *Money Under Review,* and literature quoted in Worswick and Ady,
p. 545.
[91] Douglas Fisher, 'The Objectives of British Monetary Policy, 1951–1964', *Journal of Finance,*
23 (1968) 821–31; Croome and Johnson, p. v.
[92] Bank of England and Treasury, 'The Operation of Monetary Policy since Radcliffe', in Croome
and Johnson, p. 214; Clare Group: 'Macroeconomic Policy in the UK: Is There an Alternative?'
Midland Bank Review (Autumn-Winter 1981), pp. 7–9.
[93] David Laidler and Michael Parkin, 'The Demand for Money in the United Kingdom 1956–
67: Preliminary Estimates', *Manchester School,* 38 (1970), 187–208; also see C. D. Cohen, *British
Economic Policy 1960–1969* (1971), p. 135; David Williams, C. A. E. Goodhart, D. H. Gowland,
'Money, Income and Causality: The UK Experience', *Amer. Econ. Rev.,* 66 (1976), 417–23.

asm and they also came to dominate the economic policies of the Labour Government implicitly after 1976, and those of the Conservative Government explicitly after 1979. A variant or extension of that policy, 'supply side economics'[94] was essentially a feature of the years after 1980.

With the change in the dominant theory as to how the economy worked and how it could be influenced, there also came a change in the intermediate instrumental targets. Incomes policies, operative until the later 1970s, were finally abandoned.[95] Discussions on whether inflation was due to demand-pull or cost-push,[96] the former caused by excessive demand throughout the economy and the latter by price rises of individual factors of production, particularly of labour, came to take second place to the debate about the role of the monetary sphere. Interest switched from the concern over the impact of Government income and expenditure on the national quantities of these flows, typical for the 1960s,[97] to domestic credit expansion (DCE) and ultimately to the money supply, affected directly by the Government's deficit or, more precisely, the Public Sector Borrowing Requirement (PSBR). This deficit was indeed growing very rapidly in the 1970s.[98]

On the assumption that the velocity of circulation did not change, and that the massive switches of funds in and out of the country[99] could be ignored, it seemed a reasonable proposition that the quantity of 'money' made available in one phase would determine prices (total transactions[100] divided by quantities) at some time in the future, if only all that was embraced under 'money' could be included in the calculation. Since several alternatives presented themselves, such as M1, M3, or PSL2, each moving in a different way,[101] they gave the monetary authorities, which had begun to announce targets in 1976, the opportunity to switch in their targetry from whichever showed inconvenient results

[94] David F. Lomax, 'Supply Side Economics: The British Experience', *National Westminster Bank Quarterly Review* (August 1982), 2 15; John Burton, 'The Varieties of Monetarism and their Policy Implications', *Three Banks Review*, 134 (1982) 14–31.

[95] See p. 287 above.

[96] J. C. R. Dow, *The Management of the British Economy 1945–60* (Cambridge, 1965), chapter 13; Thomas Wilson, *Inflation* (Oxford, 1961); P. A. Samuelson and R. M. Solow, 'Analytical Aspects of Anti-Inflation Policy', *Amer. Econ. Rev.*, 50 (1960); Wynne A. H. Godley, *Inflation in the United Kingdom* (University of Cambridge, Department of Applied Economics, Reprint No. 18, 1978), and criticism by Michael Parkin, pp. 476 ff.

[97] E.g., R. W. R. Price, 'Public Expenditure', in F. T. Blackaby (ed.), *British Economic Policy 1960–74* (Cambridge, 1978), pp. 105 7; *Nat. Inst. Econ. Rev.*, 96 (May 1981), 12.

[98] Below, pp. 342–3.

[99] Thus sharp rises in interest rates would attract foreign funds away from the Government to the banks, and force the Government to borrow more from the home banks, thereby *increasing* the money base, K. K. F. Zawadski, *Competition and Credit Control* (Oxford, 1981), pp. 29–30. Also see A. A. Walters, 'The Radcliffe Report – Ten Years After. A Survey of Empirical Evidence', in Croome and Johnson, p. 62.

[100] J. S. Cramer, 'The Volume of Transactions and of Payments in the United Kingdom, 1968–1977', *Oxf. Econ. P.*, 33/2 (1981), 234–55.

[101] % Changes p.a.

	1972–9	1980	1981/I	1981/II	1981/III	1981/IV
PSL2	13·75	13·5	13·5	13·5	14	11 (est)
£M3	14·5	19	18	16·5	16·5	13 (est)
M1	13·5	4	13·5	10·25	12	8 (est)

Nat. Inst. Econ. Rev., 99 (Feb. 1982), 8; also A. R. Prest and D. J. Coppock, *The UK Economy* (1978), p. 105; G. E. J. Dennis, 'Money Supply and its Control', in Peter Maunder (ed.), *The British Economy in the 1970s* (1980), pp. 49–53.

to that which, for the time being, provided a better fit. As for the 'Medium Term Financial Strategy', it 'was born only to be buried (for the time being) under an avalanche of borrowing and its targets were tumbled into the dust'.[102]

However, with all these switches in theory, the practical measures taken within the sphere of monetary policy showed very little change, except that, as time went on, the periods of 'restraint' and 'restrictions' became longer, the expansion periods between them shorter, and the squeeze to be exerted stronger. This was so even though the end of fixed exchange rates in 1972 gave the authorities considerably more freedom of manoeuvre. Tighter restraint meant that there had to be created a whole battery of measures to stiffen the traditional policies of choking off demand for credit by higher interest rates, and the supply of funds, by open market operations. Moreover, even in the early 1960s the need to manage the Government's debt operations made it advisable to supplement interest rate policy with other weapons. To this new armoury we must now turn.

Before the concept of 'money' had been widened by Radcliffe and in subsequent experience, the authorities' main concern was to control the London clearing banks, together with the Scottish and Northern Irish equivalent institutions. To ensure that traditional central bank measures would work, there had to be some stability in the reserve ratios. The long-established cash ratio of 8% was accepted in the 1950s as appropriate, and would give the authorities some control over short-term rates. For total reserves, the Bank of England had in 1951 named 28–32% as the expected ratio, with 25% as exceptional minimum. By 1955, 30% was regarded as the normal minimum, but in 1963, when the banks were under liquidity pressure at a time when the authorities did not want to restrict credit, the minimum was lowered to 28%.[103]

Meanwhile a new method of control, the 'Special Deposit', was introduced in 1960. This gave the authorities the power to require the clearing banks to deposit a certain proportion of their gross deposits with the Bank of England, thus reducing their liquidity ratio by an equal amount, and reducing their power to lend, by a multiple of that sum. Imposed in 1% and $\frac{1}{2}$% rates at a time, Special Deposits quickly reached an early peak of 3% in September 1961, and later peaks of $3\frac{1}{2}$% in October 1970 and 6% in November 1973. The rapid changes in the rates showed that the authorities used them as an important part of their armoury, but in 1967 the Bank announced that it would use them more flexibly rather than as a crisis measure. However, the joint-stock banks continued to be able, as noted above, to weaken the Bank's impact by selling their investments and maintaining their advances,[104] so that the Chancellor soon had to revert to exhortations, directives and the crude upper ceilings for bank lendings[105] when he wanted to reduce the amount of credit in the economy.

There were also periods of restrictions of new issues by the Capital Issues

---

[102] 'Annual Monetary Survey No. 32 – 1980', *Midland Bank Review*, (1981), p. 22; also see *Nat. Inst. Econ. Rev.*, 99 (Feb. 1982), 63.

[103] J. E. Maycock, 'Monetary Policy and the Clearing Banks', in Croome and Johnson, pp. 164–5.

[104] J. E. Wadsworth, 'Bank Ratios Past and Present', in C. R. Whittesley and S. S. G. Wilson (eds.), *Essays in Money and Banking in Honour of R. S. Sayers* (Oxford, 1968), pp. 244–5.

[105] J. H. B. Tew, 'Monetary Policy I', in Blackaby, *op. cit.*, pp. 219–224, 237; M. J. Artis, 'Monetary Policy II', *ibid.*, p. 261; J. C. R. Dow, *op. cit.*, p. 240.

Committee, and of occasional restriction on Building Society lending, a rapidly growing mechanism of finance. Insurance funds, another important source of finance, could not be controlled. Curiously, one of the most effective means to be discovered in this period was the restriction of hire-purchase terms, since it took effect much more quickly and directly than any of the other methods:[106] 'If we look at the actual experience of the 1950s ... we come to the conclusion that the really quick substantial effects were secured by hire-purchase controls, just those which have the most concentrated directional effects.'[107] Further, while the other methods largely cut investment, hire-purchase control largely cut consumption, though it also affected the finance of smaller firms, and it was thus the one method which did no long-term damage to the economy. In the 1950s and 1960s, every major 'package' of restrictive or relaxing measures contained statutory changes in hire-purchase provisions.

Altogether, there was thus built up in the 1950s and 1960s an impressive array of monetary weapons, grouped around the Bank Rate. This was aided by the fact that the quantity of Treasury Bills in the hands of the market rapidly declined in the 1960s, to be replaced by commercial bills, and the gilt-edged market constantly 'slid downwards'.[108] Nevertheless, control seemed always to slip out of the Treasury's grasp, as the money market developed new methods and institutions and as market conditions changed, as shown in examples quoted above.[109] The more comprehensive and efficient the restrictions on the clearing banks, the more rapidly business by-passed them by turning to other institutions where it would escape control, and which were by then expanding rapidly, above all in what became known as parallel money markets. Thus between 1958 and 1968, the share of deposits held by the clearing banks (including the Scottish and Northern Irish equivalents) had shrunk from 43·5% to a mere 27·4% of the total, whereas the share of British overseas, Commonwealth and foreign banks had risen in the same years from 4·7% to 26·4% or from little more than a tenth of the former, to virtual equality.[110]

It was therefore becoming clear that new operational methods were needed to allow the Government's monetary policy to remain effective. A major step in that direction was taken by the Bank of England in 1971 with a package of new practices summarized in a consultative document entitled *Competition and Credit Control*.[111] Its object was simultaneously to further a 'more competitive and innovatory attitude',[112] and to strengthen the Government's control over the market. To this end, the 'cartel' of interest rates among the banks was to be

---

[106] J. K. S. Gandhi, 'Estimates of Hire Purchase and its Finance, 1948–1957' *Bull. Oxf. Inst. Stat.,* 28/4 (1966); Dow, pp. 246–8; J. H. B. Tew, *loc. cit.,* pp. 226, 251; M. J. Artis, *loc. cit.,* p. 267.

[107] *Radcliffe Committee,* para 472.

[108] Nevin and Davis, *op. cit.,* p. 273; Maycock, p. 184; E. R. Shaw, *The London Money Market* (1978), pp. 20–1.

[109] Pp. 323. Also Douglas Fisher, 'The Instruments of Monetary Policy and the Generalized Trade-Off Function for Britain, 1955–1968', *Manchester School,* 38 (1970), 209–22; N. J. Gibson, 'Special Deposits as an Instrument of Monetary Policy', *ibid.* 32/3 (1964); C. D. Cohen, pp. 119–25; 'Annual Monetary Survey No. 32 – 1980', *Midland Bank Review* (1981), p. 10; F. P. R. Brechling and R. G. Lipsey, 'Trade Credit and Monetary Policy', *Econ. J.,* 73/4 (1963), 618–41.

[110] I. R. J. Clark, 'The UK Financial Sector Since Radcliffe', in Croome and Johnson, p. 134.

[111] *B. of Eng. Qtly. Bull.,* 11/2 (1971), 189.

[112] Sir Harold Wilson (Chairman), *Committee To Review the Functioning of Financial Institutions* (henceforth; *Wilson Committee*), *Evidence,* vol. 5, Bank of England written evidence, p. 219.

cancelled, and banks were to be free to vary their rates and thus also to gain some initiative as against the rest of the London Money Market. At the same time the official ceilings on bank lendings were to be abolished, but the banks were to hold $12\frac{1}{2}$% of 'eligible reserves' and the finance houses 10%, with an additional $1\frac{1}{2}$% for the London clearing banks held at the Bank of England. In other respects all financial institutions were to be treated alike. In a further set of innovations, the members of the London Discount Market agreed to keep at least 50% of their borrowed funds in public sector debt (altered later to an obligation not to extend their *non*-public sector debt beyond 20 times their capital plus reserves); they would continue to take all Treasury Bills offered, but at individual instead of syndicated prices; and for this, the Bank of England would continue as lender of last resort to them.[113]

It was the hope of the authorities that by these means they could regain full control over interest rates and over funds available, and it was certainly the case that they made the Special Deposits more effective thereby. In 1973 the Bank of England added a further special deposits scheme, known popularly as the 'corset'. Under this, the Bank specified a target rate of growth for interest-bearing 'eligible liabilities', suitably defined, for a given period, and any growth beyond this was subject to progressively higher calls for supplementary interest-free special deposits. This made expansion of the 'eligible liabilities' unprofitable, and in fact never more than 14 institutions out of 360 were ever under penalty at any one time in the following years. However, the total effect on the money market was more doubtful. The scheme was abolished in 1980.[114]

Meanwhile, it was also intended that the market should benefit by its greater freedom. The cash reserve limit of 8% for the clearing banks had been abolished[115] and in 1972 the Bank Rate was transformed into the Minimum Lending Rate (MLR), fixed no longer by the Bank, but derived from the average rate of discount of Treasury Bills, plus $\frac{1}{2}$% rounded upwards to the nearest $\frac{1}{4}$% figure. That experiment, however, was ended in 1978, the control over the MLR reverted to the directors who again led, rather than followed, the market.

That the bounds of freedom had perhaps been drawn too widely was suggested by the scandal of the property boom, ending in the so-called 'secondary banking crisis' of 1971–5. It began in 1971 when the expansion fostered by the authorities largely flowed into a highly speculative and basically unsound property market. In 1972 the banks withdrew their direct support, but large profits continued to be made by some speculators. By 1973, however, the international currency crisis and the new 'corset' began to limit liquidity, and a number of the less sound companies involved in the speculation were threatened with collapse, which in turn would have led to widespread havoc in the City.

[113] Zawadzki, pp. 33 ff.; M. J. Artis and J. M. Parkin, 'Competition and Credit Control: A General Appraisal', *The Bankers' Magazine* (September 1971); European Communities, Monetary Committee: *Monetary Policy in the Countries of the European Economic Community*. Supplement 1974: Denmark, Ireland, United Kingdom (II/213/74), Part III: *Monetary Policy Instruments of the United Kingdom*, pp. 12 ff.

[114] Zawadski, pp. 108–26; Stanley Fisher, 'Monetary Policy', in Rudiger Dornbush and Richard Layard (eds.), *The Performance of the British Economy* (Oxford, 1987).

[115] M. D. K. W. Foot, C. A. E. Goodhart, A. C. Hotson, 'Monetary Base Control', *B. of Eng. Qtly. Bull.*, 19/2 (1979), 150.

The situation was saved only by the Bank of England which stepped in and with the help of the clearing banks mounted a 'lifeboat operation' in which up to £1,200 million were committed (equal to 40% of the capital and reserves of all the English and Scottish clearing banks) plus additional funds by the Bank of England alone. By 1975 the worst was past and a major crash was averted.[116] The ease with which City firms, no matter how unsound, had access to banking funds compared with the alleged difficulties of productive industry to obtain finance, attracted much unfavourable comment.[117]

We must now turn to the sources of the savings on which the financial markets were ultimately built up. In the normalization of the monetary system in the 1950s one of the most important developments was the startlingly rapid recovery of personal savings. Their re-emergence was not only a symbol, but also part cause, of the return to more normal peaceful conditions: the post-war buying spree, the excessive velocity of circulation, had given way to a more balanced disposal of resources. In 1949–51, personal savings were still only 1–2% of GNP, but they jumped almost at once to 5%, and soon after rose to 6–7%.[118] The savings of Companies and of Public Corporations remained at about the same level, the former showing a falling, and the latter a welcome rising tendency.

As Table 8·7 shows, personal savings took a further astonishing upward turn in the course of the 1970s. The average for 1978–80 hides a further rising tendency: measured as a share of all savings, the proportions of personal savings were 47·4% in 1978, 52·6% in 1979 and 60·3% in 1980. Measured as a percentage of real disposable personal incomes, the rates rose as follows:

Table 8·7: Percentage share in total savings*

	1950	Average 1954–6	Average 1959–61	Average 1970–2	Average 1978–80
Persons	−2·8	16·5	28·6	27·7	53·4
Companies	53·0	56·5	50·2	41·7	44·3
Public corporations	5·1	6·3	6·5	8·2	10.7
Central and Local Government	42·2	18·3	16·0	29·5	−5·7
Residual error	2·5	2·5	−1·3	n.a.	n.a.
Overseas	n.a.	n.a.	n.a.	−7·1	−2·8
	100·0	100·0	100·0	100·0	99·9

* *National Income and Expenditure*; W. Beckerman and Associates, *The British Economy in 1975* (Cambridge, 1965), p. 278. The figures refer, with slight variations, to gross savings adjusted by capital transfer and increases in the value of stocks and work in progress, but *before* deduction of gross capital formation.

[116] 'The Secondary Banking Crisis and the Bank of England's Support Operations', *B. of Eng. Qtly. Bull.*, 18/2 (1978), 230–9; *Wilson Committee, Second Stage of Evidence*, vol. 4, Bank of England, pp. 97–8.

[117] E.g. *Wilson Committee Progress Report* (1977), p. 13.

[118] Richard Stone, 'Private Saving in Britain, Past, Present and Future' *Manchester School*, 32/2 (1964); *National Income and Expenditure*; R. C. O. Matthews, C. H. Feinstein, J. C. Odling-Smee, *British Economic Growth 1856–1973* (Oxford 1982), pp. 145, 150–1.

Average	1962–4	7·7%
	1966–8	8·5
	1970–2	9·3
	1976–8	12·8
	1979	14·7
	1980	15·8

The highest point was in fact reached in the third quarter of 1980, after which the ratio began to decline.[119]

This behaviour on the part of the general public has caused some surprise, since it had been assumed that in times of inflation individuals would try to buy goods rather than hold assets expressed in money terms. The explanation of the increased willingness to save may lie either in the need to hold more liquid assets in line with the price level, a transaction cost argument, or in the ultimate purpose of saving, such as provision for old age, which also requires the accumulated sums to keep pace with inflation.

It is useful in this context to distinguish between contractual savings such as insurance or pension funds, which remained stable in the 1970s, and discretionary savings, which rose from around 40% of the total in the mid-1960s to 60% in the mid-1970s and further still in the later years of the decade. Yet in 1970–7, the inflation loss on liquid assets was actually larger than the discretionary savings of households, so that there was a net loss, but it was more than balanced by the acquisition of housing, pensions and insurance. As a share of personal assets, land, buildings and other physical assets rose from 50·2% to 67·8% between 1966 and 1976, and liquid assets fell correspondingly from one-half to one-third of the total.[120]

There was also a substantial shift in the liquid assets held by the personal sector. The 1950s were marked by a revulsion against Government securities. The trend was then towards equities and away from all fixed interest securities. This lasted for about 10 years and was followed by a drastic reversal. For the decade 1966–76, the flight out of shares on the part of individuals has been

Table 8·8:   Ownership of company shares, in % of market values

	1957	1963	1969	1975
Persons	65·8	54·0	47·4	37·5
Overseas sector	n.a.	7·0	6·6	5·6
UK institutions: Insurance cos.	8·8	10·0	12·2	15·9
Pension funds	3·4	6·4	9·0	16·8
Others	22·0	22·6	24·8	24·2
	100	100	100	100
£ billion	11·6	27·5	37·8	44·6

[119] Prest and Coppock, p. 289; K. Cuthbertson, 'The Measurement and Behaviour of UK Savings Ratio in the 1970s', *Nat. Inst. Econ. Rev.*, 99 (Feb. 1982), 77; *Economic Trends*. Also see *Wilson Report, Progress Report* (1977), p. 7; Peter Falush, 'The Changing Pattern of Savings', *National Westminster Bank Quarterly Review* (August 1978), 47.

[120] K. Cuthbertson, *passim*; M. E. Blume, *loc. cit.*, pp. 292–8; Richard J. Briston and Richard Dobbins, *The Growth and Impact of Institutional Investors* (1978), p. 124.

estimated at a net £1·1 billion a year. The shares were largely bought up by insurance and pension funds and other institutional investors (see Table 8·8).[121]

Meanwhile the companies' internal sources of funds declined, largely because of the decline in trading profits, from 94% in 1952–5 to 84% in 1961–5 and 80% in 1971–6, or, by another calculation, from 64·6% in 1964 to 36·1% in 1974, the gap being made up by recourse to the banks and the capital market, as well as from abroad.[122]

The contribution of the new capital market remained modest. In 1965–6, UK share issues represented only 12·4% of new capital, and by 1975–6 this had dropped to 8·7%. The once popular preference share had virtually disappeared in this total. Equally striking was the collapse of the contribution of loans and mortgages in the capital raised. Instead, joint-stock companies turned to the banks, particularly in the high inflation and interest years of 1973 and 1974, when no less than 41% of their capital needs were raised in that way, but even in 1975–6 this amounted to 13·5% compared with 8·3% in 1965–6. In addition, a newly significant source was the foreign sector, whose share rose steadily from 7·4% to 19·7% in the same years. As a result, the 'gearing' of outside funds over own funds rose rapidly from 0·01 in 1952–4 to 0·16 in 1961–3 and 0·24 in

Table 8·9: Industrial and commercial companies: market valuation of liabilities, %

	1960	1976
Ordinary shares	78·9	59·0
Preference shares	6·7	0·7
Debentures	6·6	6·6
Bank advances	7·8	33·7
	100·0	100·0
Total values, £ billion	25,496	68,563

Table 8·10: Industrial and commercial companies, % share of funds

Averages of cycles	Capital issues at home	Capital issues overseas	Bank borrowings	Other loans and mortgages
1965–9	46·7	2·3	43·2	7·8
1970–3	10·4	2·8	75·4	11·4
1974–9	17·7	0·3	73·8	8·2

1974–6 and began to approach the ratios of other countries. The development may be summarized in the figures given in Table 8·9[123] and 8·10.[124]

[121] W. A. Thomas, *The Finance of British Industry 1918–1976* (1978), p. 144; *Wilson Committee, Progress Report* (1977), p. 21; Briston and Dobbins, pp. 122, 139; Blume, p. 294.

[122] Thomas, p. 218; 'Capital Requirements and Industrial Finance', *Midland Bank Review* (February 1976), p. 12; *Wilson Committee, Evidence*, vol. 2 (1977), CBI evidence, p. 10; K. Williams, J. Williams, D. Thomas, *Why are the British Bad at Manufacturing?* (1983), p. 59; Matthews, Feinstein and Odling-Smee, pp. 348–9.

[123] *Wilson Committee, Evidence*, vol. 2, p. 21, vol. 5, pp. 53, 61; W. A. Thomas, pp. 155, 311; J. S. Flemming, L. D. D. Price, S. A. Byers, 'The Costs of Capital Finance and Investment', *B. of Eng. Qtly. Bull.*, 16 (June 1976), 202, also *ibid.* 17 (June 1977), 158–9, 19 (June 1979), 185.

[124] T. M. Rybczynski, 'Structural Changes in the Financing of British Industry and their Implications', *National Westminster Bank Quarterly Review* (May, 1982) p. 35.

The reliance on bank advances posed particular problems for new and small firms, as had been recognized since the days of the Macmillan Committee. In the expansionary decades of the 1950s and 1960s they had little difficulty in raising bank loans, and the Government was also offering aid through the Industrial and Commercial Finance Corporation (ICFC),[125] but in the tougher 1970s they once again complained of discrimination. For longer-term capital, even medium-sized companies found it hard to float new issues. Equity Capital for Industry (1976), supported by 350 financial institutions provided some support, and several new schemes were founded in 1980–2,[126] but the main problem was that the institutional investors were not interested in small companies; yet it was precisely the institutional investors who had come to dominate the capital market in those years.

Among the most significant of them were the insurance companies, as will be evident from Table 8·8. In the 1950s, they reflected the switch into equities and away from gilt-edgeds. According to one calculation, while their total assets rose from £3,108 million in 1950 to £6,610 million in 1960, the ordinary shares they held grew more than fourfold, from £338 million to £1,417 million. In 1964 their equity holdings were up to £2,253 million, and preference shares to £409 million, out of total assets of just over £10,000 million.[127]

By 1969 their assets had reached £14·2 billion, and at the end of 1979, market values were £52·8 billion. Their heavy buying of ordinary shares reached a peak in 1972, and was replaced by mortgages and loans in 1973 and Government securities in 1975. With an annual net acquisition of £2·5 billion of British funds in those years, they had a substantial influence on capital markets. Their asset distribution changed as shown in Table 8·11.[128]

Table 8·11:   Asset distribution of insurance companies

	1966	1979
British government securities	22%	25·6%
Local authority securities	4	1·4
Ordinary shares: British	21	23·6
other		4·4
Other shares	} 20 {	4·8
Unit trusts	—	1·6
Loans and mortgages	16	6·5
Land, property, ground rents	10	21·4
Other assets, including short term	7	10·7
	100	100

[125] P. 347 below, and *Wilson Committee, The Financing of Small Firms*, Cmnd. 7503 (1979).

[126] *Wilson Committee, Progress Report* (1977), pp. 22, 33–7, vol. 3, p. 89, *Evidence*, vol. 2, 110–22, vol. 5 p. 20; Mike Jarrett and Mike Wright, 'New Initiatives in the Financing of Small Firms', *National Westminster Bank Quarterly Review*, (August 1982), 40–52.

[127] Jack Revell, *The Wealth of the Nation* (Cambridge, 1967), pp. 218–19, *passim*; E. V. Morgan, *The Structure of Property Ownership in Great Britain* (Oxford, 1960); *Annual Abstract of Statistics.*

[128] CSO, *Financial Statistics; B. of Eng. Qtly. Bull.*, 10/4 (1970), 419–22; *Wilson Committee, Evidence* vol. 3, pp. 67–9, *Second Stage Evidence*, vol. 2, pp. 13–17.

[129] *B. of Eng. Qtly. Bull.*, 10/4 (1970), p. 429; Briston and Dobbins, p. 139; *Wilson Committee,*

It is noteworthy that around 40% of their business originated abroad, directly or through subsidiaries.

Beside insurance companies, it was Pension Funds that registered the most rapid expansion in the capital market. Together these two groups absorbed £478 million from the personal sector in 1955, £1,173 in 1965 and 10 times that sum, £11,113 in 1980. Assets held by the Pension Funds rose from £4·6 billion in 1963 to £41·3 billion in 1979; those of private funds alone from £4·7 billion in 1970 to £31·5 billion in 1980. They concentrated even more than insurance companies, in fact to the extent of one-half, on ordinary shares, and in the 1970s they became the most important buyers in the market. From 1974 on, following the property collapse, they spread more widely into other securities.[129]

Investment Trusts, among the largest institutional investors at the beginning of our period, expanded more slowly, from £2·8 billion in 1963 to over £7 billion in 1980, of which 39% was held overseas. Unit Trusts provided an alternative mechanism for the public to spread their risks of shareholding: they grew much faster, from £0·35 billion to £6 billion, of which over 15% was held abroad, over the same years. In both cases, around 90% of their assets were in the form of (mostly ordinary) shares, and the rest in Government securities and short-term assets. In 1975 they held 10·3% of the shares of British-registered companies between them.[130]

The rising proportion of these large institutions in the ownership of British companies, amounting to 25% in 1966 and 40% in 1975, has given some cause for concern. In view of the dispersal of ownership, often among many thousands of shareholders in the larger companies, an individual institutional shareholder controlling perhaps no more than 1% or 2% of the capital was in a position to exercise a disproportionate influence; still more decisive would be the action of several of them combined. It has, indeed, become clear that takeover bids, mergers and reconstruction schemes normally need the backing of the institutional investors before they can be undertaken.

The traditional facilities for the small saver have been in decline: thus the Post Office Savings Bank and National Savings between them dropped from 28·5% of all deposits in 1958 to a mere 13·8% 10 years later,[131] but the Government recovered some ground with new offers, including lotteries and index-linked bonds. Nevertheless, their share in savings continued to decline (Table 8·12):[132]

Table 8·12: Distribution of small savings (%)

	1950	1960	1970	1977
National savings	46	42	29	21
Banks	45	41	35	32
Building societies	9	17	35	47
	100	100	100	100
£ billion	13·4	16·6	28 5	66 3

[129] *B. of Eng. Qtly. Bull.*, 10/4 (1970), p. 429; Briston and Dobbins, p. 139; *Wilson Committee*, vol. 3, pp. 140–2; and Table 8·8 above.

[130] Briston and Dobbin, pp. 146–7; Wilson Committee, *Second Stage Evidence*, vol. 4, p. 36.

[131] I. R. J. Clark, *op. cit.*, p. 134.

[132] *Wilson Committee*, vol. 3, p. 9 and *Second Stage Evidence*, vol. 3, p. 9.

Altogether in May 1981 National Savings totalled £17 billion and the Trustee Savings Banks, after a drastic phase of amalgamations which reduced their numbers from 67 in 1975 to 16 in 1981, held £5·7 billion of deposits.

Finally, the Building Societies resumed their pre-war triumphant advance immediately after the war, with assets worth under £800 million in 1939, £2,400 million in 1957 and £54 billion in 1980, lending by then at the rate of £10 billion a year in new mortgages. The astonishing expansion in their role as recipients of savings is evident from Table 8·12, but in recent years other institutions, including the banks, have shown an increasing interest in this profitable business while the Societies were increasingly venturing into banking. In 1970 the personal sector borrowed a net £158 million, or under 13% for house purchases from institutions other than Building Societies; by 1980 that sum had risen tenfold, to £1,570 million, and represented over 21%.[133]

Housing was in fact, the only private sector which kept its share in the non-bank market, the rest being swamped by the huge needs of Government borrowing. The summary of these changes in Table 8·13 compares 1966 and 1979:[134]

Table 8·13:   Sources and uses of funds, non-bank financial institutions, select major items

		1966	1979
Sources:	Deposits in building societies	724	5,769
	Net inflow, life and pension funds	1,241	8,969
	Deposits in trustee and savings banks	} 221	522
	National Savings Bank investment account		326
Uses:	British Government securities	} 110	6,264
	Local authorities, long-term debt	—	−130
	UK ordinary shares	} 804	1,824
	Overseas ordinary shares		563
	Loans and mortgages for house purchase	728	5,532
Totals, sources and uses (including other items)		2,340	18,064

Among the joint-stock banks which, as we have seen, bore the brunt of the Government's periodic restrictive measures at least until 1971, a further merger movement stands out. Following the Report No. 34 of the National Board for Prices and Incomes (PIB), *Bank Charges,* in 1967,[135] which stated that the authorities would not object to some bank amalgamations, the National Provincial and the Westminster merged, and soon after the National Commercial Bank (itself a merger of three banks) with the Royal Bank of Scotland. Meanwhile the major English banks had acquired stakes in the Scottish and Irish

---

[133] Margaret Wray, 'Building Society Mortgages and the Housing Market', *Westminster Bank Review* (February 1968), 31, 38; *National Income and Expenditure.*
[134] *Financial Statistics.*
[135] Cmd. 3292 (1967).

banks, and the four big clearing banks between them owned the Yorkshire Bank. However, the proposed merger of Lloyds, Barclays and Martins which would have combined nearly 50% of clearing bank deposits was vetoed and only the combination of the last two allowed. The number of London clearing banks was thus reduced from 11 to 6. The large banks also broke with tradition by entering new or expanding types of business, usually by means of subsidiaries, including HP finance, leasing, factoring, Unit Trusts, insurance broking and merchant banking, and were then said to have become more like the 'universal banks' of the continent.

After the war, the transfer from Government to private business had meant a substantial rise of advances as against investments among clearing banks. Among English and Welsh Banks, investments fell from 32·6% of assets (31·3% in Government paper) in 1949–52 to 12·5% (11·2%) in 1964–6, while non-Government loans and discounts rose from 27·3% to 52·3%. By 1980, over two-thirds of their resources were committed to lending (compared with one-third in 1957), but instead of using almost entirely the form of the overdraft, they had developed 'contractual term lending'. As for their sources, these had been expanded far beyond the deposits of their customers by tapping the expanding 'wholesale' inter-bank markets.[136] An interesting new instrument here was the 'Certificate of Deposit' (CD) available from a minimum value of £50,000 upwards, carrying a rate of interest and running for a fixed term, which had several advantages from the point of view of the banks as also of the lender. First used in 1966, the CD's were shown in the balance sheets from 1971 onward and had reached a total of £6 billion by 1973.

Yet these innovations were not able to hold up the rise of a whole new parallel or secondary banking sector to trench into much of the traditional business of the clearing banks. It was made up of the branches of foreign banks in London, of Finance Houses and of other institutions which began to proliferate in the 1960s. While in 1959–65 the deposits of the joint-stock banks rose by 5% a year, those of overseas banks registered 25% and Accepting Houses 20% a year increases. The numbers of overseas banks represented in London rose only from 53 in 1950 (of which 12 were American) to 77 (15) in 1960, but then jumped to 255 (61) in 1976 and 360 in 1981. Their market share of deposits rose from a

Table 8·14: Liabilities outstanding at year-end (£ million)

	1965	1970	1977
Inter-bank market	366	1,694	11,496
Markets in sterling CDs	—	1,089	4,641
Discount market, borrowed funds	1,381	2,259	3,610
Finance house deposits	054	000	009
Local authority temporary debt	1,740	1,879	3,013

mere 1·6% in 1958 to 20·2% in 1968. Acceptance Houses concentrated on short-term finance of which they provided £2½ billion (much of it in non-sterling

---

[136] *Wilson Committee, Evidence*, vol. 2, pp. 75 ff., vol. 5, pp. 103 ff., vol. 6, pp. 18 ff.; Nevin and Davis, Table 14; T. M. Rybczynski, pp. 31 ff.; Tew, 'Monetary Policy', pp. 241–3; David K. Sheppard, *The Growth and Role of UK Financial Institutions 1880–1962* (1971), pp. 118–19.

currencies) and £1 billion as acceptance credit in January 1977, within a total of £7½ billion credit managed by them.[137] This 'parallel money market', outside the traditional banking and discount markets, developed as shown in Table 8·14.[138]

Within these growing totals, the business in foreign currencies and with foreign borrowers and lenders was growing fastest, explaining, in turn, the growing number of foreign banking institutions in London. The most spectacular development here was that of the 'Euro-currencies'. The trade in Euro-dollars first became possible on the basis of dollars flowing to Europe as a result of the Marshall plan and the American payments deficit. It developed around 1957 because of the high bank rate and other financial constraints in London, and because of tax legislation, minimum liquidity provisions and legal interest limitation ('Regulation Q') in the USA. All these could be circumvented by the Euro-dollar trade. Since then it has spread to many other centres, though London has retained perhaps half the total business, it has taken in other currencies, and there has also developed a market in long-term securities, or 'Euro-bonds'.

The essence of a Euro-dollar deposit (which is generally of a minimum amount of $1 million) as distinct from a ' "national" dollar deposit is that it is the liability of a bank located outside the USA'.[139] As such it can be transferred between foreign (e.g. in the case of the US dollar, non-American) banks and between foreign lenders and borrowers. While at first particularly attractive because it got round irksome restrictions, the system has continued to expand even after 1974 when most of them had fallen away, because it offers favourable rates. It helped to ease American balance of payments pressure in 1968–9 and to absorb the billions of OPEC surplus petrodollars but at the same time added to the volatility and instability of international speculative switches between currencies.

Estimates of its extent are difficult to make, since multiple transfers may lead to double counting to an unknown degree. Widely accepted estimates put the business at $2 billion in 1960, $38 billion in 1970 and $67 billion in 1976. In the 1970s, central banks also entered this market, and the British Government itself borrowed $2·5 billion in the Euro-dollar market in 1973 and $1·5 billion in 1974.[140]

Overseas business liabilities among all the United Kingdom banks together increased from $2 billion in 1964 to £115 billion in 1977; between 1972 and 1976 alone, the share of foreign currency to total deposits rose from ⅓ to ⅓. The enormous size of the financial balances, as well as of long-term investments abroad, compared with actual trade in the later 1970s, will be evident from Table 8·2 on p. 307 above. The decline in investment in British industry, in particular, was matched by a sharp rise in direct investment abroad which

---

[137] Nevin and Davis, p. 214; *Wilson Committee, Evidence*, vol. 3, p. 75, vol. 5, pp. 1 ff., vol. 8, p. 31; I. R. J. Clark, p. 134, and T. Rybczynski, p. 154, both in Croome and Johnson, *op. cit.*

[138] *Wilson Committee, Second Stage Evidence*, vol. 2, p. 118. Also see E. R. Shaw, p. 80.

[139] Brian Tew, *The Evolution of the International Monetary System 1945–77* (1977), p. 154.

[140] George W. McKenzie, *The Economics of the Euro-Currency System* (1976), pp. 69, 89; *Wilson Committee, Second Stage Evidence*, vol. 2, 117–18, and vol. 4, 33–4; W. Clendenning, *The Euro-Dollar Market* (Oxford, 1970); P. Einzig, *The Euro-Dollar Market* (1973); E. R. Shaw, pp. 94–100; Geoffrey Bell, *The Euro-Dollar Market and the International Financial System* (1973).

amounted to £6·4 billion in 1969, excluding oil and insurance, but had risen to £24 billion in 1981 (net asset value); foreign holdings here exceeded £5 billion by then.[141] British currency holdings abroad totalled £10 billion and institutional investors were putting over £1·5 billion a year, or one-fifth of their new money, overseas. Some key annual figures are presented in Table 8·15.[142]

Table 8·15: International private financial transactions UK, 1965–1980

	1965	1970	1975	1980
Overseas investment in UK private sector	+238	+725	+1527	+4081
UK private investment overseas	−368	−773	−1367	−6891
Foreign currency borrowing and lending abroad by UK banks (net)	−22	+472	+253	+2024

More striking still was the recourse of the public authorities to foreign markets. Overseas holders of United Kingdom Government stock expanded their holdings as shown in Table 8·16.

Table 8·16: Market values of UK Government stocks held overseas at year-end (£ million)

	1977	1980
Held by central monetary inst's	1,341	2,234
Other holders	2,490	3,939
	3,831	6,173

The nationalized industries were similarly urged to borrow abroad, and all the major Public Corporations did so, especially from 1974 onward. Borrowings by the nine Corporations rose as shown in Table 8·17.[143]

Table 8·17: Borrowings abroad by Public Corporations (£ million)

Total of 5 years	1968–72	281
	1973	64
	1974	1,063
	1975	646
	1976	676
	1977	1,345

By 1978, some £4·3 billion was outstanding from the Public Corporations abroad, plus £0·5 billion by the Local Authorities.

[141] T. M. Rybczynzki, 'Structural Changes', p. 27; *Wilson Committee, Evidence,* vol. 3, p. 91, vol. 5, p. 13; *Bank of Eng. Qtly. Bull.,* 21/2 (1981), 203–5.
[142] *Annual Abstract of Statistics.*
[143] 'An Inventory of UK External Assets and Liabilities: End 1978', *B. of Eng. Qtly. Bull.,* 19 (1979), 163; W. A. Thomas, p. 303.

The picture that emerges, then, is a remarkable acceleration in international financial interdependence in the later 1970s. The City had always had its international links. These were now much changed in character and increased in magnitude.

9

The Government and the Economy

1 Taxation and Fiscal Policy

In the midst of the emergence of new weapons and new techniques of monetary policy, such as were described in the last chapter, the budget still retained its central importance. The budget speech, yearly at first and, as economic crises forced Governments to have emergency budgets more often, more than once a year, provided the keynote of Government plans, indicators of their strategic thinking, and statistics to back them up. The budget retained its traditional roles, such as providing finance for public expenditure, and contributing to such social aims as fairer distribution of incomes and social security. But now its substantive role was to ensure that the call on resources was matched up with the resources available in any one year, both in the economy as a whole and in the separate sectors such as labour, investment or consumption, while at the same time supporting all the other goals of Government economic policy, including full and stable employment, stabilization of the value of the currency at home and of its foreign exchange rate, economic growth and the preservation of the framework and the incentives for private enterprise.[1]

Several technical innovations were introduced into the budget. Income tax, among the most buoyant and prolific taxes during the two world wars, was largely left alone, the standard rate varying only marginally around the 8s. in the £ mark. A radical change abolished the 'standard rate' from 1972–3 onward and with it the system of charging lower income bands at lower rates, and substituted the 'basic rate', which dropped correspondingly to 30% from the last standard rate of 38·75%. It rose to a high of 35% in 1975–7, but then declined again to 30% from 1979–80 on. In that year, the top rate was reduced from its high level of 83% to 60% as part of the redistributive trend of Sir Geoffrey Howe's first budget; meanwhile, a lower rate of 25%, 5% below basic, had been introduced again for the bottom band in 1978–9.

The actual impact on incomes of these rates depended, in part, on the allowances, which were raised as inflation eroded their value, but not always fully. Family size and circumstances further altered the picture. The significance of these allowances becomes clear when it is considered that in a typical year, 1973/4, only 45% of aggregate gross income was subject to tax. Over the long term, falling real thresholds, caused by inflation and deliberate policy, tended to be compensated by lower rates. Table 9·1 provides data for a married couple with two children:[2]

[1] I. M. D. Little, 'Fiscal Policy', in G. D. N. Worswick and P. Ady, *The British Economy in the Nineteen-Fifties* (Oxford, 1962), pp. 233–4.

[2] David Piachaud, 'Taxation and Social Security', p. 69; also Chris Pond, 'Tax Expenditure and Fiscal Welfare', p. 54, both in Cedric Sandford, Chris Pond and Robert Walker (eds.), *Taxation and Social Policy* (1980).

Table 9·1:   Impact of tax rates on incomes

	Tax threshold as % of average earnings	Standard/Basic Rate start, as % of average earnings	First rate payable (p. in £)
1955/6	96·0	179·3	9
1965/6	70·5	109·8	15
1979/80	46·8	62·6	25

In view of these complications, it is not easy to determine exactly the movement of the income tax burden on equivalent real incomes over time, but the general trend is clear. Tax rates fell steadily from the early 1950s to a low in the early 1960s, and rose again thereafter erratically, to reach their initial levels in the mid-1970s. In the later 70s they fell again, experiencing a sharp drop in the budget of 1979/80.[3] 'Unearned income' continued to be taxed at higher rates throughout, but with differences in detail. Proposals for what was sometimes termed 'negative income tax', combining social payments with the tax allowance system, or alternatively for expenditure in place of income taxes, were made from time to time,[4] but were not adopted.

Profits taxes were used more flexibly and changed more drastically than taxes on incomes. The gap between distributed and undistributed profits was widened to 50%:10% in Gaitskell's budget of 1951, forming one of the main props of his deflationary policy. In 1952 rates were reduced and henceforth they changed frequently, but the gap remained until 1958, when a single flat rate of 10% was imposed. This equality in tax rates lasted for eight years. In April 1965 a new corporation tax implied a differential of 24·75% in favour of retention. In 1973 the basis of the corporation tax was changed once more to the 'imputation system', in which all profits, whether distributed or not, were subject to the same tax, which was then deemed to have been paid by the shareholders on their dividends.

While the differential lasted, it penalized equities as against loans and debentures, it penalized investment by shareholders in new ventures as against capital accumulation in existing companies and it penalized risky investments. The lowering of the tax in 1952 and the abolition of the differential in 1958 were followed by upwards jumps in the proportions of profits distributed in 1953 and 1959, and thus became significant influences on the post-war patterns of distribution.[5]

[3] F. W. Paish, 'Inflation, Personal Incomes and Taxation', *Lloyds Bank Review*, 116 (April 1975), Table 4, p. 14; Joseph A. Pechman, 'Taxation', in Richard E. Caves and Lawrence B. Krause (eds.), *Britain's Economic Performance* (Washington, 1980), Table 10, p. 247.

[4] J. E. Meade (Chairman), *The Structure and Reform of Direct Taxation* (1978); Nicholas Kaldor, *An Expenditure Tax* (1955); *Proposals for a Tax Credit System* (Green Paper), Cmnd. 5116 (1972); David Collard, 'Social Dividend and Negative Income Tax', in Sandford, Pond and Walker, *op. cit.*, pp. 190 ff.; *Report of the Committee on Turnover Taxation*, Cmnd. 2300 (1964).

[5] Little, p. 237 (footnote); *Royal Commission on the Taxation of Profits and Income, Final Report*, Cmd. 9474 (1955), esp. chapter 20.

Britain's relatively high tax rates on business were mitigated by a particularly favourable system of investment allowances. 'Initial allowances', permitting accelerated depreciation of capital installed and thus a delay in taxation and a consequent gain in interest charges, had been introduced in 1945 as a method of helping to finance investment. They were suspended in 1951, in the budget which was perhaps the most damaging of all to long-term investment, but reintroduced in 1953.[6] They were subsequently varied frequently with changes in policy, but they were temporarily replaced in 1954 by 'investment allowances', which were true tax exemptions rather than delays. Both have since been used at varying rates. In 1970 'first year allowances' were added in place of investment grants, and from the budget of November 1974 on, substantial allowances on stock appreciation were granted to deal with the distortions caused by the inflation.

A 30% capital gains tax was enacted in 1965, modified substantially in 1971; it was to be levied at the point of disposal of most types of assets. The effects of this tax have been much disputed, but it is widely believed that it discouraged saving and investment.[7] In 1978–9, a special tax was placed on land development gains over £160,000 in lieu of the capital gains tax.

National insurance contributions may be considered as a form of payroll tax. To it was added the Selective Employment Tax (SET) of 15% on payrolls in 1966. It was intended to perform a double function. In addition to the main objective which was to make labour more expensive and encourage labour-saving investment,[8] the tax had a distributional objective which largely cancelled out the first. Only the 'service industries' were to pay the tax effectively; some selected employments (e.g. hospitals) were to have the tax refunded after some delay; but manufacturing firms were in fact to gain more than they paid in. This discriminatory division into productive and unproductive employment ran against the experience of all progressive economics of a long-term growth of the tertiary occupations. Inasmuch as the tax was intended to encourage labour-saving investment, it should have been levied on manufacturing industries working for exports.[9] However, it was based on the notion that the expansion of the labour force in industry was a mainspring of the rise of productivity.[10] The effects of the tax have remained uncertain. To some extent, the distributive impact was met by the budget of 1968, which extended the effective range of the tax to all employees, but exempted the Development Areas. It was abolished in 1973 as part of the major tax reform which included the introduction of the Value Added Tax (VAT).

Expenditure taxes fell into two broad categories. One consisted of items of mass consumption, such as tobacco, alcoholic drinks and fuel oils,[11] showing a strong upward 'ratchet' effect. By contrast, purchase tax on a broad range of

[6] Changes are summarized in J. C. R. Dow, *The Management of the British Economy, 1945–1960* (Cambridge, 1965), p. 206; and in Pechman, Table 14, p. 251.

[7] A. R. Prest and D. J. Coppock, *The UK Economy* (1978), pp. 94–5.

[8] J. R. Sargent, *Out of Stagnation* (Fabian Society, 1959).

[9] J. P. Hutton and K. Hartley, 'The Selective Employment Tax and the Labour Market', *British J. of Industrial Relations*, 4/3 (1966).

[10] See pp. 298–9 above.

[11] J. C. R. Dow, 'Fiscal Policy and Monetary Policy as Instruments of Economic Control', *Westminster Bank Review* (August 1960).

other items, calculated *ad valorem*, moved up and down much more freely. In 1960 the right was granted to the Chancellor to vary during the year, and therefore free from the artificial timing of the budget proposals, purchase tax and excise duties by up to 10% either way. This was estimated to make, at its maximum, a difference of £200 million to revenue. A 10% surcharge was imposed almost at once, and since it was consolidated next year, it left the Chancellor free to use his powers again. The VAT of 1973 replaced the former purchase tax with the difference that it was also levied on services and thus ended the discrimination against commodities, while it had the further advantage that it was easier to remit on exports. Its main purpose, however, was to align the British system with that of the EEC.

There were thus numerous changes affecting the distribution of the tax burden among sections of the community,[12] but in the debate on macro-economic policy, it has been the overall weight of the 'burden' of taxation which has been given importance. This includes a varying list of other items, for example, surpluses and subsidies in the nationalized industries, as well as the more traditional taxes.

In general the Second World War had seen a rise in the share of Government expenditure as a proportion of GNP from which, as after the First World War, it did not quite fall back to its pre-war level. This 'ratchet effect' did not apply to local government, which returned after the war to the position of the late 1930s.[13] The total share of both local and central government in the country's economic activity then stayed fairly level, but with a slightly rising tendency which became more pronounced only in the 1970s, to rise to a peak in 1975 and the fall back thereafter[14] (see Table 9·2).

Table 9·2:   General government expenditure as % of GNP at market prices

	Expenditure on goods and services	Total government expenditure**
1950*	17·7	39·3
1958*	18·6	37·0
1966	21·4	37·7
1970	22·2	40·2
1975	26·7	49·3
1980	23·9	46·0

* Not strictly comparable with the later figures.
** The difference between these two columns is made up of transfer payments.

These shares were very similar to those of other western and industrialized countries, whereas the burden on employers of social payments to be added to their wage roll were in Britain well below the average of others. Nevertheless, the level of public expenditure (which might, on the part of some critics, include

---

[12] See discussion pp. 266–8 above.

[13] Alan T. Peacock and Jack Wiseman, *The Growth of Public Expenditure in the United Kingdom* (1967), pp. 107, 166.

[14] *National Income and Expenditure*; Prest and Coppock, pp. 86–7. Also R. W. R. Price, 'Public Expenditure', in F. T. Blackaby (ed.), *British Economic Policy 1960–74* (Cambridge, 1978), pp. 94 ff., and alternative figures in Jim Tomlinson, *British Macroeconomic Policy Since 1940* (1985), pp. 124, 127.

the public corporations) is commonly made responsible for the poor British economic performance.[15] It should be noted that the weight of the National Debt fell sharply because of the inflation, above all in the 1970s, precisely when its increase caused so much public concern: as a proportion of GNP it dropped from 300% in 1945 to 40% in 1975, to rise slightly thereafter. Government, in fact, was a net saver throughout this period, imparting a deflationary bias to

Table 9·3:   Public authorities income and expenditure (as % of GNP)

	Central government receipts		Public authorities current expenditure, of which:		
	Taxes on income and capital (inc. net insurance contributions)	Taxes on expenditure	Social services	Defence	Debt interest
1950	20·8	14·7	13·6	7·1	4·7
1951	20·0	14·7	12·5	8·6	4·6
1964	18·1	11·5	16·1	6·8	4·4
1965	19·3	12·2	17·1	6·8	4·4
1970	24·3	16·7	23·1	5·6	4·6
1971	23·0	16·0	22·5	5·5	4·2
1979	22·5	18·1	27·1	5·4	5·3
1980	23·8	19·3	28·6	5·9	5·8

the economy, right up to the later 1970s when the deficits predominated. Even then the returns show that while real Government expenditure had been rising by 4·9% a year in 1961–73, it rose by only 0·4% a year in 1973–8, when complaints were loudest.[16]

Table 9·3[17] shows the major items of income and expenditure. In income, the ratio of taxes on income to taxes on expenditure moved slowly in favour of the latter. Among expenditure items, it is the social services that are clearly responsible for the rise overall; defence expenditure came down and debt interest also drifted downward, only to jump in the later 1970s with renewed borrowing and high interest rates.

Fiscal policy was, throughout, one of the instruments with which the authorities sought to 'steer' the economy, in year-to-year or even more frequent changes. Within this sphere of economic management the general assumption

[15] E.g. David Smith, 'Public Consumption and Economic Performance', *National Westminster Bank Quarterly Review* (November 1975); Sir Alec Cairncross, 'The Postwar Years 1945–77', in Roderick Floud and Donald McCloskey, *The Economic History of Britain Since 1700*, vol. 2 (Cambridge, 1981), pp. 409–12; Michael Beenstock, 'Taxation and Incentives in the UK', *Lloyds Bank Review*, 134 (October 1979), p. 4; Pechman, pp. 206, 243–5; Robert Bacon and Walter Ellis, *Britain's Economic Problem: Too Few Producers* (1976).

[16] David Higham and Jim Tomlinson, 'Why Do Governments Worry About Inflation?' *National Westminster Bank Quarterly Review* (May 1982), p. 4; Andrew Glyn and John Harrison, *The British Economic Disaster* (1980), p. 128; R. C. O. Matthews, 'Why Britain Had Full Employment since the War', *Econ. J.*, 78 (1968), 556; C. V. Downton, 'The Trend of National Debt in Relation to National Income', *B. of Eng. Qtly. Bull.*, 17/3 (1977), 320; M. R. Weale, 'The Accounts of the UK Public Sector 1972–1982', *Three Banks Review*, 141, 1984, pp. 25, 27; M. Miller, 'Inflation-adjusting to the Public Sector Financial Deficit', in J. Kay (ed.), *The 1982 Budget* (Oxford, 1982).

[17] *National Income and Expenditure.*

until 1963/4 was that taxation was too high, having a negative effect on incentives,[18] so that the budget should be used only in expansionary policies by lowering taxation, whereas if restrictive policies were required, they should operate *via* the financial mechanism only.[19] In the later 1960s and in the mid-1970s, this liberal attitude to the budget was overlaid by the need to raise revenue, but it reappeared to determine Conservative policy in 1970–4. There was thus in existence a medium-term policy as well as the yearly or shorter switches.

In this period the effect of the budget on employment began to be calculated in a more sophisticated, but rather uncertain, way[20] as 'fiscal stance', i.e. not as the actual surplus or deficiency, but the rate re-calculated on the basis of full employment. In the 1950s and 1960s, when the Government was in surplus except for investment in the nationalized industries, the difference was not great. For the 1970s, the results are shown in Table 9·4:[21]

Table 9·4:   Fiscal Stance: Budget outturn and cyclically adjusted surplus (in % of GDP), 1970–1980*

	Budget Out-turn		Cyclically adjusted
1970/1	2·0	1970	5·0
1971/2	2·1	1971	3·3
1972/3	8·9	1972	1·3
1973/4	−2·3	1973	−1·0
1974/5	−0·7	1974	1·4
1975/6	1·8	1975	1·1
1976/7	3·0	1976	−0·7
1977/8	3·0	1977	1·5
1978/9	2·2	1978	−1·0
1979/80	−0·7	1979	0·9
1980/1	−3·8	1980	2·1

* Positive figures mean Government surplus (deflationary), negative are deficits (expansionary).

Overall the budgets were not only deflationary, but also destabilizing, increasing fluctuations instead of smoothing them out, as indeed was the Government's investment policy for the public sector by itself.[22] Moreover, these frequent disturbances of the budget for the sake of short-term policy switches necessarily did damage to the Government's power to perform its remaining tasks of raising revenue and redistributing incomes. It might even reasonably be held that 'it should be regarded as a confession of failure when changes in the level of public expenditure . . . are made and then reversed on a countercyclical basis', and that

[18] Such an effect has never been objectively established. E.g. Pechman, pp. 218 ff.

[19] J. M. Buchanan, 'Easy Budgets and Tight Money', *Lloyds Bank Review*, 64 (April 1962), 17–30.

[20] Prest and Coppock, p. 29; R. W. R. Price, 'Budgetary Policy', in F. T. Blackaby, *Economic Policy*, pp. 139–41.

[21] David Begg, 'Fiscal Policy', in Rudiger Dornbusch and Richard Layard (eds.), *The Performance of the British Economy* (Oxford, 1987), p. 37; also see Tomlinson, pp. 122, 127; *Nat. Inst. Econ. Rev.*, 63 (February 1973), 13 and 96 (May 1981), 12.

[22] C. D. Cohen, *British Economic Policy, 1960–1969* (1971), pp. 82–3; Price, 'Public Expenditure', p. 126. Also see note 111 below.

changes in public expenditure for the purpose of managing the economy should be used only as a last resort.[23] At the same time, it is worth noting that economic policy, including the 'stop-go' sequence, did in fact largely concern itself with marginal quantities and formed, in the long view, little more than ripples on the gently upward slope of production and incomes. Even the most drastic budget 'package' of all, the measures of 1968, were intended to cut consumption by less than £1 billion in a full year, or 3% of national income. This should be compared with unemployment rates of up to 22% in the 1930s and 12–15% in the early 1980s.

2 Forms of Direct Intervention

In addition to the indirect influence on economic affairs described in the preceding sections, the Government also intervened directly in industry and in other spheres of economic activity. The most immediate form was the control over nationalized industry, discussed in section 2 of chapter 7 above. But there were innumerable other means, many of which were expanded or transformed in our period. This section will deal with a representative sample of them.

After the preference shown for economic planning under the Labour Governments of 1945–51, the Conservative administration of the following 13 years emphasized the market and private initiative for industry, and gave industry its 'freedom' in the 1950s. Some innovations of the Labour Government, such as the Development Councils, were allowed to lapse. Direct intervention, such as the titanium agreement with ICI or the decision on the two new steel rolling mills in 1959–60, remained rare. But by the early 1960s, the signs of weakness of British industry under that regime, such as its slow growth and substantial loss of export markets, could no longer be ignored, and Government turned once again to more direct forms of action. Partly designed to deal with the repeated balance of payments crisis, the National Economic Development Council (NEDC, or 'Neddy') began working in 1962 as a common forum on which management, labour and Government and some independents could meet. It has survived the economic vicissitudes of many years; prime ministers and chancellors of the exchequer have attended its meetings, yet its exact functions and powers have never been clear.[24]

Its first task was to consider obstacles to quicker growth or greater efficiency, and a major report, published within one year, *Growth of the United Kingdom Economy 1961–6*[25] studied the implications of a 4% growth rate (compared with a 3% rate assumed by the Treasury). In December 1963 approval was given for the appointment of specialist industrial Economic Development Committees ('little Neddies'), and 21 of them were set up, engaged mainly in activities such as economic forecasting, studying the effects of such changes as decimalization, taxation and devaluation, and disseminating and exchanging information of various kinds.

[23] Ninth Report of the Expenditure Committee, *Public Expenditure, Inflation and the Balance of Payments*, H. C. 328 (1974), para. 19, p. xi.
[24] Richard Bailey, *Managing the British Economy. A Guide to Economic Planning in Britain Since 1962* (1968), pp. 9–36; Scott Newton and Dilwyn Porter, *Modernization Frustrated* (1988), pp. 132 ff; K. Middlemas, *Industry, Unions and Government; Twenty-one Years of NEDC* (1983).
[25] Published in February 1963. See also NEDC, *The Growth of the Economy* (1964).

NEDC itself, however, lacked executive powers, and when the incoming Labour Government in 1964 wanted to improve industrial performance and growth, it established a new department under a senior minister, the Department of Economic Affairs (DEA). Behind the founding of the DEA lay the belief that growth had not only not been furthered, but had actually been inhibited by deliberate Government action in the interest of short-term policies, and that a senior minister, responsible for the economy as a whole, was needed to make long-term growth plans stick. It did, indeed, publish a plan in 1965[26] for a 4% annual growth over five years, but in spite of the enthusiasm of the minister, George Brown, the DEA soon fell victim to the logic of balance of payments deficits and the inherent power of the Treasury.[27] With it fell the only real chance since the war of making growth, expansion and efficiency the major Government economic goal.

In the month in which the DEA was set up, October 1964, the Ministry of Technology was also created as part of the same drive and it began work in 1965. Among its first objects was the sponsoring of four technological industries: computers, machine tools, electronics and communications. It also took over from the Ministry of Aviation all the functions relating to aircraft production and design. These critical and vulnerable growth industries received the repeated attentions of Government thereafter.

In part, Government support took the form of offering finance and sponsoring reconstruction. In December 1966, following a white paper[28] the Labour Government established the Industrial Reorganization Corporation (IRC) with a capital of £150 million to encourage mergers on grounds of efficiency, and by the Industrial Expansion Act of 1968 it took general powers to finance industrial investment schemes without having to ask for legislation each time. The incoming Conservative Government dissolved the IRC and emasculated the Industrial Expansion Act, but was soon forced once more to commit large sums to rescuing the shipbuilding companies on the Upper Clyde in the form of the reorganized Govan Shipbuilders, and to nationalizing the Rolls Royce company, both having been in danger of bankruptcy. Further, it sponsored the Industry Act of 1972 which included provisions for tax incentives for investment as well as specific grants for capital expenditure in assisted areas and elsewhere.

Labour's Industry Act of 1975 extended these provisions and set up the National Enterprise Board (NEB). This was given large financial means, of up to £1,000 million, to continue the policy of awarding specific assistance and to extend public ownership not only to firms on the point of collapse, but also to profitable companies – a policy of 'backing winners'. Hopes nursed in some quarters that it would become part of a wider industrial strategy[29] have not been realized. However, some specific influence through the 'Accelerated Projects Scheme' of 1975, to encourage firms to bring investment projects forward in

---

[26] *The National Plan*, Cmnd. 2764 (1965).

[27] George Brown, *In My Way* (1971), pp. 95–6, 113, 119; Newton and Porter, pp. 150 ff.; Jacques Leruez, *Economic Planning and Politics in Britain* (1975), pp. 48–9; Roger Opie, 'Economic Planning and Growth', in Wilfred Beckerman (ed.), *The Labour Government's Economic Record 1964–1970* (1972), p. 171.

[28] *Industrial Reorganisation Corporation*, Cmnd. 2889 (1966).

[29] *The Regeneration of British Industry*, Cmnd. 5710 (1974); *An Approach to Industrial Strategy*, Cmnd. 6315 (1975). Also John Hughes, *Britain in Crisis* (Nottingham, 1981), p. 38.

depression years, and the 'Selective Investment Scheme', for projects that would benefit the national economy but would not be undertaken without Government assistance, did remain.

The result of this legislation was a wide net of investments in, and subsidization of, industrial firms in the 1970s.[30] In 1979–80, financial aid provided by the Department of Industry totalled £1,060 million, including £540 million for regional and general support, £140 million for scientific and technological assistance and £380 million for manufacturing directly sponsored by the Department, but excluding the nationalized industries.

Finance of a semi-official nature also continued to be available through the Finance Corporation for Industry and the Industrial and Commercial Finance Corporation; these were merged in 1973 to form Finance for Industry (FFI), which was provided by the Bank of England and the Clearing Banks with funds of up to £1,000 million. The Bank of England was also instrumental in setting up a so-called equity bank, Equity Capital for Industry, in 1976, which channelled insurance and pension funds into equities.

As far as policy on industrial location was concerned, the post-war legislation, based on assumptions of massive unemployment, was used less and less in the 1950s when that assumption proved wrong, though northeast Lancashire was added to the Scheduled Development Areas in 1953. Control was further reduced when building licensing was abolished in 1954, but then the recession of 1957–8 provided a new impetus, while the increasing traffic strangulation of London, the South-East and the Midlands, made location policy necessary for the sake of the congested as well as the depressed areas. By the Distribution of Industry (Industrial Finances) Act, the powers of the Treasury to grant loans or grants for industrial buildings were extended to all forms of business, and to places outside the Development Areas with persistently high unemployment rates of over 4%. A major, consolidating measure in 1960, the Local Employment Act, provided for a new list of localities (Development Districts), based on actual and potential unemployment of 4·5% or above to qualify for the privileges; some 160 Districts were designated and the list varied from time to time. Grants and loans were to be more freely available also. Among the early actions was the setting up of branches of the main motor manufacturers in those areas.[31]

In the Depression of 1962–3 a Secretary of State for Industry, Trade and Regional Development was appointed to deal with the disturbingly high unemployment figures in the traditional problem areas in Scotland, Wales and northern England. Regional reports worked on the assumption that the solution lay in bringing work to these areas, rather than moving people out of them, and stressed the need for positive incentives and for amenities,[32] but in fact mobility was fairly high, and in 10 years 18% of the population had moved outside their towns, and nearly 7% into another region, mostly to London and the

[30] Michael C. Fleming, 'Industrial Policy', in Peter Maunder (ed.), *The British Economy in the 1970s* (1980), pp. 145–6; Alan Whiting (ed. for Department of Industry), *The Economics of Industrial Subsidies* (1976); also see p. 262 above.

[31] P. D. Henderson, 'Government and Industry' in Worswick and Ady, pp. 337 *passim*. Also pp. 244–279 above.

[32] See also Colin Clark, 'Industrial Location and Economic Potential', *Lloyds Bank Review*, 82 (1966).

South-East.[33] The real watershed in post-war legislation came with the Local Employment Act of 1963, which provided for grants of 10% for machinery, 25% for buildings, an option of 'free' depreciation, and a more stringent use of Industrial Development Certificates (IDC) in congested areas.[34]

In July 1965, Regional Planning Councils were set up to co-ordinate industrial and social policies with the needs of whole regions in mind:[35] the object was now 'balanced regional growth' as part of overall planning, rather than curative action after the damage was done. It is doubtful if they had much effect.

The Industrial Development Act of 1966 substituted Development Areas for Development Districts, increasing the coverage to some 20% of the working population; in 1969, following the report of the Hunt Committee,[36] subsidies were extended to the so-called 'Intermediate Areas' with less severe structural and unemployment disadvantages. Finally, in this legislative period, the Regional Employment Premium (REP) was created in 1967, amounting to a subsidy of 5–7% on wages in the favoured areas, in addition to preferential rebates under the SET, which brought the subsidy up to perhaps 8%. The Local Employment Act 1970 designated two new types of area, 'Intermediate (Gray) Areas', and 'Derelict Land Clearance Areas'.[37]

In contrast to the Labour Government of 1964–70, which had seen locational policy as an aid to national economic planning,[38] the Conservative administration of 1970–4 was both averse to planning in general, and to supporting individual firms in particular. Investment grants were abolished in the mini-budget of October 1970 and replaced by allowances. IDC and Office Development Permit controls (first brought in in 1964 for London) were relaxed, and the financial grants reduced in total. The depression of 1971–2, however, forced a re-examination of the issue[39] and a return to the broad policies of the late 1960s by means of grants. Thus the Industry Act of 1972 extended the designated Intermediate Areas, so that altogether 44% of the population came under one or other special status;[40] the REP, which it had been intended to abolish in 1974, would now stay; and investment tax allowances in the budget of 1972 were given a strong regional bias.

The Labour Government that followed not only held to that commitment, but actually doubled the rate of subsidy under it. It also gave more power to the regional offices of the Department of Trade and Industry established earlier, extended the designated Development and Special Development Areas, and

[33] A. J. Harris and R. Claussen (Government Social Survey), *Labour Mobility in Great Britain, 1953–1963*, S. S. 333 (1966), pp. 10–3.

[34] A. P. Thirlwall, 'The Local Employment Acts 1960–1963: A Progress Report', *Yorkshire Bulletin*, 18/1 (1966).

[35] Ministry of Labour Gazette; Michael Stewart, *Keynes and After* (Penguin, 1967), p. 157; Paul Burrows, 'Manpower Policy and the Structure of Unemployment in Britain', *Scot. J. Pol. Econ.*, 15/1 (1968), pp. 75–7; G. McCrone, *Regional Policy in Britain* (1969).

[36] Department of Economic Affairs, *The Intermediate Areas*, Cmnd. 3998 (1969).

[37] P. J. Curwen and A. H. Fowler, *Economic Policy* (1976), p. 165; Christopher M. Law, *British Regional Development since World War 1* (1980), pp. 48–9; Ron Martin and Bob Rowthorn, *The Geography of De-Industrialisation* (1986), pp. 80–1.

[38] J. Hardie, 'Regional Policy', in W. Beckerman, *Labour Government*.

[39] Department of Trade and Industry, *Industrial and Regional Development*, Cmnd. 4942 (1972).

[40] T. Nuttall, 'The Industry Act and Regional Policy', *National Westminster Bank Quarterly Review* (November 1973), 55–68.

decided to disperse more Government Departments to the regions. In 1975 and 1976 the Scottish and Welsh Development Agencies, respectively, were set up, to deal with the high unemployment as well as to assuage the apparently growing nationalism of those regions.

Meanwhile, the problems of regional inequality were taking on new, or rather, additional forms, The Census of 1971, the results of which were becoming known in 1976, showed that migration of industry out of the large cities left a pool of unskilled and unemployed labour in the city centres, not only in traditional black spots like Glasgow and Liverpool, but also in formerly prosperous urban communities like Birmingham.[41] The Government reacted in 1977 by a policy of channelling both offices and the vulnerable small workshop industries back to the centres of conurbations, but in fact made little financial provision for this.[42] Since then the social consequences of the economic decay of the inner city areas have become more evident.

Rising unemployment in the motor industry in the late 1970s, affecting the formerly prosperous West Midlands, reduced the justification for continuing to favour the North and West. The necessary greater emphasis on cost cutting employment also worked against the high-cost Development Areas. Additionally, the strong regional policy of the EEC frowned on the REP as incompatible with its principles, and as keeping alive low-productivity firms. The new Conservative Government of 1979 added its dislike of all subsidies in principle. It announced in 1979 that by means of boundary changes the proportion of the employed population in favoured areas would be cut from over 40% to 25%, and the planned traditional regional aid programme would be cut from £609 million to £376 million by 1982–3. Meanwhile the United Kingdom has received considerable payments from the EEC Regional Fund. They have tended to be for specific projects, and to favour investment rather than subsidizing operating costs.

The new towns legislation should also be mentioned here. Some 20 towns have been built on the basis of the New Towns Act of 1946 and the Town Development Act of 1952, and others enlarged. The object was essentially to relieve the pressure on large conurbations, above all on London, and they have had some success in drawing industry with the population out to the New Towns.

The effectiveness of these regional policies as a whole is hard to gauge. Significant moves of manufacturing industry from the South-East and the West Midlands did take place, but not always to the real deficit regions, and the motives were mixed.[43] Some elements, such as the IDC's and direct subsidies, were undoubtedly effective in locating new factories,[44] but almost by definition these were high-cost units and often among the first to suffer or even close in

---

[41] Kenneth J. Button, 'Spacial Economic Policy', in Maunder, *British Economy*, p. 178.

[42] Department of the Environment, *A Policy for the Inner Cities*, Cmnd. 6845 (1977); J. S. Foreman-Peck and P. A. Gripaios, 'Inner City Problems and Inner City Policies', *Regional Studies*, 11 (1977).

[43] A. J. Brown, *The Framework of Regional Economics in the United Kingdom* (Cambridge, 1972), pp. 250 ff.

[44] J. K. Bowers and A. Gunarwardena, 'Industrial Development Certificates and Regional Policy', parts 1 and 2, *Bulletin of Economic Research*, 29 (1977) 112–22 and 30 (1978) 3–13; B. Ashcroft and J. Taylor, 'The Movement of Manufacturing Industry and the Effect of Regional Policy', *Oxf. Econ. P.*, 29/1 (1977).

depressions. The effects of REP were less clear-cut.[45] The principle, taken over from the 1930s, of bringing jobs to people rather than encouraging migration, in order to preserve the social capital of established communities, was no doubt responsible for lowering overall British efficiency, but the likelihood is that apart from certain significant exceptions, such as the motor-car industry, these cost effects of location were small.[46] On the other hand, the advantages offered have been largely on investment, which encouraged capital-intensive industries in the favoured areas and thus did little to create jobs. Large differences in regional levels of unemployment remained, and widened as rates rose (see Table 9.5), though it is not possible to say what they would have been had the battery of policies not been adopted.

Table 9·5:   Unemployment in UK regions, per cent

	December 1958–March 1961*	
London and South-East	1·21	
Central (Midlands & Yorks.)	1·21	
East and South	1·40	
South-West	1·87	
North-West	2·23	
Wales	2·70	
North	2·85	
Scotland	3·81	
Great Britain	1·83	
	1970	1980
South-East	1·6	4·8
East Anglia	2·1	5·7
East Midlands	2·2	6·4
South-West	2·8	6·7
West Midlands	1·9	7·8
Yorkshire & Humberside	2·8	7·8
North-West	2·7	9·3
Scotland	4·2	10·0
Wales	3·8	10·3
North	4·6	10·9
Northern Ireland	6·8	13·7
United Kingdom	2·6	7·4

* P. C. Cheshire, 'Regional Unemployment Differences in Great Britain', NIESR, *Regional Papers II* (Cambridge, 1973).

Finally, a further area of direct Government intervention was the promotion and support of scientific and technological research and training. These had been much boosted by the war. Government expenditure on civil research and development rose from £6·6 million in 1945–6 and £30 million in 1950–1 to an

---

[45] K. J. Button, pp. 188–9; also see A. Beacham and T. W. Buck, 'Regional Investment in Manufacturing Industries', *Yorkshire Bulletin*, 22/2 (1970); B. C. Moore and J. Rhodes, 'Evaluating the Effects of British Regional Employment Policy', *Econ. J.*, 83/1 (1973) and *idem*, 'Regional Employment Policy and the Scottish Economy', *Scot. J. Pol. Econ.*, 21/3 (1974); Gavin McCrone, *op. cit.*, pp. 151 ff., C. H. Lee, *Regional Economic Growth in the United Kingdom Since the 1880s* (Maidenhead, 1971), pp. 147 ff.

[46] A. R. Prest and D. J. Coppock, *The UK Economy* (1978), pp. 205–8; A. J. Brown, *op. cit.*, p. 302.

estimated £295 million in 1967–8, growing at a rate of 13% per annum.[47] By 1981–2, total Government expenditure on research and development (R & D) was estimated at £3,000 million, of which above one half, £1,683 million, went to the Ministry of Defence, £788 million to the Department of Education and Science, including the funds for the Universities and Research Councils, and the rest to other Departments with research interests, including Industry (£305 million), Energy (£234 million), and Agriculture, Fisheries and Food, including Scotland (£112 million). The distribution of funds and actual R & D work changed as shown in Table 9·6.

Table 9·6: Distribution of funds and R & D work

Sources of funds:	1958/9	1964	1968	1978
Government	66·9	53·6	48·6	47·0
Private industry	28·5	41·1	40·2	36·9
Other	4·6	5·2	11·2	16·6
Carrying on the work:				
Government: defence	}		11·5	9·4
other	}	27·6	13·5	12·2
Private industry		63·7	59·1	58·7
Other		8·7	15·6	19·7
Total, £ million	477·8	768·0	986·0	3510·3

The share of Government, both in providing funds and in carrying out research, therefore fell substantially in those years. The overall rising totals were caused by inflation rather than expansion. At constant (1970) prices, intramural R & D rose by only 7·5% from 1964 to 1978, and the R & D performed by the Government actually fell, from £608 million to £511 million, or by 16%.[48]

Official support for scientific research took mainly two forms: the work of the Scientific Civil Service and of Government-sponsored research institutions, and Government support for independent bodies.[49] The former were largely concerned with defence, but some, like the research activities of the Atomic Energy Authority, had important economic and industrial aspects and applications. The National Research Development Corporation, set up in 1948, had the task both of supervising the commercial exploitations of patents derived from public sponsored research and of supporting promising research which could not find industrial backers. Among the latter the development of the hovercraft was perhaps the most spectacular.

In the support of outside civil research, the Department of Scientific and Industrial Research, strengthened by a new Act in 1956, was the main agency. It subsidized research associations formed by industries and also supported research in the Universities and similar institutions. Following the Trend Report

[47] Council For Scientific Policy, *Report on Science Policy*, Cmnd. 3007 (1966), para. 9 and p. 20, and *Second Report on Science Policy*, Cmnd. 3420 (1967), para. 10.
[48] *Annual Abstract of Statistics*; Philip Gummett, *Scientists in Whitehall* (Manchester, 1980), pp. 39, 57.
[49] J. W. Grove, *Government and Industry in Britain* (1962), chapter 11.

it was abolished[50] and, in 1965, a Ministry of Technology was set up.[51] Most Government research and development activity came under the new Ministry, which began by promising massive support to the British computer industry, the NRDC undertaking to invest £5 million in International Computers and Tabulators (ICT). The Atomic Energy Authority was also permitted to engage in research outside the nuclear field. In 1967 the Ministry of Technology added the R & D functions of the Ministry of Aviation, its first real operative sections and in 1969 those of the Ministry of Power, to its competence.[52]

Under the Conservatives from 1970 on, the coolness towards Government initiatives applied to the field of sponsored research also, though the distribution of funds hardly slackened in practice. In the administrative reorganization of that year, the Department of the Environment was created as was the Department of Industry and Trade, which combined the Ministry of Technology (less some aviation) with much of the Board of Trade. In February 1974, in turn, the DTI was split again into Departments of Trade, of Industry and of Prices and Consumer Protection. Meanwhile, the newly constituted 'think tank', or Central Policy Review Staff, came out in favour of applied R & D on a customer-contractor basis, the customer stating his requirements to the scientists. Specialist 'Requirement Boards' were to bring supply and demand together. These proposals were adopted in principle, and a share of the funds allocated to the Research Councils were switched to 'customer' Government Departments.[53]

To judge the effects of the Government's involvement in industrial R & D, individual industries have to be examined in detail.[54] By such means as direct subvention, enforced amalgamation, the provision of orders and of scientific information, the Government undoubtedly helped certain firms in such sensitive industries as aircraft, electronics and machine tools, in which the bulk of the R & D expenditure occurred[55] to stay alive and remain up-to-date. Yet several of them remained ailing and vulnerable, and had to be rescued repeatedly at the taxpayer's expense.

The sums devoted in Britain, by Government and other sources together, to R & D seemed large by the standards of most other countries, but an unusually high proportion in Britain was spent on defence, or else on defence-related objects, such as that prominent loss-maker, Concorde. Further, while Britain

---

[50] *Report of the Committee of Enquiry into the Organization of the Civil Service*, Cmnd. 2171 (1963); Ian Varcoe, *Organizing for Science in Britain. A Case Study* (1974), pp. 4, 78, 81.

[51] Norman J. Vig, *Science and Technology in British Politics* (Oxford, 1968), pp. 34 ff.

[52] P. Mottershead, 'Industrial Policy' in F. T. Blackaby (ed.), *British Economic Policy 1960–74* (Cambridge, 1978), pp. 442 ff.; Vig, pp. 146 ff.; Gummett, p. 45.

[53] Civil Service Department, *A Framework for Government Research and Development*, Cmnd. 4814 (1971); *Framework for Government Research and Development*, Cmnd. 5046 (1972); Gummett, pp. 57, 132, 197, 201.

[54] Several such studies will be found in Mottershead, *loc. cit.*

[55] The leading recipients were (in % of the total):

	1972–3	1978
Electrical engineering	26·5%	32·1%
Aerospace	25·2	18·2
Chemical and allied	16·7	18·4
Motor vehicles	6·7	5·6
Mechanical engineering	6·5	7·8

No other industry received more than 4%. Prest and Coppock, p. 212; *Annual Abstract of Statistics*.

has an unusually low ratio of scientists and technologists among its higher civil service, most of those she had were, once again, engaged in defence work and she has never been able to develop a 'science policy'.[56] In any case, the gap was rapidly narrowing in the 1970s (Table 9·7).[57]

In view of the widely acknowledged shortcomings of British technical and scientific education, there was widespread demand for more education of this type superimposed on an existing upward curve of demand for all kinds of

Table 9·7: Expenditure on R & D

	Total spent on R & D % of GNP	Public sector R & D. % of GNP		Industry-funded R & D % of GDP of manu-facturing	
	1965	1970	1975	1967	1975
United Kingdom	2·3	1·25	1·18	3·3	2·7
W. Germany	1·3	0.96	1·22	2·2	2·7
France	1·5	1·24	1·16	n.a.	2·0
Italy	—	0·46	0·40	—	—
Netherlands	1·8	—	—	3·5 (1969)	3·6
USA	2·8	1·56	1·33	3·5	4·2

higher education, described most fully by the Robbins Report.[58] In 1956 the Government announced a five-year plan, estimated to cost £100 million, to expand the Technical Colleges both in their full-time and their part-time courses.[59] At a higher level, in addition to the foundation of seven new Universities, a number of Technical Colleges became Colleges of Advanced Technology and ultimately full Universities in the early 1960s, and others were elevated into a hierarchy of Polytechnics or Regional Colleges (which also offered degree courses), Area Colleges, and others. In 1964, the new Department of Education and Science was established to combine the lower and higher levels of education under one administrative control.

At a lower level, the Industrial Training Act of 1964 broke new ground.[60] Under it the Minister of Labour was given statutory power to set up Industrial Training Boards in individual industries which would be authorized to make compulsory levies from all firms and distribute them to those offering formal training facilities, thus providing a direct financial incentive to each firm to enlarge its own training activities in order to recoup its levy. By 1969, 27 Boards had been formed. Totals under vocational training rose from 4,000 in 1962 to 18,000 in 1971 and under the Training Opportunity Scheme to 40,000 in 1973; the planned total then became 100,000 a year.[61] The later phasing out of the

---

[56] *S. C. on Science and Technology, 2nd Report* (1969), pp. xxvii–xxix; Gummett, pp. 215, 233–5; Aubrey Jones, *Britain's Economy: the Roots of Stagnation* (Cambridge, 1985), p. 92.

[57] B. R. Williams, *Technology, Investment and Growth* (1967); Prest and Coppock, p. 213.

[58] *Report of the Committee on Higher Education*, Cmnd. 2154 (1963), and Appendices.

[59] *Better Opportunities in Technical Education*, Cmnd. 1254 (1961).

[60] *Industrial Training. General Proposals*, Cmnd. 1892 (1962).

[61] *Capital Investment Procedures*, Cmnd. 6106 (1975), p. 4.

Industrial Training Scheme may be taken as a sign of success rather than failure.[62]

At the beginning of 1974 the Manpower Services Commission (MSC) was set up in place of the Central Training Council. The Training Services Agency was created at the same time. The MSC had little influence on industrial training – its main concern turned out to be employment problems – and it reported in 1980 that, in spite of the emphasis of the Employment and Training Act 1973, 'in traditional crafts, it is still the passage of time rather than objectively assessed performance standards, which decide whether a trainee is accepted as skilled.'[63] More worrying was the fact that, compared with the leaders, Britain lagged badly in vocational apprenticeship of all kinds (see Table 9·8).[64]

Table 9·8:   Activities of young people after compulsory school period (%)

	Year	Full-time general education	Full-time vocational education	Appren- ticeship	Work or unem- ployed
West Germany	1980	25	18	50	7
Switzerland	1978/79	20	9	52	19
Great Britain	1977	32	10	14	44

As a proportion of GNP, education as a whole had grown from 2·5% in the 1930s to 3% in the 1950s, 5% by the mid-1960s[65] and 6%, or £11,880 million, in 1980.

3 Macro-economic Policy: Stop-go

In several of the earlier sections, the evolution of Government economic policies has been traced in broad sweeps, showing changes in emphasis, aims and methods over a 30-year period (especially chapter 8, sections 2 and 3, and chapter 9, sections 1 and 2). We have also had occasion to examine the medium-term changes in direction that arose from the replacement of one governing party by another, in 1951, 1964, 1970, 1974 and 1979. Such an approach brings out some specific aspects of British economic development and of the role of the State in economic life. But it would be wrong to suggest that behind these wide movements there lay some consistent long-term strategy.

On the contrary, as noted in numerous specific instances above, British economic policy was dominated by short-term expedients reacting to short-term crises. Whatever major movements occurred were the result of the sum of short-term policies impinging on the underlying trends in a catastrophic rather than a clearly planned manner, and in the end sacrificing long-term aims for immediate needs. Among the long-terms aims were full employment, dominating the early

[62] R. Elliott, 'Industrial Relations and Manpower Policy', in F. T. Blackaby, *Economic Policy*, pp. 606, 612.

[63] Manpower Services Commission, *Review of the Employment and Training Act 1973* (1980), para. 4.16.

[64] Ian Jones, 'The New Training Initiative – An Evaluation', *Nat. Inst. Econ. Rev.*, 99 (February 1982), 70.

[65] John Vaizey and John Sheehan, *Resources for Education. An Economic Study of Education in the United Kingdom, 1920–1965* (1968), pp. 2, 139.

post-war years, and economic growth and structural change, which occupied the leading place from the late 1950s onward. The short-term crises, which repeatedly disrupted their attainment, were caused by failures to achieve balance, above all in the foreign balance of payments, which led to the failure to keep up the international value of the pound sterling until the flow of North Sea oil had solved that problem, and failure to match home supply and demand for money, which led to inflation. At the very end of the period, crisis measures to deal with inflation appeared to have blotted out any other economic aim for material well-being whatever.

The repeated zig-zag course with which successive Governments reacted to the temporary imbalances became known, not inaptly, as 'stop-go', designating alternate phases of permitted expansion and enforced contraction. The attempted mechanism was macro-economic throughout, informed by Keynesian thinking in the earlier phases and monetarist thinking increasingly in the 1970s: that is to say, imbalances, no matter where they occurred and how limited their impact, were to be cured by subjecting the whole economy to a regime of contraction or expansion. The sequence in which this occurred will itself help to explain how the mechanism worked and why it was bound to continue without solution in an ever deteriorating spiral.

We begin with the year of 1951 which saw a sudden deterioration of the balance of payments.[66] The largest part of this deficit was caused by a sharp decline of the terms of trade,[67] to their trough of the post-war years, precipitated by the Korean War and the stockpiling of imported raw materials in expectation of further price rises, which made inventories one of the most volatile of factors. Finally, the sudden rearmament programme, decided on in August 1950, had dangerously extended the home economy, rearmament being planned to take 7% of GNP in 1951 rising to $10\frac{1}{2}$% in 1952.[68] Sharp restrictions were called for, but since the pressure was to come from rearmament, consumption cuts were not very relevant, and taxes on consumption were raised by £150 million only in the 1951 budget. The real cut was to fall on investment by such means as the suspension of 'initial allowances'.

As the crisis of 1951 turned out to be one of the foreign balance, a swing of £700 million from a surplus of £300 million in 1950 to a deficit of £400 million, the incoming Conservative Government proceeded almost at once to drastic import cuts and cuts in tourist allowances. A rise in the bank rate to $2\frac{1}{2}$% in November was to be followed by a further rise to 4% in March, 1952, accompanied by money market operations to make them effective, ushering in

[66] The year-by-year account of the following paragraphs is heavily indebted to J. C. R. Dow, *The Management of the British Economy, 1945–1960* (Cambridge, 1965); I. M. D. Little, 'Fiscal Policy', in G. D. N. Worswick and P. Ady, *The British Economy in the Nineteen-Fifties* (Oxford, 1962); the Annual Review in *Nat. Inst. Econ. Rev.; Bank for International Settlements, Report 1967–8*, pp. 3–16; R. J. Ball and T. Burns, 'Stabilization Policy in Britain 1964–81', in Michael Posner (ed.), *Demand Management* (1978); W. Beckerman (ed.), *The Labour Government's Economic Record 1964–1970* (1972); Alec Cairncross, *The Economic Section 1939–1961* (1989); F. T. Blackaby (ed.), *British Economic Policy 1960–74* (Cambridge, 1978); W. P. J. Maunder, (ed.), *The British Economy in the 1970s* (1980), esp. Tony Westaway, 'Stabilization Policy and Fiscal Reform'.

[67] Roy Harrod, *The British Economy* (New York, 1963), pp. 133–5.

[68] Alec Cairncross, *Years of Recovery. British Economic Policy 1945–51*, (1985), pp 212f; Joan Mitchell, *Crisis in Britain* (1963), pp. 33–4, 106–7.

the new 'monetary' policy.[69] The budget of 1952 continued the policy of keeping consumption level and cutting investment in order to free resources for rearmament, but it also fulfilled some election pledges by a cut in subsidies and increases in indirect taxation, as well as cuts in income and profits taxes, all designed to redistribute income to the rich and to 'enterprise'. An excess profits levy was to prevent war profiteering.

The fall in import prices, some running down of stocks and the measures taken, together afforded gratifying relief to the balance of payments in 1952. Home industrial output was cut by 3%, more sharply than had been intended, and tax revenue was also cut thereby, but the other indicators were more promising by the time of the 1953 budget. The Chancellor Butler, however, was still uncertain of the foreign balance, and the only concessions to expansion were the restoration of the initial allowances and some reduction in income and purchase taxes, calculated to add £100–150 million to consumption. As a controlled boom got under way, some import and other restrictions were removed in 1953, and the bank rate was reduced by $\frac{1}{2}$%. It was the first budget for which it was claimed that it took into account the threatened rise in unemployment.[70] The most encouraging aspect was the buoyancy of exports, so that the boom was allowed to continue into 1954, when the economy again reached full employment. The budget of 1954 made no important changes apart from turning 'initial' into 'investment' allowances to encourage investment, but food rationing and building controls were abolished. Things seemed to be getting better every year and it was at this time that Mr Butler announced his hope for a doubling of the standard of living in 25 years – the first important statement of concrete long-term growth as a major policy objective.

By the end of 1954 the boom was beginning to endanger the balance of payments, as consumption and imports exceeded the ability to produce and export. Measures early in 1955 included the raising of the bank rate in two steps from 3% to $4\frac{1}{2}$%, and some hire-purchase restrictions. But in his budget, the Chancellor, no doubt conscious of the impending election,[71] added to the expansion by an income tax cut of £150 million. By the summer, the economy was in crisis again, and the first cycle of the 1950s was completed. An autumn budget became necessary to rectify the balance of payments and to stop the speculation anticipating another devaluation. The *de facto* return to sterling convertibility about this time did not make the control of the economy any easier. There were sharp tax increases, and early in 1956 investment allowances were exchanged for the less valuable initial allowances, the bank rate was raised to $5\frac{1}{2}$%, and there were hire-purchase restrictions. This crisis also saw some of the most savage cuts of the investment plans of nationalized industries.[72]

On the whole, this credit squeeze was effective. The Budget was neutral, but contained Macmillan's best-known innovation, the premium bond to encourage saving. Output stagnated in 1956 and 1957, and so did investment, and imports actually fell, helped by a reduction in inventories. Exports showed an encour-

[69] A. J. Youngson, *Britain's Economic Growth, 1920–1966* (1967), p. 176.

[70] Jim Tomlinson, *Employment Policy 1939–1955* (Oxford, 1987), p. 146.

[71] E.g. Michael Pinto Duschinsky, 'Bread and Circuses? The Conservatives in Office 1951–1964' in Vernon Bogdanor and Robert Skidelsky (eds.), *The Age of Affluence 1951–1964* (1970), pp. 64–6.

[72] Samuel Brittan, *Steering the Economy: The Role of the Treasury* (1969), p. 125.

aging rise, and it is likely that in normal circumstances slow growth might have been resumed soon after, but instead the attack on Suez supervened at the end of 1956. The economic effects proved less destructive than might have been expected, though petrol was rationed once more, but it led, in September 1957, to a sharp speculative attack on sterling. The crisis of 1957 was thus not based on 'real' factors, which were reasonably healthy in that year. Nevertheless, it had to be met by the normal battery of squeeze measures, superimposed on a stagnant economy, and these prolonged the stagnation for another year. It was significant that the price rise, which contributed to the sterling crisis, was based on a smaller than normal wage rise, but one matched against an even smaller increase in output. Further, the budget of 1957 had encouraged consumption by cuts in direct taxes, but failed to encourage investment, except in ships.

Thus the crisis of 1957 showed itself in a drain on the reserve, rather than a payments shortfall. It was precipitated by a number of circumstances: a *de facto* devaluation of the franc, the refusal of Germany to revalue the Mark even though large quantities of gold had moved into that country, the decision to wind up the EPU, and by an attack launched from the City, led by the Governor and Deputy Governor of the Bank of England, recalling some aspects of the summer of 1931, on the alleged recklessness of the British Government in permitting credit expansion and wage increases. The Council on Prices, Productivity and Incomes, the 'Three Wise Men', had been set up in July 1957, and all seemed set for even more drastic restrictions, but in fact Mr Thorneycroft was not prepared to go much further than raise the bank rate to a sensational 7%, asking the banks to stop lending and arranging for cuts in Government spending and in the investment plans of the nationalized industries.

By early 1958 it was clear that the economy was in depression, and the budget laid the basis for only a slow expansion, since there were still fears of wage rises and another attack on the reserves. Heathcoat Amory raised 'initial' allowances, and made some moderate cuts in indirect taxes. Production stagnated but, owing to a substantial improvement in the terms of trade, Britain had the highest favourable trade balance of the post-war era, and the fall in import prices also kept home price level increases down to a low figure. With unemployment at 2·8% in January 1959, the highest since the war, Heathcoat Amory felt justified in introducing substantial boosts into the budget of 1959. Already during 1958, the ceiling on bank advances had been abolished, and hire-purchase restrictions taken off. Also sterling was made fully convertible at what looked to be an auspicious time. Now the intention was to return to full employment. Among the considerable tax cuts, purchase tax was reduced by one-sixth, the duty on beer cut, the standard income tax cut by 9*d*., and the investment allowance reinstated. Altogether, £300 million was to be added to consumers' spendable incomes in a full year, plus £70 million in a once-for-all post-war credit repayment.

For a while output increased without exceeding the labour supply, though some bottlenecks, e.g. sheet steel, began to develop. During the year, industrial output rose 10%, national output 3–4%, and final expenditure, 6%. The external balance was less favourable, though still positive, and full capacity was being reached by the end of the year. In the budget of 1960 the changes were only minor, but the bank rate had been put up to 5% in January and went up to 6% in June, and the first 1% 'Special Deposits' was called for. In consequence, the consumption rise was held back, but the reduction was greater in production and exports, while imports and investment continued strongly. In February, Macmillan as Prime Minister had resisted the clamour of the Treasury and the Bank of England to put on the 'brake'.[73] For once, the attempt was made *not* to let the inevitable squeeze fall on investments. The total result of all these influences was a sharp deterioration in the balance of payments in 1960, marking the end of the second cycle, in a form very similar to the crisis of 1955.

The budget of 1961 thus inaugurated another period of restriction and decline. There were tax increases, but these were of a kind to raise costs, and the balance of payments, while improving, was still weak. The large deficit of 1960 had been met, not by a drain on the reserves, but by more short-term loans, and now, in 1961, these turned against sterling, repeating the experience of a monetary, or speculative crisis of 1957, but this time much closer to the real deficit period which had caused it. The attack on sterling was beaten off with the help of large loans, including £323 million from the European Central Banks, and a £178 million standby credit, plus £535 million from the IMF, all of which weakened sterling still further in the long run. Meanwhile, the measures of July 1961, the 'Little Budget', included a rise of the bank rate from 5% to 7%, another 10% surcharge on customs, excise and purchase tax, a further 1% special deposit, and promises of major Government cuts in expenditure as insisted on by the IMF, heralded by an immediate attempt to stop wage rises of employees in the public sector. These were sufficient to turn the modest expansion of the first half of 1961 into a sharp decline. The losses in economic growth now began to be considered more seriously, but the simultaneous (and partly contradictory) criticism was made that the collapse had come because expansion had been allowed to proceed too quickly.

The first type of criticism was perhaps best formulated by Harold Wilson, when moving the Amendment in the House of Commons. The July measures, he alleged, were designed to keep the 'hot money' in London and, since a loan from the IMF was necessary, to satisfy the international banking community by 'massive, masochistic and irrelevant cuts in our standard of living, harmful restrictions on our production, and needless increases in our cost and price structure (in the belief that speculators are impressed only by actions which in the long term harm the economy). The Government's policies are so bankrupt that 16 years after the war we have to go for international aid. We will be a magnet again for hot money all over the world.'[74]

The budget of 1962 showed only minor changes as the Treasury overestimated the rise in demand, needlessly prolonging the depression.[75] The economy recovered but slowly, while strenuous exhortations were uttered to hold down wages, and the NEDC began working on its long-term growth plan. A world economic boom allowed exports to increase somewhat and to improve the balance so that a cautious reflationary policy could begin. By the end of the year indirect taxes had been reduced, the Special Deposits released, and investment allowances increased. However, the recovery was disappointing, industrial investment was still declining and unemployment was still substantial. For 1963 it was expected

[73] Harold Macmillan, *Pointing the Way 1959–1961* (1972), pp. 220–6.
[74] *H. of C. Debates*, vol. 645, cols. 441–2, 26 July 1961.
[75] Brittan, *Steering*, pp. 161–7.

that the economy would move towards fuller capacity, and output would rise in line with the NEDC 4% target overall.[76] Maudling's Budget was openly expansionary, and tax remissions, including income tax concessions, together with the abolition of 'Schedule A' tax were estimated to amount to £269 million. There was also greater assistance to the Development Districts. Wage increases, however, were to be limited, mainly by exhortation, to the 'guiding light' of $3\frac{1}{2}$%. In the event, the recovery was substantial, output rose by 5–6%, but private investment was still depressed and there was still spare capacity, but at least the foreign balance had stood up well to the reflation and exports were rising.

1964 became the crisis year, marking the peak of the third cycle since 1951. The budget was still hopeful. It gambled on rising output, investment and productivity to break through the export price barrier to keep up a reasonable foreign balance; this, in turn, would permit expansion to continue at the existing rate, which the NEDC and others considered a minimum. The slight deflationary indirect tax increases were intended to hold expansion down to 4%, and if there had been any intention to impose tighter restrictions and cut short the boom, it was resisted in view of the coming General Election. In the event, the gamble failed. With the rise in consumption and investment, the foreign balance collapsed, and the balance-of-payments deficit was the largest ever, reaching nearly £700 million.

The new Labour Government announced a number of crisis measures in October almost immediately on taking office,[77] including a 15% surcharge of all imports of manufactures and semi-manufactures, which raised a storm of protest abroad, and some export rebates. In November a second budget increased petrol taxes at once, and announced an income tax increase and a new Corporation Tax, from April 1965, estimated to yield £215 million in a full year. Meanwhile, to stem the panic sterling outflow, the Bank Rate went up again to 7%, and an emergency credit of $3,000 million was raised abroad.

Callaghan's April budget of 1965 was only mildly deflationary, since he still hoped to increase exports by encouraging production rises at home. Foreign central bankers, satisfied with the tough British policies, bought sterling in September to 'squeeze the bears' among the international speculators who had banked too early on a devaluation, and by February this relief, as the hot money flowed back, allowed Britain to repay a large part of the loans raised abroad.[78] However, while incomes and imports rose in the United Kingdom, exports stayed down and by the end of the year the balance was still adverse. The budget in 1966 was delayed until May because of the General Election, but when it came, its most important deflationary provision, the SET, which was calculated to bring in £315 million in the first year and to be equivalent to a £200 million purchase tax, could take effect only slowly. Meanwhile, the first half of the year had seen not only the drain on the reserves continuing, but some special features aggravating it, including the seamen's strike and a particularly heavy capital outflow matched by an unusually small inflow. There was thus a renewed run

[76] NEDC, *The National Plan*, Cmnd. 2764 (1965).

[77] Prime Minister's Office, *The Economic Situation* (1964).

[78] Robert Solomon, *The International Monetary System, 1945–1976. An Insider's View* (New York, 1977), pp. 90–1.

on sterling, which caused an even more severe application of the brake in the shape of the 'July measures'. They included severe hire-purchase restrictions; a 10% surcharge on purchase tax, petrol, and excise duties, except tobacco; savage cuts in Government spending, including investment by nationalized industries; tighter building controls; a 10% surcharge on surtax and various other measures, which together were calculated to reduce the pressure by £340 million in the current year and £516 million in a full year. The brief attempt to hold on to growth was abandoned; henceforth, the only reply to a sterling weakness would be further deflation and further squeezes.

The most controversial measure, perhaps, was the total wage freeze for six months, affecting even firms in which increases were to be paid for by increases in productivity, to be followed by a further six months of 'severe restraint'.[79] On its own premise, which was that incomes have to be cut to match productivity and not production raised to match incomes, it was a reasonable approach, though its effect was temporary, wage rises were postponed rather than abandoned and the damage done to industrial relations was incalculable. But the most significant result was that despite these most savage cuts, and five budgets in 20 months, the drain and the imbalance continued. Growth was duly slowed down, but exports did not thereby pick up. To some extent, again, there were special factors in 1967. World trade declined somewhat, while UK imports remained high and rising interest rates abroad weakened sterling; there were dock strikes in London and Liverpool; Britain's application to join the EEC renewed fears of a sterling devaluation; and the Middle East War in June again increased costs by closing the Suez Canal. This time the drain of funds out of London, particularly by speculative owners weary of three years' continuous crisis, could not be stopped by any amount of foreign lending, and in November the pound was devalued by one-seventh from $2·80 to $2·40.[80]

As noted above, the flight from sterling was not stopped by devaluation but continued, and Britain required further large foreign loans. The measures taken at once in 1967, and the full budget of March 1968, exceeded all previous cuts and tax increases in extent, and surprised even foreign bankers. Among others, SET relief was withdrawn, except for Development Areas, purchase tax, customs and excise and petrol duties increased, and Bank Rate raised from 6½% to 8% (down to 7½% in March). No less than £923 million, or 3% of GNP, was to be diverted from consumption, one half to wipe off the foreign payments deficit and the other to build up an annual positive balance, to pay off the debts accumulated since 1964, and resume economic growth. It is worthy of note that of the total negative foreign balance of £3·6 billion accumulated 1964–8, which had led to such humiliating borrowing abroad and destructive deflation at home, the actual current account deficit amounted to only £1·3 billion, or just over one-third; the rest of the deficit was caused by speculative moves of sterling holders, and by British capital exports.[81] Further, throughout these financial disasters, in which the confidence of overseas bankers and speculators had

[79] F. Blackaby and M. Artis, 'An Incomes Policy', *District Bank Review*, 165 (1968); Harold Wilson, *The Labour Government 1964–1970. A Personal Record* (1971), pp. 258–9. Also chapter 7, section 4 above.

[80] *B. of Eng. Qtly. Bull.*, 7/4 (1967), 335 and 8/1 (1968), 4–8. *Midland Bank Review* (February, 1968).

[81] C. D. Cohen, *British Economic Policy 1960–1969* (1971), p. 181.

become at least as important as the real situation of the British economy,[82] some growth in output had continued, though the 4% target had long since been abandoned.

Contrary to widespread expectations, the devaluation with its associated savage deflationary measures, offered no immediate relief to the adverse balance of payments. Apart from the well known 'J-curve' effect, caused by an early loss of foreign currency after devaluation owing to lower export unit prices before the greater quantity could outweigh the loss per unit, there were particular features in this case. The most important of these was that Britain was near full employment and there was thus no spare capacity to divert to exports; but further, one major export market, the Sterling Area, was hit by the loss in value of its sterling reserves, and/or devalued with the United Kingdom, while the other major export market, the advanced industrial world, was not very price-elastic.[83] British exports did indeed rise by 6½% in dollar value, but those of all industrial countries rose by 13%, so that Britain continued to fall behind, and her foreign drain went on. In the September Basle Group Arrangement, foreign central banks offered credits to repay the holdings of Sterling Area countries, and thus remove that millstone from British necks, but a further speculative attack on sterling followed in the belief that the Deutschmark would be revalued.

So the squeeze continued. In November 1968 HP restrictions were tightened, and the April 1969 budget increased corporation tax, SET and purchase tax. The effect on demand was to be £200–250 million, but the total Government surplus was estimated at £800 million. Unemployment continued to rise, while inflation received a boost by the devaluation.

The 1969 budget added further burdens, totalling £130 million, and the Bank Rate had been raised in February to 8%, but at last devaluation had begun to work and the foreign balance had turned positive. Wages and earnings, it is true, were rising faster, in the face of the Government's inability to hold the unions to either a statutory or a voluntary incomes policy, but the budget of 1970 set the signals to 'go', even if hesitantly. The new Conservative Government inherited a comfortable foreign surplus, but also the obligation to repay a large loan, and faced a threatened wages explosion. It reacted by asking the banks in July 1970 to limit lending, and keeping the October 1970 budget neutral.

In 1971 the combination of rising unemployment and rapidly rising prices and incomes confused the policy makers, who had hitherto looked upon these two movements as incompatible. The budget, which included some major tax reforms, was inflationary to the extent of £500 million, but of this sum only £160 million had immediate effect in the form of increased child allowances. Further relaxation followed later in the year, including tax cuts, the ending of HP restrictions, the lifting of lending ceilings, two Bank Rate cuts of 1% each, public works programmes and the repayment of the last post-war credits. Conditions were set for the great property boom. Meanwhile there was an unprecedented £1 billion surplus on foreign current account, superimposed on a £1·8 billion influx of capital, of which £1 billion had gone into private industry.

[82] 'The British Government had it brought home in no uncertain terms in late 1964, that it should not only steer the economy in what it thinks to be the right direction, but also in what foreign governments think to be the right direction.' A. R. Prest, 'The British Economy, 1945–1960', *Manchester School*, 33/2 (1965), 144.

[83] F. V. Meyer, D. C. Corner, J. E. S. Parker, *Problems of a Mature Economy* (1970), pp. 572–7.

The dollar was devalued as a consequence of American payments deficits and the world began its move towards floating exchange rates.

Thus the budget of 1972 could afford to consider unemployment, now at a temporary peak of $3\frac{1}{3}$% of the labour force. It was strongly reflationary. There were tax reductions and national and regional incentives: a total of £960 million in taxes plus £135 million in purchase tax were given away. The foreign balance was still positive, but a brief attempt to join the European currency 'snake' had to be given up, and the pound was floated in July. The budget of 1973 was neutral in effect, but included many changes in detail. The aim was to increase output and absorb the unemployed, still at 650,000. But while the pound sterling drifted down at the foreign exchanges, attention turned increasingly to the home inflation. After its *laissez-faire* attitude in 1970–2, the Government had some temporary success here with its incomes policy in 1972–3, only to end in failure in 1974.

The Conservative Government fell early in 1974, and Labour entered office committed not to impose restraints on the unions; the result was the most devastating wages explosion in British history. In the year between the second quarter of 1974 and the second quarter of 1975, average earnings were up by 28% and retail prices by 25%. With the foreign balance still precarious and rapidly being undermined by the OPEC oil price increases of 1973–4, inflation at home joined it at the centre of the stage. Policy now had to battle with these two dangers simultaneously, and in the process sacrificed all else, including in particular employment and economic growth, by measures of unprecedented severity. This was in marked contrast to 1970–4, when relaxed, if inflationary conditions, building on the investment and improved technology of the late 1960s, had seen the most sustained period of expansion in post-war history, real disposable income growing at the rate of 4·2% a year.

There were three budgets in 1974. The first, in March, was very slightly deflationary and largely distributional, taking from the rich in favour of the poor, by increasing pensions and food subsidies, and raising corporation taxes while cutting tax relief. The two later budgets reversed most of these trends, being slightly inflationary as well as favouring industry, by measures which included the relief on taxation of stock appreciation. In terms of prices also these three budgets were 'distinctly erratic. Changes in indirect taxes and subsidies tended to raise prices in March, lower them in July, and raise them again in November.'[84] What was clear was that the tendency for favouring investment and expansion, noticeable in the preceeding years, was coming to an end, and in the budget of 1975, Mr Healey for the first time openly jettisoned Keynesian remedies. Though unemployment was high and rising, he abstained from expansionary policies, for fear of worsening the foreign balance and above all the Government deficit, conventionally described as the Public Sector Borrowing Requirement (PSBR). So taxes were increased in 1975, public expenditure was to be cut in 1976 and meanwhile a tough incomes policy was to bridle inflation at home.[85]

[84] David Savage, 'Fiscal Policy, 1974/5–1980/1: Description and Measurement', *Nat. Inst. Econ. Rev.*, 99 (February 1982), 85. Also David Begg, 'Fiscal Policy', in Rudiger Dornbusch and Richard Layard (eds.), *The Performance of the British Economy* (Oxford, 1987), pp. 29–63; Andrew Glyn and John Harrison, *The British Economic Disaster* (1980).

[85] Jim Tomlinson, *British Macroeconomic Policy Since 1940* (1985), pp. 112 f.

The quite exceptional inflation rate of 1974–5 had fallen back to a still disturbing 14% by the time of the 1976 budget, and output was stagnating for the fourth year running, while unemployment reached a new high, averaging 5·76% for the year. In a somewhat bizarre move the Chancellor offered income tax reductions in return for wage restraint, but could not offer other positive incentives because the adverse foreign payments balance remained critical. The pound was allowed to drift down from $2·02 to a final $1·71, a 15% loss, to help employment at the expense of making inflation worse, thus operating directly against all the rest of the current policy package, which attempted to curb inflation at the expense of employment. Higher indebtedness abroad became necessary in the sterling crisis of 1976, when the Bank of England MLR reached 15%. There had to be a $5 billion standby loan from the central banks of the Group of Ten, plus Switzerland and the bank for International Settlements (BIS) in June, but the $3·9 billion credit, granted towards the end of the year by the IMF, carried as one of its conditions a limitation of domestic credit expansion (DCE). This helped to complete the switch to monetarist thinking which had already been evident in the announcement of monetary targets at the time of the budget earlier in the year. Budgets were now geared to medium-term DCE with limits on public expenditure, and progressive cuts in the PSBR as the main instruments. There were savage cuts in public expenditure in July, and yet again in December 1976, when there were also tax increases.

Although the foreign balance was now moving into equilibrium, there were but moderate reliefs in the three budgets of 1977. MLR moved down briskly to $12\frac{7}{8}$% in January and a low of 5% in October. By April 1978, inflation and the foreign drain had eased, whereas output and employment had stayed down: the opportunity was thus ripe for some substantial tax cuts worth £2 billion in 1978–9 and £2·5 billion in a full year, and all signals were set to 'go', but no effort was made to ensure that this benefited investment rather than consumption. The monetary quantity (sterling M3) became a six-months 'rolling target' to offer greater flexibility and perhaps quicker reactions in Government spending. Real disposal income rose by 8·3% in the year, having actually declined for three years running before, but by the end of the year the trade unions rejected all further forms of pay policy, and in the 'winter of discontent' strikes and rising inflation ruined the chances of the Callaghan Government's re-election. After a neutral Labour budget in April, the new Conservative Government set out to enforce major changes of direction in its budget of June 1979.[86]

Within a framework that was ideologically committed to reducing Government intervention, Sir Geoffrey Howe determined to cut the public sector deficit, even though the economy was clearly sliding into recession, unemployment was rising and output was actually expected to drop. The cuts were to fall mainly on investment, and it is worthy of note that at least a part of the reduction in the PSBR was to be achieved, not by genuine savings, but by the sale of national assets into private hands. In a separate move, income tax, especially for the top incomes, was cut substantially, and to make up the loss of revenue, VAT was raised from 8% to $12\frac{1}{2}$% to a standard 15%. This redistribution, switching benefits from the poor to the rich, was likely to and did indeed

[86] S. Brittan, 'A Transformation of the English Sickness', in Ralf Dahrendorf (ed.), *Europe's Economic Crisis* (1982), p. 95; Leo Pliatzky, *Getting and Spending* (Oxford, 1982), pp. 168–75.

boost inflation directly by 4–5% and indirectly by much more, in startling contradiction to the Government's declared main target, which was to *reduce* inflation. The package was completed by the plan announced in November to cut a further £3·5 billion from future public expenditure and sell an additional £1·5 billion of national assets.

By now it was clear that the monetary targets and indicators used by the Government, including M1, M3, Sterling M3, DCE and PSL 1 and 2 were too contradictory to be of much practical use. Thus in 1978–9, while £M3 had actually fallen, helping to add to the severe depression in Britain, DCE was simultaneously sharply rising, sustained in the absence of home money supplies by borrowing abroad; in 1976–7 both had moved in exactly contrary directions and were thus similarly opposite to each other.[87] Far from abandoning these indicators, however, the authorities used their erratic behaviour to switch between them, according to which looked best for the time being from their point of view. Yet in the final analysis this nimble targetry was of little account. What mattered was the solid reality of classic deflationary or 'stop' policies, applied with remarkable and unflinching consistency, and reminiscent of nothing so much as the Britain of the 1920s or the German Government after 1930.

The effects were broadly as expected. Between 1979 and 1980 total output fell by 3%, manufacturing output by 9%, investment by 9% and total employment by 2%: 418,000 jobs were lost in manufacturing alone in one year. Meanwhile, the North Sea oil, now about to come on full stream, had almost overnight solved two of the most intractable problems of the past 30 years, the balance of payments and the international value of sterling. At that point, with employment and output still falling and the foreign balance safe, all previous chancellors would have welcomed the opportunity to stop damaging the productive side of the economy further and would have reflated. Sir Geoffrey Howe however held fast to his classic deflationary strategy. The budget of 1980 brought additional increases in excise duties, petrol tax and income tax (by abolishing the reduced rate), further spending cuts and further sales of assets. The pay of employees in the public service was also to be more tightly controlled, and there were to be minor distributional changes, such as provisions to tax the unemployed and the strikers, and to reduce benefits to the latter. As the overall targets, now projected for no less than four years ahead, were once again not being met, further spending cuts and an increase in the employers' contribution to national income were imposed in November 1980. The balance of payments meanwhile had swung heavily in Britain's favour and the pound rose by a further 10% against the dollar and 9% against all currencies in the course of the year.

This depressing story of 30 years may at first sight appear confusing and without order. Closer inspection shows however that the periodic changes affecting the British economy were clearly of a cyclical nature. The cyles, which had an average duration of just under five years, were strongly influenced if not caused by the measures imposed by the authorities, which were, in turn, based on reactions to immediate crises. In the process, the repeatedly announced intentions of Governments to hold to long or medium-term plans were regularly and systematically thwarted by these needs of short-term 'management'.

---

[87] Bryan Gould, John Mills and Shaun Stewart, *Monetarism or Prosperity?* (1981), pp. 39–40. Also p. 325 above.

It is possible to construct a typical or model cycle for this period, in which all these factors come into play. Let us start with the upswing from the bottom of the trough. In that position, some resources would be unemployed and imports would be low because of low incomes and possibly some protectionist measures such as the import surcharge. Exports, encouraged by poor sales at home, would hold up better, despite the high unit costs ruling at less than full employment, and would benefit by better delivery dates, since inability to deliver at the right quality or price had helped to thwart exports in the boom. Thus there would be spare capacity and a positive balance of payments.

At this point, expansionary Government measures would gradually bring the spare capacity into play. Output could rise fairly fast and prices could stay low or rise but little as fuller use of resources reduced real costs. But to the extent that the 'go' phase brought on economic growth, the imports of the necessary raw materials would rise, and early bottlenecks would develop and become more frequent the closer full employment was approached, for it was of the essence of the preceding 'stop' phase that few additional investments had been undertaken to allow future expansion. Bottlenecks, also, had to be met by increasing imports while export delivery dates would lengthen because of capacity limitation. Thus the foreign balance would turn adverse and would lead, at once under fixed exchange rates and after some depreciation under 'floating' rates, to a drain on the reserves.

This would be the signal for panic on the part of the Bank of England and the Treasury, and all systems would go into reverse to bring the economy once more to a 'stop': Government spending cuts, incomes policies, tax rises, interest rate increases, credit curbs and import restrictions, among others, would combine to make incomes and output decline, imports drop, speculative hot money flow back, the balance of payments improve and spare capacity open up once more. The cycle was ready to begin once again *da capo*.[88]

This is the model cycle based on a crisis in the foreign balance of payments. There were also cycles in which inflation at home (caused by the relaxation under the 'go' regime) or the falling value of the pound on the international exchanges (similarly caused) would lead to, or reinforce, the panic 'stops'. In the 1980s, with the foreign balance of payments problem temporarily solved by North Sea oil, it was in fact to be inflation at home that was to be the sole justification for the destructive 'stops'.

The 'stops', imposed as the means to solve the temporary crises, became at the same time the cause of the long-term conversion of the cycle into a secular downward spiral. For it was of the essence of the 'stop' policies that it was above all investment that was held back, not personal incomes or consumption, and it was, in turn, the consequent relative decline in British productivity, or in other words, the rise in real costs relative to those of the chief competitors, that tended to price British goods out of the competitive world markets and kept exports from expanding.

[88] See S. Pollard, *The Wasting of the British Economy* (1982), pp. 47–55; John Eatwell, *Whatever Happened to Britain? The Economics of Decline* (1982), p. 95; Adrian Ham, *Treasury Rules, Recurrent Themes in British Economic Policies* (1981); Samuel Brittan, *Steering the Economy: the Role of the Treasury* (1969), p. xv.

This meant that the logic underpinning the 'stop-go' policies was flawed from the start. The reasoning appeared to be: 'Let's get the balance of payments (value of the pound, inflation) side right, and *then* we can allow healthy growth'. But if the authorities were indeed correct in their belief that high interest or high tax rates and the other paraphernalia of 'stops' were necessary to get the foreign balance (value of the pound, inflation) right, it would follow that as soon as these were relaxed, the disequilibrium was bound to reappear, and the next cycle set in motion. The only possibility of getting out of these vicious cycles was to alter some of the structural relationships. Were these affected by Treasury policy? They were indeed, but in the wrong direction, so as to make each cycle worse than the last.

Some of these tendencies could, in theory, have been counteracted by a policy of deflating the British price-level parallel with Britain's inability to keep pace with the efficiency of her rivals, but neither of the two methods of doing this, lowering prices to foreigners by devaluation, or lowering home prices by a severe incomes policy, were open to the United Kingdom. Devaluation was not permitted at all under the Bretton Woods system, and later, under floating rates, when it was brought into use, it could not be pursued to the extent necessary to match Britain's failure to reduce her real costs, because it had several adverse side effects, including accelerated inflation induced by higher import prices.[89] Incomes policies, the other means, were indeed tried, but could never be sustained for long; in any case, they were based on fundamentally mistaken assumptions, since as Table 9·9 shows strikingly, British wage rises were, if anything, below those of most other countries until the 1970s. Moreover, it came to be increasingly clear that there was an 'institutional' element in a free society enjoying full employment and strong trade unions, which raised wages by around 5% a year as a matter of course and correspondingly more in the inflationary years of the 1970s.[90] The difference between British and foreign experience was not that money wages rose here; but that these increased costs were absorbed by rising productivity elsewhere, but not in the United Kingdom. Both the devaluation of 1967 and the incomes policies were attempts to make prices reflect the relative impoverishment of Britain, rather than to remedy the causes of that impoverishment, and neither was successful even on its own misguided terms.

Thus, given common variations in input prices, like imports and wage rates, and given fixed exchange rates, Britain's failure to achieve the real cost reductions of other countries was bound to mean a relative rise in her export prices. Given the high demand elasticity, or in other words, the strongly competitive conditions in export markets, there is no alternative but to place the responsibility for the relative decline in British exports squarely on increasingly non-competitive price

[89] M. V. Posner, 'The Main Issues', in *idem, Demand Management* (1978), pp. 129–30.
[90] A. G. Hines, 'Trade Unions and Wage Inflation in the United Kingdom, 1893–1961', *Rev. Econ. Studies*, 31/88 (1964); Colin Clark, 'An International Comparison of "Overemployment" Trends in Money Wages', *Oxf. Econ. P.*, 9/2 (1957); E. V. Morgan, 'Is Inflation Inevitable', *Econ. J.*, 76/301 (1966), 6; Dow, *Management*, pp. 355–6; L. A. Dicks-Mireau and J. R. C. Dow, 'The Determinants of Wage Inflation: United Kingdom, 1946–56', *J. R. Stat. S.*, 122/2, Ser.A. (1959); K. G. J. C. Knowles, 'Wages and Productivity', in Worswick and Ady, pp. 520 ff; Eatwell, *Whatever Happened?* p. 119; Michael Nevin, *The Age of Illusions. The Political Economy of Britain 1968–1982* (1983), pp. 104–5.

Table 9·9: Hourly earnings, annual percentage growth rates[91]

	Manufacturing	All labour	Manufacturing	
	1948–63	1963–7	1967–75	1975–80
France	9·7	6·2	13·5	13·2
W. Germany	8·0	6·7	9·4	6·2
Italy	6·3	8·0	16·0	21·2
Japan	7·7	11·1	19·2	7·3
Netherlands	6·9	10·7	12·4*	—
UK	6·0	5·4	14·0	15·2
USA	4·2	3·6	6·9	8·6

* 7 years to 1974

and quality, i.e. on a failure to keep up productive efficiency.[92] The circle is thus complete: failure in productivity led to losses in exports; these led to balance of payments difficulties, and these, in turn, led to Government short-term measures which were certain, in the long term, to make the productivity failures worse and start the circle up again, in less favourable conditions, as soon as the restrictions were taken off.[93] All this was in addition to the sheer inability, noted above, of increasing output and exports in booms because of the physical limitations of existing plant.

In the case of imports, the mechanism was even simpler. The fear had been often expressed in the late 1940s that expansion of incomes would lead to a proportionate increase in imports of raw materials, food and goods that could not be produced at home according to a calculable 'propensity to import'. In the event, it was true that every expansion after 1950 led to an immediate sharp import rise; but just as the failure of exports to rise steeply was not simply due to the attractions of home demand, with which the negative correlation was weak,[94] but to a failure to produce, so this sharp rise in imports was not in commodities in which other countries enjoyed natural advantages in production, but on the contrary, the increase was greatest in machinery, steel and other capital goods, and in manufactures generally. For the economy in general in 1948–68 it was found that the elasticity of imports relative to home activity was higher for manufactures than for food.[95] Excess imports were thus largely due to non-necessities or to 'bottlenecks', i.e. failure to create sufficient capacity from home sources. To a varying extent, it was also due to a parallel sharp increase in inventories.[96] This may be put differently. Investment, the creation

[91] UN *Statistical Yearbook*; OECD, *Main Economic Indicators*.

[92] See also Youngson, *Britain's Economic Growth 1920–1966* (1967), pp. 232–5; J. R. Parkinson, 'The Progress of United Kingdom Exports' *Scot. J. Pol. Econ.*, 13/1 (1966); M. FG. Scott, *A Study of United Kingdom Imports* (Cambridge, 1963); Lynden Moore, 'Factors Affecting Demand for British Exports', *Bull. Oxf. Inst. Stat.*, 26/4 (1964), p. 347.

[93] R. W. Bacon and W. A. Eltis, 'Stop-Go and De-industrialization', *National Westminster Bank Quarterly Review* (November 1975), 31–43.

[94] R. J. Ball, J. R. Eaton and M. D. Steuer, 'The Relationship between United Kingdom Export Performance in Manufactures and the Internal Pressure of Demand', *Econ. J.*, 76/301 (1966).

[95] Klein, Ball, Hazlewood and Vandome, *An Econometric Model of the United Kingdom* (Oxford, 1961), p. 97. Also Marc Nerlove, 'Two Models of the British Economy,' *International Economic Review* 6/1 (1965), p. 165.

[96] See, e.g., NEDC, *Imported Manufactures: An Enquiry into Competitiveness* (1965); M. F. W.

of productive capacity, was at no time undertaken in a quantity to sustain a higher growth rate, so that if income growth occurred at a rate approaching the average Continental experience, it expressed itself in an import surplus rather than a commensurate growth in output. This import surplus, as noted above, resulted in measures which injured the creation of productive capacity still further. For most of the time, in periods of restriction, output was at less than capacity, preventing the full use of home resources for such objectives as improving Britain's productive potential:[97] when the brakes were taken off, capacity was then found to be too inelastic and too low.

Moreover, the progressive deterioration of British technical competitiveness meant that at each crisis, the dependence on imports increased, and the gap

Table 9·10:

Reference cycles in quarter years		changes in industrial production, %		changes in unemployment rate, in % of total employment	
Peaks	Troughs	P→T	T→P	P→T	T→P
I 1951		—		+0·5	
	III 1952		+21·4		−0·8
IV 1955		−1·2		+1·1	
	III 1958		+13·3		−0·5
III 1960		−0·4		+0·9	
	I 1963		+18·3		−1·1
I 1965		+2·6		+1·0	
	III 1967		+8·6		0·0
I 1969		−2·4		+1·6	
	I 1972		+13·7		−1·2
II 1973		−10·1		+1·4	
	III 1975		+16·5		+1·3
II 1979		(−14·1)*		(+5·0)*	
	II 1981		—		—

* Estimated

widened. While there is no clear trend in the amplitude of the swings of the post-war cycles, the overall deterioration will be clear enough from the sample series in Table 9·10.[98]

The basic difference between Britain and the other industrial nations and the

Hemming and G. F. Ray, 'Imports and Expansion', *Nat. Inst. Econ. Rev.*, 2 (1959); A. Maizels, *Industrial Growth and World Trade* (Cambridge, 1963); S. J. Wells, *Trade Policies for Britain. A Study in Alternatives* (1966), p. 92; PEP, *Growth in the British Economy* (1960), pp. 143 ff.; K. S. Lomax, 'Growth and Productivity in the United Kingdom', *Productivity Management Review*, 38 (1964), p. 14; Roy Harrod, *Towards a New Economic Policy* (Manchester, 1967), p. 25; P. M. Oppenheimer, 'Is Britain's Worsening Trade Gap due to Bad Management of the Business Cycle', *Bull. Econ. and Stat.* (formerly *Bull. Oxf. Inst. Stat.*), 27/3 (1965). M. FG. Scott, 'The Volume of British Imports', in Worswick and Ady, *op. cit.*, though published in 1962, is still wholly couched in the terms of the immediate post-war problems, and is witness to the delay in recognizing the long-term post-war trend.

[97] W. A. H. Godley and J. R. Shepherd, 'Long-term Growth and Short-term Policy', *Nat. Inst. Econ. Rev.*, 29 (1964).

[98] D. J. O'Dea, *Cyclical Indicators for the Postwar British Economy* (Cambridge, 1975), p. 39; *Nat. Inst. Econ. Rev.*, 96 (May 1981), p. 9 and 98 (November 1981) p. 7.

causes of Britain's relative decline lay therefore not so much in the existence of cycles as such, for these were found among all of them, including even the fastest growers like Germany and Japan,[99] but in the particular form taken by these cycles. While elsewhere the downward phases were caused by temporary short-falls in market demand and were used, with the strong encouragement of Government, to invest in building up the productive capacity ready for the next expansion, in Britain they were caused by the enforced deflation or *reduction* in investment, so that the next expansionary phase was condemned from the start to be throttled almost at once by inadequate capacity to sustain it. Whereas in Britain upswings were often shorter than downswings, abroad the trend was up, with but short, sharp downs to shake out the inefficient. The damage inflicted on the British economy by successive phases of Government policy thus worked essentially through cutting back the possibility and the urge to invest, and the urge to use the capital once it was installed. Inadequate investment[100] thus plays a part in all explanations of the unsatisfactory course of British economic development, though different authors assign to it differing degrees of import-ance.

Each of the cycles had well marked characteristics of its own. The first, covering approximately the years 1951–5, was still largely dominated by a seller's market and by the Korean War, and its price rises were superimposed on the price rises following from the devaluation of 1949.[101] Capacity was still stretched to the full, and demand on resources was balanced with supply by deliberately cutting investment, in order to make the particularly scarce engineering products available first for export, and secondly for rearmament.[102] Policy was concerned mainly with liquidity, the price level at home and the payments balance abroad, and long-term growth was not a major issue, since British growth was sat-isfactory by historical standards, North American growth was slow, and Con-tinental growth could be safely dismissed as a mere catching-up process after war damage.[103]

The second phase, 1955–60, which began with two years' stagnation ending in a purely financial crisis, saw substantial real income growth in its last three years. It saw the ending of controls, particularly over sterling convertibility and

[99] E.g. A. Whiting, 'An International Comparison of the Instability of Economic Growth', *Three Banks Review*, 109 (March 1976); T. Wilson, 'Instability and Growth: An International Comparison 1950–65', in D. H. Aldcroft and Peter Fearon (eds.), *Economic Growth in Twentieth-Century Britain* (1969), pp. 184–95.

[100] E.g. M. E. Blume, 'The Financial Markets', in R. E. Caves and L. B. Krause (eds.), *Britain's Economic Performance* (1980), pp. 263–4; F. T. Blackaby (ed.), *De-Industrialisation*, pp. 247–9; R. C. O. Matthews, C. H. Feinstein, J. C. Odling-Smee, *British Economic Growth 1856–1973* (Oxford, 1982), pp. 492–3; United Nations, Economic Commission for Europe, *The European Economy from the 1950s to the 1970s* (New York, 1972), pp. 12–4.

[101] Harrod, pp. 21–6; also 147–8, 165–9.

[102] 'In the long run our industries must have the equipment they need for expansion and efficiency. At the present time, however, some of them must needs be sacrificed because of the over-riding importance of increasing exports of precisely those goods for which investment demand is heaviest. The Government has therefore taken steps to divert resources on a large scale from supplying engineering goods to the home market to production for exports.' *Economic Survey 1952*, Cmd. 8509 (1952), paras. 30–1; Joan Mitchell, *Crisis in Britain* (1963); Cairncross, *Recovery*; PEP, *Growth*, pp. 139 ff.; R. Nurkse, 'The Relation between Home Investment and External Balance in the Light of British Experience, 1945–1955', *Review of Economics and Statistics*, 38/2 (1956).

[103] PEP, *Growth*, pp. 2–3.

capital movement, which the economy could not possibly sustain without major structural alteration, and it saw the peak and decline of the belief in 'monetary' means of economic control. In this period, Continental countries caught up with British absolute levels of output and income, and the first stirrings of disquiet about the slow British growth were heard.[104] Productive investment was less single-mindedly attacked by short-term policymakers than in 1951–5,[105] investment in a real sense replaced exports, and, taking the long view, the failure was less one of hitting investment thoughtlessly, but rather of allowing it too much freedom to turn into fields such as overseas companies or city centre properties which could not benefit British industrial competitiveness.

The third phase, 1960–5, was the most growth-conscious. It saw the setting up of the National Economic Development Council at the end of 1961 and its brave attempts to clear the path for a 4% growth rate.[106] The squeezes were designed to hit investment and production as little as possible, and various new encouragements to use resources productively were designed. Yet the massive backlog of investment, particularly in public utilities and capital-intensive basic industries, could not be made up in so short a space of time. Indeed, capital formation was still lower than in any other comparable country and Great Britain's productivity fell behind more and more.

The balance of payments deficit of 1964 was the largest ever, and the years 1965–9 formed one long squeeze, punctuated by several financial crises. There was no period when the balance of policy was not deflationary, and over much of it new records in deflationary pressures were set up.[107] Any plans for future growth gave way to current panic measures. NEDC and its 'Little Neddies', and the Department of Economic Affairs, both of which were dedicated to expansion and to a strengthening of the real industrial base, were effectively disarmed by the Treasury. Nevertheless, though all was sacrificed to it, the balance of payments remained obstinately negative, and year by year the burden of short-term debt and the annual interest payable on it had to be increased to finance it. When confidence fell away in the autumn of 1967, the second devaluation of sterling became inevitable, for although its immediate cause was speculative and financial, its underlying reality was that Britain's prices and costs had been left too high in relation to others by her failure to maintain similar increases in productivity. When most of the foreign private short-term capital had left, by early 1968, the total of official foreign lending (and the burden of its servicing and repayment) showed the extent to which Britain had been living beyond her means, by sustaining a quantity of foreign investment and Government

[104] 'The Government is pledged to foster conditions', the white paper on the *Economic Implications of Full Employment* declared somewhat hesitantly, 'in which the nation can, if it so wills, realize its full potentialities for growth in terms of production and living standards.' Cmd. 9725 (1956), quoted in *Radcliffe Committee Report*, para. 58.

[105] 'A check to the expansion of investment was necessary, but it was also desirable to curb consumers' expenditure, so as to make room for a healthy growth of investment and a surplus in the balance of payments.' *Economic Survey 1956*, Cmd. 9278 (1956), para. 69. Nurkse, pp. 135 ff.; W. Beckerman and Associates, *The British Economy in 1975* (Cambridge, 1965), Table 9·2, p. 271.

[106] Jim Tomlinson, *British Macroeconomic Policy Since 1940* (1985), p. 122.

[107] E.g., 'The "Neddy" Experiment', *Midland Bank Review* (February 1968); Basil Taylor, 'The NEDC after Six Years', *Westminster Bank Review* (February 1968); Sir Robert Shone, 'Problems of Planning for Growth in a Mixed Economy', *Econ. J.*, 75/297 (1965); also M. FG. Scott, 'The Balance of Payments', in P. D. Henderson, *Economic Growth in Britain* (1966), pp. 85, *passim*.

expenditure abroad for which her economic strength had provided no jus-tification. (See Table 9·11) To this $3·2 billion of indebtedness has to be added an estimated $2 billion undisclosed debt, bringing the total to $5·3 billion, matched by a reserve of $2·8 billion, not all of which was owned by Britain, so that the crude deficit was some $2·5 billion, or over £1 billion.

Table 9·11:   Disclosed debt, repayable by 1975* ($ million)

US and Canadian Government, US	
Eximbank (part of loans, repayable by 1975)	1,245
Bank for International Settlements	250
IMF (loans of 1965 and 1966)	1,521
Swiss, German and Portuguese banks	193
	3,210

* Well over half of this was repayable in 1970 or before. *Economist*, 23 March 1968, p. 70 and 30 March, 1968, p. 62.

The following cycle 1969–73 saw the last attempt to break out of the down-ward spiral by positive means. The strategy of Barber's 'dash for growth' was the basically sound one of using the temporary payments surplus and the reserves to sustain a high rate of growth for long enough to allow sufficient investment to be built up to maintain a self-reinforcing high growth and invest-ment rate thereafter; this, after all, had been the successful recipe of all the other industrial economies. The experiment foundered on two major obstacles. The first was the inadequacy of the reserves for the long haul, or at least, the loss of nerve on the part of the policy makers when the drain began to assume threat-ening proportions. The other, which would have in any case sealed the fate of the experiment, was that the freedom granted to the economy was used, not so much to invest in productive and cost reducing plant in Britain, but in property and financial speculation at home or in investment abroad. Investors had ceased to trust the promises of expansion policies, having learnt to their cost that they would be followed by contraction measures, including high interest rates and shrinking markets, just when the new plant was most vulnerable.[108] Real invest-ment was lower than in the preceding cycle.[109] It was much easier and safer to speculate in currency or in land.

Here was indeed the apotheosis of British Keynesian 'management', which had worked in macro-quantities only, without considering *what* it was that the additional purchasing power released in expansion phases should be spent on. The difference between consumption and investment was neglected, and in this it was quite unlike the policy decisions abroad where pure theory was less strongly anchored and economic policy makers were therefore less inhibited in applying common sense to growth policies. At the same time, Keynesian policies were also being undermined from quite a different direction, by a growing emphasis, especially by the foreign bankers on whom Britain now depended, on the supply of money as a steering mechanism, and inflation as the major problem.

[108] E.g., CBI evidence to *Committee to Review the Functioning of Financial Institutions* (Wilson Committee), Evidence vol. 2 (1977), p. 8.

[109] Matthews, Feinstein and Odling-Smee, pp. 126, 133, 320.

The monetarists had certainly put their finger on one increasingly troublesome phenomenon, the accelerating inflation in spite of high and rising unemployment. Expectations of ever rising prices were without a doubt beginning to play a part in the growing militancy and 'unreasonableness' of organized labour; but even more significant was the general exasperation with increasingly tough but clearly ineffective incomes policies and other restraints.

This unruliness spilled over into the final cycle of 1973–9, and tended to dominate it. For although the Labour Government succeeded in enacting a quite remarkable range of reforms in favour of the trade unions and the poor which transformed the labour market in a significant way, practically everything else went wrong for them. Inflation got out of hand, unemployment rose, output and investment stagnated, manufacturing declined, foreign indebtedness increased with ever more humiliating terms imposed by foreign lenders, and the growing deficits of the public authorities at home worsened all other troubles and hampered the Government's freedom of action. Between 1973 and 1980 output per person-hour in British manufacturing increased by no more than 6%, compared with 20% in the USA, 23% in Germany, 25% in Italy, 31% in France and 40% in Japan.[110] It was clear that without the godsend of the oil, Britain would have sunk even further and faster below the levels of her European partners.

Thus, on the face of it, British economic policy, the attempt to control the economy as a whole, proved to be astonishingly unsuccessful, particularly by comparison with other countries similarly placed. It failed to maintain stability or the value of the currency. It led to a lower rate of growth than technological improvements would have warranted. It demoralized employers and workers by periodic squeezes, discouragements to expansion and enforcements of breaches of collective agreements. It failed to preserve the Sterling Area and proved incapable of staying within the European currency agreements. And at the end of the period, it left Britain with a litter of industrial dereliction and a contrived level of unemployment, large enough to dismay even the most sanguine.

Not surprisingly, therefore, British policy came under repeated and varied attack in this period. How far has the criticism been justified? Much of the criticism was directed towards the technical handling of short-term crises, and in particular, it has frequently been alleged that the Government permitted expansion to proceed too rapidly, thus exhausting spare capacity too quickly and creating bottlenecks by-passed by high imports. It may also be said that most of the measures taken operated too slowly, so that the squeezes came only when the economy was already depressed, and the expansion effects appeared only when the resources were already over-extended.[111]

Much of this criticism seems misplaced. In technical terms, the Treasury did as well as could be expected in dealing with *ad hoc* crises and usually had the financial and economic press on its side.

The principal fault lay in ignoring long-term benefits for the sake of solving short-term problems, and this, in turn, raises the question whether there was

---

[110] *Nat. Inst. Econ. Rev.*, 101 (August 1982), 78.

[111] E.g. F. Brechling and J. N. Wolfe, 'The End of Stop-Go', *Lloyds Bank Review*, 75 (1965); P. D. Henderson, *Economic Growth in Britain* (1966), pp. 17–9; Youngson, pp. 259 ff.; Lomax, 'Growth and Productivity', pp. 14 *passim*; G. D. N. Worswick, 'Fiscal Policy and Stabilization in Britain', in A. K. Cairncross (ed.), *British Economic Prospects Reconsidered* (1971).

anything inherent in the British situation to tend towards this particular failure. Was the British relative decline, with the heartbreaking succession of crises when all our neighbours enjoyed prosperity and growth, really inevitable? Had Britain, in other words, inherited a predisposition to decline from her long-established position of economic leadership?

There were indeed several relevant unfavourable factors that were not, or not to the same extent, operative in other countries. Each of them alone might have been overcome, as they were overcome from time to time elsewhere. All of them together proved too powerful to withstand.

We may begin with the victory in the war itself. Whereas defeat and destruction on the continent and in Japan had led to low income expectations there and the unhindered devotion of large resources to reconstruction, and whereas the USA and Canada on the other side had enough resources to satisfy both a growth of incomes and of investment, in Britain the victorious outcome had induced expectations of a high standard of living[112] without the means to sustain it. The British problem, whether it appeared in the guise of an income inflation or an import surplus, may throughout be seen as pressure, not only by labour but by all income earners, to take more out of current output than their productivity warranted, and in view of the immunity or stickiness of other items, such as Government expenditure or foreign investment, the cuts fell regularly on the remaining item, productive investment at home. Secondly, arising from the same victory and preceded by a long and successful imperial tradition, Britain took on the burdens of a Great Power, including actual fighting in Korea and in several colonies before their independence, for which she no longer had the resources. Her politicians and generals failed for too long to realize to what extent Britain's earlier world leadership had depended on her economic power rather than the skills of her diplomats or field commanders. It is a sombre reflection that throughout all the crises, cuts and humiliations Britain's economy had worked up a larger and healthier surplus than even her most successful rivals, Germany and Japan; it was only the Government's expenditure abroad, to a large extent of a military nature, that turned it into a long-term deficit[113] with all its fateful consequences. The Sterling Area, another imperial burden of the past, was instrumental in inhibiting British freedom of action before it finally faded away.

Thirdly, Britain was uniquely saddled with a complex of financial interests, the 'City', which were not directly dependent on the welfare of industry, as were financiers in other countries, and with an all-powerful Treasury with inadequate access either to economic science or to industry, so that it was totally subservient to the doctrines and the appraisals of the City, transmitted by the Bank of England. Only this one-sided influence upon the Treasury can explain its failure to learn from British and other experience that growth need not mean inflation; that a 'stop' need not mean stability; and that the policy of the post-war years has led to a galloping deterioration, without even a theoretical model, let alone any practical example, that could lead one to hope for a break out of the vicious

---

[112] C. F. Carter, 'The International and Domestic Financial Policy of the United Kingdom', *Public Finance*, 8 (1953), p. 229.

[113] W. A. P. Manser, *Britain in Balance* (1971); Andrew Gamble, *Britain in Decline* (1985), p. 110; A. Shonfield, *British Economic Policy Since the War* (Harmondsworth, 1959), p. 91.

Table 9·12:   Stop-go and key indices

	Expansion periods (1953–5, 1958–60, 1962–4, 1967–9, 1972–3, 1975–9)	Stagnation periods (1955–8, 1960–2, 1964–7, 1969–72, 1973–5, 1979–80)
Annual growth rate in UK industrial production	4·9%	0·1%
Annual rise in prices:		
retail	6·6	7·5
manufactures	6·4	7·4
Annual growth in volume:		
exports	6·8	2·6
imports	7·5	1·5

circle if more of the same medicine were continued.[114] After all, the information must have been available to the Treasury, as it has been to the public at large, that it was in 'stop' periods specifically designed to hold down prices, that prices rose fastest (see Table 9·12).[115]

> It is surely very irrational indeed to tolerate 'stop' measures, lasting two years or more, causing a loss of output of perhaps 3% of the national income in the first year and 6% in the second year, merely to correct a deficit amounting to 0·85% of national income ... it is positively wrongful in relation to economic welfare.[116]

Because of the dominance of traders and financiers, protective policies never had a chance either. The policy remained that of ever sharper and ever less effective credit squeezes. It could be only a financier's mind, unfamiliar with the workings of industry, that could have thought, after 20 years of consistent failure, of responding to the problem of inadequate productivity, not with 'produce more', but with 'consume and invest less'.

Fourthly, Britain suffered not only from a higher Civil Service largely innocent of Mathematics, Technology or Economics, but also from an excess of remarkably brilliant and well trained economists who tended, for different reasons but with the same ultimately disastrous effects, to ignore the problems of productive industry in their search for satisfactory macro-economic solutions.[117] Less theoretically inclined economists elsewhere, where business studies enjoyed a higher prestige, could hardly have sustained such long years of practical failure without questioning the bases of their assumptions. Nor did matters improve when monetarists supplanted Keynesians as official advisers.

This intellectual failure was also sustained, fifthly, by the long tradition of British economic and technical leadership, going back some 200 years to the

[114] Harrod, pp. 189–207; Samuel Brittan, *The Treasury under the Tories 1951–1964* (Pelican, 1964).
[115] W. A. Eltis, 'Economic Growth and the British Balance of Payments', *District Bank Review*, 164 (1967); all figures based on *Key Statistics* and *Annual Abstract of Statistics*. See also Harrod, *Towards a New Economic Policy*, p. 13; Michael Shanks, *The Stagnant Society* (Penguin, 1961), chapter 2; Norman MacRae, *Sunshades in October* (1963).
[116] Harrod, *op. cit.*, p. 30.
[117] S. Pollard, *Wasting*, pp. 143–50.

industrial revolution. While British businessmen, technologists or civil servants were, as we have seen, willing to learn from the USA after the war, the arrogance towards the rest of the world, founded on history, survived almost to the end of our period when it had long since lost its justification, and prevented Britain not only from obtaining useful lessons from across the channel, but also from even questioning her own progress, as a first step to altering course.

Sixthly, several of the ways in which the world was changing around Britain worked to her ultimate disadvantage. Possibly the most powerful effect here was the advance of the industrial world as against the 'third world', and the benefits which the advanced countries derived from growing mutual trade and an ever more detailed international division of labour. In this way the traditional economic role of Britain as mediator between the two worlds was weakened, though it should be stressed that Britain lost ground in *all* markets and cannot therefore put much blame on the relative weakening of her traditional trade partners.

Lastly, there was necessarily a cumulative trend, or learning process, in the sum of these factors. Entrepreneurs and trade unionists learned to accommodate to stagnation and shied away from, if they were not actively hostile to, innovation. Engineers and technologists had fewer opportunities to stretch their wings by planning new schemes. Growth itself generates growth. To be sure, the argument that slower growth in Britain goes back to 1900 or even beyond, though true, is of little relevance, since all countries jumped after the war from a 1–2% annual rate to a 4–5% rate, and in the last pre-war decade British economic growth was in fact faster than most, so that the continuation of earlier trends should have favoured Britain. But it is true that it is easier to sustain a high rate, once it is started, than to switch over to it, and the rapid recovery from lower levels in the immediate post-war years may have helped some other countries by setting them on a fast growth course.

Thus the inheritance of the past had saddled the British economy with some undeniable burdens; but it also provided her with immense initial advantages after the war. Among them was a fairly intact productive apparatus, bettered only by Sweden and Switzerland in Europe, with strength in some of the key growth sectors, like vehicles, aircraft and electronics. There was also a high reputation for quality, compared, say, with German, let alone Japanese products. There was high morale at home, prestige abroad, and a degree of social and political cohesion that most other industrial countries would envy. Britain had a firm footing in many of the world's leading markets, strengthened in the later 1940s when most of her rivals were still too weak to compete. Lastly, she still had her resources advantage of location, iron ore, coal and, lately, natural gas and oil.

Perhaps all this was not enough to outweigh the long list of disadvantages. But the disadvantages became fatally operative only because policy makers chose to react repeatedly in a certain way to them, and it is difficult to believe that these reactions were, indeed, wholly inevitable.

10

A New Departure in Economic Policy 1979–1990

1 Novel Policies and Traditional Stop-go

The period 1979–90 stands in some respects apart from the preceding decades. Unlike earlier governments which tended to concern themselves with short-term expedients to meet immediate contingencies over which any long-term plans were repeatedly shelved, the Government under Mrs Thatcher had strong views, held to them firmly and undeterred by current issues and wished to be judged by the longer-term results it achieved. The period came to an end with the resignation of Mrs Thatcher on 28 November 1990. It forms a single whole, and because of the unusual significance of the role of Government policy in this period, we are beginning this chapter with a consideration of economic policy rather than leaving it to the end, after the background and the problems had been sketched in.

The policies launched after the Conservative Government took office in May 1979 had been planned in some detail in the preceding years of opposition, and bore the mark especially of Sir Keith Joseph[1] and the Conservative Centre for Policy Studies. They were based on at least three clear premises. One was that there had been something fundamentally wrong with British economic policy as a whole, to have led to such unparalleled economic relative decline, from so favourable a beginning after the war, compared with the development of other, similar economies. Secondly, among the major faults to be corrected was the repeated panic reaction to short-term issues: instead, a medium-term economic strategy was to be developed from which the Government would not be diverted by temporary difficulties. Thirdly, the problems of the British economy were not to be solved by manipulating the demand side, but were to be found in the supply side, the poor performance of the productive sectors, broadly defined.[2] Apart from some individuals in the Treasury, some theoretical economists, and most of the financial press, there would have been few to quarrel with that assessment at the time.

To overcome these basic faults, a radical change in direction was required, and that was provided by a comprehensive programme, made up of a set of

[1] Ron Martin and Bob Rowthorn, *The Geography of De-Industrialization* (1986), pp. 244, 285–6; William Keegan, *'Mrs Thatcher's Economic Experiment'* (1984), chapter 2.

[2] Kent Matthews and Patrick Minford, Mrs Thatcher's Economic Policies' 1979–1987, *Economic Policy* 5 (1987), p. 65; David Begg, 'Fiscal Policy', in Rudiger Dornbusch and Richard Layard (eds.), *The Performance of the British Economy* (Oxford, 1987), p. 39. On the advance of supply-side economics, see Bruce Bartlett and Timothy P. Roth (eds.), *The Supply-Side Solution* (Chatham, N.Y. 1983); Grahame Thompson, *The Conservatives' Economic Policy* (1986), chapter 2; Nick Gardner, *Decade of Discontent* (Oxford, 1987), pp. 144 f.

propositions that were intended to be internally consistent. One of the major premises was that the British economic performance had been held back because enterprise had been discouraged: now the entrepreneur was to be 'set free', particularly of Government interference and control. Thus a major element of the plan was to reduce the scope of Government, to abolish all restrictions on banking, international finance, and the labour market, to cut back the public sector, and to privatize the nationalized industries, though this did not receive a great deal of attention at the beginning. The role of the Government was to be limited to providing a sound currency, but here it was to be more active than previous Governments in containing the growth of the money supply, which the Thatcher Conservative Government, in faithful adherence to pure monetarist doctrine, held to be the single most important steering mechanism available to it.

Cutting Government expenditure, which the decline of interventionism might allow, moreover, would reduce the Government's annual deficit and contribute directly to containing inflation. Then taxes could be cut, stimulating enterprise: in any case, Governments usually managed matters less well than the market would. Enterprise was to be freed also from the thraldom of trade union power. Curbing the unions, and making wages more flexible downward, would, according to the same monetarist doctrine, reduce unemployment. There was also the doctrine of 'rational expectations' which implied that as soon as trade unions and traders were convinced that the Government meant business and the monetary curbs were really to be imposed, they would moderate their wage demands and their price rises. Welfare provisions were also to be pruned, in order not only to save money but also to remove the floor below wage levels and allow wages to fall in line with market demand. The market, and not incomes policies, was to settle the wage level.

Similarly, the Government would steer clear of trying to manipulate the exchange value of the pound or, indeed, the balance of payments: these also were to be left to the market, and there was therefore no wish to join the European Monetary Scheme which set out to keep the currencies concerned very closely aligned with one another by an active Central Bank policy. Perhaps most important of all, full employment would no longer be a commitment, though it was clearly still desirable.

Whether this programme, or the policies that were in fact followed by the Government, truly amounted to a revolution or even, as its supporters would claim, a turning back of the tide of history[3] is much disputed. There is also no agreement that there was, indeed, a cohesive strategy. Some have only seen 'statecraft', a response to events and to crises[4] and indeed it very soon became clear that there would be no dogmatic adherence to any preconceived line in practice. Some have even maintained that 'Thatcherism' was more 'a style than an ideology. An ideology is a consistent system of ideas whereas what (Mrs

[3] Matthews and Minford, pp. 60, 91; Leo Pliatzky, *Getting and Spending* (Oxford, 1982), p. 176; Patrick Minford, 'Mrs Thatcher's Economic Reform Programme – Past, Present and Future' in R. Skidelsky (ed.), *Thatcherism* (1988), p. 93.

[4] Andrew Gamble, *The Free Economy and the Strong State. The Politics of Thatcherism* (1988), pp. 20 f.; John Hillard, 'Thatcherism and Decline', in David Coats and John Hillard (eds.), *The Economic Decline of Modern Britain* (Brighton, 1986), pp. 352 f.; Peter Riddell, *The Thatcher Decade* (Oxford 1989), p. 5; Maurice Mullard, *The Politics of Public Expenditure* (1987), pp. 165–7, 177.

Thatcher) called her conviction politics were largely instinctive'. 'Mrs Thatcher', according to another observer, 'seems to have formulated her own somewhat homespun ideas and latched on to monetarism as a useful legitimating device.'[5]

Be that as it may, the policy in so far as there was one, or at least the direction of the thrust, was equivalent to a policy for growth, though it became obvious very soon that there would be a fundamental contradiction between 'supply-side' growth and the deflation required to cut back the money supply which enjoyed immediately the highest priority. It was this growth in output which the Government intended to achieve which would allow other desirable reforms to be implemented, just as it was the pruning of Government action which would allow the profit-making sector to enter upon a growth phase. While there might be doubt how far the analysis was based on a correct description of reality in Britain at the time, and in particular how far it was a feasible strategy given that reality, the programme, as presented in its optimistic guise, appeared plausible to many.

It need hardly be stressed that the new Government also had a pronounced radical political programme, which cannot be separated from the economic strategy sketched here. However, since the economic elements form much the most important innovative aspects of the programme as a whole, it is justifiable to treat them very largely, though never entirely, in isolation.

Although the Thatcher Government had inherited an economy steeped in crisis and would therefore face a difficult running-in period, there were several major favourable factors aiding the Government in its programme. Achieving three consecutive victories at the polls, it had a clear run of eleven years in which to 'turn the economy round'. It had a strong leader in Mrs Thatcher, who was able in the course of her premiership gradually to remove from her Cabinet those of the senior and independent-minded ministers who were not entirely in agreement with her programme, and replace them by faithful supporters, so that programmes were less watered down by compromise than is usually the case. It also conformed to the spirit of the age, in the sense that several other Governments turned to monetarist policies at about the same time. Added to this was the North Sea oil which began to flow in quantities at about the time of the accession to power of the Conservative Government, and it provided a necessary buffer for any new beginning. This was a wholly unprecedented boon for an economy which had been thwarted time and again in its efforts to take off by foreign balance of payments crises. Without the oil, the Thatcher experiment would almost certainly have been cut short as early as 1981 or 1982 after the unmitigated disasters of the first year or so of the new dispensation.

These were basically favourable circumstances, circumstances which were very much more conducive to breaking the series of deflations (which had so damaged the British economy in the whole of the post-war period) than were enjoyed in any preceding period. Given such circumstances and a determination to start afresh without being tied down by received dogma, how did the economy fare and, in particular, what were the effects of the specific Government programme and its components on the economy as a going concern?

[5] Peter Jenkins, *Mrs Thatcher's Revolution. The Ending of the Socialist Era* (1987), p. 81; Peter Holmes, 'The Thatcher Government's overall economic performance', in David S. Bell (ed.), *The Conservative Government 1979–1984* (1985), p. 15.

In economic history, such questions seldom allow a clear-cut answer. There is usually some trade off of gains against losses. Thus the Governments of the 1950s and 1960s might have argued that, as against a slow growth, they preserved full employment; and the Governments of the 1930s, that with a desperately high level of unemployment, they succeeded in accelerating growth and in initiating some measures for modernizing the industrial structure. Moreover, while laws or taxation rates can be changed rapidly, the announced aim of an 'enterprise economy',[6] changing people's attitudes, was bound to take time and thus should not be judged too hastily.

Nevertheless, for the eleven years of the Thatcher experiment there need be no ambiguity of verdict. All the signs point in the same direction: the experiment ended in almost unmitigated failure. By the end of the period, in 1990, Britain had the highest rate of inflation among advanced economies, though the curbing of the inflation had been the Government's declared priority number one. It had, correspondingly, the highest interest rates; and it also had high and rising unemployment; large-scale bankruptcies of firms in all sectors of the economy; falling output and declining national income; and the largest deficit on the current balance of payment in history. Over the period as a whole, despite the oil, Britain had, unbelievably, a slower rate of growth than in comparable periods before. In other subsidiary respects also, such as the number of hours worked in industry, environmental pollution, the morale of the Social Services, and many more, Britain was at the bottom of the developed world. There was one single exception to this sorry tale of failure. That exception was the one aim which, curiously, the Government did not stress in its statements of policy, though it clearly played a large part in its programme; the transfer of income from the poor, and especially the poorest, to the rich, and especially the richest. To this reverse Robin Hood programme it managed to hold on through all phases of the economic cycle. There was, however, also the more positive element that share ownership had risen from 3 million to 11 million, and house ownership increased further from 57% to 69% of the population. The rest of this chapter will concern itself with all these points in greater detail.

Some measures taken early on in the dash for 'freedom' went through with minimal difficulty: they included the removal of the 'corset' from the banks in 1980, the abolition of controls on hire-purchase finance in 1982, the removal of the solicitors' monopoly on conveyancing in 1986, and the abolition of all exchange controls as early as 1979. The latter led to an immediate outflow of capital: direct overseas investment doubled to £5.1 billion between 1979 and 1981, and portfolio investment rose from around £1 billion in 1979 to £16.2 billion in 1982,[7] and this withdrawal of capital from Britain may well have removed the one chance of benefiting from the oil bonanza of those years. The financial free-for-all of the 1980s which followed the removal of all restrictions led not only to the financial scandals which so damaged the image of the City of London, but also, together with the tax concessions, fuelled the credit and property boom which put an end to Mr Lawson's expansion policy and caused the second 'stop' of the Thatcher Government with all its ruinous consequences in 1989.

[6] Keith Middlemas, *Industry, Unions and Government* (1983), p. 121; Riddell, p. 96.
[7] Hillard, 'Thatcherism', p. 359; Scott Newton and Dilwyn Porter, *Modernization Frustrated* (1988), pp. 200–1.

Much more difficult than the abolition of controls was the second plank of the policy: the drive to weaken the trade unions to the point that wages became more flexible downwards. The unions were accused, even in official statements like the White Paper of 1985[8] of creating unemployment by maintaining wages at too high a level, and they were also accused of preventing technical innovation by their inflexible attitudes, as well as by insisting on overmanning and thus hindering progress.[9] The cure for the persistently high unemployment of the first half of the 1980s was to be found, according to the new dispensation, not in employment policies, but in lowering the wage level.

Table 10·1:   Consumer prices and earnings in manufacturing, 1973–87

	Average annual rates of change %	
	Consumer prices	Hourly earnings in manufacturing
1973–82	14·7	15·8
1983	4·6	9·0
1984	5·0	8·7
1985	6·1	9·1
1986	3·4	7·6
1987	4·2	8·1

The legislation of 1980, 1982 and 1984 had indeed formally contributed to weaken the market power of the trade unions (see section 3 below) and the recession with its heavy loss of jobs had not only reduced the unions' membership, but done more even than the legislation to reduce their power.[10] Yet all these forces combined had failed to curb the rise in earnings, which even in the years of the heaviest unemployment in 1985 kept well ahead of the cost of living (Table 10·1).[11] At the same time, however, the share of profits reversed its long-term declining tendency, and as a percentage of value added in manufacturing rose from a low of 9·6% in 1980 and 6·8% in 1981 to 22·0% in 1986.[12]

It was not easy to explain the paradox of the buoyancy and inflexibility of real wages in the face of the worst depression since the 1930s. Some economists had recourse to the theory of a dual labour market: firms, it was said, kept a core of skilled, unionized workers whose market power was not affected by a second group, the peripheral workers, poorly paid and organized, who were those who suffered the loss of jobs. Thus high unemployment and high wages could co-exist. The Government's supporters went further and made the power of the trade unions to hold up the wages of one group directly responsible for the rising unemployment of the other group, who paid with their jobs for the union's militancy.[13] There was, indeed, a large increase in the numbers of the long-term unemployed, the possible outsiders, as well as a gap between union

[8] Jim Tomlinson, *Employment Policy 1939–1985* (Oxford, 1987), p. 162.
[9] Andrew Gamble, *Britain in Decline* (1985), p. 150.
[10] William Brown and Sushil Wadhwani, 'The Economic Effects of Industrial Relations Legislation since 1979', *Nat. Inst. Econ. Rev.* 131 (1990), pp. 57–70.
[11] P. B. Beaumont, *Change in Industrial Relations* (1990), p. 24.
[12] Ibid., p. 176; OECD, *Economic Outlook* and *Historical Statistics*.
[13] Patrick Minford, *Unemployment, Cause and Cure* (Oxford, 1985), pp. 3–10; Also see John MacInnes, *Thatcherism at Work* (Milton Keynes, 1987), p. 113; Willem H Buiter and Marcus H Miller, 'Changing the Rules: Economic Consequences of the Thatcher Regime' *Brookings Papers*

and non-union wage levels, which varied considerably among the trades, but averaged 7·7% according to one calculation, with insignificant gaps for unskilled according to another.[14] It was not a very large difference, and there was no sign that it widened in this period.

The evidence for union obstruction to innovation was less clear-cut. Thus one enquiry among mechanical engineering firms on the unions' attitude to computer-aided installations found that of 115 firms which had installed them, only 5 had faced union opposition, and of the 102 which had not done so, only 2 blamed trade-union attitudes.[15] It is, however, possible, for obstructionism to work more subtly than that.

Altogether, the evidence is mixed. The severe depression and unemployment of the early 1980s will have had some effect on wage settlements: one enquiry, based on the official workplace Industrial Relations Survey of 1984, found that some 50–60% of settlements were influenced by profitability, productivity and the economic climate, and a similar proportion by the cost of living and comparable pay rates elsewhere, all other factors being of minor importance.[16] On the other hand, the cumulative wage increases of 1979–84 showed some of the highest rises in the most depressed regions of Wales, Scotland and the North-West, as well as in the South-East, while the prosperous East Midlands and East Anglia did worse than the average.[17] There can be no doubt that the trade unions had become more subdued and circumspect since the 'winter of discontent' of 1978–9; there were fewer strikes and they occurred in different parts of the labour market. The unemployment, the climate, the legislation and the lessons of 1979 all contributed to this. But there was no sign of a fundamental change either in trade union attitude, or in trade union power to keep wages pretty inflexible downwards.

Incomes policy, which had been relentlessly attacked in the 1970s by the Conservative leadership close to Mrs Thatcher, was of course ended at once and the Prices Commission wound up. Yet pay policy did not entirely disappear; it survived for the Government's own employees. The recommendation of the Clegg Commission, which had proposed large catching-up payments, was honoured when the Government took office, but the Commission itself was wound up in August 1980, and the Pay Research Unit for civil service pay followed in November of that year. Henceforth the imposition of severe and shrinking cash limits enforced losses of staff as well as relatively low pay settlements not only in the civil service (except for the highest ranks), but also

---

on Economic Activity 1983/2, pp. 345–6; Frank H Longstreth, 'From Corporatism to Dualism? Thatcherism and the Climacteric of British Trade Unions in the 1980s,' *Political Studies* 36 (1988), p. 427; Laurie Hunter, 'Unemployment and Industrial Relations', *British Journal of Industrial Relations* 26/2 (1988), p. 209; Tony Novak, *Poverty and the State* (Milton Keynes, 1988), p. 183.

[14] Mark B Stewart, 'Relative Earnings and Individual Union Membership in the United Kingdom', *Economica* 50/198 (1983), pp. 111–25; David Blanchflower, 'What Effects do Unions have on Relative Wages in Great Britain', *British Journal of Industrial Relations* 24/2 (1986), p. 200; Geoffrey Maynard, *The Economy under Mrs. Thatcher* (Oxford 1988), p. 127.

[15] V. G. Lintner et al., 'Trade Unions and Technological Change in the UK Mechanical Engineering Industry', *British Journal of Industrial Relations* 25/1 (1987), pp. 19–29.

[16] David G Blanchflower and Andrew J Oswald, 'Internal-External Influence upon Pay Settlements', *Ibid.* 26/3 (1988), p. 366.

[17] Mary Gregory, Peter Lobban, Andrew Thomson, 'Wage Settlement in Manufacturing 1979–84: Evidence from the CBI Pay Databank', *Ibid.* 23/3 (1985) p. 348.

among nurses, teachers and others. For their own employees, the Government refused to accept ACAS arbitration, on the grounds that it tended to split the differences between the parties and took no account of overall fiscal policies to which the spending departments were subject. Pay provision figures were set at 4% increase in 1981–2, falling to 3·5%, 3% and 3% in the following three years. Actual pay rises fell from 13–20% in 1981 to 4·5 to 6·5% by the mid-80s,[18] and the public sector, which had gained on the private pay levels up to about 1982, then fell badly behind. Staff numbers declined from 732,000 in 1979 to 569,000 in 1988, and employment in the Civil Departments alone, from 485,000 to 428,000 in the same period.

Holding down public sector pay deals served the purpose not only of exerting a downward pressure on all pay deals. It also helped to reduce Government expenditure (see below) and aided the drive for minimal Government. Not only was the Price Commission abolished, the National Enterprise Board also was emasculated and then shut down, the NEDC ('Neddy') was shunted onto a sideline, the Manpower Services Commission closed down in 1988 and 57 Quangos abolished at once.

Minimal Government also meant reduction in direct Government aid to

Table 10·2:   Expenditure on industrial support policies, 1979–88[20]

	1979–80 £ mn at current prices	1987–8 £ mn at 1979–80 prices	1987–8 £ mn at current prices
Regional and selective assistance	509	159	276
Support for industry	142	240	417
Specific industries*	338	80	139
International trade	28	26	45
Regulation of domestic trade incl. consumer protection	8	13	22
Miscell. services	63	74	128
Totals	1088	592	1027

* Includes aerospace, shipbuilding, steel, vehicle manufacture.

industry, though it proved difficult to cut it out altogether (Table 10·2). There were also, in the later 1980s, schemes to help small firms to start up: by 1987 the Government-backed loan scheme had helped 19,000 businesses at a cost of £635 million.[19]

Yet all these cuts, together with some others, failed to halt the expansion of the budget which not only rose in absolute terms, from 34·7% of GDP in 1979 to 39·1% in 1982 and to 42·6% in 1984 but also in relation to the average of the OECD countries.[21] With it, rose the burden on the taxpayer. Publically announced spending targets could not arrest the rise, which was caused mainly by two factors, the increase in unemployment and the consequent rise in national insurance and social benefits paid out to the unemployed, and the annual

[18] Beaumont, *Change,* p. 215; R. F. Elliott and P. D. Murphy, 'The Relative Pay of Public and Private Sector Employees, 1970–1984', *Cambridge Journal of Economics* 11/2 (1987), pp. 107–32.

[19] Riddell, *Decade,* pp. 75–6.

[20] James Shepherd, 'Industrial Support Policies', *Nat. Inst. Econ. Rev.* 122 (1987), p. 60.

[21] Jeremy Moon and J. J. Richardson, *Unemployment in the UK* (Aldershot, 1985), p. 21; Begg, 'Fiscal', p. 29.

increase in the defence budget agreed by NATO members. Between 1978/9 and 1985/6, public expenditure of the central Government had risen from £124 billion to £136·3 billion in 1985/6 prices.

After 1985/6, falling unemployment rates and rising incomes allowed the tax burden to be lowered. The biggest increases in real terms between 1978/9 and 1988/9 were in Defence (+18·2%), the Home Office (+55·3%), Health (+34·9%) and Social Security (+32·9%), the latter two caused largely by the increase in the proportion of older persons. There were some reductions in trade and industry and above all in housing.[22] By that time, a novel annual ritual had been initiated, in which the spending departments had to fight for their share against others before a committee of 'neutral' cabinet members known as the 'Star Chamber'. This represented, in theory if not necessarily in practice, a reformed method of arriving at the budget by fixing the overall expenditure first, on macro-economic grounds, before considering the claims of individual departments, rather than the other way round. Moreover, it could be used to shape the expenditure pattern in line with the Government's preferences and predilections.[23]

As far as financial and monetary policy was concerned, not only were most of the controls and steering mechanisms abolished, as noted above, but the balance of payments was no longer considered to be a direct concern of the Government, after having dominated British policies for over three decades. The exchange value of the pound also ceased to figure as a significant target. The Government appeared unmoved when the pound sterling appreciated from its effective rate of 84·9 in 1973 to 100·0 in 1980 and then stayed at 98·9 and 94·2 respectively in the next two years though the economy was in deep depression, only to subside again gradually to 59·0 in 1990.[24] Only later was it noticed that the Treasury had in effect begun to 'shadow' the German mark, by seeing to it that the pound stayed in a stable relation to it, from 1987 onward without, apparently, the full consent of the Prime Minister.

As all these traditional targets and indicators were demoted to insignificance, one monetary indicator was lifted up to be the major, even the single most important target of the Government's economic policy: that was the rate of inflation. The Government's concentration on the rate of inflation was based on its monetarist convictions, but its singular preoccupation with it might almost be called obsessive and was repudiated, in its extreme setting of priorities, even by most prominent monetarists. It could, however, be explained, at least partly, by the fact that its pursuit could be associated directly with another key aim, that of reducing the scope of Government.

The reasoning, broadly, went as follows: inflation is almost solely the fault and the responsibility of the monetary authorities; it is caused by an excessive money supply, which should be under the control of the Government. The British money supply had got out of hand because of Government profligacy. It was therefore imperative to cut back the public's sector's borrowing requirement

[22] M. S. Levitt and M. A. S. Joyce, *The Growth and Efficiency of Public Spending* (Cambridge, 1987), p. 25; H. M. Treasury, *The Next Ten Years, Public Expenditure and Taxation into the 1990's* (Cmnd. 9189); Riddell, *Decade*, p. 35; Michael O'Higgins, 'Inequality, Redistribution and Recession: The British Experience, 1976–1982', *Journal of Social Policy* 14/3 (1985), p. 282.

[23] Mullard, *Politics*, Introduction.

[24] *Nat. Inst. Econ. Rev.*, Statistics, based on IMF definitions.

(PSBR), and this would reduce the money supply which would, in turn, force all other agents to moderate their demand for money in line with the supply available.[25] The Medium Term Financial Strategy (MTFS) therefore had as one of its targets the systematic reduction in the annual increase of the money supply, which in the first years was taken to be 'M3', a broad measure of cash and credit instruments.[26]

Every year, in its budgetary statement, the Government would set a target for M3, as well as for the PSBR, and these annual targets could then be assembled into a medium-term strategy. Though set as a broad band, it soon became clear that the M3 target was, year by year, ludicrously out of line with reality (Table 10·3). It should be noted that the original targets were even further removed from the real world, and that those shown in the Table had already been altered upward to take account of earlier failures to predict. Thus, instead of the 8–12% for 1982/3, the original target had actually been only 5–9%, and instead of the 7–11% for 1983/4, the original target had been only 4–8%. It was clear that the Government had absolutely no control over its set target, or,

Table 10·3:   Monetary targets and outturn, 1979–87[27]
(per cent annual rate of increase of M3)

	Target	Outturn
1979–80	7–11	12
1980–1	7–11	19
1981–2	6–10	13
1982–3	8–12	11
1983–4	7–11	10
1984–5	6–10	13·5
1985–6	5–9	15·3
1986–7	11–15	20

alternatively, that the Treasury had no idea how reality operated. It is therefore not entirely surprising that M3 targets were pushed into the background, being replaced from 1982 by a mixture including M1 and PSL2, by M0 in addition from 1984 (when M0 was rising at an annual 5·5% against 9·0% for M3) and that it was quietly dropped from 1986 onward. M0, in view of the vast expansion of credit instruments at the time, was a particularly inappropriate measure to use, and from 1986 it was in fact replaced by money GDP,[28] which came very close to abandoning any monetarist approach altogether and returning to a

[25] Alan Walters, *Britain's Economic Renaissance. Margaret Thatcher's Reforms 1979–1984* (Oxford 1986), p. 4; Martin Holmes, *The First Thatcher Government 1979–1983* (Brighton, 1985), p. 33.

[26] Crude definitions might be as follows:

M0 (narrow money) – notes and coins with the public plus bank till money plus bankers operational balances with the Bank of England.

M1–M0 plus sight deposits held by the public.

sterling M3 – notes and coins with the public plus all sterling deposits (including certificates of deposits) held by UK residents, public and private sector.

M3 – sterling M3 plus bank deposits held by UK residents elsewhere. There was also M4 and M5.

PSL 2 (Private Sector Lending) – Private Sector component of £M3 (excluding deposits with original maturity of over 2 years), plus certificates of tax deposits, most building society shares, deposits in the National Savings Bank and National Savings instruments.

[27] Riddell, *Decade*, p. 30.

[28] Leo Pliatzky, *The Treasury under Mrs Thatcher* (Oxford, 1989), pp. 29–30, 130.

Keynesian way of thinking. Possibly the most remarkable aspect of this policy was the vigour with which the successive Chancellors of the Exchequer defended such obviously worthless targets or measurements or, as Mr Lawson finally declared, indications of trend (it was never quite clear which) until such time as they thought it better to drop them altogether.

Parallel with the monetary target there was also the target of the PSBR, similarly projected to decline steadily, similarly widely off the mark (Table 10·4). Here, too, it should be noted that the targets themselves were being constantly raised as experience proved them to be unrealistic: thus the projection for 1982–3 of 3·5% growth originally read 2·25%, and for 1983–4 of 3·25%, was originally

Table 10·4:   PSBR: Targets and outturns, 1979–88[29]

	Target	Nominal outturn		Outturn ignoring the income from North Sea gas, oil and the sale of nationalized industries
	% GDP	% GDP	£ bn.	£ bn.
1979–80		4·75	9·9	12·6
1980–1	3·75	5·25	12·5	16·6
1981–2	4·25	3·25	8·6	15·6
1982–3	3·50	3·25	8·9	17·2
1983–4	3·25	3·25	9·7	19·6
1984 5	2·5	3·0	10·1	24·2
1985–6	2·25	1·50	5·7	19·7
1986 7		1·0	3·4	12·7
1987–8		−0·75	−3·5	6·3
1988–9		−0·75*	−3·2*	

* Estimated

set at 1·5%. Again, the Treasury had gone hopelessly astray with its estimates. It should also be noted that the relatively successful reduction in the Government's borrowing was due far more to the oil bonanza, as well as to the sums flowing in from the privatization schemes, than to any policy measures of the Government to reduce public spending.

It will be seen that at the end of the period, and with the help of the large sums realized by major schemes of privatization, there was a negative PSBR which meant that it was possible to pay back some of the public borrowings, and thus reduce the national debt. Owing to the inflation, the national debt had in any case been falling sharply from around 81% of GNP in 1967 to around 40% by 1980. There was therefore much doubt expressed, even by sources normally friendly to the Government, as to whether, at a time of high unemployment, of closures and bankruptcies, it was sensible to impose further burdens on the economy for such a purpose as paying off the national debt. The Government saw such criticism as a sign of cowardice in the face of carrying through the necessary tough remedies.

Measurements which it have been possible to make since do indeed show a sharply deflationary true fiscal stance (see p. 344 above) in the worst years,

[29] Pliatzky, *Treasury*, p. 151; Walters, *Renaissance*, p. 80; I. Stanley Fisher, 'Monetary Policy', in Dornbusch and Layard, *Performance*, p. 13; Gardner, *Decade*, pp. 140, 207–9.

Table 10·5:   Fiscal stance, 1980–86 (per cent of GDP)

Year	Fiscal stance		Year	
	Cyclically adjusted	Weighted and cyclically adjusted		Cyclically adjusted real surplus
1980	−1·9	+0·2	1979–80	0·9
1981	−2·4	−0·9	1980–1	2·1
1982	−0·3	+0·4	1981–2	5·3
1983	+1·5	+0·8	1982–3	5·6
1984	+0·9	+0·3	1983–4	3·7
1985	−0·3	−0·5	1984–5	3·2
1986	+0.2	−0·2		

1980–2, relaxed only later in the decade (Table 10·5).[30] Next to fiscal policy as expressed in the budget, which of course had to perform various additional functions beside the macro-economic one of restoring the economy to health, it was the interest rate which became the main, and ultimately in fact the sole policy instrument of the Government. The justification was that since inflation was the villain of the piece and the crucial target, and since inflation was a monetary phenomenon, it must be combated by monetary means, and by those alone, namely, the interest rate. Thus interest rates went up in the depression years of the early 1980s, against all previous experience and against all outside advice, aggravating the crisis and certainly increasing the number of bankruptcies and lay-offs. Moreover, high interest rates helped to keep the exchange rate of the pound high, adding to the upward pressure already brought about by the North Sea oil, and thus made the task of exporters harder while encouraging imports. Interestingly enough, there were even prominent monetarists who held the reliance on interest rates as instruments of policy to be clumsy and possibly ineffective.[31]

Eventually, from about 1983, the inflation rate did begin to come down. There were many reasons for this, including a slowing-down of inflation on a world-wide basis, but there is no doubt that the drastic action of the Government in 1980–2 had contributed to it. However, the costs were enormous, in terms of manufacturing industry permanently destroyed and jobs lost, and of economic growth thwarted. Despite a relatively good performance of the economy in the mid-1980s, the loss of the crisis years was not made good, nor the previous growth curve reached again, when a second bout of inflation struck in 1987–8.

This second inflationary threat to a Government that made anti-inflationary policies its main preoccupation, was, unlike the first, entirely home-made and not matched elsewhere in the industrialized world. Among the causes was the removal of all financial controls, and the consequent development of a huge domestic credit inflation which, to make matters worse, found no home productive capacity to meet it and therefore sucked in imports to create a devastating foreign balance of payments deficit. To a considerable extent, the home consumer boom was based on competition among high street banks and building

[30] *Nat. Inst. Econ. Rev.,* November 1987, p. 41. For different calculations see Begg, in Dornbusch and Layard, *Performance,* p. 37, and Buiter and Miller, 'Changing the Rules', p. 325.
[31] Walters, *Renaissance,* p. 123.

societies, banks having begun to lend on mortgages, while building societies extended mortgage loans for purposes clearly beyond home improvements for a general spending spree: the 'leakage' of these misapplied funds was estimated at £2 billion in 1984 and had clearly risen beyond this in the following year. At the same time other consumer credit, largely by credit cards, had jumped from £3·8 billion in 1985 to £6 billion in 1987. In the ten years to November 1988, banks in the UK had increased their non-housing loans from £4 billion to £28 billion while their home loans outstanding rose from £6 billion to £63 billion. Private borrowing, it might be said, was 'crowding out' public borrowing, the PSBR.[32] The second reason for the credit explosion must be found in the two give-away budgets of 1987 and 1988, which lowered standard rates of tax to families now disposing of easy access to credit. A housing price explosion in those years completed the picture.

It was perhaps unfortunate that the illusion had taken root in Government circles that the high interest rate had single-handedly solved the 1980–2 crisis, so that it could be expected that it would do so again. It was the sole weapon used by the Chancellor, Mr Lawson, who was at the time under the further illusion that British industry had reached a position of strength, instead of having barely climbed back onto its weak growth path of earlier decades. Even supporters of the Government's doctrinal approach were warning that with the financial markets out of control, a high minimum lending rate would not be sufficient. Optimistic announcements from the Treasury about the imminent reduction of the rate of inflation because the high interest rate was beginning to bite, were month after month belied by events, and, as interest and mortgage rates rose to meet the ever rising inflation, greater distress even than in 1980–2 began to affect industry and this time also house owners with mortgages. Unemployment rose sharply, output fell, bankruptcies increased, while this time, the balance of payments went simultaneously and catastrophically into the red. The second 'stop' of the Thatcher Government, operative from 1988 onward, formed the background to the downfall of the Chancellor and finally also to that of the Prime Minister.[33] Table 10 6 indicates some of the relevant data necessary to an understanding of the changes in policy in the years 1979–90.[34]

It had been agreed early in 1979 that pending the coming election, the Spring Budget of Mr Healey would be a standstill budget, and it was left to Sir Geoffrey Howe after the Conservatives won the election to make the first moves in the new policy dispensation in his budget of 1979. In macro-economic terms, his budget was strongly deflationary, but within the total, a substantial redistribution from direct to indirect taxation was announced. The standard rate of income tax was cut from 33% to 30%, and top rates were cut from 83% to 60%, which would put a tax-free £23,000 a year into the pocket of a person

[32] Jon Shields, 'Controlling Household Credit', *Nat. Inst. Econ. Rev.* 125 (1988), p. 51; Margaret Reid, 'Mrs Thatcher and the City', in Dennis Kavanagh and Anthony Seldon (eds.), *The Thatcher Effect*, (Oxford, 1989), p. 53; Stephen Merrett with Fred Gray, *Owner-Occupation in Britain* (1982), p. 318; Alan Budd, 'Macroeconomic Aspects of the 1988 Budget' *Fiscal Studies* 9/2 (1988), pp. 8–9.

[33] Riddell, *Decade*, pp. 24–5; Pliatzky, *Treasury*, pp. 143–5; David Smith, 'Descent from Boom to Bust', *Sunday Times*, 17 March 1991, pp. Focus 11–14.

[34] *Nat. Inst. Econ. Rev.*, World Bank, *Annual Report*, 1990, p. 24.

Table 10·6: GDP, investment and prices, 1979–90

	GDP index 1985=100	Fixed investment in manufacturing, 1985=100, 1985 Prices	Stock-output ratios, 1984=100	Retail prices, annual rate of inflation %	Interest rate %††	Mortgage rate, %
1979	92·7	108·7	108	13·4	15·84	12·10
1980	90·5	96·7	119	17·9	13·13	14·95
1981	89·6	75·3	111	12·0	14·62	13·65
1982	91·2	74·1	105	8·5	9·72	12·91
1983	94·6	73·4	105	4·5	8·84	10·62
1984	96·3	86·9	100	5·1	9·12	11·38
1985	100	100	98	6·0	11·17	12·64
1986	103·6	94·0	96	3·4	10·65	11·91
1987	108·0	99·2	90	4·2	8·21	11·56
1988	112·7	112·1	85	4·9	12·51	10·97
1989	114·9	121·0	82	7·8	14·18	13·61
1990	116·0	119·2*	81*	9·4#	13·06	15·15#
1991	115·2†					

Annual Averages 1980–9
Change, % p.a.:

UK	2·6	4·3**	5·7##
G7	3·0	3·4**	4·0##

G7 = weighted average of the seven largest industrial economies
*   provisional
†   first quarter
** first three quarters of the year
\#   Gross fixed investment
\#\# GNP deflator
†† Treasury Bill Discount Rate

with an income somewhat over £100,000 a year. It was much the largest tax cut in history. The top tax rate for investment income was reduced from 98% to 75%, and the starting point raised from £1,700 to £5,000. The simultaneous raising of the tax threshold benefited the poorer taxpayer more. To compensate for the loss of revenue amounting to £4,540 million in a full year, VAT was increased from 8% and 12½% to 15% to bring in an additional £4,175 million. This increased the rate of inflation by 4 5% directly, and more indirectly by giving a further twist to the inflationary spiral through consequent wage claims and cost increases. For a Government pledged to reduce inflation as its first priority this was an astonishing action to have taken, though the Government may have received advice from one of its supporters, Professor (Sir) Alan Walters, that 'price increases *remove* inflationary pressure: they do not add to it.'[35] Presumably, by the same reasoning, it is price *cuts* which fuel inflation. At the same time the Government ended the Price Commission, increased interest rates (the MLR going up from 12% to 14%) and forced the nationalized industries to raise their prices including gas and electricity, and the local authorities to raise council rents, all adding to the upward push of prices. Inflation then rose to a peak of 22% by May 1982.

To switch from direct taxation, normally considered to be progressive, to indirect taxation, a regressive form of raising revenue which hits the poor hardest, is a normal procedure for a Government wishing to transfer income from the poor to the rich, though the extent of this switch was quite unusual. The Government defended the move on the grounds that lower income tax rates would encourage enterprise, just as excessively high tax rates had stifled it. It is a view shared by a very small minority of economists,[36] and, curiously enough, it was contradicted by the next Chancellor, Mr Lawson, in his budget speech of 1984 when reducing investment allowances. Easy profits, he stated then, encouraged laziness and complacency: it was tough conditions which forced investors to look hard for profitable action.[37]

For the longer term, substantial cuts in public expenditure were announced in order to bring down the PSBR, as well as to help meet the monetary targets noted above. Meanwhile, however, unemployment was rising, output falling while the pound remained perversely high, affecting exports. Against that background, the budget of 1980 held fast to its classic deflationary stance and the screw was tightened still further in November of that year,[38] while inflation peaked at 21·7% in May and unemployment topped 2 million in December.

Nor was there any let-up in the budget of 1981. Income taxes were to be raised by holding personal allowances and the tax threshold steady in the face of inflation. Taxes on alcohol, tobacco and petrol were up, the latter by 20p a gallon (inclusive of VAT), and among minor changes, there was to be a once for-all charge on banking deposits. There were the usual hopes expressed of throttling the money supply, and the target of the PSBR was to be tightened from the currently expected £13·5 billion to £10·5 billion in the coming year. The only sign of a let-up was the lowering of the minimum lending rate from

[35] Walters, *Renaissance*, p. 77. This might be matched by the statement by Mr Biffen for the Treasury in the Commons 1 July 1980, that pay rises did not affect the rate of inflation.
[36] Matthews and Minford, 'Policies', pp. 70–1; Thompson, *Conservatives*, pp. 157–9.
[37] *Ibid.*, p. 175.
[38] See pp. 363–4 above.

14% to 12%. In view of the fact that in 1980, output had fallen by around 10%, manufacturing output by 15% and employment by about a million, this restrictive budget ran into much opposition, including the unprecedented reaction of 364 leading economists who sent a letter of protest to the *Times* on 31 March 1981.

The Budget of 1982 saw only few changes, including the increase in alcohol and tobacco duties, and petrol duties went up by another 9p a gallon. The fall in output was halted by then, and inflation was beginning to ease up, but unemployment now exceeded 3 million. Of some importance was the lifting of hire purchase restrictions in that year. Nor was there much change in the 1983 budget, though large increases in relief and allowances reduced the burden of income tax somewhat, while alcohol and tobacco duties and petrol duties (up by 4p a gallon) were raised less than in the past. One purpose of the budget was to steady the pound after it had come down from its crisis height. There was also little change in the budget of 1984, by which time inflation had levelled off at $4\frac{1}{2}$% and output had begun to rise: alcohol duties went up by less than in the past, and petrol duty by $4\frac{1}{2}$p. per gallon. One interesting change was the reduction in investment allowances, to be abolished altogether, in stages, by 1986. This was in order to encourage productive investment in plant and machinery. By the spring of 1985, as inflation remained low, the Government at last began to consider the continuing high level of unemployment as an object of policy, without giving it undue priority. In his budget speech, the Chancellor claimed that the coal strike of 1984–5 had added some £2·5 billion to public expenditure costs, which limited his powers to grant tax relief.

It was in the 1986 budget that the first major change occurred, the standard rate of income tax being brought down from 30% to 29%, with the ultimate target of 25% in the offing. As noted above, the PSBR target was far from being met, but with the economy at last in recovery and oil revenues at their peak, the weight of the Government's policy was thrown behind tax reductions, not least because of their expected electoral impact. Shares, held on personal equity plans (PEP) to a limited amount, were to be tax free as an encouragement to small investors. The next step was taken in 1987, when the standard rate was reduced to 27%, while the stock exchange crash on 19–20 October of that year taught many of the newly wooed small holders that there are dangers, as well as joys, in share ownership.

The first major stage of the Government's plan of lowering the tax burden was completed in 1988, when standard tax came down to 25%. Even more sensationally, all the higher tax rates of hitherto 45, 50, 55 and 60% respectively were consolidated into a single top tax rate of 40%, beginning with all taxable income exceeding £19,300. For the very wealthy, with incomes exceeding £120,000 a year, this was an annual tax-free increase of £20,000 or more. Further, tax thresholds were raised more than the inflation rate.

However, this give-away tax initiative was launched in an economy in which inflationary pressures were already building up strongly, not least because of an unhindered credit explosion for consumers. House prices, in particular, were rising fast, and their rise was accelerated by the provision in the budget to grant only a single tax-free mortgage allowance of up to £30,000 for each property, and not one to each owner separately. In the scramble to beat the deadline in August, house prices were lifted even faster.

Given the strong pound, the Chancellor was reluctant to halt the inflationary pressure by raising the interest rate, which by now was the only weapon he had left. There was, however, no other way, especially since by this time the balance of payments figure was also deteriorating rapidly. Between May and December 1988 the Chancellor raised the basic interest rate no fewer than 12 times,[39] each time accompanied by the confident assertion that now the inflation was under control, which was each each time regularly belied by events.

Over the year as a whole, M3 was rising at a rate of 21%, M4 at 17%, M0 at 6·2% and bank lending at 25%. In line with the basic increases ordered by the Chancellor, mortgage rates also began to be raised in steps, to reach around 15·5% by 1990, compared with a low of 9·25% in the summer of 1988. This hit recent house purchasers doubly, since it came on top of the large price increases.

In July 1988 the fateful Act was passed introducing the community charge, or 'Poll Tax', as the new way of raising revenue for local government. Instead of being rated on an indirect valuation of property, which had some relation to income and wealth, and had the further advantage of being easily found and located, all citizens were now required to pay an identical rate per adult inhabitant, irrespective of income. It was the first time in modern times in any advanced country that a head ('poll') tax was to be levied which actually rated the rich at a very much lower share of their income than the poor: the richest could look forward to substantial cuts in their local taxation, the poor faced very substantial increases in most cases. The poll tax was defended by the Government on the grounds that it would vary directly with the local authority's expenditure, and thus bring home to all voters the need to put pressure on their local authority to spend less. There was also, and at the same time, a change in the form of rating for businesses, a common national rate being set and the payments redistributed among the local authorities.

The new tax was to be introduced in Scotland in April 1989 and in England and Wales in April 1990. It led to immediate protests, and ultimately to violent riots and widespread refusals to pay. By the end of October 1990 the Audit Commission reported that one in ten in England had not paid anything, and less than half the total had so far been collected. The Government's estimates, as usual, had proved to be wide of the mark: instead of the predicted average rate for England of £278, it turned out to be £363, and in Wales £222 instead of the estimated £173. Some local authorities setting rates higher than the Government thought proper had their rates 'capped', i.e. they were forced to reduce them, thus further undermining the independence of the elected local government. Ultimately, the tax was to be the main cause of Mrs Thatcher's resignation, which was followed by the immediate announcement that the tax would be amended, which turned out to mean abolished.

By now a full 'stop' was in force. In the budget of 1989, such other concerns as unemployment and the exchange rate were forgotten: the sole target was now the rate of inflation, to be brought down by limiting public expenditure, and above all by maintaining high interest rates. M0 growth was targeted at 1–5% compared with a 7% rise in the past year, and there was to be a further large repayment of the national debt of £14 billion, mainly out of the proceeds of

[39] Grahame Thompson, *The Political Economy of the New Right* (1990), p. 53; O.E.C.D., *Economic Surveys: United Kingdom 1989/1990* (Paris 1990), p. 11.

selling off nationalized industries. Income tax and allowances were left unchanged (allowances rising with inflation), and there was merely a slight reduction in national insurance contributions. To avoid a boost to the cost of living, there were no increases this time, in line with inflation, in alcohol, tobacco and petrol duties. By the time of the budget of 1990, it turned out that only £7 billion of the national debt had been repaid, and a similar sum was proposed for that year. Taxes again remained unchanged and allowances and excise duties went up with inflation. To encourage small savings, tax exempt savings (TESSA) were to begin in January 1991, and the ceilings for savings were raised before pensions and poll-tax relief were affected.

The hopes of containing inflation by these measures were to be disappointed. Inflation kept on rising throughout the summer to reach an annual rate of 10·9% by October 1990. At that point, contrary to repeated statements that Britain would join the European exchange rate mechanism only after her inflation rate had been brought down, Britain joined, at the par rate of £1 = 2·95 DM, with a 6% margin either side.

While the desired effects on inflation were not in sight, the negative aspects of the policy were only too evident: the rate of unemployment continued to increase, economic growth had slowed to 0·7%, investment was down by − 5·4%, bankruptcies were up for the year by 35%, to total 24,442 (compared with 5,309 in 1979), and repossession of houses rose to 14,390 for the first six months, compared with 13,740 for the whole of 1989. The balance of trade, though slightly less disastrous than in 1988 and 1989, was still negative to the extent of 2·5% of GDP. By the 5th December 1990, even the Chancellor of the Exchequer, Mr Lamont, admitted to a Commons Committee that Britain was in recession. The Treasury and Civil Service Committee of the House of Commons itself reported on the 20th that there existed a 'longer and deeper depression' than the Treasury had forecast. There was no sign of a significant let-up of the inflation into the early months of 1991; investment, output and GNP were still falling and recovery was still a long way off.

Viewing the period 1979–90 as a whole, it bears all the marks of $1\frac{1}{2}$ normal post-war stop-go cycles: it consisted of a severe stop phase 1979–82, leading in this case to actual decline in output and incomes, followed by a recovery and growth phase to 1987, which led to familiar signs of 'overheating' and the renewed imposition of a stop from 1988, once more culminating in actual declines of output and incomes. To this familiar cycle, the Government reacted in a way which may also be viewed as 'conventional' or orthodox.[40] It was an unmitigated tragedy that just at the time when the North Sea oil had removed the major cause of the repeated and damaging 'stops', namely the balance of payments deficit, which would have permitted an uninterrupted growth phase in which modernization policies might have flourished unhindered, the Government determined to make inflation its chief priority, requiring the same deflationary treatment as before (same policy, different justification). The rare gift of a second chance was thus missed. As far as this sequence of stop and go is concerned, therefore, the radical new policies had made no major discernible difference.

Nor did they affect the actual rates of growth, despite the contribution of the

---

[40] Thompson, *Conservatives*, p. 126; Hillard, 'Thatcherism', p. 355.

oil. The 1970s were, indeed, exceptionally poor years, not merely in Britain. But in comparison with earlier cycles, the Thatcher years do not stand out as particularly successful growth years (Table 10·7). Even the relatively good growth rate of investment was concentrated in the services sector: manufacturing came off relatively badly once again.

Table 10·7:   Annual growth rates in two cycles, 1973–88 (in per cent)[41]

	1950/1–1972/3	1972/3–1978/9	1978/9–1987/8
GDP (output)	2·7	1·5	2·1
Manufacturing	2·9	0·0	0·4
Services	2·5	1·9	2·7
		1973/9	1979/87
Gross domestic fixed capital formation		0·1	2·0
Of which: Manufacturing		1·7	−1·3
Distribution, catering etc		1·9	4·7
Banking, finance, leased assets		20·9	8·2
Other assets		1·4	11·5
Other services		−6·9	3·4

All the hopes of a radical new beginning, including the concentration on the medium term rather than on immediate crises and the emphasis on the supply side, seemed to have been dashed on the rock of the traditional elements in British economic policy making. There were the North Sea oil reprieve, monetarism, and Thatcherism that altered the signposts and provided a new rhetoric, yet the destructive stop-go sequence was left intact.

2 Economic Growth and Industrial Change

The population of the United Kingdom increased very slowly over this period, from an estimated 56·2 million in 1979 to 57·5 million in 1991.[42] The population of working age increased from 32·57 million in 1979 to 34·19 million in 1988 which, added to persons above retirement age still at work, meant that 34·91 million as against 33·41 million were theoretically available for work, an increase of 1·5 million. Meanwhile, unemployment had risen by just over a million, and there was also an increase of males not at work and not listed as unemployed of 700,000. Against this, the number of women of working age not at work had declined by 300,000, so that the number of people at work remained constant at almost exactly 25 million between those dates.

The replacement of men by women in the workforce was one of the most remarkable features of this decade, a development noticeable also in the preceding decades, continuing at an accelerating rate, thus between the same two dates of 1979 and 1988, the number of males in employment fell by just over 1·5 million (from 13,487,000 to 11,970,000), while the number of women increased from 9,686,000 to 10,257,000, or by not quite 600,000. The total number of men in employment actually fell by much less than the numbers of employees, by only 600,000: the difference was made up by a striking increase

---

[41] Charles Feinstein and Robin Matthews, 'The Growth of Output and Productivity in the UK: The 1980s as a Phase of the Post-war Period', *Nat. Inst. Econ. Rev.* 133 (1990), pp. 81, 86.
[42] *Annual Abstract of Statistics*.

in the numbers of self-employed men, which increased by more than 50%, from 1·9 million to virtually 3 million in this short space of time and rose further to 3·1 million in 1989. Many of these were in one-man firms or very small enterprises founded by men made redundant, living in declining industrial areas or for other reasons despairing of working at their trade again, and frequently using their redundancy payment to remain active. Others were sub-contractors for tax reasons. It was among these self-employed persons that the bankruptcies at the end of the decade were particularly high. It is also worthy of note that, according to one calculation, the increase in employment of 570,000 between March 1983 and September 1986 can be classified into 144,000 holding second jobs, 237,000 who were in special unemployment programmes and youth training schemes, and only 189,000 persons who had found genuinely new jobs.[43]

The shift to women's employment was but one aspect of the shift from manufacturing to the services, and from the northern industrial provinces to London and the South East. Of the 497,000 part-time female jobs gained in 1983–5, 157,000 were in the South East, 19,000 in East Anglia and 62,000 in the South West, making almost half the total. Many of the newly employed women, and also many men, as well as those leaving one job for another, were now in part-time jobs, often poorly paid and outside the compulsory insurance and pension schemes. Even in the 1970s, when full-time jobs had fallen by 1·7million, part-time jobs had increased by 1 million. In 1981, 5% of single women were employed part-time, but 32% of married women were so employed. By 1985, 25% of jobs were part-time.[44]

The shift from manufacturing to the services is illustrated in Table 10·8:[45]

Table 10·8:   Distribution of manpower, United Kingdom, 1979–88 (000)

	1979	1985	1988
All industries and services	22,920	21,509	22,226
All service industries	13,394	14,192	15,167
All production industries	9,159	6,976	6,745
Manufacturing industries	7,176	5,365	5,215
Of which: metal goods, engineering, vehicles	3,271	2,427	2,364
Textiles	478	244	242
Agriculture, forestry, fishing	367	341	313
Construction	1,291	1,022	1,043
Gas, water, electricity	345	589	487
Transport and communication	1,494	1,345	1,324
Distributive trades	2,826	4,340	4,427
Insurance, banking, etc.	1,233	2,083	2,467
Professional, scientific services	3,729	3,348	3,652
Miscellaneous services	2,493	1,333	1,625
Public administration and defence	1,619	1,613	1,672

[43] John MacInnes, *Thatcherism at Work* (Milton Keynes, 1987), p. 71.

[44] Felicity Henwood and Sally Wyatt, 'Women's Work, Technological Change and Shifts in the Employment Structure', in Ron Martin and Bob Rowthorn (eds.), *The Geography of De-Industrialisation* (1986); Ron Martin, 'Thatcherism and Britain's Industrial Landscape', *ibid.*, p. 285; Charles Handy, *The Future of Work* (Oxford, 1984), p. 17; P. B. Beaumont, *Change in Industrial Relations* (1990), p. 26; William Brown, 'The Changing Role of Trade Unions in the Management of Labour', *British Journal of Industrial Relations* 24/2 (1986), p. 161.

[45] *Annual Abstract of Statistics.*

It was thus among manufacturing workers, mostly male and mostly also in the north-western part of the country, that most of the jobs were lost in the slump years of the early 1980s, for whom the new jobs for females in offices and shops in the South East were little consolation. It will be noticed that even among the services there were considerable job losses in some sectors, only the distributive trades and financial and similar services showing very large rises to compensate in part for the losses of jobs elsewhere. No other period has seen such rapid changes in the distribution of the employed population.

Manufacturing labour productivity, however, showed a substantial rise in the early 1980s: the annual growth in output per head in 1979–88 in manufacturing was a remarkable 4·5%, compared with 1·1% in 1973–9, and compared with 1·8% growth in the non-manufacturing sector (excluding North Sea oil and gas and the public services) in 1979–88. At that time, for the period 1979–88, British labour productivity growth in manufacturing was ahead of all other major countries. Japan, for example, registered only 3·3% a year, Germany 1·6%, USA 3·7% and even Italy, the best of the bunch, only 4·3%, according to the OECD.[46] It was this high growth in productivity in manufacturing which made some supporters of the Government speak of an economic 'miracle' and even of having turned the economy round and having set it on a path of catching up with the rest of Europe.

This claim has given rise to considerable controversy. On the face of it, there were five possible reasons for this rise: (a) the loss of jobs and the closing down of firms occurred among the least productive, thus raising the average – the cricket 'tail-enders' argument, on the analogy that batting averages are improved (though the totals diminished) if the tail-enders are not allowed to play; (b) it was a mere catching-up process, making good the losses of the late 1970s and of the first two years of the new Government; (c) the employees were working harder or more efficiently by being given better incentives; (d) there had been better equipment or organization or greater flexibility to raise productivity per head; and (e) employers let go of previously hoarded labour. These are not necessarily mutually exclusive, and it is likely that all of them contributed to this satisfactory result. Particularly remarkable in this increase was the improvement in the steel industry, at one time the most inefficient producer in Europe, and even in the motor car industry, the problem child of British manufacturing.

Nevertheless, British manufacturing declined, not only in terms of employment but also in terms of output, and this gave rise to concern. Even in terms of cost competitiveness (unit values of UK exports) the great improvement of the fall from 109·2 in 1980 to a low of 95·5 in 1986 (1985 = 100), began to be reversed again, rising to 105·6 in 1989 and over 102 still in 1990; similarly, the

---

[46] Charles Feinstein and Robin Matthews, 'The Growth of Output and Productivity in the UK: the 1980's as a Phase of the Post-War Period', *Nat. Inst. Econ. Rev.*, 133 (1990), pp. 84, 86; Nicholas Oulton, 'Plant Closures and the Productivity "Miracle" in Manufacturing', *ibid.*, 120 (1987), pp. 53–9; Peter Riddell, *The Thatcher Decade* (Oxford, 1989), pp. 39–41; Geoffrey Maynard, 'Britain's Economic Revival and the Balance of Payments', *Political Quarterly* 60/2 (1989), pp. 156–7; G. F. Ray, 'Labour Costs in Manufacturing', *Nat. Inst. Econ. Rev.* 120 (1987); John Muellbauer, 'Productivity and Competitiveness in British Manufacturing', *Oxford Review of Economic Policy* 2/3 (1986).

relative unit labour costs, which had fallen from a high in 1981 of 124·1 to 90·3 in 1987, were up to around 98 by 1990. Other industries also showed a deterioration in the relative cost position after 1986.[47]

The share of manufacturing in value added in GDP was falling in the other advanced countries also but nowhere as fast as in the United Kingdom.[48] There were those who did not consider this a disadvantage and strongly objected to:

'the assertion ... that manufacturing has an intrinsic importance not enjoyed by other sections of the economy, such as services. The singling out of one type of activity is offensive to those of us who ... will not be bullied into accepting sheer superstition'.[49]

This view appeared to be shared also by the Treasury. A more sophisticated defence was to state that the relative fall in the British exports of manufactures, which had reached the sensational stage by 1983–4 of allowing, for the first time in recorded history, manufactured imports to exceed exports, was due not to weaknesses in manufacturing, but to the success of the exports of services and of oil.[50]

Yet even this view could not deny that Britain's de-industrialization was 'negatively' structured, determined in part by declines in real output. This point was taken up by the critics.[51] Moreover, it was not only Britain's share of the world's manufacturing output that declined year after year, but also her share in the world's manufacturing exports. Her share of these fell from 9·1% in 1979 to 7·6% in 1986, and the decline of her share of exports into the advanced world of the OECD was equally drastic. There was simultaneously a worrying increase of finished manufactures, as against raw materials and semi-manufactures, among her imports.[52]

The House of Lords Committee on Overseas Trade, reporting in October 1985, was not impressed by arguments which played down the significance of this decline in manufacturing. Imports, they noted, had risen faster than exports, and without a strong manufacturing base to sustain growth in exports, economic growth would be held back. By 1984, the trade deficit in manufacturing was of the order of £3 billion and thereafter rising fast: the import penetration of goods of foreign manufacturers was pointing up even more clearly than the export figures, the weakness of the British manufacturing sector. One study found the

[47] *Nat. Inst. Econ. Rev.*; George F Ray, 'International Labour Costs in Manufacturing, 1960–88', *Nat. Inst. Econ. Rev.* 132 (1990), p. 67.

[48] David G Mayes, 'Does Manufacturing Matter', *Nat. Inst. Econ. Rev.* 122 (1987), p. 49.

[49] Samuel Brittan, 'Now Forward to the 1960s, *Financial Times* 18 April 1991.

[50] Peter Jenkins, *Mrs Thatcher's Revolution* (1987), p. 258; R. E. Rowthorn and J. R. Wells, *De-Industrialization and Foreign Trade* (Cambridge 1987), pp. 195 ff. Evidence by P. N. Sedgwick of the Treasury to the House of Lords *S.C. On Overseas Trade*, Sess. Papers 238-II (1985), esp. QQ. 281, 319.

[51] Grazia Ietto-Gillies, 'Was Deindustrialization in the UK Inevitable? Some Comments on the Rowthorn-Wells Analysis', *International Review of Applied Economics* 4/2 (1990), and reply, pp. 209–35.

[52] Michael Chisholm, 'De-Industrialization and British Regional Policy', *Regional Studies* 19/4 (1985), p. 305; Mayes, 'Manufacturing', p. 55; Mark Smith, 'UK Manufacturing: Output and Trade Performance', *Midland Bank Review* (Autumn 1986), pp. 8–16.

share of imports in a number of consumer goods to have changed as follows in but five years:[53]

		1979	1984
(imports as	Clothing and Footwear	30	37
% of consumption)	Electrical/electronic goods	39	50
	Other household goods	18	24
	Other goods	27	40
	All goods	27	36

Comparing exports with imports, the trade balance had changed as follows (in per cent of supplies:

	1979	1985
Clothing	−9	−14
Domestic electrical	−11	−32
Furniture	−4	−11
Domestic china, earthenware	+34	+20
Wall coverings	+30	+22

By 1984, the penetration of the home market for dishwashers and wet and dry vacuum cleaners had reached 100%, of built-in ovens 80%, of irons 64%, and of other vacuum cleaners 34%. While in a group of mainly capital goods with high research intensity, imports as a percentage of home demand rose from 29% to 54%, exports as a percent of sales rose only from 37% to 52%, or by 15% between 1975 and 1985.[54]

Although it was generally more convenient to buy British, and British goods also scored well in promotion, packaging and flexibility, foreign goods scored heavily on price, style, quality and novelty. Large buyers preferred British goods also on points of delivery and performance (just), but small firms had better experience with foreign supplies on both counts. A British Insitute of Management Survey in 1986 found that the UK was still not able to meet its target of having no more than one order in four delivered late. UK branches performed significantly worse than foreign-owned plants on a comparable base in 87 cases; quality and reliability of goods were still poor, and British managers were less well trained and less skilled, particularly in managing their labour relations, than foreign ones. The British record in exports was particularly poor and worrying in the technically more sophisticated goods.[55] Investment had recovered from its slump in the early 1980s (Table 10·6 above), but had not been increased as a percentage of GDP, being 18·8% in 1979 and 18·4% in 1988.

[53] Ann D. Morgan, *British Imports of Consumer Goods. A Study of Import Penetration* (Cambridge, 1988), p. 14.

[54] Morgan, pp. 37, 49, 65, 66, 78, 87, 96; Smith, 'Manufacturing', p. 11; *S.C. (Lords) On Overseas Trade, Report*, 238-I, p. 20.

[55] Christopher Carr, *Britain's Competitiveness* (1990), pp. 254–6; Lord Aldington, 'Britain's Manufacturing Industry', *Royal Bank of Scotland Review* 151 (1986), pp. 3–13; Scott Newton and Dilwyn Porter, *Modernization Frustrated. The Politics of Industrial Decline in Britain since 1900* (1988), p. 197; Smith, 'Manufacturing', p. 13.

Since other sectors of the economy grew more slowly than the manufacturing sector, the overall growth rate for the economy was still among the slowest in the advanced countries, though not quite the slowest. The faster rate of the mid-80s merely served to put the United Kingdom back on her traditional modest growth path (Table 10·9).[56]

Table 10·9:   Growth of real GDP, major countries, 1979–90

	Growth 1979–88 (% p.a.)		1990, Index
	F & M	K & S	(1983 = 100)
Japan	4·0	4·9	138·0
USA	2·8	2·7	126·7
Germany	1·7	—	123·2
France	1·9	—	121·6 (est.)
United Kingdom	2·2	2·1	122·2
OECD (Europe)	—	2·1	—

Consequently, Britain continued to trail in absolute terms (Table 10·10).[57]

Table 10·10:   Production and productivity, major countries, using purchasing power parity exchange rates, 1985–7 (Index)

	GDP per capita, 1987	GDP per worker, 1987	Manufacturing output per worker 1985
United Kingdom	100	100	100
France	104	121	127
Germany	108	114	122
Italy	99	121	117
Japan	107	97	116
USA	149	141	167

Turning to individual industrial sectors and industries, there were considerable structural changes in the decade both in output and in productivity. Changes in the major sectors are listed in Table 10.11.[58]

Most industries, it will be noted, had by 1985 not yet recovered from the slump, but had grown considerably by 1990, as had manufacturing as a whole, though a 12% growth in 11 years for the latter is very low compared with the whole of the post-war period and reflects the difficulties of that sector of the economy. Among industries, only chemicals, and to a much lesser extent, food, drink and tobacco showed continuous growth; both were put in the shade by construction and services. The continuous decline of textiles and clothing does not reflect an actual decline in demand, but the success of import penetration and the failures in exports. By 1987, the largest industrial sectors were food, drink and tobacco (19·3% of gross output), chemicals (10·8%), electrical engineering

[56] Feinstein and Matthews, p. 87; *OECD*; Samuel Brittan, 'The Thatcher Government's Economic Policy', in Dennis Kavanagh and Anthony Seldon (eds.), *The Thatcher Effect* (Oxford 1989), p. 14; also Ken Coutts and Wynn Godley, 'The British Economy under Mrs Thatcher', *Political Quarterly* 60/2 (1989), pp. 137–9.
[57] Brittan, 'Policy', p. 19.
[58] Recalculated from *Nat. Inst. Econ. Rev.*

Table 10·11:   Production index, seasonally adjusted, 1979–1990 (1979 = 100)

	1985	1990 (3rd quarter)
Energy	119·5	102·6
Manufacturing	94·8	112·4
Metals	85·6	106·2
Building materials	85·3	96·6
Chemicals	107·1	124·9
Engineering and allied	96·5	115·4
Food, drink, tobacco	100·3	108·2
Textiles, clothing	86·4	82·9
Other manufacturing	88·5	118·7
Consumer goods	95·7	109·5
Investment goods	98·4	118·7
Intermediate goods	104·4	106·2
Construction	106·2	134·7
Services	111·6	135·3

(10·8%), mechanical engineering (9·6%) and paper, printing and publishing (8·6%), while motor vehicles and parts were down to 6·9%. Energy and water supply delivered 12·5%, and construction 13·9%.

Productivity, as distinct from total output, showed gratifying improvements in the mid-80s. The larger firms in most fields were among the most successful, or most ruthless, in shedding labour and thus improving their productivity performance. Among the most prominent were the following, showing the reduction in their labour force between 1977 and 1983:

British Steel	−61%
British Leyland	−53%
Courtaulds	50%
TI	−59%
Dunlop	−54%
Talbot	−69%
BSR International	68%[59]

As far as other sectors were concerned, labour productivity in agriculture increased at the same rate between 1979 and 1988 as in manufacturing, by 4·2%, and in energy and water by 6·6%, but in other sectors by less. Transport and communication improved by 3·6% a year, construction by 2·4%, finance by 2·3%, distribution and similar services by 2·0 and 'other services' declined by −1·7%; it was the latter which helped to pull down the average for the whole economy to 2·14% over the period. Since the average growth of capital inputs was lowered by an above average rate of retirement of capital, it follows that in terms of total factor productivity the 1980s performed even better than labour productivity in comparison with the preceding decade.[60]

Coal continued on its secular decline, despite enormous subsidies paid to the National Coal Board and despite other measures, such as the obligation on the Central Electricity Generating Board to use a minimum of 95% of British coal,

[59] Ron Martin, in Martin and Rowthorn, *Geography*, p. 261.
[60] Feinstein and Matthews, *passim*.

at a time when foreign coal was much cheaper. Production fell from 122 million tonnes in 1979 (130 million in 1980) to around 93 million tonnes in 1990, but since the share of open-cast mining had meanwhile risen from around 8 million tonnes to 18 million, the decline of deep mining was faster still. The number of pits fell from 219 in 1980 to 94 in 1988, and the number of wage earners from 231,000 to 59,000 in 1990 but output per manshift shot up from 2·32 tonnes to 3·97 tonnes in that period. Thus closures of mines and redundancies for miners became the order of the day. The strike of 1984/5, fought against closures determined on purely economic grounds, certainly accelerated the process. All over north-western Europe mines were closing also, though not in Spain or overseas, and coal imports from low-cost areas rose to 10–13 million tonnes a year in 1986–8, while exports declined to a mere 2 million tonnes, so that in this area also, Britain became a net importer. Large investments in modern mines, especially in Yorkshire, promised higher productivity and easier working conditions for the future. In Selby, it was planned that 4,000 men should produce as much as 30,000 miners elsewhere. Although the industry was internationally in the forefront of technical innovation and research, the decline of coal could not be halted in this period.[61]

The motor industry, already in serious decline in the 1970s, suffered near collapse in the slump of the early 1980s. British Leyland, the only British mass-produced-car maker left, had to be rescued once again by an injection of £990 million in 1981, very much against the current Government philosophy, bringing the total state aid for 1975–84 up to some £2,411 million. Since then, under vigorous management as a nationalized undertaking, the firm has steadied at around 40% of British production, and its profitable part, Jaguar Cars, has been privatized. Also, the Japanese car makers Honda, Nissan and Toyota were beginning to invest in British car-making capacity, no doubt largely as a means of entering the EC market over and above the direct Japanese car imports permitted under agreement. The early 1980s saw a rapid rise in productivity per man from an abysmally low starting level, Austin Rover's increased by 25% between 1979 and 1986, Jaguar's by 310% and Ford's by 90%. In 1989, BL's output was 435,000 cars (plus 21,000 car derived vans); closely followed by Ford (383,000 + 50,000), though Ford transferred the production of the popular Sierra to Belgium in mid-1990. Vauxhall (208,000 + 29,000) was some way behind. Nissan by that time were producing 77,000 cars and Peugeot 107,000. Total output in 1989 was 1,267,000 + 100,000, up from around a million vehicles a year in the early 1980s, equivalent to 76% of capacity. This equalled around one-third of the output rate of Germany, France or Italy. With imports valued at £7·5 billion and exports at £2·5 billion, the trading deficit was £5 billion in 1989, to which has to be added a trading deficit of £928 million for commercial vehicles.[62] No other major industrial country has anything approaching this poor result. The plight of the British car industry has been widely blamed on Government policy, yet Government aid, beside the direct subsidies to BL, Ford, DeLorean, Talbot and others, included support for the development of

[61] George F. Ray, 'British Coal', *Nat. Inst. Econ. Rev.* 130 (1989), pp. 75–84; Barry Thomas, 'Coal', in Peter Johnson (ed.), *The Structure of British Industry* (1988), p. 63; Amin Rajan and Richard Pearson (eds.), *UK Occupation and Employment Trends 1990* (1986), p. 44.

[62] D. G. Rhys, 'The Motor Industry and the Balance of Payments', *Royal Bank of Scotland Review* 168 (1990), pp. 11–27; idem, 'Motor Vehicles', in Johnson, *Structure*, pp. 164–87.

new technology.[63] Other factors in the decline have been poor management, complacency, poor industrial relations, an over-fragmented industrial structure, unhelpful financial institutions and a relatively stagnant home market.[64]

Import penetration, measured by imports c.i.f. as a proportion of home demand plus exports, exceeded 33% also in metal manufactures, instrument engineering, office machinery and electrical engineering, as well as in textiles, and it was not much below that in chemicals and mechanical engineering. Several sectors had virtually collapsed by then, including the making of motor cycles, cameras, colour TV, cash registers, dishwashers and shipbuilding. After two decades of yard closures, gross tonnage of merchant shipping launched still amounted to 707,000 g.t. in 1979. By 1988 it was a mere 31,000 g.t.[65]

The steel industry, declining from an output level of 27 million tonnes in the early 1970s, to a mere 14 m.t. in 1984 recovered again to reach almost 19 m.t. in 1988. Following a disastrous 13-week strike in 1980, which cost British makers a large part of their markets in an internationally highly competitive industry, productivity rose almost miraculously in parallel with the shedding of labour. From an output per man-hour of half the German level, and lower than any other industry in Europe in 1979, British productivity improved to equal the German by the mid-1980s. Curiously enough, the heaviest investment had been made in the years 1975–7, rather than in the years after 1980. After losing over £1 billion a year in 1980 and 1981, financial results also improved, to leave the industry in surplus in 1986/7 after meeting all charges. The industry was privatized at the end of 1988.[66] Almost alone among the makers of goods of sophisticated technology, the munitions industry held its own even in the bad years and indeed was not starved of research and development (R & D) expenditure by the Government, which channelled relatively far more resources in that direction than any other advanced industrial nation. The two industries mostly concerned, aerospace and electronic capital goods, suffered a general employment loss from 212,000 to 169,000 between 1978 and 1989, but the numbers of scientists and engineers employed increased from 15,260 to 23,100 in those years. Their share of manufacturing output doubled between 1978 and 1984 from 6 to 12%, and while the arms market declined with the easing of the cold war by the end of the decade, the Government made great efforts to sustain the industry's exports.[67] In the installation of numerically controlled machine tools Britain also held her own, being behind Germany but ahead of France, and the same applied to automatic-flexible factory systems, though in the use of industrial robots the United Kingdom was well behind both, not to mention Japan and the USA, by 1985.[68]

[63] Peter J. S. Dunnett, *The Decline of the British Motor Industry* (1980); K. Baskar, with G. Rhys, *The Future of the British Motor Industry* (1979).

[64] Stephen Wilks, *Industrial Policy and the Motor Industry* (Manchester 1984), pp. 272–3.

[65] Christopher Carr, *Britain's Competitiveness: The Management of the Vehicle Components Industry* (1990), p. 11; Daniel Todd, *The World Shipbuilding Industry* (1985), p. 123.

[66] Anthony Cockerill, 'Steel', in Johnson, *Structure*, pp. 70–93.

[67] John Lovering, 'Military Expenditure and the Restructuring of Capitalism: the Military Industry in Britain', *Cambridge Journal of Economics* 14/4 (1990), pp. 453–67; Grahame Thompson, *The Political Economy of the New Right* (1990), pp. 106 f.; idem, *The Conservatives' Economic Policy* (1986), pp. 186–91.

[68] George F. Ray, 'The Diffusion of Innovation: an Update', *Nat. Inst. Econ. Rev.* 126 (1988), 51–6; Paul Stoneman, 'Information Technology', in Johnson, *Structure*, pp. 140–63.

Among the consumer goods industries, clothing and footwear increased their output in the 1980s, but by less than the rise in consumption, and import penetration increased, as a proportion of consumption plus exports, from 11% in 1979 to 18% in 1984. A detailed study revealed that British makers, unlike the German, had failed to turn to high-grade production, and in the poorer qualities were being driven out of their markets by low-wage countries. High quality, in turn, could be produced in Germany, not so much because of better machines, but because of a more highly trained labour force.[69]

This very brief review of particular industries reveals, broadly, and with some variations, that the overall statistics present a generally true picture: slow growth of output, rapid loss of employment, and a consequent improvement in output per head.[70] The investment statistics confirm the impression gained by detailed examination on the ground that the improved per capita productivity, which even at the end rarely approached that of the continent in absolute terms, was achieved by the ending of overmanning, by harder work and better use of existing machinery rather than by substantially increased investment.

North Sea oil deserves special mention, not only because it provided a measurable boost to national income, but because unlike the earlier development of North Sea gas, which merely replaced home coal as a source of energy, oil had profound effects on the balance of payments, turning a substantial deficit item into an important export surplus. Moreover, oil is a commodity in which, at any realistic level of output, users are prepared to pay far more than the level of costs, so that there is a potential surplus to be tapped. Consequently, oil has given rise all over the world to huge revenues to the Governments of states fortunate enough to possess it. This was the case in the United Kingdom as well, the Government 'take' being around 70% of the net revenues.[71]

Statistics of output, foreign trade and revenues relating to oil are shown in Table 10·12.[72] Output was rising very fast in the late 1970s and it will be seen that it began to exceed consumption from 1980 onward. The decline in consumption was in part due to energy saving, and in part to the decline in production, particularly of heavy energy users such as the iron and steel industry.[73] The peak of production was reached in the mid-1980s. It is evident that the Government's revenue was heavily dependent not only on quantities, but also on prices which began to falter in the second half of the decade and then fell from over $30 to $10–15 per barrel. At its highest point, British output was equivalent to 6% of the output of the Western World (4·5% of world output), making Britain the world's fifth largest producer and contributing around 6% of GDP. The fall in revenues thereafter subtracted around $\frac{1}{2}$% a year from the growth rate of the economy.

The production of North Sea oil, emerging as it did with such extraordinary

---

[69] Hilary Steedman and Karin Wagner, 'Productivity, Machinery and Skills: Clothing Manufacture in Great Britain and Germany', *Nat. Inst. Econ. Rev.* 128 (1989), pp. 40–57; Morgan, *Imports*, pp. 14, 49.

[70] Chisholm, 'De-Industrialization', p. 309.

[71] Colin Robinson and Danny Hann, 'North Sea Oil and Gas', in Johnson, *Structure*, p. 45.

[72] *Monthly Digest of Statistics*; Department of Energy, *Development of Oil and Gas Resources of the United Kingdom* (1990); Leo Pliatzky, *The Treasury under Mrs Thatcher* (Oxford 1989), p. 151.

[73] Richard Bending and Richard Eden, *UK Energy, Structure, Prospects and Policies* (Cambridge, 1984); Rowthorn and Wells, *De-Industrialization*, pp. 120–3.

Table 10·12:   North Sea oil: output, trade and revenues, 1979–90

	Production m. tonnes	Consumption m. tonnes	Petroleum and products Exports less imports £bn.	Taxes and royalties from N. Sea oil and gas £bn.*
1979	77·9	84·6	−1·1	0·6
1980	80·5	71·2	+0·1	2·3
1981	89·5	66·3	+2·9	3·7
1982	103·2	67·2	+4·4	6·5
1983	115·0	64·5	+6·8	7·8
1984	126·1	81·4	+6·6	8·8
1985	127·6	69·8	+7·8	12·0
1986	127·1	69·2	+3·7	11·3
1987	123·3	67·7	+4·0	4·8
1988	114·4	71·6	+2·1	3·2
1989	91·8	73·0	—	3·2
1990	92·1+	74·9+	—	2·3

* fiscal year ending in the year shown
+ based on the first three quarters of the year

speed, exerted its influence on the behaviour of the economy as a whole. There has been a considerable debate on the nature of that influence. Many economists thought they could detect signs of the 'Dutch disease', the problems faced by the Netherlands after the opening up of that country's natural gas resources: a temporary boom which raised costs and prices, made industry less competitive at home and abroad and led to unemployment and shrinkage in the productive sectors. This effect would be reinforced in the British case if foreigners expected the pound sterling, as a petro-currency, to rise, and bought sterling bonds, sold by British citizens who then bought goods.[74] Agreement on these issues was not made easier by the fact that the upward push which the oil would give to the pound sterling occurred at the same time as the Government's severe deflationary policy, including high interest rates, which would also tend to drive up the exchange value of sterling, and it has not been easy to separate out these two influences.

One view was that the end effect would be to shift employment from the secondary to the service trades in Britain which were unaffected by world prices. Others stressed that rising prices at home would counteract the upward pressure on sterling. For some, the effects one way or the other had altogether been exaggerated, and in any case, the oil had at least the advantage that it greatly improved the balance of payments.[75]

Economic opinion thus tended to emphasize the negative aspects of the oil

[74] W. M. Corden, 'The Exchange Rate, Monetary Policy and North Sea Oil: The Economic Theory of a Squeeze on Tradeables', *Oxf. Econ. P.* 33, Special Issue (1981), pp. 36–7.

[75] Peter D. Spencer, 'The Effect of Oil Discoveries on the British Economy', *Econ. J.* 94/375 (1984), pp. 633–44; Charles Bean, 'The Impact of North Sea Oil', in Rudiger Dornbursch and Richard Layard, (eds.), *The Performance of the British Economy* (Oxford 1987), pp. 70–4; Alan Walters, *Britain's Economic Renaissance* (Oxford, 1986), pp. 162–3; Marian E. Bond and Adalbert Knöbl, 'Some Implications of North Sea Oil for the UK Economy', *IMF Staff Papers*, 29/3, (1982), pp. 363–97; P.J. Forsyth and J.A. Kay 'The Economic Implications of North Sea Oil Revenues', *Fiscal Studies* 113 (1980), pp. 1–28; *Bank of England Quarterly Bulletin* 20/4 (1980), pp. 443–54 and 22/1 (1982), pp. 56–73.

bonanza. Few stressed that a new, rich source of income had been opened up, that there would be a downward effect on inflation, that the threat of a balance of payments deficit, which in the past had led to repeated and destructive 'stops' was now removed, as was the need to deflate to cope with the concurrent world oil price rise. Even fewer urged that the additional income and the breathing space thus gained should be used in a major drive to modernize and re-equip British industry.[76] As a matter of historic fact, no attempt was made in the latter direction. On the contrary, the high sterling exchange rate was boosted further by a severe deflationary policy, industry was allowed to shrink dramatically, output was allowed to fall, and the increased Government revenues were used first, to reduce the annual deficits, and later to pay back part of the National Debt. Not even the nationalized industries received any direct benefit from that remarkable gift of nature in the 1980s.

In the regional distribution of industries, the tendencies of the 1970s were continued: the relative decline of the North West as against the relative gain of the South East, including East Anglia as a particularly favoured growth area. There was one major change: with the decline of the motor industry, the West Midlands had now joined the ranks of the relatively depressed areas, whereas

Table 10·13:   Regional changes in output and employment 1979–84

	Change in output	Change in employment		Confirmed redundancies per 1000 employees
	1979–83, %	1979–84, %	1982–4, %	1979–82
South East	−6·1	−17·5	−2·8	28·1
East Anglia	−3·0	−14·5	12·2	31·0
South West	−4·5	−16·7	2·8	42·1
West Midlands	−23·3	−28·5	2·0	47·5
East Midlands	−12·4	−19·7	4·5	42·8
Yorkshire and Humberside	−18·3	−28·0	−1·6	61·5
North West	−19·3	−29·0	−4·6	65·2
North	−15·7	−29·8	−1·5	64·3
Wales	−20·0	−33·0	−5·3	84·3
Scotland	−14·0	−27·7	−3·2	69·2
Great Britain	−13·3	−23·6		49·1

the East Midlands were distinctly among the growth regions. The shift was particularly dramatic in the years of the slump in the early 1980s (Table 10·13).[77] In the second slump of the Thatcher years, however, the South East was affected as much as the rest of the country.

[76] Terry Barker, 'De-Industrialisation, North Sea Oil and an Investment Strategy for the United Kingdom', in Terry Barker and Vladimir Brailovsky, *Oil or Industry* (1981), pp. 191–224; F. J. Atkinson, S. J. Brooke, S. G. F. Hall, 'The Economic Effects of North Sea Oil', *Nat. Inst. Econ. Rev.* 104 (1983) pp. 38–44; Nick Garden, *Decade of Discontent* (Oxford, 1987), p. 193; M. FG. Scott, 'The Unemployment Policy Discussion in the UK in the 1970's', in Angus Maddison and Bote Wilpstra (eds.), *Unemployment: The European Perspective* (1982), pp. 2–3, 28–30, House of Lords, S.C. on Overseas Trade, Report, 238-I (1985), p. 43–4.

[77] Ron Martin, 'Thatcherism and Britain's Industrial Landscape', in Martin and Rowthorn, *Geography*, pp. 262–3; John MacInnes, *Thatcherism at Work* (Milton Keynes, 1987), p. 73. Also see John Creedy and Richard Disney, *Social Insurance in Transition* (Oxford, 1985), p. 121.

Given its general attitude to State initiative, it was not surprising that the new Government was highly critical of many aspects of regional policy. As early as 1979, the areas classified as needing assistance were reduced from 44% to 27·5% of the country's surface, and many of the existing ones were downgraded to lower status, in order to cut down expenditure. In the first years expenditure rose nonetheless, but by 1987–8 it had been reduced to £159 million from £509 in 1979–80 at constant prices. The White Paper on Regional Industrial Development of 1983 proposed further severe cuts, though the Government relented to the extent of giving the West Midlands Intermediate Area status, even if not full Development Area designation, while it was now the inner cities which were attracting attention and funds.

Some of the criticisms of regional policies were well founded. The industries favoured were often capital-intensive, thus affording few jobs. The extension of existing firms would tend to help older industries; wholly new ones very rarely grew fast enough to employ much labour. Within the framework of the new Regional and Selective Assistance Scheme, which was discretionary rather than automatic, the guidelines were to exclude replacement capital, and to foster new enterprises that created relatively large numbers of jobs. 'Regional' as such ceased to be a major operating concept.[78]

Agriculture experienced a further sustained increase in output (2·7% a year between 1978–9 and 1987–8) as well as in labour productivity (4·2%), both well above the growth rate of the economy as a whole. Employment declined, mainly of hired workers while the number of part-time and seasonal workers, of farmers and managers, remained constant. Fixed capital formation declined also.[79] The average size of holdings increased further, and so did the average farmer's indebtedness. There was little change in the distribution of land use or in the animals held, except that the number of sheep increased considerably. Farming policies were by now dictated by the vagaries of the Common Market agricultural policy (CAP), which rewarded the milk producer and encouraged higher output in general. Thus the degree of self-sufficiency of soft wheat in Britain increased from 68% in 1976–80 to 102% in 1981–4, and of sugar, from 40% to 55% in the same period. For cereals as a whole, self-sufficiency rose from 88% in 1980 to 109% in 1984, for butter from 23% to 62%, and for 'other milk products' from 120% to 159%. Total cereal production rose by 41% between 1978–80 and 1986–8, and total agricultural output by 11%.[80]

Among the services, it was distribution in the wider sense, and financial services which saw the fastest increase in employment. Distribution, in spite of all its innovations, had a low rate of productivity increase, employed many young people and part-timers, had a low value added per head and showed, in comparison with Germany, poor training and poor productivity.[81] There was a

[78] James Shepherd, 'Industrial Support Policies', *Nat. Inst. Econ. Rev.* 122 (1988), pp. 59–71.

[79] Feinstein and Matthews, pp. 81, 85, 86; Brian Hill, 'Agriculture', in Johnson, *Structure*, p. 8.

[80] Rajan and Pearson, pp. 34–6; Francesco Giavazzi, 'The Impact of EEC Membership', in Dornbusch and Layard, *Performance*, pp. 102–3; Rowthorn and Wells, *De-Industrialization*, p. 106; *Annual Abstract of Statistics*.

[81] Feinstein and Matthews, p. 85; Stuart Eliot, 'Retailing', in Johnson, *Structure*, p. 235; A. D. Smith and D. M. W. Hitchens, *Productivity in the Distributive Trades* (Cambridge, 1985), pp. 5–6; S. J. Prais, Valerie Jarvis, Karin Wagner, 'Productivity and Vocational Skills in Services in Britain and Germany: Hotels', *Nat. Inst. Econ. Rev.* 130 (1989), pp. 52–74; Rajan and Pearson, pp. 83, 109.

remarkable extension of multiple chain retailing and of hyper-markets and shopping centres. In 1975–9, 157 schemes of shopping centres were launched with almost 27 million square feet of floor-space; in 1980–6 it was 176 schemes, with 22 million sq. ft. By 1987, multiples (excluding the co-ops) provided 78% of food sales, as against 57% in 1976, and the five largest chains alone, Tesco, Sainsbury, Gateway, Argyll and Asda, controlled 57% of food sales between them. In 1984, the largest 10 companies also had 41% of the alcoholic drink trade, 53% of footwear, 46% of men's and boys' clothing and 23·8% of retail sales overall.[82]

Government had begun by removing virtually all controls from the financial sector, but its freedom was somewhat reduced after a series of City scandals and by the decision of the Director General of Fair Trading in 1979 to investigate the Stock Exchange, and particularly its fixed commission charge. Afraid of being reorganized from the outside and conscious of losing much trade abroad, the Exchange decided to reform itself, and the 'Big Bang' of 1986 ended many ancient traditions in the City. It deregulated the trading system, made dealing in commission competitive, and abolished the division between brokers and jobbers, which had been largely subverted in practice in any case. The Big Bang forced the bankers to spend some £3 billion in modernizing their equipment and in buying up other firms, and the resulting low profitability was not helped by the (worldwide) stock exchange crash in October 1987, in which share prices tumbled. The Financial Services Act of 1986 created a watchdog in the shape of the Securities and Investment Board (SIB) assisted by 5 self-regulating organizations, which became four after one amalgamation. The Bank of England, for its part, having had to provide aid after the collapse of the Johnson Matthey Bank which had brought with it widespread losses to small investors, instituted the Board of Banking Supervisors in 1985 to act as its own watchdog.[83] Financial services remained a positive item in the balance of payments; but tourism and shipping, which had formerly also been positive, turned heavily negative in the 1980s.

The Government's attempts to encourage the setting up of new small firms had some success, particularly in the service trades. An enquiry covering the years 1980–5 found that 38% of those asked had positive reasons for setting up on their own, while 34% did so to avoid unemployment, or to join members of the family or friends. In many sectors, as in retailing, there continued a strong tendency for the largest firms to grow at the expense of the rest. Among industrial firms there were 339 mergers a year in 1975–9 and 338 a year in 1980–5, but while the first period averaged £695 million per annum, in the second this had risen to £2,639 million. The really spectacular mergers and acquisitions occurred in the financial field, among other services and among holding companies. Acquisitions averaged under £2 billion a year in the ten years to 1983; they then rose to £5·9 billion in 1984, £7·2 billion in 1985 and levelled out at around £15 billion in 1986 and 1987, all at constant 1986 prices.[84] At the same time compan-

[82] Stuart Eliot, pp. 240, 243; Carl Gardner and Julie Sheppard, *Consuming Passion. The Rise of the Retail Culture* (1989), pp. 97, 155, 163; Morgan, *Imports*, pp. 20, 24, 29.

[83] Margaret Reid, *All-Change in the City* (1988); eadem, 'Mrs Thatcher and the City', in Dennis Kavanagh and Anthony Seldon (eds.), *The Thatcher Effect* (Oxford 1989), pp. 49–63.

[84] Donald Hay and John Vickers, 'The Reform of Competition Policy', *Nat. Inst. Econ. Rev.* 125 (1988), p. 62; Rajan and Pearson, p. 132; P. B. Beaumont, *Change in Industrial Relations* (1990), p. 81.

ies, such as insurance companies, tended to increase at the expense of the individual shareholder. The multi-nationals received much bad publicity when it was found that their massive sackings in the United Kingdom in the slump of the early 1980s were matched by increases of employment in their branches abroad.[85]

The Government's attitude to monopolies and restrictive practices was less strict than one might have expected from those dedicated to the advantages of competitive markets. Possibly they were persuaded that free imports, as well as settlements of multinationals in this country mitigated the effects of local cartels: formally, policy increasingly tended to look for actual effects on markets rather than for nominal control of market shares. By the Competition Act of 1980 the Director of Fair Trading was given power to investigate cases of restrictive practice and refer them to the Monopolies Commission, and an active policy was in fact pursued, including the investigation of several nationalized industries. There was also a Merger Panel to consider the referral of mergers. In the event, however, few cases were held up by this mechanism, and Government ministers several times intervened to let a merger go through.[86] It was the EC which by the later 1980s curbed monopolies and exacted fines: thus in 1986 15 chemical companies, including ICI, were fined heavily for having fixed polypropylene prices. However, the EC could intervene only if there were effects on international trade.[87]

Without a doubt the most important change in industrial structure which occurred in the 1980s was the privatization of a large part of the publically owned sector. Whereas in 1979, state-owned enterprises represented 11·5% of GDP, by June 1987 their share had dropped to 5·5%[88] and the largest privatization schemes were yet to come.

Privatization had not played a major part in the early days of the Government. Only parts of enterprises were sold off at first, and the sums raised were moderate, receipts keeping well below £500 million a year in 1979–83. With the sale of 51% of British Telecom in November 1984, a new phase began and the programme was accelerated. By 1984–6, over £2 billion a year came in, £4·4 billion in 1986–7, £5·2 billion in 1987–8, and even larger sums thereafter.[89] Among the most important enterprises privatized were British Aerospace (1981 and 1985), Cable and Wireless (1981, 1983, 1985), Jaguar (1984), British Telecom (1984), British Gas (1986), British Airways (1987), Rolls Royce (1987), British Airports Authority (1987), British Steel (1988), Electricity Generating Board (1990) and the water authority (1989).

Gradually, privatization also came to occupy a more important place in the Government's ideological armoury. Probably the most prominent reason for

[85] MacInnes, *Thatcherism*, p. 80; Grazia Ietto-Gillies, 'Some Indicators of Multinational Domination of National Economies'. *International Review of Applied Economics* 3/1 (1989), pp. 25–45; Martin, 'Thatcherism', p. 264.

[86] M. A. Utton and A. D. Morgan, *Concentration and Foreign Trade* (Cambridge 1983), pp. 1–2; Hay and Vickers, p. 58; Thompson, *Conservatives*, pp. 17, 121 f.

[87] *Economist*, 6–12 April 1991, p. 11.

[88] John Vickers and George Yarrow, *Privatization; an Economic Analysis* (Cambridge, Mass. 1988), pp. 1, 140–1.

[89] Riddell, *Decade*, p. 92; John Kay and David Thompson, 'Policy for Industry', in Dornbusch and Layard, *Performance*, p. 191; Leo Pliatzky, *The Treasury under Mrs Thatcher* (Oxford, 1989), p. 105; Cento Veljanovski, *Selling the State: Privatization in Britain* (1987).

the policies put forward was an improvement in efficiency, on the grounds that private enterprise would normally be more efficient than public monopolies. This claim was backed by data showing considerable rises in productivity and profitability after the units were privatized.[90] However, both had begun to improve before privatization, and also went up in the rest of industry at the time, and the differences do not seem to be significant, so that the efficiency argument does not carry too much weight. Rather, the consensus seems to be that it is not the form of ownership, but the framework which may explain changes in efficiency,[91] and the nationalized undertakings were freed from many burdensome restraints once they became privately owned, while they still kept their monopoly powers. There was much criticism, also from the Right, about the decision to leave the units in large, monopolistic market control, obviated only very little by permitting Mercury to compete with Telecom, and by splitting electricity generating into two, as well as by the appointment of consumer watchdogs like OFGAS and OFTEL.[92] One major reason for not breaking up these large monopolies was the need to keep the goodwill of their managers and workers.

A second incentive for the privatization programme was the yield to the Exchequer. The sums received for the public undertakings were registered as income and used to reduce the PSBR, a policy to which the Government had committed itself. Technically, this was a bizarre procedure since, if the Government used the funds acquired by selling state-owned industries to pay off an equivalent amount of the national debt, the public merely exchanged one debt paper for another[93] and the State lost a source of income by getting rid of a source of expenditure; but it suited the Government to present its policy of reducing the PSBR as having been successful.

There was also a political gain in the process of privatization. For one thing, it acquainted millions of people who had never before done so, with the holding of shares. Moreover, since the shares were generally sold much under their value, millions of new shareholders sold them at once at a profit, and it could be assumed that, having done so, they would be less inclined to object to the large fortunes made in the financial world for similarly adding nothing to the national income, while they would also be less inclined to listen to the Labour Party's criticism of such profiteering. The Labour Party, indeed, soon ceased to threaten to re-nationalize the undertakings concerned, and the later schemes went through with remarkably little comment. The underpricing of the shares on issue did, however, cause much adverse comment. Thus, on the opening day of free trading, the Telecom shares sold at 85% over the issue price, British Airways at 68%, Rolls Royce at 73% and British Gas at 25%. The Government's advisers were seen to have made grotesque misjudgements, and in the sales to

[90] Kavanagh and Seldon, *Effect*, pp. 28, 43; Matthews and Minford, pp. 67–9; Grahame Thompson, *The Political Economy of the New Right* (1990), pp. 143–4.

[91] Vickers and Yarrow, pp. 142, 159; Riddell, pp.88, 93–5; Thompson, p. 156; Ben Fine, 'Scaling the Commanding Heights of Public Enterprise Economics', *Cambridge Journal of Economics* 14/2 (1990), p. 129; Matthew Bishop and John Kay, *Does Privatization Work?* (1988), pp. 12–15; Jonathan Aylen, 'Privatization of the British Steel Corporation', *Fiscal Studies* 10/2 (1989), pp. 3–4.

[92] Vickers and Yarrow, pp. 185–6; Patrick Minford, 'Mrs. Thatcher's Economic Reform Programme – Past, Present and Future' in R. Skidelsky (ed.), *Thatcherism* (1988), p. 100.

[93] Ibid., pp. 160–3, 177; Pliatzky, p. 109.

1987 alone, the Exchequer lost some £3 billion by their incompetence.

A fourth reason may have been the opportunities the sale provided for enormous profits by the City firms handling them. This would be in line with the interest which the Government in general had shown in the well-being of the City. Set at between 4·5% and 6·5% of the sales proceeds, the issuing expenses were approaching those of small private issues whereas they should have been much less in view of their size.[94]

By the end of 1990 the programme was not quite completed, though there was by then little left to sell off other than such loss-making enterprises as the railways and the coal mines. At most, there has been some talk of separating out the profitable parts of these for privatization. It is still too early to offer an opinion on the success or otherwise of the programme of privatization as a whole.

3 Trade Unions and the Welfare Services

The membership of trade unions, after growing for many years to a peak of 13,289,000 in 1979, declined drastically thereafter, falling to 10,238,000 in 1988. As a proportion of the working population, this meant a fall from 51·1% to 37·6%. Measured against those in work only, however, the decline would be less severe. At the same time, there was a decline in the number of independent unions, mainly by mergers, from 453 in 1979 to 330 in 1987. Among the most significant mergers were the creation of Manufacturing, Science, Finance Union, out of ASTMS and TASS, a white collar union, and the National Union of Civil and Public Servants out of the Civil Service Union and the Society of Civil and Public Servants, both in 1987.[95]

The decline in membership was only in part due to the hostile legislation of those years. It arose also out of the loss of their jobs by many former members, compensated only in part by the remarkable growth of white collar and particularly of civil service unionism. Trade union density had traditionally been high in the public services, where membership was often encouraged. At its inception in 1979, the Government had been saddled with the so-called Clegg award, providing for large increases in the public services to catch up with equivalent wages in the private sector. Thereafter, increases in wages in the public services were kept below those outside, causing much bitterness and strikes among groups not normally known to be militant, such as nurses and teachers, and politicizing them. In 1984, 88% of the working days lost in strikes were lost in the public service, which furnished only about 44% of trade unionists.[96]

It was noted above (p. 380) that despite the loss of members and the high level of unemployment in the 1980s, trade unions were not noticeably impaired in their ability to keep wages well ahead of the cost of living and thus channel part of the increased productivity gain of the country to their members. While there

[94] Vickers and Yarrow, p. 183; Riddell, p. 108; Kavanagh and Seldon, p. 53.

[95] P. B. Beaumont, *Change in Industrial Relations* (1990), pp. 50, 61 ff.; idem, *The Decline of Trade Union Organization* (Beckenham, 1987), pp. 2–3.

[96] Beaumont, *Change*, p. 212 and *Decline*, pp. 148–51, 165; William Brown, 'The Changing Role of Trade Unions in the Management of Labour', *British Journal of Industrial Relations* 24/2 (1986), p. 166.

were some employers who went all out to use their temporary superiority of bargaining power to weaken the unions, others were content to keep to their former routine, maintain the position of their shop stewards and even accept the closed shop where it had been traditional, though the closed shop itself was in retreat. The numbers of shop stewards in fact rose, especially in the public services and among white-collar unions as total membership fell.[97]

A major change in industrial relations was the increased tendency for wage bargains to be struck with individual works, or even teams of workers rather than with a whole industry. National wage agreements still served as guidelines and were thus of critical importance, but the agreements at local level did tend, to some extent, to shift loyalty to the firm rather than to the union, and this was particularly so when jobs were lost and redundancy payments were in question.[98] In some cases this was taken a step further in what many called a 'new realism': the negotiation of single union agreements, with a no-strike clause, for individual works. The Electrical, Electronics, Telecommunications and Plumbing Union (EETPU), which was in the lead in this field, was ultimately expelled from the TUC for, among other reasons[99], this policy. But other unions, in particular the Amalgamated Engineering Union, were not far behind.

The Government's offensive against the trade unions began with the Employment Act of 1980. This excluded secondary picketing, i.e. the picketing of works with which the worker was not himself in dispute, from protection, and generally restricted immunity for secondary action. It provided for compensation for those unreasonably excluded from a closed shop, and a new closed shop henceforth had to have the agreement of four-fifths of the workers covered. Government money was to be made available for union ballots. The Act also repealed the provision of the Act of 1975, under which a union could claim recognition and the application of recognized working terms if it made a case to ACAS which was accepted.

The Act of 1982 was considerably tougher. There was more compensation for unfair dismissal under the closed shop; unions could be made liable for damages for unlawful actions during a dispute; and lawful actions were restricted to pay, conditions of work, and jobs, in the firms under dispute. The next Act, passed two years later, provided for the re-election of all members of a union's executive committee by secret ballot every five years; the legal immunities during a dispute were to apply only if the strike had been supported by a secret ballot

[97] David Coates, *The Crisis of Labour. Industrial Relations and the State in Contemporary Britain* (Oxford, 1989), p. 141; John Kelly, 'Trade Unions Through the Recession 1980–1984', *British Journal of Industrial Relations* 25/2 (1987), pp. 275–82; Michael Terry, 'How Do We Know if Shop Stewards are Getting Weaker', *ibid.* 24/2 (1986), pp. 169–79; Eric Batstone and Stephen Gourlay, *Unions, Unemployment and Innovation* (Oxford, 1986), pp. 1–2, 61–4; Beaumont, *Change*, p. 56; Michael Fogarty and Douglas Brooks, *Trade Unions and British Industrial Development* (1989), p. xxiv.

[98] William Brown, 'Pay Determination: British Workplace Industrial Relations 1980–84', *British Journal of Industrial Relations* 25/2 (1987), p. 292; *idem*, 'Changing Role', p. 163; Beaumont, *Change* pp. 117–8; John MacInnes, *Thatcherism at Work* (Milton Keynes, 1987), p. 3; Frank H Longstreth, 'From Corporatism to Dualism? Thatcherism and the Climacteric of British Trade Unions in the 1980's', *Political Studies* 36 (1988), pp. 413–432; Keith Sisson and William Brown, 'Industrial Relations in the Private Sector', in G. S. Bain (ed.), *Industrial Relations in Britain* (Oxford 1983), p. 141.

[99] MacInnes, loc. cit.; Beaumont, *Change*, p. 48; Peter Riddell, *The Thatcher Decade* (Oxford, 1989), p. 54.

beforehand; there was a tightening up of records and of complaints procedures, and there was to be a ballot every ten years before funds could be applied for political purposes. Finally, the Act of 1988 gave individual union members power to take court action to stop their union calling a strike without a ballot; it also prevented the union from disciplining a member for failure to join a strike; it made non-membership of a union automatically a ground for unfair dismissal; and extended the obligation to be re-elected to the General Secretary, the President and all non-voting members of the Executive. It also strengthened internal accountability and election procedure, and established a Commissioner for the Rights of Trade Union Members.[100] These last were clearly a reaction to the coal strike of 1984–5.

Other measures to weaken trade unions and wage earners included the repeal in 1983 of the Fair Wages Resolution of 1891, a Victorian measure which had limited Government contracts to firms paying recognized wages and conditions; the clause in the Social Security Act of 1980 which reduced by £12–16 the weekly payments to the families of strikers; and the Wages Act of 1986 which limited the power of Wages Councils to set a minimum hourly and overtime rate, for adults over the age of 21.[101]

Most spectacular was the prohibition of trade union membership in the Government's Communications Headquarters (GCHQ) in Cheltenham in 1984: this was taken to the European court, which upheld the Government's decision.

The effects of this mass of legislation are in dispute. The objectives included, on the one hand, the weakening of the unions vis-à-vis their employers, and on the other, the reduction in power of the union leadership over their members, who were believed by the Government to be less militant than their leaders. Supporters of the Government thought the legislation to have been effective.[102] Others have found the evidence less convincing. It was clear that the legislation itself had proceeded very cautiously, that many employers, who would have to enforce much of it by taking their workers to court, were unhappy with it, and that in many cases the discrimination against them and the enforced ballots strengthened the resolve and the unity of the workers concerned. The attempt to prevent trade-union funds going to the Labour Party turned out to be a humiliating failure.[103] Compared with the legal position in most other countries, British unions were still in a relatively privileged position.

Even under the new legislation the trade unions were by no means inhibited from striking. On the contrary, comparing the years 1980–8 with the 1970s, the number of strikes was halved, but the number of workers involved was much the same, though the working days lost per thousand had fallen from 569 to

[100] Riddell, *Decade*, pp. 47–8.

[101] Beaumont, *Decline*, p. 161; Coates, *Crisis*, p. 124; B.C. Roberts, 'Trade Unions' in Dennis Kavanagh and Anthony Seldon (eds.), *The Thatcher Effect* (Oxford, 1989), p. 69; David Deaton, 'The Labour Market and Industrial Relations Policy of the Thatcher Government' in David S. Bell (ed.), *The Conservative Government 1979–84* (1985), pp. 33–48; Steve Winyard, 'Low Pay', *ibid.*, pp. 58–9.

[102] Kent Matthews and Patrick Minford, 'Mrs Thatcher's Economic Policies 1979–1987' *Economic Policy* 5 (1987), pp. 65–7.

[103] William Brown and Sushil Wadhwani, 'The Economic Effects of Industrial Relations Legislation since 1979', *Nat. Inst. Econ. Rev.* 131 (1990), pp. 57–70; Mairi Steele, Kenneth Miller, John Gennard, 'The Trade Union Act: Political Fund Ballots', *British Journal of Industrial Relations* 24/3 (1986), pp. 443–67.

371.[104] These figures were necessarily affected by the 'winter of discontent' of 1978–9, on the one hand, and the great coal strike of 1984–5, on the other. Until the latter date, workers frequently had at least partial success as a result of coming out on strike, as in the steel strike of 1980, the docks dispute of 1980, the dispute of the civil service workers in 1981 and of the health workers in 1982. In 1981, the mere threat of a strike by the miners resulted in larger subsidies for mines working at a loss.[105]

The single most important dispute was the miners' strike of 1984–5. It had so many unusual features that it may be misleading to fit it into the statistics of more 'normal' strikes. For one thing, it had strong political overtones. The Government was committed to defeat the strike, and had made numerous preparations, including the setting up of the 'National Reporting Centre' to co-ordinate police forces from other areas to help those in the coal districts. It had also backed the accumulation of large coal stocks, especially at the power stations. The miners' leadership, for its part, was consciously seeking to under-mine an elected democratic 'capitalistic' Government by action in the streets. Both were looking to the disputes of 1972 and 1974, when the Yorkshire 'flying pickets' had scored successes against a helpless police force, and Yorkshire's leader then, Arthur Scargill, was now President of the National Union of Mineworkers.

At another level, the Government was seeking to weaken the trade unions' power by confronting the strongest of them; Arthur Scargill, on the other hand, appeared to want a strike at all costs, no matter what the cause. He had tried unsuccessfully to bring out his men, for a variety of reasons, three times before 1984–5 as well as several times since then. The strike itself was forced upon an unwilling minority, and possibly even a majority of miners, and it was launched by a manipulation of the union's rules which the courts repeatedly declared to be incompatible with the rulebook. Finally, the coal industry was once again picked as the arena in which the Government's downward pressure on the wage level was to make its breakthrough, as in 1926.

Though there were many trouble spots in the industry, the immediate cause was the closure of pits: logical and necessary from the point of view of the Coal Board and the Government, destructive of whole communities from the point of view of the NUM. The form of the proposed closure of the Cortonwood Colliery in Yorkshire, which sparked off the strike, was clearly in breach of the agreed procedure, but the fault was procedural: closures of that kind would normally be accepted, with the usual redundancy payments for the older miners and transfer to other pits for the rest. In this case, both sides appeared to be spoiling for a fight and only too eager to grasp the opportunity offered, though there were also many peaceful voices on both sides. Mr Scargill's demand that no pit should ever be closed on economic grounds alone, but only when the coal had given out completely was clearly absurd if taken literally; but the miners' exasperation at the job losses, particularly when there were few older men left to be paid off in redundancies, was real enough, and the miners had a good case

[104] Paul Edwards, 'Industrial Action 1980–1984', *British Journal of Industrial Relations* 25/2 (1987), p. 287; Beaumont, *Change*, p. 149.

[105] MacInnes, *Thatcherism*, p. 93; Jock Bruce-Gardyne, *Mrs Thatcher's First Administration* (1984), pp. 127–9.

against the NCB's system of accounting and neglect of costs.

The irregular way in which the strike was called, the refusal of the leadership to permit a ballot on the grounds that they might lose it, and the violence exerted by Yorkshire flying pickets, especially in neighbouring Nottingham, caused much opposition even in mining communities, and the strike was at no point complete. Much of Nottingham continued at work, as did smaller pockets elsewhere. Perhaps more importantly, other unions which were in any case not too eager to make sacrifices to defend the miners' jobs when those of their own members were being lost in large numbers, could use this breach of rules as a pretext for being very sparing with concrete support, though unstinting in their rhetorical enthusiasm at TUC and Labour Party Congresses and elsewhere. The TUC had, in addition, been rebuffed in the early weeks of the strike by the NUM which was not inclined to share its control with any outside body.

There can be doubt of the loyalty, the devotion, the suffering and the courage of the miners on strike and of their families,[106] and they enjoyed widespread sympathy among the public, even among those who considered the strike to be wrong. Against this, the leadership, and in particular Arthur Scargill himself, an overpowering personality without whom the strike may well never have taken place, had a good deal less public support, in spite of much favourable TV exposure. Nor did the scenes of violence, especially the pitched battles outside Orgreave coke plant, organized by the Yorkshire men in order to stop the fuel supply, and thus close down the important Scunthorpe steelworks, gain the miners much sympathy. Among other unusual features of the strike was the legal impounding of the NUM funds which were thereupon spirited away abroad outside the reach of British courts. The intransigence of the NUM leadership was matched by that of the tough stance of the recently appointed chairman of the NCB, Ian MacGregor. A more flexible approach by either of them might have brought an earlier end to the strike on more than one occasion.

The miners began to drift back to work early in 1985, and the strike was effectively over by the end of February after eleven months. In logical parallel with its unorthodox beginnings, the strike ended without any sort of formal agreement: work just returned more or less to normal. The cost to the miners on strike was the loss of almost a year's wages, or 26·1 million working days. The Coal Board estimated its loss at £1·7 billion (£3·3 billion lost output less £1·6 billion in cost savings). The cost to the economy has been estimated at £2– £3 billion;[107] that it was no higher was due to the fact that the rest of the country continued to work normally. The Nottinghamshire miners and those of South Derbyshire and County Durham seceded from NUM in October 1985 to form their own union, the Union of Democratic Mineworkers (UDM). The terms negotiated by the UDM for its members were applied henceforth to NUM members also, although the latter's leaders refused to negotiate at the side of the UDM.

The violence engineered on the streets in the miners' strike was not the only example of such tactics. Similar scenes were enacted in a printing dispute in

---

[106] Raphael Samuel et al. (eds.), *The Enemy Within: Pit Villages and the Miners' Strike of 1984– 5* (1986).

[107] Barry Thomas, 'Coal', in Peter Johnson, (ed.), *The Structure of British Industry* (1988), p. 64. Among many accounts of the strike, see Peter Wilsher et al., *Strike: Thatcher, Scargill and the Miners* (1985); Geoffrey Goodman, *The Miners' Strike* (1985).

Warrington in 1983, and worse violence, involving something akin to set battles, was perpetrated by the print workers of Rupert Murdoch's London newspapers belonging to the NGA and SOGAT 82 unions in defence of their out-of-date technology and their overmanning practices: they were defeated only by the removal of the printing to a building structured like a fortress and defended by large police forces for almost a year. Black sheep may be found everywhere: the noteworthy aspect of these developments was that neither the trade union movement, nor its many sympathisers, officially condemned such plainly illegal actions of terrorism against individuals[108] (most of whom were not even concerned in the dispute) which they would certainly have condemned, had any other social group acted in a similar manner. The assumption that trade unionists are above the law and may commit almost any outrage in furtherance of a trade dispute has largely contributed to the ease with which the legislation of the 1980s, hostile to the trade unions, has been accepted.

The Government's programme of trade-union reform was accompanied also by plans to undertake fundamental revision of the social services, though to reduce expenditure on them turned out to be rather more difficult than the Government had hoped. At constant prices, expenditure on the health service increased by about a third between 1978–9 and 1989–90; expenditure on social security, affected by the higher unemployment level, increased rather more; and educational expenditure was also up a little. Only housing was almost cut out of existence, to a mere fifth of its earlier level. Yet even in 1980, social expenditure in Britain was much below that of the OECD (Europe), at 22·1% of GDP against 28·3%. Transfer payments, however, were near the average.[109]

Health expenditure was bound to rise, simply because of the ageing of the population and the development of new, more costly treatment and equipment. If total expenditure rose by less than was necessary to keep pace with these two factors, it was quite possible for hospital closures and lengthening waiting lists to go hand in hand with an absolute rise in expenditure. Actual expenditure increased by 2·8% in real terms between 1979 and 1987, or by 1·2% more than GNP, but was clearly inadequate to maintain existing standards. Britain also made a poor showing in comparison with other countries. According to the OECD, the United Kingdom spent 6·2% of her GNP on health services in 1983, against the USA 10·8%, Germany 8·2%, France 9·3% and even Spain 6·3%. In terms of expenditure per head, the United Kingdom was the sixth lowest out of 23 OECD countries, only Spain, Greece, Ireland, Portugal and New Zealand spending less. At the same time, considerable efforts were made to boost private health provision.[110]

As far as the network of social security benefits was concerned, the new Government tried from the beginning to economize by reducing benefits. The Social Security Act of 1980 laid down that in future benefits would go up with

[108] Samuel Brittan, *A Restatement of Economic Liberalism* (1988), pp. 236–9.

[109] OECD, *Social Expenditure 1960–1990* (Paris, 1985), p. 21; Riddell, *Decade*, p. 128; M. S. Levitt and M. A. S. Joyce, *The Growth and Efficiency of Public Spending* (Cambridge 1987), p. 25; Alan Sked, *Britain's Decline. Problems and Perspectives* (Oxford, 1987), p. 74.

[110] OECD, *Measuring Health Care 1960–1983* (Paris, 1985), p. 11; Riddell, *Decade*, p. 140; Anthony Atkinson, John Hills, Julian LeGrand, 'The Welfare State,' in R. Dornbusch and R. Layard, *The Performance of the British Economy* (Oxford, 1987), p. 218; Charles Webster, 'The Health Service', in Kavanagh and Seldon, *Effect*, pp. 166–82.

prices, not wages; thus the beneficiaries were no longer to share in the rise in national incomes. Various means-tested benefits were to be cut or abolished altogether, and child benefit payments were no longer to be automatically uprated.

In 1982 it was decided to phase out the earnings-related supplement to sickness and unemployment pay. By the Social Security and Housing Benefit Act of that year, sickness benefit was replaced by 'statutory sick pay', to be paid by the employer who would later be reimbursed. The object was to make sure that total benefits, including those paid by occupational schemes within the firm, did not exceed normal pay.

A further review in 1985 led to the reduction in value of the State Earnings-Related Pension Scheme (SERPS) only 7 years after its inauguration. A major review of the social services, *Reform of Social Security*[111] was issued as a Green Paper by Mr Fowler in that year and became the basis of the important Social Security Act of 1986: its changes mostly became operative in 1988.[112] Its main objective was clearly to save money. Supplementary Benefits were re-named 'Income Support' and were greatly simplified. Family Income Supplement was likewise replaced by Family Credit. None of this, however, entirely removed the so-called 'poverty trap', describing a situation where family income over a significant range was affected by taxes and benefits in such a way that increased earnings led to no increases in real incomes. Dilnot and Stark found that of 575,000 'tax units' in that category, 115,000, mostly single-parent families, were actually worse off by earning an extra £1. The others lost over 60% of their additional earnings.[113]

The unemployed derived their income mainly from two sources: unemployment insurance for an initial period of up to one year, and benefit thereafter, supplemented in both cases, if necessary, by supplementary benefits or income support. For the period 1979–88, no fewer than 38 significant changes in these benefits have been recorded.

As far as the supplementary benefits/income support changes were concerned, two out of the 17 changes were favourable to the claimant, three were mixed, and 12 were unfavourable. Similar proportions were found also in the other changes.[114] Under the Act of 1986, various fringe benefits were abolished or transferred to a new Social Fund, which was limited to a global sum, and grants from which were discretionary.[115]

Housing subsidies were the only item which it proved possible to cut substantially. However, not all housing expenditure appeared as part of the social

[111] Cmnd. 9517 (1985). Also see Ruth Lister, 'The Politics of Social Security: An Assessment of the Fowler Review' in Andrew Dilnot and Ian Walker (eds.), *The Economics of Social Security* (Oxford, 1989); Michael Beenstock and Valerie Brasse, *Insurance for Unemployment* (1986); John Creedy and Richard Disney, *Social Insurance in Transition. An Economic Analysis* (Oxford, 1985).

[112] John Creedy and Richard Disney, 'The New Pension Scheme in Britain', in Dilnot and Walker, pp. 224–38; Andrew Dilnot and Stephen Webb, 'The 1988 Social Security Reform', in *ibid.*, pp. 239–67; Michael Hill, *Social Security Policy in Britain* (Aldershot, 1990).

[113] Andrew Dilnot and Graham Stark, 'The Poverty Trap, Tax Cuts and the Reform of Social Security', in Dilnot and Walker, pp. 169–78; Michael Beenstock and Associates, *Work, Welfare and Taxation* (1987); Creedy and Disney, *Transition*, pp. 190 f.

[114] Tony Atkinson and John Micklewright, 'Turning the Screw: Benefits for the Unemployed 1979–88' in Dilnot and Walker, pp. 27, 40–1.

[115] Tony Novak, *Poverty and the State* (Milton Keynes, 1988), p. 192.

services vote. Thus for 1987–8 it was estimated that about £4 billion was spent via the social security network, including rent rebates, allowances and some income support for paying mortgage interest; £1·3 billion was spent on 'brick and mortar' subsidies through the local authorities and the housing associations; but at the same time a further £4·8 billion was accounted for by tax relief for mortgage payments of owner-occupiers.[116] Meanwhile the rent restrictions on private lettings were greatly loosened.

Table 10·14:   Social security expenditure estimates, 1989–90

	Amounts £ bn.	Recipients, 000
Retirement pensions	19·4	9735
Invalidity benefit	3·4	1040
Unemployment benefit	1·1	755
Widows' benefit	0·9	395
All other insurance benefits	0·7	
Total insurance	25·6	
Income support	7·7	4925
Family credit	0·4	470
Housing benefit	3·8	4465
Social fund	0·2	
Total means-tested	12·1	
Child benefit	4·5	12015
Attendance, invalidity care allowances	1·2	770
Mobility allowances	0·7	540
Other contingent benefits	1·1	
Total contingent benefits	7·5	
Administration and misc.	2·4	
Total	47.6	

Altogether, by the end of the period, the Government envisaged spending over half its social security disbursements on insurance benefits, about one quarter on means-tested benefits, and 16% on contingent benefits, the rest going on administration and miscellaneous spending (Table 10·14).[117]

Unemployment rose from the 1·3 million (5·6%) inherited in 1979 to over 3·1 million (13·2%) at its peak in the third quarter of 1983, only to decline to 6·8% in 1990, and rise again thereafter as a consequence of the severe deflationary measures then taken (Table 10·15). The statistical basis of these official figures has, however, been widely questioned, since it was subjected to numerous changes in those years, most of which would tend to understate the real rate. In particular, the restriction of the category of the 'unemployed' to those receiving relief only, at a time when conditions for such relief were severely tightened, was said to have 'doctored' the official figures by a substantial amount. Some critics maintained that the real figures were 500,000–6,000,000, and up to one million higher than the official ones in the recession of the mid-80s.[118]

[116] Richard Berthoud, 'Social Security and the Economics of Housing', in Dilnot and Walker, p. 88. Also Maurice Mullard, *The Politics of Public Expenditure* (1987), p. 173; Alan Murie, 'Housing and the Environment', in Kavanagh and Seldon, *Effect*, pp. 213–25.

[117] Hill, *Policy*, p. 79, based on Cmnd. 615 of 1989.

[118] Riddell, *Decade*, p. 28; MacInnes, *Thatcherism*, pp. 63, 71–2; Andrew Gamble, *The Free Economy and the Strong State* (1988), p. 117; *Economist*, 14 Feb 1987, pp. 46–50.

Table 10·15: Unemployment in the United Kingdom, 1979–1991[119]

	Per cent (OECD) standardized)	Numbers (000)
1979	5·4	1089
1980	6·8	1186
1981	10·6	2068
1982	12·3	2477
1983	13·1	2767
1984	11·7	2879
1985	11·2	3037
1986	11·1	3115
1987	10·3	2954
1988	8·5	2403
1989	6·9	1856
1990	6·2	1626
1991 (March)	6·7	2093

It was noticeable that in this spectacular rise from one to three million, the rate of inflow of the newly out-of-work did not change: instead the stock of the unemployed went up because the average duration out of work was longer. Unemployment affected men more than women, and, in the early eighties at least, found far more victims in the older industrial areas of the North and West than in the South East. Thus in 1984 the rate stood at 13% in the North, 12·6% in Scotland and 13·8% in the North West, compared with 7·8% in the South East and 7·9% in East Anglia.[120] The job losses at the end of the decade, by contrast, were more evenly distributed over the regions.

Unemployment at those levels had become a major political issue, and the debate as to how far the trade unions and the high benefit rates, respectively, were responsible was conducted in the 1980s with even greater vigour than in the 1970s. While the monetarist doctrine held that Government could not affect unemployment, only the inflation rate, there were those who thought they could measure the effects of benefits and of trade union power and membership on the unemployment rate down to a percentage point.[121] Others were less convinced by the notion that the receipt of benefit stopped men from looking for work. It was pointed out that many older persons and those unemployed for a longer period would take any job, while econometric studies appeared to show that most of the rise in the 1980s was due to the lack of demand rather than to changes in the labour supply, and indeed the 'replacement ratio' of benefits to earned income had not changed since the 1970s yet unemployment had trebled.[122]

[119] OECD; *Annual Abstract of Statistics.*

[120] Jonathan Bradshaw and Meg Huby, 'Trends in Dependence on Supplementary Benefit', in Dilnot and Walker, *Economics*, p. 77; Ron Martin and Bob Rowthorn, *The Geography of De-Industrialisation* (1986), p. 240; Stephen Nickell, Wiji Narendrathan, Jon Stern, *The Nature of Unemployment in Britain* (Oxford 1989), p. 1; Laurie Hunter, 'Unemployment and Industrial Relations', *British Journal of Industrial Relations* 26/2 (1988), pp. 203–28.

[121] Patrick Minford, *Unemployment: Cause and Cure* (Oxford, 1985); Peter Holmes, 'The Thatcher Government's Overall Economic Performance', in David S. Bell (ed.), *The Conservative Government 1979–84* (1985), p. 17; Nick Gardner, *Decade of Discontent* (Oxford 1987), pp. 163–4.

[122] H. G. Layard and S. J. Nickell, 'Unemployment in Britain', *Economica* 53/210, (Supplement 1986), pp. S. 121–69; *idem*, 'The Causes of British Unemployment', *Nat. Inst. Econ. Rev.* 111 (1985), pp. 62–85; Nickell, *Nature*, pp. 13, 71; Willem H. Buiter and Marcus H. Miller, 'Changing the

It did seem, however, that the participation rate of wives in the paid labour force increased when the husband became unemployed.[123]

Against the persistent, if only partly successful, efforts to reduce spending on the social services, spending on defence and on law and order was increased as a matter of policy: thus the defence budget rose from 4·75% of GDP in 1979 to 5·25% in 1983 (raised much more during the Falkland War), and Law and Order from 1·53% to 1·85% in the same years. In the later 1980s, as the Cold War receded, defence was reduced in real terms, but law and order expenditure continued to rise, as did the crime rate.[124] At the same time the powers of the police were increased by such legislation as the Criminal Justice Act of 1982, the Police and Criminal Evidence Act of 1984 and the Public Order Act of 1986.

Education was among the expenditures on which the Government economized. The level of educational provision was a good deal lower than in other comparable countries; thus the UK was 16th out of 23 OECD countries in terms of 15–19 year olds enrolled in any form of education, and 49% of boys and 44% of girls left British schools without a single O Level or GCSE Grade 1 in 1981. Nevertheless, the share of education in the GDP was brought down from 5·5% to 4·8% in the Thatcher years. This was achieved in part by starving the schools of books and equipment, in part by neglecting maintenance, and in part by keeping teachers' salaries below other income increases which led to a series of costly disputes in 1984–7 and the abolition of the teachers' negotiating rights.[125] Spending cut-backs were particularly severe in the University area, where a cut of 10% in real terms was enforced, at a time when 65,000 more students were admitted. Yet the proportion of young people in higher education was already the lowest among all comparable large countries: the total number of students per 100,000 in 1987 was 1913 in the UK compared with 2779 in Germany, 2655 in France and 5438 in the United States.[126] Other Colleges of Higher Education were gradually eased out of local authority control. In 1989 University funding was transferred to a new Universities Funding Council, and funds were distributed as contracts rather than as grants, though it did not seem to make much difference, at any rate in the first year. For other institutions of tertiary education a College Funding Council was made the channel of the distribution of funds. The universities did indeed succeed in making up some of the shortfall by raising money themselves, from 37% of the

---

Rules: Economic Consequences of the Thatcher Regime', *Brookings Papers in Economic Activity*, 1983, No. 2, pp. 305–65; S. G. B. Henry, J. M. Payne, C. Trinder, 'Unemployment and Real Wages: The Role of Unemployment, Social Security Benefits and Unionisation', *Oxf. Econ. P.* 37/2 (1985), pp. 330–8; Geoffrey Maynard, *The Economy under Mrs. Thatcher* (Oxford 1989), pp. 124–5.

[123] J. Garcia, 'Incentive and Welfare Effects of Reforming the British Benefit System', in Nickell and others, *Nature*, p. 172.

[124] John Alderson, 'Law and Order', in Bell, *Government*, pp. 125–41; Mullard, *Politics*, pp. 171–2; M. S. Levitt and M. A. S. Joyce, *The Growth and Efficiency of Public Spending* (Cambridge, 1987), pp. 17, 25; Michael O'Higgins, 'Inequality, Redistribution and Recession: the British Experience, 1976–1982' *Journal of Social Policy* 14/3 (1985), p. 282.

[125] Charles Handy, *The Future of Work* (Oxford, 1984), pp. 133, 143; J. R. G. Tomlinson, 'The Schools', in Kavanagh and Seldon, *Effect*, p. 185.

[126] Riddell, *Decade*, pp. 142 f.; Peter Scott, 'Higher Education', in Kavanagh and Seldon, pp. 198–9; Peter Jenkins, *Mrs Thatcher's Revolution* (1987), p. 271; Unesco, *Statistical Yearbook* 1990.

total in 1979 to 45% in 1987–8, but at the cost of diverting highly trained personnel to the activity of money raising, of demoralizing the academic staff and of accelerating the brain drain abroad of some of the best academics. In the expenditure on Research and Development, Britain continued to trail behind other advanced countries, and the gap was widening.[127] Also, while 49·2% of it was spent on defence here, that proportion was only 8·0% in Japan, 13·2% in Germany and 36·5% in France. Only the USA, at 64·3%, exceeded the British proportion.

Apart from the sheer saving of money, these changes also had an ideological basis in the belief that schools and colleges would work better when exposed to the 'market place'. Thus parental power was increased, as was that of the headmasters of schools who were expected to budget like managers in private firms, and the powers of the local authorities (many of which were Labour-controlled) were reduced. Some schools were encouraged to take themselves out of local authority control altogether, and various attempts were made to increase 'competition' for pupils between them. At the same time the Public Schools were to be helped by providing assisted places in order to channel some of the most promising pupils from the State sector into them.[128]

As far as vocational training was concerned, the comparative position was, if anything, still bleaker, and some earlier starts of Government aid to industrial training schemes were cut back in this period, 20 of the 27 Industrial Training Boards having been abolished by 1985. Employer dominated Training and Enterprise Councils (TECs) were planned to take their place later. The National Institute of Economic Research undertook a number of enquiries into the training for foremen and skilled workers in Britain, in comparison with other countries, with uniformly dismal results. Among the more important of these studies were those comparing English and Japanese schools, office workers in France and Britain, mechanical and electrical craftsmen in France and Britain, engineering in Britain and other advanced countries, clothing manufacture in Britain and Germany and foremen in Britain and Germany.[129]

In 1982 the Manpower Services Commission initiated a Youth Training Scheme, in part to reduce the widespread unemployment among the young. Planned at first to last one year, it was later extended to a two-year training period, though the training given compared poorly even then with the training provided for a similar group of young people in Germany. By 1986, about one million people had been covered. It was available as of right to all young people

[127] Levitt and Joyce, *Efficiency*, p. 83; Unesco, *Statistical Yearbook* 1990.

[128] Peter Gosden, 'Education Policy 1979–84', in Bell, *Conservative Government* pp. 105–22; Riddell, *Decade*, p. 142.

[129] All published in the *Nat. Inst. Econ. Rev.*: S. J. Prais: 'Educating for Productivity: Japanese and English Schooling and Vocational Preparation', 119 (1987); Hilary Steedman, 'Vocational Training in France and Britain: Office Work', 120 (1987); *eadem*, 'Vocational Training in France and Britain: Mechanical and Electrical Craftsmen', 126 (1988); S. J. Prais, 'Qualified Manpower in Engineering: Britain and Other Industrially Advanced Countries', 127 (1989); Hilary Steedman and Karin Wagner, 'Productivity, Machinery and Skills: Clothing Manufacture in Great Britain and Germany' 128 (1989); S. J. Prais and Karin Wagner, 'Productivity and Management: the Training of Foreman in Britain and Germany', 123 (1988); *idem*, 'Some Practical Aspects of Human Capital Investment: Training Standards in Five Occupations in Britain and Germany', 105 (1883). Also William Brown, 'The Changing Role of Trade Unions', p. 162; HMSO, *Aspects of Vocational Education and Training in the Federal Republic of Germany* (1991).

over 16. However, it was criticized as paying low wages, and was unprotected by health or safety regulation or trade union agreement. Lord Young also started a Technical and Vocational Initiative (TVEI) to influence classroom teaching in the direction of providing a vocational slant. By 1986, 65,000 children in 600 schools were covered by this scheme.[130]

There was also an Employment (or Job) Training Scheme for those over 18 to take up to 100,000 at a time, and a Young Workers' Scheme in 1981-6, in which employers were paid up to £15 per week per young worker on condition they employed them at low wages. Altogether in 1986-7, 801,000 individuals were covered by seven training schemes compared with just over 300,000 in 1979-80, while in 1989-90 the expenditure on employment, training and related measures had risen to £4 billion. Critics maintained that the object was to remove young people from the streets and from the unemployment register, rather than provide a valuable, thought-out vocational training for them.[131]

Personal disposable income rose in this period from £222 billion in 1979 at constant 1985 prices to about £300 billion in 1990, or by 35% in eleven years. Consumers' expenditure on durable goods rose by 69% in those years, and expenditure on non-durable goods by 40%. The volume of retain sales went up from an index of 86 to 123 (1985 = 100) in the same years, or by 43%.[132]

There was a clear trend in this period towards a less equal distribution of incomes, in part because of the rise in profits,[133] but largely because of the measures taken by the Government, including the cuts in income tax, especially at the higher rates, and the savings in the social services. As for the first, the gross earnings of the top 10% of earners rose by 22% in real terms between 1979 and 1986, those of the bottom 10% by only 4%. After tax, the top 10% improved their position between 1979 and 1987 by 28%, the bottom 10% by only 5%, while in the 1970s their increase had been equal, at 8% each. To take a different measure, between 1978/9 and 1988/9 a single person earning five times the national average benefited from a tax reduction from 52·2% to 36·1% of gross income, and an equally well-off married couple with two children benefited by a reduction from 46·7% to 33·8%. By contrast, the share in income paid in taxes by tax payers earning only half the national average, actually rose. The Gini coefficient in inequality (the higher, the more unequal), showed a rise from 35 to 40 for gross income between 1979 and 1987, and a rise from 32 to 36 for final income, including taxes and benefits.[134] As the rich reaped the benefits

[130] Jenkins, *Revolution*, pp. 270–1; Novak, *Poverty*, p. 194; Steedman and Wagner, loc. cit.

[131] Beaumont, *Change*, p. 23; Coates, *Crisis*, pp. 147–8; Hill, *Policy*, pp. 136–7; Winyard, 'Low Pay', p. 60; OECD *Economic Surveys: United Kingdom 1989–1990* (Paris 1990), p. 45.

[132] *Nat. Inst. Econ. Rev.*.

[133] Andrew Henley, 'Aggregate Profitability and Income Distribution in the UK Corporate Sector 1963–1985', *International Review of Applied Economics* 3/2 (1989), pp. 183–4; Beaumont, *Change*, p. 176; Riddell, *Decade*, p. 152; Samuel Brittan, 'The Thatcher Government's Economic Policy', In Kavanagh and Seldon, *Effect*, p. 34; idem, *Liberalism*, p. 268.

[134] *Economic Trends*, No. 439 (1990), p. 118; Riddell, *Decade*, p. 153; O'Higgins, 'Inequality', p. 287; Leo Pliatzky, *The Treasury under Mrs Thatcher* (Oxford, 1989), p. 147; Nick Morris and Ian Preston, 'Inequality, Poverty and the Distribution of Income', *Bulletin of Economic Research* 38/4 (1986), p. 307; Paul Johnson and Graham Stark, 'Ten Years of Mrs Thatcher: the Distributional Consequences; *Fiscal Studies* 10/2 (1989), p. 33. According to a Bristol University Study, over 1979–89, the top 20% of incomes were up by almost 40%, or £7,986, while the bottom 20% were *down* by almost 5–6%, or –£160. Report in the *Independent*, 24 June 1991.

of lower income tax to 1·9 million families in 1987, the proportion of the population living below the income support level increased, higher council housing rents were enforced, and ways were found to tax some very low incomes.[135]

There was, at the same time, an increase in house ownership, rising from 57% in 1979 to 69% in 1990. This was part of a continuing trend, but was aided by the sale of council houses to their occupiers on favourable terms, by the expansion of lending on mortgage on the part of the banks, and by the effect of deaths, occurring at this time, among large cohorts of first generation house owners of the 1930s, which allowed their heirs to buy their own houses in turn. In a sample of testators, dying in Glasgow in 1983, it was found that between 40% and 50% of the wealth left by those with estates of between £10,000 and £100,000, consisted of dwellings net of mortgages.[136]

There was also a considerable increase in the number of people holding shares in companies. This was partly the result of the mass sales of shares in the privatized industries at very favourable terms, and it was fostered also by tax concessions to employee share ownership schemes. By 1988, there were estimated to be 9 million adult shareholders, but as many of the shares of privatized undertakings were re-sold again, that number may have rapidly slumped to $5\frac{1}{2}$– 6 million, still double the figure of 1979.[137] To that extent, the Government had had some success in moving towards its goal of a 'property-owning democracy'.

4 Relations with the World Outside

The period opened with a favourable balance of payments year by year, caused by the impact of the oil flows on a reasonably balanced underlying position, as well as by the drastic deflationary policies pursued by the Government. This positive balance deteriorated dramatically from 1986 onwards, to create the largest balance of payments deficit in British history. The cushion of North Sea oil exports which had created the surplus had been worn away with astonishing speed by a vast spending spree in Britain unmatched by an equivalent improvement in the productive sectors of the economy, while the international competitive position of British export products deteriorated further. Some details are presented in Table 10·16.

The signs were that this dramatic turn-round had caught the Government and its advisers by surprise. However, in contrast to previous occasions when the brakes would be applied, bringing the economy to a screeching 'stop', even with an adverse balance of payments a fraction of the size of the 1988–90 figure, the Government, on this occasion viewed the inability of the British economy to pay its way in the world with remarkable equanimity and no direct measures were taken to counteract it. It must be remembered, however, that the high

[135] Steve Winyard, 'Low Pay', in Bell, *Government*, p. 53; MacInnes, *Thatcherism*, p. 57; Stephen Merrett with Fred Gray, *Owner-Occupation in Britain* (1982), p. 295; Paul Johnson and Stephen Webb, Low Income Families, 1979–87', *Fiscal Studies* 11/4 (1990), pp. 44–62.

[136] Riddell, *Decade,* p. 113; Merrett, op. cit.; Moira Munro, 'Housing Wealth and Inheritance', *Journal of Social Policy* 17/4 (1988), p. 421.

[137] Pliatzky, *Treasury*, p. 113; Beaumont, *Change*, p. 245; Grahame Thompson, *The Political Economy of the New Right* (1990), pp. 143–6.

Table 10·16: UK balance of payments, 1979–1990. (in £– bn).[138]

	Exports	Imports	Visible balance	Services balance	Interest profits dividends	Transfers balance	Current balance	Current balance as % GDP
1979	40·5	43·8	−3·3	+3·8	+1·2	−2·2	−0·5	−0·3
1980	47·1	45·8	+1·4	+3·7	−0·2	−2·0	+2·8	1·2
1981	50·7	47·4	+3·3	+3·8	+1·3	−1·5	+6·7	2·7
1982	55·3	53·4	+1·9	+3·0	+1·5	−1·7	+4·6	1·7
1983	60·7	62·2	−1·5	+4·1	+2·9	−1·6	+3·8	1·2
1984	70·3	75·6	−5·3	+4·5	+4·4	−1·7	+1·8	0·6
1985	78·0	81·3	−3·3	+6·7	+2·5	−3·1	+2·7	0·9
1986	72·7	82·1	−9·5	+6·7	+4·9	−2·2	0	0
1987	79·4	90·7	−11·2	+6·6	+3·7	−3·4	−4·3	−0·9
1988	80·8	101·9	−21·1	+4·5	+4·8	−3·5	−15·3	−3·2
1989	92·8	116·6	−23·8	+4·7	+4·1	−4·6	−19·6	−4·1
1990	102·7	120·7	−17·9	+4·4	+5·1	−4·4	−12·8	−2·4

[138] *Nat. Inst. Econ. Rev.*

interest rates maintained in order to bring down inflation would have a side-effect on the international payments figure as well.

It will be noticed that both imports and exports had a share in the deterioration. The growth in exports came to an abrupt halt over the four years 1985–8, implying a sharp reduction in volume in the light of rising prices. Imports also slowed in 1985–6, but then expanded dramatically both in monetary and in real terms. At the same time, the balance for the services and interest and dividends also ceased to grow from 1984 and 1985 onwards, respectively, again implying a fall in real terms.

The volume of manufactured and semi-manufactured exports continued to grow throughout: it was the relative decline of fuel exports, i.e. oil, that in 1986, halted for a time and thereafter slowed overall export growth. Imports of manufactures rose very much faster than exports, however, while, equally significantly, imports of basic materials increased but slowly. In terms of volume (index 1985 = 100), manufacturing exports rose between 1980 and 1990 from 91 to 143, or by 57%, but by the same token manufactured imports rose by no less than 115%, while the imports of basic materials increased by only 16%.[139] Apart from the worrying factor that British manufacturing exports were growing only at half the rate of manufacturing imports, there was also the dangerous sign that Britain did particularly badly in the richer markets and in the more sophisticated goods. Thus the United Kingdom share of OECD imports fell from 7·0% in 1975 to 6·7% in 1980 and a mere 5·3% in 1984. In some of the more complex or high-tech goods, the fall was even more drastic: the share of motor vehicles imported into the OECD from Britain fell between 1975 and 1984 from 5·0% to 2·3%, or by more than half; of electrical machinery from 6·4% to 4·4%, and of non-electrical machinery from 10·0% to 7·0%.

There was a similar increase in import penetration overall. Between 1979 and 1988 the percentage of imports over home demand plus exports, rose for chemicals from 21 to 28, for mechanical engineering from 19 to 28, for electrical engineering from 23 to 35, for motor vehicles from 31 to 40 and for textiles from 26 to 38: these were signs of a very serious deterioration in so short a period of time. Only timber and its products, paper, printing and publishing, and office machinery stayed fairly level. By contrast, exports as a proportion of manufacturers' sales and imports rose very slightly, if at all. For electrical engineering (25 to 18) and for mechanical engineering, (33 to 29) they even fell.[140] In the later 1980s, from 1985 to 1989, the excess of imports over exports in machinery increased from 2% to 14%, and in transport equipment from 29% to 41%. In chemicals, where there was an excess of exports, that shrank from 26% to 18% in the same period. Only textile yarn, fabrics, etc. improved slightly: the excess of imports fell from 77% to 71%. Altogether, for the first time in recorded history, manufactured imports began to exceed manufactured exports in 1983. The rising import penetration among various groups of consumer goods has been noted above.[141] The terms of trade changed little in this period, except for

[139] *Nat. Inst. Econ. Rev.*

[140] *Department of Trade and Industry*; Mark Smith, 'UK Manufacturing: output and trade performance', *Midland Bank Review* (Autumn 1986), pp. 9, 11. Also Christopher Carr, *Britain's Competitiveness* (1990), p. 11.

[141] Based on *Monthly Digest of Statistics*. See also pp. 396–7 above and A. D. Morgan, *British Imports of Consumer Goods* (Cambridge, 1988).

a sharp drop between 1985 and 1986, made good again in part in the following years.

The Government was not alone in remaining calm over these signs of deterioration in British competitive ability at the existing exchange rate, and over the threat to the reserves and to the pound implied by such drastic deterioration in the international position. Others found reason to point to the rising exports (though they were rising at a lesser rate than manufactured imports), or held to the idea, against all the evidence, that the deteriorating balance was due, not to the supply side, but to excessive demand. A particularly optimistic version of this view was the belief that Britain's balance had deteriorated merely because there was an investment boom in progress, which would of course have been very desirable. Whilst it was true that investment was rising in the late 1980s, this was from the very low levels to which it had sunk in the late 1970s, and investment was still low by comparison with earlier years, let alone with most other countries.[142]

There was also a more sophisticated version of the above interpretation: it treated the deterioration in the manufactured goods balance as part of a long-term structural change in the British economy which should by no means be judged as negative. In Britain, it was asserted, the service sectors had attracted a rising share of employment and output at the expense of manufacturing, as indeed they had in all the advanced countries. Britain enjoyed a healthy export surplus in services, as well as a positive balance in the transfer of interest and dividends from abroad. Given the declining relative need for raw materials from abroad, the oil exports, and the dramatic fall in the imports of food, there had to be a falling, and ultimately negative balance on manufactures to balance the accounts, which otherwise would show an unmanageable surplus in Britain's favour. The problem, then, was not so much Britain's inability to pay her way, but the need to reduce her overwhelming positive balance.[143] Unlike Japan and Germany, which managed to thrive on large payments surpluses year by year on the basis of their irresistible manufactured exports, Britain had chosen the right path in balancing her accounts by a negative balance in manufacturing.

There are good grounds for supporting each of these steps in the argument individually. It was indeed true that the imports of food had fallen from 6·0% of GDP in 1950 to 2·5% in 1970 and to a mere 1·0% in 1983, while beverages fell from 0·5% to 0·0% and 0·0%, and tobacco from 0·3% to 0·1% and 0·0% respectively. Fuel, meanwhile, had turned into a positive item. Basic materials imports had also fallen from 1·3% of GNP in 1973–4 to 0·9% in 1982–3. Among the reasons for this was the replacement of natural textile fibres by artificial ones, the replacement of timber pitprops by steel ones, and the enlarged production of woodpulp at home, as well as the reduced imports of ores and the greater use of scrap and recycling. Aluminium and oil seed for cattle feed, however, were

---

[142] Geoffrey Maynard, 'Britain's Economic Revival and the Balance of Payments', *Political Quarterly* 60/2 (1989), pp. 152–63; Michael Chisholm, 'De-Industrialization and British Regional Policy', *Regional Studies* 19/4 (1985), p. 307; Brittan, 'Economic Policy', p. 16.

[143] R. E. Rowthorn and J. R. Wells, *De-Industrialization and Foreign Trade* (Cambridge 1987), on which the following paragraphs are also based. For a critical view see Grazia Ietto-Gillies, 'Was De-Industrialization in the United Kingdom Inevitable?, *International Review of Applied Economics* 4/2 (1990), and reply, pp. 209–35.

up, so that the whole picture was complex, but tending downward. Reduced energy consumption at home helped Britain to achieve a positive balance on fuel account, based largely on the North Sea oil exports.

As far as services were concerned, high and rising earnings in financial services, in construction overseas and in 'other' services helped to counteract the drastic falls in shipping earnings and in tourism; the latter had turned from a positive to a large negative item, and would continue to do so as prosperity at home continued. In civil aviation, the debits were also growing faster than the credits.

As for trade in manufactured goods, there was some substance in the argument that it was not necessarily a sign of failure to sell less to the richer countries and to 'trade down' to the less developed regions to market British goods. There was, in effect, a triangularity in British trade. Britain had a surplus (in 1983) in all commodity trade with the USA, the OPEC countries and the less developed world; she was in surplus in primary goods with the other industrialized countries (where formerly, before the oil, she had a surplus of manufactures); and she was then balanced with the rest of the world, including the white Dominions, Japan and the newly industrialized countries (NIC) and the centrally planned economies. The change, then, did not come from the decline in manufactures, but from the growing self-sufficiency in primary goods.

However, even this optimistic view had to admit that the British decline in manufacturing output and employment was faster than that of any other country. There were three possible explanations for this: (a) the maturity thesis, implying that the very small agricultural sector could lose no more people to the services, so that the rise of the latter had to be met entirely from the resources of manufacturing; (b) the specialization thesis, referring to the need for very large manufacturing exports after the war to pay for food and raw material imports, for which a much lower rate of manufacturing exports was now required; (c) the failure thesis: the fall was due to the inability to compete. Had industrial output been greater, the manufacturing base might have carried an even larger service sector and there would have been less unemployment.

The study by Rowthorn and Wells, of which this is a very inadequate summary, faced with these three possible causes, came to the conclusion that there were elements of all three to be observed in reality, but while the first two were unambiguously present, the last was more doubtful: had manufacturing been more efficient and productive, they thought, its share would have fallen even more.

In theory, such a conclusion might stand, though there is nothing in it to exclude the opposite explanation of a fall in industrial efficiency and a consequent loss of export markets. In practice, fate has dealt unkindly with the thesis: the failure of British manufacturing exports, the sharply deteriorating balance of payments (instead of the postulated danger of a surplus) almost as soon as the book was published, and the evidence that a shrinking volume and revenue from oil was not compensated by a revival of manufacturing or other exports, fitted the 'failure' thesis better than either of the other two. For a service-based economy with a shrinking manufacturing base to be deemed successful, the latter, even if small, would have to be efficient – what might be called the Swiss model. Clearly, the United Kingdom was very far from that situation.

There were, however, two other aspects of the trade balance in the 1980s which made it different from earlier current account situations. One was the share of foreign trade now conducted *within* the multinational companies, and the other was the greatly enlarged role of capital movements across borders. For the first, motor car manufacturers might be taken as an example. Nowadays they commonly distribute their work over several countries, so that the finished cars contain components made overseas, and components made in one country appear as exports of another. Moreover, the values put on the components' exports may arbitrarily diverge from their real values for the company's accounting or tax-avoiding purposes. According to one estimate, more than half the visible trade of the USA and Japan in the mid-80s consisted of this kind of export and import between firms and their overseas affiliates.[144] The trade figures therefore do not fully reflect the real state of affairs.

As for the second, capital transactions are nowadays so large that they may easily be able to absorb imbalances in trade. Short-term needs can be dealt with by mobile international capital where once reserves had to be run down and home economic policy altered to take account of imbalances. More important still is the vast expansion of foreign direct and portfolio investment. This means that much of every country's production accrues to foreigners who own the firms in that country. Companies establishing businesses abroad affect and distort what appears to be a country's foreign trade transactions. Thus it has been estimated that if 'trade' is taken on the basis of the companies' ownership rather than residence, the American visible trade deficit in 1986 of $144 billion would be transformed into a surplus of $57 billion. Conversely, the local sales of American-owned firms in the United Kingdom were almost seven times as large as the imports from the United States.[145]

After a reduction in direct foreign investment in the 1970s, the 1980s saw an enormous expansion, at a rate some four times as fast as the growth in GNP. Its direction changed to some extent, a large part of the British as well as other foreign investment being directed into the USA, and much of the rest to other advanced countries. There was also a substantial increase in the service sector among these direct investments, though not in the case of British investments abroad, where the sector had been large to begin with.[146]

In Britain, exchange restrictions in operation up to 1979 had required Bank of England permission before capital could be invested abroad. This had become increasingly less effective, as much for foreign investment could be financed from earnings abroad outside the control of the British authorities. In 1981–2, an equivalent of two-thirds of foreign investment was financed from foreign earnings, and in 1983–4 this had risen to three-quarters.[147]

Some data relating to the British external capital position are presented in Table 10. The stock of investments, it should be noted, will alter in value with shifts in the value of currencies, inventory revaluations and other factors;

---

[144] However, this estimate counts any holding of 10% and over by a foreign firm as direct foreign investment and may therefore exaggerate its importance. De-Anne Julius, *Global Companies and Public Policy* (1990), pp. 3, 74. Also *eadem*, 'British Interests and the International Economy', *International Affairs* 63/3 (1987), pp. 375–93.

[145] 'Tricks of the Trade', *Economist* 5 April 1991, p. 61; Julius, p. 77.

[146] Julius, pp. 5, 31; OECD, Tokyo Round Table, *International Direct Investment and the New Economic Environment* (Paris, 1989), p. 23.

[147] David Shepherd, 'Assessing the Consequences of Overseas Investment', *Royal Bank of Scotland Review* (1986), p. 24; David Shepherd, Aubrey Silberston, Roger Strange, *British Manufacturing Investment Overseas* (1985), p. 26.

Table 10·17: United Kingdom: Overseas investment, 1979–89 (in £Bn)[148]

| | Total private sector investments (stock) | | | Capital transactions* | | | | |
| | | | | UK investment overseas | | Overseas investment in UK | | Total capital transactions incl. other items |
	UK investments abroad	Overseas investments in UK	Balance	Direct	Portfolio	Direct	Portfolio	
1979	43·6	26·4	17·2	−5·9	−0·9	3·0	1·5	−0·7
1980	52·2	31·5	20·7	−4·9	−3·3	4·4	1·5	−3·9
1981	70·1	35·3	34·8	−6·0	−4·5	2·9	0·3	−7·4
1982	83·3	39·1	44·2	−4·1	−7·6	3·0	0·2	−2·4
1983	105·0	46·8	58·2	−5·4	−7·2	3·4	1·9	−4·4
1984	139·2	53·3	85·9	−6·0	−9·9	−0·2	1·4	−7·8
1985	144·0	62·8	81·2	−8·8	−19·4	3·8	7·1	−9·5
1986	195·9	75·2	120·6	−11·3	−23·1	4·8	8·1	−11·1
1987	175·3	86·8	83·5	−18·6	−2·7	8·1	10·4	−7·7
1988	228·9	120·5	103·4	−15·2	−9·7	7·3	4·6	+2·3
1989	324·5	164·2	160·3	−19·5	−30·3	18·3	11·4	

* A minus figure means British investment abroad

[148] *United Kingdom Balance of Payments*; Grahame Thompson, *The Political Economy of the New Right* (1990), based on the *Bank of England Quarterly Review*.

changes in these balances are therefore not equivalent to the investment activity listed on the right hand side of the Table. Enormous sums are involved, and the direct and portfolio long-term investments are, in turn, put in the shade by short-term financial transactions. Thus, in 1987, when just over £21 billion was invested long term, overseas lending by United Kingdom banks amounted to over £50·3 billion, and borrowing from overseas banks was estimated at £52·8 billion. Year-by-year changes in the balance of payments are therefore quite easily absorbed in the short term by the financial sector.

Portfolio investments are those in which the British owners do not exert dominant control over the companies concerned, and they would include also the holdings of foreign government loans. Direct investment would nowadays almost always involve the multinational companies setting up branches abroad. There are many reasons for such investment overseas. In some cases, investment is made in order to move into territory protected by tariffs, or other means, to gain access to raw materials, use cheap labour, use local know-how, safeguard against currency fluctuations, or for tax purposes. In the later 1980s, the use of robots, computers and automatic control, as well as energy saving methods, may have, temporarily at least, reduced the attractiveness of low-wage countries and contributed to the shift of foreign direct investments to develop economies.[149] In some of the more recent moves, the hope for capital gains, and the pursuit of power, monopoly or otherwise, may have played an even bigger part. The aggressive acquisition of several major American firms by British buyers, and some of the foreign acquisition in the UK, may have had mainly such motivations.

Whether such capital exports were harmful or beneficial to the British economy has been much debated, particularly in the early 1980s when their increase was accompanied by sharply rising unemployment.[150] Given the large number of workers thrown out of their jobs, the capital would certainly have provided much needed work if it had stayed at home. Moreover, in view of the numerous backward and inefficient units in the British productive sector, the benefits of foreign investment would have to be extremely high to outweigh the lost opportunities at home. Against this, it has been argued, the capital invested abroad brought a very high return and helped to stabilize the British economy. Thus in 1988, with an unprecedented balance of payments deficit, the value of the external assets actually increased from £90 to £94 billion: some of the balancing item was foreign short-term capital in Britain, attracted by the high interest rates and by the facilities of the City of London. Thus, it was said, it paid to be a net borrower of financial assets and 'a net investor in a diversified portfolio of real assets' abroad.[151]

It is easy to paint a glowing picture of the money to be made by using other

---

[149] See p. 309 above. Also OECD, *International*, pp. 109–10; Julius, pp. 50 f.; Shepherd et al., p. 86; Robert Z. Aliber, 'A Theory of Direct Foreign Investment', in C. P. Kindleberger, (ed.), *The International Corporation* (Cambridge, Mass. 1970), pp. 17–34.

[150] See pp. 379, 403 above.

[151] Julius, p. 89, quoting the *Financial Times*. (There was a sharp reduction in net assets in 1990: *Bank of England Quarterly's Bulletin* 30/4 (1990), pp. 487). Also see Shepherd, 'Assessing'; Riddell, *Decade*, p. 81; Ron Martin and Rob Rowthorn, *The Geography of De-Industrialization* (1986), pp. 264–5.

nation's financial assets and investing them in productive enterprises abroad yielding higher returns than the cost of the capital. But, on the other hand, the dangers of borrowing short and lending, or investing long, are well known, particularly if the inward borrowing depends on the maintenance of higher rates of interest than prevail elsewhere and the assets abroad are subject to the vagaries of foreign governments. There is also a distributional effect involved in the export of capital. While the owners of capital may well achieve higher returns abroad than at home, workers at home remain unemployed, and equipment remains unmodernized. As far as the direct manufacturing investments abroad are concerned, the question may be asked whether British investors were fleeing the country because they despaired of Britain's ability to match the low costs or the quality achieved by industry abroad. Thus there may well be a gain to owners of capital, but a loss to everyone else.

The freedom for Britain to enage in commercial policies abroad had been much reduced over the years by membership of GATT (The General Agreement on Tariffs and Trade). More importantly, economic (as well as political) relationships with foreign countries were in this period increasingly dominated by the European Economic Community. While the ratios of imports and exports to GDP increased overall and, with them, the economic interdependence of countries, the ratios of trade within the Community showed much the largest rates of increase, especially the ratio of imports into Britain. The one important exception was agriculture, where the Common Market incentives led to a large increase in the self-sufficiency of British food production. Nevertheless, the Common Agricultural Policy (CAP) has never met with British approval. This is because it is extremely expensive, accounting for some two-thirds of the Community budget, and is the main reason why Britain is a large net payer to the Community despite being one of the poorer members. Repeated attempts by Britain have, despite the occasional support by other countries, so far been unable to change the methods of assessment or of subsidisation of agriculture. In 1991 the farm budget was expected to rise by 10%, and in 1992 by as much as 30%. If this happened, it would mean that, together with the regional policy aid to the poorer countries, mainly those along the Mediterranean, the ceiling of a contribution of 1·2% of GDP by each country to the EC, established only with great difficulty from the original ceiling of 1%, would most likely be exceeded again.

In the later 1980s, the main attention within the Community moved from trading and the budget to the monetary mechanism. The probable reason for this was that it appeared to many that the latter was the most likely road to effective political unification. The ultimate political unification of Europe had been a formal aim of the Community from the beginning, but movement towards it had stalled for some time, especially after the accession of Greece (1981) and of Spain and Portugal (both in 1986). Here, in the monetary sphere, lay new hope.

The first steps were taken with the inauguration of the European Monetary System (EMS) in 1979.[152] This consisted of four parts, of which Britain elected to participate in three. The first was the establishment of a European Currency Unit, the ECU, in place of the former mere unit of account (EUA). Like the

[152] Brian Tew, *The Evolution of the International Monetary System, 1945–88* (1988), pp. 253 ff.

latter, it was based on a basket of European currencies, weighted according to a quota related roughly to the economic stature of the member countries. Thus, by the weighting established in 1989, the Deutschmark accounted for 30·1% of its weight, the French franc for 19·0%, the pound sterling for 13·0%, and the Italian lira for 10·15%. The ECU is the denominator of debts and claims between central banks, of the community budget and its expenditure, and is also used for other intra-Community purposes. It was created as a counterpart to the 20% of the gold and foreign exchange reserves which the member countries paid into the European Monetary Co-operation Fund (EMCF) of 1973. The initial creation yielded about 26 billion ECUs, then worth some $29 billion.

Secondly, the EMS took over and expanded three previously existing EEC credit mechanisms, for very short-term financing, short-term financing and for medium-term financial assistance respectively. Together, these added up to about 20% of the members' official reserves. Thirdly, there was the EMCF, mentioned above, intended as the forerunner of a future European Monetary Fund.

The fourth provision of 1979 was the European Exchange Rate Mechanism (ERM), in which Britain decided at the time not to take part. It derived from the earlier 'snake' of currencies, of which the pound sterling had briefly been a member in 1972, and consisted of fixed exchange rates settled between each pair of members and therefore also between each and the ECU. Members agreed to keep within a narrow margin of these parities (±2·25%, and ±6% in the case of Italy), and to take steps to return to them as soon as there was any movement of currency values away from these parities. Should a change of parity become necessary, it would have to be effected by agreement with the Governments of the member countries. In practice, as noted above (p. 383) the British Treasury decided that, from 1987 onward, it would follow the central currency of the ERM, the Deutschmark, as if Britain were a member of the ERM, but without any formal undertaking.

In June 1989 the Prime Minister, Mrs Thatcher, declared that Britain would join the ERM only after a number of conditions had been met. These included the following:

(a) the remaining capital movement restrictions, especially by France, must be ended;
(b) full liberalization of financial services must be implemented by all;
(c) the EC competition policy must be strengthened;
(d) the internal free market must actually be completed;
(e) the British inflation rate (which then stood at 8%) must be substantially reduced.

This negative stance did not find universal support, and was strongly opposed even within the Cabinet, the Chancellor of the Exchequer, Mr Lawson, having favoured joining the ERM some years earlier. On 5th October 1990 it was announced that Britain had decided to join at once at the target exchange rate of 2·95 DM to the pound, but with a 6% band plus or minus. This was part of a package which also included the lowering of the Minimum Lending Rate in London by 1% to 14%. Britain's accession to the ERM caused some surprise, since several of the Prime Minister's clearly stipulated conditions had not been met. Although France had now freed her capital movements, and others were about to do so, the internal market of the EC was not yet free and above all, British inflation, far from having been lowered, was a good deal higher, standing at 10·9%, well above the average level in the EC. The move was justified at the time on the grounds that conditions were moving in the right direction, and especially that inflation was on its way down, though this turned out to be a somewhat premature. In view of the implausibility of that explanation, it has been generally assumed that the reasons for the move must be sought in the political rather than the economic sphere. The new Chancellor, who entered his office after Mr Major had been appointed Prime Minister, hastened to stress that joining the ERM implied even tighter monetary discipline and would require even tougher deflationary action than had been necessary before, since devaluation was no longer an option.

Meanwhile, the EC was about to take a much bigger step forward on a parallel and related road in the form of the Delors plan, made public in April 1989. This plan for economic and monetary union (EMU) envisaged three stages, though without naming a timetable for them. In stage one, all EC countries would participate in the ERM as a strong expression of commitment to further integration. Realignment of EMS parities would still be possible, but other mechanisms would be preferred. A Committee of Central Bank Governors would be formed empowered to have direct access to the Council of Ministers. Common economic and monetary policies were to be strengthened through existing institutions. This stage was accepted by the United Kingdom, as by the others, and came into operation on 1 July 1990.

In the second stage the Council would progressively set limits to national budget deficits and to their financing, though these would not be binding as yet. The limits within which currencies might vary, ±2·25% at that time, might be tightened, with EMS realignments as last resort. The Committee of Central Bankers was to be institutionalized as the European System of Central Banks (ESCB), with a separate new central bank, but ultimate decision-making on economic and monetary policy was still to remain with the national Governments.

In stage three a full economic and monetary union would be accomplished. Exchange rates would be 'irrevocably locked' with a single European currency, and the convertibility of the currencies made total and irreversible. Banking transactions would be completely liberalized, and the ESCB would manage member states' reserves and would decide on exchange market interventions outside the EC. The Council would be able to enforce certain budgetary policies 'to the extent necessary to prevent imbalances that might threaten monetary stability.'[153]

The British Government objected at once to stages two and three on the grounds that by taking decisions on economic policy, including budgetary policy, out of the hands of existing Governments, member countries would in effect give up their sovereignty and accede to a political union which Britain was not willing to contemplate. By June 1990, a more gradualist alternative was set out by the British Government. On the one hand, further steps should be taken after stage one to promote the convergence of economic performances, low inflation

[153] *Keesing's Record of World Events* (1989), p. 36598.

and stable currencies. For this purpose, the ECU should be strengthened and become a real currency, to be used even in the form of bank notes for payments abroad. This would require the creation of a European Monetary Fund (EMF) as a currency exchange institution. As a next stage, the European currency would become a 'hard ECU', no longer consisting of a basket of European currencies, but a genuine international currency in its own right. The EMF would exchange it for other currencies, and set its own interest rate. Detailed measures to prevent these institutions having an inflationary effect were also suggested. Karl Otto Pöhl, Governor of the German Bundesbank who had meanwhile been elected chairman of the newly-instituted Committee of Central Bankers, seemed to favour something like the slower British approach. At the same time he stressed that the EMU would require economic and financial convergence among member states, including anti-inflation policies and con-tractually enforced budget discipline, and that ultimately the new Central Banking System should enjoy independence (akin to that of his own bank) and be able to impose sanctions on Governments which breached budgetary discipline. He did, however, envisage a lengthy period of adaptation, and thought that countries with high inflation rates would find it hard to join the full EMU.

By October 1990, in spite of some serious divergences of views among them, the other eleven members had agreed to proceed to stage two on 1 January 1994, once certain conditions had been met, Britain alone preferring an alternative approach to greater economic union and towards a common currency, including the 'hard ECU'.

There were two quite separate reasons for Britain's reluctance to enter upon a path of inescapable ultimate political union. One was political: it was Britain's differing historical experience, and especially the link with the English-speaking world outside Europe, compared with the continental countries which had been through Fascism, occupation and other common sufferings, which made her more fearful of giving up some of her sovereignty.

The other reason was economic. If British inflation was higher than that of the others, this might be considered a short-term problem. But it represented a more fundamental inability, evident since the war,[154] to contain imbalances, be they internal or external, and it was reflected in a balance of payments position, which in 1988–90 was wholly out of control, as well as in a frightening rise in import penetration. This, in turn, was caused by the backwardness, the uncompetitiveness and the inefficiency of much of the British productive sector, and the inability of her institutions to contain demands for incomes which exceeded the power to produce them. For the time being, the British economy was too weak to stand up to full integration. Would control from outside, as envisaged by Karl Otto Pöhl, effect a cure, or would it hasten Britain's relative economic decline? Britain's reluctance to entrust her economic fate to others was a reflection of the fact that those who controlled her economic affairs were not sure of the answer.

---

[154] C. Goodhart 'An Assessment of EMU'; *Royal Bank of Scotland Review* 170 (June 1991), pp. 3–25.

Further Reading

This bibliography contains only a few titles of general works which the reader may find useful. For the rest of the recommended reading, students are referred to the Preface, pp. v–vii.

The only work covering most of the period considered here is A. J. Youngson, *Britain's Economic Growth 1920–1966* (1967), This is essentially a series of essays, mostly on economic policy, and requires some knowledge of the economic controversies of these years. Comprehensive volumes of statistics are now available in B. R. Mitchell and Phyllis Deane, *Abstract of British Historical Statistics* (Cambridge, 1962), and R. C. O. Matthews, C. H. Feinstein and J. C. Odling-Smee, *British Economic Growth 1856–1973* (Oxford, 1982).

For the years up to 1939, an elementary introduction will be found in M. W. Thomas (ed.), *A Survey of English Economic History* (1960 ed.), and a more advanced treatment in W. Ashworth, *An Economic History of England 1870–1939* (1960). For the inter-war years specifically, W. A. Lewis, *Economic Survey 1919–1939* (1949), S. N. Broadberry, *The British Economy between the Wars. A Macroeconomic Survey* (Oxford, 1986); Derek H. Aldcroft, *The British Economy. Vol. 1, The Years of Turmoil* (New York, 1986), and Sean Glyn and John Oxborrow, *Interwar Britain: A Social and Economic History* (1976) are strongly recommended.

The best account of the years of the Second World War is in the main volume of the official series of war histories, W. K. Hancock and M. M. Gowing, *British War Economy* (1949), The most comprehensive study made to date, of the immediate post-war years in the collective work, edited by G. D. N. Worswick and P. H. Ady, *The British Economy 1945–1950* (Oxford, 1952). This contains a valuable bibliography, as do most of the other works mentioned here. Also recently available is Alec Cairncross, *Years of Recovery. British Economic Policy 1945–51* (1985).

For the years since 1950, see G. D. N. Worswick and P. H. Ady (ed.), *The British Economy in the Nineteen-Fifties* (1962); W. Beckerman and Associates, *The British Economy in 1975* (Cambridge, 1965); J. C. R. Dow, *The Management of the British Economy 1945–60* (Cambridge, 1965); F. T. Blackaby (ed.), *British Economic Policy 1960–74* (Cambridge, 1978); W. Beckerman (ed.), *The Labour Government's Economic Record 1964–1970* (1972); W. P. J. Maunder (ed.), *The British Economy in the 1970s* (1980); Jim Tomlinson, *British Macroeconomic Policy Since 1940* (1985); Rudiger Dornbush and Richard Layard, *The Performance of the British Economy* (Oxford, 1987); A. R. Prest and D. J. Coppock, *The UK Economy. A Manual of Applied Economics* (latest edition).

The best account of the 1980s will be found in Peter Riddell, *The Thatcher Decade. How Britain has Changed During the 1980s* (Oxford, 1989).

Index